LONDON CIGARETTE C.

CIGARETTE & TRADE CARD CATALOGUE

(INCLUDING LIEBIG & REPRINT SERIES)

2022 edition

FIRST CATALOUGE PRODUCED IN 1929

ISBN 978-1-906397-23-4

Compiled by

IAN A. LAKER & Y. BERKTAY

Published by

LONDON CIGARETTE CARD CO. LTD
Sutton Road, Somerton, Somerset, England TA11 6QP

Telephone: 01458-273452 • Fax: 01458-273515
International Calls: Telephone: ++44 1458-273452 • Fax: ++44 1458-273515
e-mail: cards@londoncigcard.co.uk

www.londoncigcard.co.uk

Cards illustrated on back cover are from:
Brooke Bond Tropical Birds - blue back 1961 (back and front)
The River Group USA - The Beatles Collection 1992
John Players & Sons Uniforms of the Terrirorial Army 1939
W D & H O Wills Cricketers 2nd Series 1929

CARD COLLECTORS CLUB BY THE LCCC

Join Now

A club for collectors from all over the world!!

With this prestigious club you will receive:

- Each month savings on over 100 sets
- 12 Free copies of Card Collectors News
- Free Type Cards with every issue
- Free Monthly Auction Catalogue
- A Special Discount on a Set of the Month
- Details on New Issues and Additions to Stock
- Reduced Handling Fees on orders
- Priority Order Despatch
- Reduced Price on our Cigarette and Trade Card Catalogues
- Loyalty Vouchers
- Competitions with Prizes
- Handy Membership Card with your own membership ID & renewal date.
- Free Newsletters via Email

ALL THIS CAN BE YOURS FOR JUST

£27 for UK Members
£54 for European Members
£66 for the Rest of the World

You can even become a **Digital Member** to this club for a cost of just **£20** regardless where you are in the world

(T & C's apply)

CONTENTS

Card Collectors Club	ii
Card Collecting	iv
Card Collectors News Monthly Magazine	viii
Albums	ix
Our Website	xii
Greeting Cards	xiii
Books for the Collector	xiv
Cartophilic Reference Books	xvii
Auctions	xviii
How to Use the Catalogue	xix
How to Order	xx
Additional Information	xxi
A Guide to Condition	xxii
Index of Brands	xxiii
Index of Inscriptions	xxvi
Card Sizes	xxvii
Starter Collections	xxviii
Section 1 — BRITISH TOBACCO ISSUERS	**1**
Section 2 — FOREIGN TOBACCO ISSUERS	**147**
Section 3 — REPRINT SERIES	**186**
Illustrations of Cigarette Cards	197
Illustrations of Trade Cards	198
Section 4 — TRADE CARD ISSUES	**199**
Section 5 — LIEBIG CARD ISSUES	**389**

FREE E-MAIL NEWSLETTER

Sign up to our Free E-mail Newsletter via our website for extra special offers and latest news about the LCCC and card collecting.

www.londoncigcard.co.uk

CARD COLLECTING

When you mention cigarette cards, most people think of cricketers, footballers and film stars of the 1930s. This was the heyday of cigarette card issues when virtually every packet contained a little picture and the major companies like Wills and Players had their own studios and artists devoted entirely to the production of cigar ette cards. It was big business, and massive print-runs often ran into hundreds of millions for each series. That's why there are still lots of them around today — sets can still be bought for around £20 upwards in very good condition, which is a major reason for their popularity for those of us wishing to indulge in nostalgia for Hollywood legends, sporting heroes, military hardware, famous trains and graceful ocean liners from a golden age.

Players
Film Stars
Third Series
(1938)

Wills
Cricketers
2nd Series
(1929)

In The Beginning

In fact the hobby goes back to the 1890s, to a time when cigarettes were wrapped in paper packets. Manufacturers began inserting pieces of card to protect the contents, quickly realising that these would be useful for advertising their products. Soon these were followed by pictorial sequences, which would build up into sets. The object was to encourage repeat purchases and establish brand loyalty, and the subjects chosen were those most likely to appeal to the predominantly male customer base. Beautiful young women, sportsmen and soldiers dom inated the earliest series, followed by ever more diverse topics in the early 20th century as companies competed for trade by offering something new. Remember this was before the days of cinema, Radio or TV, let alone the modern tech nological wonders we now take for granted. Newspapers carried few illustrations, and living standards were much lower. For most smokers, therefore, the cards they collected from their packets were their window on the world, serving to educate, excite or amuse—they were colourful, informative and free! Many of these early cards were from firms whose names would mean nothing to a non-collector, little companies which went out of business or were swallowed up by the big boys before World War I. And it is these cards, few of which have survived, which are often the most valuable.

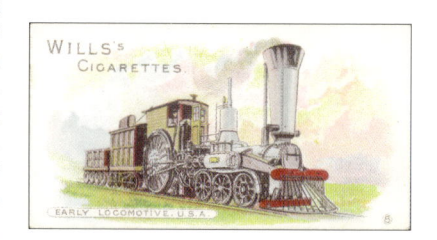

Wills, Locomotive Engines
and Rolling Stock (1901)

The 1920s and 1930s

The 1920s and 1930s are generally regarded as the golden age of cards. Competition was fierce and rival firms were constantly looking for something different to stand out from the crowd. Players and Wills went in for adhesive-backed cards and offered special albums to stick them in. So many were produced that there are still loads around today, and they fetch only a few pounds. Another idea was cards that made up into a sectional picture of a work of art, a map or an historic event like the 1937 Coronation Procession. Some makers developed cards with push-out sections which could be made into models, whilst others came out with sequences of silk embroidered flowers, cards in miniature frames, bronze plaques, metal charms to hang on a bracelet — even little gramophone records which could actually be played!

Players
Motor Cars Second Series (1937)

A New Dawn

Paper shortages halted card production in 1940. Cigarette cards would never be issued on the same scale as before the war, but even so there have been quite a few over the years, starting with the blue and white pictures of film stars and footballers printed in the sliding trays in Turf Cigarettes, and progressing to many series of popular cards in packets of Tom Thumb, Doncella and Grandee Cigars. Recent anti-smoking legislation has ended any hope of new cards with tobacco products, but we will continue to welcome new trade card issues.

Trade cards, or 'trading cards' as they are often called, are picture cards issued with non-tobacco products and they have a distinguished history which pre-dates even the earliest cigarette cards. On the continent of Europe, one of the first to recognise the sales potential of cards was the Liebig Meat Extract Company, which over a period of 120 years from 1872 onwards issued no fewer than 1,800 different series. In the 1920s and '30s firms like chocolate makers Frys and Cadburys, tea companies such as Typhoo, periodical publishers etc. mimicked their tobacco counterparts by producing a regular flow of picture cards. But it was in the post-war environment that trade cards really came into their own, filling the gap left by the demise of cigarette cards.

From the 1950s onwards came a flood of 'trade' cards issued with tea, confectionery, biscuits, cereals, ice cream and so on. Among them were companies such as A & B C Gum, Bassetts and Brooke Bond, who regularly released one set after another year after year. I expect many of you will remember collecting them — and there has been a notable trend for this age group to begin collecting again, which can be satisfyingly inexpensive with some Brooke Bond cards from the 1960s and '70s priced at around £4 or £5 for a mint set.

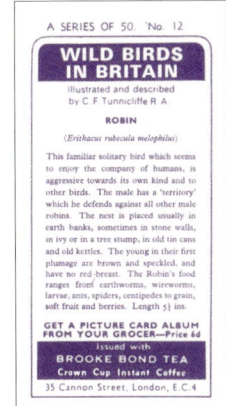

Brooke Bond Tea
Wild Birds in Britain (blue back) (1965)

Cards at War

During World War I many patriotic collections were issued — 'Recruiting Posters', 'Infantry Training', 'Modern War Weapons', 'Military Motors', 'Allied Army Leaders', 'Britain's Part in The War' and so on. All were subject to Government scrutiny to ensure no secrets reached the enemy, and 'passed for publication by the Press Bureau' is printed on many of these cards. In the run-up to World War II, out came cards demonstrating the nation's apparent military strength and preparedness for action — 'Britain's Defences', the 'R.A.F. at Work' and 'Life in the Royal Navy' to name a few. 'Aircraft of the R.A.F.' cards showed our latest fighters, the Spitfire and Hurricane ('the performance of this machine is an official secret' we are warned). It is rumoured that German agents were buying up Player's 1939 'British Naval Craft' in London to send back to U-Boat crews. Meanwhile the authorities sponsored a series of 'Air Raid Precautions', 'cigarette cards of national importance', endorsed by Home Secretary Samuel Hoare, with useful hints on how to put on a gas-mask or extinguish an incendiary bomb. How effective or otherwise these proved in the blitz we shall never know, but they raised public awareness.

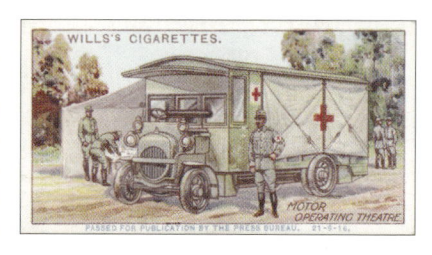

Wills
Military Motors (1916)

The Cards That Never Were

The Wagner cards were not the only ones never to see the light of day. Britain's biggest maker, W. D. & H. O. Wills of Bristol prepared a series of 50 cards to celebrate Wellington's victory over Napoleon at the Battle of Waterloo, but when the date for issue came up in 1915 their release was cancelled so as not to offend the French who were our allies fighting the Germans. And in a series of 'Musical Celebrities' all the German subjects were withdrawn and substituted by lesser-known individuals from other nationalities. Another Wills casualty was a series of 50 cards prepared to mark the coronation of King Edward VIII. Edward's abdication in 1936 put paid to this and the cards were destroyed — all except, that is, for a handful of sets presented to the firm's directors and top management.

Unstoppable Cards
The Avengers 50 (2012)

Wills
Waterloo
(c1916)

Today's Hobby

Remember *The Saint*, *The Avengers*, *The Prisoner*, *Thunderbirds*, *Captain Scarlet* and *Doctor Who*? They all have huge followings and collectors are snapping up new sets as they come onto the market. The same goes for *Star Trek*, Buffy, Disney, Harry Potter and *The Lord of the Rings*. Cult TV series and blockbuster movies are sure to be pictured on cards. That goes for football too. There are hundreds of different sets to chose from, some going back to the days of Matthews, Finney and Lofthouse, others bringing us right up to date with the latest Premiership players and stars like Marcus Rashrord and Kieran Trippier. The thing is, card collecting is a living hobby with many new series being produced each year attracting a new generation of collectors. Whatever your age or interests, you're going to be pleasantly surprised by what cards can offer. Collecting cards has come a long way since its pre-war image and people from all walks of life are now keen collectors.

Inkworks The World Is Not Enough James Bond 007 1999

London Cigarette Card Company

In 2017 the London Cigarette Card Company celebrated its 90th anniversary. The firm's remarkable history as the world's first company devoted solely to the needs of card collectors began in 1927 when Colonel C.L. Bagnall D.S.O, M.C., set up business at 47 Lionel Road, Brentford with a capital of just £500. The enterprise proved popular with collectors, and card stocks quickly grew to the point where an extension had to be built to house them, and the first catalogue was published in 1929. Four years later came another momentous event — the launch of the monthly magazine *Cigarette Card News* now renamed **Card Collectors News** and still being published today. By 1933, the business had expanded to such a degree that larger premises were essential and, in October of that year, the L.C.C.C. moved to Wellesley Road, Chiswick, their address until 1977 when they moved again, this time to Somerset. Today, the company's headquarters in Sutton Road, Somerton houses one of the world's largest stocks of cigarette cards and trade cards — **MORE THAN 50 MILLION** — and serves collectors around the world. In September 1999 they set up their website (**www.londoncigcard.co.uk**) which now offers over 9,000 different series, all with sample colour illustrations.

For many years we have published the hobby's essential reference catalogues as three independent catalogues for Cigarette, Trade and Liebig issues. In 2015, after extensive market research and speaking with many collectors it was decided to amalgamate all three catalogues mentioned above into one volume. The 2022 Catalogue now contains prices for over 17,150 different series on every subject imaginable, thus making it the most definitive guide to collecting available today.

In 2017 we introduced a brand new Card Collectors Club. Membership starts from £20.00 a year (see page ii), which includes the monthly *Card Collectors News* magazine (see page viii), which keeps everyone up to date with news about the latest card issues, stories and features.

For further information contact:
London Cigarette Card Company Ltd, Sutton Road, Somerton, Somerset TA11 6QP
telephone 01458-273452   e-mail cards@londoncigcard.co.uk
Website www.londoncigcard.co.uk

CARD COLLECTORS NEWS MAGAZINE BACK COPIES

Back Copies

Pre 1965 .... £2.50 each

Issues from January 1966 to December 1975 .... £1.50 each

Issues from January 1976 to December 2012 .... £1.25 each

Issues from January 2013 to Present .... £2.25 each

We don't have copies of every single magazine ever published, but we do have a good selection. Please check our website for availability.

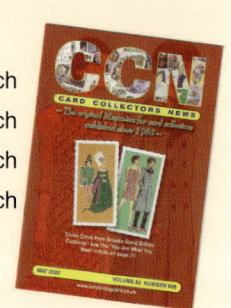

www.londoncigcard.co.uk

A5 Magazine Binders

Keep your magazines safe in a purpose designed luxury binder to hold 12 copies in a choice of blue and maroon covers with gold lettering for.. **£11.95 each**

(L.C.C.C Card Collectors Club Members Price £10.95 each)

LUXURY ALBUMS

LUXURY BINDER
with 30 leaves
size 275 x 187mm
£14.50

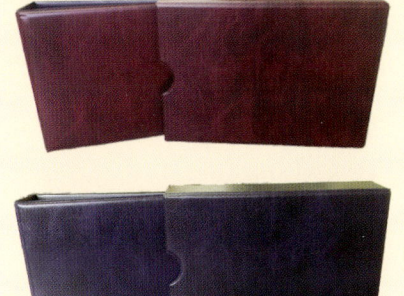

MATCHING SLIP-CASE £6.50
(only supplied with binder)

EXTRA LEAVES 19p EACH

☆ **GREY CARD INTERLEAVES**
— **30 FOR £4.50** ☆

Orders are sent post free to UK addresses, but PLEASE NOTE orders under £25.00 (Club members under £15.00) will incur a handling fee of £2.00.

Overseas postage is charged at cost and there is no handling fee.

Full display, front and back, is given to your cards in top quality transparent leaves held in a luxurious binder. The leaves are made from a tough, clear optical film. Binders are available in a choice of blue or maroon covers (with matching slip-cases as an optional extra) and each is supplied complete with 30 leaves, of which various sizes are available as listed below.

Page Ref.	Suitable for	Pockets Per Page	Pocket size (mm) wide x deep
A	Standard size cards	10	43 x 83
M	Medium size cards	8	55 x 83
D	Doncella/Grandee/Typhoo size cards	6	111 x 55
L	Large size cards	6	73 x 83
X	Extra large cards	4	111 x 83
P	Postcards	2	111 x 170
C	Cabinet size cards, booklets etc.	1	224 x 170
K	Miniature size cards	15	43 x 55

Remember to state which colour (blue or maroon) and which page reference/s you require.

Order by telephone (01458-273452), fax (01458-273515), e-mail (cards@londoncigcard.co.uk) or through our website (www.londoncigcard.co.uk) 24 hours a day, 7 days a week using your credit or debit cards, or you can order by post.

ALBUMS FOR LARGE TRADE CARDS

- An album designed specifically for modern trade cards like Skybox, Comic Images, Rittenhouse, Inkworks, Topps etc
  - The ideal way to display your large modern trade cards to their best advantage
  - 3-ring luxury padded binders in a choice of maroon or blue size 316 x 276mm

There are two types of leaves:
9 pockets per sheet size 91 x 68mm, reference LT
6 pockets per sheet size 138 x 66mm, reference WV

Orders are sent post free to UK addresses, but PLEASE NOTE orders under £25.00 (Club members under £15.00) will incur a handling fee of £2.00. Overseas postage is charged at cost and there is no handling fee.

**COMPLETE ALBUM WITH 30 LEAVES
IN A CHOICE OF 'LT' OR 'WV' LEAVES £21.00 • EXTRA LEAVES 32p EACH**

☆ COLLECTORS' ACCESSORIES ☆

A neat and tidy way for you to deal with incomplete sets is to use our
numbered, printed 'wants' lists

30 adhesive lists numbered 1 to 50 . . . . **75p**

The professional way to wrap sets with our translucent
glascine wrapping strips

200 strips size 123 x 68 mm for standard size cards . . **£5.50**
200 strips size 175 x 83mm for large cards **£6.00**
200 strips size 228 x 83mm for extra-large cards **£6.50**

Tweezers (including cover case) **£5.95**

Quality manufactured nickel tweezers with straight smooth tips, They come with a plastic cover case for safe storage, a perfect addition to your collecting accessories.

EXTRA LARGE ALBUMS FOR CARDS

- Luxury 4-ring padded binder, size 415 x 333mm
- Albums include 20 leaves of your choice, 'XLA' or 'XLLT' or 'XLC'
- Ideal for storing large volumes of cards, both cigarette and trade
- A choice of maroon or blue
- Three types of leaves available:
  30 pocket page, pocket size 72 x 40mm, ref XLA
  15 pocket page, pocket size 72 x 90mm, ref XLLT
  2 pocket page, pocket size 186 x 273mm ref XLC

Album with 20 leaves
(XLA, XLLT or XLC) £35.00

Slipcases available
£18 (maroon or blue)

Extra packs of 20 leaves
(XLA, XLLT or XLC) £15.00

Orders are sent post free to UK addresses, but please note orders under £25 (Club members under £15.00) will incur a handling fee of £2.00.

Overseas postage is charged at cost and there is no handling fee.

Our Website
www.londoncigcard.co.uk

Quite Possibly the best Website for collecting both Cigarette and Trade Cards in the UK, with huge stocks over 9,000 items online!!

What's on our website

An impressive list of sets available to purchase with images to complement them and descriptions of the sets.

Subject lists (Thematic lists) covering interesting matter such as:

- Sci-fi
- Films
- Animals
- Sport (Football, Rugby, Tennis, Speedway etc)
- Military
- Music (Pop Stars and Singers)
- General Interests etc.

And so much more. Why don't you look for yourself?

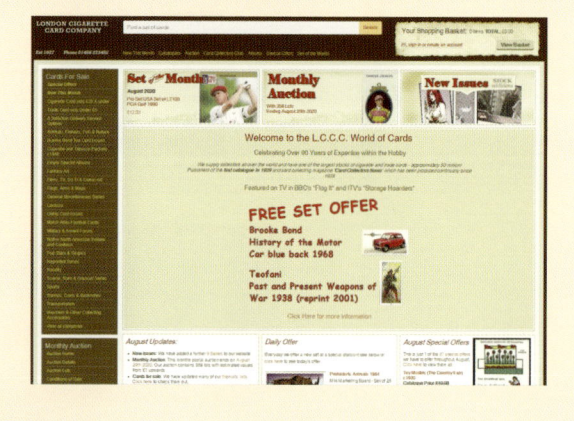

The website also includes

- Information about our company
- History of collecting cards
- New card issues into stock every month from various manufacturers
- Availability of albums, reference books, magazines and catalogues
- Information on how to value and sell your collection

Why not try our Monthly Auctions?

We have auctions every month, at least 350 lots in each, starting from as low as £2. Just pop onto our website to view the list (hard copies are available on request).

Discounts Discounts Discounts!!!!

Our website offers discounts every month on various different sets and you can get up to 33% off selected sets, so why wait log on now?!

Come on in you might be surprised!!!
www.londoncigcard.co.uk

GREETING CARDS
A CARD FOR EVERY OCCASION

Only £1.75 each
Choose from 72 subjects

Greetings cards which feature cigarette cards on all manner of different subjects, beautifully printed in colour, and with the bonus of early packet designs from the firms which issued the cards reproduced on the back. The insides are blank so that they can be used for any and every occasion. This is a brilliant idea for collectors. Send them to friends or relatives, include them with gifts, or just collect them yourself.

Aesop's Fables	Aircraft	Alpine Flowers	Astronomy
Aviators	Bats	Batsmen	Bowling
Boxing	Boy Scouts	Brahms & Liszt	Butterflies
Cars	Celebrated Oils	Cinema Stars	Composers
Cycling (Lady Cyclists)	Cycling (3 Profiled Bikes)	Deer	Derby Winners
Dogs (Hounds)	Dogs (Terriers)	Elizabethan Mis-Quotes	Film Stars
Fire Appliances	Firefighters	Flowering Trees	Flowers in Pots
Freshwater Fish	Frogs and Toads	Gilbert & Sullivan	Golfers
Grand National Winners	Hares & Rabbits	Highland Regiments	Highway Code
Jovial Golfers (Humorous)	Keep Fit	Lighthouses	Lizards
Marine Life (Jellyfish etc)	Marine Life (Penguin etc)	Marine Mammals	Medals
Merchant Ships	Mice	Mis-Quotes	Motor Cycles
Mythology	Newts	Old English Flowers	Owls
Parrots	Polar Exploration	Poultry	Predatory Mammals
Proverbs	Railway Engines	Red Indians (Pocahontas)	Red Indians (Geronomo)
Roses	Rowing	Sea Shells	Small Mammals
Snakes	Speed Boats	Teaching	Tennis (Men's Shots)
Warships	Wicketkeeping	Wild Flowers	Wildlife (Badger etc)

TOP QUALITY, DISTINCTIVE AND EYE-CATCHING CARDS WHICH STAND OUT FROM ALL THE OTHERS AS SOMETHING COMPLETELY DIFFERENT — SIZE 150 x 100mm
ONLY £1.75 EACH INCLUDING ENVELOPE
Order direct from
LONDON CIGARETTE CARD COMPANY LIMITED
SUTTON ROAD, SOMERTON, SOMERSET TA11 6QP • TELEPHONE: 01458-273452

BOOKS FOR THE COLLECTOR

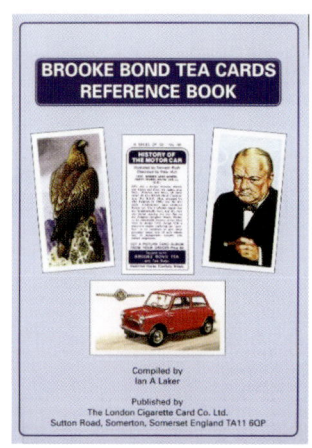

Brooke Bond Tea Cards Reference Book
by Ian A. Laker

This definitive 104 page reference book with 319 colour illustrations of cards and albums covers all 55 British issues from 1954 to 1998 as well as details of their double card issues and black back re-issue series, plus details of their overseas issues including Canada, USA, Africa and Ireland and their Italian Liebig issues. Also included are details of miscellaneous issues, playing cards, advert cards and inserts up to 2005. The colour illustrations show examples of the fronts and backs of the cards including their different printings and also pictures album covers. Published in 2007. . . . . **SOLD OUT**
(BRAND NEW BROOK BOND REFERENCE BOOK TO BE PUBLISHED LATE 2021)

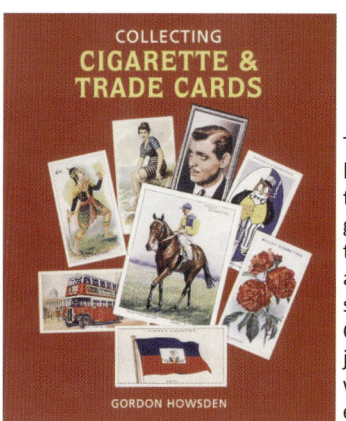

Collecting Cigarette & Trade Cards
by Gordon Howsden

Traces the history and development of cards from their beginning to the present day and includes the background of the issuing firms, thematic collecting, printing and production, grading, pricing and so on. Authoritatively written in an easy-to-read style and beautifully illustrated in colour, the book approaches the subject from a fresh angle which will appeal to seasoned collectors and newcomers alike. Cigarette & Trade Cards is not only an indispensable reference work but also a joy to read or just browse through. 152 large-format pages with 220 colour illustrations featuring 750 cards and related ephemera. **£17.50**

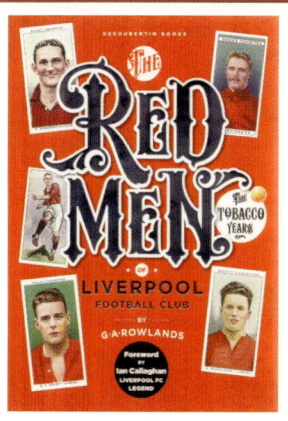

The Red Men of Liverpool Football Club by G.A. Rowlands

This excellent colourful and well researched book is packed with pictures and gives details of Liverpool players who appear on cigarette cards and information on card issuers and their sets as well as a brief general card collecting history. George Rowlands has been a life-long card collector and fan of the club and his 168-page book lists over 330 cards issued between 1892 and 1952 and includes a foreword by former Liverpool player Ian Callaghan. This is an interesting book for any football fan, particularly supporters of The Reds. Published 2017. . . . . **£14.99**

BOOKS FOR THE COLLECTOR

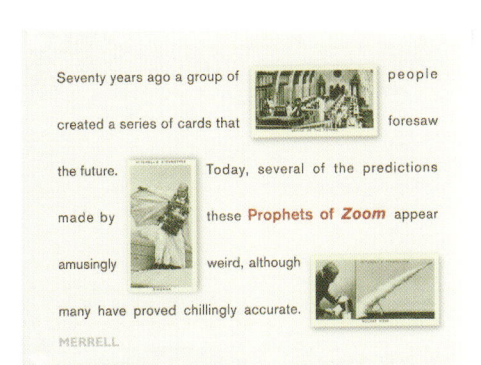

Prophets of Zoom

An unusual but fascinating book, *Prophets of Zoom*, with 112 pages, reproduces the front and back of each card in Mitchell's 1936 series of 50 The World of Tomorrow, opposite which ispictured a modern equivalent – and it's surprising how many of the predictions have become true!

From author Alfredo Marcantonio's introduction, we learn that the card set was inspired by a book called *The World of Tomorrow* and drew upon images from contemporary films, in particular Alexanda Korda's *Things to Come*, as well as inventions then at the cutting edge of technology. The individual predictions range from the amazing to the amusing, and together they paint a unique picture of the world we live in now, as pre-war Britain imagined it would be.

To take just one example. The very first card informs us that 'coal-mines and oil-wells will not last forever. We shall have to gain the energy we need, not from fuel, but from the inexhaustible forces of nature', and the set forecasts wind turbines, atomic energy and solar motors as being the power sources of the future. From space travel and giant television screens, robots and bullet trains, to London's skyscraper skyline, this is highly entertaining stuff, and excellent value. **£8.50**

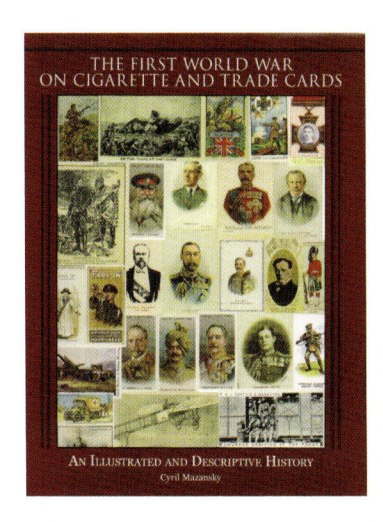

The First World War On Cigarette and Trade Cards

By Dr Cyril Mazansky
Published in 2015

What a wonderful advertisement for our hobby! *The First World War on Cigarette and Trade Cards* is a book illustrated with 941 cards, mostly issued at the time and including many rarities. This is no mere picture book. It is an authoritative history of the war written by an expert on the subject, employing cards from a collection built up over a period of more than thirty years. The result is a richly illustrated descriptive tapestry of this great conflict, using cards and silks to great effect both as a source of information and also as a means of showing how events, personalities and various aspects of the war were presented to the public at the time. The book is split into chapters dealing with particular topics such as Military Leaders, Armaments, War Scenes, Army Life, VC Heroes and The Home Front, plus a special section on the History of Card Collecting. The author, Dr Cyril Mazansky, will be familiar to readers of *Card Collectors News* magazine as he has contributed many articles. We cannot recommend this book too highly. It is a marvellous production, well researched, well written in a style which involves the reader in 'The War to End All Wars', and impeccably illustrated with a magnificent array of cards. **£39.95**

BOOKS FOR THE COLLECTOR

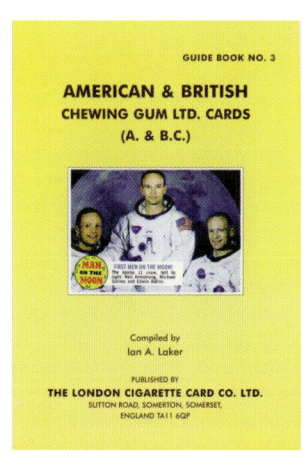

The Card Issues of A & BC Chewing Gum Reference Book 2004 Edition

Compiled by I. A Laker 52 pages (3rd Revised Edition 2004) First published in 1981 A & B C produced their first cards in 1953, during a period of more than twenty years they were to become one of the most popular and prolific sources of cards. They issued well over a hundred different series, usually in a large format, and covering a variety of subjects, although football and entertainment were dominant. Several of their series were produced under licence from Topps USA who eventually took over ownership and are still issuing cards today under the Topps name. This booklet is the third revised edition published in 2004. It lists on pages 1 to 40 alphabetically all the series issued by A & BC giving a comprehensive subject-listing where necessary, together with details of varieties, etc. Illustrations have been used where appropriate. On pages 41 to 50 contain new information that has come to light since the original publication in 1981. Also since this was published new information has come to light regarding the actual issuing name. It has long been referred to as American & British Chewing Gum Limited, but in fact new information has established that the actual name was taken from the initials of the actual founders and should in fact be A & B C Chewing Gum Limited. **£4.50**

REGIMENTAL BOOKS

The following series of books featuring the different Regiments and Corps of the British Army illustrated on Cigarette and Trade cards, contain History, Uniforms, Badges, Regimental Colours, Victoria Cross Winners and Personalities. Approximately 200 illustrations in each book, 56 pages with 16 in full colour, all produced by David J. Hunter.

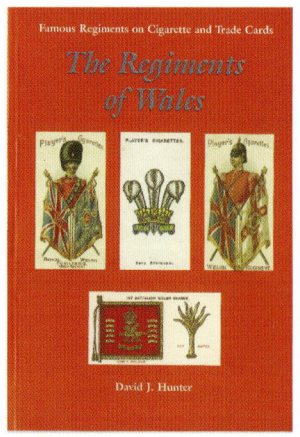

The Coldstream Guards	£8.50
The Gordon Highlanders	£8.50
Queen's Own Highlanders (Seaforth & Camerons)	£8.50
The Queen's Royal Lancers	£8.50
The Regiments of Wales (The Welsh Guards, The Royal Welsh Fusiliers & The Royal Regiment of Wales)	£8.50
The Royal Army Medical Corps	£8.50
The Royal Marines	£8.50
The Royal Regiment of Fusiliers — Part 1 (The Royal Northumberland Fusiliers & The Royal Warwickshire Regiment)	£8.50
The Royal Regiment of Fusiliers — Part 2 (The Royal Fusiliers (City of London Regiment) & The Lancashire Fusiliers)	£8.50
The Scots Guards	£8.50
The Worcestershire & Sherwood Foresters Regiment	£8.50

CARTOPHILIC REFERENCE BOOKS

British Tobacco Issues Handbook (updated 2003 edition). Updates the original Handbooks Parts I & II, but excludes Ogden, Wills and Godfrey Phillips Group of Companies. 369 pages . . **£24.00**
Handbook Part II (1920 to 1940) British Tobacco Issues. Updated by the above book, but includes Phillips Silks. 164 pages, illustrated. Published at £12.00 . . . . **Special Offer Price £6.00**
The Card Issues of Abdulla/Adkin/Anstie (reprint, originally published 1943). 20 pages **£4.50**
The Card Issues of Ardath Tobacco (reprint, originally published 1943). 28 pages **£4.50**
The Card Issues of W.A. & A.C. Churchman (reprint, originally published 1948). 36 pages **£4.50**
The Card Issues of W. & F. Faulkner (reprint, originally published 1942). 12 pages **£4.50**
The Card Issues of Gallaher (reprint, originally published 1944). 40 pages **£4.50**
The Card Issues of R. & J. Hill (reprint, originally published 1942). 28 pages **£4.50**
The Card Issues of Lambert & Butler (reprint, originally published 1948). 32 pages **£4.50**
The Card Issues of Ogdens (reprint 2015 paperback edition includes 2 pages of additions and corrections from the updated 2005 edition). 333 pages **£24.00**
The Card Issues of Godfrey Phillips (reprint, originally published 1949). 40 pages . . . . **Out of Print**
The Card Issues of Godfrey Phillips & Associated Companies (updated 2008 edition). Includes Cavanders, Drapkin, Millhoff and Muratti. 256 pages **£28.00**
The Card Issues of John Player & Sons (reprint, originally published 1950). 44 pages **£4.50**
Guide Book No. 2, F. & J. Smith Cards (published 1980). 36 pages **£4.50**
The Card Issues of Taddy (reprint, originally published 1948). 32 pages **£4.50**
The Card Issues of W.D. & H.O. Wills (updated 2011 Edition). 214 pages **£25.00**
The Card Issues of Wills and B.A.T. combined (published 1942-1952, reprinted as one volume in 1998). 402 pages **£20.50**
Directory of British Tobacco Issuers (reprint, originally published 1946). 36 pages **£4.50**
World Tobacco Card Index & Handbook Part I & Part II . . . . **Out of Print**
World Tobacco Card Index & Handbook Part III. Supplement to Index I & II. 504 pages **£25.50**
World Tobacco Card Index & Handbook Part IV. Supplement to Index I, II & III. 688 pages **£19.00**
World Tobacco Card Index & Handbook Part V. Supplement to Index I, II, III & IV (published 1990). 552 pages **£19.00**
World Tobacco Issues Part 1. Issuers A to K. 344 pages **£23.00**
World Tobacco Issues Part 2. Issuers L to Z, plus Anonymous. 344 pages **£23.00**
The above two books, updated to August 2000, are a revision of the World Tobacco Indexes Parts I to V combined (but not the Handbooks) with many additions & amendments. They do not contain the Handbook and therefore do not have subject listings.
Handbook of Worldwide Tobacco and Trade Silk Issues. updated 2016 Edition with colour illustrations. 366 pages **£30.00**
Australian and New Zealand Card Issues Part 1 . . . . **Out of Print**
Australian and New Zealand Card Issues Part 2 (published 1993). 257 pages **£16.00**
The New 'Tobacco War' Reference Book (updated 1999 edition). 236 pages **£20.50**
Glossary of Cartophilic Terms (reprint, originally published 1948). 40 pages **£4.50**
British Trade Card Index Part I, Part II & Part III . . . . **Out of Print**
British Trade Card Index Part IV (1986-1994 issues). 412 pages **£20.50**
British Trade Card Index Issues up to 1970 (2006 edition). 516 pages **£27.50**
British Trade Card Handbook Issues up to 1970 (2006 edition). 542 pages **£27.50**
Brooke Bond Tea Cards Reference Book (2007 edition) 104 pages **(New Book to be published late 2021)** . . . . **Sold Out**
Guide Book No. 1, Typhoo Tea Cards (published 1976). 36 pages **£4.50**
Guide Book No. 3, A. & B.C. Gum Cards (updated 2004 edition). 52 pages **£4.50**

xvii

2022 AUCTIONS

We have been auctioning for over 80 years cards to suit every collector

Monthly 360-lot postal auctions of cigarette and trade cards and associated items with estimated values from as little as £1 up to many hundreds. Lots to interest every collector and suit their pocket.

Postal Auctions for 2022 are as follows:

Tuesday,	4th January	Saturday,	25th June
Saturday,	29th January	Saturday,	30th July
Saturday,	26th February	Saturday,	27th August
Saturday,	26th March	Saturday,	24th September
Saturday,	30th April	Saturday,	29th October
Saturday,	28th May	Saturday,	26th November

Each postal auction finishes at midnight on the above dates.

A guide to how we assess condition and how to bid can be found on our bidding sheet which comes with the free auction catalogue, so it couldn't be easier if you are an 'auction beginner'. (Auction date could be subject to change.)

There are no additional charges to bidders for buyer's premium, so bidding is straightforward, with no 'hidden extras'.

Each lot is described with an estimate of its value reflecting the condition of the cards, ranging from poor right through to mint condition, and for over 80 years collectors have bid with complete confidence, knowing that every effort is made to describe the lots accurately.

Each auction contains a selection of rare sets, rare and scarce individual cards, pre-1918 issues, 1920-40 series, old and modern trade issues including Brooke Bond, errors and varieties, silks, albums, books, Liebigs, cigarette packets etc – in fact plenty to interest everyone.

Auction catalogues are available **FREE OF CHARGE**, 4 weeks before the date of sale from London Cigarette Card Company Limited, Sutton Road, Somerton, Somerset TA11 6QP
Telephone: 01458-273452   Fax: 01458-273515
E-mail: auctions@londoncigcard.co.uk

The Auction Catalogue can also be found on our website, which contains a preview of each auction as well as facilities for on-line bidding – visit **www.londoncigcard.co.uk** for further details or why not sign up to our **FREE E-mail Newsletter** to be reminded when new auctions become available online.

Also a copy of the auction catalogue is automatically sent each month to members of our Card Collectors Club
(membership details on page ii)

HOW TO USE THE CATALOGUE

This catalogue is published in five sections. Section 1 covers the cigarette card issues of British tobacco manufacturers for the home market with overseas series. Section 2 deals with cards issued by foreign tobacco manufacturers. Section 3 covers reprinted series of cigarette and trade cards. Section 4 covers trade card manufacturers excluding Liebig card issues, which are covered in Section 5.

In Sections 1 to 4 manufacturers are featured in alphabetical order and the issues of each firm are also catalogued alphabetically. Section 1 is also divided into appropriate sub-divisions i.e. 'British Issues', 'Overseas Issues', 'Silks' etc. Section 2 also has sub-divisions such as 'With Brand Name', 'Without Brand Name', 'Silks' etc. In Section 4 all British and overseas issues are listed in one alphabetical listing except Brooke Bond overseas issues, where these are listed under the company's code to show chronological sequence of issue. In Section 5 the issues of Liebig are listed in the same order as shown in the Italian-language *Fada Liebig Catalogue* officially recognised by the Liebig Company. However, for ease of use for collectors using Sanguinetti references, these are also listed. Where a brand name but no maker's name is shown on the card, reference should be made to the Index of Brands. Anonymous British tobacco issues are listed at the end of Section 1 and Anonymous trade card issues are listed at the end of Section 4.

Information is given in the columns from left to right as follows:

Size
(a) Sections 1 and 3 (British manufacturers and reprint series): the code letter refers to the size of the card as indicated in the chart on page xxvii. A number 1 or 2 after the letter means that the card is slightly larger or smaller than shown.

(b) Sections 2 and 4 (Foreign Tobacco manufacturers and Trade Card issuers): the absence of a code letter indicates that the series is of standard size. A code letter 'L' defines the card as being large (about 80 × 62 mm). Other codes are 'K' = smaller than standard, 'M' = between standard and large, and 'EL' = larger than large, and in the Trade Card section 'LT' = large trade (size 89 x 64mm).

Printing
(a) Sections 1 and 3 (British manufacturers and reprint series): the code indicates the printing on the front of the card. 'BW' = black-and-white; 'C' = coloured; 'CP' = colour photograph; 'P' = photograph; 'U' = uncoloured (monochrome).

(b) Sections 2 and 4 (Foreign Tobacco manufacturers and Trade Card issuers): the letter 'P' is used to show that a series consists of photographs.

Number in Set
This figure gives the number of cards in the series. A question mark alongside shows the exact number is unknown.

Title and Date
Where a series title is printed on the cards, this is used in the catalogue. For cards which do not exhibit a series title, an 'adopted' title is shown (indicated by an asterisk in the British section). Where a firm issued more than one series with the same title, these are distinguished by the addition of 'Set 1', 'Set 2', etc, or a code letter. The date of issue, where known, is shown in brackets, otherwise an approximate date is shown prefixed by 'C'.

Reference Code
(a) British issues: un-numbered series, series issued by more than one manufacturer, and different series of the same title issued by a single firm, have been given an 'H', 'OG', 'GP' or 'W' number cross-referencing them to provide further information.
  'H' refers to *The British Tobacco Issues Handbook* 2003 Edition.
  'OG' refers to *The Ogdens Reference Book* 2005 Edition.
  'GP' refers to *The Godfrey Phillips & Associated Companies Reference Book* 2008 Edition.
  'W' refers to *The W.D. & H.O. Wills Reference Book* 2011 Edition.

(b) Foreign issues: References H and W as above. 'RB.118' or 'RB.21' followed by a number refers to the Tobacco War reference book or the British American Tobacco reference book respectively. 'WI' or 'RB.23'and 'WII' refer to World Tobacco Index Part I and Part II respectively. (Details of these publications will be found on page xvii.)

(c) Trade Card issues: reference codes in this section all relate to Cartophilic Reference Book No. 126 – The British Trade Card Handbook.

Code Letters Used After the Set Title
In Some Early series a code word has been created. This is to help identify the various manufactures that printed the same set, i.e. Actresses, Beauties, Boer War Celebrities etc. For example: Beauties 'PAC' was issued by **P**ritchard & Burton, **A**dkin and **C**ope. Some series may not include all manufactures within the coded word, therefore for full listing please use the appropriate reference number in the catalogue with their respective reference books. For Example: Beauties 'PAC' – see H.2 in the *British Tobacco Issues Handbook*.

The Definition of Multi-Backed & Vari-Backed
Where each number in the set can be collected in each advertisement back these are listed in the catalogue.
Multi-Backed: If only certain cards can be collected within a set with the same advertisement these are referred to as multi-backed. For instance in Wills Sports of All Nations numbers 1 to 9 can be collected with a Three Castles or Traveller back but not a complete set in these advertisement backs.
Vari-Backed: The term vari-backed means you can only collect one advertisement back of each card for instance numbers 1 to 9 of a set would only be available in one advertisement back and number 10 to 19 in another back and so on.

Prices and Condition of Cards
Value Added Tax where applicable is included in all prices shown, at the current rate.
Sections 1 and 2: the last two columns show the London Cigarette Card Company's selling prices for odd cards, complete sets or albums in very good condition; post-1955 issues are priced as Finest Collectable Condition to Mint.
Section 3: gives a price for complete sets in mint condition.
Section 4: gives prices for odd cards, complete sets and albums the majority of which are in finest collectable to mint condition except for pre-1955 cards which are very good condition.
Section 5: the prices quoted are for cards in good average condition (the more recent series will be of a higher quality).
Please note: For sections 1 and 2, when ordering 'end' numbers, for example Nos. 1 and 50 of a set of fifty, the following applies. For series catalogued up to £1 per card, end cards are charged at treble price. For series catalogued from £1 to £3 per card, end cards are charged at £3 per card. For series catalogued at more than £3 per card there is no additional charge for end numbers.
Please note: Album prices quoted in this catalogue are for empty albums without corner mounts or cards stuck in. When albums have corner mounts or cards stuck in they would in most cases be at a much reduced price.

HOW TO ORDER

Availability
We have one of the world's largest stocks of cards and the chances are that we will be able to supply your requirements for most series at the prices shown in the catalogue. However, certain odd cards, particularly from rarer series, may not be available in top condition and in such cases it is helpful if you indicate whether cards of a lower standard are acceptable at reduced prices. If a complete set is not in stock, we may be able to offer a part set, with one or two cards missing, at the appropriate fraction of full catalogue price. In some instances we can supply sets on request in fair to good condition at half catalogue price. If in doubt, please e-mail or write for a quotation, enclosing a stamped, self-addressed envelope.

End Numbers (Sections 1 and 2)
When ordering 'end' numbers, for example Nos. 1 and 50 of a set of fifty, please note that the following applies. For series catalogued up to £1 per card, end cards are charged at treble price. For series catalogued from £1 to £3 per card, end cards are charged at £3 per card. And for series catalogued at more than £3 per card there is no additional charge for end numbers.

Postage and Handling Fee
Orders are sent post free to UK addresses, but **please note** orders under £25.00 will incur a handling fee of £2.00. Overseas postage is charged at cost and there is no handling fee.

Ordering and Payment
Please ensure that your name and full address are clearly shown. State the maker's name and the set title required (with 'first series', 'second series', date of issue, etc. as appropriate). For odds, please list each individual number wanted. Make your crossed cheque or postal order payable to London Cigarette Card

Company Limited and enclose with order. Notes and coins should be registered. Overseas payments can only be accepted by Sterling cheque drawn on a British bank or by credit/debit card. We accept Mastercard, Visa credit/debit cards, Visa Delta, Electron, JCB, American Express. Quote the 16 card number on the front your expiry date and the card security code (which is the last three numbers in the signature strip for American Express it is the four numbers on the front); also now accepting Paypal. Please allow 14 days for delivery. Send your order to:

London Cigarette Card Co. Ltd, Sutton Road, Somerton, Somerset TA11 6QP, England

Please note (subject to change): Orders sent to addresses outside the United Kingdom will have the current UK tax deducted off card and album prices.

24-Hour Telephone Order Line (01458-273452)

For the convenience of customers, an answering machine is in operation to receive orders when the office is closed. Just leave your order, name and address with credit or debit card number, expiry date, and the card security code, which is the last three numbers on the signature strip (and, for Maestro cards, the issue number, if one is shown, or start date). Your order will be dealt with as soon as possible. Please note that we can only deal with general enquiries in office hours. Telephone number: **01458-273452** (international ++44 1458-273452).

Fax Machine (01458-273515)

Our fax machine is on 24 hours a day to receive orders. Just place your order stating your name, address, credit or debit card number, expiry date and the card security code, which is the last three numbers on the signature strip (and, for Maestro cards, the issue number, if one is shown, or start date). The fax number is **01458-273515** (international ++44 1458-273515).

Website – www.londoncigcard.co.uk

Over 9,000 series are listed on our website, each one with a sample illustration. Orders can be placed direct via our website.

E-Mail – cards@londoncigcard.co.uk

Remember that your cards will look their best when displayed in one of our albums: please see pages xviii to xix.

Guarantee

In the unlikely event that you, the collector, are not satisfied with the cards supplied, we guarantee to replace them or refund your money, provided the goods are returned within 14 days of receipt. This guarantee does not affect your statutory rights.

OPENING TIMES AT SUTTON ROAD

Collectors are welcome to call at our offices in Sutton Road, Somerton, where you will be able to purchase your requirements direct from the massive stocks held at the premises – sets, albums, books and accessories plus odd cards. We do not have items on display, but we are more than happy to get things out for you to view.

**Our offices are open to customers Monday to Friday
9.30am-12.30pm and 2.30pm-4.30pm**

SALE OF COLLECTIONS

Our buying department welcomes offers of collections (whether large or small), particularly early and rare cards, but please note that we are mainly interested in cards in very good condition. If in doubt please get in touch before sending anything.

NEW ISSUES

We have new issues (mostly trade card issues) added to stock each month, and if you wish to keep up to date why not join our LCCC Card Collectors Club, which includes the *Card Collectors News* monthly magazine, in which the magazine editior, gives a description of all new additions and includes sample illustrations of most of them. A sample of the back and front of each new issues can also be found on our website each month **(www.londoncigcard.co.uk).**

A GUIDE TO CONDITION

When valuing cards condition is of paramount importance regardless of age.
Please use the guide below to help you assess condition.

MINT — Uncirculated cards direct from the packet or the printer.

FCC — Finest Collectable Condition – perfect cards which have been handled with extreme care.

VERY GOOD — Clean undamaged cards with sharp corners, edges showing slight signs of handling.

GOOD — One or two minor blemishes may be visible, corners may be marked or slightly rounded, no creases.

FAIR — Showing signs of considerable handling, such as rounded corners, slight damage along edges or a minor crack.

POOR — Prominently cracked or with some surface damage, often with rounded corners and a degree of soiling.

VERY POOR — Cards with serious cracks, a piece missing, soiled, damaged, badly worn or cut.

Cards in sub-standard condition will have their value considerably reduced from prices stated in this catalogue.

Please see index page viii under 'Prices and Condition of Cards' for more information.

See Examples below of Very Good Condition, Fair Condition and Very Poor Condition, and also see the section headed 'Availability' under 'How to Order'.

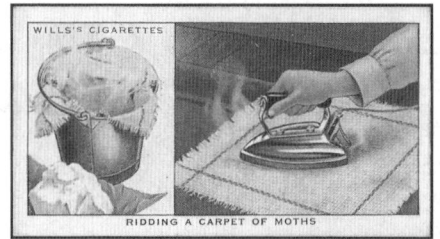

Very Good Condition 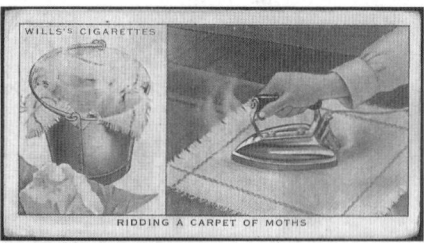   Fair Condition

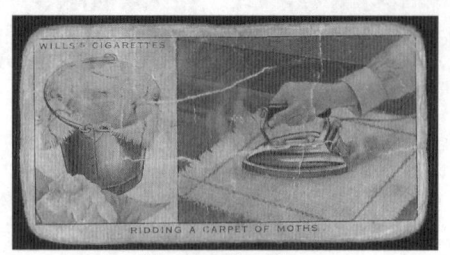

Very Poor Condition

INDEX OF BRANDS

The following is a list of the cases so far known where cards appear without the name of issuer, but inscribed with a brand name or other indication which is the collector's only clue to the identity of the issuer. (1), (2) or (4) indicates in which section of the catalogue the manufacturer appears

GENERAL NOTE: Where no brand name appears on the cards in a lot of cases they were issued by British American Tobacco Co., Imperial Tobacco Company of Canada Ltd or United Tobacco Companies (South) Ltd which all appear in Section 2. As regards to plain back cards, in a lot of cases they will be listed under Anonymous Series (in Section 1) or British American Tobacco Co. section 'F' Plain Backs (in Section 2).

Admiral Cigarettes — see National Cigarette & Tobacco Co. (2)
Adventure – see D.C. Thomson (4)
Airmail Cigarettes — see Hill (1)
Albert Cigarettes — see British American Tobacco Co. (2)
All Arms Cigarettes — see Ray & Co. (1)
Amblin – see Bassetts (4)
Ambrosia – see J. Pascall (4)
S. Anargyros — see American Tobacco Co. (2)
BDV Cigarettes — see Godfrey Phillips (1)
THE B.I. Co. — see Burnstein Isaacs (1)
Bandai – see Cereal Partners (4)
BEA — see Benson & Hedges (1)
Bell Boy – see Anglo-American Gum (4)
Bandmaster Cigarettes — see Cohen, Weenen & Drapkin (1)
Between the Acts — see American Tobacco Co. (2)
Big Gun Cigarettes — see Sandorides (1)
Big Run Cigarettes — see American Tobacco Co. (2)
Black & White Whisky – see R. & J. Hill (1)
Black Cat Cigarettes — see Carreras (1)
Black Spot Cigarettes — see Scerri (2)
Blush of Day Cigarettes — see Robinson & Barnsdale (1)
Borneo Queen Cigars — see B. Morris (1)
Bouquet Cigarettes — see I.T.C. of Canada (2)
British Consuls — see Macdonald (2)
Broadleaf Cigarettes — see American Tobacco Co. (2)
Broadway Novelties — see Teofani (1)
The Buffs — see Drapkin (1)
Bulldog Cigars — see Elliot (1)
Buster – see IPC Magazines (4)
Buster and Jet – see IPC Magazines (4)
Bouquet Cigarettes – see I.T.C. of Canada (2)
C.T. Ltd — see United States Tobacco Co. (2)
Cairo Monopol Cigarettes — see American Tobacco Co. (2)
Cake Walk Cigarettes — see Pezaro (1)
Canary and Cage Bird Life – see Feathered World (4)

Caps The Lot — see Bewlay (1)
Carolina Brights — see American Tobacco Co. (2)
Casket and Critic Cigarettes — see Pattreiouex (1)
Castella Cigars — see W.D. & H.O. Wills (1)
Chairman Cigarettes — see R.J. Lea (1)
The Challenge Flat Brilliantes — see Gloag (1)
Champion – see Amalgamated Press (4)
Chantler & Co., Bury — see Lea (1)
Citamora Cigarettes — see Gloag (1)
Club Member Cigarettes — see Pattreiouex (1)
Club Mixture Tobaccos — see Continental Cigarette Factory (1)
Colin Campbell Cigars — see Robinson & Barnsdale (1)
Copain Cigarettes — see British American Tobacco Co. (2)
Coronet Cigarettes — see Sniders & Abrahams (2)
Crowfoot Cigarettes — see Hill (1)
Cycle Cigarettes — see American Tobacco Co. (2)
Cymax Cigarettes — see Coudens (1)

Derby Little Cigars — see American Tobacco Co. (2)
Discworld – see Cunning Articifer (4)
Doctor Tea – see Harden Brothers (4)
Domino Cigarettes — see British American Tobacco Co. (2)
Double Ace Cigarettes — see Ardath (1)

'Eagle, Cork' — see Lambkin (1)
Eat More Fish – see Fish Marketing Board (4)
Egyptienne Luxury — see American Tobacco Co. (2)
Eldona Cigars — see Drapkin & Millhoff (1)
Emblem Cigarettes — see American Tobacco Co. (2)
Erinmore Cigarettes — see Murray (1)
Explorer Cigars — see Drapkin & Millhoff (1)

The Favourite Magnums Cigarettes — see Teofani (1)

xxiii

Fez Cigarettes — see American Tobacco Co. (2)
The Flor de Dindigul Cigar — see Bewlay (1)
Forecasta — see B. Morris (1)
Four Square — see Dobie (1)
Fresher Cigarettes — see Challis (1)
Fume Emblem — see Westminster Tobacco Co. (2)
Futera – see Futura or Trade Cards (Europe) Ltd (4)
GP — see Godfrey Phillips (1)
Gainsborough Cigarettes — see Cohen Weenen (1)
General Favourite Onyx — see E. Robinson (1)
Gibson Girl Virginia, Madrali Turkish and Hungarian — see Golds (1)
Gold Coin Tobacco — see Buchner (2)
Gold Flake Cigarettes — see Hill (1)
Gold Flake, Honeydew and Navy Cut Medium Cigarettes — see Hill (1)
The Greys Cigarettes — see United Kingdom Tobacco Co. (1)
Guards Cigarettes — see Carreras (1)

Hard-a-Port – see Moore & Calvi (2)
Hassan Cigarettes — see American Tobacco Co. (2)
Havelock Cigarettes — see Wills (Overseas) (2)
Hawser, Epaulet and Honey Flake Cigarettes — see Wholesale Tobacco Supply Syndicate (1)
Heart's Delight Cigarettes — see Pritchard & Burton (1)
Helmar Cigarettes — see American Tobacco Co. (2)
Herbert Tareyton Cigarettes — see American Tobacco Co. (2)
Hindu Cigarettes — see American Tobacco Co. (2)
Hoffman House Magnums — see American Tobacco Co. (2)
Honest Long Cut — see Duke or American Tobacco Co. (2)
Hornet – see D.C. Thomson (4)
Hotspur – see D.C. Thomson (4)
Hustler – see J. Knight (4)
Hustler Little Cigars — see American Tobacco Co. (2)

Imperial Tobacco Limited (Castella) — see W.D. & H.O. Wills (1)
Islander, Fags, Specials, Cubs — see Bucktrout (2)

Jack Rose Little Cigars — see American Tobacco Co. (2)
Jag – see Fleetway Publications (4)
Jersey Lily Cigarettes — see Wm. Bradford (1)
Jibco – see J.I. Batten (4)
Cigarette Job — see Societe Job (1)
Jolly Sailor – see Cunning Articifer (4)
Jubbly – see Freshmaid Ltd (4)
Junior Member Cigarettes — see Pattreiouex (1)
Just Suits Cut Plug — see American Tobacco Co. (2)

K The B – see Local Authorities Caterers' Association (4)
Kensitas Cigarettes — see J. Wix (1)
King Edward VII Cigarettes — see Cabana (1)
King Features – see Authentix (4)
Kopec Cigarettes — see American Tobacco Co. (2)

L. & Y. Tobacco Co. — see Lancs. and Yorks. Tobacco Manufacturing Co. (1)
V.G. Langford — see Vincent Graphics (4)
Laughing Cow — see Bel UK (4)
Lego — see Sainsburys (4)
Lennox Cigarettes — see American Tobacco Co. (2)
Leon de Cuba Cigars — see Eldons (1)
Le Roy Cigars — see Miller (2)
Levant Favourites — see B. Morris (1)
Life Ray Cigarettes — see Ray & Co. (1)
Lifeboat Cigarettes — see United Tobacco Co. (2)
Lion – see Fleetway Publications & IPC Magazines (4)
Lion and Thunder – see IPC Magazines (4)
Lord Nielson – see Mister Softee Ltd (4)
Lotus Cigarettes — see United Tobacco Co. (2)
Lucana Cigarettes — see Sandorides (1)
Lucky Strike Cigarettes — see American Tobacco Co. (2)
Luxury Cigarettes — see American Tobacco Co. (2)
Magpie Cigarettes — see Schuh (2)
Manikin Cigars — see Freeman (1)
Mascot Cigarettes — see British American Tobacco Co. (2)
Matossian's Cigarettes — see Henley & Watkins (1)
Max Cigarettes — see A. & M. Wix (1)
Mayblossom Cigarettes — see Lambert & Butler (1)
Mecca Cigarettes — see American Tobacco Co. (2)
Mickey Mouse Weekly – see Caley (4)
Mills — see Amalgamated (1)
Milo Cigarettes — see Sniders & Abrahams (2)
Miners Extra Smoking Tobacco — see American Tobacco Co. (2)

Mogul Cigarettes — see American Tobacco Co. (2)
Murad Cigarettes — see American Tobacco Co. (2)

Natural American Spirit — see Santa Fe Natural Tob. Co. (2)
Nebo Cigarettes — see American Tobacco Co. (2)
New Hotspur – see D.C. Thomson (4)
New Orleans Tobacco — see J. & T. Hodge (1)

OK Cigarettes — see African Tobacco Mfrs. (2)
Obak Cigarettes — see American Tobacco Co. (2)
Officers Mess Cigarettes — see African Tobacco Mfrs. (2)
Old Gold Cigarettes — see American Tobacco Co. (2)
Old Judge Cigarettes — see Goodwin (2)
Old Mills Cigarettes — see American Tobacco Co. (2)
1a, 27 & 33 Leigh Road, Eastleigh — see Ingram's (1)
One of the Finest — see Buchner (2)
Oracle Cigarettes — see Tetley (1)
Orient Line Steamships — see Singleton & Cole (1)
Our Little Beauties — see Allen & Ginter (2)
Oxford Cigarettes — see American Tobacco Co. (2)

Pan Handle — see American Tobacco Co. (2)
Park Drive — see Gallaher (1)
Perfection Cigarettes — see American Tobacco Co. (2)
Peter Pan Cigarettes — see Sniders & Abrahams (2)
Pibroch Virginia — see Fryer (1)
Piccadilly — see Carreras (1)
Picadilly Little Cigars — see American Tobacco Co. (2)
Pick-Me-Up Cigarettes — see Drapkin & Millhoff (1)
Piedmont Cigarettes — see American Tobacco Co. (2)
Pinhead Cigarettes — see British American Tobacco Co. (2)
Pinnace — see Godfrey Phillips (1)
Pioneer Cigarettes — see Richmond Cavendish (1)
Pirate Cigarettes — see Wills (Overseas) (2)
PO Box 5744, Johannesburg — see A. & M. Wix (1)
Polo Bear Cigarettes — see American Tobacco Co. (2)
Polo Mild Cigarettes — see Murray (1)

Private Seal Tobacco — see Godfrey Phillips (1)
Pure Virginia Cigarettes — see Thomson & Porteous (1)
Puritan Little Cigars — see American Tobacco Co. (2)
Purple Mountain Cigarettes — see Wills (Overseas) (2)

QV Cigars — see Webster (1)

RS — see Robert Sinclair (1)
Recruit Little Cigars — see American Tobacco Co. (2)
Red Cross — see Lorillard or American Tobacco Co. (2)
Reina Regenta Cigars — see B. Morris (1)
De Reszke Cigarettes — see Millhoff and Godfrey Phillips (1)
Richmond Gem Cigarettes — see Allen & Ginter (2)
Richmond Straight Cut Cigarettes — see American Tobacco Co. (2)
Ringers Cigarettes — see Edwards, Ringer & Bigg (1)
Rock City Tobacco — see Carreras (1)
Roseland Cigarettes — see Glass (1)
Rover – see D.C. Thomson (4)
Roxy – see Fleetway Publications (4)
Royal Bengal Little Cigars — see American Tobacco Co. (2)

St Dunstan's — see Carreras (1)
St Leger Little Cigars — see American Tobacco Co. (2)
Scorcher – see IPC Magazines (4)
Scorcher and Score – see IPC Magazines (4)
Scoreboard – see Merlin (4)
Scots Cigarettes — see African Tobacco Mfrs (2)
Scrap Iron Scrap — see American Tobacco Co. (2)
Senator Cigarettes — see Scerri (2)
Senior Service Cigarettes — see Pattreiouex (1)
Sensation Cut Plug — see Lorillard (2)
Shredded Wheat/Shreddies – see Nabisco Foods or Cereal Partners (4)
Sifta Sam – see Palmer Mann & Co. (4)
Silko Cigarettes — see American Tobacco Co. (2)
Skipper – see D.C. Thomson (4)
Smash – see IPC Magazines (4)
Sovereign Cigarettes — see American Tobacco Co. (2)
Spinet Cigarettes or The Spinet House — see Hill (1)

Sportsman — see Carreras (Overseas) (2)
The Spotlight Tobaccos — see Hill (1)
Springbok Cigarettes — see United Tobacco Co. (2)
Standard Cigarettes — see Carreras or Sniders & Abrahams (2)
Star of the World Cigarettes — see JLS (1)
State Express Cigarettes — see Ardath (1)
Stimorol Gum – see Scanlen (4)
Strato Gum — see Myers & Metreveli (4)
Sub Rosa Cigarros — see American Tobacco Co. (2)
Subbuteo – see P.A. Adolf (4)
Sultan Cigarettes — see American Tobacco Co. (2)
Summit — see International Tobacco Co. (1)
Sunlight Soap – see Lever Brothers (4)
Sunripe Cigarettes — see Hill (1)
Sunspot Cigarettes — see Theman (1)
Superkings – see J. Player & Sons (1)
Sweet Alva Cigarettes — see Drapkin (1)
Sweet Caporal — see Kinney or American Tobacco Co. or ITC Canada (2)
Sweet Lavender — see Kimball (2)

TSS — see Tobacco Supply Syndicate (1)
Tatley's Cigarettes — see Walker's Tobacco Co. (1)
Teal Cigarettes — see British American Tobacco Co. (2)
Three Bells Cigarettes — see J. & F. Bell (1)
Tiger – see Fleetway Publications & IPC Magazines (4)
Tiger Cigarettes — see British American Tobacco Co. (2)
Tipsy Loo Cigarettes — see H.C. Lloyd (1)
Tokio Cigarettes — see American Tobacco Co. (2)
Tolstoy Cigarettes — see American Tobacco Co. (2)
Tom Thumb — see Players (1)
Top Flight – see T.P.K. Hannah (4)

Topsy Cigarettes — see Richards & Ward (1)
Trawler, Critic and King Lud Cigarettes — see Pattreiouex (1)
Trebor Bassett – see Bassett (4)
Trebor/Topps – see Topps (UK) (4)
Triumph – see Amalgamated Press (4)
Trumps Long Cut — see Moore & Calvi (2)
Turf Cigarettes — see Carreras (1)
Turkey Red Cigarettes — see American Tobacco Co. (2)
Turkish Trophy Cigarettes — see American Tobacco Co. (2)
Twelfth Night Cigarettes — see American Tobacco Co. (2)

U.S. Marine — see American Tobacco Co. (2)
Uzit Cigarettes — see American Tobacco Co. (2)

Val Footer Gum – see Klene (4)
Valiant – see IPC Magazines (4)
Vanguard – see D.C. Thomson (4)
Vanity Fair Cigarettes — see Kimball (2)
Vice Regal Cigarettes — see Wills (Overseas) (2)
Victor – see D.C. Thomson (4)
Victory Bubble Gum – see Trebor Ltd (4)
Virginia Brights Cigarettes — see Allen & Ginter (2)

WTC — see Walker's Tobacco Co. (1)
Wagon Wheels – see Burtons (4)
Wings Cigarettes — see Brown & Williamson (2)
Wizard – see D.C. Thomson (4)
Woman's Realm – see Brooke Bond Tea (4)
Wow Gum – see Myers & Metreveli (4)

Yankee Doodle and Pilot – see British Australasian Tobacco Co (2)
Yankee Doodle and Champion – see British Australasian Tobacco Co (2)

Zip Bubble Gum – see Trebor Ltd (4)

INDEX OF INSCRIPTIONS found on British issues of cards

'The Cigarettes with which these Picture Cards are issued are manufactured in England and are Guaranteed Pure' — see Hill
'England expects that Every Man will do his duty — By Purchasing these Cigarettes you are supporting British labour' — issuers unknown, see Anonymous
'Issued with these Famous Cigarettes' — see Teofani
'Issued with these Fine Cigarettes' — see Teofani
'Issued with these High Grade Cigarettes' — see Teofani
'Issued with these Well-known Cigarettes' — see Teofani
'Issued with these World Famous Cigarettes' — see Teofani
'Presented with these well-known choice cigarettes' — see Teofani
'Smoke these cigarettes always' — see Teofani
'These Cigarettes are Guaranteed Best British Manufacture' — see Hill.

CARD SIZES (applies to Sections 1 & 3). Please note: (card size) *album leaf size*

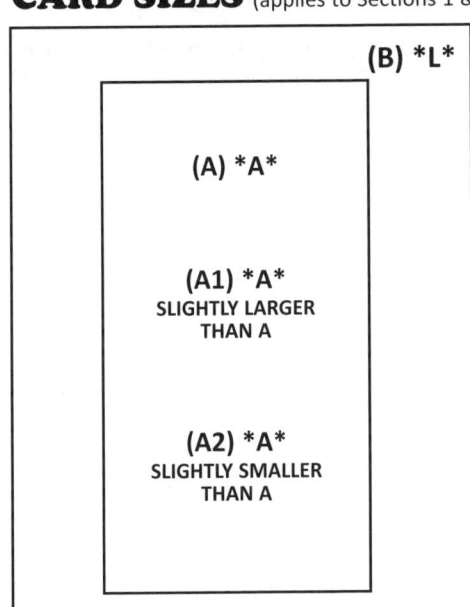

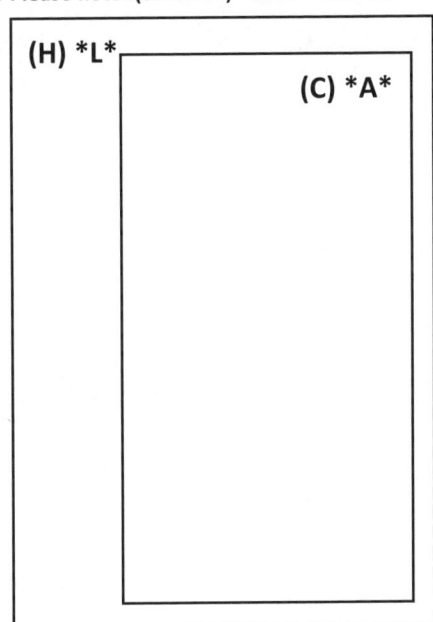

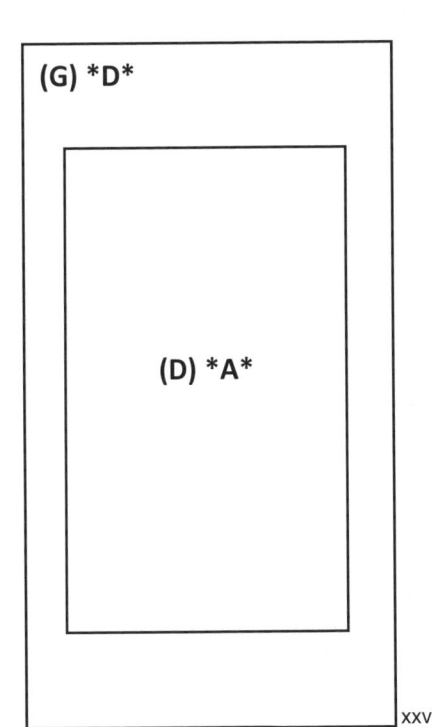

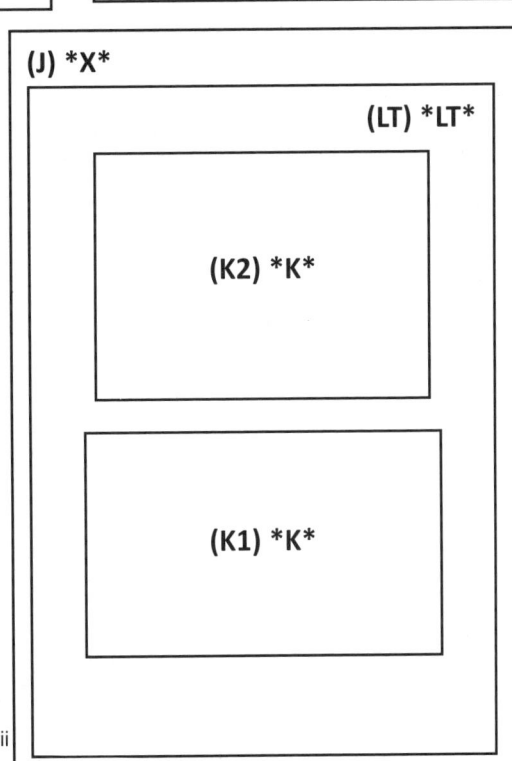

(B) *L*

(A) *A*

(A1) *A*
SLIGHTLY LARGER
THAN A

(A2) *A*
SLIGHTLY SMALLER
THAN A

(H) *L*

(C) *A*

(G) *D*

(D) *A*

(J) *X*

(LT) *LT*

(K2) *K*

(K1) *K*

xxvii

STARTER COLLECTIONS

Ideal for the new collector. We have put together two bargain offers of sets of cards in mint condition saving well over 50% off catalogue prices.

* BARGAIN 10 OFFER *
10 sets for £35.00

Ten Sets selected from Section 1, British Tobacco Issuers, issued between 1936 and 1979. These are all original sets and not reprints, in top condition, catalogued at £93.00, for a bargain price of £35.00. Sets included in this bargain offer are:

CARRERAS 50 British Birds 1976
CARRERAS 50 Military Uniforms 1976
CARRERAS 50 Sport Fish 1978
CARRERAS 50 Vintage Cars 1976
CARROLL 25 Birds 1940
MURRAY 40 Bathing Belles 1939
MURRAY 50 The Story of Ships 1940
PLAYERS 24 The Golden Age of Motoring 1975
TEOFANI 12 London Views 1936
WILLS 25 Pond and Aquarium 1st Series 1950

Ask for 'Bargain 10' when ordering

* BARGAIN 20 OFFER *
20 sets for £30.00

We have selected 20 sets from Section 4, Trade Card Issuers, issued between the 1950s and 1990s, chosen for their wide variety of interesting subjects. All in top condition. Each set is individually catalogued at £3.00 or more, so this collection represents a huge saving on normal prices.

Ask for 'Bargain 20' when ordering

* SAMPLER COLLECTIONS *

We have taken one card from each of 450 post-1945 card series and assembled them into nine different groups of 50. These are particularly useful for the collector who wishes to see sample cards before buying complete sets, and are also a great foundation for a type card collection. Each group of 50 costs only £7.00.

Order one collection from groups A, B, C, D, E, F, G, H or I for £7.00 each or all nine groups for £63.00

SECTION 1
BRITISH TOBACCO ISSUERS

Prices are for **Very Good** condition; post-1955 issues are priced as **Finest Collectable Condition** to **Mint**

Size	Print-ing	Number in set	BRITISH TOBACCO ISSUERS	Handbook reference	Price per card	Complete set
			ABDULLA & CO. LTD, London			
			20 page reference book (combined with Adkin & Anstie) — £4.50			
A	BW	50	Beauties of To-Day (1938)	GP.20	£4.50	—
	?	4	Bridge Rule Cards (various sizes) (c1935)	GP.311	£16.00	—
A	C	25	British Butterflies (1935)	GP.42	£1.60	£40.00
A	P	52	Cinema Stars Set 1 (c1933)	GP.306	£4.00	—
A2	U	30	Cinema Stars Set 2 (c1933)	GP.51	£6.00	—
A2	U	30	Cinema Stars Set 3 (c1933)	GP.52	£4.00	—
A2	U	32	Cinema Stars Set 4 (c1933)	GP.53	£3.00	£95.00
A2	C	32	Cinema Stars Set 5 (c1933)	GP.54	£3.00	£95.00
A2	C	30	Cinema Stars Set 6 (c1933)	GP.55	£3.60	—
—	C	2	Commanders of the Allies (127 x 67mm) (c1915)	GP.313	£140.00	—
D	C	25	Feathered Friends (1935)	GP.70	£1.60	£40.00
A2	C	50	Film Favourites (1934)	GP.71	£4.00	—
A	C	50	Film Stars (1934)	GP.73	£8.00	—
—	C	24	*Film Stars — No. ... of a series of 24 cards (128 x 89mm) (1934)	GP.74	£10.00	—
—	C	24	*Film Stars — No. ... of a series of cards Nd 25-48 (128 x 89mm) (1935)	GP.75	£10.00	—
—	C	24	*Film Stars — No. ... of a series of cards, vivid backgrounds (128 x 89mm) (1936)	GP.76	£10.00	—
—	BW	3	Great War Gift Packings Cards (78 x 48mm) (1916)	GP.314	£100.00	—
A	U	18	Message Cards (letters of the alphabet) (c1936):	GP.315		
			A Back in blue		£16.00	—
			B Back in green		£16.00	—
			C Back in orange		£16.00	—
K2	U	18	Message Cards (letters of the alphabet) (c1936):	GP.315		
			A Last line 'may be used'		£16.00	—
			B Last line 'of Jokers may be...'		£16.00	—
A	C	25	Old Favourites (1936) (Flowers)	GP.106	90p	£22.50
—	C	1	Princess Mary Gift Card (67 x 49mm) (1914)	GP.317	—	£30.00
A	C	40	Screen Stars (1939):	GP.307		
			A Without 'Issued by the Successors to...' back		£1.25	£50.00
			B With 'Issued by the Successors to ...' back		£2.50	—
A2	C	50	Stage and Cinema Beauties (1935)	GP.135	£4.00	—
A	—	30	Stars of the Stage and Screen (c1934):	GP.308		
			A Black and White		£4.00	—
			B Coloured		£6.00	—
			ADCOCK & SON, Norwich			
A1	U	12	Ancient Norwich (1928)		—	£140.00
			11 different, minus No. 6 (Mousehold Heath)		£3.00	£33.00

Size	Printing	Number in set		Handbook reference	Price per card	Complete set

ADKIN & SONS, London
20 page reference book (combined with Abdulla & Anstie) — £4.50

Size	Printing	Number in set	Description	Handbook ref	Price per card	Complete set
D	BW	25	*Actresses — French. Nd. 126-150 (c1898)	H.1	£260.00	—
A	C	15	*Beauties 'PAC', multi-backed (c1898)	H.2	£350.00	—
A	C	50	Butterflies and Moths (1924)	H.80	£3.00	£150.00
		12	Character Sketches:	H.3		
A2	C		A Black printing on back (1901)		£9.00	£110.00
A2	C		B Green printing on back (1902)		£9.00	£110.00
—	C		C Premium issue (145 x 103mm) (1901)		£110.00	—
—	C	4	*Games — by Tom Browne, postcard back (135 x 85mm) (c1900)	H.4	£325.00	—
		12	A Living Picture (c1901):	H.5		
A2	C		A 'Adkin & Sons' at top back			
			(i) crimson		£9.00	£110.00
			(ii) scarlet		£9.00	£110.00
A2	C		B 'These cards are ...' at top back		£9.00	£110.00
—	C		C Premium issue (145 x 103mm)		£110.00	—
A	BW	25	Notabilities (1915)		£5.60	£140.00
A1	C	12	Pretty Girl Series (Actresses) (c1897)	H.7	£75.00	—
A2	C	12	*Pretty Girl Series 'RASH' (1897):	H.8		
			A Calendar back		£75.00	—
			B Advertisements back		£50.00	—
			C Figure and verse back		£45.00	—
D	C	12	A Royal Favourite (1900)	H.9	£15.00	£180.00
A	BW		Soldiers of the Queen (1899-1900):	H.10		
			A Series of 50:			
		24	(a) Nos. 1-24 '... and exclusively with'		£30.00	—
		50	(b) Nos. 1-50 and variety '... and issued with ...'		£6.50	£325.00
		59	B Series of 60, plus No. 61 (Nos 28, 33 not issued)		£6.50	—
A	BW	31	*Soldiers of the Queen and Portraits (1901)	H.11	£7.50	—
A	C	30	Sporting Cups and Trophies (1914)		£20.00	—
A	BW	25	War Trophies (1917)		£5.60	£140.00
A	C	50	Wild Animals of the World (1922)	H.77	£2.00	£100.00

AIKMAN'S, Montrose

Size	Printing	Number in set	Description	Handbook ref	Price per card	Complete set
D	C	30	*Army Pictures, Cartoons, etc. (c1916)	H.12	£160.00	—

H.J. AINSWORTH, Harrogate

Size	Printing	Number in set	Description	Handbook ref	Price per card	Complete set
D	C	30	*Army Pictures, Cartoons, etc (1916)	H.12	£160.00	—

ALBERGE & BROMET, London

Size	Printing	Number in set	Description	Handbook ref	Price per card	Complete set
A	C		*Boer War and General Interest (c1900):	H.13		
		? 11	A 'Bridal Bouquet' and 'El Benecio' wording on green leaf design back		£160.00	—
		? 2	B 'La Optima' and 'Federation' wording on green leaf design back		£220.00	—
		? 8	C 'Bridal Bouquet' and 'El Benecio' wording on brown leaf design back		£160.00	—
		? 1	D 'La Optima' and 'Federation' wording on brown leaf design back		£260.00	—
DI	C	40	*Naval and Military Phrases (c1904):	H.14		
			A 'Bridal Bouquet' and 'El Benecio'		£130.00	—
			B 'La Optima' and 'Federation'		£130.00	—
DI	C	30	*Proverbs (c1903)	H.15	£130.00	—

Size	Print-ing	Number in set	BRITISH TOBACCO ISSUERS	Handbook reference	Price per card	Complete set
			PHILLIP ALLMAN & CO. LTD, London			
A	C	50	Coronation Series (1953)		£1.20	£60.00
			Pin-up Girls (1953):	H.851		
A1	C		A First 12 subjects:			
		12	Ai Unnumbered, 'For men only'		£5.50	£65.00
		12	Aii Numbered, 'Ask for Allman always'		£5.50	£65.00
		12	Aiii Unnumbered, 'Ask for Allman always'		£5.50	£65.00
A1	C	12	B Second 12 subjects		£6.00	—
A1	C	24	C Inscribed '1st series of 24'		£10.00	—
—	C	24	D Large size (75 x 68mm)		£6.00	—

AMALGAMATED TOBACCO CORPORATION LTD ('Mills' Cigarettes)

Size	Printing	Number in set	Title	Handbook reference	Price per card	Complete set
—	C	25	Famous British Ships 'Series No. 1' (75 x 48mm) (1952)		20p	£4.50
—	C	25	Famous British Ships 'Series No. 2' (75 x 48mm) (1952)		20p	£5.00
—	C	50	History of Aviation (75 x 48mm) (1952):			
			A Nos. 1 to 16, 18 to 25 and 27		£2.20	—
			B Nos. 17, 26 and 28 to 50		30p	£7.50
A	C	25	Kings of England (1954)		£2.00	£50.00
A	C	25	Propelled Weapons (1953)		20p	£5.00

OVERSEAS ISSUES

Size	Printing	Number in set	Title	Handbook reference	Price per card	Complete set
A	C	25	Aircraft of the World (1958)	H.852	£1.00	£25.00
A	C	25	Animals of the Countryside (1957)	H.853	32p	£8.00
A	C	25	Aquarium Fish (1960)	H.854	32p	£8.00
A	C	25	Army Badges — Past and Present (1960)		£1.20	£30.00
A	C	25	British Coins and Costumes (1958)	H.855	50p	£12.50
A	C	25	British Locomotives (1961)	H.856	80p	£20.00
A	C	25	British Uniforms of the 19th Century (1957)	H.857	£1.00	£25.00
A	C	25	Butterflies and Moths (1957)	H.858	50p	£12.50
A	C	25	Cacti (1960)	H.859	50p	£12.50
A	C	25	Castles of Britain (1961)	H.860	£1.20	£30.00
A	C	25	Coins of the World (1960)	H.861	24p	£6.00
A	C	25	Communications (1961)	H.862	£1.00	£25.00
A	C	25	Dogs (1958)	H.863	90p	£22.50
A	C	25	Evolution of the Royal Navy (1957)	H.864	90p	£22.50
A	C	25	Football Clubs and Badges (1961)	H.865	£1.60	—
A	C	25	Freshwater Fish (1958)	H.866	32p	£8.00
A	C	25	Guerriers à Travers les Ages (French text) (1961)	H.882	80p	£20.00
A	C	25	Historical Buildings (1959)	H.867	£1.00	£25.00
A	C	25	Histoire de l'Aviation, 1st series (French text) (1961)	H.868	36p	£9.00
A	C	25	Histoire de l'Aviation, 2nd series (French text) (1962)	H.868	£1.00	£25.00
A	C	25	Holiday Resorts (1957)	H.869	20p	£5.00
A	C	25	Interesting Hobbies (1959)	H.870	60p	£15.00
A	C	25	Into Space (1958)	H.871	40p	£10.00
A	C	25	Les Autos Modernes (French text) (1961)	H.875	60p	£15.00
A	C	25	Medals of the World (1959)	H.872	40p	£10.00
A	C	25	Merchant Ships of the World (1961)	H.873	£1.00	£25.00
A	C	25	Merveilles Modernes (French text) (1961)	H.876	50p	£12.50
A	C	25	Miniature Cars and Scooters (1959)	H.874	£1.60	—
A	C	25	Nature Series (1958)	H.877	20p	£4.50
A	C	25	Naval Battles (1958)	H.878	70p	£17.50
A	C	25	Ports of the World (1957)	H.869	20p	£5.00
A	C	25	Ships of the Royal Navy (1961)	H.879	80p	£20.00
A	C	25	Sports and Games (1958)	H.880	£1.20	£30.00
A	C	25	Tropical Birds (1959)	H.881	£1.20	—
A	C	25	Weapons of Defence (1961)	H.883	£1.20	£30.00

Size	Print-ing	Number in set	BRITISH TOBACCO ISSUERS	Handbook reference	Price per card	Complete set
			AMALGAMATED TOBACCO CORPORATION LTD (Overseas Issues continued)			
A	C	25	Wild Animals (1958)	H.884	20p	£5.00
A	C	25	The Wild West (1960)	H.885	£1.20	£30.00
A	C	25	World Locomotives (1959)	H.886	£1.20	£30.00
			THE ANGLO AMERICAN CIGARETTE MAKING CO. LTD, London			
A	C	20	Russo-Japanese War Series (1906)	H.100	£525.00	—
			THE ANGLO CIGARETTE MANUFACTURING CO., London			
A	C	36	Tariff Reform Series (1909)	H.16	£40.00	—

E. & W. ANSTIE, Devizes
20 page reference book (combined with Abdulla & Adkin) — £4.50

Size	Print-ing	Number in set		Handbook reference	Price per card	Complete set
A2	C	25	Aesop's Fables (1934)	H.518	£3.20	£80.00
A	C	16	*British Empire Series (1904)	H.17	£15.00	£240.00
A	BW	40	Nature Notes (1939)		£10.00	—
A	U	50	People of Africa (1926)		£4.50	£225.00
A	U	50	People of Asia (1926)		£4.50	£225.00
A	U	50	People of Europe (1925)		£4.50	£225.00
A2	BW	40	Places of Interest (1939):			
			A Varnished front		90p	£36.00
			B Unvarnished front		£3.00	—
—	C	8	Puzzles (26 x 70mm) (1902)	H.18	£240.00	—
A	C	50	*Racing Series (1922):			
			1-25 — Racing Colours		£5.00	—
			26-50 — Horses, Jockeys, Race-courses, etc		£7.00	—
—	C	5	Royal Mail (70 x 50mm) (1899)	H.19	£350.00	—
A	C	50	Scout Series (1923)		£4.00	£200.00
A2	C		Sectional Series:			
		10	Clifton Suspension Bridge (1938)	H.519-1	£3.20	£32.00
		10	Stonehenge (1936)	H.519-2	£3.20	£32.00
		10	The Victory (1936)	H.519-3	£4.50	—
		20	Wells Cathedral (1935)	H.519-4	£3.00	£60.00
		20	Wiltshire Downs (1935)	H.519-6	£3.00	£60.00
		10	Windsor Castle (1937)	H.519-5	£3.20	£32.00
A2	BW	40	Wessex (1938)		£1.75	£70.00
A	U	50	The World's Wonders (1924)		£2.00	£100.00

SILKS. Anonymous unbacked woven silks. Width sizes only are quoted as the silks were prepared in ribbon form and length sizes are thus arbitrary.

—	C	10	*Flags, large (width 95mm) (c1915)	H.495-1	£12.00	—
—	C	36	*Flags, small (width 42mm) (c1915)	H.495-1	£3.00	—
—	C	85	*Regimental Badges (width 32mm) (c1915)	H.495-3	From £2.00	—
—	C		*Royal Standard and Portraits (c1915):	H.495-2		
		1	Royal Standard (width 95mm)		—	£16.00
		1	King George V:			
			(a) Large (width 71 mm), black frame		—	£70.00
			(b) Large (width 71mm), gold frame		—	£60.00
			(c) Small (width 32mm)		—	£70.00
		1	Queen Mary:			
			(a) Large (width 71 mm)		—	£60.00
			(b) Small (width 32mm)		—	£75.00
		1	Lord French (width 71mm)		—	£85.00
		1	Lord Kitchener (width 71mm)		—	£20.00

Size	Print-ing	Number in set	BRITISH TOBACCO ISSUERS	Handbook reference	Price per card	Complete set
			H. ARCHER & CO., London			
C	C		*Actresses — Selection from 'FROGA A and B' (c1900):	H.20		
		? 20	A 'Golden Returns' back		£75.00	—
		? 13	B 'M.F.H.' back		£75.00	—
C			*Beauties — 'CHOAB' (c1900):	H.21		
	U	50	A 'Bound to Win' front		£32.00	—
	C	? 4	B 'Golden Returns' back		£80.00	—
	C	? 5	C 'M.F.H.' back		£80.00	—
C	C	20	*Prince of Wales Series (c1912)	H.22	£32.00	—
			ARDATH TOBACCO CO. LTD, London			
			28 page reference book — £4.50			
A1	C	50	*Animals at the Zoo (export) (c1924):	H.520		
			A Back with descriptive text		£2.50	—
			B Back without description, 'Double Ace' issue		£25.00	—
A	C	96	Ardath Modern School Atlas (export) (c1935)		£1.60	—
A2	P	54	Beautiful English Women (1928) (export)		£4.50	—
A	C	25	Big Game Hunting (export) (c1930):			
			A Back in blue		£4.50	—
			B Back in black		£15.00	—
—	U	30	Boucher Series (77 x 62mm) (c1915)		£3.30	—
A	U	50	Britain's Defenders (1936)		£1.00	£50.00
	U	50	British Born Film Stars (export) (1934):			
A2			A Small size, back white semi-glossy		£2.00	—
A2			B Small size, back cream matt		£2.00	—
—			C Medium size (67 x 53mm)		£3.00	—
	U		Camera Studies (c1939):	H.644		
—		36	A Small size (70 x 44mm)		£1.50	£55.00
—		45	B Large size (79 x 57mm)		£1.40	£65.00
—	C	25	Champion Dogs (95 x 67mm) (1934)		£2.40	£55.00
A	C	50	Cricket, Tennis and Golf Celebrities (1935):			
			A Home issue, grey back		£1.80	£90.00
			B Export issue, brownish-grey back, text revised		£2.60	£130.00
—	U	25	Dog Studies (95 x 68mm) (1938)		£5.00	£125.00
A	C	25	Eastern Proverbs (export) (c1930)	H.521	£2.00	£50.00
A	C	48	Empire Flying-Boat (sectional) (1938)		£1.80	£90.00
			Album		—	£40.00
A	C	50	Empire Personalities (1937)		90p	£45.00
A	C	50	Famous Film Stars (1934)		£1.20	£60.00
A	C	50	Famous Footballers (1934)		£1.80	£90.00
A	C	25	Famous Scots (1935)		£1.60	£40.00
—	C	25	Fighting and Civil Aircraft (96 x 68mm) (1936)		£3.20	£80.00
A	C	50	Figures of Speech (1936)		£1.50	£75.00
A	C	50	Film, Stage and Radio Stars (1935)		£1.20	£60.00
—	C	25	Film, Stage and Radio Stars (96 x 68mm) (1935) ...		£1.40	£35.00
—	BW	? 22	Film Stars (postcard size) (c1935)	H.645	£30.00	—
—	U	40	Franz Hals Series, Dutch back (70 x 60mm) (c1916):			
			A Without overprint		£15.00	—
			B With overprint		£25.00	—
—	C	50	From Screen and Stage (96 x 65mm) (1936)		£2.00	£100.00
—	U	30	Gainsborough Series (77 x 62mm) (c1915)	H.714	£3.30	—
—	C	30	Girls of All Nations (78 x 66mm) (c1916)		£20.00	—
A1	U	50	Great War Series (c1916)		£8.50	—
A1	U	50	Great War Series 'B' (c1916)		£8.50	—
A1	U	50	Great War Series 'C' (c1916)		£8.50	—

Size	Printing	Number in set	BRITISH TOBACCO ISSUERS	Handbook reference	Price per card	Complete set
			ARDATH TOBACCO CO. LTD, London (continued)			
A2	P	35	Hand Shadows (c1930) (export)		£36.00	—
—	BW	25	Historic Grand Slams (folders) (101 x 70mm) (c1935)		£36.00	—
			Hollandsche Oude Meesters, Dutch back (70 x 60mm) (c1916):			
—	U	25	A First 25 subjects		£16.00	—
—	U	25	B Second 25 subjects		£16.00	—
J2	U	48	How to Recognise the Service Ranks (holed for binding) (c1939)	H.642	£7.00	—
			Industrial Propaganda Cards (c1942):	H.914		
—	C	2	A Black background Size 96 x 66mm		£8.00	£16.00
—	C	4	B Coloured background Size 89 x 61mm		£8.00	£32.00
—	C	11	C White background Size 89 x 65mm		£4.00	£45.00
J2	U	? 171	Information Slips (holed for binding) (1938)	H.643	£3.50	—
A	U	50	Life in the Services (1938):			
			A Home issue, adhesive		90p	£45.00
			B Export issue, non-adhesive		£1.50	£75.00
			Ministry of Information Cards (1941-3):			
J2	U	5	A Calendar — 'It all depends on me'		£4.00	£20.00
J2	U	1	B Greeting Card — 'It all depends on me'		—	£10.00
—	C	24	C 'It all depends on me' (80 x 63mm)	H.913	£1.25	£30.00
—	C	1	D Union Jack Folder (60 x 46mm)		—	£10.00
—	C	1	E 'On the Cotton Front' (80 x 63mm)	H.913	—	£3.50
—	BW	1	F 'On the Kitchen Front' (70 x 55mm)	H.913	—	£3.50
A	C	50	National Fitness (1938):			
			A Home issue, adhesive		70p	£35.00
			B Export issue, non-adhesive		£1.00	£50.00
A2	CP	50	New Zealand Views (1928) (export)		£3.00	—
A	U	50	Our Empire (export) (c1937)	H.522	£1.50	£75.00
A	C		Proverbs (c1936):			
		25	A Home issue Nos 1-25		£1.60	£40.00
		25	B Export issue Nos 26-50		£3.60	—
—	U	30	Raphael Series (77 x 62mm) (c1915)		£3.30	—
—	U		Rembrandt Series (1914):			
		30	A Large size (77 x 62 mm), English back		£4.00	—
		40	B Large size (77 x 62mm), Dutch back		£16.00	—
		30	C Extra-large size (101 x 62mm)		£6.00	—
—	U	30	Rubens Series (77 x 61 mm) (c1915):			
			A English 'State Express' back		£3.00	—
			B English 'Winfred' back		£18.00	—
			C Dutch back		£18.00	—
			D New Zealand 'State Express' back		£18.00	—
	U	100	Scenes from Big Films (export) (1935):			
A			A Small size, white back		£2.50	—
A			B Small size, cream back		£4.00	—
—			C Medium Size (67 x 52mm)		£4.50	—
—	BW	20	Ships of The Royal Navy (Double Ace Cigarettes Slides) (c1955)	H.887	£20.00	—
A	C	50	Silver Jubilee (1935)		80p	£40.00
			Album		—	£35.00
A	C	50	Speed — Land, Sea and Air (1935):			
			A Home issue, 'Issued with State Express'		£1.60	£80.00
			B Export issue, Ardath name at base		£2.50	—
—	C	25	Speed — Land, Sea and Air (95 x 68mm) (1938) ...		£2.00	£50.00
A	C	50	Sports Champions (1935):			
			A Home issue, 'State Express' at base		£1.20	£60.00
			B Export issue, 'Ardath' at base		£2.40	£120.00

Size	Print-ing	Number in set	BRITISH TOBACCO ISSUERS	Handbook reference	Price per card	Complete set
			ARDATH TOBACCO CO. LTD, London (continued)			
A	C	50	Stamps — Rare and Interesting (1939)		£1.60	£80.00
A	C	50	Swimming, Diving and Life-Saving (1937) (export)	H.523	£2.50	—
A	C	50	Tennis (1937) (export)	H.524	£2.50	—
A	C	48	Trooping the Colour (sectional) (1939)		£2.00	£100.00
			Album		—	£35.00
—	C	12	Types of Smokers (c1910):	H.716		
			A Size 77 x 64mm		£85.00	—
			B Size 102 x 64mm		£85.00	—
—	U	30	Valasquez Series (c1915):			
			A Large size (77 x 62mm)		£3.50	—
			B Extra-large size (101 x 62mm)		£6.00	—
A	C	50	Who is This? (1936) (Film Stars)		£1.80	£90.00
J2	U	? 5	Wonderful Handicraft (c1935)	H.717	£45.00	—
—	BW	24	World Views (No. 13 not issued) (95 x 68mm) (1937)		60p	£15.00
A	C	50	Your Birthday Tells Your Fortune (1937)		80p	£40.00

PHOTOGRAPHIC ISSUES

H	P		Photocards — Numbered Series (1936)*:			
		110	'A' — Football Clubs of North West Counties		£2.00	£220.00
		110	'B' — Football Clubs of North East Counties		£2.40	—
		110	'C' — Football Clubs of Yorkshire		£2.00	£220.00
		165	'D' — Football Clubs of Scotland		£2.00	£330.00
		110	'E' — Football Clubs of Midlands		£2.00	£220.00
		110	'F' — Football Clubs of London and Southern Counties		£2.00	£220.00
		99	'Z' — General Interest (Sports):			
			Nos. 111-165		80p	£45.00
			Nos. 166-209 (Cricket etc)		80p	£35.00
		11	'A.s' (1), 'C.s' (2-3), 'E.s' (4-10), 'F.s' (11) — Football Clubs (supplementary)		£5.50	£60.00
		?	Selected cards from the above 8 series:			
			A With red overprint		£7.00	—
			B Thin paper attached to back covering front of card advertising Ardath 'Kings'		£7.00	—
	P		Photocards — 'A Continuous Series of Topical Interest' (1937):	H.525		
		22	Group A — Racehorses and Sports		£1.50	£33.00
		22	Group B — Coronation and Sports		—	£40.00
			21 Different (minus Walter Neusel)		£1.00	£21.00
		22	Group C — Lancashire Personalities		—	£45.00
			21 Different (minus Gracie Fields)		£1.25	£25.00
		22	Group D — Sports and Miscellaneous		£1.50	£33.00
		22	Group E — Film Stars and Sports		£1.50	£33.00
		22	Group F — Film Stars and Sportsmen		£1.50	£33.00
		66	'G.S.' — Miscellaneous subjects (export)		£3.00	—
H	P		Photocards — 'A Continuous Series of General interest', with Album offer (1938):	H.526		
		11	Group G — Australian Cricketers		£26.00	—
		22	Group H — Film, Radio and Sporting Stars		£1.50	£33.00
		22	Group I — Film Stars and Miscellaneous		£1.50	£33.00
	P		Photocards — 'A Continuous Series of General Interest', without Album offer — uncoloured (1938):	H.527		
H		22	Group J — Film Stars and General Interest		£1.35	£30.00
H		22	Group K — Film, Radio and Sporting Stars:			
			1 With 'Kings' Clause		£1.25	£27.50
			2 Without 'Kings' Clause (export)		£1.60	—
H		44	Group L — Film Stars and Miscellaneous		90p	£40.00

Size	Printing	Number in set	BRITISH TOBACCO ISSUERS	Handbook reference	Price per card	Complete set

ARDATH TOBACCO CO. LTD, London (Photographic Issues continued)

Size	Printing	Number in set	Description	Handbook ref	Price per card	Complete set
		45	Group M — Film Stars and Miscellaneous:			
C			1 Small size		£1.10	£50.00
—			2 Large size (80 x 69 mm), with 'Kings' Clause ...		£1.10	£50.00
—			3 Large size (80 x 69mm), without 'Kings' Clause		£1.10	£50.00
	P	45	Group N — Film, Stage and Radio Stars:			
C			1 Small size		£1.10	£50.00
—			2 Large size (80 x 69mm)		£1.10	£50.00
H	CP		Photocards — 'A Continuous Series of General Interest', without Album offer — Hand coloured (export) (1938):	H.528		
		22	Group 1 — Views of the World		£1.00	£22.00
		22	Group 2 — Views of the World		£1.00	£22.00
		22	Group 3 — Views of the World		80p	£17.50
			Real Photographs:			
	P	45	Group O — 'A Continuous Series of General Interest' — Films, Stage and Radio Stars (1939) ...	H.529	£1.00	£45.00
C	P	45	'1st Series of 45' — Film and Stage Stars (1939) ...		£1.10	—
C	P	54	'2nd Series of 54' — Film and Stage Stars (1939) ...		£1.10	—
J2	P	18	'First Series' — Views (1937)		£2.50	—
J2	P	18	'Second Series' — Film and Stage Stars (1937)		£2.50	—
J2	P	18	'Third Series' — Views (1937)		£2.50	—
J2	P	18	'Fourth Series' — Film and Stage Stars (1937)		£2.50	—
J2	P	18	'Fifth Series' — Views (1938)		£2.50	—
J2	P	18	'Sixth Series' — Film and Stage Stars (1938)		£2.50	—
H	P	44	'Series One' 'G.P.1' — Film Stars (export) (1939) ...		£1.00	£45.00
H	P	44	'Series Two' 'G.P.2' — Film Stars (export) (1939) ...		45p	£20.00
H	P	44	'Series Three' 'G.P.3' — Film Stars (export) (1939)		£3.00	—
H	CP	44	'Series Three' 'C.V.3' — Views (export) (1939)		£1.00	£45.00
H	CP	44	'Series Four' 'C.V.4' — Views (export) (1939)		45p	£20.00
J2	P	36	'Series Seven' — Film and Stage Stars (1938)		£1.00	—
J2	P	54	'Series Eight' — Film and Stage Stars (1938)		80p	£45.00
	P	54	'Series Nine' — Film and Stage Stars (1938):			
H			A Medium size		80p	£45.00
J2			B Extra-large size		80p	£45.00
	P	54	'Series Ten' — Film and Stage Stars (1939):			
—			A Large size (80 x 69mm)		80p	£45.00
J2			B Extra-large size		£1.00	£55.00
	P	54	'Series Eleven' — Film and Stage Stars (1939):			
—			A Large size (80 x 69mm)		80p	£45.00
J2			B Extra-large size		£1.20	—
	P	54	'Series Twelve' — Film and Stage Stars (80 x 69mm) (1939)		80p	£45.00
—	P	54	'Series Thirteen' — Film and Stage Stars (80 x 69mm) (1939)		80p	£45.00
	P	36	'Of Famous Landmarks' (1939):			
—			A Large size (80 x 69 mm), titled 'Real Photographs'		£3.50	—
J2			B Extra-large size, titled 'Real Photographs of Famous Landmarks'		£1.70	£60.00
	P	36	'Of Modern Aircraft' (1939):			
—			A Large size (80 x 69mm)		£4.50	—
J2			B Extra-large size		£3.50	—

SILKS

Size	Printing	Number in set	Description	Handbook ref	Price per card	Complete set
—	C	1	Calendar for 1937 (silk) (138 x 102mm)	H.508	—	£150.00
—	C	1	Calender for 1938 (silk) (160 x 102mm)	H.508	—	£150.00

Size	Printing	Number in set	BRITISH TOBACCO ISSUERS	Handbook reference	Price per card	Complete set
			THE ASSOCIATED TOBACCO MANUFACTURERS LTD			
C2	C	25	Cinema Stars (export) (c1926):	H.530		
			A 'Issued with Bond Street Turkish Cigarettes' …		£38.00	—
			B 'Issued with John Bull Virginia Cigarettes' …		£38.00	—
			C 'Issued with Club Virginia Cigarettes' …… …		£38.00	—
			D 'Issued with Heliopolis Turkish Cigarettes' …		£38.00	—
			E 'Issued with Sports Turkish Cigarettes' ……		£38.00	—
			A. ATKINSON, London			
D	C	30	*Army Pictures, Cartoons, etc (c1916) …… …… …	H.12	£160.00	—
			AVISS BROTHERS LTD, London			
D1	C	40	*Naval and Military Phrases (c1904) …… …… …	H.14	£240.00	—
			J.A. BAILEY, Swansea			
D1	C	40	*Naval and Military Phrases (c1904) …… …… …	H.14	£300.00	—
			A. BAKER & CO. LTD, London			
A	BW	20	*Actresses — 'BLARM'(c1900):	H.23		
			A Long design back (64mm) …… …… ……		£38.00	—
			B Design altered and shortened (58mm) …… ……		£38.00	—
A	BW	10	*Actresses — 'HAGGA' (c1900) …… …… ……	H.24	£38.00	£380.00
	BW		*Actresses 'Baker's 3-sizes' (c1900):	H.25		
A		25	A Small cards … …… …… …… …… ……		£40.00	—
—		25	B Extra large cards (67 x 127mm) …… ……		£250.00	—
—	BW	25	Actresses 'Baker's 3 sizes' (56 x 75mm) (c1900) …	H.25	£60.00	—
C	BW	? 41	*Baker's Tobacconists' Shops (c1901):	H.26		
			A 'Try our 3½d Tobaccos' back … …… ……		£300.00	—
			B 'Cigar, Cigarette, etc. Manufacturers' back …		£180.00	—
C	C	25	Beauties of All Nations (c1900):	H.27		
			A 'Albert Baker & Co. (1898) …' back …… ……		£24.00	£600.00
			B 'A. Baker & Co. …' back …… …… ……		£20.00	£500.00
C	BW	16	*British Royal Family (c1902) …… …… ……	H.28	£50.00	—
A1	BW	20	Cricketers Series (1901) …… …… …… ……	H.29	£380.00	—
A1	C	25	*Star Girls (c1898) …… …… …… …… ……	H.30	£250.00	—
			BAYLEY & HOLDSWORTH			
A	C	26	*International Signalling Code (c1910) …… …… …		£200.00	
			E.C. BEESTON, Wales			
D	C	30	*Army Pictures, Cartoons etc (c1916) …… …… …	H.12	£160.00	—
			BELFAST SHIPS STORES CO. LTD, Belfast			
	C	1	*Dickens' Characters (79 x 40mm) (c1895) …… …	H.31	£1100.00	—
			J. & F. BELL LTD, Glasgow			
A	BW	10	*Actresses — 'HAGGA' ('Three Bells Cigarettes') (c1900) … …… …… …… …… …… ……	H.24	£80.00	—
C	C	25	*Beauties — Tobacco Leaf Back (c1898):	H.32		
			A 'Bell's Scotia Cigarettes' back …… …… …		£120.00	—
			B 'Three Bells Cigarettes' back …… …… ……		£120.00	—
A	C	25	Colonial Series (c1901) …… …… …… ……		£50.00	—
A	BW	30	*Footballers (1901) …… …… …… …… ……		£100.00	—
A	C	25	Scottish Clan Series No. 1 (c1903) …… …… …	H.33	£20.00	£500.00

Size	Print-ing	Number in set	BRITISH TOBACCO ISSUERS	Handbook reference	Price per card	Complete set

J. & F. BELL LTD, Glasgow (continued)

OVERSEAS ISSUES

| A | C | 60 | Rigsvaabner (Arms of Countries) (c1925) .... | | £30.00 | — |
| A | C | 60 | Women of Nations (1924) .... | | £30.00 | — |

B. BELLWOOD, BRADFORD

| C | C | 18 | Motor Cycle Series (c1912) .... | H.469 | £160.00 | — |

RICHARD BENSON LTD, Bristol

	U	24	Old Bristol Series:			
—			A Original issue (80 x 70mm) (c1925):			
			i 23 different, minus No. 8		£3.00	£70.00
			ii Number 8		—	£30.00
—			B Re-issue (88 x 78-83mm) (1946)		£2.00	£50.00

BENSON & HEDGES, London

A2	C	1	Advertisement Card, The Original Shop (1973)		—	£2.00
B	C	10	B.E.A. Aircraft (1958)	H.888	£11.00	—
—	C	50	Friendly Games (75 x 45mm) (c1970)		£1.50	—

OVERSEAS ISSUES (CANADA)

| A2 | C | 48 | Ancient and Modern Fire Fighting Equipment (1947) | | £6.50 | — |
| — | BW | 12 | Oxford University Series (90 x 50mm) (c1912) ...... | | £40.00 | — |

FELIX BERLYN, Manchester

	C	25	Golfing Series (Humorous) (c1910):			
A1			A Small size		£550.00	—
—			B Post card size (139 x 87mm)		£650.00	—

BERRY, London

| D | U | 20 | London Views (c1905) .... | H.34 | £275.00 | — |

BEWLAY & CO. LTD, London

D1	U		Bewlay's War Series (Generals, etc) (c1915):	H.477		
		12	A 'Caps the Lot' Smoking Mixture		£15.00	—
		6	B Try Bewlay's 'Caps the Lot' Mixture		£15.00	—
		6	C Try Bewlay's 'Modern Man' Mixture		£15.00	—
D1	U	25	Bewlay's War Series (Photogravure War Pictures) (c1915):	H.35		
			A 'Modern Man' Mixtures etc		£15.00	—
			B 'Modern Man' Cigarettes		£15.00	—
			C 'Two Great Favourites'		£15.00	—
A	C	6	*Comic Advertisement Cards (1909)	H.36	£200.00	—
—	C	6	*Comic Advertisement Cards (140 x 88mm) (c1909)	H.36	£100.00	—

W.O. BIGG & CO., Bristol

A	C	37	*Flags of All Nations (c1904):	H.37		
			A 'Statue of Liberty' back, 4d oz		£11.00	—
			B As A:— (a) altered to 4½d by hand		£11.00	—
			(b) 4½d red seal over 4d		£11.00	—
			C Panel design 'New York' Mixture		£11.00	—
A	C	50	Life on Board a Man of War (c1905)	H.38	£13.00	£650.00

JAS. BIGGS & SONS, London

| C | C | 26 | *Actresses — 'FROGA A' 'Two Roses' in white (c1900) .... | H.20 | £50.00 | — |

10

Size	Printing	Number in set	BRITISH TOBACCO ISSUERS	Handbook reference	Price per card	Complete set
			JAS. BIGGS & SONS, London (continued)			
C	C	52	*Actresses — 'FROGA A & B' 'Two Roses' in black (c1900)	H.20	£55.00	—
A	C		*Beauties, with frameline — 'CHOAB' (c1900):	H.21		
		25	A Blue typeset back		£85.00	—
		50	B Overprinted in black on Bradford cards		£80.00	—
C	C		*Beauties, no framelines — selection 'BOCCA' (c1900):	H.39		
		25	A Blue back		£80.00	—
		25	B Black back		£80.00	—
C	C	30	*Colonial Troops (c1901)	H.40	£50.00	—
C	C	30	*Flags and Flags with Soldiers (c1903)	H.41	£40.00	—
A1	C	25	*Star Girls (c1900)	H.30	£300.00	—
			J.S. BILLINGHAM, Northampton			
D	C	30	*Army Pictures, Cartoons etc (c1916)	H.12	£160.00	—
			R. BINNS, Halifax			
A	U	? 17	*Halifax Footballers (c1924)	H.531	£200.00	—
			BLANKS CIGARETTES			
A	C	50	Keystrokes in Break-Building (c1935)	H.647	£500.00	—
			THE BOCNAL TOBACCO CO., London			
A2	U	25	Luminous Silhouettes of Beauty and Charm (1938)		£3.00	£75.00
A2	C	25	Proverbs Up-to-Date (1938)		£2.40	£60.00
			ALEXANDER BOGUSLAVSKY LTD, London			
—	C	12	Big Events on the Turf (133 x 70mm) (1924)		£50.00	—
A2	C	25	Conan Doyle Characters (1923):			
			A Back in black, white board		£7.00	—
			B Back in grey, cream board		£7.00	—
			C Back in green		£7.00	—
A2	C	25	Mythological Gods and Goddesses (1924)		£3.00	£75.00
A	C	25	*Sports Records, Nd. 1-25 (1925)		£2.80	£70.00
A	C	25	Sports Records, Nd. 26-50 (1925)		£2.80	£70.00
	C	25	Winners on the Turf (1925):			
A			A Small size, captions 'sans serif'		£5.00	£125.00
A			B Small size, captions with 'serif'		£6.00	—
B			C Large size		£7.00	—
			R. & E. BOYD LTD, London			
—	U	25	Places of Interest (c1938):			
			A Size 67 x 35mm		£75.00	—
			B Size 71 x 55mm		£75.00	—
—	U	25	Wild Birds at Home (75 x 57mm) (c1938)	H.626	£75.00	—
			WM. BRADFORD, Liverpool			
C	C	50	*Beauties 'CHOAB' (c1900)	H.21	£50.00	—
D	U	? 7	Beauties — 'Jersey Lily Cigarettes' (c1900)	H.488	£650.00	—
D2	BW	20	Boer War Cartoons (c1901)	H.42	£170.00	—
			T. BRANKSTON & CO., London			
C	C	30	*Colonial Troops (c1901):	H.40		
			A Golf Club Mixture		£38.00	
			B Red Virginia		£38.00	
			C Sweet as the Rose		£38.00	

Size	Print-ing	Number in set	BRITISH TOBACCO ISSUERS	Handbook reference	Price per card	Complete set
			T. BRANKSTON & CO., London (continued)			
A2	C	12	*Pretty Girl Series 'RASH' (c1900)	H.8	£400.00	—
			BRIGHAM & CO., Reading			
B	U	16	Down the Thames from Henley to Windsor (c1912)		£170.00	—
A	U	16	Reading Football Players (c1912)		£500.00	—
—	BW	3	Tobacco Growing in Hampshire (89 x 79mm) (1915)	H.470	£16.00	£50.00
			BRITANNIA ANONYMOUS SOCIETY			
—	C	? 32	*Beauties and Scenes (60 x 40mm) (c1914)	H.532	£80.00	
			BRITISH & COLONIAL TOBACCO CO., London			
A1	C	25	*Armies of the World (c1900)	H.43	£260.00	
			J.M. BROWN, Derby			
D	C	30	*Army Pictures, Cartoons etc (c1916)	H.12	£160.00	—
			ROBERT BRUCE LTD, Birmingham & Wolverhampton			
A	C	18	Motor Cycle Series (c1912)	H.469	£300.00	—
			JOHN BRUMFIT, London			
A	C	50	The Public Schools' Ties Series (Old Boys) (1925) ...		£4.00	£200.00
			G.A. BULLOUGH, Castleford			
D	C	30	*Army Pictures, Cartoons etc (c1916)	H.12	£160.00	—
			BURSTEIN, ISAACS & CO., London			
			(The BI-CO Company, B.I. & Co. Ltd)			
D	BW	25	Famous Prize-Fighters, Nd. 1-25 (1923):			
			A Front caption upper and lower case lettering		£8.00	—
			B Front caption small capital letters		£8.00	—
D	BW	25	Famous Prize-Fighters, Nd. 26-50 (1924):			
			A Front caption upper and lower case lettering		£8.00	—
			B Front caption small capital letters		£8.00	—
D	P	28	London View Series (1922)		£4.00	—
			BYRT WOOD & CO., Bristol			
A2	U	? 37	*Pretty Girl Series — 'BAGG' (c1900)	H.45	£150.00	
			CABANA CIGAR CO., London			
—	BW	2	Advertisement Card — 'Little Manturios'			
			(63 x 49mm) (1905)	H.719	£350.00	—
A2	C	40	*Home and Colonial Regiments (c1900)	H.69	£350.00	—
			PERCY E. CADLE & CO. LTD, Cardiff			
A1	BW	20	*Actresses 'BLARM' (c1900)	H.23	£40.00	
C	U	26	*Actresses — 'FROGA A' (c1900):	H.20		
			A Printed Back		£40.00	
			B Rubber — Stamped Back		£200.00	
C	C	26	*Actresses — 'FROGA B' (c1900)	H.20	£55.00	—
C	BW	12	*Boer War and Boxer Rebellion Sketches (c1901) ...	H.46	£80.00	—
C	BW	10	*Boer War Generals — 'FLAC' (c1901)	H.47	£90.00	—
A	BW	20	*Footballers (c1904)	H.48	£90.00	—

Size	Printing	Number in set	BRITISH TOBACCO ISSUERS	Handbook reference	Price per card	Complete set
			CARRERAS LTD, London			
A	CP	24	Actresses and Their Pets (1926) (export)	H.648	£5.00	—
	C	48	Alice in Wonderland (1930):			
A			A Small size, rounded corners		£1.70	£85.00
A			B Small size, square corners		£3.50	—
B2			C Large size		£1.80	£90.00
		1	D Instruction Booklet		—	£20.00
A	C	50	Amusing Tricks and How to Do Them (1937)		£1.60	£80.00
	C		Battle of Waterloo (1934):	H.533		
C		1	1 Paper insert, with instructions		—	£12.00
—		15	*2 Soldiers and Guns, large size (67 x 70mm)		£4.00	—
A			*3 Soldiers and Guns, small size:			
		10	Soldiers — Officers' Uniforms		£2.00	—
		12	Soldiers and Guns		£2.00	—
C1	C	50	Believe it or Not (1934)		80p	£40.00
A	C	50	Birds of the Countryside (1939)		£1.10	£55.00
D1	BW	200	The Black Cat Library (Booklets) (c1910)		£12.00	—
A	C	50	Britain's Defences (1938)		80p	£40.00
A	C	50	British Birds (1976)		20p	£5.00
			Album		—	£12.00
	C	25	British Costumes (1927):			
C2			A Small size		£1.40	£35.00
B2			B Large size		£1.40	£35.00
A	P	27	British Prime Ministers (1928) (export)		£2.00	£55.00
A1	C	1	Calendar for 1934		—	£30.00
A	C	50	Celebrities of British History (1935):			
			A Brown on cream back (two shades of ink)		90p	£45.00
			B Pale brown on bluish back		90p	£45.00
			Album		—	£35.00
A	C	25	Christie Comedy Girls (1928) (export)		£2.40	£60.00
A	U		Cricketers (1934):			
		30	A 'A Series of Cricketers'		£3.50	£105.00
		50	B 'A Series of 50 Cricketers':			
			1 Front in brown and white		£3.50	£175.00
			2 Front in black and white		£38.00	—
A	BW	50	Dogs and Friend (1936)		50p	£25.00
A	C	50	Do You Know? (1939)		35p	£17.50
A	C	50	Famous Airmen and Airwomen (1936)		£1.70	£85.00
	C		Famous Escapes (1926):			
A		25	A Small size		£1.60	£40.00
B2		25	B Large size		£1.40	£35.00
—		10	C Extra-large size (133 x 70mm)		£3.00	£30.00
A2	C	96	Famous Film Stars (1935)	H.534	£1.50	£145.00
A	C		Famous Footballers (1935):			
		48	A Set of 48		£1.70	£85.00
		24	B Nos. 25-48 redrawn		£2.00	£50.00
A	C	25	Famous Men (1927) (export)		£1.80	£45.00
B2	P	24	Famous Naval Men (1929) (export)		£2.20	£55.00
—	C	6	Famous Posters (folders) (65 x 41mm) (1923)	H.606	£26.00	—
B2	P	12	Famous Soldiers (1928) (export)		£6.00	£75.00
A	P	27	Famous Women (1929) (export)		£1.65	£45.00
A	C	25	Figures of Fiction (1924)		£2.20	£55.00
	P	54	Film and Stage Beauties (1939):			
A2			A Small size		50p	£27.00
—			B Medium size (70 x 60mm):			
			(a) Without full stop after 'Carreras Ltd'		80p	£42.00
			(b) With full stop after 'Carreras Ltd.'		90p	£50.00

Size	Print-ing	Number in set	BRITISH TOBACCO ISSUERS	Handbook reference	Price per card	Complete set
			CARRERAS LTD, London (continued)			
	P	36	Film and Stage Beauties:			
B1			A Large size (1939)		£1.00	£36.00
J2			B Extra-large size (1938)		£1.50	£55.00
A	C	50	Film Favourites (1938)		£1.50	£75.00
A	P	54	Film Stars — 'A Series of 54' (1937)		£1.00	£55.00
	P	54	Film Stars (1938):			
A			A Small size, 'Second Series of 54'		60p	£32.50
—			B Medium size (68 x 60mm), 'A Series of 54'		£1.10	£60.00
J2	P		Film Stars (export):			
		36	'A Series of 36' (c1935)		£3.00	—
		36	'Second Series of 36' (c1936)		£3.00	—
		36	'Third Series of 36' (c1937)		£3.00	—
		36	'Fourth Series of 36' (c1938)		£3.00	—
A2	C	50	Film Stars, by Florence Desmond (1936)		£1.00	£50.00
—		72	Film Stars, oval (70 x 30mm) (1934):			
	P		A Inscribed 'Real Photos'		£2.50	—
	U		B Without 'Real Photos'		£1.50	£110.00
			Album		—	£35.00
A	C	60	Flags of All Nations (unissued) (c1960)		50p	£30.00
—	C		*Flags of the Allies (shaped) (c1915):	H.49		
		1	Grouped Flags:'Black Cat' Cigarettes		£75.00	—
		5	Allies Flags: 'Black Cat' Cigarettes		£75.00	—
A	C	50	Flowers (1936)		50p	£25.00
A	C	50	Flowers All the Year Round (1977)		20p	£10.00
			Album		—	£15.00
A2	C	75	*Footballers (1934):			
			A 'Carreras Cigarettes' on front 27mm long		£2.25	£170.00
			B 'Carreras Cigarettes' on front 26mm long		£2.25	£170.00
	C	36	'Fortune Telling' (1926):			
A			A Small size:			
			1 Card inset		75p	£27.00
			2a Head inset, black framelines		75p	£27.00
			2b Head inset, brown framelines		£1.25	£45.00
B2			B Large size:			
			1 Card inset		75p	£27.00
			2 Head inset		75p	£27.00
		1	C Instruction Booklet:			
			1 Address 23 New North Street		—	£22.00
			2 Address 12 Bath Street		—	£14.00
	P		Glamour Girls of Stage and Films (1939):			
A2		54	A Small size		60p	£32.50
—		54	B Medium size (70 x 60mm)		65p	£35.00
—		36	C Large size (76 x 70mm)		£1.00	£36.00
J2		36	D Extra-large size		£1.25	£45.00
	C	50	'Gran-Pop' by Lawson Wood (1934):			
C1			A Small size		50p	£25.00
B			B Large size		40p	£20.00
	C	52	Greyhound Racing Game (1926):			
A			A Small size		30p	£15.00
B2			B Large size		30p	£15.00
		1	C Instruction Leaflet		—	£12.00
—	C		Guards Series (68 x 50mm):			
		4	A Military Mug Series (1971)		£1.50	—
		8	B Order Up the Guards (1970)		£1.50	—
		16	C Send for the Guards (1969)		£1.50	—
D1	BW	5	The Handy Black Cat English-French Dictionary (Booklets) (1915)		£25.00	—

Size	Printing	Number in set	BRITISH TOBACCO ISSUERS	Handbook reference	Price per card	Complete set
			CARRERAS LTD, London (continued)			
	C	48	Happy Family (1925):			
A1			A Small size		40p	£20.00
B2			B Large size		40p	£20.00
A	C	25	Highwaymen (1924)		£2.60	£65.00
A	C	50	History of Army Uniforms (1937)		£1.50	£75.00
A	C	50	History of Naval Uniforms (1937)		£1.00	£50.00
	C		Horses and Hounds (1926)			
A		25	A Small size		£2.20	£55.00
B2		20	B Large size		£2.25	£45.00
—		10	C Extra-large size (133 x 70mm)		£4.50	£45.00
	C	50	Kings and Queens of England (1935):			
A			A Small size		£1.80	£90.00
B2			B Large size		£2.50	£125.00
			Album (To suit either size of cards)		—	£35.00
A	C	50	Kings and Queens of England (1977)		40p	£20.00
			Album		—	£15.00
A	U	50	A 'Kodak' at the Zoo 'Series of Fifty' (1924)		£1.00	£50.00
A	U	50	A 'Kodak' at the Zoo '2nd Series' (1925)		£1.00	£50.00
A	P	27	Malayan Industries (1929) (export)		80p	£20.00
	P	24	Malayan Scenes (1928):			
A			A Small size		£3.00	—
—			B Medium size (70 x 60mm)		75p	£18.00
A	C	50	Military Uniforms (1976)		20p	£5.00
			Album		—	£12.00
—	C	7	Millionaire Competition Folders (68 x 30mm) (1971)		£2.25	—
—	C	53	*Miniature Playing Cards (44 x 32mm) (c1935)	H.535-1A	20p	£9.00
	C	50	The 'Nose' Game (1927):			
A			A Small size		50p	£25.00
B2			B Large size		50p	£25.00
		1	C Instruction Leaflet		—	£12.00
	C	50	Notable MPs (1929):			
A			A Small size		£1.30	£65.00
—			B Medium size (69 x 60mm)		60p	£30.00
A	P	25	Notable Ships — Past and Present (1929) (export)		£1.60	£40.00
	C		Old Staffordshire Figures (1926):			
A		24	A Small size		£1.40	£35.00
—		12	B Extra-large size (134 x 71mm)		£3.00	£36.00
B	C	24	Old Staffordshire Figures (different subjects) (1926)		£1.50	£36.00
	C	24	Orchids (1925):			
A			A Small size		£1.00	£25.00
B			B Large size		£1.00	£25.00
—			C Extra-large size (133 x 70mm)		£3.40	—
A	C		Our Navy (1937):			
		20	A Thick card, selected numbers		£1.20	£24.00
		50	B Thin card		£1.20	£60.00
C1	C	50	Palmistry (1933)		70p	£35.00
A	C	50	Palmistry (1980)		£1.00	—
			Album		—	£15.00
A	P	27	Paramount Stars (1929) (export)		£1.85	£50.00
A	C	25	Picture Puzzle Series (1923)	H.649	£1.60	£40.00
—	C	53	Playing Cards (68 x 42mm) (c1925)	H.535-1B	£1.20	—
	C		*Playing Cards and Dominoes (1929):	H.535-1C		
C		52	A Small size:			
			(a) Numbered		60p	—
			(b) Unnumbered		60p	—
—		26	B Large size (77 x 69mm):			
			(a) Numbered		£1.15	£30.00
			(b) Unnumbered		£1.15	£30.00

15

Size	Print-ing	Number in set	BRITISH TOBACCO ISSUERS	Handbook reference	Price per card	Complete set
			CARRERAS LTD, London (continued)			
A	C	48	Popular Footballers (1936):			
			A White back		£1.40	£70.00
			B Cream back		£1.40	£70.00
—	C		Popular Personalities, oval (70 x 30mm) (1935):	H.629		
		72	1 Normal issue		90p	£65.00
			Album		—	£35.00
		10	2 Replaced subjects (Nos. 1-10) for issue in Eire		£20.00	—
	C		Races — Historic and Modern (1927):			
A		25	A Small size		£2.60	£65.00
B		25	B Large size		£2.60	£65.00
—		12	C Extra-large size (133 x 69mm)		£5.00	£60.00
A	U	50	Radio & Television Favourites (unissued) (c1955)		£8.00	—
A	C	140	Raemaekers War Cartoons (1916):			
			A 'Black Cat' Cigarettes		£1.50	£210.00
			B Carreras Cigarettes		£4.20	—
	C		Regalia Series (1925):			
A		25	A Small size		50p	£12.50
B		20	B Large size		60p	£12.00
—		10	C Extra-large size (135 x 71mm)		£2.00	£20.00
—	C	50	'Round the World' Scenic Models (folders) (83 x 73mm) (c1930)		80p	£40.00
	C		School Emblems (1929):			
A		50	A Small size		90p	£45.00
B		40	B Large size		75p	£30.00
—		20	C Extra-large size (134 x 76mm)		£2.25	£45.00
A	C	50	The Science of Boxing (c1916):			
			A 'Black Cat' back		£3.20	£160.00
			B 'Carreras Ltd' back		£6.00	—
A	C	50	Sport Fish (1978)		20p	£5.00
			Album		—	£12.00
C1	C	48	Tapestry Reproductions of Famous Paintings (sectional) (1938)		80p	£40.00
A	C	50	Tools — And How to Use Them (1935)		£2.20	£110.00
A	C	80	Types of London (1919)		£1.70	£135.00
A	P	27	Views of London (1929) (export)		45p	£12.00
A	P	27	Views of the World (1927) (export)		80p	£22.00
A	C	50	Vintage Cars (1976):			
			A With word 'Filter' in white oval:			
			i Thin card, bright red oblong at top		20p	£10.00
			ii Thick card, bright red oblong at top		20p	£7.50
			iii Thin card, dull red oblong at top		50p	—
			B Without word 'Filter' in white oval		20p	£5.00
			Album		—	£12.00
A	C	25	Wild Flower Art Series (1923)		£1.60	£40.00
A	C	50	Women on War Work (c1916)		£10.00	£500.00

TURF SLIDE ISSUES

Size	Printing	Number in set		Handbook reference	Price per card	Complete set
A	U	50	British Aircraft (1953)		£2.00	£100.00
A	U	50	British Fish (1954)		£1.20	£60.00
A	U	50	British Railway Locomotives (1952)		£2.00	£100.00
A	U	50	Celebrities of British History (1951)		£1.50	£75.00
A	U	50	Famous British Fliers (1956)		£8.00	—
A	U	50	Famous Cricketers (1950)		£6.50	—
A	U	50	Famous Dog Breeds (1952)	H.889	£2.00	£100.00
A	U	50	Famous Film Stars (1949)		£3.20	—
A	U	50	Famous Footballers (1951)		£5.00	—
A	U	50	Film Favourites (1948)		£4.50	

Size	Print-ing	Number in set	BRITISH TOBACCO ISSUERS	Handbook reference	Price per card	Complete set
			CARRERAS LTD, London (Turf Slide Issues continued)			
A	U	50	Film Stars (1947)		£3.20	—
A	U	50	Footballers (1948)		£5.00	—
A	U	50	Olympics (1948)		£8.00	—
A	U	50	Radio Celebrities (1950)		£1.40	£70.00
A	U	50	Sports Series (1949)		£4.00	—
A	U	50	Zoo Animals (1955)		60p	£30.00
			(N.B. These prices are for the full slides. If only the cut slides are required these will be half Catalogue price.)			

SILKS

			Lace Motifs (c1915):	H.506		
—	—	79	A Size 63 x 63mm		£10.00	—
—	—	15	B Size 125 x 63mm		£45.00	—
—	—	7	C Size 125 x 125mm		£85.00	—
—	C	12	Miscellaneous Series Cabinet size (1915)	H.505-18	£200.00	—

OVERSEAS ISSUES (AUSTRALIA & CANADA)

—	C	20	Canadian Fish (69 x 50mm) (1985)		£3.00	—
—	C	20	Canadian Wild Animals (69 x 50mm) (1984):			
			A Complete set		£2.00	—
			B 15 Different		40p	£6.00
C2	U	72	Film Star Series (1933):			
			A Smile Away back		£3.50	—
			B Standard back		£1.80	—
C2	C	72	Football Series (1933)		£3.00	—
C2	C	24	Personality Series (Sports) (1933)		£3.00	—
C2	U	72	Personality Series Film Stars (1933)		£1.80	—
C2	C	72	Personality Series Footballers (1933)		£3.00	—
—	C	216	Sportsman's Guide — Fly Fishing (Package Issue) (c1955):			
			A 25 Package (103 x 75mm)		£2.00	—
			B 20 Package (82 x 75mm)		£2.00	—

CARRICK & CO., Hull

D	C	12	*Military Terms (1901)	H.50	£90.00	—
—	U	1	Queen Victoria Jubilee 1887 (105 x 67mm)	H.720	—	£300.00

P.J. CARROLL & CO. LTD, Dundalk, Glasgow and Liverpool

D	C	25	Birds (prepared but not issued) (c1940)	H.537	70p	£17.50
D	C	25	British Naval Series (c1915)	H.51	£50.00	—
A	P	20	County Louth G.R.A. Team and Officials (1913)		£40.00	—
D	BW	25	*Derby Winners (1914-15):	H.52		
			A Back in black		£120.00	—
			B Back in green		£120.00	—
K2	BW	26	Grand Slam Spelling Bee Cards (c1935)		£17.00	—
D	C	25	Ship Series (1937)		£12.00	£300.00
D	U	24	Sweet Afton Jig-Saw Puzzles (1935)	H.650	£22.00	—

THE CASKET TOBACCO & CIGARETTE CO. LTD, Manchester

A2	U	? 1	Bowling Fixture Cards, Coupon Back (1907)	H.53	£600.00	—
A2	U	? 5	Cricket Fixture Cards, Coupon back (1905-10)	H.53	£650.00	—
A2	U	? 2	Cyclists Lighting-up Table (1909-10)		£600.00	—
A2	U	? 18	*Football Fixture Cards, Coupon back (1905-11)	H.53	£650.00	—
A2	BW	? 7	Road Maps (c1910)	H.54	£600.00	—

S. CAVANDER & CO., London and Portsea

D	BW	50	*Beauties — selection from 'Plums' (1898)	H.186	£600.00	—

Size	Printing	Number in set	BRITISH TOBACCO ISSUERS	Handbook reference	Price per card	Complete set
			CAVANDERS LTD, London and Glasgow			
A	C	25	Ancient Chinese (1926)		£1.80	£45.00
A	C	25	Ancient Egypt (1928)		£1.60	£40.00
B	C	25	Ancient Egypt (different subjects) (1928)		£1.60	£40.00
A	P	36	Animal Studies (1936)		40p	£14.00
	CP	50	Beauty Spots of Great Britain (1927):			
A			A Small size		50p	£25.00
—			B Medium size (76 x 52mm)		50p	£25.00
	CP		Camera Studies (1926):			
A		54	A Small size		38p	£20.00
—		56	B Medium size (77 x 51mm)		36p	£20.00
A	C	30	Cinema Stars — Set 6 (1934)	GP.55	£1.35	£40.00
—	CP	30	The Colonial Series (77 x 51mm) (1925):	GP.330		
			A Small caption, under 1mm high on front		50p	£15.00
			B Larger caption, over 1mm high on front		50p	£15.00
—	C	25§	Coloured Stereoscopic (77 x 51mm) (1931)		70p	£35.00
D	C	25	Feathered Friends or Foreign Birds (1926):	GP.70		
			A Titled 'Feathered Friends'		£2.60	—
			B Titled 'Foreign Birds'		£1.60	£40.00
—	C	25§	Glorious Britain (76 x 51mm) (1930)		60p	£30.00
			The Homeland Series (1924-26):	GP.333		
A			Small size:			
	CP	50	A Back in blue		£1.20	£60.00
	CP	50	B Back in black, glossy front		£1.00	£50.00
	CP	54	C Back in black, matt front		45p	£25.00
			Medium size (77 x 51mm):			
	CP	50	D Back inscribed 'Hand Coloured Real Photos'		40p	£20.00
	CP	56	E As D, with 'Reprinted ...' at base		50p	£28.00
	CP	56	F Back inscribed 'Real Photos'		50p	£28.00
	P	56	G Back inscribed 'Real Photos'		70p	£40.00
A	C	25	Little Friends (1924)	GP.89	£1.20	£30.00
—	C	25	The Nation's Treasures (77 x 51mm) (1925)		70p	£17.50
	P		Peeps into Many Lands — 'A Series of ...' (1927):			
D		36§	A Small size		50p	£36.00
—		36§	B Medium size (75 x 50mm)		85p	£60.00
—		36	C Extra-large size (113 x 68mm)		£2.20	—
	P	36§	Peeps into Many Lands — 'Second Series ...' (1928):			
D			A Small size		£1.00	£75.00
—			B Medium size (75 x 50mm)		£1.00	£75.00
	P	24§	Peeps into Many Lands — 'Third Series ...' (1929):			
D			A Small size		40p	£20.00
—			B Medium size (75 x 50mm)		90p	£45.00
—			C As B, but inscribed 'Reprinted by Special Request'		£1.50	£75.00
	P	24§	Peeps into Prehistoric Times — 'Fourth Series ...' (1930):			
D			A Small size		£1.00	£50.00
—			B Medium size (75 x 50mm)		£1.40	£65.00
—	P		*Photographs (54 x 38mm) (1924):	GP.337		
		30	1 Animal Studies		£1.50	—
		3	2 Royal Family		£3.50	—
—	C	48	Regimental Standards (76 x 70mm) (c1924)	GP.245	£16.00	—
C	C	25	Reproductions of Celebrated Oil Paintings (1925) ...	GP.338	£1.40	£35.00
	CP	108	River Valleys (1926):			
A			A Small size		40p	£45.00
—			B Medium size (75 x 50mm)		40p	£45.00

Size	Print-ing	Number in set	BRITISH TOBACCO ISSUERS	Handbook reference	Price per card	Complete set
			CAVANDERS LTD, London and Glasgow (continued)			
A	C	25	School Badges (1928):	GP.121		
			A Back in dark blue		£1.00	£25.00
			B Back in light blue		£1.00	£25.00
—	CP	30	Wordsworth's Country (76 x 51mm) (1926)		£1.20	£36.00

§ Stereoscopic series, consisting of a Right and a Left card for each number, a complete series is thus **double** the number shown.

R.S. CHALLIS & CO. LTD, London

Size	Print	Num		Ref	Price	Set
D1	C	50	Comic Animals (1936)		80p	£40.00
A	BW	44	Flickits (Greyhound Racing Flickers) (1936)	Ha.589-1	£40.00	—
D1	U	36	Wild Birds at Home (1935):	H.626		
			A Inscribed 'Issued with Baldric Cigarettes'		70p	£25.00
			B Above wording blocked out in black		£1.40	£50.00

H. CHAPMAN & Co.

D	C	30	*Army Pictures, Cartoons, etc (c1916)	H.12	£230.00	—

CHARLESWORTH & AUSTIN LTD, London

C	U	50	*Beauties — 'BOCCA' (c1900)	H.39	£35.00	—
C	BW	16	*British Royal Family (1902)	H.28	£50.00	—
C	C		Colonial Troops (c1900):	H.40		
		50	A Black back		£40.00	—
		30	B Brown back		£40.00	—
A1	BW	20	Cricketers Series (1901)	H.29	£375.00	—
C	C	30	*Flags and Flags with Soldiers (c1903)	H.41	£40.00	—

CHESTERFIELD CIGARETTES

—	C	6	Chesterfield Collection (76 x 45mm) (1979)		£3.00	—
—	C	6	Cocktails (76 x 45mm) 1980		50p	£3.00

CHEW & CO., Bradford

D	C	30	*Army, Pictures, Cartoons etc (c1916)	H.12	£160.00	—

W.A. & A.C. CHURCHMAN, Ipswich

36 page reference book — £4.50

C	C	26	*Actresses — 'FROGA A' (c1900)	H.20	£40.00	—
C	C	26	*Actresses — 'FROGA B' (c1900)	H.20	£50.00	—
C	U	24	*Actresses, 'For the Pipe' back (c1900)	H.55	£90.00	—
—	C	48	Air-Raid Precautions (68 x 53mm) (1938)	H.544	60p	£30.00
A	C	25	Army Badges of Rank (1916)	H.56	£6.00	£150.00
A	U	50	Association Footballers (1938)		80p	£40.00
A	U	50	Association Footballers, 2nd series (1939)		£1.20	£60.00
A	C	12	*Beauties — 'CERF' (1904)	H.57	£75.00	—
			*Beauties — 'CHOAB' (c1900):	H.21		
—	C	3	I Circular cards, 55mm diameter		£1800.00	—
C	C	25	II Five different backs		£150.00	—
C	U	25	*Beauties — 'FECKSA'(c1902)	H.58	£100.00	—
C	C	25	*Beauties — 'GRACC' (c1900)	H.59	£100.00	—
A	C	50	Birds and Eggs (1906)	H.60	£10.00	£500.00
D	BW	20	*Boer War Cartoons (c1901)	H.42	£130.00	—
		20	*Boer War Generals' — 'CLAM' (c1901):	H.61		
A2	BW		A Black front		£40.00	—
A	U		B Brown front		£40.00	—
A	C	25	Boxing (1922)	H.311	£6.00	—
A	U	50	Boxing Personalities (1938)		£1.80	£90.00

Size	Printing	Number in set	BRITISH TOBACCO ISSUERS	Handbook reference	Price per card	Complete set
			W.A. & A.C. CHURCHMAN, Ipswich (continued)			
A	C	50	Boy Scouts (1916)	H.62	£8.00	£400.00
A	C	50	Boy Scouts, 2nd series (1916)	H.62	£8.00	£400.00
A	C	50	Boy Scouts, 3rd series (1916):	H.62		
			A Brown back		£8.00	£400.00
			B Blue back		£12.00	—
A	U	25	British Film Stars (1934)		£2.60	£65.00
A	C	55	Can You Beat Bogey at St Andrews? (1933):			
			A Without overprint		£3.00	—
			B Overprinted in red 'Exchangeable'		£3.00	—
	U		Cathedrals and Churches (1924):	H.545		
A		25	A Small size		£2.60	£65.00
J		12	B Extra-large size		£15.00	—
A	C	50	Celebrated Gateways (1925)	H.347	£2.00	£100.00
D	P	41	*Celebrities — Boer War Period (c1901)	H.63	£25.00	—
—	BW	1	Christmas Greetings Card (68 x 53mm) (1938)		—	£3.00
A	C	25	Civic Insignia and Plate (1926)		£2.20	£55.00
A	C	50	Contract Bridge (1935)		90p	£45.00
A	C	50	Cricketers (1936)		£4.00	£200.00
	C		Curious Dwellings:			
A		25	A Small size (1926)		£2.20	£55.00
B		12	B Large size (1925)		£7.00	—
A	C	25	Curious Signs (1925)		£2.20	£55.00
A	C	38	Dogs and Fowls (1908)	H.64	£10.00	—
	C		Eastern Proverbs:	H.521		
			A Small size:			
A		25	1 'A Series of 25' (1931)		80p	£20.00
A		25	2 '2nd Series of 25' (1932)		£1.40	£35.00
			B Large size:			
B		12	1 'A Series of 12' (1931)		£4.00	—
B		12	2 '2nd Series of 12' (1933)		£3.00	£36.00
B		12	3 '3rd Series of 12' (1933)		£3.00	£36.00
B		12	4 '4th Series of 12' (1934)		£1.65	£20.00
A		50	East Suffolk Churches:			
	BW		A Black front, cream back (1912)		£2.20	£110.00
	BW		B Black front, white back (1912)		£2.20	£110.00
	U		C Sepia front (1917)		£2.20	£110.00
A	C	50	Empire Railways (1931)		£2.60	£130.00
A	C	25	Famous Cricket Colours (1928)		£4.00	£100.00
	U		Famous Golfers:			
A		50	A Small size (1927)		£15.00	—
			B Large size:			
B		12	1 'A Series of 12' (1927)		£60.00	—
B		12	2 '2nd Series of 12' (1928)		£60.00	—
	C		Famous Railway Trains:			
A		25	A Small size (1929)		£3.00	£75.00
			B Large size:			
B		12	1 'Series of 12' (1928)		£7.00	—
B		12	2 '2nd Series of 12' (1929)		£7.00	—
A	C	50	Fish and Bait (1914)	H.65	£7.00	£350.00
A	C	50	Fishes of the World (1911):	H.66	—	£300.00
			30 cards as re-issued 1924		£1.65	£50.00
			20 cards not re-issued		£12.50	—
A	C	50	Flags and Funnels of Leading Steamship Lines (1912)	H.67	£7.50	—
A	C	50	Football Club Colours (1909)	H.68	£15.00	£750.00
A	U	50	*Footballers — Photogravure Portraits (c1913)		£45.00	—

Size	Printing	Number in set	BRITISH TOBACCO ISSUERS	Handbook reference	Price per card	Complete set
			W.A. & A.C. CHURCHMAN, Ipswich (continued)			
A	C	50	Footballers — Action Pictures & Inset (1914)		£25.00	—
A	C	52	'Frisky' (1935)		£3.50	—
A	C	50	History and Development of the British Empire (1934)		£2.00	£100.00
			Album		—	£40.00
—	U	48	Holidays in Britain (Views and Maps) (68 x 53 mm) (1937)		60p	£30.00
—	C	48	Holidays in Britain (views only) (68 x 53mm) (1938)		60p	£30.00
C	C	40	*Home and Colonial Regiments (1902)	H.69	£55.00	—
A	C	25	The Houses of Parliament and Their Story (1931)		£2.20	£55.00
	C		Howlers:			
A		40	A Small size (1937)		50p	£20.00
B		16	B Large size (1936)		50p	£8.00
A	C	25	The Inns of Court (1932)		£3.00	£75.00
A	C	50	Interesting Buildings (1905)	H.70	£8.00	£400.00
A	C	25	Interesting Door-Knockers (1928)		£2.60	£65.00
A	C	25	Interesting Experiments (1929)		£1.80	£45.00
A	C	50	'In Town To-night' (1938)		40p	£20.00
B	C	12	Italian Art Exhibition, 1930 (1931)		£2.50	£30.00
B	C	12	Italian Art Exhibition, 1930 — '2nd Series' (1931)		£2.50	£30.00
	C		The King's Coronation (1937):			
A		50	A Small size		30p	£15.00
B		15	B Large size		£1.00	£15.00
A	U	50	Kings of Speed (1939)		60p	£30.00
	C		Landmarks in Railway Progress:			
A		50	A Small size (1931)		£3.00	£150.00
			B Large size:			
B		12	1 '1st Series of 12' (1932)		£6.00	£75.00
B		12	2 '2nd Series of 12' (1932)		£6.00	£75.00
	U		Lawn Tennis (1928):	H.546		
A		50	A Small size		£4.00	£200.00
B		12	B Large size		£12.50	—
	C		Legends of Britain (1936):			
A		50	A Small size		£1.00	£50.00
B		12	B Large size		£1.50	£18.00
	C		Life in a Liner (1930):			
A		25	A Small size		£1.80	£45.00
B		12	B Large size		£6.00	—
A	C	50	*Medals (1910)	H.71	£8.00	£400.00
	C		Men of the Moment in Sport:			
A		50	A Small size (1928):			
			1 40 Different		£4.00	—
			2 10 Different Golfers (Nos. 24 to 33)		£18.00	—
			B Large size:			
B		12	1 '1st Series of 12' (1929):			
			A 10 Different		£14.00	—
			B Nos. 7 and 8 (Golfers)		£125.00	—
B		12	2 '2nd Series of 12' (1929):			
			A 10 Different		£14.00	—
			B Nos. 7 and 8 (Golfers)		£125.00	—
—	C	48	Modern Wonders (68 x 53mm) (1938)		40p	£20.00
A	C	25	Musical Instruments (1924)	H.547	£3.80	£95.00
	C		Nature's Architects (1930):			
A		25	A Small size		£1.40	£35.00
B		12	B Large size		£2.50	£30.00
—	U	48	The Navy at Work (68 x 53mm) (1937)		50p	£24.00

Size	Print-ing	Number in set		Handbook reference	Price per card	Complete set

BRITISH TOBACCO ISSUERS

W.A. & A.C. CHURCHMAN, Ipswich (continued)

Size	Printing	Number in set	Description	Handbook ref	Price per card	Complete set
—	U	55	Olympic Winners Through The Years (Package Designs, 30 small, 25 large) (1960)	H.891	£3.00	—
A	C	50	*Phil May Sketches (1912):	H.72		
			A 'Churchman's Gold Flake Cigarettes'		£7.00	£350.00
			B 'Churchman's Cigarettes'		£8.00	—
A	C	25	Pipes of the World (1927)		£3.00	£75.00
	C		Prominent Golfers (1931):			
A		50	A Small size:			
			1 49 Different		£14.00	—
			2 No. 25 Bobby Jones		£125.00	—
B		12	B Large size:			
			1 11 Different		£36.00	—
			2 No. 5 Bobby Jones		£250.00	—
	C		The 'Queen Mary' (1936):			
A		50	A Small size		£1.60	£80.00
B		16	B Large size		£3.50	£55.00
A	C	50	Racing Greyhounds (1934)		£3.00	£150.00
—	C	48	The RAF at Work (68 x 53mm) (1938)		90p	£45.00
	C		Railway Working:	H.548		
			A Small size:			
A		25	1 'Series of 25' (1926)		£4.00	£100.00
A		25	2 '2nd Series of 25' (1927)		£2.60	£65.00
			B Large size:			
B		12	1 'Series of 12' (1926)		£12.00	—
B		13	2 '2nd Series, 13' (1927)		£12.00	—
B		12	3 '3rd Series, 12' (1927)		£12.00	—
A	C	50	*Regimental Colours and Cap Badges (1911)	H.73	£7.00	£350.00
A	BW	50	Rivers and Broads (1922):			
			A Titled 'Rivers & Broads'		£7.00	—
			B Titled 'Rivers & Broads of Norfolk & Suffolk'		£6.00	—
A	C	50	Rugby Internationals (1935)		£2.00	£100.00
A	C	50	Sectional Cycling Map (1913)	H.74	£6.50	£325.00
A	C	50	Silhouettes of Warships (1915)		£11.00	—
A	C	50	Sporting Celebrities (1931):			
			A 43 Different		£3.00	—
			B 7 Different Golfers (Nos. 30 to 36)		£12.00	—
	C		Sporting Trophies (1927):			
A		25	A Small size		£3.00	£75.00
B		12	B Large size		£7.00	—
A	C	25	Sports and Games in Many Lands (1929):			
			A 24 Different minus No. 25		£4.00	£100.00
			B Number 25 (Babe Ruth)		—	£70.00
	C		The Story of London (1934):			
A		50	A Small size		£2.00	£100.00
B		12	B Large size		£3.00	£36.00
	C		The Story of Navigation:			
A		50	A Small size (1936)		40p	£20.00
B		12	B Large size (1935)		£1.25	£15.00
A	C		3 Jovial Golfers in search of the perfect course (1934):			
		36	A Home issue		£4.00	£145.00
		72	B Irish issue, with green over-printing		£10.00	—
A	C	50	A Tour Round the World (1911)	H.75	£8.00	£400.00
	C		Treasure Trove:			
A		50	A Small size (1937)		40p	£20.00
B		12	B Large size (1935)		£1.50	£18.00
A1	C	25	*Types of British and Colonial Troops (c1900)	H.76	£55.00	

Size	Print-ing	Number in set	BRITISH TOBACCO ISSUERS	Handbook reference	Price per card	Complete set
			W.A. & A.C. CHURCHMAN, Ipswich (continued)			
	C		Warriors of All Nations:			
A		25	A Small size (1929)		£3.00	£75.00
			B Large size:			
B		12	1 'A Series of 12' (1929)		£4.00	£50.00
B		12	2 '2nd Series of 12' (1931)		£4.00	£50.00
	C		Well-known Ties (1934):			
A		50	A Small size		90p	£45.00
			B Large size			
B		12	1 'A Series of 12'		£2.00	£24.00
B		12	2 '2nd Series of 12'		£1.75	£21.00
A	C	50	Well-known Ties, '2nd Series' (1935)		70p	£35.00
A	U	25	Wembley Exhibition (1924)		£3.00	£75.00
A	U	50	West Suffolk Churches (1919)		£2.00	£100.00
A	C	50	Wild Animals of the World (1907)	H.77	£8.00	£400.00
—	C	48	Wings Over the Empire (68 x 53mm) (1939)		40p	£20.00
	C		Wonderful Railway Travel (1937):			
A		50	A Small size		60p	£30.00
B		12	B Large size		£1.65	£20.00
—	U	40	The World of Sport (Package Designs, 30 small, 10 large) (1961)	H.892	£2.50	—
A	C	50	World Wonders Old and New (prepared but not issued) (c1955)		40p	£20.00

OVERSEAS ISSUES (CHANNEL ISLANDS)

(All cards without I.T.C. clause)

—	C	48	Air Raid Precautions (68 x 53) (1938)	H.544	£2.00	—
—	U	48	Holidays in Britain (68 x 53) (1937)		£2.00	—
—	C	48	Holidays in Britain (68 x 53) (1938)		£2.00	—
—	C	48	Modern Wonders (68 x 53) (1938):			
			A I.T.C. clause blocked out in silver		£5.00	—
			B Reprinted without I.T.C. clause		£2.00	—
—	U	48	The Navy at Work (68 x 53) (1937)		£2.00	—
—	C	48	The RAF at Work (68 x 53) (1939)		£2.00	—
—	C	48	Wings Over the Empire (68 x 53) (1939)		£2.00	—

WM. CLARKE & SON, Liverpool and London

A	C	25	Army Life (1915)	H.78	£18.00	£450.00
A1	BW	16	*Boer War Celebrities — 'CAG' (c1901)	H.79	£35.00	—
A	C	50	Butterflies and Moths (1912)	H.80	£12.00	£600.00
A	BW	30	Cricketer Series (1901)		£250.00	—
A1	BW	66	Football Series (1902)	H.81	£50.00	—
A	C	25	Marine Series (1907)		£20.00	£500.00
A	C	50	Royal Mail (1914)	H.82	£15.00	£750.00
	C	50	Sporting Terms (38 x 58mm) multi-backed (c1900):	H.83		
			14 Cricket Terms		£75.00	—
			12 Cycling Terms		£75.00	—
			12 Football Terms		£75.00	—
			12 Golf Terms		£75.00	—
—	C	20	*Tobacco Leaf Girls (shaped) (c1898)	H.84	£520.00	—
—	C	25	Well-known Sayings (71 x 32mm) (c1900)	H.85	£28.00	£700.00

J. CLAYTON, Wakefield

—	C	? 6	*Play Up Sporting Shields (c1895)	H.718	£175.00	—

Size	Print-ing	Number in set	BRITISH TOBACCO ISSUERS	Handbook reference	Price per card	Complete set

J.H. CLURE, Keighley

Size	Print-ing	Number in set		Handbook reference	Price per card	Complete set
D	C	30	*Army Pictures, Cartoons, etc (c1900):	H.12		
			A 'These Cigarettes' back		£160.00	—
			B 'Try Clure's Havana Mixture' back		£160.00	—
A	U	50	War Portraits (1916)	H.86	£120.00	—

J. LOMAX COCKAYNE, Sheffield

A	U	50	War Portraits (1916)	H.86	£120.00	—

COHEN WEENEN & CO. LTD, London

Size	Print-ing	Number in set		Handbook reference	Price per card	Complete set
—	P	40	*Actresses, Footballers and Jockeys (26 x 61mm) (c1901)	GP.350	£65.00	—
A1	U	26	*Actresses — 'FROGA A' (c1900)	H.20/GP.351	£70.00	—
A	C	25	*Beauties — selection from 'BOCCA' (c1900)	H.39/GP.353	£75.00	—
A1	C	25	*Beauties — 'GRACC' (c1900)	H.59/GP.354	£130.00	—
D2	BW	25	*Boxers (c1912):	H.721/GP.362		
			A Black back		£20.00	
			B Green back		£14.00	£350.00
			C *Without Maker's Name*		£20.00	—
A	BW		*Celebrities — Black and white (1901):	GP.356		
		65	A 'Sweet Crop, over 250 ...' back		£7.00	—
		? 20	B 'Sweet Crop, over 500 ...' back		£12.00	—
A	C		*Celebrities — Coloured (1901):			
		45	I 1-45 Boer War Generals etc. 'Sweet Crop, over 100 ...' back:	GP.355		
			A Toned back		£7.50	—
			B White back		£7.50	—
			C *Plain Back*		£10.00	—
		121	II 1-121 Including Royalty, etc. 'Sweet Crop, over 250 ...' back:			
			1-45 as in I	GP.355	£11.00	—
			46-121 additional subjects	GP.357	£7.00	—
—	C		*Celebrities — 'GAINSBOROUGH I' (1901):	GP.358		
—		? 21	A In metal frames (46 x 67mm)		£100.00	—
D2		39	B 'Sweet Crop, over 250 ...' back		£50.00	—
D		30	C 'Sweet Crop, over 400 ...' back		£15.00	£450.00
D1		2	D 1902 Calendar Back gilt border to front		£130.00	—
D1		39	E Plain Back, *white border*		£12.00	£475.00
D1		? 40	F Plain back, *gilt border to front*		£100.00	—
	P	? 177	*Celebrities — 'GAINSBOROUGH II' (c1901):	GP.359		
—			A In metal frames (46 x 67mm)		£18.00	—
D2			B *Without frames showing Frame Marks*		£6.00	—
D2			C *Without Frames no Frame Marks (as issued)*		£10.00	—
D2	U	25	*Cricketers (1926)		£24.00	—
A2	C	20	*Cricketers, Footballers, Jockeys (c1900):	GP.361		
			A Caption in brown		£28.00	£560.00
			B Caption in grey-black		£28.00	£560.00
D	C	40	Fiscal Phrases (c1905):	GP.363		
			A 'Copyright Regd.' on front		£12.50	£500.00
			B Without 'Copyright Regd.'		£12.50	£500.00
A2	C	60	Football Captains, 1907-8 — Series No. 5	GP.364	£17.00	—
A2	BW	100	*Heroes of Sport (c1898)	GP.365	£110.00	—
A	C	40	*Home and Colonial Regiments (c1901):	H.69/GP.366		
			A 'Sweet Crop, over 100 ...' back		£12.00	£480.00
			B 'Sweet Crop, over 250 ...' back		£16.00	—
			C *1902 Calendar Back Gilt Border*		£150.00	—

Size	Print-ing	Number in set	BRITISH TOBACCO ISSUERS	Handbook reference	Price per card	Complete set
			COHEN WEENEN & CO. LTD, London (continued)			
A2	C	20	*Interesting Buildings and Views (1902):	GP.367		
			A No Framelines		£12.00	£240.00
			B *Gilt Framelines 1902 Calendar back*		£140.00	—
K2	C	52	*Miniature Playing Cards — Bandmaster Cigarettes (c1910)		£4.00	—
D2	C		*Nations:	GP.369		
		20	A Blue 'Sweet Crop, over 250 ...' back (c1902)		£12.00	£240.00
		20	B *Plain back — gilt border* (c1902)		£100.00	—
		? 1	C 1902 Calender back (c1902)		£140.00	—
		20	D Text back (1923)		£5.00	£100.00
D	C	40	Naval and Military Phrases (c1904):	H.14/GP.370		
			A Red back, 'Series No. 1'		£25.00	—
			B 'Sweet Crop, over 250 ...' back:			
			i White Border		£34.00	—
			ii Gilt Border		£140.00	—
D2	C	50	Owners, Jockeys, Footballers, Cricketers — Series No. 2 (c1906)	GP.371	£18.00	£900.00
D2	C	20	Owners, Jockeys, Footballers, Cricketers — Series No. 3 (c1907)	GP.372	£20.00	£400.00
D	C	30	*Proverbs, 'Sweet Crop, over 400 ...' back (c1905)	H.15/GP.373	£16.00	—
A	C	20	Russo-Japanese War Series (1904)	H.100/GP.120	£22.00	—
A	BW	25	*Silhouettes of Celebrities (c1905)	GP.374	£16.00	£400.00
D1	C	50	Star Artistes — Series No. 4 (c1905):	GP.375		
		20	With stage background		£12.00	£240.00
		30	No stage, plain background		£12.00	£360.00
D	C	50	V.C. Heroes (of World War I), Nd. 51-100 (1915):			
			51-75 — dull greyish card		£14.00	£350.00
			Without Maker's Name on back		£17.00	—
			76-100 — glossy white card		£14.00	£350.00
D	U	50	*War Series (World War I) (1915):	H.103/GP.376		
			1-25 Admirals and Warships:			
			A Thick card		£14.00	£350.00
			B *Thin card*		£14.00	£350.00
			26-50 Leaders of the War:			
			A Maker's Name on back		£14.00	£350.00
			B *Without Maker's Name on back*		£17.00	—
D1	C	30	Wonders of the World:	GP.378		
			A Inscribed 'Series 6', white borders (c1908) ...		£7.00	£210.00
			B Without 'Series 6', gilt borders (1923)		£3.00	£90.00
SILKS						
—	C	16	*Victoria Cross Heroes II (72 x 70mm) (paper-backed) (c1915)	GP.251	£50.00	—
			T.H. COLLINS, Mansfield			
Al	U	25	Homes of England (1924):			
			A Dark mauve front		£6.00	£150.00
			B Grey front		£20.00	—
A	C	25	Sports and Pastimes — Series I (1923)	H.225	£12.00	£300.00
			F. COLTON Jun., Retford			
D	C	30	*Army Pictures, Cartoons, etc (c1916):	H.12		
			A 'Best House' back		£160.00	—
			B 'Our Hand-filled Cigarettes' back		£160.00	—
A	U	50	War Portraits (1916)	H.86	£120.00	—

Size	Print-ing	Number in set		BRITISH TOBACCO ISSUERS	Handbook reference	Price per card	Complete set
				T.W. CONQUEST, London			
D	C	*30	Army Pictures, Cartoons etc (c1916)		H12	£160.00	—
				THE CONTINENTAL CIGARETTE FACTORY, London			
A	C		Charming Portraits (c1925):		H.549		
		25	A	Back in blue, with firm's name		£5.00	—
		25	B	Back in blue, inscribed 'Club Mixture Tobacco'		£7.00	—
		4	C	Back in brown, inscribed 'Club Mixture Tobacco'		£12.00	—
		25	*D	Plain back		£5.00	—
				COOPER & CO'S STORES LTD, London			
A	BW	25	*Boer War Celebrities — 'STEW' (c1901):		H.105		
			A	'Alpha Mixture' back		£170.00	—
			B	'Gladys Cigars' back		£170.00	—
				COOPERATIVE WHOLESALE SOCIETY LTD, Manchester			
A2	C	? 6	*Advertisement Cards (c1915)		H.106	£450.00	—
A	C	24	African Types (1936)			50p	£12.00
—	C	? 2	*Beauties (102 x 68mm) (c1915)		H.722	£100.00	—
—	U	50	Beauty Spots of Britain (76 x 51mm) (1936)			50p	£25.00
A2	C	50	Boy Scout Badges (1939)			£1.80	£90.00
A	C	25	Boy Scout Series (c1915)			£50.00	—
A	C	48	British and Foreign Birds (1938)			£1.10	£55.00
A	C	50	British Sport Series§ (c1914)			£45.00	—
D	C	25	*Cooking Recipes (1923)			£2.60	£65.00
A	C	28	*Co-operative Buildings and Works (c1914)		H.107	£16.00	£450.00
A	C	24	English Roses (1924)			£4.00	£100.00
A	C	50	Famous Bridges (48 + 2 added) (1937)			£1.10	£55.00
A	C	48	Famous Buildings (1935)			80p	£40.00
A2	C	25	How to Do It (1924):				
			A	'Anglian Mixture' back		£3.00	—
			B	'Equity Tobacco' back		£3.00	—
			C	'Jaycee Brown Flake' back		£3.00	—
			D	'Raydex Gold Leaf' back		£3.00	—
A	C	48	Musical Instruments (1934)			£4.00	£200.00
A	C	25	Parrot Series (1910)			£60.00	—
A	C	48	Poultry (1927)			£10.00	£500.00
A	C	48	Railway Engines (1936)			£4.00	£200.00
A	C	24	Sailing Craft (1935)			£1.60	£40.00
A	C	18	War Series (c1915)			£34.00	—
A2	C	48	Wayside Flowers, brown back (1923)			£2.00	£100.00
A2	C	48	Wayside Flowers, grey/green back (1928)			80p	£40.00
A2	C	48	Wayside Woodland Trees (1924)			£2.50	£125.00
A	C	24	Western Stars (1957)			80p	£20.00

§Note: Cards advertise non-tobacco products, but are believed to have been packed with cigarettes and/or tobacco.

				COPE BROS. & CO. LTD, Liverpool			
	BW	20	*Actresses — 'BLARM' (c1900):		H.23		
A1			A	Plain backs. Name panel ¼" from border		£40.00	—
A1			B	Black design back. Name ¼" from border		£40.00	—
D			C	Black design back. Name panel ¹⁄₁₆" from border		£40.00	—
A	U	? 6	*Actresses — 'COPEIS' (c1900)		H.108	£350.00	—
A	U	26	*Actresses 'FROGA A' (c1900)		H.20	£90.00	—
D1	P	50	*Actresses and Beauties (c1900)		H.109	£20.00	—

Size	Print-ing	Number in set	BRITISH TOBACCO ISSUERS	Handbook reference	Price per card	Complete set
			COPE BROS. & CO. LTD, Liverpool (continued)			
K1	P	? 46	*Beauties, Actors and Actresses (c1900)	H.110	£38.00	—
A	C	52	*Beauties — P.C. inset (c1898)	H.111	£45.00	—
A	C	15	*Beauties 'PAC' (c1898)	H.2	£80.00	—
A1	C	50	Boats of the World (c1910)		£16.00	£800.00
D2	BW	126	Boxers (c1915):			
			1-25 Boxers		£26.00	£650.00
			26-50 Boxers		£24.00	£600.00
			51-75 Boxers		£24.00	£600.00
			76-100 Boxers		£27.00	£675.00
			101-125 Army Boxers		£24.00	£600.00
			Unnumbered 'New World Champion' Jess Willard		—	£65.00
D	BW	25	Boxing Lessons (1935)		£4.00	£100.00
A1	C	35	*Boy Scouts and Girl Guides (c1910)	H.132	£14.00	£500.00
—	C	25	Bridge Problems (folders) (85 x 50mm) (1924)		£30.00	—
D	BW	25	British Admirals (c1915)	H.103	£18.00	£450.00
A2	C	50	British Warriors (c1912):			
			A Black on white backs		£10.00	£500.00
			B Grey on toned backs		£12.00	£600.00
A1	U	25	Castles§ (1939)		£1.20	£30.00
A1	U	25	Cathedrals§ (May, 1939)		£1.60	£40.00
A	C	50	Characters from Scott (c1900):			
			A Wide card		£13.00	£650.00
			B Narrow card — officially cut		£13.00	—
	U	115	Chinese Series (c1903):			
A1			Nos 1-20		£14.00	—
A1			Nos-2I-40:			
			A 'Bond of Union Tobacco' back		£14.00	—
			B 'Cope's Courts' back		£14.00	—
			C 'Golden Cloud' back		£14.00	—
			D 'Golden Magnet' back		£14.00	—
			E 'Solace' back		£14.00	—
			Nos 41-65:			
D			A Picture 56mm long		£14.00	—
A1			B Picture 58mm long		£14.00	—
A2			Nos 66-115:			
			A 'Bond of Union'/'Bond of Union' back		£14.00	—
			B 'Bond of Union'/'Golden Magnet' back		£14.00	—
			C 'Golden Magnet'/'Golden Magnet' back		£14.00	—
			D 'Golden Magnet'/'Bond of Union' back		£14.00	—
—	C	6	*Comic Hunting Scenes (c1890)	H.723	£300.00	—
A	C	50	Cope's Golfers (1900):			
			A Wide card		£85.00	—
			B Narrow card — officially cut		£85.00	—
—	C	25	Dickens' Character Series (75 x 58mm) (1939)		£1.20	£30.00
—	C	50	Dickens' Gallery (1900):			
A			A Back listed		£12.00	£600.00
—			B Size 70 x 43mm, 'Solace' back		£120.00	—
A	C	50	Dogs of the World (by Cecil Aldin) (c1910)		£15.00	£750.00
A	C	25	Eminent British Regiments Officers' Uniforms (c1908):		—	£425.00
			A Yellow-brown back		£17.00	—
			B Claret back		£17.00	—
A2	C	30	*Flags of Nations (c1903):	H.114		
			A 'Bond of Union' back		£15.00	£450.00
			B *Plain back*		£12.00	—
D	C	24	*Flags, Arms and Types of Nations (c1904):	H.115		
			A Numbered		£10.00	£240.00
			B Unnumbered		£100.00	—

Size	Print-ing	Number in set	BRITISH TOBACCO ISSUERS	Handbook reference	Price per card	Complete set
			COPE BROS. & CO. LTD, Liverpool (continued)			
—	C	25	The Game of Poker§ (75 x 58mm) (1936)		60p	£15.00
—	C	50	General Knowledge§ (70 x 42mm) (1925)		£4.00	—
—	BW	32	Golf Strokes (70 x 44mm) (1923)		£24.00	—
A1	C	60	'Happy Families' (1937)		£1.65	£100.00
—	C	50	Household Hints§ (advertisement fronts) (70 x 45mm) (1925)		£1.80	£90.00
—	U	20	*Kenilworth Phrases (80 x 70mm) (c1910)	H.116	£500.00	—
C	BW	30	Lawn Tennis Strokes (1924):			
			A Numbers 1 to 25		£8.00	—
			B Numbers 26 to 30		£26.00	—
—	U	50	Modern Dancing (folders) (74 x 43mm) (1926)		£16.00	—
A2	C	50	Music Hall Artistes (c1910):			
			A Inscribed 'Series of 50'		£35.00	—
			B Without the above		£13.00	£650.00
A	U	472	Noted Footballers — 'Clips Cigarettes' (c1910):	H.474		
		1	Unnumbered — Wee Jock Simpson		—	£70.00
		120	Series of 120:			
			A Greenish-blue frame		£30.00	—
			B Bright blue frame		£30.00	—
		162	Series of 282:			
			A Greenish-blue frame		£30.00	—
			B Bright blue frame		£30.00	—
		471	Series of 500. Bright blue frame		£30.00	—
D	P	195	Noted Footballers — 'Solace Cigarettes' (c1910) ...	H.474	£30.00	—
A	C	24	*Occupations for Women (1897)	H.117	£120.00	—
—	C	6	*Phases of the Moon (111 x 74mm) (c1890)	H.725	£300.00	—
—	C	24	Photo Albums for the Million (c1898):	H.119		
			12 Buff cover (25 x 39mm)		£20.00	—
			12 Green cover (25 x 39mm)		£20.00	—
A2	C	25	Pigeons (c1926)		£10.00	£250.00
A	C	52	*Playing Cards. Blue backs (c1902):			
			A Rounded Corners		£16.00	—
			B Square Corners		£12.00	—
—	C	7	The Seven Ages of Man (114 x 78mm) (c1885)	H.726	£300.00	—
A	C	50	Shakespeare Gallery (c1900):			
			A Wide card		£14.00	£700.00
			B Narrow card — officially cut		£14.00	—
A2	C	25	Song Birds (c1926)		£7.00	£175.00
A1	C	25	Sports and Pastimes (1925)	H.55I	£5.00	£125.00
—	C	25	Toy Models (The Country Fair) (73 x 66mm) (c1930)	H.552	50p	£12.50
A1	C	25	*Uniforms of Soldiers and Sailors (c1900):	H.120		
			A Circular Medallion back, wide card		£30.00	—
			B Square Medallion back, wide card		£60.00	—
			C Square Medallion back, narrow card, officially cut		£28.00	—
D	BW		VC and DSO Naval and Flying Heroes:			
		50	Unnumbered (1916)	H.121	£11.00	£550.00
		25	Numbered 51-75 (1917)		£11.00	£275.00
D	BW	20	*War Pictures (1915)	H.122	£18.00	£360.00
D	BW	25	*War Series (War Leaders and Warships) (c1915) ...	H.103	£18.00	—
A1	C	25	Wild Animals and Birds (c1908)		£18.00	—
A	C	25	The World's Police (c1935)		£5.00	£125.00
			§Joint Cope and Richard Lloyd issues.			
OVERSEAS ISSUES						
A2	C	30	Flags of Nations (c1903)		£80.00	—
A	C	50	Jordklodens Hunde (1912)		£40.00	—

Size	Print-ing	Number in set	BRITISH TOBACCO ISSUERS	Handbook reference	Price per card	Complete set
			COPE BROS. & CO. LTD, Liverpool (Overseas Issues continued)			
D	C	30	Scandinavian Actors and Actresses (1910)		£40.00	—
A	C	35	Speider Billeder I Hver Pakke (1910)		£35.00	—
A	C	25	Uniformer A F Fremragende Britiske Regimenter (1908)		£40.00	—
A	C	25	Vilde Dyr Og Fugle (1907)		£40.00	—
			E. CORONEL, London			
A	C	25	*Types of British and Colonial Troops (1900)	H.76	£80.00	—
			DAVID CORRE & CO., London			
—	C	1	Advertisement Card — The New Alliance (70 x 42mm) (c1915)		—	£400.00
D	C	40	*Naval and Military Phrases (1900):	H.14		
			A With border		£100.00	—
			B Without border		£100.00	—
			JOHN COTTON LTD, Edinburgh			
—	C	50	*Bridge Hands (folders) (82 x 66mm) (1934)		£14.00	—
A1	U	50	*Golf Strokes — A/B (1936)		£11.00	—
A1	U	50	*Golf Strokes— C/D (1937)		£12.00	—
A1	U	50	*Golf Strokes— E/F (1938)		£18.00	—
A1	U	50	*Golf Strokes — G/H (1939)		£500.00	—
A1	U	50	*Golf Strokes — I/J (1939)		£500.00	—
			A. & J. COUDENS LTD, London			
A1	P	60	British Beauty Spots (1923):	H.553		
			A Printed back, numbered		£1.70	£100.00
			B Printed back, unnumbered		£2.50	—
			*C Back rubber stamped 'Cymax Cigarettes …'		£4.00	—
			*D Plain back		£4.00	—
A	P	60	Holiday Resorts in East Anglia (1924)		£1.25	£75.00
A2	BW	25	Sports Alphabet (1924)	H.551	£12.00	£300.00
			THE CRAIGMILLAR CREAMERY CO. LTD, Midlothian			
H	C	1	*Views of Craigmillar (c1901)	H.727	—	£1300.00
			W.F. DANIELL, Bristol			
—	BW	? 1	*Puzzle Cards (108 x 73mm) (c1900)	H.729	£700.00	
			W.R. DANIEL & CO., London			
—	C	1	Advertisement Card (85 x 55mm) (c1901)	H.728	—	£600.00
A2	C	30	*Colonial Troops (c1902):	H.40		
			A Black back		£110.00	—
			B Brown back		£110.00	—
A2	C	25	*National Flags and Flowers — Girls (c1901)	H.123	£160.00	—
			W.T. DAVIES & SONS, Chester			
A	C	50	*Actresses — 'DAVAN' (c1902)	H.124	£100.00	—
A2	U	42	Aristocrats of the Turf (1924):	H.554		
			1 Nos 1-30 — 'A Series of 30'		£8.00	—
			2 Nos 31-42 — 'A Series of 42'		£24.00	—

Size	Print-ing	Number in set	BRITISH TOBACCO ISSUERS	Handbook reference	Price per card	Complete set
			W.T. DAVIES & SONS, Chester (continued)			
A2	U	36	Aristocrats of the Turf, Second Series (1924)	H.554	£7.00	—
A	C	25	Army Life (1915)	H.78	£16.00	—
A	BW	12	*Beauties (1903)	H.125	£70.00	—
A	C	25	Boxing (1924)	H.311	£4.80	£120.00
A	C	50	Flags and Funnels of Leading Steamship Lines (1913)	H.67	£12.00	—
A	BW	? 13	Newport Football Club (c1904)	H.126	£475.00	—
A	BW	5	Royal Welsh Fusiliers (c1904)	H.127	£475.00	—
			S.H. DAWES, Luton			
D	C	30	*Army Pictures, Cartoons, etc (c1916)	H.12	£160.00	—
			J.W. DEWHURST, Morecambe			
D	C	30	*Army Pictures, Cartoons, etc (c1916)	H.12	£160.00	—
			R.I. DEXTER & CO., Hucknall			
D2	U	30	*Borough Arms (1900)	H.128	£1.30	£40.00
			A. DIMITRIOU, London			
—	C	? 3	Advertisement Cards (100 x 65mm) (c1930)		£125.00	—
			GEORGE DOBIE & SON LTD, Paisley			
—	C	? 22	Bridge Problems (folders) (circular 64mm diameter) (c1933)		£50.00	—
—	C	32	Four-Square Book (Nd 1-32) (75 x 50mm) (1959)		£2.00	—
—	C	32	Four-Square Book (Nd 33-64) (75 x 50mm) (1959)		£2.00	—
—	C	32	Four-Square Book (Nd 65-96) (75 x 50mm) (1960)		£1.70	£55.00
A	C	25	Weapons of All Ages (1924)		£10.00	£250.00
			DOBSON & CO. LTD			
A	C	8	The European War Series (c1917)	H.129	£50.00	—
			THE DOMINION TOBACCO CO. (1929) LTD, London			
A	U	25	Old Ships (1934)		£2.60	£65.00
A	U	25	Old Ships (Second Series) (1935)		£1.00	£25.00
A	U	25	Old Ships (Third Series) (1936)		£1.00	£25.00
A	U	25	Old Ships (Fourth Series) (1936)		£2.60	£65.00
			JOSEPH W. DOYLE LTD, Manchester			
—	P	18	*Beauties, Nd X.1-X.18 (89 x 70mm) (c1925)	H.653	£16.00	—
D	P	12	Dirt Track Riders Nd. CC.A.1-CC.A.12 (c1925)	H.635	£65.00	—
D	P	12	Views Nd. CC.B.1-CC.B.12 (c1925)	H.635	£35.00	—
D	P	12	Views Nd CC.C.1-CC.C.12 (c1925)	H.635	£35.00	—
D	P	12	*Beauties Nd. CC.D.1-CC.D.12 (c1925)	H.635	£35.00	—
D	P	12	*Beauties Nd CC.E.1-CC.E.12 (c1925)	H.635	£35.00	—
			MAJOR DRAPKIN & CO., London			
D	BW	12	*Actresses 'FRAN' (c1910)	H.175/GP.400	£9.00	—
C	C	8	*Advertisement Cards (c1925):	GP.401		
			1 Packings (4)		£9.00	£36.00
			2 Smokers (4)		£8.00	£32.00
—	BW	? 1	*Army Insignia (83 x 46mm) (c1915)	GP.402	£1000.00	—

Size	Printing	Number in set	BRITISH TOBACCO ISSUERS	Handbook reference	Price per card	Complete set
			MAJOR DRAPKIN & CO., London (continued)			
	BW	50	Around Britain (1929) (export):			
C			A Small size		£1.50	£75.00
B1			B Large size		£3.00	—
	C	50	Around the Mediterranean (1926) (export):	GP.404		
C			A Small size		£1.50	£75.00
B1			B Large size		£3.00	—
A2	P	40	Australian and English Test Cricketers (1928)		£2.25	£90.00
—	—	? 111	'Bandmaster' Conundrums (58 x 29mm) (c1910) ...	GP.352	£10.00	—
A2	BW	? 32	Boer War Celebrities 'JASAS' — 'Sweet Alva Cigarettes' (c1901)	H.133	£180.00	—
A1	U	25	British Beauties (1930) (export)		£3.00	£75.00
A1	P		*Celebrities of the Great War (1916):	GP.409		
		36	A Printed back		£1.10	£40.00
		34	B *Plain back*		£1.10	£38.00
—	BW	96	Cinematograph Actors (42 x 70mm) (1913)	GP.410	£16.00	—
	C	15	Dogs and Their Treatment (1924):			
A			A Small size		£6.00	£90.00
B2			B Large size		£7.00	£105.00
A	C	40	The Game of Sporting Snap (1928)		£5.00	—
			Instruction Leaflet		—	£12.00
	C	50	Girls of Many Lands (1929):			
D			A Small size		£4.00	—
—			B Medium size (76 x 52mm)		50p	£25.00
A	C	1	'Grey's' Smoking Mixture Advertisement Card (plain back) (c1935)		—	£7.00
A	C	25	How to Keep Fit — Sandow Exercises (c1912):	H.136		
			A 'Drapkin's Cigarettes'		£16.00	£400.00
			A1 'Drapkin's Cigarettes' short cards, cut officially		£16.00	—
			B 'Crayol Cigarettes'		£16.00	£400.00
A2	BW	54	Life at Whipsnade Zoo (1934)	GP.415	50p	£27.00
D2	C	50	'Limericks' (1929):	GP.416		
			A White card		£2.00	—
			B Cream card		£2.00	—
A2	P	36	National Types of Beauty (1928)	GP.417	£1.00	£36.00
	C	25	Optical Illusions (1926):			
A			A Small size. Home issue, name panel (23 x 7mm)		£3.40	£85.00
A			B Small size. Export issue, name panel (26 x 10mm)		£3.20	£80.00
B2			C Large 'size. Home issue		£3.60	£90.00
	C	25	Palmistry:			
A			A Small size (1927)		£3.20	£80.00
B			B Large size (1926)		£3.20	£80.00
D	U	48	Photogravure Masterpieces (1915)	GP.420	£10.00	—
	C	25	Puzzle Pictures (1926):			
A			A Small size		£5.00	£125.00
B			B Large size		£5.00	£125.00
—	C	25	*Soldiers and Their Uniforms, die cut (1914):	H.138/GP.423		
			A 'Drapkin's Cigarettes':			
			i 23 Different		£1.00	—
			ii 1st Life Guards		£30.00	—
			iii South Wales Borderers		£30.00	—
			B 'Crayol Cigarettes':			
			i 22 Different		£1.00	£22.00
			ii Durham Light Infantry		£20.00	—
			iii 1st Life Guards		£30.00	—
			iv South Wales Borderers		£30.00	—

Size	Print-ing	Number in set	BRITISH TOBACCO ISSUERS	Handbook reference	Price per card	Complete set

MAJOR DRAPKIN & CO., London (continued)

Size	Print-ing	Number in set		Handbook reference	Price per card	Complete set
A2	P	36	Sporting Celebrities in Action (1930) (export):			
			A 32 Different ...		£5.00	—
			B Nos. 4,5 and 6 (Golfers) ...		£20.00	—
			C No. 18 withdrawn ...		£125.00	—
D	BW		*Views of the World (c1912):	H.176/GP.425		
		12	A Caption in two lines ...		£6.00	£75.00
		8	B Caption in one line ...		£32.00	—
D	BW	8	*Warships (c1912) ...	GP.426	£15.00	—
SILKS						
—	C	40	Regimental Colours and Badges of the Indian Army (70 x 50mm) (paper-backed) (c1915):	H.502-5/GP.422		
			A The Buffs' back ...		£6.00	—
			B No brand back ...		£36.00	—

DRAPKIN & MILLHOFF, London

Size	Print-ing	Number in set		Handbook reference	Price per card	Complete set
A	U		*Beauties 'KEWAI' (c1898):	H.139-1		
		? 2	A 'Eldona Cigars' back ...		£350.00	—
		? 1	B 'Explorer Cigars' back ...		£350.00	—
A	BW	25	*Boer War Celebrities — 'PAM' (c1901):	H.140		
			A With PTO on front 'Pick-Me-Up Cigarettes', multi-backed ...		£38.00	—
			B Without PTO on front 'Pick-Me-Up Cigarettes', multi-backed ...		£38.00	—
			C Plain back ...		£75.00	—
C	C	30	*Colonial Troops, multi-backed (c1902) ...	H.40	£65.00	—
—	BW	? 7	*'Pick-me-up' Paper Inserts (112 x 44mm) (c1900) ...		£300.00	—
—	U	? 2	*Portraits (48 x 36mm) (c1900) ...	H.461	£300.00	—
A2	U	? 3	*Pretty Girl Series — 'BAGG' (c1900) ...	H.45	£350.00	—

J. DUNCAN & CO. LTD, Glasgow

Size	Print-ing	Number in set		Handbook reference	Price per card	Complete set
D1	C	50	'Evolution of the Steamship' (c1925) ...	H.559	—	£85.00
			47 different ...		£1.00	£47.00
			'Olympia II' ...		£30.00	—
			'Castalia' and 'Athenia' ...		£12.00	—
D1	C	48	*Flags, Arms and Types of Nations (c1910):	H.115		
			A Back in Blue ...		£35.00	—
			B Back in Green ...		£50.00	—
A	C	20	Inventors and Their Inventions (c1915) ...	H.213	£60.00	—
A	C	30	Scottish Clans, Arms of Chiefs and Tartans (c1910):	H.142		
			A Back in black ...		£250.00	—
			B Back in green ...		£20.00	—
—	C		Scottish Gems: (58 x 84mm):	H.143		
—	C	72	1st series (c1912) ...		£13.00	—
—	C	50	2nd series (c1913) ...		£13.00	—
—	C	50	3rd series (c1914) ...		£13.00	—
H1	BW	50	Scottish Gems (known as '4th Series') (c1925) ...	H.143	60p	£30.00
D	C	25	*Types of British Soldiers (c1910) ...	H.144	£70.00	—

G. DUNCOMBE, Buxton

Size	Print-ing	Number in set		Handbook reference	Price per card	Complete set
D	C	30	*Army Pictures, Cartoons, Etc (c1916) ...	H.12	£160.00	—

ALFRED DUNHILL LTD, London

Size	Print-ing	Number in set		Handbook reference	Price per card	Complete set
			Dunhill Kingsize Ransom (75 x 45mm) (1985):			
—	U	25	A Back reading top to bottom ...		£2.00	—
—	U	25	B Back reading bottom to top ...		£2.00	—

Size	Print-ing	Number in set	BRITISH TOBACCO ISSUERS	Handbook reference	Price per card	Complete set
			EDWARDS, RINGER & CO., Bristol			
—	BW	50	How to Count Cribbage Hands (79 x 62mm) (c1908)		£400.00	—
			EDWARDS, RINGER & BIGG, Bristol			
A	U	25	Abbeys and Castles — Photogravure series (c1912):			
			A Type-set back		£10.00	£250.00
			B 'Statue of Liberty' back		£10.00	£250.00
			C 'Stag Design' back		£10.00	£250.00
A	U	25	Alpine Views — Photogravure series (c1912):			
			A 'Statue of Liberty' back		£10.00	£250.00
			B 'Stag Design' back		£10.00	£250.00
A	C	12	*Beauties — 'CERF' (1905)	H.57	£75.00	—
A	U	25	*Beauties — 'FECKSA', 1900 Calendar back	H.58	£50.00	—
A	C	50	*Birds and Eggs (1906)	H.60	£16.00	£800.00
A	BW	? 2	Boer War and Boxer Rebellion Sketches (c1901)	H.46	£200.00	—
A	BW	25	*Boer War Celebrities — 'STEW' 1901 Calendar back	H.105	£50.00	—
A	C	25	British Trees and Their Uses (1933)	H.654	£2.80	£70.00
A	C	1	Calendar for 1899	H.730	—	£600.00
A	C	1	Calendar (1905), Exmore Hunt Stag design back	H.730	—	£450.00
A	C	2	Calendar (1910)	H.730	£450.00	—
A	C	50	Celebrated Bridges (1924)	H.346	£2.50	£125.00
	U		Cinema Stars (1923):			
A2		50	A Small size		£2.00	£100.00
—		25	B Medium size (67 x 57mm)		£2.00	£50.00
A	U	25	Coast and Country — Photogravure series (1911):			
			A 'Statue of Liberty' back		£10.00	£250.00
			B 'Stag Design' back		£10.00	£250.00
A	C	23	*Dogs series (1908):	H.64		
			A 'Exmoor Hunt' back		£10.00	—
			B 'Klondyke' back		£5.50	£125.00
A	C	3	Easter Manoeuvres of Our Volunteers (1897)	H.146	£375.00	—
A	C	25	Flags of All Nations, 1st series (1906)	H.37	£10.00	£250.00
A	C	12	Flags of All Nations, 2nd series (1907)	H.37	£13.00	£155.00
A	C	37	*Flags of All Nations (1907) (All Exmoor Hunt backs):	H.37		
			A Globe and Grouped Flags back		£10.00	—
			B With Price back:			
			i 4½d per oz		£10.00	—
			ii Altered to 5d by hand		£10.00	—
			iii 5d label added		£11.00	—
			C 'Stag' design back		£10.00	—
			D Upright titled back		£10.00	—
A	C	25	Garden Life (1934)	H.449	£3.20	£80.00
A	C	25	How to Tell Fortunes (1929)		£4.00	£100.00
A	C	50	Life on Board a Man of War (1905)	H.38	£12.00	—
—	C	1	'Miners Bound for Klondyke' (41 x 81mm) (1897)		—	£500.00
A	C	50	Mining (1925)	H.450	£2.50	£125.00
A	C	25	Musical Instruments (1924)	H.547	£4.00	£100.00
A	C	25	Optical Illusions (1936)	H.560	£3.20	£80.00
A	C	25	Our Pets (1926)	H.561	£2.60	£65.00
A	C	25	Our Pets, 2nd series (1926)	H.561	£2.60	£65.00
A	C	25	Past and Present (1928)		£3.60	£90.00
A	C	10	Portraits of His Majesty the King in Uniforms of the British and Foreign Nations (1902)	H.147	£45.00	£450.00
A	C	25	Prehistoric Animals (1924)		£5.00	£125.00
A	C	25	Sports and Games in Many Lands (1935):			
			A 24 Different minus No. 25		£6.00	—
			B Number 25 (Babe Ruth)		—	£60.00

Size	Printing	Number in set	BRITISH TOBACCO ISSUERS	Handbook reference	Price per card	Complete set
			EDWARDS, RINGER & BIGG, Bristol (continued)			
A	C	50	A Tour Round the World (Mar. 1909)	H.75	£12.00	£600.00
A	C	56	War Map of the Western Front (1916)		£15.00	—
A	U	54	War Map of the Western Front, etc Series No. 2 (1917):			
			A 'Exmoor Hunt' back		£15.00	—
			B 'New York Mixture' back		£15.00	—
			S. EISISKI, Rhyl			
D	U	? 25	*Actresses 'ANGOOD' (c1900)	H.187	£400.00	—
A	U	? 6	*Actresses — 'COPEIS' (c1900)	H.108	£400.00	—
A	U	? 23	*Beauties — 'FENA' (c1900)	H.148	£400.00	—
A	U	? 2	*Beauties — 'KEWA I', back inscribed 'Eisiski's New Gold Virginia Cigarettes' (c1900)	H.139	£400.00	—
A	U	? 2	*Beauties — 'KEWA I', back inscribed 'Eisiski's Rhyl Best Bird's Eye Cigarettes' (c1900)	H.139	£400.00	—
A	U	? 2	*Beauties — 'KEWA I' Rubber-stamped back (c1900)	H.139	£400.00	—
			ELDONS LTD			
A1	C	30	*Colonial Troops — 'Leon de Cuba' Cigars (c1900)	H.40	£180.00	—
			R.J. ELLIOTT & CO. LTD, Huddersfield			
A2	C	? 2	Advertisement Card — Bulldog (c1910)		£300.00	—
			EMPIRE TOBACCO CO., London			
D	C	? 6	Franco-British Exhibition (1908)	H.471	£375.00	—
			THE EXPRESS TOBACCO CO. LTD, London			
—	U	50	'How It is Made'(Motor Cars) (76 x 51mm) (1931)		£4.00	—
			L. & J. FABIAN, London			
—	P		The Elite Series (Beauties) (c1935):			
D1		24	A Numbered LLF 1 to 24		£40.00	—
A1		? 47	B Plain Numerals		£40.00	—
			FAIRWEATHER & SONS, Dundee			
A	C	50	Historic Buildings of Scotland (c1914)		£50.00	—
			W. & F. FAULKNER, London			
			12 page reference book — £4.50			
C	C	26	*Actresses — 'FROGA A' (c1900)	H.20	£60.00	—
A	C	25	Angling (1929)	H.655	£12.00	—
D2	C	12	*'Ation Series (1901)		£25.00	—
C	C	25	*Beauties (c1898)	H.150	£80.00	—
A	U	49	*Beauties — 'FECKSA' (1901)	H.58	£30.00	—
A	BW	16	*British Royal Family (1901)	H.28	£40.00	—
A	C	50	Celebrated Bridges (1925)	H.346	£3.00	£150.00
D2	C	12	*Coster Series (1900)	H.151	£34.00	—
A	BW	20	Cricketers Series (1901)	H.29	£400.00	—
D2	C	12	Cricket Terms (1899)	H.152	£110.00	—
D2	C	12	Football Terms, 1st Series (1900)	H.153	£55.00	—
D2	C	12	Football Terms, 2nd Series (1900)	H.153	£55.00	—
D2	C	12	*Golf Terms (1901)	H.155	£130.00	—
D2	C	12	Grenadier Guards (1899)	H.156	£34.00	—
A2	C	40	*Kings and Queens (1902)	H.157	£26.00	—

Size	Print-ing	Number in set	BRITISH TOBACCO ISSUERS	Handbook reference	Price per card	Complete set
			W. & F. FAULKNER, London (continued)			
D2	C	12	Kipling Series (1900)	H.158	£27.00	—
D2	C	12	The Language of Flowers (1900):	H.159		
			A 'Grenadier' Cigarettes		£32.00	—
			B 'Nosegay' Cigarettes		£32.00	—
D2	C	12	*Military Terms, 1st series (1899)	H.50	£34.00	—
D2	C	12	*Military Terms, 2nd series (1899)	H.160	£34.00	—
D2	C	12	*Nautical Terms, 1st series (1900)	H.161	£30.00	—
D2	C	12	*Nautical Terms, 2nd series (1900):	H.161		
			A 'Grenadier' Cigarettes		£30.00	—
			B 'Union Jack Cigarettes'		£30.00	—
A	C	25	Old Sporting Prints (1930)	H.563	£4.00	£100.00
A	C	25	Optical Illusions (1935)	H.560	£3.60	£90.00
D2	C		'Our Colonial Troops' (1900):			
			A Grenadier Cigarettes:			
		30	i With copyright Nos 1-30		£36.00	—
		90	ii Without copyright Nos 1-90		£20.00	—
		60	B Union Jack Cigarettes Nos 31-90		£22.00	—
A	C	20	Our Gallant Grenadiers, 1-20:	H.163		
			A Without I.T.C. clause (1901):			
			i Thick card		£20.00	£400.00
			ii Thin card		£20.00	£400.00
			B With I.T.C. clause, thin card (1902)		£30.00	£600.00
A	C	20	Our Gallant Grenadiers, 21-40 (1903)		£30.00	£600.00
A	C	25	Our Pets (1926)	H.561	£3.20	£80.00
A	C	25	Our Pets, 2nd series (1926)	H.561	£3.00	£75.00
D2	C	12	*Police Terms (1899)	H.165	£34.00	—
D2	C	12	*Policemen of the World (1899):	H.164		
			A 'Grenadier' Cigarettes		£220.00	—
			B 'Nosegay' Cigarettes		£40.00	—
A	C	25	Prominent Racehorses of the Present Day (1923)		£4.00	£100.00
A	C	25	Prominent Racehorses of the Present Day, 2nd series (1924)		£5.40	£135.00
D2	C	12	*Puzzle series (1897):	H.166		
			A 'Grenadier' Cigarettes		£240.00	—
			B 'Nosegay' Cigarettes		£75.00	—
A	BW	25	*South African War Scenes (1901)	H.167	£20.00	—
D2	C	12	Sporting Terms (1900)	H.168	£50.00	—
D2	C	12	Street Cries (1902)	H.169	£25.00	—
			FIELD FAVOURITES CIGARETTES			
D	P	? 1	*Footballers (c1895)	H.731	£2500.00	—
			THE FIGARO CIGARETTE			
—	C	12	Caricatures of Celebrities (101 x 57mm) (c1880)	H.732	£800.00	—
			FINLAY & CO. LTD, Newcastle-on-Tyne and London			
D1	BW	? 28	Our Girls (c1910)	H.170	£175.00	—
A	U	30	World's Aircraft (c1912)		£90.00	—
			FLYNN, Dublin			
A	C	26	*Beauties — 'HOL' (c1900)	H.192	£650.00	—
			C.D. FOTHERGILL, St Helens			
—	C	? 1	*'Play Up' Sporting Shields (c1895)	H.718	£175.00	—

Size	Printing	Number in set	BRITISH TOBACCO ISSUERS	Handbook reference	Price per card	Complete set

FRAENKEL BROS., London

Size	Printing	Number in set		Handbook reference	Price per card	Complete set
A2	C	? 2	*Beauties — 'Don Jorg (c1898)	H.733	£800.00	—
A	U	? 23	*Beauties — 'FENA' (c1898)	H.148	£130.00	—
A	C	25	*Beauties — 'GRACC' (c1898)	H.59	£160.00	—
A	U	24	*Beauties — 'HUMPS' (c1900)	H.222	£150.00	—
A	U	26	*Music Hall Artistes (c1900):	H.171		
			A Pink card		£130.00	—
			B White card		£130.00	—
A2	C	25	*Types of British and Colonial Troops (c1900)	H.76	£85.00	—

FRANKLYN, DAVEY & CO., Bristol

Size	Printing	Number in set		Handbook reference	Price per card	Complete set
A	C	12	*Beauties — 'CERF' (1905)	H.57	£80.00	—
D2	C	50	*Birds (c1895)		£80.00	—
A2	BW	10	*Boer War Generals — 'FLAC' (1901)	H.47	£100.00	—
A	C	25	Boxing (1924)	H.311	£4.00	£100.00
A	C	25	Ceremonial and Court Dress (Oct. 1915)	H.145	£12.00	—
A	C	50	Children of All Nations (1934)	H.656	90p	£45.00
—	C	? 1	Comic Dog Folder (opens to 183 x 65mm) (1898)	H.490	—	£700.00
A	C	50	*Football Club Colours (1909)	H.68	£25.00	—
A	C	50	Historic Events (1924)	H.464	£3.00	£150.00
A	U	25	Hunting (1925)		£1.20	£30.00
A	U	50	Modern Dance Steps (1929)		£5.00	£250.00
A	U	50	Modern Dance Steps, 2nd series (1931)		£1.00	£50.00
A	C	50	Naval Dress and Badges (1916)	H.172	£15.00	—
A	C	50	Overseas Dominions (Australia) (1923)	H.451	£5.00	£250.00
A	C	25	*Star Girls (c1898)	H.30	£260.00	—
A	C	10	Types of Smokers (c1898)		£60.00	£600.00
A	C	50	Wild Animals of the World (c1902)	H.77	£13.00	£650.00

A.H. FRANKS & SONS, London

Size	Printing	Number in set		Handbook reference	Price per card	Complete set
D1	BW	56	*Beauties — 'Beauties Cigarettes' (c1900)	H.173	£75.00	—
D	C	24	*Nautical Expressions (c1900)	H.174	£80.00	—
A1	C	25	*Types of British and Colonial Troops (c1900)	H.76	£80.00	—

J.J. FREEMAN, London

Size	Printing	Number in set		Handbook reference	Price per card	Complete set
D	BW	12	*Actresses — 'FRAN' (c1912)	H.175	£45.00	—
D	BW	12	*Views of the World (c1910)	H.176	£45.00	—

J.R. FREEMAN, London

Size	Printing	Number in set		Handbook reference	Price per card	Complete set
C1	U	33	Football Challenge (1969)		£8.00	—
—	U	12	*'Manikin' Cards (77 x 49mm) (c1920)	H.481	£75.00	—

C. FRYER & SONS LTD, London

Size	Printing	Number in set		Handbook reference	Price per card	Complete set
A2	C		*Boer War and General Interest: (c1900):	H.13		
		? 10	A Brown leaf design back		£220.00	—
		? 5	B Green leaf design back		£220.00	—
		? 2	C Green daisy design back		£220.00	—
—	—	50	Clan Sketches (101 x 74mm) (paper folders with wording only) — 'Pibroch Virginia' (c1936)		£15.00	—
D	C	40	*Naval and Military Phrases (c1905)	H.14	£70.00	—
A2	BW	? 14	*'Vita Berlin' series (c1902)	H.177	£500.00	—

FRYER & COULTMAN, London

Size	Printing	Number in set		Handbook reference	Price per card	Complete set
D	BW	50	*Beauties — PLUMS (c1900)	H.186	£800.00	—
—	C	12	*French Phrases, 1893 Calendar back (96 x 64 mm)	H.178	£800.00	—

Size	Print-ing	Number in set	BRITISH TOBACCO ISSUERS	Handbook reference	Price per card	Complete set
			J. GABRIEL, London			
A	BW	10	*Actresses — 'HAGG A' (1900)	H.24	£85.00	—
A2	C	25	*Beauties — 'GRACC' (c1898)	H.59	£220.00	—
A	BW	20	Cricketers series (1901)	H.29	£550.00	—
A	C	40	*Home and Colonial Regiments (c1902)	H.69	£90.00	—
A	U	? 56	*Pretty Girl series — 'BAGG' (c1898)	H.45	£75.00	—
A2	C	25	*Types of British and Colonial Troops (c1900)	H.76	£80.00	—

			GALLAHER LTD, Belfast and London			
			40 page reference book — £4.50			
D	P	110	*Actors and Actresses (c1900)	H.179	£6.00	—
D	C	48	Aeroplanes (1939)		90p	£45.00
A2	C	25	Aesop's Fables (1931):	H.518		
			A Inscribed 'Series of 25'		£1.60	£40.00
			B Inscribed 'Series of 50'		£1.40	£35.00
D	C	25	The Allies Flags: (1914):			
			A Toned card		£6.00	—
			B White card		£6.00	—
D	C	100	Animals and Birds of Commercial Value (1921)		90p	£90.00
D	C	48	Army Badges (1939)		80p	£40.00
—	U	24	Art Treasures of the World (76 x 56mm) (1930)		90p	£22.50
D	C	100	Association Football Club Colours (1910):			
			A Grey border		£11.00	—
			B Brown border		£11.00	—
A	C	52	*Beauties (c1900):	H.180		
			A Without inset		£16.00	—
			B With Playing Card inset		£13.00	—
—	P	48	Beautiful Scotland (77 x 52mm) (1939)	H.564-1	90p	£45.00
D	C	50	*Birds and Eggs (c1905):	H.60		
			A 'Gallaher Ltd' Label		£50.00	—
			B 'Manufactured by Gallaher' Label		£12.00	—
D	C	100	Birds' Nests and Eggs series (1919):			
			A White card		£2.00	£200.00
			B Toned card		£2.00	—
D	C		Boy Scout Series grey-green back (1911):	H.630		
		100	A 'Belfast and London'		£3.00	£300.00
		86	B 'London and Belfast'		£3.20	—
D	C	100	Boy Scout Series brown back (1922)	H.630	£2.80	£280.00
D	C	48	British Birds (1937)		50p	£25.00
D	C	100	British Birds by Rankin (1923):	H.537		
			A 'By Rankin'		£25.00	—
			B 'By George Rankin'		£1.80	£180.00
D	C	75	British Champions of 1923 (1924)		£2.20	£165.00
D	U	50	British Naval series (1914)		£6.00	£300.00
D	C	48	Butterflies and Moths (1938)		40p	£20.00
D	C	25	Champion Animals & Birds of 1923 (1924)		£2.40	£60.00
D	C	48	Champions (1934):			
			A Front without letterpress		90p	£45.00
			B Front with captions, subjects re-drawn		80p	£40.00
D	C	48	Champions, 2nd Series (1935)		60p	£30.00
D	C	48	Champions of Screen & Stage (1934):			
			A Red back		70p	£35.00
			B Blue back, 'Gallaher's Cigarettes' at base		£1.20	£60.00
			C Blue back, 'Gallaher Ltd' at base		£2.00	£100.00
D	U	100	Cinema Stars (1926)	H.658	£1.80	£180.00
—	P	48	Coastwise (77 x 52mm) (1938)	H.564-2	£1.10	£55.00

Size	Print-ing	Number in set	BRITISH TOBACCO ISSUERS	Handbook reference	Price per card	Complete set

GALLAHER LTD, Belfast and London (continued)

Size	Print-ing	Number in set	Description	Handbook reference	Price per card	Complete set
	C	24	Dogs (1934):			
			A Captions in script letters on front:			
D			1 Small size		£2.20	£55.00
B			2 Large size		£2.20	£55.00
			B Captions in block letters on front:			
D			1 Small size		£1.25	£30.00
B			2 Large size		£1.50	£36.00
D	C	48	Dogs (1936)		60p	£30.00
D	C	48	Dogs Second Series (1938)		50p	£24.00
D	P	100	English and Scotch Views (c1910)		£4.00	£400.00
D	C	100	Fables and Their Morals:			
			A Numbered Outside Set Title Panel (1912) ...		£1.75	£175.00
			B & C numbered in set title panel			
			B Thin numerals 'The Moral' 16mm long (1922)			
			1 White card		£1.25	£125.00
			2 Yellow card		£1.25	£125.00
			C Thick numerals 'The Moral' 12mm long (1922)		£1.25	£125.00
D	U	100	Famous Cricketers (1926)		£4.00	£400.00
D	C	48	Famous Film Scenes (1935)		70p	£35.00
D	U	100	Famous Footballers, green back (1925)		£3.00	£300.00
D	C	50	Famous Footballers, brown back (1926)		£3.00	£150.00
D	C	48	Famous Jockeys (1936):			
			A Blue text		£1.30	£65.00
			B Mauve text:			
			1 Nos 1 to 24		£3.00	—
			2 Nos 25 to 48		£5.00	—
D	C	48	Film Episodes (1936)		70p	£35.00
D	C	48	Film Partners (1935)		80p	£40.00
—	P	48	Flying (77 x 52mm) (1938)	H.564-3	£2.00	—
D	C	100	Footballers, red back (1928):	H.659		
			1 Nos. 1-50 — Action pictures		£4.00	£200.00
			2 Nos. 51-100 — Portraits		£4.00	£200.00
D	C	50	Footballers in Action (1928)		£3.60	£180.00
D	C	48	Garden Flowers (1938)		25p	£12.50
D	C	100	The Great War series (1915)		£3.00	£300.00
D	C	100	The Great War series — Second Series (1916)		£3.00	£300.00
D	C		The Great War, Victoria Cross Heroes (1915-16):	H.735		
		25	1st series 1-25		£6.00	£150.00
		25	2nd series 26-50		£6.00	£150.00
		25	3rd series 51-75		£6.00	£150.00
		25	4th series 76-100		£6.00	£150.00
		25	5th series 101-125		£6.00	£150.00
		25	6th series 126-150		£6.00	£150.00
		25	7th series 151-175		£6.00	£150.00
		25	8th series 176-200		£6.00	£150.00
—	C	20	£½ Million Berkeley Star Competition (90 x 33mm) (1995)		£1.50	—
D	C	100	How to do it (1916)		£4.00	£400.00
D		100	Interesting Views:			
	P		A Uncoloured, glossy (1923)		£2.00	£200.00
	CP		B Hand-coloured, matt (1925)		£3.00	£300.00
D			Irish View Scenery (c1910):	H.181		
	BW	400	1-400, matt:			
			A Numbered on back		£2.00	—
			B Unnumbered, plain back		£3.00	—

Size	Print-ing	Number in set		Handbook reference	Price per card	Complete set

BRITISH TOBACCO ISSUERS

GALLAHER LTD, Belfast and London (continued)

Size	Print-ing	Number in set	Description	Handbook reference	Price per card	Complete set
	P	400	1-400, glossy	H.181-A		
			A Black photo		£1.10	£440.00
			B Brown photo		£4.00	—
			C As A, but series title and No. omitted		£2.00	—
			D Numbered 1-200 plain back		£3.00	—
	P	600	1-600, glossy	H.181-B		
			A Nos 1 to 500		£1.10	£550.00
			B Nos 501 to 600		£6.00	—
B2	P	48	Island Sporting Celebrities (Channel Islands) (1938)		£3.00	—
D	C	100	'Kute Kiddies' series (1916)		£5.00	£500.00
D	P	50	Latest Actresses (1910):			
			A Black photo		£15.00	—
			B Chocolate photo		£22.00	—
D	C	50	Lawn Tennis Celebrities (1928)		£6.50	£325.00
A	C	24	Motor Cars (1934)		£5.00	£125.00
D	C	48	My Favourite Part (1939)		60p	£30.00
D	C	48	The Navy (1937):			
			A 'Park Drive ...' at base of back		60p	£30.00
			B 'Issued by ...' at base of back		£1.40	£70.00
—	P	48	Our Countryside (72 x 52mm) (1938)	H.564-4	£1.40	—
D	C	100	Plants of Commercial Value (1923)		£1.00	£100.00
D	C	48	Portraits of Famous Stars (1935)		£1.00	£50.00
D	C	48	Racing Scenes (1938)		60p	£30.00
D	C	100	The Reason Why (1924)		£1.00	£100.00
A	C	50	*Regimental Colours and Standards (Nd 151-200) (1899)		£9.00	£450.00
D	C	100	Robinson Crusoe (1928)		£2.25	£225.00
A	C	50	Royalty series (1902)		£8.00	£400.00
B2	P	48	Scenes from the Empire (1939) (export)	H.565	30p	£15.00
—	P	24	Shots from the Films (77 x 52mm) (1936)	H.566	£3.60	—
D	C	48	Shots from Famous Films (1935)		60p	£30.00
D	C	48	Signed Portraits of Famous Stars (1935)		£3.00	—
C1	C	20	Silk Cut Advertisements (1993)		£1.50	—
A	C	111	The South African series (Nd 101-211) (1901):			
			A White back		£6.00	—
			B Cream back		£6.00	—
D	C	48	Sporting Personalities (1936)		40p	£20.00
D	C	100	'Sports' series (1912)		£7.00	£700.00
D	U	? 98	*Stage and Variety Celebrities (collotype) (c1898):	H.182		
			A 'Gallager' back		£90.00	—
			B 'Gallaher' back		£90.00	—
			C As B but larger lettering, etc		£90.00	—
D	C	48	Stars of Screen & Stage (1935):			
			A Back in green		60p	£30.00
			B Back in brown		£1.60	£80.00
—	C	5	Telemania (1989):			
			A Size 90 x 33mm		£2.00	—
			B Size 90 x 45mm		£2.00	—
D	C	48	Trains of the World (1937)		£1.00	£50.00
D	C	100	Tricks and Puzzles Series, green back (1913)		£7.50	£750.00
D	C	100	Tricks & Puzzles Series, black back (1933):			
			Nos. 1-50		£1.00	£50.00
			Nos. 51-100		£1.00	£50.00
A	C	50	*Types of the British Army — unnumbered (1897):	H.183		
			A 'Battle Honours' back		£14.00	—
			B 'The Three Pipe ...' — green back		£14.00	—

Size	Printing	Number in set	BRITISH TOBACCO ISSUERS	Handbook reference	Price per card	Complete set
			GALLAHER LTD, Belfast and London (continued)			
A	C	50	*Types of the British Army — Nd 1-50 (1898):	H.183		
			A 'The Three Pipe ...' — brown back		£12.00	—
			B 'Now in Three ...' — brown back		£12.00	—
A	C	50	*Types of British and Colonial Regiments — Nd 51-100 (1900):			
			A 'The Three Pipe ...' — brown back		£12.00	—
			B 'Now in Three ...' — brown back		£12.00	—
D	C	100	Useful Hints series (1915)		£3.50	£350.00
	C	20	Views – Berkeley Superkings Panoramic (1994):			
G2			A Blue border (90 x 45mm)		£1.50	
—			B Blue border (90 x 33mm)		£1.50	
G2			C Green border (90 x 45mm)		£1.50	
—			D Green border (90 x 33mm)		£1.50	
G2			E Red border (90 x 45mm)		£1.50	
—			F Red border (90 x 33mm)		£1.50	
D	U	25	Views in North of Ireland (1912)		£60.00	—
D	C	50	Votaries of the Weed (1916)		£8.00	£400.00
D	C	100	'Why is it?' series (1915):			
			A Green back		£3.50	£350.00
			B Brown back		£3.50	£350.00
D	C	48	Wild Animals (1937)		40p	£20.00
D	C	48	Wild Flowers (1939)		70p	£35.00
D	C	100	Woodland Trees series (1912)		£5.50	£550.00
D	C	100	The 'Zoo' Aquarium (1924)		£1.30	£130.00
D	C	50	'Zoo' Tropical Birds, 1st Series (1928)		£1.70	£85.00
D	C	50	'Zoo' Tropical Birds, 2nd Series (1929)		£1.70	£85.00
SILKS						
—	C	25	Flags — Set 1 (68 x 48mm) (paper-backed) (1916)	H.501-1	£9.00	—
			SAMUEL GAWITH, Kendal			
—	BW	25	The English Lakeland (90 x 70mm) (1926)		£25.00	—
			F. GENNARI LTD, London			
A	U	50	War Portraits (1916)	H.86	£120.00	—
			LOUIS GERARD LTD, London			
D1	U	50	Modern Armaments (1936):	H.567		
			A Numbered		£1.10	£55.00
			B Unnumbered		£1.30	£65.00
D1	U	24	Screen Favourites (1937):	H.568		
			A Inscribed 'Louis Gerard & Company'		£4.00	—
			B Inscribed 'Louis Gerard Limited'		£4.00	—
D1	C	48	Screen Favourites and Dancers (1937):	H.569		
			A Matt front		£2.50	£125.00
			B Varnished front		£4.00	—
			W.G. GLASS & CO. LTD, Bristol			
A	BW	20	*Actresses — 'BLARM' (c1900)	H.23	£90.00	—
A2	BW	10	*Actresses — 'HAGG A' (c1900)	H.24	£90.00	—
A	U	25	*Beauties — 'FECKSA' (c1901)'	H.58	£140.00	—
D1	BW	20	*Boer War Cartoons ('Roseland Cigarettes') (c1901)	H.42	£140.00	—
A	BW	25	*Boer War Celebrities — 'STEW' (c1901)	H.105	£100.00	—
A	BW	16	*British Royal Family (1901)	H.28	£80.00	—
A2	BW	20	Cricketers Series (1901)	H.29	£475.00	—

Size	Print-ing	Number in set	BRITISH TOBACCO ISSUERS	Handbook reference	Price per card	Complete set
			W.G. GLASS & CO. LTD, Bristol (continued)			
D	C	40	*Naval and Military Phrases (c1902)	H.14	£130.00	—
A	BW	19	*Russo-Japanese Series (1904)	H.184	£80.00	—

R.P. GLOAG & CO, London

(Cards bear advertisements for 'Citamora' and/or 'The Challenge Flat Brilliantes' without maker's name)

Size	Print-ing	Number in set		Handbook reference	Price per card	Complete set
A2	U	? 9	*Actresses — 'ANGLO' (c1896):	H.185		
			A 'Citamora' on front		£450.00	—
			B 'The Challenge Flat' on front		£450.00	—
D			*Beauties — Selection from 'Plums' (c1898):	H.186		
	BW	60	A 'The Challenge Flat' front in black and white ...		£100.00	—
			B 'Citamora' front:			
	BW	? 10	(a) front in black and white		£130.00	—
	U	? 11	(b) front in brown printed back		£250.00	—
	U	? 10	(c) front in brown, plain back		£250.00	—
A	C	40	*Home and Colonial Regiments (c1900)	H.69	£60.00	—
D	C	30	*Proverbs (c1901)	H.15	£110.00	—
A2	C	25	*Types of British and Colonial Troops (c1900)	H.76	£80.00	—

GLOBE CIGARETTE CO.

D	BW	25	*Actresses — French (c1900)	H.1	£400.00	—

GOLDS LTD, Birmingham

A2	BW	1	Advertisement Card (Chantecler) (c1905)	H.737	—	£750.00
C	C	18	Motor Cycle Series (c1914):	H.469		
			A Back in blue, numbered		£60.00	—
			B Back in grey, numbered		£70.00	—
			C Back in grey, unnumbered		£70.00	—
—	BW	? 21	*Prints from Noted Pictures (68 x 81mm) (c1908):	H.216		
			A With firm's name, 5 brands listed back		£140.00	—
			B With firm's name, 3 brands listed back		£140.00	—
			C Without firm's name, 'Gibson Girl' back		£140.00	—

T.P. & R. GOODBODY, Dublin and London

—	U	? 4	*Actresses — 'ANGOOD' (36 x 60mm) (c1898)	H.187	£400.00	—
A2	U	? 10	*Beauties — 'KEWA' (c1898):	H.139		
			A Back rubber stamped in mauve		£320.00	—
			B Back rubber stamped in red		£320.00	—
D	BW		*Boer War Celebrities — 'CAG' (1901):	H.79		
		25	See H.79 — Fig. 79-B		£45.00	—
		16	See H.79 — Fig. 79-C		£45.00	—
		16	See H.79 — Fig. 79-D		£45.00	—
		16	See H.79 — Fig. 79-E		£45.00	—
	C	50	Colonial Forces (c1900):	H.188		
A2			A Brown back		£95.00	—
A2			B Black back		£95.00	—
—			C Size 80 x 50mm		£550.00	—
—	U	? 67	*Dogs (1910) (36 x 60mm):	H.189		
			A 'Brown Flake' back		£110.00	—
			B 'Celebrated Greenville Plug' back		£110.00	—
			C 'Eblana Flake' back		£110.00	—
			D 'Furze Blossom Cigarettes' back		£110.00	—
			E 'Furze Blossom Navy Cut' back		£110.00	—
			F 'Golden Flake' back:			
			i Text 44mm deep		£110.00	—
			ii Text 50mm deep		£110.00	—
			G 'Silk Cut Cigarettes' back		£110.00	—

Size	Print-ing	Number in set	BRITISH TOBACCO ISSUERS	Handbook reference	Price per card	Complete set
			T.P. & R. GOODBODY, Dublin and London (continued)			
			*Dogs (1910) (36 x 60mm) (continued)			
			H 'Specialities in Tins & Packets' back		£110.00	—
			I 'Two Flakes' back:			
			i Text 44mm deep		£110.00	—
			ii Text 50mm deep		£110.00	—
C	C	26	Eminent Actresses — 'FROGA A' (c1900):	H.20		
			A Front 'Goodbody' at base		£55.00	—
			B Front 'Goodbody' at top		£250.00	—
C	C	20	Irish Scenery (c1905):	H.190		
			A 'Donore Castle' back		£45.00	—
			B 'Fuze Blossom' back		£45.00	—
			C 'Primrose' back		£45.00	—
			D 'Royal Wave' back		£45.00	—
			E 'Straight Cut' back		£45.00	—
A2	U	? 14	*Pretty Girl Series — 'BAGG' (c1898):	H.45		
			A 10 'Gold and Silver Medals' back		£320.00	—
			B 'Furze Blossom':			
			i Mauve back		£320.00	—
			ii Red back		£320.00	—
			iii Grey back		£320.00	—
D	C	50	Questions & Answers in Natural History (1924)		£5.00	£250.00
A	C	25	Sports & Pastimes — Series 1 (1925)	H.225	£10.00	£250.00
A	C	25	Types of Soldiers (c1914)	H.144	£65.00	—
D	U	20	*War Pictures (c1915)	H.122	£42.00	—
C	C	12	'With the Flag to Pretoria' (c1901)	H.191	£130.00	—
			GORDON'S, Glasgow			
A2	BW	? 4	Billiards — By George D. Gordon (c1910)		£1000.00	—
			F. GOUGH, Blackley			
—	C	? 1	*Play Up Sporting Shields (c1895)	H.718	£125.00	—
			GRAVESON, Mexboro'			
A2	C	30	*Army Pictures, Cartoons, Etc (c1916):	H.12		
			A 'Wholesale Tobacconist' back		£160.00	—
			B 'Wholesale and Retail Tobacconist' back		£160.00	—
			C 'Wholesale and Retail Tobacconist Flash Cards etc.' back		£160.00	—
A	U	50	War Portraits (1916)	H.86	£120.00	—
			FRED GRAY, Birmingham			
A	C	25	*Types of British Soldiers (c1914)	H.144	£160.00	—
			GRIFFITHS BROS., Manchester			
—	P	18	*Beauties (89 x 70mm) (c1925)	H.653	£150.00	—
			W.J. HARRIS, London			
A2	C	26	*Beauties 'HOL' (c1900)	H.192	£45.00	—
C	C	30	*Colonial Troops (c1900)	H.40	£120.00	—
A1	C	25	*Star Girls (c1898)	H.30	£350.00	—
			JAS. H. HARRISON, Birmingham			
C	C	18	Motor Cycle Series (c1914)	H.469	£120.00	—

Size	Print-ing	Number in set	BRITISH TOBACCO ISSUERS	Handbook reference	Price per card	Complete set
			HARVEY & DAVY, Newcastle-on-Tyne			
D1	C	50	*Birds and Eggs (c1905)	H.60	£6.00	£300.00
A1	C	35	*Chinese and South African Series (c1901)	H.193	£150.00	—
C	C	30	*Colonial Troops (c1900)	H.40	£95.00	—
A1	C	25	*Types of British and Colonial Troops (c1901)	H.76	£95.00	—
			HARVEY'S NAVY CUT			
—	C	? 3	*Play Up Sporting Shields (c1895)	H.718	£125.00	—
			W. & H. HEATON, Birkby			
—	BW	? 6	Birkby Views (70 x 39mm) (c1912)	H.226	£400.00	—
			HENLY & WATKINS LTD, London			
A1	C	25	Ancient Egyptian Gods — 'Matossian's Cigarettes' (1924)	H.570		
			*A Plain back		£8.00	£200.00
			B Back in blue		£8.00	£200.00
			HIGNETT BROS. & CO., Liverpool			
A	C	50	Actors — Natural and Character Studies (1938)	H.571-1	£1.60	£80.00
C	C	26	*Actresses — 'FROGA A' (c1900)	H.20	£70.00	—
A2	U	25	*Actresses — Photogravure (c1900)	H.194	£50.00	—
D1	BW	28	*Actresses — 'PILPI I' (c1901)	H.195	£20.00	—
D1	P	50	*Actresses — 'PILPI II' (c1901)	H.196	£13.00	—
—	C	? 3	Advertisement Cards. (c1885)		£600.00	—
A	C	50	A.F.C. Nicknames (1933)	H.571-2	£8.00	—
A	C	50	Air-Raid Precautions (1939)	H.544	£1.50	£75.00
—	C	60	Animal Pictures ... (38 x 70mm) (c1900)	H.197	£36.00	—
A	C	50	Arms and Armour (1924)	H.273	£4.00	£200.00
C	C	? 25	*Beauties — 'CHOAB' (c1900)	H.21	£250.00	—
D	U	50	*Beauties — gravure (c1898):	H.198		
			A 'Cavalier' back		£85.00	—
			B 'Golden Butterfly' back		£85.00	—
—	C	? 8	*Beauties, multi-backed (168 x 109mm) (c1900)	H.708	£420.00	—
A	C	50	British Birds and Their Eggs (1938)	H.571-3	£4.00	—
A	U	50	Broadcasting (1935)	H.571-4	£3.00	—
A1	C	19	Cabinet, 1900	H.199	£100.00	—
A	C	25	Cathedrals and Churches (1909)	H.545	£5.00	£125.00
A	U	50	Celebrated Old Inns (1925)		£3.20	£160.00
A	C	50	Champions of 1936 (1937)	H.571-5	£4.00	£200.00
A	C	25	Common Objects of the Sea-Shore (1924)		£2.40	£60.00
A	C	25	Company Drill (1915)		£5.00	£125.00
A	C	50	Coronation Procession (sectional) (1937)	H.571-6	£3.00	—
—	BW	6	Diamond Jubilee 1897 (156 x 156mm)	H.740	£600.00	—
A	C	50	Dogs (1936)	H.571-7	£2.60	£130.00
A	C	50	Football Caricatures (1935)	H.571-8	£5.00	£250.00
A	C	50	Football Club Captains (1935)	H.571-9	£5.00	£250.00
A	C	25	Greetings of the World (1907 — re-issued 1922)		£4.00	£100.00
A	U	25	Historical London (1926)		£3.00	£75.00
A	C	50	How to Swim (1935)	H.571-10	£1.50	£75.00
A	C	50	Interesting Buildings (1905)	H.70	£7.00	£350.00
A	C	25	International Caps and Badges (1924)		£5.00	£125.00
A	C	25	Life in Pond & Stream (1925)		£3.40	£85.00
—	C	40	*Medals (34 x 72mm) (1901):	H.200		
			A 'Butterfly Cigarettes'		£32.00	—
			B Officially cut for use in other brands		£32.00	—

Size	Print-ing	Number in set	BRITISH TOBACCO ISSUERS	Handbook reference	Price per card	Complete set

HIGNETT BROS. & CO., Liverpool (continued)

Size	Print-ing	Number in set		Handbook reference	Price per card	Complete set
A	BW	25	Military Portraits (1914)	H.201	£8.00	£200.00
A	C	50	Modern Railways (1936)	H.571-11	£3.00	£150.00
A	C	25	Modern Statesmen (1906):			
			A 'Butterfly' back		£5.00	£125.00
			B 'Pioneer' back		£5.00	£125.00
A	C	20	*Music Hall Artistes (c1900)	H.202	£70.00	—
A	C	50	Ocean Greyhounds (1938)	H.571-12	£1.60	£80.00
	U	1	Oracle Butterfly (shaped) (c1898):			
			A Orange gold cellophane:			
			i Size 65 x 57mm		£125.00	—
			ii Size 51 x 40mm		£125.00	—
			iii Size 49 x 43mm		£125.00	—
			B Yellow and gold cellophane, size 51 x 38mm		£125.00	—
			C Purple and gold cellophane, size 48 x 38mm		£125.00	—
A	C	25	Panama Canal (1914)		£6.00	£150.00
A2	C	12	*Pretty Girl Series — 'RASH' (c1900)	H.8	£60.00	—
A	U	25	*The Prince of Wales' Empire Tour (1924)		£3.00	£75.00
A	U	50	Prominent Cricketers of 1938 (1938)	H.571-13	£5.00	£250.00
A	C	50	Prominent Racehorses of 1933 (1934)	H.571-14	£3.00	£150.00
A	C	50	Sea Adventure (1939)	H.571-15	60p	£30.00
A	C	25	Ships Flags & Cap Badges (1926)		£5.00	£125.00
A	C	25	Ships Flags & Cap Badges, 2nd Series (1927)		£5.00	£125.00
A	C	50	Shots from the Films (1936)	H.571-16	£3.50	—
—	C	6	*Story of a Boy Who Robs a Stork's Nest (118 x 88mm) (c1890)	H.742	£600.00	—
A	C	50	Trick Billiards (1934)	H.571-17	£7.00	—
A	U	25	Turnpikes (1927)		£2.80	£70.00
—	BW	25	*V.C. Heroes (35 x 72mm) (1901)	H.203	£85.00	—
A	C	20	*Yachts (c1902):	H.204		
			A Gold on black back		£75.00	—
			B Black on white back		£75.00	—
A	C	50	Zoo Studies (1937)	H.571-18	£1.00	£50.00

OVERSEAS ISSUES (NEW ZEALAND)

D1	P	50	Beauties, Set 1 (1926):			
			A Back without framelines, no brand mentioned		£2.00	—
			B Back with framelines, 'Chess Cigarettes'		£1.60	£80.00
D1	P	50	Beauties, Set 2 (1927)		£2.00	£100.00

R. & J. HILL LTD, London

28 page reference book — £4.50

A	C	26	*Actresses — 'FROGA A' (c1900)	H.20	£60.00	—
D	BW	30	*Actresses, Continental (c1905):	H.205		
			A 'The Seven Wonders' back		£18.00	—
			B 'Black and White Whisky' back		£25.00	—
			C Plain back		£18.00	—
D	BW	16	*Actresses — 'HAGG B' (c1900):	H.24		
			A 'Smoke Hill's Stockrider ...'		£35.00	—
			B 'Issued with Hill's High Class'		£35.00	—
—	BW	25	*Actresses (Belle of New York Series) (1899):	H206		
			A White back (41 x 75mm)		£26.00	—
			B Toned back, thick card (39 x 74mm)		£26.00	—
D1	U	20	*Actresses, chocolate tinted (1917):	H.207		
			A 'Hill's Tobaccos' etc back		£20.00	—
			B 'Issued with Hill's ...' back		£22.00	—
			C Plain back		£20.00	—

Size	Print-ing	Number in set	BRITISH TOBACCO ISSUERS	Handbook reference	Price per card	Complete set
			R. & J. HILL LTD, London (continued)			
C	U	30	The All Blacks (1924)		£9.00	—
C	C	20	*Animal Series (1909):	H.743		
			A 'R. & J. Hill Ltd.' back		£28.00	—
			B 'Crowfoot Cigarettes' back		£28.00	—
			C 'The Cigarettes with which ...' back		£34.00	—
			D Space at back		£28.00	—
			E Plain Back		£28.00	—
A	BW	25	Aviation Series (1934):			
			A 'Issued by R. & J. Hill ...'		£3.60	£90.00
			B 'Issued with "Gold Flake Honeydew" ...'		£3.80	£95.00
A	BW	? 18	*Battleships (c1914):	H.208		
			A 'For the Pipe Smoke Oceanic ...' back		£400.00	—
			B Plain back		£50.00	—
A	C	25	*Battleships and Crests (1901)		£26.00	£650.00
D2	C	12	*Boer War Generals ('Campaigners') (c1901)	H.209	£50.00	£600.00
A1	C	20	Breeds of Dogs (1914):	H.211		
			A 'Archer's M.F.H.' back		£26.00	—
			B 'Hill's Badminton' back		£26.00	—
			C 'Hill's Verbena Mixture' back		£26.00	—
			D 'Spinet Tobacco' back		£26.00	—
D1	BW	? 48	*British Navy Series (c1902)	H.210	£32.00	—
	U	50	Caricatures of Famous Cricketers (1926):			
C			A Small size		£4.00	£200.00
B1			B Large size		£4.00	£200.00
A	BW	? 1	*Celebrated Pictures (c1905)	H.744	£900.00	—
D1	C	50	Celebrities of Sport (1939):			
			A 'Issued by R. & J. Hill ...'		£3.00	£150.00
			B 'Issued with "Gold Flake Honeydew" ...'		£6.00	—
A2	C	35	Cinema Celebrities (1936):	H.572		
			A Inscribed 'These Cigarettes are guaranteed' ...		£1.30	£45.00
			B Inscribed 'The Spinet House'		£1.45	£50.00
C	C		*Colonial Troops (c1900):	H.40		
		30	A i 'Hill's Leading Lines ...' back		£26.00	—
		30	A ii 'Perfection vide Dress ...' back		£26.00	—
		50	B 1-50. 'Sweet American' back		£26.00	—
D1	BW	40	Crystal Palace Souvenir:			
			A Front matt (1936)		£2.50	£100.00
			B Front varnished (1937)		£2.00	£80.00
D1	C	48	Decorations and Medals (1940):			
			A 'Issued by R. & J. Hill ...'		£2.00	£100.00
			B 'Issued with Gold Flake Cigarettes'		£3.00	—
	P		Famous Cinema Celebrities (1931):			
—		? 48	Set 1:			
			A Medium size (74 x 56mm) inscribed 'Series A':			
			1 'Kadi Cigarettes' at base of back		£5.00	—
			2 Space at base of back blank		£4.50	—
A			B1 Small size, inscribed 'Spinet Cigarettes'		£4.50	—
A			B2 Small size, without 'Spinet Cigarettes'		£4.50	—
		50	Set 2:			
—			C Small size (66 x 41mm) inscribed 'Series C':			
			1 'Devon Cigarettes' at base of back		£7.00	—
			2 'Toucan Cigarettes' at base of back		£7.00	—
			3 Space at base of back blank		£4.50	—
			D Medium size (74 x 56mm) inscribed 'Series D':			
			1 'Kadi Cigarettes' at base of back		£4.50	—
			2 Space at base of back blank		£4.50	—

Size	Printing	Number in set	BRITISH TOBACCO ISSUERS	Handbook reference	Price per card	Complete set
			R. & J. HILL LTD, London (continued)			
D1	U	28	Famous Cricketers Series (1912):			
			A Red back, blue picture		£90.00	—
			B Deep blue back, brown picture		£90.00	—
			C Blue back, black picture		£90.00	—
C	U	40	Famous Cricketers (1923)	H.633	£6.00	£240.00
	U	50	Famous Cricketers, including the S. Africa Test Team — 'Sunripe Cigarettes' (1924):			
C			A Small size		£6.50	£325.00
B1			B Large size		£6.50	£325.00
A	U	50	Famous Dog Breeds 1954 (Airmail Cigarettes Slides)	H.889	£9.00	—
—	C	30	Famous Engravings — Series XI (80 x 61mm) (c1920)		£5.00	—
A2	BW	40	Famous Film Stars (1938):	H.634-1		
			A Text in English		£1.25	£50.00
			B *Text in Arabic, caption in English on back (see also Modern Beauties)*		£1.00	£40.00
D1	BW	20	Famous Footballers Series (1912)		£30.00	£600.00
C	U	50	Famous Footballers (1923)		£4.50	£225.00
D	C	50	Famous Footballers (1939):	H.574		
			A Shoreditch address		£3.50	£175.00
			B 'Proprietors of Hy. Archer ...'		£3.60	£180.00
D	C	25	Famous Footballers, Nd. 51-75 (1939)		£3.60	£90.00
—	U	25	Famous Pictures: (41 x 70mm) (c1912):			
			A 'Prize Coupon' back		£4.00	£100.00
			B Without 'Prize Coupon' back		£4.00	£100.00
D	C	50	Famous Ships:			
			A Front matt (1939)		£1.20	£60.00
			B Front varnished (1940)		90p	£45.00
D	C	48	Film Stars and Celebrity Dancers (1935)		£1.80	£90.00
C	C	30	*Flags and Flags with Soldiers (c1902)	H.41	£32.00	
—	C	24	*Flags, Arms and Types of Nations, 'Black & White' Whisky advert back (41 x 68mm) (c1910)	H.115	£15.00	£360.00
D	BW	20	Football Captain Series. Nd. 41-60 (1906):			
			A Small title		£75.00	
			B Larger title, back re-drawn		£80.00	—
—		10	Fragments from France (38 x 67mm) (1916):	H.212		
	C		A Coloured, caption in script		£27.50	£275.00
	U		B Sepia-brown on buff, caption in block		£30.00	£300.00
	U		C As B, but black and white		£100.00	—
—	C	10	Fragments from France, different subjects, caption in block (38 x 67mm) (1916)	H.212	£27.50	£275.00
A1	U	25	Hill's War Series (c1916)	H.35	£18.00	£450.00
	C		Historic Places from Dickens' Classics (1926):			
D		50	A Small size		80p	£40.00
B1			B Large size:			
		25	1 Nos. 2-26, small numerals under 2mm high		70p	£17.50
		50	2 Nos. 1-50, large numerals over 2mm high		60p	£30.00
	U	50	Holiday Resorts (1925):			
C			A Small size:			
			1 Back in grey		£1.00	£50.00
			2 Back in brown		£1.50	—
B1			B Large size:			
			1 Back in grey		£1.00	£50.00
			2 Back in brown		£1.60	—
—	C	20	Inventors and Their Inventions Series, Nd. 1-20, (1907):	H.213		
			A Black back, white card (68 x 38mm)		£5.00	£100.00
			B Black back, toned card (66 x 38mm)		£6.00	—

Size	Printing	Number in set	BRITISH TOBACCO ISSUERS	Handbook reference	Price per card	Complete set
			R. & J. HILL LTD, London (continued)			
C2	C	20	Inventors and Their Inventions Series, Nd. 21-40, (1907)		£8.00	£160.00
A	BW	20	*Inventors and Their Inventions (plain back) (1934)	H.213	£1.50	£30.00
—			*Japanese Series (40 x 66mm) (1904):	H.214		
	C	15	A 'Hills' on red tablet		£65.00	—
	C	1	B 'Hills' on blue tablet		£300.00	—
	BW	15	C 'Hills' on black tablet:			
			i With 'E F Lind Sydney'		£300.00	—
			ii Without 'E·F Lind Sydney'		£60.00	—
—	C	20	Lighthouse Series — without frame lines to picture (42 x 68mm) (c1903)		£35.00	—
—	C	30	Lighthouse Series — with frame line. Nos. 1-20 re-touched and 10 cards added (c1903)		£35.00	—
			Magical Puzzles — see 'Puzzle Series'			
A2	BW		Modern Beauties (1939):	H.634-2		
		50	A Titled 'Modern Beauties'. Text in English		£1.00	£50.00
		40	B Titled 'Famous Film Stars' (selection):			
			i Text in Arabic, No Captions, Numbered		£2.00	—
			ii Text in Arabic, No Captions, Unnumbered		£12.00	—
	C	30	Music Hall Celebrities — Past and Present (1930):			
D1			A Small size		£3.00	£90.00
B1			B Large size		£3.00	£90.00
D	C	20	National Flag Series (1914):	H.473		
			A Printed back		£10.00	£200.00
			B Plain back		£9.00	—
D	C	30	Nature Pictures — 'The Spotlight Tobaccos' (c1930)		£1.70	£50.00
C2	C	30	Nautical Songs (1937)		£1.70	£50.00
—	BW	25	*Naval Series unnumbered (42 x 64mm) (1901)	H.215	£50.00	—
D1	BW	30	Naval Series Nd. 21-50 (1902):	H.215		
			A Numbered 21-40		£16.00	—
			B Numbered 41-50		£65.00	—
	U	30	'Our Empire' (1929):			
D1			A Small size		50p	£15.00
B1			B Large size		£1.00	£30.00
—	BW		Popular Footballers — Season 1934-5 (68 x 49mm):			
		30	'Series A' — Nd. 1-30		£4.00	£120.00
		20	'Series B' — Nd. 31-50		£4.00	£80.00
C	C	20	Prince of Wales Series (1911)	H.22	£12.50	£250.00
	U		Public Schools and Colleges (1923):	H.575		
		50	A 'A Series of 50':			
C			1 Small size		£1.00	£50.00
B1			2 Large size		£1.00	£50.00
		75	B 'A Series of 75':			
C			1 Small size		£1.20	£90.00
B1			2 Large size		£1.20	£90.00
A1	C	50	Puzzle Series:	H.660		
			A Titled 'Puzzle Series' (1937)		£1.30	£65.00
			B Titled 'Magical Puzzles' (1938)		£2.60	£130.00
	U	50	The Railway Centenary — 'A Series of 50' (1925):			
C			A Small size		£1.60	£80.00
B1			B Large size:			
			1 Back in brown		£1.60	£80.00
			2 Back in grey		£4.20	—
	U	25	The Railway Centenary — '2nd Series — 51 to 75' (1925):			
C			A Small size		£2.20	£55.00
B1			B Large size		£2.20	£55.00

Size	Printing	Number in set	BRITISH TOBACCO ISSUERS	Handbook reference	Price per card	Complete set
			R. & J. HILL LTD, London (continued)			
C2	P	42	Real Photographs — Set 1 (Bathing Beauties) (c1930):	H.576-1		
			A 'London Idol Cigarettes' at base of back:			
			1 Front black and white, glossy		£2.85	—
			2 Front brown, matt		£2.85	—
			B Space at base of back blank:			
			1 Front black and white, glossy		£2.85	—
			2 Front brown, matt		£2.85	—
C2	P	42	Real Photographs — Set 2 (Beauties) (c1930)	H.576-2	£3.20	—
—	BW	20	Rhymes — black and white sketches (c1905)	H.217	£36.00	—
			The River Thames — see 'Views of the River Thames'			
D1	P	50	Scenes from the Films (1932):			
			A Front black and white		£3.50	—
			B Front sepia		£3.50	—
A2	BW	40	Scenes from the Films (1938)		£1.00	£40.00
D1		35	Scientific Inventions and Discoveries (1929)	H.213		
	C		A Small size, 'The Spinet House ...' back		£1.40	£50.00
	BW		B Small size, 'The Spotlight Tobaccos ...' back		£1.40	£50.00
B1	C		C Large size		£1.40	£50.00
DI	P	50	Sports (1934):			
			A Titled 'Sports', numbered front and back		£6.50	—
			B Titled 'Sports Series', numbered front only		£16.00	—
			*C Untitled, numbered front only		£17.00	—
A1	BW	30	*Statuary — Set 1 (c1900):	H.218-1		
			A Black and white front, matt		£55.00	—
	BW		B Black and white front, varnished		£13.00	—
A	BW	30	*Statuary — Set 2 (c1900)	H.218-2	£11.00	£330.00
C1	BW		*Statuary — Set 3 (c1900):	H.218-3		
		? 26	A Name panel white lettering on black background		£25.00	—
		? 4	B Name panel black lettering on grey background		£50.00	—
		? 26	C Name panel black lettering on white background		£50.00	—
D1	C	100	*Transfers (c1935)		£8.50	—
D	C	20	*Types of the British Army (1914):			
			A 'Badminton' back		£38.00	—
			B 'Verbena' back		£38.00	—
B2	CP		Views of Interest:			
		48	'A First Series ...' Nd. 1-48 (1938):			
			A 'The Spinet House ...' back		35p	£17.50
			B 'Sunripe & Spinet Ovals ...' back		30p	£15.00
		48	'Second Series ...' Nd. 49-96 (1938)		30p	£15.00
		48	'Third Series ...' Nd. 97-144 (1939)		30p	£15.00
		48	'Fourth Series ...' Nd. 145-192 (1939)		50p	£25.00
		48	'Fifth Series ...' Nd. 193-240 (1939)		60p	£30.00
			Album (1st to 5th Series Combined)		—	£35.00
B2	CP		Views of Interest — British Empire Series:			
		48	'1st Issue — Canada — Nos. 1-48' (1940)		50p	£25.00
		48	'2nd Issue — India — Nos. 49-96' (1940)		£3.00	£150.00
	U	50	Views of London (1925):	H.577		
C			A Small size		£1.30	£65.00
B1			B Large size		£1.30	£65.00
	C	50	Views of the River Thames (1924):			
D			A Small size:			
			Nos. 1-25		£2.00	£50.00
			Nos. 26-50		£1.60	£40.00
B1			B Large size:			
			1 Back in green (thin card)		£1.60	£80.00
			2 Back in green and black (thick card)		£1.60	£80.00

Size	Print-ing	Number in set	BRITISH TOBACCO ISSUERS	Handbook reference	Price per card	Complete set
			R. & J. HILL LTD, London (continued)			
	U	50	Who's Who in British Films (Nov. 1927):			
A2			A Small size		£1.80	£90.00
B2			B Large size		£1.80	£90.00
C	C	84	Wireless Telephony (1923)		£1.60	£135.00
B1	U	20	Wireless Telephony — Broadcasting Series (1923)		£2.50	£50.00
A	U	25	World's Masterpieces — 'Second Series' (c1915) …		£2.00	£50.00
	U	50	Zoological Series (1924):	H.578		
C			A Small size:			
			1 Back in light brown		£1.00	£50.00
			2 Back in grey		£1.10	£55.00
B1			B Large size:			
			1 Back in light brown		£1.10	£55.00
			2 Back in dark brown		£1.10	£55.00

CANVASES. Unbacked canvases. The material is a linen fabric, glazed to give the appearance of canvas. Specimens are found rubber stamped in red on back 'The Pipe Tobacco de Luxe Spinet Mixture'.

—	C	30	'Britain's Stately Homes' (78 x 61mm) (c1915)		£4.00	—
—	C		*Canvas Masterpieces — Series 1 (73 x 61mm) (c1915):			
			A 'Badminton Tobacco Factories …' back:			
		40	1 'H.T. & Co., Ltd., Leeds' at right base …		£2.20	—
		20	2 Cardigan Press, Leeds' at right base			
			(Nos. 21-40)		£2.20	—
		10	3 Without printers' credit (Nos. 21-30) … …		£2.20	—
		3	4 As 3, but size 73 x 53mm (Nos. 23-25) …		£2.20	—
		40	B 'The Spinet House …' back		£2.00	£80.00
—	C	40	*Canvas Masterpieces — Series 2, Nd. 41-80			
			(73 x 61mm) (c1915)	H.509	£2.50	£100.00
—	C	10	*Canvas Masterpieces — Series 2, Nd. 1-10 (c1915):			
			Nos. 1 to 5		£2.40	£12.00
			Nos. 6 to 10		£3.60	£18.00
—	C	5	Chinese Pottery and Porcelain — Series 1			
			(132 x 108mm) (c1915)		—	£50.00
			4 Different (minus No. 5)		£1.00	£4.00
—	C	11	Chinese Pottery and Porcelain — Series 2			
			(107 x 62mm) (c1915)		£6.00	—
—	C	23	*Great War Leaders — Series 10 (73 x 60mm) (1919)		£11.00	—

OVERSEAS ISSUE

A2	C	10	Chinese Series (c1912)		£90.00	—

L. HIRST & SON, Leeds

—	C	? 5	*Soldiers and their Uniforms (cutouts) (c1915) … …	H.138	£260.00	—

J.W. HOBSON, Huddersfield

C2	C	18	Motor Cycle Series (c1914)	H.469	£130.00	—

J. & T. HODGE, Glasgow

—	C	? 5	*British Naval Crests (70 x 38mm) (c1896) … …	H.219	£900.00	—
A	BW	16	British Royal Family (c1901)	H.28	£325.00	—
—	U		*Scottish Views (c1898):	H.220		
		? 11	A Thick card (74 x 39mm)		£220.00	—
		? 33	B Thin card (80 x 45mm)		£220.00	—

HOOK OF HOLLAND CIGARETTES

A	U	? 5	*Footballers (c1905)	H.745	£900.00	—

Size	Print-ing	Number in set	BRITISH TOBACCO ISSUERS	Handbook reference	Price per card	Complete set

HUDDEN & CO. LTD, Bristol

Size	Print-ing	Number in set		Handbook reference	Price per card	Complete set
C	C	26	*Actresses — 'FROGA A' (c1900)	H.20	£70.00	—
C	C	25	*Beauties — 'CHOAB' (c1900)	H.21	£70.00	—
A2	U	20	*Beauties — 'Crown Seal Cigarettes' (c1898)	H.221	£160.00	—
A	U	24	*Beauties — 'HUMPS' (c1898):	H.222		
			A Blue scroll back		£75.00	
			B Orange scroll back		£60.00	
			C Typeset back in brown		£400.00	
D1	C	? 12	Comic Phrases (c1900)	H.223	£120.00	—
D	U	25	Famous Boxers (1927)	H.721	£45.00	—
A	C	25	*Flags of All Nations (c1905)	H.37	£28.00	£700.00
—	C	48	*Flowers and Designs (55 x 34mm) (c1900):	H.224		
			A 'Hudden Cigarettes' back		£100.00	
			B 'Hudden's — Dandy Dot' back		£220.00	
A	C	18	*Pretty Girl Series — 'RASH' (c1900)	H.8	£100.00	—
C	U	50	Public Schools and Colleges (c1925)	H.575	£2.80	£140.00
A	C	25	Soldiers of the Century, Nd. 26-50 (1901)		£75.00	—
A	C	25	Sports and Pastimes Series 1 (c1925)	H.225	£60.00	—
A	C	25	*Star Girls (c1900)	H.30	£130.00	—
A	C	25	Types of Smokers (c1903)		£60.00	—

HUDSON

Size	Print-ing	Number in set		Handbook reference	Price per card	Complete set
D	U	? 1	*Actresses — 'ANGOOD' (c1900)	H.187	£650.00	—
C	C	25	*Beauties — selections from 'BOCCA' (c1900)	H.39	£550.00	—

HUNTER, Airdrie

Size	Print-ing	Number in set		Handbook reference	Price per card	Complete set
A	BW	? 11	*Footballers (c1910)	H.227	£2500.00	—

J.T. ILLINGWORTH & SONS, Kendal

Size	Print-ing	Number in set		Handbook reference	Price per card	Complete set
—	P	48	Beautiful Scotland (77 x 52mm) (1939)	H.564-1	£2.00	—
C1	C	25	*Cavalry (1924)		£7.00	£175.00
—	P	48	Coastwise (77 x 52mm) (1938)	H.564-2	£1.00	£50.00
A	C	25	'Comicartoons' of Sport (1927)		£8.00	£200.00
—	P	48	Flying (77 x 52mm) (1938)	H.564-3	£1.80	£90.00
A	C	25	*Motor Car Bonnets (1925)		£10.00	£250.00
A	C	25	*Old Hostels (1926)		£6.00	£150.00
—	P	48	Our Countryside (77 x 52mm) (1938)	H.564-4	£2.00	£100.00
—	P	24	Shots from the Films (1937)	H.566	£5.00	—
A	BW	25	Views from the English Lakes (c1895)	H.228	£250.00	—

THE IMPERIAL TOBACCO CO. (of Great Britain & Ireland) Ltd, Bristol

Size	Print-ing	Number in set		Handbook reference	Price per card	Complete set
A	C	50	British Birds (c1910)	H.229	£6.50	—
C	C	1	Focus on What's What (see Wills Post-1965) Folder — Coronation of His Majesty King Edward VII (1902)		—	£100.00
—	C	10	Out of the Blue — Richmond Adverts (2002):			
			A Size 75 x 32mm		£2.00	—
			B Size 80 x 47mm		£2.00	—
			C Size 90 x 47mm		£1.50	—
G2	C	12	Supertrivia — Superkings Adverts (2002)		£2.00	—

INGRAM'S, 1A, 27 & 33 Leigh Road, Eastleigh

Size	Print-ing	Number in set		Handbook reference	Price per card	Complete set
D	C	30	*Army Pictures, Cartoons, etc (1916)	H.12	£160.00	—

Size	Print-ing	Number in set	BRITISH TOBACCO ISSUERS	Handbook reference	Price per card	Complete set
			INTERNATIONAL TOBACCO CO. LTD, London			
—	C	28	Domino cards (58 x 35mm) (1938)		50p	£14.00
	U		*Famous Buildings and Monuments of Britain (1934)			
			(bronze metal plaques without envelopes):	H.580		
		50	'Series A':			
A1			1 Nos. 1-30, small size		£1.20	£36.00
H2			2 Nos. 31-50, large size		£1.20	£24.00
		50	'Series B':			
A1			1 Nos. 51-80, small size		£2.00	£60.00
H2			2 Nos. 81-100, large size		£2.00	£40.00
—	—	100	Empty envelopes with text for numbers 1 to 100		£1.00	—
			*The same plaques were also used for an export issue, with envelopes inscribed 'International Tobacco (Overseas), Ltd.'			
A2	C	100	Film Favourites (c1937):	H.581		
			A Back in grey		£2.50	—
			B Back in black		£2.50	—
—	C	100	'Gentlemen! The King!' — (60 small, 40 large) (1937):	H.582		
			A Back in blue		50p	£50.00
			B Back in black		20p	£20.00
A	C	50	International Code of Signals (1934)		£1.00	£50.00
D	C	48	Screen Lovers — 'Summit' (unissued) (c1940)		£3.80	—
			J.L.S. TOBACCO CO., London			
			('Star of the World' Cigarettes)			
D	BW	20	*Boer War Cartoons (1901)	H.42	£170.00	—
B2	BW	? 32	*Boer War Celebrities — 'JASAS' (c1901)	H.133	£260.00	—
A2	C	30	*Colonial Troops (c1901)	H.40	£130.00	—
			PETER JACKSON, London			
	P		Beautiful Scotland (1939):	H.564-1		
D		28	A Small size		£1.35	£40.00
—		48	B Medium size, 77 x 52mm		£1.00	£50.00
	P		Coastwise (1938):	H.564-2		
D		28	A Small size		£1.35	£40.00
—		48	B Medium size, 77 x 52mm		£1.25	£60.00
D	P	28	Famous Film Stars (1935)		£3.50	£100.00
D	P	27	Famous Films (1934)		£3.50	£100.00
D	P	28	Film Scenes (1936)		£3.50	£100.00
B	P	28	Film Scenes (1936)		£4.50	£125.00
	P		Flying (1938):	H.564-3		
D		28	A Small size		£3.50	—
—		48	B Medium size (77 x 52mm)		£3.50	—
—	C	100	'Gentlemen! The King!' (60 small, 40 large) (1937):	H.582		
			A Overprinted on International black back		£1.00	£100.00
			B Overprinted on International blue back		£1.00	—
			C Reprinted with Jackson's name at base:			
			i Back in black		£1.00	—
			ii Back in blue		£2.00	—
			Album		—	£35.00
D	P	28	Life in the Navy (1937)		£2.00	£55.00
B	P	28	Life in the Navy (1937)		£2.50	£70.00
	P		Our Countryside (1938):	H.564-4		
D		28	A Small size		£1.00	£28.00
—		48	B Medium size (77 x 52mm)		£1.25	£60.00

Size	Print-ing	Number in set	BRITISH TOBACCO ISSUERS	Handbook reference	Price per card	Complete set
			PETER JACKSON, London (continued)			
—	C	150	The Pageant of Kingship — 90 small, 60 large (1937):			
			A Inscribed 'Issued by Peter Jackson' ……………		50p	£75.00
			B Inscribed 'Issued by Peter Jackson (Overseas), Ltd.':			
			1 Printed on cream matt board …………		50p	£75.00
			2 Printed on white glossy board …………		50p	£75.00
			3 Printed on white glossy paper …………		40p	£60.00
			Album ………………………………………………		—	£35.00
	P		Shots from the Films (1937):	H.566		
D		28	A Small size ………………………………		£3.20	£90.00
—		24	B Medium size (77 x 52mm) ……………………		£3.25	£80.00
—	C	250	Speed — Through the Ages (170 small, 80 large) (1937) ………………………………………	H.583	30p	£75.00
D	P	28	Stars in Famous Films (1935) ……………………		£3.50	£100.00
			JACOBI BROS. & CO. LTD, London			
A	BW	? 32	*Boer War Celebrities — 'JASAS' (c1901):	H.133		
			A Black and white front ………………………		£250.00	—
			B As A, but mauve tinted ……………………		£250.00	—
			JAMES & CO. (Birmingham) LTD			
—	C	20	Arms of Countries (c1915):			
			A Size 70 x 40mm ………………………………		£170.00	—
			B Size 70 x 49mm ………………………………		£170.00	—
			JAMES'S (GOLD LEAF NAVY CUT)			
A	U	? 11	Pretty Girl Series — 'BAGG' (c1898) …………	H.45	£400.00	—
			J.B. JOHNSON & CO., London			
A	C	25	*National Flags and Flowers — Girls (c1900) ……	H.123	£400.00	—
			JOHNSTON'S CIGARETTES			
A	U	? 3	*British Views (c1910) …………………………	H.746	£700.00	—
			JONES BROS., Tottenham			
A	BW	20	*Spurs Footballers:	H.230		
			A 12 Small titles (1911):			
			i 10 Different ………………………………		£18.00	—
			ii F Bentley ………………………………		£100.00	—
			iii H Middlemiss …………………………		£150.00	—
			B 6 Large titles (1912):			
			i 4 Different ………………………………		£18.00	—
			ii E J Lightfoot …………………………		£200.00	—
			iii R McTavish …………………………		£150.00	—
			C 1 Team Group of 36 (1910-11) ……………		£1600.00	—
			D 1 Team Group of 34 (1911-12) ……………		£1600.00	—
			A.I. JONES & CO. Ltd, London			
—	C	1	*Advertisement Card — Alexia Mixture (80 x 46mm) (c1900) ………………………………………	H.748	—	£750.00
D	C	12	Nautical Terms (c1905) …………………………	H.231	£50.00	—
			A.S. JONES, Grantham			
D	C	30	Army Pictures, Cartoons, etc (c1916) …………	H.12	£160.00	—

Size	Print-ing	Number in set	BRITISH TOBACCO ISSUERS	Handbook reference	Price per card	Complete set
			ALEX. JONES & CO., London			
D2	U		*Actresses — 'ANGOOD' (c1898):	H.187		
		? 15	A Front in brown		£275.00	—
		? 1	B Front in green		£500.00	—
A	BW	1	Portrait of Queen Victoria 1897		—	£150.00
			T.E. JONES & CO., Aberavon			
D	C	? 2	*Conundrums (c1900)	H.232	£250.00	—
A2	C	50	*Flags of All Nations (c1899)	H.233	£85.00	—
D	C	12	Well-known Proverbs (c1900)	H.235	£250.00	—
—	BW	52	Welsh Rugby Players (64 x 34mm) (1899)	H.234	£270.00	—
			C.H. JORDEN LTD, London			
—	P	? 12	*Celebrities of the Great War (c1915) (35 x 64mm)	H.236	£100.00	—
			J. & E. KENNEDY, Dublin			
A	U	25	*Beauties — 'FECKSA' (c1900)	H.58	£55.00	—
			RICHARD KENNEDY, Dundee			
—	C	? 25	*Naval & Military Cartoons (130 x 90mm) (c1905) ...	H.701	£850.00	—
A	U	50	War Portraits (1916)	H.86	£120.00	—
			KINNEAR LTD, Liverpool			
A	C	? 13	*Actresses (c1898)	H.237	£125.00	—
D1	BW	? 15	*Australian Cricketers (1897)	H.238	£320.00	—
—	BW	? 1	Cricket Fixture Folder (89 x 69mm) (1903)	H.750	£2000.00	—
A	C	? 18	*Cricketers (c1895)	H.269	£600.00	—
A2	C	25	*Footballers and Club Colours (c1898)	H.239	£300.00	—
—	U	1	The Four Generations (Royal Family) (65 x 70mm) (1897)	H.749	—	£500.00
—	BW	1	'A Gentleman in Kharki' (44 x 64mm) (1900)		—	£90.00
A	C		*Jockeys (1896):	H.240		
		12	— see H.240—I-1		£80.00	—
		1	— see H.240—I-2		£140.00	—
		25	— see H.240—II-A		£140.00	—
		4	— see H.240—II-B		£140.00	—
A	C	? 2	*Prominent Personages (c1902)	H.479	£850.00	—
D1	U	13	*Royalty (1897)	H.241	£60.00	—
—	U	? 32	Views (49 x 35mm) (c1899)	H.751	£425.00	—
			B. KRIEGSFELD & CO., Manchester			
—	C	1	*Advertisement Card— Apple Blossom (c1900)	H.752	—	£1600.00
A2	U		*Beauties — 'KEWA' (c1900):	H.139		
		? 63	A Matt surface		£90.00	—
		? 6	B Glossy surface		£160.00	—
A	C	? 10	Celebrities (c1900):	H.242		
			A Backs Horizontal Format		£220.00	—
			B Backs Vertical Format		£220.00	—
A	C	50	*Flags of All Nations (c1900)	H.233	£80.00	—
A	C	50	*Phrases and Advertisements (c1900)	H.243	£125.00	—
			A. KUIT LTD, Manchester			
—	C	? 12	Arms of Cambridge Colleges (17 x 25mm) (c1914)	H.458	£120.00	—
—	C	? 12	Arms of Companies (30 x 33mm) (c1914)	H.459	£120.00	—
—	C	30	British Beauties — oval card (36 x 60mm) (c1914) ...	H.244	£60.00	—
—	P	? 44	*'Crosmedo'Bijoucards (55 x 37mm) (c1915)	H.245	£140.00	—

Size	Print-ing	Number in set		Handbook reference	Price per card	Complete set
			A. KUIT LTD, Manchester (continued)			
A	U	25	Principal Streets of British Cities and Towns (1916)		£110.00	—
A	CP	50	Types of Beauty (c1914)	H.246	£110.00	—
			LAMBERT & BUTLER, London			
			32 page reference book — £4.50			
A1	BW	20	*Actresses — 'BLARM' (c1900)	H.23	£40.00	£800.00
—	C	10	*Actresses and Their Autographs (c1898):	H.247		
			A Wide card (70 x 38mm): 'Tobacco' back		£175.00	—
			B Narrow card (70 x 34mm): 'Cigarettes' back ...		£150.00	—
A2	BW	50	*Admirals (1900):	H.248		
			A 'Flaked Gold Leaf Honeydew' back		£22.00	—
			B 'May Blossom' back		£22.00	—
			C 'Prize Medal Bird's Eye' back		£22.00	—
			D 'Viking' back		£27.00	—
—	C	12	Advertisement Cards — Facts about Lambert & Butler (2002):			
			A Size 75 x 32mm		£2.00	—
			B Size 80 x 47mm		£1.50	£18.00
C	C	1	*Advertisement Card — Spanish Dancer (1898)	H.249	—	£500.00
A	C	50	Aeroplane Markings (1937)		£2.00	£100.00
A	C	40	Arms of Kings and Queens of England (1906)		£6.00	£240.00
A	C	25	Aviation (1915)		£5.60	£140.00
A2	C	26	*Beauties — 'HOL' (c1900):	H.192		
			A 'Flaked Gold Leaf Honey Dew' back		£36.00	—
			B 'Log Cabin' back		£36.00	—
			C 'May Blossom' back		£36.00	—
			D 'Viking Navy Cut' back		£36.00	—
A	C	50	Birds and Eggs (1906)	H.60	£5.00	£250.00
C	BW	25	*Boer War and Boxer Rebellion — Sketches (1904) ...	H.46	£38.00	—
C	U	20	*Boer War Generals — 'CLAM' (1900):	H.61		
			I 10. No frame lines to back:			
			A Brown back		£45.00	
			B Black back		£45.00	
			II 10. With frame lines to back:			
			A Brown back		£45.00	
			B Black back		£45.00	
C	B	10	*Boer War Generals — 'FLAC' (1901)	H.47	£45.00	—
C	U	1	*Boer War Series — 'The King of Scouts' (Col. R.S.S. Baden-Powell) (1901)	H.753	—	£650.00
A	C	25	British Trees and Their Uses (1927)	H.654	£3.00	£75.00
A	C	25	Common Fallacies (1928)		£2.00	£50.00
—	C	50	*Conundrums (38 x 57mm) (1901):	H.250		
			A Blue back — thick card		£24.00	—
			B Green back		£20.00	—
A2	C	12	Coronation Robes (1902)	H.251	£22.00	£265.00
A	C	25	Dance Band Leaders (1936)		£4.00	£100.00
A	C	50	Empire Air Routes (1936)		£2.00	£100.00
A	BW	25	Famous British Airmen and Airwomen (1935)		£2.40	£60.00
A	U	25	Fauna of Rhodesia (1929)		£1.40	£35.00
A	C	50	Find Your Way:			
			A Address 'Box No. 152, London' (1932)		£1.60	£80.00
			B Address 'Box No. 152, Drury Lane, London' (1932)		£1.60	£80.00
			C Overprinted in red (1933)		£1.60	£80.00
A	BW	1	D Joker Card:			
			i Without overprint (1932)		—	£14.00
			ii With overprint (1933)		—	£14.00

Size	Print-ing	Number in set	BRITISH TOBACCO ISSUERS	Handbook reference	Price per card	Complete set
			LAMBERT & BUTLER, London (continued)			
A	C	50	Footballers 1930-1 (1931)		£5.50	—
A	C	25	Garden Life (1930)	H.449	£1.20	£30.00
A	C	25	Hints and Tips for Motorists (1929)		£5.00	£125.00
A	U	25	A History of Aviation:			
			A Front in green (1932)		£2.20	£55.00
			B Front in brown (1933)		£3.20	£80.00
A	C	50	Horsemanship (1938)		£2.50	£125.00
A	C	25	How Motor Cars Work (1931)		£2.20	£55.00
A	C	50	Interesting Customs and Traditions of the Navy, Army and Air Force (1939)		£1.30	£65.00
A	C	25	Interesting Musical Instruments (1929)		£3.00	£75.00
A	C	50	Interesting Sidelights on the Work of the GPO (1939)		£1.50	£75.00
A	C	20	International Yachts (1902)		£80.00	—
A	C	25	Japanese Series (1904):			
			A Thick toned card		£8.00	£200.00
			B Thin white card		£8.00	£200.00
—	C	4	*Jockeys, no frame lines (35 x 70mm) (c1903)	H.252	£60.00	£240.00
—	C	10	*Jockeys with frame lines (35 x 70mm) (c1903)	H.252	£60.00	£600.00
A	C	50	Keep Fit (1937)		£1.00	£50.00
A	C	25	London Characters (1934):			
			A With Album Clause		£2.40	£60.00
			B Without Album Clause		£20.00	—
			Album		—	£40.00
A	C	1	*Mayblossom Calendar, 1900		—	£800.00
A	C	25	Motor Car Radiators (1928)		£6.00	£150.00
A	C	25	Motor Cars — 'A Series of 25', green back (1922)		£3.00	£75.00
A	C	25	Motor Cars — '2nd Series of 25' (1923)		£3.00	£75.00
A	C	50	Motor Cars — '3rd Series of 50' (1926)		£4.00	£200.00
A	C	25	Motor Cars — 'A Series of 25', grey back (1934)		£3.60	£90.00
A	C	50	Motor Cycles (1923)		£4.00	£200.00
A	C	50	Motor Index Marks (1926)		£3.20	£160.00
A	C	25	Motors (1908):	H.703		
			A Green back		£32.00	—
			B Plain back		£32.00	—
A	BW	25	Naval Portraits (1914)		£4.40	£110.00
A	BW	50	Naval Portraits, incl. above 25 (1915)		£4.50	£225.00
—	C	3	Packet Redesign of The Pack (1998):			
			A Size 75 x 32mm		£2.00	—
			B Size 80 x 47mm		£2.00	—
A	C	25	Pirates and Highwaymen (1926)		£1.80	£45.00
A	U	25	Rhodesian Series (1928)		£1.40	£35.00
A	C	50	The Thames from Lechlade to London:	H.754		
			A Small numerals about 1mm high (1907)		£7.00	£350.00
			B Large numerals about 2mm high (1908)		£7.00	£350.00
			C Plain back (unnumbered)		£7.00	—
A	U	25	Third Rhodesian Series (1930)		70p	£17.50
—	C	12	Total Experience Total Trivia (1999):			
			A Size 75 x 32mm		£2.00	—
			B Size 80 x 47mm		£2.00	—
—	C	4	*Types of the British Army & Navy (35 x 70mm) (c1897):	H.254		
			A 'Specialities' back in brown		£80.00	—
			B 'Specialities' back in black		£80.00	—
			C 'Viking' back in black		£80.00	—
A	C	25	*Waverley series (1904)	H.255	£16.00	£400.00
A	C	25	Winter Sports (1914)		£5.00	£125.00

Size	Print-ing	Number in set	BRITISH TOBACCO ISSUERS	Handbook reference	Price per card	Complete set
			LAMBERT & BUTLER, London (continued)			
A	C	25	Wireless Telegraphy (1909)		£5.40	£135.00
A	C	25	Wonders of Nature (1924)		£1.00	£25.00
A	C	25	World's Locomotives, Nd. 1-25 (1912)		£5.40	£135.00
A	C	50	World's Locomotives Nd. 1-50 (1912)		£6.00	£300.00
A	C	25	World's Locomotives, Nd. 1A-25A (c1913)		£5.40	£135.00
OVERSEAS ISSUES						
D2	U	50	Actors and Actresses — 'WALP' (1905)	W.32	£5.00	—
		250	Actresses — 'ALWICS' (1905):	W.33		
D2	U		A Portraits in black, border in red:			
			i Scout back		£5.00	—
			ii With firm's name		£5.00	—
D2	BW		B Portraits and border in black		£7.50	—
D2	U	50	Beauties red tinted (1908):	W.146		
			A Scout back		£4.50	—
			B With firm's name		£4.50	—
A	C	83	Danske Byvaabner (c1915)		£16.00	—
	BW	26	Etchings of Dogs (1926):			
A			A Small size		£30.00	—
—			B Medium size (80 x 54mm)		£30.00	—
D2	C	25	Flag Girls of All Nations (1908)	W.64	£15.00	—
A2	P	50	Homeland Events (1928)		£2.50	£125.00
A	P	50	London Zoo (1927)		£1.50	—
A	C	50	Merchant Ships of the World (1924)		£2.50	—
D2	BW	30	Music Hall Celebrities (1916)	W.269	£7.00	—
A	P	50	Popular Film Stars (1926):			
			A Series title in one line, no brand quoted		£1.50	£75.00
			B Series title in two lines, inscribed 'Varsity Cigarettes'		£2.50	—
			C Series title in two lines, no brand quoted		£1.50	£75.00
A	P	50	The Royal Family at Home and Abroad (1927)		£1.60	£80.00
A	BW	100	Royalty, Notabilities and Events 1900-1902 (1902)	W.28	£16.00	—
D2	BW	100	Russo Japanese series (1905)		£8.50	—
D	P	50	Types of Modern Beauty (1927)		£1.50	£75.00
A	P	50	Who's Who in Sport (1926)		£4.00	£200.00
A	P	50	The World of Sport (1927)		£2.50	£125.00
A	U	50	Zoological Studies (c1928)		£10.00	—
			LAMBKIN BROS., Cork			
A	C	36	*Country Scenes — Small size (1924) (6 sets of 6):			
			Series 1 — Yachting		£10.00	—
			Series 2 — Country		£10.00	—
			Series 3 — Far East		£10.00	—
			Series 4 — Sailing		£10.00	—
			Series 5 — Country		£10.00	—
			Series 6 — Country		£10.00	—
C	C	36	*Country Scenes — Large size (1924) (6 sets of 6):			
			Series 7 — Yachting		£10.00	—
			Series 8 — Country		£10.00	—
			Series 9 — Far East		£10.00	—
			Series 10 — Sailing		£10.00	—
			Series 11 — Country		£10.00	—
			Series 12 — Windmill Scenes		£10.00	—
—	C	? 9	*Irish Views, anonymous. inscribed 'Eagle, Cork' (68 x 67mm) (c1925)	H.585	£45.00	—
—	C	? 5	*'Lily of Killarney' Views (73 x 68mm) (c1925)	H.586	£230.00	—

Size	Print-ing	Number in set	BRITISH TOBACCO ISSUERS	Handbook reference	Price per card	Complete set
			LANCS & YORKS TOBACCO MANUFACTURING CO. LTD, Burnley (L. & Y. Tob. Mfg. Co.)			
C	C	26	*Actresses — 'FROGA A' (c1900)	H.20	£500.00	—
			C. & J. LAW, Hertford			
A	C	25	*Types of British Soldiers (c1914)	H.144	£40.00	—
A	U	50	War Portraits (1916)	H.86	£120.00	—
			R.J. LEA LTD, Manchester			
A	C	1	*Advertisement Card — Swashbuckler (c1913)		—	£1000.00
A1	C	50	Chairman Miniatures 1-50 (1912):			
			A No border		£3.20	£160.00
			B Gilt border		£3.20	£160.00
			Album		—	£40.00
A1	C	50	Chairman and Vice Chair Miniatures, 51-100 (1912)		£3.20	£160.00
—	C	1	Chairman Puzzles Picture No 1 (diamond shaped 54 x 31mm) (c1910)	H.755	£325.00	—
—	C	12	Chairman Puzzles Picture No 2 (60 x 21mm) (c1910)	H.755	£325.00	—
A1	BW	25	Chairman War Portraits (marked 'War Series' on front) (1915)		£7.00	£175.00
A	C	70	Cigarette Transfers (Locomotives) (1916)		£15.00	—
A	BW	25	Civilians of Countries Fighting with the Allies (1914)		£20.00	—
A2	P	48	Coronation Souvenir (1937):			
			A Small size, glossy:			
			1 Lea's name		60p	£30.00
			2 'Successors to ...'		45p	£22.00
A2	BW		B Small size, matt:			
			1 Lea's name		£1.00	£50.00
			2 Successors to		50p	£25.00
—	P		C Medium size (77 x 51mm)		60p	£30.00
A2	C	50	Dogs (1923):			
			1 Nos. 1-25 — A White card		£5.00	—
			B Cream card		£5.00	—
			2 Nos. 26-50		£7.50	—
A2	C	25	English Birds (1922):			
			A Glossy front		£3.60	£90.00
			B Matt front		£6.00	—
A2	C	25	The Evolution of the Royal Navy (1925)		£3.00	£75.00
A2	P	54	Famous Film Stars (1939)		£1.30	£70.00
	CP	48	Famous Racehorses of 1926 (1927):			
A2			A Small size		£4.00	£200.00
			B Medium size (75 x 50mm)		£8.00	—
		48	Famous Views (1936):			
A2	P		A Small size — 1 Glossy		40p	£20.00
	BW			2 Matt		£1.00	£50.00
—	P		B Medium size (76 x 51mm)		50p	£25.00
A2	P	36	Film Stars — 'A First Series ...' (1934)		£3.40	£120.00
A2	P	36	Film Stars — 'A Second Series ...' (1934)		£3.00	£110.00
A2	C	25	Fish (1926)		£3.00	£75.00
A1	C	50	Flowers to Grow (The Best Perennials) (1913)		£4.50	£225.00
A2		48	Girls from the Shows (1935):			
	P		A Glossy front		£2.40	£120.00
	BW		B Matt front		£2.60	£130.00
			Album		—	£45.00
A1	C	50	Modern Miniatures (1913)	H.756	—	£435.00
			46 different, less 1, 8, 12, 32		£2.50	£115.00

Size	Print-ing	Number in set	BRITISH TOBACCO ISSUERS	Handbook reference	Price per card	Complete set
			R. J. LEA LTD, Manchester (continued)			
A1	C	12	More Lea's Smokers (1906):	H.256		
			A Green borders		£90.00	—
			B Red borders		£130.00	—
			Album		—	£50.00
A1	C	50	Old English Pottery and Porcelain, 1-50 (1912)		£3.00	£150.00
			Album		—	£35.00
A1	C	50	Old Pottery and Porcelain, 51-100 (1912):			
			A 'Chairman Cigarettes'		£2.50	£125.00
			B 'Recorder Cigarettes'		£6.00	—
			Album		—	£35.00
A1	C	50	Old Pottery and Porcelain, 101-150 (1912):			
			A 'Chairman Cigarettes'		£2.50	£125.00
			B 'Recorder Cigarettes'		£6.00	—
			Album		—	£35.00
A1	C	50	Old Pottery and Porcelain, 151-200 (1913)		£2.50	£125.00
			Album		—	£35.00
A1	C	50	Old Pottery and Porcelain, 201-250 (1913)		£2.50	£125.00
			Album		—	£35.00
—	C	24	Old English Pottery and Porcelain (138 x 89mm) ...	H.257	£6.00	—
			(Inscribed Chairman Cigarette Series or other firms' names, postcard format back) (c1910)			
A2		54	Radio Stars (1935):			
	P		A Glossy front		£2.40	£130.00
	BW		B Matt front		£3.00	£160.00
A2	C	50	Roses (1924)		£1.80	£90.00
A2	C	50	Ships of the World (1925)		£2.00	£100.00
A	BW	25	War Pictures (1915)		£7.00	£175.00
		48	Wonders of the World (1938):			
A2	P		A Small size — 1 Glossy		70p	£35.00
	BW		2 Matt		£1.50	£75.00
	P		B Medium size (76 x 50mm)		60p	£30.00
SILKS. All paper-backed.						
—	C		*Butterflies and Moths III (c1925):	H.505-7		
		12	1 Small size (70 x 44mm)		£4.50	£55.00
		12	2 Large size (70 x 88mm)		£4.00	£50.00
		6	3 Extra-large size (143 x 70mm)		£4.50	£27.00
—	C	54	*Old Pottery — Set 1 (68 x 38mm) (c1915)	H.505-14	£1.50	£80.00
—	C	72	*Old Pottery — Set 2 (61 x 37mm) (c1915)	H.505-14	£1.50	£110.00
—	C	50	Regimental Crests and Badges — Series I (48mm sq.) (c1920)	H.502-4	£2.60	—
—	C	50	Regimental Crests and Badges — Series II (48 mm sq.) (c1920)	H.502-4	£2.60	—

ALFRED L. LEAVER, London

	U	12	Manikin Cards (79 x 51mm) (c1925)	H.481	£150.00	—

J. LEES, Northampton

A	C	? 21	Northampton Town Football Club (No. 301-321) (c1912)		£150.00	

A. LEWIS & CO. (WESTMINSTER) LTD, London

A2	C	52	Horoscopes (1938)	H.587	£1.00	£50.00

Size	Print-ing	Number in set	BRITISH TOBACCO ISSUERS	Handbook reference	Price per card	Complete set

H.C. LLOYD & SON, Exeter

Size	Print-ing	Number in set		Handbook reference	Price per card	Complete set
A	U	28	Academy Gems, multi-backed (c1900):	H.258		
			A Red-brown tint		£50.00	—
			B Purple tint		£50.00	—
			C Green tint		£50.00	—
D	BW	? 26	*Actresses and Boer War Celebrities (c1900)	H.260	£45.00	—
—	BW		*Devon Footballers and Boer War Celebrities (c1901):	H.259		
		? 42	Set 1 — Without framelines (70 x 41mm)		£70.00	—
		? 6	Set 2 — With framelines (70 x 45mm)		£280.00	—
A1	C	25	*Star Girls — 'Tipsy Loo Cigarettes' (c1898):	H.30		
			A Brand name in capitals:			
			i Black		£450.00	—
			ii Blue		£450.00	—
			iii Red		£450.00	—
			B Brand name in upper and lower case		£450.00	—
—	BW	36	War Pictures (73 x 69mm) (c1914)		£400.00	—

RICHARD LLOYD & SONS, London

Most cards inscribed 'Branch of Cope Bros. & Co., Ltd.' See also under 'Cope Bros'.

Size	Print-ing	Number in set		Handbook reference	Price per card	Complete set
A	C	25	Atlantic Records (1936)		£3.40	£85.00
—	BW	25	*Boer War Celebrities (35 x 61mm) (1899)	H.261	£50.00	—
A2	P	27	Cinema Stars, glossy — 'A Series of 27', Nd. 1-27 (c1934)		£7.00	—
A2	P	27	Cinema Stars, glossy — 'A Series of 27', Nd. 28-54 (c1934)		£3.00	£80.00
A2	P	27	Cinema Stars, glossy — 'Third Series of 27', Nd. 55-81 (1935)		£7.00	—
A2	U	25	Cinema Stars, matt — 'A Series of 25' (c1937)		£2.40	£60.00
A	BW	25	*Famous Cricketers (Puzzle Series) (1930)	H.661	£10.00	—
—	U	? 23	*General Interest — Actresses, Celebrities and Yachts (62 x 39mm) (c1900)	H.262	£120.00	—
A1	C	96	*National Types, Costumes and Flags (c1900)	H.263	£38.00	—
D	C		Old Inns:			
		25	A1 Titled 'Old English Inns' (1923)		£2.00	£50.00
		25	A2 Titled 'Old Inns — Series 2' (1924)		£3.00	£75.00
		50	B Titled 'Old Inns' (1925)		£1.60	£80.00
A	C	10	Scenes from San Toy (c1905)	H.462	£12.00	£120.00
A	BW	25	Tricks and Puzzles (1935)		£1.20	£30.00
A2	U	25	Types of Horses (1926):			
			A Back in light brown		£4.00	£100.00
			B Back in dark brown		£4.00	£100.00
A2	U	25	'Zoo' Series (1926)	H.588	£1.20	£30.00

A. LOWNIE, Abroath

Size	Print-ing	Number in set		Handbook reference	Price per card	Complete set
A	C	30	*Army Pictures, Cartoons, etc. (c1916)	H.12	£160.00	—

LUSBY LTD, London

Size	Print-ing	Number in set		Handbook reference	Price per card	Complete set
D	C	25	Scenes from Circus Life (c1900)	H.264	£150.00	—

HUGH McCALL, Edinburgh, Glasgow and Aberdeen

Size	Print-ing	Number in set		Handbook reference	Price per card	Complete set
C	C	? 1	*RAF Advertisement Card (c1924)	H.594	£400.00	—

D. & J. MACDONALD, Glasgow

Size	Print-ing	Number in set		Handbook reference	Price per card	Complete set
A	C	? 10	*Actresses — 'MUTA' (c1891)	H.265	£140.00	—
A	BW	25	*Cricketers (c1902)	H.266	£600.00	—

Size	Printing	Number in set	BRITISH TOBACCO ISSUERS	Handbook reference	Price per card	Complete set
			D. & J. MACDONALD, Glasgow (continued)			
—	BW	? 24	*Cricket and Football Teams (71 x 69mm) (c1902):	H.267		
			A 'Winning Team' Cigarettes		£600.00	—
			B 'Tontine' Cigarettes		£600.00	—
—	C	? 1	County Cricket Team (71 x 69mm) (1900)	H.267	£3500.00	—
			MACKENZIE & CO., Glasgow			
—	P	50	*Actors and Actresses (32 x 58mm) (c1902)	H.268	£26.00	—
—	U	50	Victorian Art Pictures — Photogravure (32 x 58mm) (c1908)		£26.00	—
A	BW	50	The Zoo (c1910)		£30.00	—
			WM. M'KINNELL, Edinburgh			
A	C	12	European War Series (1915)	H.129	£80.00	—
A	U	50	War Portraits (1916)	H.86	£120.00	—
			MACNAUGHTON, JENKINS & CO. LTD, Dublin			
—	C	50	Castles of Ireland (1924):	H.662		
			A Size 76 x 45mm		£4.00	£200.00
			B Size 74 x 44mm		£4.50	—
D	C	50	Various Uses of Rubber (1924)		£3.00	£150.00
			A. McTAVISH, Elgin			
D	C	30	*Army Pictures, Cartoons etc (c1916)	H.12	£160.00	—
			McWATTIE & SONS, Arbroath			
D	C	30	*Army Pictures, Cartoons etc (c1916)	H.12	£160.00	—
			THE MANXLAND TOBACCO CO., Isle of Man			
D	BW	? 10	*Views in the Isle of Man (c1900):	H.491		
			A Varnished front		£500.00	—
			B Matt front		£500.00	—
			MARCOVITCH & CO., London			
A2	P	18	*Beauties (anonymous with plain backs, numbered left base of front) (1932)	GP.490	£1.00	£18.00
			The Story in Red and White (1955):	GP.494		
A	U	6	A Standard size		£4.00	—
—	U	7	B Size 75 x 66mm		£2.00	£14.00
			MARCUS & CO., Manchester			
A	C	? 18	*Cricketers, 'Marcus Handicap Cigarettes' (1895) ...	H.269	£750.00	—
A	C	25	*Footballers and Club Colours (1896)	H.239	£300.00	—
—	BW	1	The Four Generations (Royal Family) (65 x 70mm) (1897)	H.749	—	£350.00
			T.W. MARKHAM, Bridgwater			
—	BW	? 28	Views of Bridgwater (68 x 44mm) (c1906)	H.709	£120.00	—
			MARSUMA LTD, Congleton			
A	BW	50	*Famous Golfers and Their Strokes (c1914)		£65.00	—

Size	Print-ing	Number in set	BRITISH TOBACCO ISSUERS	Handbook reference	Price per card	Complete set
			C. MARTIN, Moseley			
D	C	30	*Army Pictures, Cartoons etc. (c1916)	H12	£160.00	—
			MARTINS LTD, London			
A	C	1	"Arf a Mo', Kaiser!' (c1915)		—	£85.00
—	U		Carlyle Series — folding card (c1918):	H.270		
			A Second page 'Martin Bros.'			
		? 3	i Size 83 x 38mm		£150.00	—
		? 14	ii Size 83 x 78mm		£150.00	—
		? 5	B Third page 'Martin Bros.'		£150.00	—
		? 3	C Second Page 'Martin's Ltd'		£150.00	—
—	U	? 781	The Performer Tobacco Fund Photographs – Celebrities (140 x 88mm) (c1916)		£7.00	—
D	U	25	*VC Heroes (c1916)		£36.00	£900.00
			R. MASON & CO., London			
C	C	30	*Colonial Troops (c1902)	H.40	£75.00	—
D2	C	40	*Naval and Military Phrases (c1904):	H.14		
			A White Border		£55.00	—
			B No Border		£55.00	—
			JUSTUS VAN MAURIK			
—	C	12	*Dutch Scenes (108 x 70mm) (c1920)	H.622	£175.00	—
			MAY QUEEN CIGARETTES			
—	C	12	Interesting Pictures (68 x 48mm) (c1960)		£1.00	
			MENTORS LTD, London			
—	C	32	Views of Ireland (42 x 67mm) (c1912)	H.271	£15.00	—
			J. MILLHOFF & CO. LTD, London			
	CP		Antique Pottery (1927):			
A2		54	A Small size		90p	£50.00
—		56	B Medium size (74 x 50mm)		90p	£50.00
	C		Art Treasures:			
D		30	A Small size (1927)		£1.00	£30.00
B		50	B Large size (1926)		70p	£35.00
B	C	25	Art Treasures — '2nd Series of 50', Nd. 51-75 (1928)		£1.20	£30.00
B	C	25	England, Historic and Picturesque — 'Series of 25' (1928)		£1.40	£35.00
B	C	25	England, Historic and Picturesque — 'Second Series ...'(1928)		£1.20	£30.00
A2	P	27	Famous Golfers (1928)		£24.00	—
	P	27	Famous 'Test' Cricketers (1928):			
A2			A Small size		£6.50	—
			B Medium size (76 x 51mm)		£6.50	—
—	C	24	Film Stars – postcard format back (128x 89mm) (1934)	GP.74	£10.00	—
—	C	25	Gallery Pictures (76 x 51mm) (1928)		£1.60	£40.00
A2	C	50	'Geographia' Map Series (sectional) (1931)	GP.506	£2.00	£100.00
	CP		The Homeland Series (1933):	GP.333		
A2		54	A Small size		40p	£20.00
—		56	B Medium size (76 x 51mm)		50p	£28.00
A2	P	36	In the Public Eye (1930)		£2.00	£75.00
D	C	25	Men of Genius (1924)		£5.00	£125.00
B	C	25	Picturesque Old England (1931)		£1.60	£40.00

Size	Print-ing	Number in set	BRITISH TOBACCO ISSUERS	Handbook reference	Price per card	Complete set
			J. MILLHOFF & CO. LTD, London (continued)			
A2	P	27	Real Photographs: 'A Series of 27' —	GP.7		
			A Matt front (c1931)		£1.00	£27.00
			B Glossy front (c1931)		50p	£13.50
		27	'2nd Series of 27' (c1931)		80p	£22.00
		27	'3rd Series of 27' (c1932)		50p	£13.50
		27	'4th Series of 27' (c1932)		80p	£22.00
		27	'5th Series of 27' (c1933)		£1.10	£30.00
		27	'6th Series of 27' (c1933)		£1.10	£30.00
C	C	25	Reproductions of Celebrated Oil Paintings (1928)	GP.338	£1.60	£40.00
—	U		'RILETTE' Miniature Pictures (60 x 45mm) (c1925):	GP.512		
		20	A Inscribed Series of 20		£3.50	—
		25	B Inscribed Series of 25		£3.50	—
		30	C Inscribed Series of 30		£3.50	—
		42	D Inscribed Series of 42		£3.50	—
		43	E Inscribed Series of 43		£3.50	—
		56	F Inscribed Series of 56		£3.50	—
		74	G Inscribed Series of 74		£3.50	—
B	C	25	Roses (1927)		£3.00	£75.00
			Theatre Advertisement Cards, multi-backed (c1905):			
—	BW	? 9	A Medium size (83 x 56mm)		£180.00	—
—	BW	? 2	B Large size (108 x 83mm)		£250.00	—
A2	C	50	Things to Make — 'De Reszke Cigarettes' (1935)		60p	£30.00
A2	C	50	What the Stars Say — 'De Reszke Cigarettes' (1934)		£1.00	£50.00
A2	P	36	Zoological Studies (1929)		50p	£18.00
			MIRANDA LTD, London			
A	C	20	Dogs (c1925)	H.211	£12.00	—
A	C	25	Sports and Pastimes — Series I (c1925)	H.225	£12.00	£300.00
			STEPHEN MITCHELL & SON, Glasgow			
C	C	51	*Actors and Actresses — Selection from 'FROGA B and C' (c1900)	H.20	£28.00	—
C	U	25	*Actors and Actresses — 'FROGA C' (c1900)	H.20	£28.00	—
C	U	50	*Actors and Actresses — 'FROGA D' (c1900)	H.20	£28.00	—
C	U	26	*Actresses — 'FROGA B' (c1900)	H.20	£28.00	—
A	U	1	Advertisement Card 'Maid of Honour' (c1900)		—	£800.00
A	C	50	Air Raid Precautions (1938)	H.544	£1.00	£50.00
A	C	25	Angling (1928)	H.655	£8.00	£200.00
A	C	50	Arms and Armour (1916)	H.273	£4.00	£200.00
A	C	25	Army Ribbons and Buttons (1916)		£4.40	£110.00
C	BW	25	*Boxer Rebellion — Sketches (c1904)	H.46	£34.00	—
D1	BW	25	British Warships, 1-25 (1915)		£9.00	£225.00
D1	BW	25	British Warships, Second series 26-50 (1915)		£9.00	£225.00
A	C	50	Clan Tartans — 'A Series of 50' (1927)	H.663	£2.00	£100.00
A	C	25	Clan Tartans — '2nd Series, 25' (1927)		£1.20	£30.00
A	C	25	Empire Exhibition, Scotland, 1938 (1938)		£1.00	£25.00
			Album		—	£40.00
A2	C	25	Famous Crosses (1923)		80p	£20.00
A	C	50	Famous Scots (1933)		£2.00	£100.00
A	U	50	First Aid (1938)		£1.40	£70.00
A	U	50	A Gallery of 1934 (1935)		£3.00	£150.00
			Album		—	£40.00
A	U	50	A Gallery of 1935 (1936)		£2.50	£125.00
A	C	50	Humorous Drawings (1924)	H.590	£3.00	£150.00
A	C	50	Interesting Buildings (1905)	H.70	£9.00	£450.00

Size	Printing	Number in set	BRITISH TOBACCO ISSUERS	Handbook reference	Price per card	Complete set
			STEPHEN MITCHELL & SON, Glasgow (continued)			
A	C	40	London Ceremonials (1928)		£1.50	£60.00
A	C	25	Medals (1916)	H.71	£5.00	£125.00
A	C	30	A Model Army (cut-outs) (1932)		£1.20	£36.00
A	C	25	Money (1913)		£5.00	£125.00
A	C	25	Old Sporting Prints (1930)	H.563	£1.80	£45.00
A	U	50	Our Empire (1937)	H.522	60p	£30.00
A	C	25	*Regimental Crests, Nicknames and Collar Badges (1900)	H.274	£16.00	£400.00
A	C	70	River and Coastal Steamers (1925)		£4.50	—
A	C		A Road Map of Scotland (1933):			
		50	A Small numerals		£3.50	£175.00
		50	B Large numerals in circles		£3.50	£175.00
		50	C Overprinted in red		£4.50	£225.00
		1	D Substitute card (Blue)		—	£16.00
A	C	50	Scotland's Story (1929)		£3.00	£150.00
A	C	25	Scottish Clan Series No. 1 (1903)	H.33	£14.00	£350.00
A	U	50	Scottish Football Snaps (1935)		£3.50	£175.00
			Album		—	£40.00
A	U	50	Scottish Footballers (1934)		£3.50	£175.00
			Album		—	£40.00
A	C	25	Seals (1911)		£5.00	£125.00
A	C	25	Sports (1907)	H.275	£16.00	£400.00
A	C	25	Stars of Screen and History (1939)		£3.00	£75.00
A	C	25	Statues and Monuments (1914)		£5.00	£125.00
—	C	25	Village Models Series (1925):	H.664		
A			A Small size		£2.80	£70.00
			B Medium size (68 x 62mm)		£5.60	£140.00
—	C	25	Village Models Series — 'Second' (1925):	H.664		
A			A Small size:			
			1 Inscribed 'Second Series'		£2.80	£70.00
			2 Not inscribed 'Second Series'		£5.60	—
			B Medium size (68 x 62mm)		£5.60	£140.00
A	U	50	Wonderful Century (1937)		70p	£35.00
A	U	50	The World of Tomorrow (1936)		£2.00	£100.00
			MOORGATE TOBACCO CO., London			
—	BW	30	The New Elizabethan Age (20 small, 10 large) (1953):			
			A Matt front		£3.50	—
			B Varnished front		£2.00	£60.00
			B. MORRIS & SONS LTD, London			
—	BW	30	*Actresses (41 x 68mm) (1898)	H.276	£2.00	£60.00
C	U	26	*Actresses — 'FROGA A (c1900):	H.20		
			A 'Borneo Queen' back		£36.00	—
			B 'Gold Seals' back		£36.00	—
			C 'Morris's Cigarettes' back		£36.00	—
			D 'Tommy Atkins' back		£85.00	—
—	C	? 4	*Actresses — selection from 'FROGA B' — 'Morris's High Class Cigarettes' on front (76 x 66mm) (c1900)	H.20	£1600.00	—
A1	P	1	*Advertisement Card (Soldier and Girl) (c1900)	H.758	—	£2000.00
A1	C	50	Animals at the Zoo (1924):	H.520		
			A Back in blue		80p	£40.00
			B Back in grey		90p	£45.00
A1	C	35	At the London Zoo Aquarium (1928)		50p	£17.50
A1	BW	25	Australian Cricketers (1925)		£4.00	£100.00

Size	Print-ing	Number in set	BRITISH TOBACCO ISSUERS	Handbook reference	Price per card	Complete set
			B. MORRIS & SONS LTD, London (continued)			
A	C	50	*Beauties — 'CHOAB' (c1900):	H.21		
			A 'Gold Flake Honeydew' back		£50.00	—
			B 'Golden Virginia' back		£50.00	—
			C 'Levant Favourites' back		£50.00	—
			D 'Reina Regenta' back		£50.00	—
A	U	? 53	*Beauties — Collotype, multi-backed (c1897)	H.278	£200.00	—
A	U	21	*Beauties — 'MOM' (c1900):	H.277		
			A 'Borneo Queen' back		£36.00	—
			B 'Gold Seals' back		£36.00	—
			C 'Morris's Cigarettes' back		£36.00	—
			D 'Tommy Atkins' back		£85.00	—
A	C	20	Boer War, 1900 (VC Heroes)	H.279	£50.00	—
A	BW	25	*Boer War Celebrities — 'PAM' (c1901)	H.140	£40.00	—
A2	C	25	Captain Blood (1937)		£1.20	£30.00
D	U	50	Film Star Series (1923)		£3.50	—
A	C	30	*General Interest — six cards each entitled (c1910):	H.280		
			i Agriculture in the Orient		£7.00	£42.00
			ii Architectural Monuments		£7.00	£42.00
			iii The Ice Breaker		£7.00	£42.00
			iv Schools in Foreign Countries		£7.00	£42.00
			v Strange Vessels		£7.00	£42.00
D	U	25	Golf Strokes Series (1923)		£8.00	£200.00
A1	—	12	Horoscopes (wording only) (1936):			
			A White card		£1.20	—
			B Cream card		80p	£10.00
A2	C	25	How Films are Made (1934):			
			A White card		£1.20	£30.00
			B Cream Card		£1.40	£35.00
A1	BW	50	How to Sketch (1929)		£1.20	£60.00
D	BW	20	London Views (c1905):	H.34		
			A 'American Gold' back		£34.00	—
			B 'Morris's Gold Flake' back		£34.00	—
			C 'Smoke Borneo Queen' back		£34.00	—
			D 'Smoke Reina Regenta' back		£34.00	—
A	C	25	Marvels of the Universe Series (c1912)	H.281	£4.40	£110.00
A1	C	25	Measurement of Time (1924)		£1.60	£40.00
D	U	25	Motor Series (Motor parts) (1922)		£6.00	£150.00
D	C	50	National and Colonial Arms (1917)	H.704	£6.00	£300.00
A1	C	25	The Queen's Dolls' House (1925)		£3.20	£80.00
D	U	25	Racing Greyhounds — 'Issued by Forecasta' (1939)		£1.60	£40.00
A1	BW	24	Shadowgraphs (1925)		£3.20	£80.00
A1	C	13	Treasure Island (1924)		£2.25	£30.00
A1	C	50	Victory Signs (1928)		70p	£35.00
C	U	25	War Celebrities (1915)		£9.00	£225.00
D	C	25	War Pictures (1916)	H.51	£11.00	£275.00
A	C	25	Wax Art Series (1931)		60p	£15.00
A	C	25	Whipsnade Zoo (1932)		60p	£15.00
D	C	25	Wireless Series (1923)		£5.00	£125.00
SILKS						
—	C	24	Battleship Crests (70 x 50mm) (paper backed) (c1915)	H.504-3	£50.00	—
—	C		English Flowers (78 x 56mm) (paper backed) (c1915):	H.505-4		
		25	A Series of 25:			
			i Back text 5th line with 'Crewel'		£4.60	—
			ii Back text 5th line overprinted with 'Cruel'		£9.00	—
			iii Back Without 'Crewel' or 'Cruel'		£7.00	—
		50	B Series of 50		£5.00	—

Size	Print-ing	Number in set	BRITISH TOBACCO ISSUERS	Handbook reference	Price per card	Complete set

B. MORRIS & SONS LTD, London (Silks continued)

—	C	25	English and Foreign Birds (78 x 56mm) (paper backed) (c1915) ... H.505-1		£6.00	£150.00
—	C	25	*Regimental Colours IV (75 x 55m) (unbacked and anonymous (c1915)) ... H.502-9		£5.50	—
—	C	4	*Regimental Colours (210 x 190mm) (c1915) ... H.502-13		£80.00	—

PHILIP MORRIS & CO. LTD, London

	U	50	British Views (1924):			
C			A Small size ...		£3.20	—
—			B Large size (79 x 67mm) ...		£3.20	—
C	—	72	Motormania (75 x 45mm) (1986) ...		£1.50	—
C	—	108	Raffles Classic Collection (90 x 47mm) (1985) ... H.894		£1.25	—

P. MOUAT & CO., Newcastle-on-Tyne

C	C	30	*Colonial Troops (c1902) ... H.40		£340.00	—

MOUSTAFA LTD, London

D2	CP	50	Camera Studies (1923):	GP.541		
			A Front with number and caption, back in black		£3.50	—
			*B Front without letterpress, plain back ...		£3.50	—
D2	C	25	Cinema Stars — Set 8 (1924) ...	GP.542	£6.00	—
A2	C	40	Leo Chambers Dogs Heads (1924) ...		£3.50	£140.00
D2	C	25	Pictures of World Interest (1923) ...		£3.60	—
A2	P	25	Real Photos (Views) (1925) ...		50p	£12.50

MUNRO, Glasgow

C	C	30	Colonial Troops (c1900) ...		£500.00	—

B. MURATTI, SONS & CO. LTD, Manchester and London

—	U	? 24	*Actresses, cabinet size, collotype (106 x 69mm) (c1898) ...	GP.551	£140.00	—
C	C	26	*Actresses — 'FROGA A' (c1900):	H.20		
			A 'To the Cigarette Connoisseur' back ...		£30.00	—
			B 'Muratti's Zinnia Cigarettes' back ...		£36.00	—
—	C		*Actresses and Beauties — Green Corinthian column framework — 'Neb-Ka' vertical backs (117 x 67mm) (c1900):			
		? 18	Actresses — selection from 'FROGA C' ...	H.20	£170.00	—
		? 3	Beauties — selection from 'MOM' ...	H.277/GP.555	£300.00	—
—	C		*Actresses and Beauties — brown and yellow ornamental framework (117 x 67mm) (c1900):			
			I 'Neb-Ka' horizontal backs:			
		26	i Actresses — selection from 'FROGA A'	H.20	£160.00	—
		50	ii Beauties — selection from 'CHOAB' ...	H.21	£160.00	—
		25	II Rubber stamped back. Beauties — selection from 'CHOAB' ...	H.21	£160.00	—
		25	III Plain back — Beauties — selection from 'CHOAB' ...	H.21	£160.00	—
—	C		*Advertisement Cards, Globe design back (88 x 66mm) (c1900):	GP.552		
		? 10	i Brown borders to front ...		£400.00	—
		? 19	ii White borders to front ...		£400.00	—
A2	P	24	Australian Race Horses (export) (c1930) ...		£1.20	£30.00
C	C	50	*Beauties — 'CHOAB' (Zinnia back) (c1900):	H.21/GP.554		
			A Black printing on back ...		£55.00	—
			B Olive green printing on back ...		£65.00	—

Size	Print-ing	Number in set		BRITISH TOBACCO ISSUERS	Handbook reference	Price per card	Complete set

B. MURATTI, SONS & CO. LTD, Manchester and London (continued)

Size	Print-ing	Number in set		Description	Handbook reference	Price per card	Complete set
—	C	? 66		*Beautiful Women, Globe design back (54 x 75mm) (c1900)	H.284/GP.32	£100.00	—
—	BW	20		*Boer War Generals — 'CLAM' (35 x 61mm) (c1901)	H.61/GP.556	£45.00	—
—	C	15		*Caricatures (42 x 62mm) (c1903):	GP.558		
			A	'Sole Manufacturers of …' brown back		£32.00	—
			B	'Muratti's Zinnia Cigarettes' brown back		£35.00	—
			C	'Muratti's Zinnia Cigarettes' black back		£32.00	—
			D	'Muratti's Vassos Cigarettes' (not seen)		—	—
			E	As D, but 'Vassos' blocked out, brown back		£60.00	—
—	C	35		Crowned Heads (53 x 83mm) (c1913)		£17.00	—
C	C	52		*Japanese Series, Playing Card inset (c1904)	GP.560	£20.00	—
				Plain back		£17.00	—
—	P			Midget Post Card Series (1902):	GP.561		
		? 124	A	Matt Front (90 x 70mm)		£11.00	—
		? 18	B	Matt Front (80 x 65mm)		£11.00	—
			C	Glossy front (85 x 65mm few 75-80 x 65mm):			
		? 96		i With serial numbers		£11.00	—
		? 136		ii Without serial numbers		£11.00	—
—	P	? 127		'Queens' Post Card Series (90 x 70mm) (c1902):	GP.562		
			A	Front in black/sepia		£15.00	—
			B	Front in reddish brown		£15.00	—
A1	BW	19		*Russo-Japanese Series (1904)	H.184/GP.563	£18.00	—
A1	C	25		*Star Girls (c1898)	H.30	£250.00	—
A	U	? 51		*Views of Jersey (c1912):	GP.564		
			A	Plain back		£20.00	—
			B	'Opera House, Jersey' back		£20.00	—
A	U	25		*War Series — 'MURATTI I', white card (1916)	GP.565	£28.00	—
A	U	50		*War Series — 'MURATTI II', toned card (1917)			
				Nos. 1-25 (and alternative cards)	H.290/GP.566	£20.00	—

SILKS

Size	Print-ing	Number in set	Description	Handbook reference	Price per card	Complete set
—	C		*Flags — Set 3 (70 x 52mm) (paper backed) (c1915):			
		25	1st Series — Series C, Nd. 20-44	GP.579	£4.00	—
		24	2nd Series:			
			Series A, Nd. 26-49	GP.578	£4.00	—
			Series E, Nd. 48-72, paper backing in grey (No. 52 unissued)	GP.582	£4.00	—
			Series E, Nd. 48-72, paper backing in green (No. 52 unissued)	GP.582	£4.00	—
—	C		*Flags — Set 8 (paper backed) (c1915):			
		3	Series A, Nd. 1-3 (89 x 115mm)	GP.577	£12.00	—
		1	Series B, Nd. 19 (70 x 76mm)	GP.586	—	£14.00
		18	Series C, Nd. 1-18 (89 x 115mm)	GP.580	£12.00	—
		3	Series D, Nd. 45-47 (89 x 115mm)	GP.581	£12.00	—
		6	Series F, Nd. 73-78 (89 x 115mm)	GP.583	£12.00	—
—	C	18	*Great War Leaders — Series P (89 x 115mm) (paper backed) (c1916)	GP.584	£22.00	—
—	C		*Regimental Badges I (paper backed) (c1915):	H.502-1		
		25	Series A, Nd. 1-25 (70 x 52mm)	GP.585	£5.50	—
		48	Series B, Nd. I-48 (76 x 70mm)	GP.587	£7.00	—
		15	Series B, Nd. 4-18 (76 x 70mm)	GP.586	£7.00	—
		16	Series G, Nd. 79-94 (76 x 70mm)	GP.588	£9.00	—
—	C	25	*Regimental Colours I — Series CB (76 x 70mm) (paper backed) (c1915)	GP.589	£12.00	—
—	C	72	*Regimental Colours V — Series RB (70 x 52 mm) (paper backed) (c1915)	GP.590	£7.00	—

Size	Print-ing	Number in set	BRITISH TOBACCO ISSUERS	Handbook reference	Price per card	Complete set

B. MURATTI, SONS & CO. LTD, Manchester and London (continued)

CANVASES. Unbacked canvases. The material is not strictly canvas, but a linen fabric glazed to give the tappearance of canvas.

Size	Print	Num	Description	Handbook	Price	Complete
—	C	40	Canvas Masterpieces — Series M (71 x 60mm) (c1915):	H.509/GP.575		
			A Shaded back design, globe 12mm diam		£6.00	—
			B Unshaded back design, globe 6mm diam		£2.50	£100.00
—	C	16	Canvas Masterpieces — Series P (114 x 90mm) (c1915)		£15.00	—

MURRAY, SONS & CO. LTD, Belfast

Size	Print	Num	Description	Handbook	Price	Complete
A	BW	20	*Actresses — 'BLARM' (c1900):	H.23		
			A 'Pineapple Cigarettes' back		£90.00	—
			B 'Special Crown Cigarettes' back		£100.00	—
D1	P	22	Bathing Beauties (1929)		£7.50	—
A1	BW	40	Bathing Belles (1939)	H.592	45p	£18.00
C	C	15	Chess and Draughts Problems — Series F (1912)	H.291	£90.00	—
D1	P	22	Cinema Scenes (1929)		£6.50	—
A	BW	54	*Cricketers and Footballers — Series H (c1912):	H.292		
			20 Cricketers. A Thick card		£90.00	—
			B Thin card		£90.00	—
			C Brown Printing		£275.00	—
			34 Footballers. A Thick card		£70.00	—
			B Thin card		£70.00	—
A1	BW	25	Crossword Puzzles (c1925)		£350.00	—
D1	P	26	Dancers (1929)		£6.00	—
D	P		Dancing Girls (1929):			
		25	A 'Belfast-Ireland' at base		£3.60	£90.00
		25	B 'London & Belfast' at base		£3.60	£90.00
		26	C Inscribed 'Series of 26'		£3.60	—
—	C	? 29	Football Flags (shaped) (60 x 32mm) (c1905):	H.759		
			A Maple Cigarettes		£95.00	—
			B Murray's Cigarettes		£95.00	—
C	C	25	*Football Rules (c1911)		£45.00	—
A	BW	104	*Footballers — Series J (c1910)	H.293	£65.00	—
A	C	20	Holidays by the LMS (1927)	H.593	£12.50	—
A1	C	20	Inventors Series (1924)	H.213	£5.00	£100.00
C	U	25	*Irish Scenery Nd. 101-125 (1905):			
			A 'Hall Mark Cigarettes'		£25.00	—
			B 'Pine Apple Cigarettes'		£25.00	—
			C 'Special Crown Cigarettes'		£25.00	—
			D 'Straight Cut Cigarettes'		£25.00	—
			E 'Yachtsman Cigarettes'		£25.00	—
C	BW	25	Polo Pictures — E Series (1911)	H.294	£30.00	—
—	U	50	Prominent Politicians — B Series (41 x 70mm) (1909):	H.295		
			A Without '… in two strengths' in centre of back		£18.00	—
			B With '… in two strengths' in centre of back		£3.50	£175.00
—	C	50	Puzzle Series (1925):	H.660		
A1			A With coupon attached at top		£20.00	—
			B Without coupon		£10.00	—
C	U	25	Reproductions of Famous Works of Art — D Series (1910)	H.296	£26.00	£650.00
C	U	24	Reproductions of High Class Works of Art — C Series (1910)	H.297	£28.00	—
D2	C	50	Stage and Film Stars — 'Erinmore Cigarettes' (c1926)		£5.00	£250.00
A1	BW	25	Steam Ships (1939)		£1.80	£45.00

Size	Print-ing	Number in set	BRITISH TOBACCO ISSUERS	Handbook reference	Price per card	Complete set
			MURRAY, SONS & CO. LTD, Belfast (continued)			
A1	C	50	The Story of Ships (1940)		45p	£22.50
A2	C	25	Types of Aeroplanes (1929)		£1.80	£45.00
C	C	20	Types of Dogs (1924):	H.211		
			A Normal back		£7.00	—
			B Normal back, with firm's name rubber-stamped in red		£7.00	—
A1	C	35	*War Series — Series K (1915)	H.298	£34.00	—
C2	U	25	*War Series — Series L, Nd. 100-124 (c1916):			
			A Sepia		£5.00	£125.00
			B Grey-brown		£5.00	—
			C Purple-brown		£5.00	—
SILKS						
—	C	? 16	*Flags, small (70 x 42mm) — 'Polo Mild Cigarettes' (plain paper backing) (c1915)	H.498-1	£25.00	—
—	C	? 3	*Flags and Arms, large (102 x 71mm) — 'Polo Mild Cigarettes' (plain paper backing) (c1915)	H.498-2	£80.00	—
—	C	? 31	*Orders of Chivalry II, 'Series M' (70 x 42mm) (paper backed, Nd. 35-65) (c1915)	H.504-15	£20.00	—
—	C	? 25	*Regimental Badges (70 x 42mm) — 'Polo Mild Cigarettes' (plain paper backing) (c1915)	H.498-3	£20.00	—
			H.J. NATHAN, London			
D	C	40	Comical Military and Naval Pictures (c1905):	H.14		
			A White Border		£80.00	—
			B No Border		£80.00	—
			JAMES NELSON, London			
A	P	? 23	*Beauties — 'FENA' (c1899)	H.148	£1000.00	—
			NETTLETON AND MITCHELL, Ossett			
A	C	30	*Army Pictures, Cartoons, etc. (c1916)	H.12	£180.00	—
			THE NEW MOSLEM CIGARETTE CO., London			
D	C	30	*Proverbs (c1902)	H.15	£140.00	—
			E.J. NEWBEGIN, Sunderland			
—	P	50	*Actors and Actresses (39 x 60mm) (c1902)	H.299	£65.00	—
A	BW	10	*Actresses — 'HAGG A' (c1900)	H.24	£200.00	—
D	C	? 4	Advertisement Cards (c1900)	H.761	£1100.00	—
A	BW	20	Cricketers Series (1901)	H.29	£650.00	—
A	BW	19	*Russo-Japanese Series (1904)	H.184	£170.00	—
D	C	12	Well-Known Proverbs (c1905)	H.235	£170.00	—
D	C	25	Well-Known Songs (c1905)	H.300	£170.00	—
			W.H. NEWMAN, Birmingham			
C	C	18	Motor Cycle Series (c1914)	H.469	£130.00	—
			THOS. NICHOLLS & CO., Chester			
A	C	50	Orders of Chivalry (1916)	H.301	£10.00	£500.00
			THE NILMA TOBACCO COY., London			
A	C	40	*Home and Colonial Regiments (c1903)	H.69	£140.00	—
D	C	30	*Proverbs (c1903)	H.15	£130.00	—

Size	Print-ing	Number in set	BRITISH TOBACCO ISSUERS	Handbook reference	Price per card	Complete set

M.E. NOTARAS LTD, London

| A2 | P | 36 | National Types of Beauty (c1925) .... | GP.417 | £1.25 | £45.00 |
| — | U | 24 | *Views of China (68 x 43mm) (1925) .... | | 80p | £20.00 |

A. NOTON, Sheffield

| — | U | 12 | 'Manikin' Cards (79 x 51mm) (c1920) .... | H.481 | £120.00 | — |

OGDENS LTD, Liverpool

333 page reference book (updated paperback 2015 Edition) – £24.00

Home Issues (*excluding 'Guinea Gold' and 'Tabs', but including some early issued abroad*).

A	C	25	ABC of Sport (1927)		£5.00	£125.00
A	C	50	Actors — Natural and Character Studies (1938)	H.571-1	£1.00	£50.00
C	C	25	*Actresses — coloured, 'Ogden's Cigarettes contain no glycerine' back (c1895):	OG.3		
			A Titled in black		£100.00	—
			B Titled in brown		£100.00	—
D2	U	? 1	*Actresses — green, green borders (c1900)	OG.4	£1300.00	—
D1	U	50	*Actresses — green photogravure (c1900)	OG.5	£15.00	—
D	P	? 589	*Actresses — 'Ogden's Cigarettes' at foot (c1900) ...	OG.6	£5.00	—
D	P		*Actresses and Beauties — collotype (c1895):	OG.12		
		? 83	i named:			
			A *Plain back*		£90.00	—
			B 'Midnight Flake' back		£80.00	—
		? 21	ii unnamed:			
			A *Plain back*		£90.00	—
			B 'Midnight Flake' back:			
			i blue back		£80.00	—
			ii red back		£140.00	—
D	P		*Actresses and Beauties — collotype, 'Ogden's Cigarettes' back (1895):	OG.12		
		? 54	i named		£80.00	—
		? 45	ii unnamed		£80.00	—
A	P	? 205	*Actresses and Beauties — woodbury-type (c1894)	OG.13	£48.00	—
A	C	50	AFC Nicknames (1933)	H.571-2	£5.00	£250.00
A	C	50	Air-Raid Precautions (1938)	H.544	£1.00	£50.00
A	C	50	Applied Electricity (1928)		£1.30	£65.00
—	C	192	Army Crests and Mottoes (39 x 59mm) (c1902)	OG.20	£7.00	—
			Album		—	£50.00
A	U	36	Australian Test Cricketers, 1928-29	OG.21	£4.50	£160.00
A	C	28	*Beauties — 'BOCCA' (c1900)	H.39/OG.23	£30.00	—
—	C	50	*Beauties — 'CHOAB' (c1900):	H.21/OG.24		
			Nos 1-25 (size 65 x 36mm)		£30.00	—
			Nos 26-50 (size 67 x 37mm)		£30.00	—
A	C	26	*Beauties — 'HOL' (c1900):	H.192/OG.25		
			A 'Guinea Gold' red rubber stamp back		£275.00	—
			B Blue Castle Design back		£26.00	£675.00
A2	C	52	*Beauties — 'Playing Card' series (c1900):	OG.26		
			A 52 with playing card inset		£34.00	—
			B 26 without playing card inset		£38.00	—
A2	C	52	*Beauties and Military — PC inset (c1898)	OG.29	£40.00	—
—	P	50	Beauty Series, numbered, 'St. Julien Tobacco' (36 x 54mm) (c1900)	OG.30	£3.20	£160.00
D	P	? 83	Beauty Series, unnumbered, issued Australia (c1900)	OG.31	£75.00	—
A	C	50	Billiards, by Tom Newman (1928)	OG.33	£3.00	£150.00
A	C	50	Birds' Eggs (1904):			
			A White back		£2.60	£130.00
			B Toned back		£2.40	£120.00

Size	Print-ing	Number in set	BRITISH TOBACCO ISSUERS	Handbook reference	Price per card	Complete set
			OGDENS LTD, Liverpool (continued)			
A	C	50	Bird's Eggs (cut-outs) (1923)		£1.20	£60.00
A	C	50	The Blue Riband of the Atlantic (1929)		£2.50	£125.00
D	P	? 142	*Boer War and General Interest — 'Ogden's Cigarettes' at foot (c1900)	OG.38	£6.00	—
H2	P	? 68	*Boer War and General Interest — 'Ogden's Cigarettes' at foot (c1900)	OG.38	£55.00	—
—	P	? 3	*Boer War & General Interest (Liners) 'Ogdens Cigarettes' at foot (72 x 55mm) (c1900)	OG.38	£200.00	—
A	C	50	Boxers (1915)		£9.00	£450.00
A	C	25	Boxing (1914)	H.311/OG.40	£6.00	£150.00
—	C	? 6	*Boxing Girls (165 x 94mm) (c1895)	OG.69	£650.00	—
A	C	50	Boy Scouts (1911):	H.62/OG.41		
			A Blue back		£4.50	£225.00
			B Green back		£5.50	£275.00
A	C	50	Boy Scouts, 2nd series (1912):	H.62/OG.42		
			A Blue back		£4.50	£225.00
			B Green back		£5.50	£275.00
A	C	50	Boy Scouts, 3rd series (1912):	H.62/OG.43		
			A Blue back		£4.50	£225.00
			B Green back		£5.50	£275.00
A	C	50	Boy Scouts, 4th series, green back (1913)		£4.50	£225.00
A	C	25	Boy Scouts, 5th series, green back (1914)		£4.60	£115.00
A	C	50	Boy Scouts (1929)	OG.46	£3.00	£150.00
A	C	50	British Birds:	H.229/OG.47		
			A White back (1905)		£2.60	£130.00
			B Toned back (1906)		£2.40	£120.00
A	C	50	British Birds, Second Series (1908)		£2.80	£140.00
A	C	50	British Birds (Cut-Outs) (1923)	OG.49	£1.00	£50.00
A	C	50	British Birds and Their Eggs (1939)	H.571-3	£3.00	£150.00
A	C	50	British Costumes from 100 BC to 1904 (1905)	OG.51	£6.00	£300.00
A	U	50	Broadcasting (1935)	H.571-4	£1.80	£90.00
A	C	50	By the Roadside (1932)		£1.20	£60.00
A	C	44	Captains of Association Football Clubs and Colours (1926)		£5.00	£220.00
A	U	50	Cathedrals and Abbeys (1936):			
			A Cream card		£1.20	£60.00
			B White card		£1.20	£60.00
A	C	50	Champions of 1936 (1937)	H.571-5	£2.50	£125.00
A	C	50	Children of All Nations (cut-outs) (1923)	H.656/OG.58	£1.00	£50.00
A	C	50	Club Badges (1914)		£5.00	£250.00
A	C	50	Colour in Nature (1932)		£1.00	£50.00
—	C	? 27	*Comic Pictures (1890-95) (size varies)	OG.62	£360.00	—
A	C	50	Construction of Railway Trains (1930)		£2.50	£125.00
A	C	50	Coronation Procession (sectional) (1937)	H.571-6	£1.80	£90.00
			Album		—	£40.00
A	U	50	Cricket, 1926		£3.00	£150.00
A2	C	12	*Cricket and Football Terms — Women (c1896)	OG.69	£500.00	—
D2	U	50	*Cricketers and Sportsmen (c1898)	OG.70	£120.00	—
A	C	25	Derby Entrants, 1926		£2.80	£70.00
A	C	50	Derby Entrants, 1928		£2.80	£140.00
A	U	50	Derby Entrants, 1929		£2.80	£140.00
A	C	50	Dogs (1936)	H.571-7	£2.50	£125.00
A	U	28	*Dominoes — Actresses — 'FROGA' back (c1900):	H.20/OG.75A		
			A Mitred corners (7 backs)		£26.00	—
			B Unmitred corners (7 backs)		£26.00	—
A	U	56	*Dominoes — Beauties — 'MOM' back (c1900)	H.277/OG.75B	£26.00	

Size	Print-ing	Number in set	BRITISH TOBACCO ISSUERS	Handbook reference	Price per card	Complete set
			OGDENS LTD, Liverpool (continued)			
A2	BW	55	*Dominoes — black back (1909)		£2.00	£110.00
A	C	25	Famous Dirt-Track Riders (1929)		£6.00	£150.00
A	C	50	Famous Footballers (1908)		£5.50	£275.00
A	U	50	Famous Rugby Players (1926-27)		£3.00	£150.00
A	C	50	Flags and Funnels of Leading Steamship Lines (1906)	H.67/OG.81	£4.00	£200.00
A	C	50	Football Caricatures (1935)	H.571-8	£3.50	£175.00
—	C	43	*Football Club Badges (shaped for buttonhole) (c1910)	OG.85	£11.00	—
A	C	50	Football Club Captains (1935)	H.571-9	£3.00	£150.00
			Album		—	£40.00
A	C	51	Football Club Colours (1906):	H.68/OG.86		
			Nos. 1-50		£4.50	£225.00
			No. 51		—	£6.00
A	C	50	Foreign Birds (1924)		90p	£45.00
A	C	50	Fowls, Pigeons and Dogs (1904)	H.64/OG.88	£4.00	£200.00
A	U	25	Greyhound Racing — '1st Series ...' (1927)		£4.40	£110.00
A	U	25	Greyhound Racing — '2nd Series ...' (1928)		£4.40	£110.00
—	C	1	*History of the Union Jack (threefold card)			
			(51 x 37mm closed) (1901)	OG.102	—	£225.00
A	C	50	How to Swim (1935)	H.571-10	£1.00	£50.00
A	BW	50	Infantry Training (1915)	OG.105	£3.00	£150.00
A	C	50	Jockeys, and Owners' Colours (1927)		£2.50	£125.00
A	C	50	Jockeys 1930 (1930)		£2.50	£125.00
A	C	50	Leaders of Men (1924)		£2.00	£100.00
A	C	25	Marvels of Motion (1928)		£2.40	£60.00
K2	C	52	*Miniature Playing Cards — Actresses and Beauties			
			back (c1900):	OG.115		
			I Unnamed, no numeral (76 backs known)		£5.00	—
			II Unnamed, 'numeral 40' (26 backs known)		£5.00	—
			III Named, 'numeral 46' (26 backs known)		£5.00	—
			IV Named, no numeral (26 backs known)		£5.00	—
K2	C	52	*Miniature Playing Cards, blue Tabs 'Shield and			
			Flower' design back (1909)	OG.118	£3.00	—
K2	C	52	*Miniature Playing Cards, yellow 'Coolie Cut Plug'			
			design back:	OG.116		
			A Yellow back (1904)		£3.00	—
			B Yellow back with white border (1904)		£4.00	—
A	C	50	Modern British Pottery (1925)		£1.10	£55.00
A	C	50	Modern Railways (1936)	H.571-11	£2.40	£120.00
A	BW	50	Modern War Weapons (1915):	OG.122		
			A Original numbering		£4.00	£200.00
			B Numbering re-arranged		£11.00	—
A	C	25	Modes of Conveyance (1927)		£2.60	£65.00
A	C	50	Motor Races 1931 (1931)		£3.00	£150.00
A	C	50	Ocean Greyhounds (1938)	H.571-12	£1.20	£60.00
A	C	25	Optical Illusions (1923)	H.560/OG.127	£3.60	£90.00
A	C	50	Orders of Chivalry (1907)		£4.00	£200.00
A	C	25	Owners, Racing Colours and Jockeys (1914)		£4.40	£110.00
A	C	50	Owners, Racing Colours and Jockeys (1906)		£3.50	£175.00
A	C	25	Picturesque People of the Empire (1927)		£1.40	£35.00
A	U	50	Picturesque Villages (1936)		£1.50	£75.00
A	C	25	Poultry (1915):			
			A 'Ogden's Cigarettes' on front		£5.60	£140.00
			B Without 'Ogden's Cigarettes' on front		£5.60	£140.00
A	C	25	Poultry, 2nd series, as 'B' above (1916)		£5.60	£140.00
A	C	25	Poultry Alphabet (1924)		£4.80	£120.00
A	C	25	Poultry Rearing and Management — '1st Series ...'			
			(1922)		£3.00	£75.00

Size	Print-ing	Number in set	BRITISH TOBACCO ISSUERS	Handbook reference	Price per card	Complete set
			OGDENS LTD, Liverpool (continued)			
A	C	25	Poultry Rearing and Management — '2nd Series …' (1923)		£3.00	£75.00
A	U	50	Prominent Cricketers of 1938 (1938)	H.571-13	£2.60	£130.00
A	C	50	Prominent Racehorses of 1933 (1934)	H.571-14	£2.00	£100.00
A	C	25	Pugilists and Wrestlers, Nd. 1-25 (1908)		£6.00	£150.00
A	C	25	Pugilists and Wrestlers, Nd.26-50:			
			A White back (1909)		£6.00	£150.00
			B Toned back (1908)		£6.00	£150.00
A	C	25	Pugilists and Wrestlers, 2nd series, Nd. 51-75 (1909)		£8.00	£200.00
A	U	50	Pugilists in Action (1928)		£4.00	£200.00
A	C	50	Racehorses (1907)		£4.00	£200.00
A	C	50	Racing Pigeons (1931)		£4.00	£200.00
A	C	25	Records of the World (1908)		£4.00	£100.00
A	C	50	Royal Mail (1909)	H.82/OG.147	£5.00	£250.00
A	C	50	Sea Adventure (1939)	H.571-15	50p	£25.00
A	C	50	Sectional Cycling Map (1910)	H.74/OG.150	£3.20	£160.00
A	C	50	*Shakespeare Series (c1903):	OG.151		
			A Unnumbered		£13.00	£650.00
			B Numbered		£13.00	£650.00
A	C	50	Shots from the Films (1936)	H.571-16	£2.00	£100.00
A	U	25	Sights of London (1923)		£2.00	£50.00
A	C	50	Smugglers and Smuggling (1932)		£2.40	£120.00
A	C		Soldiers of the King (1909):	OG.156		
		50	A Grey printing on front		£6.00	£300.00
		25	B Brown printing on front		£7.00	—
A	U	50	Steeplechase Celebrities (1931)		£2.00	£100.00
A	C	50	Steeplechase Trainers, and Owners' Colours (1927)		£2.00	£100.00
A	C	50	The Story of Sand (1934)		£1.00	£50.00
A	C	50	Swimming, Diving and Life-Saving (1931)	H.523/OG.161	£1.50	£75.00
D	C	25	*Swiss Views, Nd. 1-25 (c1905)		£4.00	£100.00
D	C	25	*Swiss Views, Nd. 26-50 (c1905)		£5.00	£125.00
A	C	25	Trainers, and Owners' Colours — '1st Series …' (1925)		£2.60	£65.00
A	C	25	Trainers, and Owners' Colours — '2nd Series …' (1926)		£3.20	£80.00
A	C	50	Trick Billiards (1934)	H.571-17	£1.60	£80.00
A	C	50	Turf Personalities (1929)		£2.40	£120.00
D	C	48	Victoria Cross Heroes, multi-backed (1901)	OG.168	£22.00	—
A	C	25	Whaling (1927)		£3.00	£75.00
A	C	50	Yachts and Motor Boats (1930)		£2.50	£125.00
A	C	50	Zoo Studies (1937)	H.571-18	60p	£30.00

'GUINEA GOLD' SERIES

(The Set …S and X numbers represent the reference numbers quoted in the original Ogden's Reference Book).

D	P	1148	1-1148 Series (c1901):	OG.330S		
			Nos. 1-200		£1.20	£240.00
			Nos. 201-500		£2.20	—
			Nos. 501-900, excl. 523 and 765		£2.20	—
			Nos. 901-1000, excl. 940, 943, 947 and 1000		£2.40	—
			Nos. 1001-1148, excl. 1003, 1006-8, 1024, 1030, 1033, 1034, 1037, 1040, 1042, 1048, 1066, 1081, 1082, 1088		£2.40	
			Scarce Nos: 523, 940, 943, 947, 1000, 1003, 1007, 1008, 1024, 1030, 1033, 1034, 1037, 1040, 1042, 1048, 1066, 1088		£75.00	—
			Very scarce Nos. 765, 1006, 1081, 1082		From £400.00	—

Size	Print-ing	Number in set	BRITISH TOBACCO ISSUERS	Handbook reference	Price per card	Complete set

OGDENS LTD, Liverpool ('Guinea Gold' Series continued)

Size	Print-ing	Number in set	Description	Handbook reference	Price per card	Complete set
D	CP	?	Selected numbers from 1-1148 Series (c1900)		£5.00	—
D	P	400	New Series I (c1902)		£1.50	—
D	P	400	New Series B (c1902)		£1.50	—
D	P	—	Boxing, Cricket & Football cards from above set 'New Series B'		£10.00	—
D	P	300	New Series C (c1902)		£1.50	—
D	P	? 323	Set 73S Base B Actresses (c1900)	OG.340S	£4.00	—
			Set 75S Base D (c1900):	OG.350S		
D	P	? 318	List DA — White Panel Group		£1.50	—
D	P	? 58	List DB — The Denumbered Group		£3.20	—
D	P	? 62	List DC — The Political Group		£1.60	—
D	P	? 193	List DD — Boer War etc		£1.60	—
D	P	? 46	List DE — Pantomime and Theatre Group		£4.50	—
D	P	? 376	List DF — Actors and Actresses		£2.75	—
D	P	? 40	Set 76S Base E Actors and Actresses (c1900)	OG.355S	£4.25	—
D	P	? 59	Set 77S Base F Boer War etc (c1901)	OG.360S	£1.60	—
			Set 78S Base I (c1900):	OG.365S		
			List IA — The small Machette Group:			
D	P	83	I Actors and Actresses		£2.20	—
D	P	14	II London Street Scenes		£4.00	—
D	P	32	III Turner Pictures		£2.50	—
D	P	11	IV Cricketers		£20.00	—
D	P	18	V Golf		£50.00	—
D	P	10	VI Views and Scenes Abroad		£2.00	—
D	P	30	VII Miscellaneous		£2.00	—
D	P	639	List IB — The Large Machette Group		£2.75	—
D	P	5	List IC — The White Panel Group		£6.50	—
D	P	30	Set 79S Base J Actresses (c1900)	OG.370S	£4.50	—
D	P	238	Set 80S Base K Actors and Actresses (c1900)	OG.375S	£4.50	—
D	P	216	Set 81S Base L Actors and Actresses (c1900)	OG.380S	£3.00	—
			Set 82S Base M (c1901):	OG.385S		
D	P	3	List Ma Royalty		£3.25	£10.00
D	P	77	List Mb Cricketers		£35.00	—
D	P	50	List Mc Cyclists		£7.00	—
D	P	150	List Md Footballers		£30.00	—
D	P	50	List Me Pantomime and Theatre Group		£7.00	—
D	P	33	List Mf Footballers and Cyclists		£18.00	—
D	P	27	List Mg Boer War and Miscellaneous		£1.75	—
D	P ?	2951	List Mh Actors and Actresses		£2.20	—

Guinea Gold Series, Large and Medium

Size	Print-ing	Number in set	Description	Handbook reference	Price per card	Complete set
H	P	77	Set 73X Actresses Base B (c1900)	OG.340X	£20.00	—
H2	P	1	Set 74X Actress Base C (c1900)	OG.345X	—	£50.00
—	P	55	Set 75X Actresses Base D List DX1 medium size (73 x 55mm) (c1901)	OG.350X	£18.00	—
			Set 75X Base D large size (c1901):	OG.350X		
H	P	50	List DB – The Denumbered Group		£5.00	—
H	P	158	List DD – Boer War etc.		£2.50	—
H	P	45	List DE – Pantomime and Theatre Group		£6.50	—
H	P	270	List DX2 – Actors and Actresses		£2.50	—
H	P	24	Set 78X Actresses Base I (c1900)	OG.365X	£50.00	—
H	P	406	Set 82X Actors, Actresses, Boer War Etc Base M (c1901)	OG.385X	£2.50	—

'TABS' SERIES

(The listing includes both home and overseas 'Tabs' issues.)

Size	Print-ing	Number in set	Description	Handbook reference	Price per card	Complete set
D	BW	200	*Actresses (c1900)	OG.7	£3.50	—
D	BW	200	*Actresses and Foreign Views (c1900)	OG.14	£2.50	—

Size	Printing	Number in set		Handbook reference	Price per card	Complete set

BRITISH TOBACCO ISSUERS

OGDENS LTD, Liverpool ('Tabs' Series continued)

Size	Printing	Number in set	Description	Handbook reference	Price per card	Complete set
D	BW ?	331	*Composite Tabs Series, with 'Labour Clause' (1901)	OG.63		
		1	General de Wet		—	£5.00
		1	General Interest		—	£6.50
		17	Heroes of the Ring		£10.00	—
		1	HM the Queen		—	£5.00
		2	HRH the Prince of Wales		£4.00	£8.00
		14	Imperial Interest		£1.50	£21.00
		106	Imperial or International Interest		£1.40	—
		3	International Interest		£2.00	£6.00
		14	International Interest or a Prominent British Officer		£1.50	£21.00
		22	Leading Athletes		£3.50	—
		15	Leading Favourites of the Turf		£5.00	—
		54	Leading Generals at the War		£2.50	—
		2	Members of Parliament		£3.50	£7.00
		11	Notable Coursing Dogs		£10.00	—
		12	Our Leading Cricketers		£25.00	—
		17	Our Leading Footballers		£12.00	—
		37	Prominent British Officers		£1.50	£55.00
		1	The Yacht 'Columbia'		—	£7.00
		1	The Yacht 'Shamrock'		—	£7.00
D	BW ?	71	*Composite Tabs Series, without 'Labour Clause' (c1900):	OG.64		
		40	General Interest		£27.00	—
		31	Leading Artists of the Day		£25.00	—
D	BW ?	114	*Composite Tabs Series, Sydney issue (c1900):	OG.65		
		1	Christian de Wet		£10.00	—
		1	Corporal G. E. Nurse, VC		£10.00	—
		15	English Cricketer Series		£90.00	—
		1	Imperial Interest		£10.00	—
		29	Imperial or International Interest		£9.00	—
		6	International Interest		£9.00	—
		1	Lady Sarah Wilson		£12.00	—
		41	Leading Generals at the War		£9.00	—
		13	Prominent British Officers		£9.00	—
D	BW	150	General Interest, Series 'A' (1901)	OG.89	£1.50	—
D	BW	200	General Interest, Series 'B' (1902)	OG.90	£1.50	—
D	BW	470	General Interest, Series 'C' (1902):			
			C.1-200	OG.91	£1.50	—
			C.201-300		£3.00	—
			C.301-350		£2.00	—
			No Letter, Nd 1-120		£1.80	—
D	BW	200	General Interest, Series 'D' (1902)	OG.92	£1.50	—
D	BW	120	General Interest, Series 'E' (1902)	OG.93	£2.00	—
D	BW	420	General Interest, Series 'F' (1902):	OG.94		
			F.1-200		£2.00	—
			F.201-320		£2.00	—
			F.321-420		£3.50	—
D	BW	—	General Interest Series A to F Boxing, Cricket & Football cards (1902)		£10.00	—
D	BW ?	400	General Interest, Sydney issue (c1902):	OG.99		
			Nd 1-100 on front		£4.50	—
			Nd 101-400 on back		£4.50	—
		? 106	Unnumbered, mostly similar numbered cards 101-200		£7.00	—
D	BW	196	*General Interest, unnumbered, similar style C.201-300 (1902):	OG.95		
		76	Stage Artistes		£1.50	—
		41	Celebrities		£1.50	—
		56	Footballers		£4.00	—
		23	Miscellaneous		£1.50	—

Size	Print-ing	Number in set	BRITISH TOBACCO ISSUERS	Handbook reference	Price per card	Complete set
			OGDENS LTD, Liverpool ('Tabs' Series continued)			
D	BW	100	*General Interest, unnumbered, similar style C.301-350 (1902):	OG.96		
			28 Actresses		£1.50	—
			40 Castles		£1.50	—
			12 Dogs		£2.00	—
			20 Miscellaneous		£2.50	—
D	BW	300	*General Interest, unnumbered, similar style F.321-420 (1903):	OG.97		
			A 100 with full stop after caption		£1.80	—
			B Without full stop after caption:			
			79 I Stage Artistes		£1.50	—
			21 II Cricketers		£12.00	—
			25 III Football		£9.00	—
			15 IV Golf		£50.00	—
			10 V Cyclists		£6.00	—
			9 VI Fire Brigades		£6.00	—
			5 VII Aldershot Gymnasium		£3.50	—
			36 VIII Miscellaneous		£1.50	—
D	BW?	111	*General Interest, 'oblong' back (c1900)	OG.98	£20.00	—
D	BW	? 75	*Leading Artistes of the Day, numbered 126-200, plain backs (c1900)	H.1/OG.109	£16.00	—
D	BW	? 71	Leading Artistes of the Day with 'Labour Clause' (c1900):	OG.110		
			A Type-set back		£2.00	—
			B Plain back		£24.00	—
D	BW	? 25	Leading Artistes of the Day, without 'Labour Clause' (c1900):	OG.111-1		
			A With caption, type-set back		£16.00	—
			B With caption, plain back		£16.00	—
			C Without caption, type-set back		£16.00	—
D	BW	? 91	Leading Artistes of the Day, without 'Labour Clause' (c1900):	OG.111-2		
			A Type-set back		£15.00	—
			B Plain back		£15.00	—
D	BW	25	Leading Generals at the War, with descriptive text (c1900):	OG.112		
			A 'Ogden's Cigarettes' back		£3.00	—
			B 'Ogden's Tab Cigarettes' back		£2.50	—
D	BW		Leading Generals at the War, without descriptive text (c1900):	OG.113		
		? 47	A 'Ogden's Tab Cigarettes' back (47 known) ...		£2.50	—
		? 25	B 'Ogden's Lucky Star' back (25 known)		£8.00	—
D	BW	50	*Stage Artistes and Celebrities (c1900)	OG.157	£4.00	—

OVERSEAS ISSUES

Size	Print-ing	Number in set		Handbook reference	Price per card	Complete set
D2	BW	51	Actresses, black and white Polo issue (1906)	OG.10	£4.00	—
D	U	30	Actresses, unicoloured Polo issue (1908):	OG.11		
			A Tin foil at back white		£3.60	£110.00
			B Tin foil at back shaded		£4.00	—
D2	C	17	Animals Polo issue (1916)	OG.18	£13.00	—
A1	C	60	Animals — cut-outs:	OG.17		
			A Ruler issue (1912)		£3.50	—
			B Tabs issue (1913):			
			i With captions		£3.50	—
			ii Without captions		£5.00	—
D2	C	50	Aviation series Tabs issue (1912):	OG.22		
			A Ogdens at base		£8.00	—
			B Ogdens England at base		£8.00	—

Size	Print-ing	Number in set	BRITISH TOBACCO ISSUERS	Handbook reference	Price per card	Complete set
			OGDENS LTD, Liverpool (Overseas Issues continued)			
			Beauties green net design back 1901:	OG.27		
D	BW	? 66	A Front black & white		£18.00	—
D	C	? 98	B Front coloured		£32.00	—
D2	C	45	Beauties Picture Hats Polo issue (1911)	OG.28	£7.00	—
D	C	50	Best Dogs of Their Breed Polo issue (1916):	OG.32		
			A Back in red		£9.00	—
			B Back in blue with Eastern characters		£9.00	—
			C Back in blue without Eastern characters		£9.00	—
D	C	52	Birds of Brilliant Plumage Ruler issue (1914):	OG.36		
			A Fronts with framelines		£3.60	—
			B Fronts without framelines		£3.60	—
A	C	25	British Trees and Their Uses, Guinea Gold issue (1927)	OG.52	£3.00	£75.00
D	C	25	China's Famous Warriors, Ruler issue (1913)	OG.59	£6.00	—
A	C	25	Famous Railway Trains, Guinea Gold issue (1928)	OG.79	£3.20	£80.00
D2	C	20	Flowers, Polo issue (1915):	OG.82		
			A Without Eastern inscription		£6.00	—
			B With Eastern inscription		£6.00	—
D2	U	25	Indian Women, Polo issue (1919):	OG.104		
			A Framework in light apple green		£7.00	—
			B Framework in dark emerald green		£7.00	—
—	C	52	Miniature Playing Cards, Polo issue (56 x 38mm) (c1910)	OG.117	£13.00	—
D2	BW		Music Hall Celebrities (1911):	OG.125		
		30	A Polo issue		£6.50	—
		50	B Tabs issue		£6.50	—
A	C	50	Riders of the World, Polo issue (1911)	OG.146	£4.00	—
D2	U	50	Russo-Japanese series (1905)	OG.148	£22.00	—
D2	C	36	Ships and Their Pennants, Polo issue (1911)	OG.153	£6.50	—
D2	C	32	Transport of the World, Polo issue (1917)	OG.165	£6.50	—
			THE ORLANDO CIGARETTE & CIGAR CO., London			
A	C	40	*Home & Colonial Regiments (c1901)	H.69	£600.00	—
			OSBORNE TOBACCO CO. LTD, Portsmouth & London			
A	U	50	Modern Aircraft (1953):	H.895		
			A Dark Blue back:			
			i Firm's name in one line		70p	£35.00
			ii Firm's name in two lines		£2.00	—
			B Light Blue back		£1.50	—
			C Brown back		70p	£35.00
			W.T. OSBORNE & CO., London			
D	C	40	*Naval and Military Phrases (c1904):	H.14		
			A White Border		£65.00	—
			B No Border		£65.00	—
			PALMER & CO., Bedford			
—	U	12	'Manikin' Cards (79 x 51mm) (c1920)	H.481	£120.00	—
			J.A. PATTREIOUEX, Manchester			
	P		Beautiful Scotland (1939):	H.564-1		
D		28	A Small size		£1.25	£35.00
—		48	B Medium size (77 x 52mm)		40p	£20.00
—	P	48	The Bridges of Britain (77 x 52mm) (1938)		40p	£20.00
—	P	48	Britain from the Air (77 x 52mm) (1939)		35p	£17.50

Size	Print-ing	Number in set	BRITISH TOBACCO ISSUERS	Handbook reference	Price per card	Complete set
			J.A. PATTREIOUEX, Manchester (continued)			
A	C	50	British Empire Exhibition Series (1924)		£3.00	£150.00
—	P	48	British Railways (77 x 52mm) (1938)		70p	£35.00
A	C	50	Builders of the British Empire (c1929)		£3.50	£175.00
—	C	24	Cadet's Jackpot Jigsaws (90 x 65mm) (1969)		£2.00	—
A	C	50	Celebrities in Sport (c1930):			
			A 46 Different		£4.00	—
			B Nos. 39,40 and 41 (Golfers)		£20.00	—
			C No. 38 Bobby Jones		£50.00	—
	P		Coastwise (1939):	H.564-2		
D		28	A Small size		£1.40	£40.00
—		48	B Medium size (77 x 52mm)		35p	£17.50
A	C	75	Cricketers Series (1926)	H.665	£15.00	—
A	C	50	Dirt Track Riders (1929)		£12.00	—
D	P	54	Dirt Track Riders (1930):			
			A Descriptive back		£12.00	—
			* B Non-descriptive back		£35.00	—
—	P	48	Dogs (76 x 51mm) (1939)		50p	£25.00
A	C	30	Drawing Made Easy (c1930)		£2.50	£75.00
A	C	52	The English and Welsh Counties (c1928)		£2.20	£115.00
	P		Flying (1938):	H.564-3		
D		28	A Small size		£2.00	—
—		48	B Medium size (77 x 52mm)		70p	£35.00
A2	P	78	Footballers in Action (1934)		£4.50	—
A	C		Footballers Series (1927):			
		50	A Captions in blue		£11.00	—
		100	B Captions in brown		£11.00	—
—	P .	48	Holiday Haunts by the Sea (77 x 52mm) (1937)		40p	£20.00
A	C	25	'King Lud' Problems (c1935)	H.638	£20.00	—
A	C	26	Maritime Flags (c1932)		£10.00	—
—	P	48	The Navy (1937):			
			A Large captions on back, text width 36mm		70p	£35.00
			B Smaller captions on back, text width 35mm ...		80p	£40.00
	P		Our Countryside (1938):	H.564-4		
D		28	A Small size		£1.75	£50.00
—		48	B Medium size (77 x 52mm)		35p	£17.50
A	U	25	Photos of Football Stars (c1930)	H.666	£42.00	—
D	C	50	Railway Posters by Famous Artists (c1930)		£12.00	—
A2	P	54	Real Photographs of London (1936)		£2.50	—
D	P	28	Shots from the Films (1938)	H.566	£2.75	—
—	P	48	Sights of Britain — 'Series of 48' (76 x 51 mm) (1936)		50p	£25.00
—	P	48	Sights of Britain — 'Second Series ...' (76 x 51mm) (1936):			
			A Large captions on back 2mm high		30p	£15.00
			B Smaller captions on back 1mm high		35p	£17.50
—	P	48	Sights of Britain — 'Third Series ...' (76 x 51mm) (1937)		50p	£25.00
—	P	48	Sights of London — 'First Series ...' (76 x 51mm) (1935)		£1.25	£60.00
—	P	12	Sights of London — 'Supplementary Series of 12 Jubilee Pictures' (76 x 51mm) (1935)		£1.25	£15.00
A2	P	54	Sporting Celebrities (1935)		£5.00	—
—	P	96	Sporting Events and Stars (76 x 50mm) (1935):			
			A 92 Different		£2.00	—
			B Nos. 18, 20 and 21 (Golfers)		£12.00	—
			C No. 19 Bobby Jones		£45.00	—
A	C	50	Sports Trophies (c1931)		£3.50	£175.00
—	C	24	Treasure Island (65 x 45mm) (1968)		£2.00	—

Size	Printing	Number in set	BRITISH TOBACCO ISSUERS	Handbook reference	Price per card	Complete set

J.A. PATTREIOUEX, Manchester (1920s Photographic Series continued)

Size	Printing	Number in set	Description	Handbook reference	Price per card	Complete set
A2	CP	51	*Views (c1930)	H.597	£1.30	£65.00
A2	P	54	Views of Britain (1937)		£1.70	—
—	P	48	Winter Scenes (76 x 52mm) (1937)		30p	£15.00

1920s PHOTOGRAPHIC SERIES Listed in order of letters and/or numbers quoted on cards.

Size	Printing	Number in set	Description	Handbook reference	Price per card	Complete set
H2	P	50	*Animals and Scenes — unnumbered 'Junior Member' back (c1925)	H.595-1	£2.20	—
H2	P	50	Animals and Scenes, Nd 1-50 (c1925)		£2.20	—
H2	P	50	*Scenes, Nd 201-250 'Junior Member' back (c1925)		£1.80	—
C	P	96	Animals and Scenes, Nd 250-345 (c1925):	H.595-2B		
			A 'Casket/Critic' back (i) grey		£2.00	—
			(ii) brown		£2.00	—
			* B 'Junior Member' back		£2.00	—
C	P	96	Animals and Scenes, Nd 346-441 (c1925):			
			A 'Casket/Critic' back		£2.00	—
			B 'Club Member' back		£2.00	—
			* C 'Junior Member' back		£2.00	—
H	P	50	*Animal Studies, Nd A42-A91 'Junior Member' back (c1925)		£2.00	—
H	P	50	*Animal Studies, Nd A92-A141 'Junior Member' back (c1925)		£2.00	—
H	P	50	*Animal Studies, Nd A151-A200 'Junior Member' back (c1925)		£2.00	—
C	P		*Natives and Scenes (c1925):	H.595-2G		
		36	A 'Series 1/36 B' on front, Nd 1-36 'Junior Member' back		£1.80	—
		96	B 'Series 1/96 B' on front, Nd 1-96 'Junior/Club Member' back		£1.80	—
C	P	96	*Foreign Scenes, Nd 1/96C-96/96C (c1925)		£1.80	—
C	P	96	Cricketers, Nd C1-C96, 'Casket Cigarettes' on front (c1925):	H.595-2C		
			A Printed back		£70.00	—
			* B Plain back		£70.00	—
C	P	96	*Animals — 'Series Nos CA1 to 96'. Back 7 (c1925)	H.595-2A	£2.00	—
C	P	96	*Natives and Scenes (c1925):			
			A 'C.B.1 to 96' on front.'Club/Critic Member' back:			
			1 Nd 1-96		£1.80	—
			2 Nd C.B.1-C.B.96		£1.80	—
			B 'J.S. 1 to 96' on front. 'Junior Member' back		£1.80	—
C	P	96	*Animals and Scenes — 'CC1 to 96' on front (c1925)		£2.00	—
H2	P	50	*British Scenes — 'Series C.M.1-50.A' on front (c1925)		£1.80	—
H2	P	50	*Foreign Scenes (c1925):			
			A 'Series CM. 1/50 B' on front		£1.80	—
			B 'J.M. Series 1/50' on front		£1.80	—
H2	P	50	*Foreign Scenes (c1925):	H.595-2H		
			A 'Series C.M. 101-150.S' on front		£1.80	—
			B Nd S.101-S.150 on front		£1.80	—
C	P	96	*Foreign Scenes, Nd 1/96D-96/96D (c1925)		£2.20	—
H2	P	50	*Foreign Scenes, Nd 1/50E-50/50E (c1925)		£1.80	—
H2	P	50	*Foreign Scenes, Nd 1/50F-50/50F (c1925)		£1.80	—
C	P	96	Footballers, Nd F.1-F.96. 'Casket' and 'Critic' back (c1922)		£16.00	—
C	P	95	Footballers, Nd F.97-F.191. 'Casket' and 'Critic' back styles (c1922)		£16.00	—
H	P	50	Football Teams, Nd F.192-F.241. ('Casket' and 'Critic') (1922)	H.595-2F	£65.00	—
C	P	96	*Footballers — 'Series F.A. 1/96' on front (c1922)		£13.00	—

Size	Print-ing	Number in set	BRITISH TOBACCO ISSUERS	Handbook reference	Price per card	Complete set
			J.A. PATTREIOUEX, Manchester (1920s Photographic Series continued)			
C	P	96	*Footballers — 'Series F.B. 1/96' on front (1922) ...	H.595-2D	£13.00	—
C	P	96	*Footballers — 'Series F.C. 1/96' on front (c1922) ...	H.595-2E	£13.00	—
H2	P	50	*Scenes — 'G. 1/50' on front (c1925)		£1.80	—
H2	P	50	*Scenes — '1/50. H' on front (c1925)	H.595-2J	£1.80	—
H2	P	50	*Animals and Scenes, Nd I.1-I.50 (c1925)		£2.00	—
H2	P	50	Famous Statues — 'J.C.M. 1 to 50 C' on front (c1925)............................		£2.30	—
H2	P	50	*Scenes, Nd JCM 1/50D-JCM 50/50D (c1925):			
			A 'Junior/Club Member' back		£1.80	
			B 'Junior Member' back		£1.80	
B1	P	30	Child Studies, Nd J.M. No. 1-J.M. No. 30 (c1925) ...		£5.00	—
B1	P	30	*Beauties, Nd J.M.1-J.M.30 (c1925)		£5.00	—
H2	P	50	*Foreign Scenes — 'J.M. 1 to 50 A' on front (c1925)	H.595-2I	£1.80	—
H2	P	50	British Empire Exhibition 'J.M. 1 to 50 B' on front (c1925)............................		£2.50	—
C	P	96	*Animals and Scenes — 'J.S. 1/96A'on front (c1925)		£2.00	—
H2	P	50	*Scenes, Nd S.1-S.50.' Junior Member' back (c1925)		£1.80	—
H2	P	50	*Scenes, Nd S.51-S.100.' Junior Member' back (c1925)		£1.80	—
B1	P	50	*Cathedrals and Abbeys, Nd S.J. 1-S.J. 50. Plain back (c1925)............................		£3.50	—
B1	P	50	*British Castles. Nd S.J. 51-S.J. 100. Plain back (c1925)............................		£3.50	—
H2	P	4	*Scenes, Nd V.1-V.4. 'Junior Member' back (c1925)	H.595-1	£5.00	—
			W. PEPPERDY			
A	C	30	*Army Pictures, Cartoons, etc (c1916)	H.12	£160.00	—
			M. PEZARO & SON, London			
D	C	25	*Armies of the World (c1900):	H.43		
			A Cake Walk Cigarettes		£150.00	—
			B Nestor Virginia Cigarettes		£150.00	—
D	C	? 19	Song Titles Illustrated (c1900)	H.323	£350.00	—
			GODFREY PHILLIPS LTD, London			
			The Card Issues of Godfrey Phillips & Associated Companies (2009 Edition) reference book, 256 pages — £28.00			
D1	C	25	*Actresses 'C' Series, Nd 101-125 (c1900):	GP.1		
			A Blue Horseshoe design back		£38.00	—
			B Green back, 'Carriage' Cigarettes		£38.00	—
			C Blue back, 'Teapot' Cigarettes		£100.00	—
			D Blue back, 'Volunteer' Cigarettes		£100.00	—
			E Blue back, 'Derby' Cigarettes		£100.00	—
			F Blue back 'Ball of Beauty' Cigarettes		£100.00	—
—	C	50	*Actresses — oval card (38 x 62mm) (1916):	GP.2		
			A With name		£8.00	—
			B Without Maker's and Actress's Name		£6.00	£300.00
A2	C	1	*Advertisement Card — 'Grand Cut' (1934)	GP.2	—	£15.00
A2	C	1	*Advertisement Card — 'La Galbana Fours' (1934)	GP.2	—	£15.00
A	C	50	Aircraft (1938)	GP.5	£2.20	£110.00
A2	C	54	Aircraft — Series No. 1 (1938):	GP.4		
			A Millhoff and Philips names at base		£4.00	—
			B Phillips and Associated Companies at base:			
			1 Front varnished		£3.00	£160.00
			2 Front matt		60p	£32.00
D	C	40	Animal Series (c1905)		£7.00	£280.00
—	C	30	Animal Studies (61 x 53mm) (1936)		33p	£10.00

Size	Print-ing	Number in set	BRITISH TOBACCO ISSUERS	Handbook reference	Price per card	Complete set
			GODFREY PHILLIPS LTD, London (continued)			
A2	C	50	Annuals (1939):	GP.9		
			A Home issue		30p	£15.00
			B New Zealand issue (dates for planting 4-6 months later). See Overseas Issues			
B	C	25	Arms of the English Sees (1924)		£5.00	£125.00
A	BW		B.D.V. Package Issues (1932-34):			
		17	Boxers	GP.161	£8.00	—
		55	Cricketers	GP.162	£9.00	—
		68	Film Stars	GP.168	£3.00	—
		136	Footballers	GP.163	£7.00	—
		19	Jockeys	GP.164	£5.00	—
		21	Speedway Riders	GP.165	£10.00	—
		28	Sportsmen	GP.166	£7.00	—
D1	C	25	*Beauties, Nd B.801-825 (c1902)	GP.12	£12.00	£300.00
A1	U	24	*Beauties, collotype — 'HUMPS' (c1895):	H.222/GP.24		
			A 'Awarded 7 Gold Medals 1895' on front		£110.00	—
			B 'PLUMS' on front		£650.00	—
A	C	30	*Beauties, 'Nymphs' (c1896)	GP.14	£110.00	—
D			*Beauties — 'PLUMS' (1897):	H.186/GP.16		
	BW	?60	A Front in black and white		£180.00	—
	C	50	B Plum-coloured background		£80.00	—
	C	50	C Green background		£80.00	—
DA	C	44	Beauties of Today, small — 'A Series of 44 ...' (1937)		£1.60	—
A	C	50	Beauties of Today, small — 'A Series of 50 ...' (1938)	GP.20	£1.20	£60.00
A2	P	54	Beauties of Today, small — 'A Series of Real Photographs ...' (1939)		£1.40	£75.00
A	C	36	Beauties of Today, small — 'A Series of 36 ... Second Series' (1940)		£1.10	£40.00
—	P		Beauties of Today, large (83 x 66mm) (c1938):	GP.24		
		36	First arrangement, known as 'Series A'		£3.50	—
		36	Second arrangement, known as 'Series B'		£6.50	—
J2	P	36	Beauties of Today, extra-large, unnumbered (1937)	GP.25	£1.65	£60.00
J2	P	36	Beauties of Today, extra-large — 'Second Series' (1938)		£1.25	£45.00
J2	P	36	Beauties of Today, extra-large — 'Third Series' (1938)		£1.25	£45.00
J2	P	36	Beauties of Today, extra-large — 'Fourth Series' (1938)		£1.25	£45.00
J2	P	36	Beauties of Today, extra-large — 'Fifth Series' (1938)		£1.25	£45.00
J2	P	36	Beauties of Today, extra-large — 'Sixth Series' (1939)		£1.25	£45.00
J2	P	36	Beauties of Today, extra-large — Unmarked (1939):	GP.31		
			A Back 'Godfrey Phillips Ltd'		£1.10	£40.00
			B Back 'Issued with B.D.V. Medium Cigarettes ...'		50p	£18.00
A2	BW	36	Beauties of the World — Stage, Cinema, Dancing Celebrities (1931)		£1.65	£60.00
A2	C	36	Beauties of the World — Series No. 2 — Stars of Stage and Screen (1933)		£1.65	£60.00
A1	C	50	Beautiful Women (c1905):	H.284/GP.32		
			A Inscribed 'W.I. Series'		£12.00	—
			B Inscribed 'I.F. Series'		£12.00	—
—	C	50	Beautiful Women, Nd W.501-550 (55 x 75mm) (c1905)	H.284/GP.32	£24.00	—
—	C	30	Beauty Spots of the Homeland (126 x 89mm) (1938)		50p	£15.00
A	C	50	Bird Painting (1938)		£1.00	£50.00
D1	C	25	*Boxer Rebellion — Sketches (1904)	H.46/GP.35	£32.00	—
—	C	30	*British Beauties — Oval Card (36 x 60mm) Plain back (c1910)	H.244/GP.15	£3.00	£90.00

Size	Printing	Number in set	BRITISH TOBACCO ISSUERS	Handbook reference	Price per card	Complete set
			GODFREY PHILLIPS LTD, London (continued)			
D	U	50	'British Beauties' photogravure (c1916)	GP.38	£8.00	£400.00
—	PC	76	British Beauties (37 x 51mm) (c1916)		£3.50	£265.00
A	C	54	British Beauties Nd 1-54 (1914):	GP.36		
			(a) Blue back, grey-black, glossy front		£2.75	£150.00
			(b) *Plain back, grey-black, glossy front*		£3.50	—
			(c) *Plain back, sepia, matt front*		£3.50	—
A	C	54	British Beauties Nd 55-108 (1914):	GP.37		
			A Blue back, grey-black, semi-glossy front		£2.75	£150.00
			B Blue back, grey-black matt front		£2.75	£150.00
			C *Plain back, grey-black matt front*		£3.50	—
A	C	50	British Birds and Their Eggs (1936)		£1.50	£75.00
D1	C	30	British Butterflies, No. 1 issue (1911)		£6.50	£195.00
A	C	25	British Butterflies:	GP.42		
			A Back in pale blue (1923)		£1.60	£40.00
			B Back in dark blue (1927)		£1.20	£30.00
			C 'Permacal' transfers (1936)		80p	£20.00
A2	C	25	British Orders of Chivalry and Valour (1939):	GP.43		
			A Back 'Godfrey Phillips Ltd'		£4.00	£100.00
			B Back 'De Reszke Cigarettes' (no maker's name)		£4.00	£100.00
D1	U	25	British Warships, green photo style (1915)		£11.00	£275.00
L	U	25	British Warships, green photo style (1915)		£50.00	—
A1	P	80	British Warships, 'real photographic' (c1916)	GP.45	£20.00	—
D1	C	50	*Busts of Famous People (1906):			
			A Pale green back, caption in black		£30.00	—
			B Brown back, caption in black		£50.00	—
			C Green back, caption in white		£8.00	£400.00
—	C	36	Characters Come to Life (61 x 53mm) (1938)		£1.00	£36.00
D1	C	25	*Chinese Series (c1910):	GP.48		
			A Back in English		£8.00	£200.00
			B 'Volunteer' Cigarettes back		£10.00	£250.00
—	P	25	*Cinema Stars — Circular (57mm diam.) (1924)	GP.49	£3.60	—
A	P	52	Cinema Stars — Set 1 (1929)	GP.50	£3.00	—
A2	U	30	Cinema Stars — Set 2 (1924)	GP.51	£3.00	—
A2	BW	30	Cinema Stars — Set 3 (1931)	GP.52	£1.70	£50.00
A2	C	32	Cinema Stars — Set 4 (1934)	GP.53	£2.00	£65.00
A2	BW	32	Cinema Stars — Set 5 (1934)	GP.54	£1.75	£55.00
A	C	50	*Colonial Troops (1904)	H.40/GP.56	£32.00	—
	C		Come to Life Series — see 'Zoo Studies' Coronation of Their Majesties (1937):	GP.57		
A2		50	A Small size		30p	£15.00
—		36	B Medium size (61 x 53mm)		30p	£11.00
—		24	C Postcard size (127 x 89mm):			
			i Back with postcard format		£1.60	£40.00
			ii Back without postcard format		£4.00	—
	P		Cricketers (with 'c' after numeral) (1924):	GP.58		
K2		198	*A Miniature size, 'Pinnace' photos (selected Nos)		£12.00	—
D		192	B Small size, brown back (selected Nos)		£11.00	—
B1	?	157	*C Large size, 'Pinnace' photos (selected Nos) ...		£60.00	—
B1	?	25	D Large size, brown back (selected Nos)		£26.00	—
—	?	180	*E *Cabinet size* (selected Nos)		£60.00	—
D	BW	1	Cricket Fixture Card (Radio Luxembourg) (1936) ...		—	£7.00
D	C	25	Derby Winners and Jockeys (1923)		£4.00	£100.00
D1	C	30	Eggs, Nests and Birds, No. 1 issue (1912):			
			A Unnumbered	GP.60	£7.00	£210.00
			B Numbered		£7.00	£210.00
D1	C	25	Empire Industries (1927)	GP.61	£1.40	£35.00

Size	Print-ing	Number in set	BRITISH TOBACCO ISSUERS	Handbook reference	Price per card	Complete set
			GODFREY PHILLIPS LTD, London (continued)			
A2	C	50	Evolution of the British Navy (1930)		—	£125.00
			49 different (minus No 40)		£1.50	£75.00
D	C	25	Famous Boys (1924)		£3.00	£75.00
D	C	32	Famous Cricketers (1926)		£8.00	—
A	C	25	Famous Crowns (1938)		50p	£12.50
A2	C	50	Famous Footballers (1936)	GP.66	£2.50	£125.00
—	C	36	Famous Love Scenes (60 x 53mm) (1939)		70p	£25.00
A2	C	50	Famous Minors (1936)		35p	£17.50
—	C	26	Famous Paintings (128 x 89mm) (1938)	GP.69	£1.30	£35.00
D	C	25	Feathered Friends (1928)	GP.70	£1.80	£45.00
A2	C	50	Film Favourites (1934)	GP.71	70p	£35.00
A2	C	50	Film Stars (1934)	GP.73	80p	£40.00
—	C	24	*Film Stars — '... No. ... of a series of 24 cards ...' (128 x 89mm) (1934):	GP.74		
			A Postcard format back		£3.00	£75.00
			B Back without postcard format		£4.00	£100.00
—	C	24	*Film Stars — '... No. ... of a series of cards', Nd 25-48 (128 x 89mm) (1935):	GP.75		
			A Postcard format back		£3.00	—
			B Back without postcard format		£6.00	—
—	C	24	*Film Stars '... No. ... of a series of cards', vivid backgrounds (128 x 89mm) (1936):	GP.76		
			A Postcard format back		£2.00	—
			B Back without postcard format		£3.00	—
D	C	25	First Aid Series, green back (1914)	GP.78	£8.00	£200.00
D	C	50	First Aid, black back (1923)	GP.77	£1.70	£85.00
D	C	25	*Fish (1924)		£3.40	£85.00
	C	30	Flower Studies (1937):			
—			A Medium size (61 x 53mm)		30p	£9.00
—			*B Postcard size (128 x 89mm)		70p	£21.00
K2	P	2462	Footballers — 'Pinnace' photos (1922-24): A Miniature size (prices shown apply to numbers 1 to 940, for numbers above 940 prices are doubled):	GP.155		
		112	1a 'Oval' design back, in brown		£5.00	—
		400	1b 'Oval' design back, in black		£3.00	—
		? 388	2 Double-lined oblong back		£3.00	—
		? 890	3 Single-lined oblong back, address 'Photo'		£2.00	—
		? 2350	4 Single-lined oblong back, address 'Pinnace' photos		£2.00	—
—			B Large size (83 x 59mm):	GP.156		
		? 400	1 'Oval' design back		£5.00	—
			2 Double-lined oblong back:			
		? 63	a Address 'Photo'		£14.00	—
		? 2462	b Address 'Pinnace' photos		£5.00	—
—		? 2462	C Cabinet size (153 x 111mm)	GP.157	£22.00	—
—		? 24	D Football Teams (153 x 111mm)	GP.157	£600.00	—
—	C	30	Garden Studies (128 x 89mm) (1938)		50p	£15.00
A	C	13	*General Interest (c1895)	GP.83	£45.00	£600.00
—	BW	100	*Guinea Gold Series, unnumbered (64 x 38mm) Inscribed 'Phillips' Guinea Gold', matt (1899)	GP.87	£6.50	—
—	BW	90	*Guinea Gold Series, numbered 101-190 (68 x 41mm). Inscribed 'Smoke Phillips ...' (1902):	GP.88		
			A Glossy		£5.00	
			B Matt		£5.00	

Size	Print-ing	Number in set	BRITISH TOBACCO ISSUERS	Handbook reference	Price per card	Complete set
			GODFREY PHILLIPS LTD, London (continued)			
			*Guinea Gold Series, unnumbered (63 x 41mm) (c1900):	GP.89		
			Actresses:			
	BW	135	A Black front		£5.00	—
	U	100	B Brown front		£10.00	—
	BW	26	Celebrities, Boer War		£5.00	—
A2	C	25	Home Pets (1924)	GP.90	£2.20	£55.00
A2	U	25	How to Build a Two Valve Set (1929)		£2.60	£65.00
D1	C	25	How to Do It Series (1913)		£8.00	£200.00
D	C	25	How to Make a Valve Amplifier ..., Nd 26-50 (1924)		£3.20	£80.00
A	C	25	How to Make Your Own Wireless Set (1923)		£3.00	£75.00
D	C	25	Indian Series (1908)		£16.00	—
A2	C	54	In the Public Eye (1935)		70p	£38.00
A2	C	50	International Caps (1936)	GP.66	£2.00	£100.00
A2	C	37	Kings and Queens of England (1925):			
			Nos 1 and 4		£30.00	—
			Other numbers		£2.00	£70.00
A2	U	25	Lawn Tennis (1930)		£3.80	£95.00
K1	C	52	*Miniature Playing Cards (c1905)	GP.99	£120.00	—
K2	C	53	*Miniature Playing Cards (1932-34):	GP.100		
			A Back with exchange scheme:			
			1 Buff. Offer for 'pack of playing cards'		60p	—
			2 Buff. Offer for 'playing cards, dominoes or chess'		60p	£30.00
			3 Buff. Offer for 'playing cards, dominoes or draughts'		60p	£30.00
			4 Lemon		60p	—
			5 White, with red over-printing		60p	—
			B *Blue scroll back*		60p	£30.00
A2	C	25	Model Railways (1927)	GP.101	£3.60	£90.00
D1	C	30	Morse and Semaphore Signalling (1916):	GP.102		
			'Morse Signalling' back		£12.00	£360.00
			'Semaphore Signalling' back		£12.00	£360.00
D	C	50	Motor Cars at a Glance (1924)		£4.50	£225.00
D	C	20	Novelty Series (1924)		£17.00	—
A2	C	48	The 'Old Country' (1935)		80p	£40.00
A	C	25	Old Favourites (1924)	GP.107	£2.00	£50.00
—	C	36	Old Masters (60 x 53mm) (1939)		55p	£20.00
A	U	36	Olympic Champions Amsterdam, 1928		£2.75	£100.00
A	C	25	Optical Illusions (1927)		£2.60	£65.00
	C		'Our Dogs' (1939):	GP.110		
A2		36	A Small size (export)		£1.60	£60.00
—		30	B Medium size (60 x 53mm)		60p	£18.00
—		30	*C Postcard size (128 x 89mm)		£3.40	—
—	BW	48	'Our Favourites' (60 x 53mm) (1935)		30p	£15.00
—	C	30	Our Glorious Empire (128 x 89mm) (1939)		70p	£21.00
	C	30	'Our Puppies' (1936):	GP.113		
—			A Medium size (60 x 53mm)		£1.65	£50.00
—			*B Postcard size (128 x 89mm)		£1.80	£55.00
A2	C	25	Personalities of Today (Caricatures) (1932)		£2.20	£55.00
A2	C	25	Popular Superstitions (1930)		£1.60	£40.00
J2		20	'Private Seal' Wrestling Holds (export) (c1920)		£35.00	—
A	C	25	Prizes for Needlework (1925)	GP.116	£2.20	£55.00
D	C	25	Railway Engines (1924)		£3.60	£90.00
—	P	27	Real Photo Series — Admirals and Generals of the Great War. Cut-outs for buttonhole (28 x 40mm) (c1915)	GP.118	£9.00	—

Size	Printing	Number in set	BRITISH TOBACCO ISSUERS	Handbook reference	Price per card	Complete set
			GODFREY PHILLIPS LTD, London (continued)			
D	C	25	Red Indians (1927)	GP.119	£3.60	£90.00
A	C	20	Russo-Japanese War Series (1904)	H.100/GP.120	£350.00	—
A	C	25	School Badges (1927)	GP.121	£1.20	£30.00
A	C		Screen Stars (1936):			
		48	First arrangement, known as 'Series A':	GP.122		
			i Frame embossed		£1.20	£60.00
			ii Frame not embossed		£1.60	£80.00
		48	Second arrangement, known as 'Series B'	GP.123	£1.00	£50.00
A2	C		A Selection of B.D.V. Wonderful Gifts:			
		48	'... based on 1930 Budget' (1930)	GP.84	£1.40	—
		48	'... based on 1931 Budget' (1931)	GP.85	£1.40	—
		48	'... based on 1932 Budget' (1932)	GP.86	£1.20	£60.00
		30	Semaphore Signalling — see 'Morse and Semaphore Signalling'			
D	C	25	Ships and Their Flags (1924)	GP.124	£3.00	£75.00
—	C	36	Ships that have Made History (60 x 53mm) (1938)		60p	£22.00
—	C	48	Shots from the Films (60 x 53mm) (1934)	GP.126	80p	£40.00
A2	C	50	Soccer Stars (1937)	GP.66	£2.00	£100.00
A2	C	36	Soldiers of the King (1939):	GP.127		
			A Inscribed 'This surface is adhesive'		£1.60	—
			B Without the above:			
			1 Thin card		70p	£25.00
			2 Thick card		70p	£25.00
	C		Special Jubilee Year Series (1935):	GP.128		
—		20	A Medium size (60 x 53mm)		60p	£12.00
—		12	B Postcard size (128 x 89mm)		£2.00	£24.00
A2	U	30	Speed Champions (1930)		£2.30	£70.00
A2	U	36	Sporting Champions (1929)		£3.00	£110.00
D1	C	25	Sporting Series (c1910)	GP.131	£30.00	—
D	C	25	Sports (1923):	GP.131		
			A White card		£5.00	—
			B Grey card		£5.00	—
A2	C	50	*Sportsmen — 'Spot the Winner' (1937):			
			A Inverted back		£1.10	£55.00
			B Normal back		£1.50	£75.00
A	BW		Sports Package Issues:			
		25	Cricketers (1948)	GP.171	£10.00	—
		25	Cricketers (1951)	GP.177	£10.00	—
		25	Footballers (1948)	GP.172	£8.00	—
		50	Footballers (1950)	GP.176	£8.00	—
		25	Footballers (1951)	GP.178	£8.00	—
		25	Football & Rugby Players (1952)	GP.180	£8.00	—
		25	Jockeys (1952)	GP.179	£6.00	—
		25	Radio Stars (1949)	GP.175	£4.00	—
		50	Sportsmen (1948)	GP.173	£6.00	—
		25	Sportsmen (1949)	GP.174	£6.00	—
		25	Sportsmen (1953)	GP.181	£6.00	—
		25	Sportsmen (1954)	GP.182	£6.00	—
A2	C		Stage and Cinema Beauties (1933):			
		35	First arrangement — known as 'Series A'	GP.133	£1.40	£50.00
		35	Second arrangement — known as 'Series B'	GP.134	£1.40	£50.00
A2	C	50	Stage and Cinema Beauties (1935)	GP.135	£1.20	£60.00
A	U	?	Stamp Cards (four colours, several wordings) (c1930)	GP.287	£2.50	—
A2	CP	54	Stars of the Screen — 'A Series of 54' (1934)		£1.20	£65.00

Size	Print-ing	Number in set	BRITISH TOBACCO ISSUERS	Handbook reference	Price per card	Complete set
			GODFREY PHILLIPS LTD, London (continued)			
A2	C	48	Stars of the Screen — 'A Series of 48' (1936):			
			A Frame not embossed		£1.00	£50.00
			B Frame embossed		£1.00	£50.00
			C In strips of three, per strip		£2.50	£40.00
D1	C	25	*Statues and Monuments (cut-outs) (1907):	GP.139		
			A Provisional Patent No. 20736		£9.00	£225.00
			B Patent No. 20736		£9.00	£225.00
D	C	25	*Territorial Series (Nd 51-75) (1908)		£34.00	—
A	U	25	The 1924 Cabinet (1924)		£2.40	£60.00
A	C	50	This Mechanized Age — First Series (1936):			
			A Inscribed 'This surface is adhesive'		32p	£16.00
			B Without the above		36p	£18.00
A	C	50	This Mechanized Age — Second Series (1937)		60p	£30.00
A1	C	25	*Types of British and Colonial Troops (1899)	H.76/GP.145	£50.00	—
D1	C	25	*Types of British Soldiers (Nd M.651-75) (1900)	H.144/GP.146	£34.00	—
A	C	63	*War Photos (1916)	GP.149	£10.00	—
—	C	30	Zoo Studies — Come to Life Series (101 x 76mm) (1939)		£1.50	£45.00
			Spectacles for use with the above		—	£8.00

SILKS Known as 'the B.D.V. Silks'. All unbacked. Inscribed 'B.D.V. Cigarettes' or 'G.P.' (Godfrey Phillips), or anonymous. Issued about 1910-25. 'Ha' prefix refers to original Handbook Part II. Nos 201 to 253 refer to new Godfrey Phillips Reference Book.

—	C	62	*Arms of Countries and Territories (73 x 50mm) — Anonymous	Ha.504-12/201	£4.00	—
—	C	32	*Beauties — Modern Paintings (B.D.V.):	Ha.505-13/202		
			A Small size (70 x 46mm)		£12.00	—
			B Extra-large size (143 x 100mm)		£45.00	—
—	C	100	*Birds II (68 x 42mm) — B.D.V	Ha.505-2/203	£3.50	—
—	C	12	*Birds of the Tropics III — B.D.V.:	Ha.505-3/204		
			A Small size (71 x 47mm)		£12.00	—
			B Medium size (71 x 63mm)		£13.00	—
			C Extra-large size (150 x 100mm)		£18.00	—
—	U	24	*British Admirals (83 x 76mm) — Anonymous	Ha.504-5/205	£8.00	—
—	C		*British Butterflies and Moths II — Anonymous:	Ha.505-6/206		
		40	Nos 1-40. Large size, 76 x 61mm		£7.50	—
		10	Nos 41-50. Medium size. 70 x 51mm		£7.50	—
—	C	108	*British Naval Crests II:	Ha.504-4/207		
			A B.D.V., size 70 x 47mm		£2.75	—
			B Anonymous, size 70 x 51mm		£2.75	—
—	C	25	*Butterflies I (70 x 48mm) — Anonymous	Ha.505-5/208	£12.00	—
—	C	47	Ceramic Art — B.D.V.:	Ha.505-16/209		
			A Small size (70 x 43mm)		£1.00	£47.00
			B Small size (70 x 48mm)		£1.00	—
			C Medium size (70 x 61mm)		£2.00	—
—	C		*Clan Tartans:	Ha.505-15/210		
			A Small size (71 x 48mm):			
		49	1 Anonymous		£1.20	£60.00
		65	2 B.D.V		£1.20	£75.00
		56	B Medium size (70 x 60mm) — B.D.V		£3.20	—
		12	C Extra-large size (150 x 100mm) B.D.V. (selected Nos.)		£6.00	—
—	C	108	*Colonial Army Badges (71 x 50mm) — Anonymous	Ha.502-3/211	£4.00	—
—	C	17	County Cricket Badges (69 x 48mm):	Ha.505-8/212		
			A Anonymous		£24.00	—
			B B.D.V		£24.00	—

Size	Print-ing	Number in set	BRITISH TOBACCO ISSUERS	Handbook reference	Price per card	Complete set
			GODFREY PHILLIPS LTD, London (Silks continued)			
—	C	108	*Crests and Badges of the British Army II:	H.502-2/213		
			A1 Small size (70 x 48mm) Anonymous:			
			(a) Numbered		£1.50	£160.00
			(b) Unnumbered		£1.50	£160.00
			A2 Small size (70 x 48mm) — B.D.V.		£1.50	£160.00
			A3 Medium size (70 x 60mm):			
			(a) Anonymous		£1.80	—
			(b) B.D.V.		£1.80	—
—	C		*Flags — Set 4 — Anonymous:	Ha.501-4/214		
		? 143	A 'Long' size (82 x 53mm)		£1.70	—
			B 'Short' size (70 x 48mm):			
		? 143	1 First numbering arrangement (as A)		£1.40	—
		? 108	2 Second numbering arrangement		£1.00	—
		? 113	3 Third numbering arrangement		£1.00	—
—	C		*Flags — Set 5 — Anonymous:	Ha.501-5/215		
			A Small size (70 x 50mm):			
		20	1 With caption		£1.20	—
		6	2 Without caption, flag 40 x 29mm		£1.50	—
		? 6	3 Without caption, flag 60 x 41mm		£1.50	—
		? 8	B Extra-large size (155 x 108mm)		£14.00	—
—	C	18	*Flags — Set 6 — Anonymous:	Ha.501-6/216		
			A Size 69 x 47mm		£1.10	£20.00
			B Size 71 x 51mm		£1.10	£20.00
—	C	20	*Flags — Set 7 (70 x 50mm) — Anonymous	Ha.501-7/217	£1.10	—
—	C	50	*Flags — Set 9 — ('5th Series') (70 x 48mm) — Anonymous	Ha.501-9/218	£1.80	£90.00
—	C		*Flags — Set 10:	Ha.501-10/219		
		120	'7th Series' (70 x 48mm) — Anonymous		£1.00	—
		120	'10th Series' (70 x 62mm) — Anonymous		£1.00	—
		120	'12th Series' (70 x 48mm) — Anonymous		£1.00	—
		65	'15th Series' (70 x 62mm) (selected Nos.) — B.D.V.		£1.20	—
		65	'16th Series' (70 x 62mm) (selected Nos.) — B.D.V.		£1.20	—
			'20th Series' (70 x 48 mm) — B.D.V.:			
		132	A B.D.V. in brown		£1.00	—
		48	B B.D.V. in orange		£2.50	—
		126	'25th Series' (70 x 48mm) — B.D.V.		£1.00	—
		62	'25th Series' '(70 x 62mm) (selected Nos.) — B.D.V.		£3.00	—
			'26th Series' (70 x 48mm) — B.D.V.:			
		112	A 26th Series in brown		£1.00	—
		55	B 26th Series in blue		£4.00	—
		70	'28th Series' (70 x 48mm) (selected Nos.) — B.D.V.		£1.00	—
—	C		*Flags — Set 12:	Ha.501-12/220		
		1	A 'Let 'em all come' (70 x 46mm) — Anonymous		—	£11.00
			B Allied Flags (grouped):			
		1	Four Flags — Anonymous:			
			1 Small size (70 x 46mm)		—	£12.00
			2 Extra-large size (163 x 120mm)		—	£40.00
		1	Seven Flags (165 x 116mm):			
			1 Anonymous		—	£12.00
			2 B.D.V. in brown or orange		—	£12.00
		1	Eight Flags (165 x 116mm) — B.D.V.		—	£40.00
—	C		*Flags — Set 13:	Ha.501-13/221		
		? 23	A Size 163 x 114mm — Anonymous		£2.50	—
		? 27	B Size 163 x 114mm — B.D.V. in brown, orange, blue, green or black		£2.50	—
		? 17	C Size 150 x 100mm — B.D.V.		£2.50	—

Size	Print-ing	Number in set		BRITISH TOBACCO ISSUERS	Handbook reference	Price per card	Complete set
			GODFREY PHILLIPS LTD, London (Silks continued)				
—	C	26		*Flags — Set 14 ('House Flags') (68 x 47mm) —			
				Anonymous ...	Ha.501-14/229	£10.00	—
—	C	25		*Flags — Set 15 (Pilot and Signal Flags) (70 x 50mm):	Ha.501-15/244		
			A	Numbered 601-625 — Anonymous ...		£4.40	£110.00
			B	Inscribed 'Series II' — B.D.V. ...		£3.00	£75.00
—	C			*Football Colours:	Ha.505-9/222		
		? 21	A	Anonymous. size 68 x 49mm ...		£9.00	—
		? 86	B	B.D.V., size 68 x 49mm ...		£7.50	—
		? 78	C	B.D.V., size 150 x 100mm ...		£8.50	—
—	C	126		G.P. Territorial Badges (70 x 48mm) ...	Ha.502-12/223	£2.50	—
—	U	25		*Great War Leaders II (81 x 68mm) — Anonymous	Ha.504-7/224	£8.00	—
—	U	50		*Great War Leaders III and Warships, sepia, black or blue on white or pink material (70 x 50mm) —			
				Anonymous ...	Ha.504-10/225	£8.00	—
—	C			*Great War Leaders IV and Celebrities:	Ha.504-11/226		
		3	A	Small size (70 x 48mm) — Anonymous ...		£8.00	—
		4	B	Small size (70 x 48mm) — B.D.V. ...		£8.00	—
		3	C	Medium size (70 x 63mm) — Anonymous ...		£8.00	—
		2	D	Medium size (70 x 63mm) — B. D.V. ...		£8.00	—
		? 18	E	Extra-large size (150 x 100mm) — B.D.V. ...		£8.00	—
		? 4	F	Extra-large size (150 x 110mm) — Anonymous		£8.00	—
		? 1	G	Extra-large size (150 x 110mm) — B.D.V. ...		—	£16.00
		? 25	H	Extra-large size (163 x 117mm) — Anonymous		£8.00	—
		? 44	I	Extra-large size (163 x 117mm) — B.D.V. ...		£8.00	—
—	C			Heraldic Series — B.D.V.:	Ha.504-17/228		
		25	A	Small size (68 x 47mm) ...		£1.40	£35.00
		25	B	Small size (68 x 43mm) ...		£1.40	£35.00
		25	C	Medium size (68 x 60mm) ...		£3.00	—
		12	D	Extra-large size (150 x 100mm) (selected Nos)		£6.00	—
—	C	10		*Irish Patriots — Anonymous:	Ha.505-11/230		
			A	Small size (67 x 50mm) ...		£13.00	—
			B	Large size (83 x 76mm) ...		£13.00	—
			C	Extra-large size (152 x 110mm) ...		£17.00	—
—	C	1		*Irish Republican Stamp (70 x 50mm) ...	Ha.505-12/231	—	£2.00
—	C	10		Miniature Rugs (89 x 55mm) (c1920) ...	GP.232	£10.00	—
—	C	54		*Naval Badges of Rank and Military Headdress (70 x 47mm) — Anonymous ...	Ha.504-9/233	£7.00	—
—	C	40		*Old Masters — Set 1 (155 x 115mm) — B.D.V. ...	Ha.503-1/235	£32.00	—
—	C	20		*Old Masters — Set 2 (150 x 105mm):	Ha.503-2/236		
			A	Anonymous ...		£4.00	—
			B	B.D.V. wording above picture ...		£4.00	—
			C	B.D.V. wording below picture ...		£7.00	—
—	C			*Old Masters — Set 3A (70 x 50mm):	Ha.503-3A/237		
		40	A	B.D.V. ...		£3.00	—
		55	B	Anonymous ...		£2.50	—
—	C	30		*Old Masters — Set 3B (70 x 50mm) — Anonymous	Ha.503-3B/237	£2.50	—
—	C	120		*Old Masters — Set 4 (70 x 50mm) — Anonymous	Ha.503-4/238	£2.50	—
—	C			*Old Masters — Set 5 (70 x 50mm):	Ha.503-5/239		
		20	A	Unnumbered — Anonymous ...		£3.00	—
		60	B	Nd. 1-60 — B.D.V ...		£1.20	£72.00
		20	C	Nd. 101-120 — Anonymous:			
				1 Numerals normal size ...		£2.00	—
				2 Numerals very small size ...		£2.00	£40.00
		20	D	Nd. 101-120 — B.D.V. ...		£1.80	£36.00
—	C	50		*Old Masters — Set 6 (67 x 42mm) — B.D.V. ...	Ha.503-6/240	£1.30	£65.00
—	C	50		*Old Masters — Set 7, Nd. 301-350 (67 x 47mm) — Anonymous ...	Ha.503-7/241	£2.50	—

Size	Print-ing	Number in set	BRITISH TOBACCO ISSUERS	Handbook reference	Price per card	Complete set
			GODFREY PHILLIPS LTD, London (Silks continued)			
—	C	50	*Orders of Chivalry I (70 x 48mm) — Anonymous ...	Ha.504-14/242	£3.50	—
—	C	24	*Orders of Chivalry — Series 10 (70 x 50mm):	Ha.504-16/243		
			A Nd. 1-24 — B.D.V.		£3.00	£75.00
			B Nd. 401-424 — G.P		£3.00	£75.00
—	C	72	*Regimental Colours II (76 x 70mm) — Anonymous	Ha.502-7/245	£4.50	—
—	C		*Regimental Colours and Crests III:	Ha.502-8/246		
			A Small size (70 x 51mm):			
		40	1 Colours with faint backgrounds — Anonymous		£2.50	
		120	2 Colours without backgrounds — Anonymous		£2.50	—
		120	3 Colours without backgrounds — B.D.V.		£2.50	—
		120	B Extra-large size (165 x 120mm):			
			1 Anonymous — unnumbered		£7.50	—
			2 B.D.V. — numbered		£7.50	—
—	C	50	*Regimental Colours — Series 12 (70 x 50mm) — B.D.V.	Ha.502-11/247	£3.00	—
—	C	10	*Religious Pictures — Anonymous:	Ha.505-10/248		
			A Small size (67 x 50mm)		£18.00	—
			B Large size (83 x 76 mm)		£20.00	—
			C Extra-large size (155 x 110mm)		£27.00	—
—	C	75	*Town and City Arms — Series 30 (48 unnumbered, 27 numbered 49-75) — B.D.V.:	Ha.504-13/250		
			A Small size (70 x 50mm)		£2.00	—
			B Medium size (70 x 65mm)		£3.00	—
—	C	25	*Victoria Cross Heroes I (70 x 50mm) — Anonymous	Ha.504-1/251	£18.00	—
—	C	? 25	*Victoria Cross Heroes II (70 x 50mm) — Anonymous	Ha.504-2/252	£18.00	—
—	C	90	*War Pictures (70 x 48mm) — Anonymous	Ha.504-8/253	£9.00	—
OVERSEAS ISSUES (AUSTRALIA AND NEW ZEALAND)						
A2	U	50	*Animal Studies (c1930)	GP.7	£2.00	—
A2	C	50	Annuals (1939) (New Zealand issue)	GP.9	£1.75	£85.00
D	BW	50	Australian Sporting Celebrities (1932)		£3.50	—
D	BW	50	Film Stars (1934)		£2.00	—
D	C	50	Stars of British Films (1934):			
			A Back 'B.D.V. Cigarettes'		£2.00	—
			B Back 'Grey's Cigarettes ...'		£2.00	—
			C Back 'De Reszke Cigarettes'		£2.00	—
			D Back 'Godfrey Phillips (Aust)'		£2.00	—
D	BW	38	Test Cricketers, 1932-1933:			
			A 'Issued with Grey's Cigarettes'		£5.00	—
			B 'Issued with B.D.V. Cigarettes'		£5.00	—
			C Back 'Godfrey Phillips (Aust.)'		£5.00	—
D2	C		Victorian Footballers (1933):			
		50	1 'Series of 50':			
			A 'Godfrey Phillips (Aust.)'		£5.00	—
			B 'B.D.V. Cigarettes ...'		£5.00	—
			C 'Grey's Cigarettes'		£5.00	—
		75	2 'Series of 75':			
			D 'B.D.V. Cigarettes ...'		£7.00	—
D	BW	50	Victorian League and Association Footballers (1934)		£7.00	—
A2	C	100	*Who's Who in Australian Sport (1933)	GP.150	£4.50	—

JOHN PLAYER & SONS, Nottingham
44 page reference book — £4.50
NOTE: The Imperial Tobacco Co. clause (I.T.C. clause) appears on Home issues dated between 1902 and 1940, excluding those issued in the Channel Islands. For series without I.T.C. clause, see the Overseas section.

Size	Printing	Number in set	BRITISH TOBACCO ISSUERS	Handbook reference	Price per card	Complete set
			JOHN PLAYER & SONS, Nottingham (continued)			
A	C	25	*Actors and Actresses (1898)	H.337	£30.00	—
A1	BW	50	*Actresses (c1897)	H.339	£30.00	—
A	C		*Advertisement Cards (1893-1894):	H.338		
		2	Beauties:			
			A Player's Navy Cut Cigarettes back		£350.00	—
			B Copy of Unsolicited Testimonial back		£350.00	—
		2	'Old Salt' Men with Pipes:			
			A Player's Navy Cut Cigarettes back		£350.00	—
			B Copy of Unsolicited Testimonial back		£350.00	—
		1	Poster — Girl three quarter length		£850.00	—
		2	Cigarette Packings vertical		£1100.00	—
		1	Cigarette Packing horizontal		£2500.00	—
	C	1	*Advertisement Card (Sailor) (c1930):			
A			A Small size		—	£5.00
B			B Large size		—	£20.00
B	BW	1	Advertisement Card — Wants List (1936)		—	£1.00
A	C	50	Aeroplanes (1935):			
			A Home issue — titled 'Aeroplanes (Civil)'		£1.10	£55.00
			Album (with price)		—	£25.00
			B Irish issue — titled 'Aeroplanes'		£1.70	£85.00
A	C	50	Aircraft of the Royal Air Force (1938):			
			A Home issue — with I.T.C. clause		£1.00	£50.00
			Album		—	£25.00
			B Channel Islands issue — without I.T.C. clause		£1.60	£80.00
J	C	10	Allied Cavalry or Regimental Uniforms:	H.340		
			Allied Cavalry (1914)		£12.00	£120.00
			Regimental Uniforms (1914)		£11.00	£110.00
A	C	50	Animals of the Countryside (1939):			
			A Home issue — adhesive, with I.T.C. clause		30p	£15.00
			Album		—	£25.00
			B Irish issue — non-adhesive, green numerals overprinted		£1.60	—
			C Channel Islands issue — adhesive, without I.T.C. clause		£1.00	£50.00
B	C	25	Aquarium Studies (1932)		£2.00	£50.00
B	C	25	Architectural Beauties (1927)		£2.20	£55.00
A	C	50	Arms and Armour (1909):	H.273		
			A Home issue — with I.T.C. clause		£2.60	£130.00
			B Overseas issue — without I.T.C. clause — see Overseas section			
A	C	50	Army Corps and Divisional Signs, 1914-1918 (1924)		60p	£30.00
A	C	100	Army Corps and Divisional Signs, 1914-1918, '2nd Series' (1925):			
			Nos. 51-100		80p	£40.00
			Nos. 101-150		80p	£40.00
A	C	25	Army Life (1910)	H.78	£2.20	£55.00
J	C	12	Artillery in Action (1917)		£6.00	£75.00
A	U	50	Association Cup Winners (1930)	H.667	£1.80	£90.00
A	C	50	Aviary and Cage Birds:			
			A Small size (1933):			
			1 Cards		£1.00	£50.00
			2 Transfers		60p	£30.00
			Album		—	£30.00
B		25	B Large size (1935)		£3.60	£90.00
A	C	50	Badges and Flags of British Regiments (1904):	H.341		
			A Brown back, unnumbered		£2.50	£125.00
			B Brown back, numbered		£2.50	£125.00

Size	Print-ing	Number in set	BRITISH TOBACCO ISSUERS	Handbook reference	Price per card	Complete set
			JOHN PLAYER & SONS, Nottingham (continued)			
A	C	50	Badges and Flags of British Regiments (1903):			
			A Green back, thick card		£2.50	£125.00
			B Green back, thin card		£2.50	£125.00
A	C	50	Birds and Their Young (1937):			
			A Home issue — adhesive, with I.T.C. clause		30p	£15.00
			Album			
			A Cream Cover		—	£25.00
			B Grey Cover		—	£25.00
			B Irish issue:			
			1 Adhesive, with large green numerals		£1.20	—
			2 Non-adhesive, with large green numerals		£1.60	—
			C Channel Islands issue — adhesive, without I.T.C. clause		90p	£45.00
A	C	25	Birds and Their Young, 1st series (unissued) (1955)		24p	£6.00
A	C	25	Birds and Their Young, 2nd series (unissued) (1955)		20p	£5.00
—	P	10	*Bookmarks — Authors (139 x 51mm) (1905)		£70.00	—
A	C	25	Boxing (1934)		£7.00	—
			Album		—	£40.00
A	C	50	Boy Scout and Girl Guide Patrol Signs and Emblems (1933):			
			A Cards		60p	£30.00
			B Transfers		60p	£30.00
			Album		—	£30.00
B	C	25	British Butterflies (1934)		£4.40	£110.00
A	C	50	British Empire Series (1904):	H.343		
			A Grey-white card, matt		£1.40	£70.00
			B White card, semi-glossy		£1.60	£80.00
	C	25	British Livestock:			
A			A Small card (1915)		£3.00	£75.00
			B Medium card — see Overseas section			
J			C Extra-large card, brown back (1916)		£5.00	£125.00
J			D Extra-large card, blue back (1923)		£5.00	£125.00
B	C	25	British Naval Craft (1939)		£1.00	£25.00
J	C	20	British Pedigree Stock (1925)		£5.00	£100.00
B	C	25	British Regalia (1937)		£1.20	£30.00
A	C	50	Butterflies (1932):			
			A Cards		£1.30	£65.00
			B Transfers		60p	£30.00
			Album		—	£30.00
A	C C	50	Butterflies and Moths (1904)	H.80	£2.00	£100.00
			Bygone Beauties:			
A		25	A Small card (1914)		£1.60	£40.00
J		10	B Extra-large card (1916)		£5.00	£50.00
—	U	? 32	*Cabinet Size Pictures, 1898-1900 (220 x 140mm):	H.476		
			A Plain back		£100.00	—
			B Printed back		£100.00	—
A	C	20	Castles, Abbeys etc (c1894):	H.345		
			A Without border		£30.00	£600.00
			B White border		£30.00	£600.00
B	C	24	Cats (1936)		£7.00	—
A	C	50	Celebrated Bridges (1903)	H.346	£3.00	£150.00
A	C		Celebrated Gateways (1909):	H.347		
		50	A Thick card		£1.80	£90.00
		25	B Thinner card (26-50 only)		£2.00	—
A	C	25	Ceremonial and Court Dress (1911)	H.145	£1.80	£45.00
B	C	25	Championship Golf Courses (1936)		£8.00	£200.00

Size	Print-ing	Number in set	BRITISH TOBACCO ISSUERS	Handbook reference	Price per card	Complete set
			JOHN PLAYER & SONS, Nottingham (continued)			
	C		Characters from Dickens:	H.348		
A		25	Small card, 1st series (1912)		£2.40	£60.00
J		10	Extra-large card (1912)..		£6.00	£60.00
A	C	25	Characters from Dickens, 2nd series (1914)	H.348	£2.40	£60.00
A	C	50	Characters from Dickens (1st & 2nd series combined) (1923)	H.348	£1.40	£70.00
B	C	25	Characters from Fiction (1933)		£4.00	£100.00
A	C	25	Characters from Thackeray (1913)		£1.60	£40.00
A	C	50	Cities of the World (1900):			
			A Grey-mauve on white back		£5.00	—
			B Grey-mauve on toned back		£5.00	—
			C Bright mauve on white back		£5.00	—
B	C	20	Clocks — Old and New (1928)		£5.00	£100.00
A	C	25	Colonial and Indian Army Badges (1916)		£1.40	£35.00
A	C	50	Coronation Series Ceremonial Dress (1937):			
			A Home issue — with I.T.C. clause		40p	£20.00
			Album		—	£25.00
			B Channel Islands issue — without I.T.C. clause		£1.20	—
A	C	25	*Counties and Their Industries:	H.349		
			A Unnumbered (c1910)		£2.60	£65.00
			B Numbered (1914)		£2.60	£65.00
A	C	50	*Countries — Arms and Flags:			
			A Thick card (1905)		90p	£45.00
			B Thin Card (1912)		£1.10	£55.00
A	C	50	*Country Seats and Arms (1906)		£1.00	£50.00
A	C		*Country Seats and Arms, 2nd series (1907):			
		25	A Nd. 51-75 First printing		£1.60	£40.00
		50	B Nd. 51-100 Second printing		£1.00	£50.00
A	C	50	*Country Seats and Arms, 3rd series (1907)		£1.00	£50.00
B	C	25	Country Sports (1930)		£6.00	£150.00
A	C	50	Cricketers, 1930 (1930)		£1.50	£75.00
A	C	50	Cricketers, 1934 (1934)		£1.20	£60.00
A	C	50	Cricketers, 1938 (1938):			
			A Home issue — with I.T.C. clause		£1.00	£50.00
			Album		—	£25.00
			B Channel Islands issue — without I.T.C. clause		£2.00	£100.00
A	C	50	Cricketers, Caricatures by 'Rip' (1926)		£2.00	£100.00
	C		Cries of London:	H.350		
A		25	Small cards, 1st series (1913)		£2.00	£50.00
J		10	Extra-large cards, 1st series (1912)		£4.50	£45.00
J		10	Extra-large cards, 2nd series (1914)		£4.00	£40.00
A	C	25	Cries of London, 2nd series (1916):			
			A Blue back		£1.00	£25.00
			B Black back (unissued)		£8.00	—
A	C	50	Curious Beaks (1929)		90p	£45.00
A	C	50	Cycling (1939):			
			A Home issue — adhesive, with I.T.C. clause		90p	£45.00
			Album		—	£25.00
			B Irish issue:			
			1 Adhesive, with large green numerals		£2.00	—
			2 Non-adhesive, with large green numerals		£2.00	—
			C Channel Islands issue — adhesive, without I.T.C. clause		£1.80	—
	C		Dandies (1932):			
A		50	A Small size		50p	£25.00
B		25	B Large size		£2.00	£50.00

Size	Print-ing	Number in set	BRITISH TOBACCO ISSUERS	Handbook reference	Price per card	Complete set
			JOHN PLAYER & SONS, Nottingham (continued)			
A	C	50	Decorations and Medals (unissued) (c1940)		£2.00	£100.00
A	C	50	Derby and Grand National Winners (1933):			
			A Cards		£1.70	£85.00
			B Transfers		60p	£30.00
			Album		—	£30.00
	C		Dogs (1924) — Scenic backgrounds:			
A		50	A Small size		£1.20	£60.00
J		12	B Extra-large size		£3.50	£42.00
	C		Dogs — Full length:	H.668		
A		50	A Small size (1931):			
			1 Cards		90p	£45.00
			2 Transfers		60p	£30.00
			Album		—	£30.00
B		25	B Large size (1933)		£2.60	£65.00
	C		Dogs — Heads:			
A		50	A Small size — Home issue (1929)		£1.00	£50.00
A		25	B Small size — Irish issue, 'A Series of 25', with I.T.C. clause (1927)		£2.20	£55.00
A		25	C Small size — Irish issue, '2nd Series of 25', with I.T.C. clause (1929)		£2.20	£55.00
			D Small size — Overseas issue, without I.T.C. clause (1927) — see Overseas section			
B		20	E Large size — Home issue, 'A Series of 20' (1926)		£2.75	£55.00
B		20	F Large size — Home issue, '2nd Series of 20' (1928)		£2.75	£55.00
A	C	50	Dogs' Heads (silver-grey backgrounds) (1940)		£3.20	—
A	C	50	Dogs' Heads by Biegel (unissued) (c1955)		90p	£45.00
B	C	25	Dogs — Pairs and Groups (unissued) (c1955)		£1.40	£35.00
A	C	50	Drum Banners and Cap Badges (1924):			
			A Base panel joining vertical framelines		£1.20	£60.00
			B Fractional space between the above		80p	£40.00
A	C	25	Egyptian Kings and Queens, and Classical Deities (1911)		£2.00	£50.00
J	C	10	Egyptian Sketches (1915)	H.351	£4.50	£45.00
	C	25	*England's Military Heroes (1898):	H.352		
A1			A Wide card		£48.00	—
A1			A1 Wide card plain back		£48.00	—
—			B Narrow card (68 x 28mm)		£38.00	—
—			B2 Narrow card, plain back (68 x 28mm)		£35.00	—
	C	25	England's Naval Heroes (1897):	H.353		
A1			A Wide card		£45.00	—
—			B Narrow card (68 x 28mm)		£30.00	£750.00
	C	25	England's Naval Heroes (1898), descriptive on back:	H.353		
A1			A Wide card		£45.00	—
A1			A2 Wide card, plain back		£45.00	—
—			B Narrow card (68 x 29mm)		£30.00	£750.00
—			B2 Narrow card, plain back (68 x 29mm)		£30.00	—
A	C	25	Everyday Phrases by Tom Browne (1901):	H.354		
			A Thick card		£20.00	£500.00
			B Thin card		£20.00	£500.00
B	BW	25	Fables of Aesop (1927)		£2.60	£65.00
	C	20	Famous Authors and Poets (1902):			
A			A Wide card		£32.00	£640.00
—			B Narrow card (67 x 30mm)		£22.00	£440.00

Size	Print-ing	Number in set	BRITISH TOBACCO ISSUERS	Handbook reference	Price per card	Complete set
			JOHN PLAYER & SONS, Nottingham (continued)			
B	C	25	Famous Beauties (1937):			
			A Home issue — with I.T.C. clause		£1.80	£45.00
			B Channel Islands issue — without I.T.C. clause		£2.60	£65.00
A	C	50	Famous Irish-Bred Horses (1936)		£4.00	£200.00
			Album		—	£45.00
A	C	50	Famous Irish Greyhounds (1935)		£5.50	—
			Album		—	£45.00
J	C	10	Famous Paintings (1913)	H.355	£4.00	£40.00
A	C	50	Film Stars — 'Series of 50' (1934)		£1.30	£65.00
			Album		—	£25.00
A	C	50	Film Stars — 'Second Series ...':			
			A Home issue — Album 'price one penny' (1934)		£1.00	£50.00
			Album (with price)		—	£25.00
			B Irish issue — Album offer without price (1935)		£1.60	£80.00
			Album (without price)		—	£45.00
A	C	50	Film Stars — Third Series:			
			A Home issue — titled 'Film Stars — with I.T.C. clause (1938)		90p	£45.00
			Album		—	£25.00
			B Irish issue — titled 'Screen Celebrities' (1939)		£2.20	—
			C Channel Islands issue — titled 'Film Stars', without I.T.C. clause (1938)		£1.80	—
B	BW	25	Film Stars — Large size (1934):			
			A Home issue — with Album offer		£3.20	£80.00
			Album		—	£35.00
			B Irish issue — without Album offer		£7.00	—
A	C	50	Fire-Fighting Appliances (1930)		£1.60	£80.00
A	C	50	Fishes of the World (1903)	H.66	£2.50	£125.00
A	C	50	Flags of the League of Nations (1928)		50p	£25.00
A	C	50	Football Caricatures by 'Mac' (1927)		£1.40	£70.00
A	C	50	Footballers Caricatures by 'Rip' (1926)		£1.40	£70.00
A	C	50	Footballers, 1928 (1928)		£1.80	£90.00
A	C	25	Footballers, 1928-9 — '2nd Series' (1929)		£1.80	£45.00
—	C	?	Football Fixture Folders (1935-61)		£16.00	—
	C		Fresh-Water Fishes:			
A		50	A Small size, Home issue:			
			1 Pink card (1933)		£1.50	£75.00
			2 White card (1934)		£1.70	£85.00
			Album (titled British Fresh-Water Fishes)		—	£25.00
B		25	B Large size, Home issue — adhesive (1935) ...		£3.00	£75.00
B		25	C Large size, Irish issue — non-adhesive (1935)		£5.00	£125.00
A	C	25	From Plantation to Smoker (1926)		50p	£12.50
	C	50	Gallery of Beauty (1896):	H.356		
			A Wide Card:			
A			I Set of 50		£25.00	—
A			II 5 Alternative Pictures (Nos 20, 24, 25, 48, 49)		£70.00	—
			B Narrow Card official cut:			
—			I Set of 50		£22.00	—
—			II 5 Alternative Pictures (Nos 20, 24, 25, 48, 49)		£65.00	—
	C		Game Birds and Wild Fowl:			
A		50	A Small size (1927)		£1.50	£75.00
B		25	B Large size (1928)		£5.00	£125.00

Size	Print-ing	Number in set	BRITISH TOBACCO ISSUERS	Handbook reference	Price per card	Complete set
			JOHN PLAYER & SONS, Nottingham (continued)			
A	C	25	Gems of British Scenery (1914)		£1.20	£30.00
	C		Gilbert and Sullivan — 'A Series of ...':			
A		50	A Small size (1925)		£1.20	£60.00
J		25	B Extra-large size (1926)		£3.40	£85.00
	C		Gilbert and Sullivan — '2nd Series of ...':			
A		50	A Small size (1927)		£1.20	£60.00
B		25	B Large size (1928)		£4.00	£100.00
B	C	25	Golf (1939):			
			A Home issue — with I.T.C. clause		£7.50	£190.00
			B Channel Islands issue — without I.T.C. clause		£7.00	£175.00
A	C	25	Hidden Beauties (1929)		40p	£10.00
A	C	25	Highland Clans (1908)		£5.00	£125.00
A	C	50	Hints on Association Football (1934)	H.669	£1.00	£50.00
			Album		—	£25.00
J	C	10	Historic Ships (1910):			
			A Thick card		£6.00	£60.00
			B Thin card		£6.00	£60.00
	C		History of Naval Dress:			
A		50	A Small size (1930)		£1.20	£60.00
B		25	B Large size (1929)		£2.00	£50.00
A	C	50	International Air Liners:			
			A Home issue — Album 'price one penny', with I.T.C. clause (1936)		50p	£25.00
			Album (with price)		—	£25.00
			B Irish issue — Album offer without price, with I.T.C. clause (1937)		£1.20	£60.00
			Album (without price)		—	£45.00
			C Channel Islands issue — without Album offer or I.T.C. clause (1936)		£1.40	£70.00
A	C	25	Irish Place Names — 'A Series of 25' (1927)		£3.20	£80.00
A	C	25	Irish Place Names — '2nd Series of 25' (1929)		£3.20	£80.00
A	C	1	Joker Card – Card Scheme (1937)		—	£5.00
	C	50	Kings and Queens of England (1935):	H.670		
A			A Small size		£1.60	£80.00
			Album		—	£25.00
B			B Large size		£3.00	£150.00
			Album		—	£35.00
A	C	50	Life on Board a Man of War in 1805 and 1905 (1905)	H.38	£2.50	£125.00
A	C	25	Live Stock (1925)		£4.00	£100.00
A	C	50	Military Head-Dress (1931)		£1.20	£60.00
A	C	50	Military Series (1900)		£25.00	—
A	C	50	Military Uniforms of the British Empire Overseas (1938):			
			A Home issue — adhesive, with I.T.C. clause		80p	£40.00
			Album		—	£25.00
			B Channel Islands issue:			
			1 Adhesive, without I.T.C. clause		£1.60	£80.00
			2 Non-adhesive, without I.T.C. clause		£1.60	£80.00
A	C	25	Miniatures (1916)		50p	£12.50
A	C	50	Modern Naval Craft (1939):			
			A Home issue — adhesive, with I.T.C. clause		50p	£25.00
			Album		—	£25.00
			B Irish issue — non-adhesive		£1.20	—
			C Channel Islands issue — adhesive, without I.T.C. clause		£1.20	£60.00

Size	Printing	Number in set	BRITISH TOBACCO ISSUERS	Handbook reference	Price per card	Complete set
			JOHN PLAYER & SONS, Nottingham (continued)			
A	C	50	Motor Cars — 'A Series of 50' (1936):			
			A Home issue — Album 'price one penny'		£1.50	£75.00
			Album (with price)		—	£25.00
			B Irish issue — Album offer without price		£2.40	—
			Album (without price)		—	£45.00
			C Channel Islands issue — without Album offer		£2.00	£100.00
A	C	50	Motor Cars — 'Second Series ...' (1937):			
			A Home issue — with I.T.C. clause		£1.00	£50.00
			Album		—	£25.00
			B Channel Islands issue — without I.T.C. clause		£2.00	£100.00
B	U	20	Mount Everest (1925)		£5.00	£100.00
A	C	25	Napoleon (1915)	H.364	£2.20	£55.00
A	C	50	National Flags and Arms:			
			A Home issue — Album 'price one penny' (1936) ...		50p	£25.00
			Album (with price)		—	£25.00
			B Irish issue — Album offer without price (1937) ...		£1.20	£60.00
			Album (without price)		—	£45.00
			C Channel Islands issue — without Album offer (1936)		£1.20	£60.00
B	C	25	The Nation's Shrines (1929)		£2.20	£55.00
	C		Natural History:			
A		50	A Small size (1924)		50p	£25.00
J		12	B Extra-large size — 'A Series of 12' (1923) ...		£1.25	£15.00
J		12	C Extra-large size — '2nd Series of 12' (1924)		£1.25	£15.00
B	C	24	A Nature Calendar (1930)		£6.00	£150.00
	C		Nature Series:			
A		50	Small card (1908)		£1.60	£80.00
J		10	Extra-large card (Birds) (1908)		£12.00	—
J		10	Extra-large card (Animals) (1913)		£7.00	£70.00
A	C	50	Old England's Defenders (1898)		£25.00	—
B	C	25	'Old Hunting Prints' (1938):			
			A Home issue — with I.T.C. clause		£3.00	£75.00
			B Channel Islands issue — without I.T.C. clause		£4.40	—
B	C	25	Old Naval Prints (1936):			
			A Home issue — with I.T.C. clause		£2.60	£65.00
			B Channel Islands issue — without I.T.C. clause		£4.00	—
J	BW	25	Old Sporting Prints (1924)		£4.40	£110.00
B	C	25	Picturesque Bridges (1929)		£3.00	£75.00
B	C	25	Picturesque Cottages (1929)		£3.60	£90.00
B	C	25	Picturesque London (1931)		£5.00	£125.00
A	C	25	Players — Past and Present (1916)		£1.00	£25.00
A	C	25	Polar Exploration (1915)		£2.80	£70.00
A	C	25	Polar Exploration, 2nd series (1916)		£2.40	£60.00
B	C	25	Portals of the Past (1930)		£2.20	£55.00
A	C	50	Poultry (1931):	H.671		
			A Cards		£1.80	£90.00
			B Transfers		60p	£30.00
			Album		—	£30.00
A	C	25	Products of the World:			
			A Thick card (1909)		90p	£22.50
			B Thin card (1908)		£1.20	£30.00
A	C	50	Products of the World — Scenes only (1928)		40p	£20.00
A	C	25	Racehorses (1926)		£5.40	£135.00
A	U	40	Racing Caricatures (1925)		90p	£36.00
B	C	25	Racing Yachts (1938):			
			A Home issue — with I.T.C. clause		£3.80	£95.00
			B Channel Islands issue — without I.T.C. clause		£5.00	—

Size	Printing	Number in set	BRITISH TOBACCO ISSUERS	Handbook reference	Price per card	Complete set
			JOHN PLAYER & SONS, Nottingham (continued)			
A	C	50	RAF Badges (1937):			
			A Home issue — with I.T.C. clause:			
			1 Without motto		60p	£30.00
			2 With motto		60p	£30.00
			Album		—	£25.00
			B Channel Islands issue — without I.T.C. clause		£1.20	£60.00
A	C	50	*Regimental Colours and Cap Badges (1907) — title box with side indent	H.73	£1.30	£65.00
A	C	50	*Regimental Colours and Cap Badges — Territorial Regiments (1910) — title box without side indent:			
			A Blue back		£1.30	£65.00
			B Brown back		£1.30	£65.00
A	C	50	Regimental Standards and Cap Badges (1930)		80p	£40.00
J	C	10	Regimental Uniforms — see 'Allied Cavalry'			
A	C	50	Regimental Uniforms (1-50):			
			A Blue back (Jul. 1912)		£2.20	£110.00
			B Brown back (Jul. 1914)		£2.40	£120.00
A	C	50	Regimental Uniforms (51-100) (1914)		£1.40	£70.00
A	C	50	Riders of the World:	H.358		
			A Thick grey card (1905)		£1.70	£85.00
			B Thinner white card (1914)		£1.70	£85.00
—	P	6	The Royal Family (101 x 154mm) (1902)	H.359	—	£270.00
—	C	1	The Royal Family (55 x 66mm) (1937)		—	£3.00
—	P	? 30	Rulers and Views (101 x 154mm) (1902)	H.363	£110.00	—
			Screen Celebrities — see Film Stars			
A	C	50	Sea Fishes:			
			A Home issue — Album 'price one penny', with I.T.C. clause (1935)		40p	£20.00
			Album (with price)		—	£25.00
			B Irish issue — Album offer without price, with I.T.C. clause (1937)		£1.20	—
			Album (without price)		—	£45.00
			C Channel Islands issue — without Album or I.T.C. clause (1935)		£1.20	£60.00
A	C	50	A Sectional Map of Ireland (1937)		£3.50	—
A	U	1	A Sectional Map of Ireland Joker (1937)		—	£15.00
A	C	25	Shakespearean Series (1914)		£1.80	£45.00
B	C	20	Ship-Models (1926)		£3.00	£60.00
A	C	50	Shipping (unissued) (1960)		£1.50	£75.00
A	C	25	Ships' Figureheads (1912):			
			A Numerals 'sans serif'		£2.80	£70.00
			B Numerals with serif		£2.60	£65.00
B	C	25	Ships' Figure-Heads (1931)		£2.00	£50.00
—	C	8	Snap Cards (93 x 65mm) (c1930)	H.672	£7.00	—
A	C	50	Speedway Riders (1937)		£1.80	£90.00
			Album:			
			A Cream Cover		—	£30.00
			B Grey Cover		—	£30.00
A	BW ?	148	Stereoscopic Series (c1900)	H.357	£125.00	—
A	C	50	Straight Line Caricatures (1926)		60p	£30.00
A	C	25	Struggle for Existence (1923)		40p	£10.00
A	C	50	Tennis (1936)	H.524	90p	£45.00
			Album		—	£25.00
A	C	25	Those Pearls of Heaven (1914)		£1.40	£35.00
A	BW	66	Transvaal Series (1902):	H.360		
			A Black front		£6.50	—
			B Violet-black front		£6.50	—

Size	Print-ing	Number in set	BRITISH TOBACCO ISSUERS	Handbook reference	Price per card	Complete set
			JOHN PLAYER & SONS, Nottingham (continued)			
B	C	25	Treasures of Britain (1931)		£1.80	£45.00
A	C	25	Treasures of Ireland (1930)		£2.00	£50.00
B	C	25	Types of Horses (1939):			
			A Home issue — with I.T.C. clause		£4.00	£100.00
			B Channel Islands issue — without I.T.C. clause		£4.60	—
A	C	50	Uniforms of the Territorial Army (Oct. 1939)		90p	£45.00
			Album		—	£25.00
A	C	50	Useful Plants and Fruits (1904)	H.361	£2.50	£125.00
A	C	25	Victoria Cross (1914)		£3.00	£75.00
A	C	90	War Decorations and Medals (1927)		90p	£80.00
	C		Wild Animals:	H.673		
A		50	A Small size — 'Wild Animals' Heads' (1931)		70p	£35.00
A		25	B Small transfers, number in series not stated (1931)		£2.20	—
A		50	C Small transfers — 'A Series of 50' (1931)		60p	£30.00
			Album		—	£30.00
B		25	D Large size — 'Wild Animals — A Series of ...' (1927)		£2.00	£50.00
B		25	E Large size — 'Wild Animals — 2nd Series ...' (1932)		£2.00	£50.00
A	C	50	Wild Animals of the World (1902):	H.77		
			A 'John Player & Sons Ltd.'		£3.00	£150.00
			B 'John Player & Sons, Branch, Nottingham'		£5.00	—
			C1 As B, 'Branch' omitted but showing traces of some or all of the letters		£5.00	—
			C2 As B. New printing with 'Branch' omitted		£3.00	£150.00
A2	C	45	Wild Animals of the World, narrow card (1902):	H.77		
			A 'John Player & Sons Ltd.'		£6.00	£270.00
			B 'John Player & Sons, Branch, Nottingham'		£7.00	—
			C1 As B, 'Branch' omitted but showing traces of some or all of the letters		£6.00	—
			C2 As B. New printing with 'Branch' omitted		£6.00	£270.00
	C		Wild Birds:			
A		50	A Small size (1932):			
			1 Cards		50p	£25.00
			2 Transfers		60p	£30.00
			Album		—	£30.00
B		25	B Large size (1934)		£3.00	£75.00
B	C	25	Wild Fowl (1937)		£3.40	£85.00
A	C	50	Wonders of the Deep (1904)	H.365	£2.20	£110.00
A	C	25	Wonders of the World:	H.362		
			A Blue back (1913)		80p	£20.00
			B Grey back (1926)		£1.40	£35.00
J	C	10	Wooden Walls (1909):			
			A Thick card		£6.00	£60.00
			B Thin card		£6.00	£60.00
A	C	25	Wrestling and Ju-Jitsu:			
			A Blue back (1911)		£2.40	£60.00
			B Grey back (1925)		£1.60	£40.00
A	C	26	Your Initials (transfers) (1932)		70p	£18.00
B	C	25	Zoo Babies (1938):			
			A Home issue — with I.T.C. clause		80p	£20.00
			B Channel Islands issue — without I.T.C. clause		£2.00	—
POST-1960 ISSUES						
G	C	30	African Wildlife (1990)		50p	£15.00
			Album		—	£15.00
—	BW	9	Basket Ball Fixtures (114 x 71mm) (1972)		£6.00	—

Size	Printing	Number in set	BRITISH TOBACCO ISSUERS	Handbook reference	Price per card	Complete set
			JOHN PLAYER & SONS, Nottingham (Post-1960 Issues continued)			
	C	44	Black Jack (1984):	H.896		
—			A Size 75 x 35mm		£1.00	—
—			B Size 80 x 47mm		60p	—
G2			C Size 90 x 47mm		60p	—
G	C	32	Britain's Endangered Wildlife:			
			A Grandee Issue (1984)		25p	£8.00
			Album		—	£15.00
			B Doncella Issue (1984)		30p	£9.00
			Album		—	£15.00
H2	C	30	Britain's Maritime History (1989)		40p	£12.00
			Album		—	£12.00
G	C	30	Britain's Nocturnal Wildlife:			
			A Grandee Issue (1987)		27p	£8.00
			Album		—	£15.00
			B Doncella Issue (1987)		£1.00	£30.00
			Album		—	£15.00
G	C	30	Britain's Wayside Wildlife (1988)		30p	£9.00
			Album		—	£15.00
G	C	30	Britain's Wild Flowers:			
			A Grandee Issue (1986)		25p	£7.50
			Album		—	£15.00
			B Doncella Issue (1986)		60p	£18.00
			Album		—	£15.00
G	C	32	British Birds (1980)		60p	£18.00
			Album/Folder		—	£15.00
G	C	32	British Butterflies:			
			A Grandee Issue (1983)		40p	£13.00
			Album		—	£15.00
			B Doncella Issue (1984)		60p	£19.00
			Album		—	£15.00
G	C	30	British Mammals:			
			A Grandee Issue (1982):			
			1 Imperial Tobacco Ltd		27p	£8.00
			2 Imperial Group PLC		50p	£15.00
			Album		—	£15.00
			B Doncella Issue (1983)		50p	£15.00
			Album		—	£15.00
G	C	32	Country Houses and Castles (1981)		33p	£10.00
			Album/Folder		—	£15.00
—	U	116	Corsair Game (63 x 38mm) (1965)	H.897	£1.20	—
H2	C	32	Exploration of Space (1983)		22p	£7.00
			Album		—	£10.00
G	C	28	Famous MG Marques (1981)		90p	£25.00
			Album/Folder		—	£15.00
G	C	24	The Golden Age of Flying (1977)	H.898	25p	£6.00
			Album/Folder		—	£15.00
G	C	1	The Golden Age of Flying Completion Offer (1977)	H.898	—	£4.00
G	C	24	The Golden Age of Motoring (1975):	H.899		
			A With set completion offer		£4.00	—
			B Without set completion offer		27p	£6.50
			Album/Folder		—	£15.00
G	C	24	The Golden Age of Sail (1978)		27p	£6.50
			Album/Folder		—	£12.00
G	C	1	The Golden Age of Sail Completion Offer (1978)		—	£4.00
G	C	24	The Golden Age of Steam (1976)	H.900	27p	£6.50
			Album/Folder		—	£15.00
G	C	1	The Golden Age of Steam Completion Offer (1976)	H.900	—	£4.00

Size	Print-ing	Number in set	BRITISH TOBACCO ISSUERS	Handbook reference	Price per card	Complete set
			JOHN PLAYER & SONS, Nottingham (Post-1960 Issues continued)			
G	U	7	Grandee Limericks (1977)		£12.00	—
H2	C	30	History of Britain's Railways (1987)		80p	£24.00
			Album		—	£15.00
H2	C	30	History of British Aviation (1988)		80p	£24.00
			Album		—	£15.00
H2	C	30	History of Motor Racing (1986):			
			A Imperial Tobacco Ltd		90p	£27.00
			B Imperial Group PLC		£1.20	£36.00
			Album		—	£15.00
G	C	24	History of the VC (1980)		£1.00	£24.00
			Album/Folder		—	£15.00
G	C	1	History of the VC completion offer (1980)		—	£5.00
—	BW	5	Jubilee Issue (70 x 55mm) (1960)	H.901	£1.60	£8.00
G	C	30	The Living Ocean:			
			A Grandee Issue (1985)		25p	£7.50
			Album		—	£15.00
			B Doncella Issue (1985)		40p	£12.00
			Album		—	£15.00
H2	C	32	Myths and Legends (1982)		£1.10	£35.00
			Album/Folder		—	£15.00
G	C	24	Napoleonic Uniforms (1979)		30p	£7.50
			Album/Folder		—	£15.00
G	C	1	Napoleonic Uniforms Completion Offer (1979)		—	£4.00
G	C	7	Panama Puzzles (1975)		£7.00	—
G	BW	6	Play Ladbroke Spot-Ball (1975)		£7.00	—
G	C	6	Play Panama Spot Six (1977)		£7.00	—
G1	C		Player Clues:	H.902		
		?	A Closing Date 30-1-87, red headings		£1.00	—
		?	B Closing Date 31-7-87, blue headings		£1.00	—
G1	C		Player Games:	H.903		
		?	A Closing Date 28-1-83		£1.00	—
		?	B Closing Date 29-7-83		£1.00	—
		?	C Closing Date 30-12-83		£1.00	—
		?	D Closing Date 30-4-84		£1.00	—
		?	E Closing Date 31-8-84		£1.00	—
		?	F Closing Date 31-1-85		£1.00	—
G1	C	?	Player Prize Closing Date 29-1-88	H.904	£1.00	—
G1	C		Player Quiz:	H.905		
		?	A Closing Date 31-7-85, green headings		£1.00	—
		?	B Closing Date 28-2-86, red headings		£1.00	—
		?	C Closing Date 31-7-86 blue headings		£1.00	—
	C	50	Supercars (1987):	H.906		
—			A Size 90 x 35mm		70p	—
G2			B Size 90 x 47mm		70p	—
	C	60	Superdeal (1985):	H.907		
—			A Size 75 x 35mm		60p	—
—			B Size 80 x 47mm		60p	—
—			C Size 90 x 35mm		60p	—
G2			D Size 90 x 47mm		60p	—
	C	108	Superyear 88 (1988):	H.908		
—			A Size 90 x 35mm		70p	—
G2			B Size 90 x 47mm		70p	—
—	U	4	Tom Thumb Record Breakers (82 x 65mm) (1976)	H.909	£7.00	—
G	C	25	Top Dogs (1979)		£1.20	£30.00
			Album/Folder		—	£15.00
—	C	4	Vanguard Limericks (80 x 45mm) (1981)	H.910	£3.00	—

Size	Printing	Number in set	BRITISH TOBACCO ISSUERS	Handbook reference	Price per card	Complete set

JOHN PLAYER & SONS, Nottingham (Post-1960 Issues continued)

Size	Printing	Number in set		Handbook reference	Price per card	Complete set
H2	C	32	Wonders of the Ancient World (1984)		40p	£12.50
			Album		—	£15.00
H2	C	30	Wonders of the Modern World (1985)		30p	£9.00
			Album		—	£15.00
G	C	6	World of Gardening (1976)		£13.00	—
	C	156	World Tour (1986):	H.911		
—			A Size 80 x 35mm		70p	—
—			B Size 80 x 47mm		70p	—
—			C Size 90 x 35mm		70p	—
G2			D Size 90 x 47mm		70p	—

OVERSEAS ISSUES

A	C	50	Aeroplane Series (1926)		£2.50	—
A	C	50	Arms and Armour (1926)		£3.00	£150.00
		50	Beauties 1st series (1925):			
—	P		A Black and white fronts (63 x 41mm)		£1.70	£85.00
—	PC		B Coloured fronts (63 x 44mm)		£1.90	£95.00
—	PC	50	Beauties 2nd series (63 x 41mm) (1925)		£1.70	£85.00
D2	C	52	Birds of Brilliant Plumage (1927)		£3.50	—
A	C	25	Bonzo Dogs (1923)		£6.00	—
A	C	50	Boy Scouts (1924)		£4.00	—
—	C	25	British Live Stock (80 x 54mm) (1924)		£8.00	—
A	C	50	Butterflies (Girls) (1928)		£7.50	—
A	C	25	Dogs (Heads) (1927)		£1.60	£40.00
D	C	32	Drum Horses (1911)		£9.00	—
D2	C	25	Flag Girls of All Nations (1908)		£9.00	—
A	C	50	Household Hints (1928-29)		£1.20	£60.00
A	C	50	Lawn Tennis (1928)		£5.00	—
A	C	50	Leaders of Men (1925)		£2.50	£125.00
A	U	48	Pictures of the East (1931)		£2.50	£125.00
A	C	25	Picturesque People of the Empire (1928)		£2.40	£60.00
—	C	53	Playing Cards (68 x 45mm) (1929)		£1.40	—
A	U	50	Pugilists in Action (1928)		£5.50	—
A	C	50	Railway Working (1926)		£2.20	£110.00
A	P	50	The Royal Family at Home and Abroad (1927)		£3.00	—
A	C	50	Ships Flags and Cap Badges (1930)		£2.20	£110.00
A	C	50	Signalling series (1926)		£2.20	—
A	C	25	Whaling (1930)		£3.00	£75.00

JAS. PLAYFAIR & CO., London

A	C	25	How to Keep Fit — Sandow Exercises (c1912)	H.136	£40.00	—

THE PREMIER TOBACCO MANUFACTURERS LTD, London

D	U	48	Eminent Stage and Screen Personalities (1936)	H.569	£2.20	—
K2	C	52	*Miniature Playing Cards (c1935)		£7.50	—
—	BW		Stage and Screen Personalities (57 x 35mm) (1937):	H.674		
		100	A Back in grey		£2.20	—
		50	B Back in brown (Nos. 51-100)		£2.75	—

PRITCHARD & BURTON LTD, London

A2	C	51	*Actors and Actresses — 'FROGA B and C' (c1900)	H.20		
			A Blue back		£28.00	—
			B Grey-black back		£85.00	—
A	C	15	*Beauties 'PAC' (c1900)	H.2	£75.00	—
D	BW	20	*Boer War Cartoons (1900)	H.42	£150.00	—

Size	Print-ing	Number in set	BRITISH TOBACCO ISSUERS	Handbook reference	Price per card	Complete set
			PRITCHARD & BURTON LTD, London (continued)			
A1	C		*Flags and Flags with Soldiers (c1902):	H.41		
			A Flagstaff Draped:			
		30	1st printing		£22.00	£660.00
		15	2nd printing		£24.00	—
		15	B Flagstaff not Draped (Flags only)		£24.00	—
D	U	25	*Holiday Resorts and Views (c1902)	H.366	£22.00	—
A	C	40	*Home Colonial Regiments (c1901)	H.69	£65.00	—
D	U	25	*Royalty Series (1902)	H.367	£25.00	—
D	U	25	*South African Series (1901)	H.368	£25.00	—
A2	C	25	*Star Girls (c1900)	H.30	£250.00	—
			G. PRUDHOE, Darlington			
C	C	30	*Army Pictures, Cartoons, etc (c1916)	H.12	£160.00	—
			JAMES QUINTON LTD, London			
A	C	26	*Actresses — 'FROGA A' (c1900)	H.20	£230.00	—
			RAY & CO. LTD, London			
—	C		*Flags of The Allies (Shaped) (c1915):	H.49		
		1	A Grouped Flag 'All Arms' Cigarettes		£85.00	—
		5	B Allies Flags 'Life Ray' Cigarettes		£85.00	—
A	BW	25	War Series — 1-25 — Battleships (c1915)	H.472	£22.00	—
A	C	75	War Series — 26-100 — British and Foreign Uniforms (c1915)	H.472	£16.00	—
A	C	24	War Series — 101-124 — British and Dominion Uniforms (c1915)	H.472	£32.00	—
			RAYMOND REVUEBAR, London			
—	P	25	Revuebar Striptease Artists (72 x 46mm) (1960) ...		£20.00	—
			RECORD CIGARETTE & TOBACCO CO., London			
—	U	? 2	Gramophone Records (100mm Diameter) (c1935) ...	H.675	£110.00	—
—	U	? 34	The 'Talkie' Cigarette Card — (gramophone record on reverse) (70mm square) (c1935):			
			A Back 'Record Tobacco Company'		£60.00	—
			B Back 'Record Cigarette Company'		£60.00	—
			J. REDFORD & CO., London			
A	BW	20	*Actresses — 'BLARM' (c1900)	H.23	£80.00	—
A2	C	25	*Armies of the World (c1901)	H.43	£70.00	—
A2	C	25	*Beauties — 'GRACC' (c1899)	H.59	£150.00	—
A2	C	30	*Colonial Troops (c1902)	H.40	£70.00	—
D	C	24	*Nautical Expressions (c1900)	H.174	£80.00	—
D2	C	40	*Naval and Military Phrases (c1904)	H.14	£75.00	—
A	C	25	Picture Series (c1905)	H.369	£75.00	—
A	C	25	Sports and Pastimes Series 1 (c1905)	H.225	£90.00	—
D1	BW	50	Stage Artistes of the Day (c1908)	H.370	£25.00	—
			RELIANCE TOBACCO MFG. CO. LTD			
A2	C	24	British Birds (c1935)	H.604	£5.50	—
A2	C	35	*Famous Stars* (c1935)	H.572	£5.50	—
			RICHARDS & WARD			
A1	P	? 13	*Beauties — 'Topsy Cigarettes' (c1900)	H.371	£750.00	—

Size	Print-ing	Number in set	BRITISH TOBACCO ISSUERS	Handbook reference	Price per card	Complete set
			A.S. RICHARDSON, Luton			
—	U	12	*Manikin Cards (82 x 51mm) (c1920)	H.481	£120.00	—
			THE RICHMOND CAVENDISH CO. LTD, London			
A2	C	26	*Actresses — 'FROGA A' (c1900)	H.20	£35.00	—
D2	BW	28	*Actresses — 'PILPI I' (c1902)	H.195	£18.00	—
D	P	50	*Actresses 'PILPI II' (c1902)	H.196	£14.00	—
A	U		*Actresses Photogravure, 'Smoke Pioneer Cigarettes' back (c1905):	H.372		
		50	A Reading bottom to top		£10.00	£500.00
		? 179	B Reading top to bottom. Different subjects		£10.00	—
		? 13	C Plain back		£12.00	—
A	C	14	*Beauties 'AMBS' (1899):	H.373		
			A 'The Absent Minded Beggar' back:			
			i '1st Verse' back		£60.00	—
			ii '2nd Verse' back		£60.00	—
			iii '3rd Verse' back		£60.00	—
			iv '4th Verse' back		£60.00	—
			v 'Chorus (1st verse)' back		£60.00	—
			vi 'Chorus (2nd verse)' back		£60.00	—
			vii 'Chorus (3rd verse)' back		£60.00	—
			viii 'Chorus (4th verse)' back		£60.00	—
			B 'The Soldiers of The Queen' back:			
			i '1 Britons once did' back		£60.00	—
			ii '2 War clouds gather' back		£60.00	—
			iii '3 Now we're roused' back		£60.00	—
			iv 'Chorus' back		£60.00	—
A	C	52	*Beauties — 'ROBRI' playing card inset (c1898)	H.374	£55.00	—
—	C	40	*Medals (34 x 72mm) (c1900)	H.200	£26.00	—
A2	C	20	Music Hall Artistes (c1902)	H.202	£50.00	—
A	C	12	*Pretty Girl Series — 'RASH' (c1900)	H.8	£50.00	—
A	C	20	*Yachts (c1900):	H.204		
			A Gold on black back		£75.00	—
			B Black on white back		£75.00	—
OVERSEAS ISSUES						
D	C	28	Chinese Actors and Actresses (1922)	W.361	£4.00	—
A	P	50	Cinema Stars (1926)		£4.00	—
			RIDGWAYS, Manchester			
—	C	? 2	*Play Up' Sporting Shields (c1895)	H.718	£150.00	—
			R. ROBERTS & SONS, London			
A2	C	26	*Actresses — 'FROGA A' (c1900)	H.20	£85.00	—
A	C	25	*Armies of the World (c1900):	H.43		
			A 'Fine Old Virginia' back		£60.00	—
			B Plain back		£60.00	—
A2	C	50	*Beauties — 'CHOAB' (c1900):	H.21		
			1-25 without borders to back		£75.00	—
			26-50 with borders to back		£90.00	—
—	C	50	*Beautiful Women (60 x 43mm) (c1900)	H.284	£300.00	—
A2	C	50	*Colonial Troops (c1902)	H.40	£50.00	—
A	BW	28	*Dominoes (c1905)		£80.00	—
K1	C	52	*Miniature Playing Cards (c1905):			
			A Blue background		£65.00	—
			B Pink background		£65.00	—
			C Yellow background		£65.00	—

Size	Print-ing	Number in set	BRITISH TOBACCO ISSUERS	Handbook reference	Price per card	Complete set
			R. ROBERTS & SONS, London (continued)			
D2	C	24	*Nautical Expressions (c1900):	H.174		
			A 'Navy Cut Cigarettes' on front		£70.00	—
			B Firm's name only on front		£70.00	—
A2	C	70	Stories without words (c1905)		£60.00	—
A2	C	25	*Types of British and Colonial Troops (c1900)	H.76	£65.00	—
			ROBINSON & BARNSDALE LTD, London			
—	C	1	*Advertisement Card — Soldier, 'Colin Campbell Cigars' (29 x 75mm) (c1897):	H.764		
			A With equal 'E' back		—	£200.00
			B With unequal 'E' back		—	£150.00
—	BW	? 24	*Actresses, 'Colin Campbell Cigars' (c1898):	H.375		
			A Size 43 x 70mm		£150.00	—
			B Officially cut narrow — 32 x 70mm		£150.00	—
A	P	? 33	*Actresses, 'Cupola' Cigarettes (c1898)	H.376	£250.00	—
A1	P		*Beauties — collotype (c1895):	H.377		
		? 9	A 'Our Golden Beauties' back in black		£260.00	—
		? 18	B 'Nana' back in red on white		£260.00	—
		? 1	C 'Nana' back in vermillion on cream		£260.00	—
A	C	? 1	*Beauties — 'Blush of Day' (c1898)		£350.00	—
—	C	? 16	*Beauties — 'Highest Honors' (44 x 73mm) (c1895)	H.379	£350.00	—
A2	U	? 3	Beauties 'KEWA II' (c1895)	H.139	£350.00	—
			E. ROBINSON & SONS LTD, Stockport			
A1	C	10	*Beauties 'ROBRI' (c1900):	H.374		
			A 'Forget-Me-Not Mixture' back		£70.00	—
			B 'Gold Flake Honeydew' back		£70.00	—
			C 'Gold Leaf Navy Cut' back		£70.00	—
			D 'Jack's Best Tobacco' back		£70.00	—
			E 'Jack Tar Navy Cut' back		£70.00	—
			F 'Man Friday Mixture' back		£70.00	—
			G 'Reliable Tobaccos' back		£70.00	—
			H 'Stockport Snuff' back		£70.00	—
			I 'Thin Twist & Thick Twist' back		£70.00	—
			J 'Three Decker Cigarettes' back		£70.00	—
A	BW	50	Derbyshire and the Peak (c1905)	H.380	£250.00	—
A2	C	25	Egyptian Studies (c1914)		£32.00	—
A	C	25	King Lud Problems (c1934)	H.638	£25.00	—
A	C	6	Medals and Decorations of Great Britain (c1905):	H.484		
			A Vertical back with firm's name		£300.00	—
			B Horizontal back with 'General Favourite Onyx'		£500.00	—
A2	C	40	Nature Studies (c1912)		£28.00	—
A2	C	25	Regimental Mascots (1916)		£75.00	—
A	C	25	Types of British Soldiers (1900)	H.144	£400.00	—
A2	C	25	Wild Flowers (c1915)		£22.00	£550.00
			ROMAN STAR CIGARS			
C	C	26	*Actresses 'FROGA A' (c1900)	H.20	£200.00	—
A	C	25	*Beauties 'BOCCA' (c1900)	H.39	£200.00	—
			ROTHMAN'S LTD, London			
	C		Beauties of the Cinema (1936):	H.605		
D1		40	A Small size		£2.00	£80.00
—		24	B Circular cards, 64mm diam:			
			1 Varnished		£4.40	£110.00
			2 Unvarnished		£4.40	£110.00

Size	Printing	Number in set	BRITISH TOBACCO ISSUERS	Handbook reference	Price per card	Complete set
			ROTHMAN'S LTD, London (continued)			
A2	P	24	Cinema Stars — Small size (c1925)		£1.80	£45.00
B	P	25	Cinema Stars — Large size (c1925)		£1.20	£30.00
—	C	30	Country Living (Consulate) (112 x 102mm) (1973)		—	£24.00
—	C	6	Diamond Jubilee Folders (127 x 95mm) (1950)		£12.00	—
C2	C	50	Football International Stars (unissued) (1984)	H.912	60p	£30.00
C	U	36	Landmarks in Empire History (c1936)		£1.25	£45.00
			Album		—	£50.00
		?	Metal Charms (c1930)		£4.00	—
D1	U	50	Modern Inventions (1935)		£1.20	£60.00
B2	P	54	New Zealand (c1930)		£1.00	£55.00
			Album		—	£50.00
D1	U	24	Prominent Screen Favourites (1934)	H.568	£1.20	£30.00
A2	BW	50	'Punch Jokes' (c1935)		60p	£30.00
A1	C	5	Rare Banknotes (1970)		£4.00	—
			Album		—	£12.00
			WM. RUDDELL LTD, Dublin and Liverpool			
K	U	? 3	*Couplet Cards (c1925)	H.676	£32.00	—
D	C	25	Grand Opera Series (1924)		£8.00	£200.00
A2	C	25	Rod and Gun (1924)		£8.00	£200.00
D	C	50	Songs that will Live for Ever (c1925)		£5.00	£250.00
			RUTHERFORD			
A	BW	? 8	Footballers (c1900)	H.765	£2500.00	—
			I. RUTTER & CO., Mitcham			
D	BW	15	*Actresses — 'RUTAN' (c1900):	H.381		
			A Rubber-stamped on plain back		£100.00	—
			B Red printed back		£65.00	—
			C Plain back		£35.00	—
A	BW	1	Advertisement Card 'Tobacco Bloom' (1899)	H.485	—	£1200.00
A	BW	7	*Boer War Celebrities (c1901)	H.382	£75.00	—
D1	C	54	*Comic Phrases (c1905)	H.223	£23.00	—
A	BW	20	Cricketers Series (1901)	H.29	£325.00	—
C	C		*Flags and Flags with Soldiers (c1902):	H.41		
		15	A Flagstaff Draped, 2nd printing		£36.00	—
		15	B Flagstaff not Draped (Flags only)			
			(a) white back		£36.00	—
			(b) cream back		£36.00	—
C	C	24	*Girls, Flags and Arms of Countries (c1900):	H.383		
			A Blue back		£35.00	—
			B Plain back		£25.00	—
A	C	25	Proverbs (c1905):	H.384		
			A Green Seal on front		£45.00	—
			B Red Seal on front		£45.00	—
A	C	25	*Shadowgraphs (c1905)	H.44	£45.00	—
			S.D.V. TOBACCO CO. LTD, Liverpool			
A	BW	16	British Royal Family (c1901)	H.28	£600.00	—
			ST. PETERSBURG CIGARETTE CO. LTD, Portsmouth			
A	BW	? 17	Footballers (c1900)	H.410	£2000.00	—

Size	Print-ing	Number in set	BRITISH TOBACCO ISSUERS	Handbook reference	Price per card	Complete set
			SALMON & GLUCKSTEIN LTD, London			
—	C	1	*Advertisement Card ('Snake Charmer' Cigarettes) (73 x 107mm) (c1897)	H.767	—	£500.00
C	C	15	*Billiard Terms (c1905):			
			A Small numerals about 2mm high		£90.00	—
			B Larger numerals about 3mm high		£90.00	—
A	C	12	British Queens (c1897)	H.480	£50.00	—
—	C	30	*Castles, Abbeys and Houses (76 x 73mm) (c1906):			
			A Brown back		£20.00	—
			B Red back		£26.00	—
C	C	32	*Characters from Dickens (c1903)	H.385	£32.00	—
A	C	25	Coronation Series (1911)		£15.00	£375.00
—	U	25	*Famous Pictures — Brown photogravure (57 x 76mm) (c1910)	H.386	£12.00	£300.00
—	U	25	*Famous Pictures — Green photogravure (58 x 76mm) (c1910)	H.387	£11.00	£275.00
A2	C	6	Her Most Gracious Majesty Queen Victoria (1897):	H.388		
			A Thin card		£50.00	£300.00
			B Thick card		£50.00	£300.00
A	C	50	The Great White City (c1908)		£16.00	£800.00
C	C	40	Heroes of the Transvaal War (1901)	H.389	£22.00	£880.00
D2	C	25	Magical Series (1923)		£8.00	£200.00
C	C	30	*Music Hall Celebrities (c1902)		£55.00	—
—	C	25	*Occupations (64 x 18mm) (c1898)	H.390	£650.00	—
C	C	20	'Owners and Jockeys' Series (c1900)	H.392	£95.00	—
—	C	48	*The Post in Various Countries (41 x 66mm) (c1900)	H.391	£28.00	—
A2	C	6	*Pretty Girl Series — 'RASH' (c1900)	H.8	£70.00	—
—	C	22	Shakespearian Series (c1902):	H.393		
			A Large format, frame line back (38 x 69mm)		£35.00	—
			B Re-drawn, small format, no frame line back (37 x 66mm)		£35.00	—
A	C	25	*Star Girls (c1900):	H.30		
			A Red back		£140.00	—
			B Brown back, different setting		£140.00	—
A	C	25	Traditions of the Army and Navy (c1917):			
			A Large dome above number 2mm wide		£18.00	£450.00
			B Small dome above number 1mm wide		£18.00	£450.00
A2	C	25	Wireless Explained (1923)		£6.00	£150.00
SILKS						
—	C	50	*Pottery Types (paper-backed) (83 x 55mm) (c1915):	H.505-17		
			A Numbered on front and back		£5.00	—
			B Numbered on back only		£5.00	—

W. SANDORIDES & CO. LTD, London

	U	25	Aquarium Studies from the London Zoo (1925):	H.607		
C2			A Small size:			
			1 Small lettering on back		£3.60	£90.00
			2 Larger lettering on back		£3.60	£90.00
B1			B Large size		£3.60	£90.00
	C	25	Cinema Celebrities (1924):	H.530		
C2			A Small size		£2.80	£70.00
—			B Extra-large size (109 x 67mm)		£4.00	£100.00
	C	25	Cinema Stars (export) (c1924):	H.530		
C2			A Small size, with firm's name at base of back		£6.00	—
C2			B Small size, 'Issued with Lucana Cigarettes		£6.00	—
C2			C Small size, 'Issued with Big Gun Cigarettes …'		£8.00	—

Size	Print-ing	Number in set	BRITISH TOBACCO ISSUERS	Handbook reference	Price per card	Complete set
			W. SANDORIDES & CO. LTD, London (continued)			
			Cinema Stars (export) (c1924) (continued)			
—			D Extra-large size (109 x 67mm) 'Issued with Big Gun Cigarettes		£2.60	£65.00
—			E Extra-large size (109 x 67mm) issued with Lucana 66		£8.00	—
	U	50	Famous Racecourses (1926) — 'Lucana':	H.608		
C2			A Small size		£6.00	£300.00
B1			B Large size		£6.00	£300.00
C2	U	50	Famous Racehorses (1923):	H.609		
			1A Back in light brown		£4.00	£200.00
			1B Back in dark brown		£4.00	£200.00
			2 As 1A, with blue label added, inscribed 'Issued with Sandorides Big Gun Cigarettes ...' ...		£13.00	
—	BW	12	London Views (57 x 31mm) (c1936) — see Teofani			
A	C	25	Sports & Pastimes — Series 1 — 'Big Gun Cigarettes (c1924)	H.225	£16.00	—
			SANSOM'S CIGAR STORES, London			
—	P	? 2	*London Views (52 x 37mm) (c1915)	H.768	£800.00	—
			NICOLAS SARONY & CO., London			
	C	50	Around the Mediterranean (1926):	GP.404		
C2			A Small size		£1.20	£60.00
			Album		—	£30.00
B1			B Large size		£1.20	£60.00
—	U	? 7	Boer War Scenes (67 x 45mm) (c1901)	GP.701	£900.00	—
	U	25	Celebrities and Their Autographs, Nd 1-25 (1923):			
C1			A Small size		£1.20	£30.00
B1			B Large size		£1.20	£30.00
	U	25	Celebrities and Their Autographs, Nd 26-50 (1924):			
C1			A Small size:			
			1 Small numerals		£1.20	£30.00
			2 Large numerals		£1.20	£30.00
B1			B Large size:			
			1 Small numerals		£1.20	£30.00
			2 Large numerals		£1.20	£30.00
	U	25	Celebrities and Their Autographs. Nd 51-75 (1924):			
C1			A Small size		£1.20	£30.00
B1			B Large size		£1.20	£30.00
	U	25	Celebrities and Their Autographs, Nd 76-100 (1925):			
C1			A Small size		£1.20	£30.00
B1			B Large size		£1.20	£30.00
A2	U	50	Cinema Stars — Set 7 (1933)	GP.703	£1.50	£75.00
—	U		Cinema Stars — Postcard size (137 x 85mm):			
		38	'of a Series of 38 Cinema Stars' (1929)		£9.00	—
		42	'of a second Series of 42 Cinema Stars' (c1930)		£5.00	£210.00
		50	'of a third Series of 50 Cinema Stars' (c1930) ...		£5.00	£250.00
		42	'of a fourth Series of 42 Cinema Stars' (c1931) ...		£5.00	£210.00
		25	'of a fifth Series of 25 Cinema Stars' (c1931)		£5.00	£125.00
D	U	25	Cinema Studies (1929)		£1.20	£30.00
	C	25	A Day on the Airway (1928):			
C2			A Small size		£1.40	£35.00
B2			B Large size		£1.40	£35.00
A2	P	54	Life at Whipsnade Zoo (1934)	GP.415	60p	£32.50

Size	Print-ing	Number in set	BRITISH TOBACCO ISSUERS	Handbook reference	Price per card	Complete set
			NICOLAS SARONY & CO., London (continued)			
	BW	25	Links with the Past — First 25 subjects, Nd 1-25 (1925):	GP.711		
C1			A Small size		70p	£17.50
B			B Large size		80p	—
	BW	25	Links with the Past — Second 25 subjects (1926):	GP.711		
C			A Home issue, Nd 26-50:			
B			1 Small size		70p	£17.50
B			2 Large size, descriptive back		50p	£12.50
			3 Large size, advertisement back		£2.20	—
			B Sydney issue, Nd 1-25:			
C			1 Small size		£1.00	£25.00
B			2 Large size		£1.00	£25.00
			C Christchurch issue, Nd 1-25:			
C			1 Small size		£1.00	£25.00
B			2 Large size		50p	£12.50
	BW	25	Museum Series (1927):	GP.712		
			A Home issue:			
C2			1 Small size		32p	£8.00
B			2 Large size, descriptive back		32p	£8.00
B			3 Large size, advertisement back		£1.00	£25.00
			Booklet Cover for large size		—	£4.00
B			B Sydney issue, large size		80p	£20.00
			C Christchurch issue:			
C2			1 Small size		60p	£15.00
B			2 Large size		80p	£20.00
	P	36	National Types of Beauty (1928):	GP.417		
A2			A Small size		60p	£22.00
—			B Medium size (76 x 51mm)		50p	£18.00
	C	15	Origin of Games (1923):			
A			A Small size		£9.00	£135.00
B2			B Large size		£9.00	£135.00
	C	50	'Saronicks' (1929):	GP.414		
D2			A Small size		40p	£20.00
—			B Medium size (76 x 51 mm)		40p	£20.00
	C	50	Ships of All Ages (1929):			
D			A Small size		90p	£45.00
—			B Medium size (76 x 52mm)		£1.20	£60.00
D	C	25	Tennis Strokes (1923)		£4.40	£110.00
			T.S. SAUNT, Leicester			
D	C	30	*Army Pictures, Cartoons etc (c1916)	H.12	£160.00	—
			SCOTTISH COOPERATIVE WHOLESALE SOCIETY LTD, Glasgow ('S.C.W.S.')			
A2	C	25	Burns (1924):	H.611		
			A Printed back:			
			1 White card		£3.20	—
			2 Cream card		£2.00	£50.00
			*B Plain back		£8.00	—
C	C	20	Dogs (1925)	H.211	£16.00	—
A2	C	25	Dwellings of All Nations (1924):	H.612		
			A Printed back:			
			1 White card		£3.50	—
			2 Cream card		£2.40	£60.00
			*B Plain back		£7.50	—
B	C	25	Famous Pictures (1924)		£8.00	—

Size	Print-ing	Number in set		BRITISH TOBACCO ISSUERS	Handbook reference	Price per card	Complete set
			SCOTTISH COOPERATIVE WHOLESALE SOCIETY LTD, Glasgow ('S.C.W.S.') (continued)			
H2	C	25		Famous Pictures — Glasgow Gallery (1927):			
			A	Non-adhesive back		£2.40	£60.00
			B	Adhesive back		£1.60	£40.00
H2	C	25		Famous Pictures — London Galleries (1927):			
			A	Non-adhesive back		£2.40	£60.00
			B	Adhesive back		£1.60	£40.00
A2	C	50		Feathered Favourites (1926):			
			A	Grey borders		£2.50	£125.00
			B	White borders:			
				1 Non-adhesive back		£2.50	£125.00
				2 Adhesive back		£2.00	£100.00
A	C	25		Racial Types (1925)		£8.00	£200.00
A2	C	50		Triumphs of Engineering (1926):			
			A	Brown border		£2.50	£125.00
			B	White border		£2.60	—
A2	C	50		Wireless (1924)		£5.00	£250.00
				SELBY'S TOBACCO STORES, Cirencester			
—	U	12		'Manikin' Cards (79 x 51mm) (c1920)	H.481	£120.00	—
				SHARPE & SNOWDEN, London			
A	U	? 1		*Views of England (c1905)	H.769	£800.00	—
A	U	? 23		*Views of London (c1905)	H.395	£400.00	—
				W.J. SHEPHERD, London			
A	U	25		*Beauties — 'FECKSA' (c1900)	H.58	£120.00	—
				SHORT'S, London			
—	BW			*Short's House Views (c1925):	H.562		
		? 13		1 Numbered (75 x 60mm)		£65.00	—
		? 6		2 Unnumbered (77 x 69mm)		£45.00	—
				JOHN SINCLAIR LTD, Newcastle-on-Tyne			
D2	U	? 92		*Actresses (42 x 63 mm) (c1900)	H.396	£90.00	—
—	P			*Birds (1924):	H.613		
C		? 41	A	Small size, back 'Specimen Cigarette Card'		£8.50	—
C		48	B	Small size, descriptive back:			
				1 White front		£4.00	—
				2 Pinkish front		£4.00	—
—		50	C	Large size (78 x 58mm)		£7.00	—
A	C	50		British Sea Dogs (1926)		£6.50	£325.00
	P			Champion Dogs — 'A Series of ...' (1938):			
A2		54	A	Small size		75p	£40.00
B2		52	B	Large size		75p	£40.00
	P			Champion Dogs — '2nd Series ...' (1939):			
A2		54	A	Small size		£3.50	£190.00
B2		52	B	Large size		£3.75	—
A2	P	50		English and Scottish Football Stars (1935)		£1.80	£90.00
A	P	54		Film Stars — 'A Series of 54 Real Photos' (1934)		£2.20	£120.00
A	P	54		Film Stars — 'A Series of Real Photos', Nd 1-54 (1937)		£1.80	£95.00
A	P	54		Film Stars — 'A Series of Real Photos', Nd 55-108 (1937)		£1.50	£80.00

Size	Print-ing	Number in set	BRITISH TOBACCO ISSUERS	Handbook reference	Price per card	Complete set
			JOHN SINCLAIR LTD, Newcastle-on-Tyne (continued)			
	P		*Flowers and Plants (1924):	H.614		
C		? 37	A Small size, back 'Specimen Cigarette Card' …		£7.50	—
C		96	B Small size, descriptive back:			
			1 White front ……………………………		£2.50	—
			2 Pinkish front ……………………………		£2.50	—
D	P	? 52	Football Favourites (c1910) ……………………		£230.00	—
A	BW	4	*North Country Celebrities (c1905) ……………	H.397	£75.00	£300.00
D	P	? 55	Northern Gems (c1902) ………………………		£75.00	—
A	C	50	Picture Puzzles and Riddles (c1910) …………		£30.00	—
A	P	54	Radio Favourites (1935) ………………………		£1.50	£80.00
K2	C	53	Rubicon Cards (miniature playing cards) (1933):			
			A Without overprint …………………………		£6.00	—
			B With red overprint ………………………		£8.00	—
A	C	50	Trick Series (c1910) …………………………		£32.00	—
A	BW	50	Well-Known Footballers — North Eastern Counties (1938) ………………………………………		£1.20	£60.00
A	BW	50	Well-Known Footballers — Scottish (1938) ……		£1.20	£60.00
D2	C	50	World's Coinage (c1915) ………………………	H.398	£24.00	—
SILKS						
—	C	? 1	The Allies (140 x 100mm) (numbered 37) (c1915) …	H.501-2	—	£45.00
—	C		*Flags — Set 2 (70 x 52mm) (unbacked and anonymous) (c1915):	H.501-2		
		? 12	A Numbered Nos 25-36 ………………………		£15.00	—
			B Unnumbered:			
		? 24	1 Caption in red …………………………		£10.00	—
		? 24	2 Caption in myrtle-green ………………		£9.00	—
		? 24	3 Caption in bright green ………………		£9.00	—
		? 24	4 Caption in blue ………………………		£10.00	—
		? 25	5 Caption in black ………………………		£14.00	—
—	C		*Flags — Set 11 (unbacked and anonymous) (c1915):	H.501-11		
		50	'Fourth Series' (49 x 70mm) ………………		£7.00	—
		50	'Fifth Series' (49 x 70mm) …………………		£7.00	—
		50	'Sixth Series':			
			1 Nos 1-25 (49 x 70mm) ………………		£8.00	—
			2 Nos 26-50 (68 x 80mm) ……………		£8.00	—
		? 10	'Seventh Series' (115 x 145mm) ……………		£65.00	—
—	C	50	*Regimental Badges I (paper backed) (70 x 52mm) (c1915) ………………………………………	H.502-1	£7.00	—
—	C	? 24	*Regimental Colours II (unbacked and anonymous) (c1915):	H.502-7		
			1 Nos 38-49 (No. 49 not seen) (76 x 70mm) …		£16.00	—
			2 Nos 50-61 (65 x 51mm) …………………		£16.00	—
			ROBERT SINCLAIR TOBACCO CO. LTD, Newcastle-on-Tyne			
C2	C		Billiards by Willie Smith (1928):			
		10	1 First set of 10 …………………………		£12.00	£120.00
		15	2 Second Set of 15 ………………………		£14.00	£210.00
		3	3 Third Set of 25 (Nos 26-28 only issued) ……		£20.00	£60.00
A2	U	28	Dominoes (c1900) ………………………………		£60.00	—
			*Footballers (c1900):	H.399		
A2	U	? 4	A Mauve Collotype …………………………		£1800.00	—
D2	BW	? 16	B Black & White Collotype …………………		£1200.00	—
D	C	12	*Policemen of the World (c1899) ……………	H.164	£245.00	—
	C	12	The 'Smiler' Series (1924):			
A			A Small size (inscribed '… 24 cards'), ………		£10.00	—
H			B Large size ………………………………		£15.00	—

109

Size	Printing	Number in set	BRITISH TOBACCO ISSUERS	Handbook reference	Price per card	Complete set

ROBERT SINCLAIR TOBACCO CO. LTD, Newcastle-on-Tyne (continued)

SILKS. Unbacked silks, inscribed with initials 'R.S.' in circle.

—	C	4	*Battleships and Crests (73 x 102mm) (c1915)	H.499-1	£70.00	—
—	C	10	*Flags (70 x 51 mm) (c1915)	H.499-2	£26.00	—
—	C	6	*Great War Area — Cathedrals and Churches (140 x 102mm) (c1915)	H.499-3	£60.00	—
—	C	10	*Great War Heroes (70 x 51 mm) (c1915)	H.499-4	£45.00	—
—	C	1	*Red Cross Nurse (73 x 102mm) (c1915)	H.499-5	—	£60.00
—	C	5	*Regimental Badges (70 x 51 mm) (c1915)	H.499-6	£38.00	—

J. SINFIELD, Scarborough

A	U	24	*Beauties — 'HUMPS' (c1900)	H.222	£1500.00	

SINGLETON & COLE LTD, Shrewsbury

A	C	50	*Atlantic Liners (1910)		£28.00	—
A	C	25	Bonzo Series (1928)	H.678	£9.00	£225.00
D1	BW	50	*Celebrities — Boer War Period (c1901):	H.400		
		25	Actresses		£25.00	£625.00
		25	Boer War Celebrities		£25.00	£625.00
A2	BW	35	Famous Boxers (1930):			
			A Numbered		£20.00	—
			B Unnumbered		£50.00	—
A2	BW	25	Famous Film Stars (1930)		£12.00	—
A	BW	35	Famous Officers — Hero Series (1915):			
			A1 'Famous Officers' on back toned card		£16.00	£560.00
			A2 'Famous Officers' thin white card		£36.00	—
			B 'Hero Series' on back		£425.00	—
D1	BW	50	*Footballers (c1905)		£200.00	—
C	C	40	*Kings and Queens (1902)	H.157	£25.00	—
—	U	12	'Manikin' Cards (77 x 49mm) (c1920)	H.481	£120.00	—
A	C	25	Maxims of Success (c1905):	H.401		
			A Orange border		£30.00	—
			B Lemon yellow border		£250.00	—
A	BW		Orient Royal Mail Line (c1905):	H.402		
		8	A 'Orient-Pacific Line' front, Manager's back		£75.00	—
		8	B 'Orient Royal Mail Line' front, Singleton and Cole back		£55.00	—
		10	C 'Orient Line' front, Manager's back (5 ports)		£55.00	—
		10	D 'Orient Line' front, Manager's back (11 ports)		£55.00	—
A	C	25	Wallace Jones — Keep Fit System (c1910)		£26.00	—

SILKS

—	C	110	Crests and Badges of the British Army (paper-backed) (66 x 40mm) (c1915)	H.502-2	£5.00	—

F. & J. SMITH, Glasgow

36 page reference book — £4.50

A	C	25	*Advertisement Cards (1899)	H.403	£275.00	—
A	C	50	Battlefields of Great Britain (1913):			
			A 'Albion Gold Flake Cigarettes' back		£20.00	—
			B 'Auld Brig Flake' back		£20.00	—
			C 'Cut Golden Bar Twilight Brand' back		£20.00	—
			D 'Glasgow Mixture Cigarettes' back		£20.00	—
			E 'Glasgow Mixture Tobacco' back		£20.00	—

Size	Print-ing	Number in set	BRITISH TOBACCO ISSUERS	Handbook reference	Price per card	Complete set
			F. & J. SMITH, Glasgow (continued)			
			Battlefields of Great Britain (1913) (continued)			
			F 'Goodwill Virginia' back		£20.00	—
			G 'Kashan Cigarettes' back		£20.00	—
			H 'No. 1 Mixture' back		£20.00	—
			I 'Orchestra Cigarettes' back		£20.00	—
			J 'Pinewood Cigarettes' back		£20.00	—
			K 'Pinewood Mixture' back		£20.00	—
			L 'Squaw Thick Black Tobacco' back		£20.00	—
			M 'Studio Cigarettes' back		£20.00	—
			N 'Sun Cured Mixture' back		£20.00	—
			O 'Wild Geranium Cigarettes' back		£20.00	—
A1	BW	25	*Boer War Series 'Studio' Cigarettes back (1900) ...		£90.00	—
A	C	50	*Boer War Series (1900)		£40.00	—
D	BW		*Champions of Sport (1902):	H.404		
		50	A Red back. Numbered, multi-backed		£110.00	—
		50	B Blue back. Unnumbered		£110.00	—
A	C	25	'Cinema Stars' (1920):	H.615		
			A 'Compeer Cigarettes' back		£12.00	—
			B 'Glasgow Mixture Mild, Medium & Full' back		£12.00	—
			C 'Kashan Cigarettes' back		£12.00	—
			D 'Luxury Mixture' back		£12.00	—
			E 'Orchestra Cigarettes, Mild & Medium' back ...		£12.00	—
			F 'Pinewood Cigarettes' back		£12.00	—
			G 'Studio Cigarettes' back		£12.00	—
			H 'Sun Cured Mixture' back		£12.00	—
A	U	50	Cricketers (1912)		£24.00	£1200.00
A	U	20	Cricketers, 2nd Series, Nd 51-70 (1912)		£32.00	£640.00
A	U	50	Derby Winners (1913)		£16.00	£800.00
A	C	50	Famous Explorers (1911)		£18.00	£900.00
A	C	50	Football Club Records, 1913 to 1917 (1918)		£18.00	£900.00
A	C	50	Football Club Records, 1921-22 (1922)		£18.00	£900.00
D	U	120	*Footballers, brown back (1902)		£50.00	—
A	U	50	*Footballers, blue back Nd 1-52 (Nos 1 and 13 not issued) (1910):			
			A Black portrait		£16.00	—
			B Brown portrait		£16.00	—
A	U	50	*Footballers, blue back. Nd 55-104 (Nos 53 and 54 not issued) (1910):			
			A Black portrait		£16.00	—
			B Brown portrait		£16.00	—
A	U	150	*Footballers, yellow frame line (1914):			
			A Pale blue back		£16.00	—
			B Deep blue back		£16.00	—
A	C	50	Fowls, Pigeons and Dogs (1908)	H.64	£12.00	£600.00
A	C	25	Holiday Resorts (1925)		£8.00	£200.00
A	C		*Medals:	H.71		
		20	A Unnumbered — thick card (1902)		£18.00	£360.00
		50	B Numbered. 'F. & J. Smith' thick card, multi-backed (1902)		£15.00	£750.00
		50	C Numbered. 'The Imperial Tobacco Co.' very thin card (1903)		£36.00	—
		50	D Numbered. 'The Imperial Tobacco Company' thin card, multi-backed (1906)		£15.00	£750.00
A	C	50	Nations of the World (1923)	H.454	£7.50	£375.00
A	C	50	Naval Dress and Badges:	H.172		
			A Descriptive back, multi-backed (1911)		£12.00	£600.00
			B Non-descriptive back, multi-backed (1914) ...		£12.00	£600.00

Size	Printing	Number in set		BRITISH TOBACCO ISSUERS	Handbook reference	Price per card	Complete set
			F. & J. SMITH, Glasgow (continued)				
A	C	50	Phil May Sketches:		H.72		
			A Blue-grey back, multi-backed (1908)			£10.00	—
			B Brown back (1924):				
			1 'Albion (Empire Grown) Smoking Mixture' back			£8.00	—
			2 'Glasgow Smoking Mixture' back			£8.00	—
			3 'High Class Virginia Cigarettes' back ...			£8.00	—
			4 'Seal Virginia Cigarettes' back			£8.00	—
A	C	25	Prominent Rugby Players (1924)			£12.00	£300.00
A	C	40	Races of Mankind (1900):		H.483		
			A Series title on front, multi-backed			£50.00	—
			*B Without series title, multi-backed			£70.00	—
A	C	25	Shadowgraphs (1915):				
			A 'Glasgow Mixture, Mild, Medium & Full' back			£10.00	—
			B 'Orchestra Cigarettes' back			£10.00	—
			C 'Pinewood Cigarettes' back			£10.00	—
			D 'Pinewood Mixture' back			£10.00	—
			E 'Squaw Thick Black Tobacco' back			£10.00	—
			F 'Studio Cigarettes' back			£10.00	—
			G 'Sun Cured Mixture' back			£10.00	—
A	C	50	*A Tour Round the World:				
			A Script Advertisement back (1904)			£25.00	—
			B Post-card format back (1905)			£45.00	—
A	C	50	A Tour Round the World (titled series, multi-backed) (1906)		H.75	£12.00	£600.00
A	BW	25	War Incidents (1914):				
			A White back			£10.00	£250.00
			B Toned back			£10.00	£250.00
A	BW	25	War Incidents, 2nd series (1915):				
			A White back			£10.00	£250.00
			B Toned back			£10.00	£250.00
			SNELL & CO., Plymouth and Devonport				
A	BW	25	*Boer War Celebrities — 'STEW' (c1901)		H.105	£260.00	—
			SOCIETE JOB, London (and Paris)				
A	C	25	British Lighthouses (c1925)			£10.00	£250.00
—	U		*Cinema Stars (c1926):		H.616		
		48	A Unnumbered size (58 x 45mm):				
			1 Complete Set			—	£75.00
			2 46 different (minus Love, Milovanoff) ...			£1.00	£46.00
		43	B Unnumbered size (58 x 36mm)			£3.00	—
		?	C Numbered 100-192 (56 x 45mm) (sepia)			£4.00	—
		? 1	D Numbered 39 (57 x 45mm) (reddish brown) ...			£10.00	—
D	BW	25	*Dogs (1911)		H.406	£30.00	£750.00
D	BW	25	*Liners (1912)		H.407	£36.00	—
D1	C	52	*Miniature Playing Cards (c1925)			£7.00	—
A2	C	25	Orders of Chivalry (1924)			£5.00	£125.00
A2	C	25	Orders of Chivalry (Second series) (1927)			£5.00	£125.00
A2	C	3	Orders of Chivalry (unnumbered) (1927)			£10.00	£30.00
D	BW	25	*Racehorses — 1908-09 Winners (1909)		H.408	£26.00	£650.00
			LEON SOROKO, London				
—	U	6	Jubilee series (1935):				
			A Small size (75 x 41mm)			£200.00	
			B Large size (83 x 73mm)			£200.00	

Size	Print-ing	Number in set	BRITISH TOBACCO ISSUERS	Handbook reference	Price per card	Complete set
			SOUTH WALES TOB. MFG CO. LTD, Newport and London			
A	BW	? 91	Game of Numbers (c1910)		£80.00	—
A	U	25	*Views of London (c1910)	H.409	£30.00	£750.00
			SOUTH WALES TOBACCO CO. (1913) LTD, Newport			
D	C	30	*Army Pictures, Cartoons, etc. (c1916)	H.12	£160.00	—
			S.E. SOUTHGATE & SON, London			
A1	C	25	*Types of British and Colonial Troops (c1900)	H.76	£150.00	—
			T. SPALTON, Macclesfield			
D	C	30	*Army Pictures, cartoons etc (c1916)	H.12	£160.00	—
			SPIRO VALLERI & CO.			
A	BW	? 10	Noted Footballers (c1905)	H.772	£2200.00	—
			G. STANDLEY, Newbury			
—	U	12	'Manikin' Cards (77 x 49mm) (c1920)	H.481	£120.00	—
			A. & A.E. STAPLETON, Hastings			
—	U	12	*'Manikin' Cards (79 x 51mm) (c1920)	H.481	£120.00	—
			H. STEVENS & CO., Salisbury			
A1	C	20	*Dogs (1923)	H.211	£14.00	—
A1	U	25	*Zoo series (1926)	H.588	£7.50	—
			A. STEVENSON, Middleton			
A	U	50	War Portraits (1916)	H.86	£120.00	—
			ALBERT STOCKWELL, Porthcawl			
D	C	30	*Army Pictures, Cartoons, etc (c1916).	H.12	£160.00	—
			STRATHMORE TOBACCO CO. LTD, London			
—	U	25	British Aircraft (76 x 50mm) (1938)		£3.20	£80.00
			PETER STUYVESANT			
—	C	4	Discover the World (80 x 45mm) (1986)		£3.00	—
—	C	4	Skyline Competition (80 x 45mm) (1984)		£3.00	—
			TADDY & CO., London			
			32 page reference book — £4.50			
—	U	? 72	*Actresses — collotype (40 x 70mm) (c1897)	H.411	£130.00	—
A	C	25	*Actresses — with Flowers (c1900)		£90.00	—
A	BW	37	Admirals and Generals — The War (c1915):			
			A 25 Commoner Cards	H.412	£20.00	
			B 12 Scarce Cards (Nos 8, 9, 10, 13, 14, 17, 18, 21, 22, 23, 24, 25)		£42.00	
A	BW	25	Admirals and Generals — The War (South African printing) (c1915)	H.412	£40.00	—
A	C	25	Autographs (c1910)	H.413	£24.00	£600.00
A	C	20	Boer Leaders: (c1901)			
			A White back		£30.00	£600.00
			B Cream back		£30.00	—
A	C	50	British Medals and Decorations — Series 2 (c1905)		£16.00	£800.00
A	C	50	British Medals and Ribbons (c1903)		£16.00	£800.00
A	C	20	*Clowns and Circus Artistes (c1915)	H.414	£1000.00	—

Size	Printing	Number in set	BRITISH TOBACCO ISSUERS	Handbook reference	Price per card	Complete set
			TADDY & CO., London (continued)			
C2	C	30	Coronation series (1902):			
			A Grained card		£25.00	—
			B Smooth card		£25.00	—
A	BW	238	County Cricketers (c1907)	H.415	£75.00	—
A	C	50	Dogs (c1900)	H.487	£38.00	—
C	U	5	*English Royalty — collotype (c1898)	H.416	£1100.00	—
A	C	25	Famous Actors — Famous Actresses (c1903)		£24.00	£600.00
A	BW	50	Famous Horses and Cattle (c1912)		£130.00	—
A2	C	25	Famous Jockeys (c1905):	H.417		
			A Without frame line — blue title		£38.00	—
			B With frame line — brown title		£34.00	—
A	BW	50	Footballers (export issue) (c1906)	H.418	£120.00	—
A	C	25	'Heraldry' series (c1910)		£24.00	£600.00
A	C	25	Honours and Ribbons (c1910)		£30.00	£750.00
C	C	10	Klondyke series (c1900)		£80.00	£800.00
C	BW	60	Leading Members of the Legislative Assembly (export issue) (c1900)		£1000.00	—
A	C	25	*Natives of the World (c1900)	H.419	£80.00	—
A	C	25	Orders of Chivalry (c1911)	H.301	£25.00	£650.00
A	C	25	Orders of Chivalry, second series (c1912)	H.301	£30.00	£750.00
A	BW		Prominent Footballers — Grapnel and/or Imperial back:	H.420		
		? 596	A Without 'Myrtle Grove' footnote (1907)		£32.00	—
		? 403	B With 'Myrtle Grove' footnote (1908-9)		£32.00	—
A	BW	? 409	Prominent Footballers — London Mixture back (1913-14)	H.420	£60.00	—
—	C	20	*Royalty, Actresses, Soldiers (39 x 72mm) (c1898)	H.421	£260.00	—
A	C	25	'Royalty' series (c1908)		£20.00	£500.00
A	C	25	*Russo-Japanese War (1-25) (1904)		£25.00	£625.00
A	C	25	*Russo-Japanese War (26-50) (1904)		£30.00	£750.00
A	BW	16	South African Cricket Team 1907	H.422	£75.00	—
A	BW	26	South African Football Team 1906-07	H.423	£30.00	—
A	C	25	Sports and Pastimes — Series 1 (c1912)	H.225	£30.00	£750.00
A	C	25	Territorial Regiments — Series 1 (1908)		£26.00	£650.00
A	C	25	Thames series (c1903)		£38.00	£950.00
C	C	20	Victoria Cross Heroes (1-20) (c1900)		£80.00	—
C	C	20	Victoria Cross Heroes (21-40) (c1900)		£80.00	—
A	C	20	VC Heroes — Boer War (41-60) (1901):			
			A White back		£30.00	—
			B Toned back		£30.00	£600.00
A	C	20	VC Heroes — Boer War (61-80) (1901):			
			A White back		£30.00	—
			B Toned back		£30.00	£600.00
A	C	20	VC Heroes — Boer War (81-100) (1902):			
			A White back		£30.00	—
			B Toned back		£30.00	£600.00
A	C	25	Victoria Cross Heroes (101-125) (1905)		£75.00	—
A2	BW	2	*Wrestlers (c1910)	H.424	£320.00	—
			TADDY & CO., London and Grimsby			
—	C	8	Advertisement Cards, three sizes (1980)		75p	£6.00
A	C	26	Motor Cars, including checklist (1980):			
			A 'Clown Cigarettes' back		50p	£12.50
			B 'Myrtle Grove Cigarettes' back		50p	£12.50
A	C	26	Railway Locomotives including checklist (1980):			
			A 'Clown Cigarettes' back		80p	£20.00
			B 'Myrtle Grove Cigarettes' back		50p	£12.50

Size	Print-ing	Number in set	BRITISH TOBACCO ISSUERS	Handbook reference	Price per card	Complete set
			W. & M. TAYLOR, Dublin			
A	C	8	European War series (c1915):	H.129		
			A 'Bendigo Cigarettes' back		£50.00	—
			B 'Tipperary Cigarettes' back		£50.00	—
A	U	25	*War series — 'Muratti II' (c1915):	H.290		
			A 'Bendigo Cigarettes' back		£60.00	—
			B 'Tipperary Cigarettes' back		£24.00	£600.00
			TAYLOR WOOD, Newcastle			
C	C	18	Motor Cycle series (c1914)	H.469	£130.00	—
			TEOFANI & CO. LTD, London			
			(Cards mostly without Teofani's name.)			
C2	U	25	Aquarium Studies from the London Zoo ('Lucana' cards with green label added, inscribed 'Issued with Teofani Windsor Cigarettes') (c1925)	H.607	£12.00	—
D1	U	50	Cinema Celebrities (c1928):			
			A 'Presented with Broadway Novelties'		£5.50	—
			B 'Presented with these well-known ...'		£5.00	—
	C	25	Cinema Stars (c1928):	H.530		
			1 Anonymous printings:			
C2			A Small size		£7.50	—
			B Extra-large size (109 x 67mm)		£7.50	—
			2 Teofani printings:			
C2			A Small size — 'Issued with Blue Band Cigarettes		£7.50	—
C2			B Small size — 'Three Star Cigarettes' ...		£7.50	—
C2			C Small size — 'Three Star Magnums' ...		£7.50	—
C2			D Small Size — 'The Favourite Cigarettes'		£7.50	—
—			E Extra-large size (109 x 67mm) — 'Three Star Magnums'		£7.50	—
D	U	25	*Famous Boxers — 'Issued with The 'Favourite Magnums ...' (c1925)	H.721	£17.00	—
C2	P	32	Famous British Ships and Officers — 'Issued with these High Grade Cigarettes' (1934)		£5.00	£160.00
B1	U	50	Famous Racecourses ('Lucana' cards with mauve label added, inscribed 'Issued with The Favourite Cigarettes' (c1926)	H.608	£22.00	—
A	U	? 24	Famous Racehorses (c1925)	H.609	£15.00	—
—	BW	12	*Film Actors and Actresses (56 x 31mm) (plain back) (1936)	H.618	£1.50	£18.00
C2	C	20	Great Inventors (c1924)	H.213	£5.00	—
A	C	20	*Head Dresses of Various Nations (plain back) (c1925)		£16.00	—
—	BW	12	*London Views (57 x 31mm) (c1936):	H.620		
			A Plain back		50p	£6.00
			B Back 'Our Agent Raoul Savon' with brand name:			
			i 'Big Gun' back		£5.00	—
			ii 'Fine' back		£5.00	—
			iii 'Hudavend' back		£5.00	—
			iv 'K.O.G.' back		£5.00	—
			v 'Lucana 66' back		£5.00	—
			vi 'Lucana C.T.' back		£5.00	—
			vii 'Palace' back		£5.00	—
			viii 'Pharoah's' back		£5.00	—
			ix 'Teofani No. 1' back		£5.00	—
			x 'Three Dogs' back		£5.00	—
			xi 'Three Star' back		£5.00	—
			xii 'West End' back		£5.00	—

Size	Printing	Number in set	BRITISH TOBACCO ISSUERS	Handbook reference	Price per card	Complete set
			TEOFANI & CO. LTD, London (continued)			
D2	U	48	Modern Movie Stars and Cinema Celebrities (1934)	H.569	£1.20	£60.00
A	C	50	*Natives in Costume (plain back) (c1925)		£20.00	—
A2	C	24	Past and Present — Series A — The Army (1938):			
			A With framelines		£2.00	£50.00
			B Without framelines		£1.80	£45.00
A2	C	24	Past and Present — Series B — Weapons of War (1938)		£1.00	£25.00
A2	C	4	Past and Present — Series C — Transport (1940) ...	H.679	£6.00	—
C	U	50	Public Schools and Colleges — 'Issued with these Fine Cigarettes' (c1924)	H.575	£3.60	—
D	C	50	Ships and Their Flags — 'Issued with these well-known cigarettes' (c1925)	GP.124	£4.00	£200.00
A	C	25	Sports and Pastimes Series I — 'Smoke these cigarettes always' (c1925)	H.225	£16.00	—
—	P	22	*Teofani Gems I — Series of 22 (53 x 35mm) (plain back) (c1925)		£3.00	—
—	P	28	*Teofani Gems II — Series of 28 (53 x 35mm) (plain back) (c1925)		£1.20	—
—	P	36	*Teofani Gems III — Series of 36 (53 x 35mm) (plain back) (c1925)		£3.00	—
—	P	2	Teofani Gems — unnumbered (53 x 35mm) (plain back) (c1925)		£3.00	£6.00
A2	P	36	Views of the British Empire — 'Issued with these Famous Cigarettes' (c1928):			
			A Front in black and white		£1.25	£45.00
			B Front in light brown		£1.25	£45.00
C	U	50	Views of London — 'Issued with these World Famous Cigarettes' (c1925)	H.577	£4.00	—
C2	U	24	Well-Known Racehorses (c1924)	H.609	£15.00	—
A	C	50	*World's Smokers (plain back) (c1925)		£20.00	—
	U	50	Zoological Studies (c1924):	H.578		
C			A Standard Size		£4.00	—
B1			B Large Size		£7.00	—
OVERSEAS ISSUE						
H1	BW	50	Teofani's Icelandic Employees (1930)		£7.00	—
H	P	50	Theatre Artistes and Scenes (c1930)		£25.00	—
			TETLEY & SONS LTD, Leeds			
A2	C	1	*'The Allies' (grouped flags) (c1915)	H.425	—	£1400.00
A	U	50	War Portraits (c1916)	H.86	£120.00	—
D	C	25	World's Coinage (1914)	H.398	£70.00	—
			THEMANS & CO., Manchester			
A	—	55	Dominoes (Sunspot brand issue) (c1914)		£80.00	—
C	C	18	Motor Cycle series (c1914)	H.469	£110.00	—
A	C	? 2	Riddles and Anecdotes (c1913)	H.426	£1200.00	—
A	U	50	*War Portraits (1916)	H.86	£90.00	—
—	C	14	War Posters (63 x 41 mm) (c1916)	H.486	£425.00	—

SILKS

Anonymous silks with blue border, plain board backing. Reported also to have been issued with firm's name rubber stamped on backing.

—	C		*Miscellaneous Subjects (c1915):	H.500		
		? 8	Series B1 — Flags (50 x 66mm)		£10.00	—
		? 3	Series B2 — Flags (50 x 66mm)		£10.00	—
		? 12	Series B3 — Regimental Badges (50 x 66mm) ...		£8.00	—

Size	Print-ing	Number in set	BRITISH TOBACCO ISSUERS	Handbook reference	Price per card	Complete set

THEMANS & CO., Manchester (continued)

Silks, *Miscellaneous Subjects (c1915) (continued)

		? 12	Series B4 — Ship's Badges (50 x 66mm)		£20.00	—
		? 7	Series B5 — British Views and Scenes (50 x 66mm)		£20.00	—
		? 48	Series B6 — Film Stars (50 x 66mm)		£10.00	—
		? 2	Series C1 — Flags (65 x 55mm)		£12.00	—
		? 3	Series C2 — Flags (70 x 65mm)		£12.00	—
		? 4	Series C3 — Regimental Badges (64 x 77mm)		£10.00	—
		? 2	Series C4 — Crests of Warships (64 x 77mm)		£10.00	—
		? 1	Series D1 — Royal Standard (138 x 89mm)		£15.00	—
		? 1	Series D2 — Shield of Flags (138 x 89mm)		£15.00	—
		? 1	Series D3 — Regimental Badge (138 x 89mm)		£15.00	—
		? 1	Series D5 — British Views and Scenes (138 x 89mm)		£20.00	—
		? 14	Series D6 — Film Stars (138 x 89mm)		£10.00	—

THOMSON & PORTEOUS, Edinburgh

D2	C	50	Arms of British Towns (c1905)		£20.00	—
A	BW	25	*Boer War Celebrities — 'STEW' (c1901)	H.105	£75.00	—
A	C	20	European War series (c1915)	H.129	£20.00	£400.00
A	C	25	*Shadowgraphs (c1905)	H.44	£50.00	—
A	C	41	VC Heroes (c1915):	H.427		
			A Front with firm's name at base:			
			i 40 Different (minus No. 6)		£16.00	£640.00
			ii Number 6		—	£70.00
			B Front with firm's name at top		£60.00	—
			C Without firm's name, with 'Pure Virginia Cigarettes		£16.00	£650.00

TOBACCO SUPPLY SYNDICATE, London (T.S.S.)

D	C	24	*Nautical Expressions (c1900)	H.174	£120.00	—

TOM NODDY

—	C	12	Children of the Year Series (140 x 90mm) (1904)		£100.00	—

TURKISH MONOPOLY CIGARETTE CO. LTD

—	C	? 16	*Scenes from the Boer War (113 x 68mm, folded in three) (c1901)	H.478	£600.00	—

UNITED KINGDOM TOBACCO CO., London

A	C	50	Aircraft — 'The Greys Cigarettes' (1938)	GP.5	£1.80	£90.00
—	U	48	Beautiful Britain — 'The Greys Cigarettes' (140 x 90mm) (1929)	GP.406	£1.80	£90.00
—	U	48	Beautiful Britain — Second series 'The Greys Cigarettes' (140 x 90mm) (1929)	GP.407	£1.60	£80.00
A2	C	25	British Orders of Chivalry and Valour — 'The Greys Cigarettes' (1936)	GP.43	£1.80	£45.00
A	U	24	Chinese Scenes (1933)		75p	£18.00
A2	U	32	Cinema Stars — Set 4 (1933)	GP.53	£1.90	£60.00
A2	U	50	Cinema Stars — Set 7 (1934):	GP.703		
			A Anonymous back		£2.60	£130.00
			B Back with firm's name		£1.80	£90.00
A2	C	36	Officers Full Dress (1936)		£2.20	£80.00
A2	C	36	Soldiers of the King — 'The Greys Cigarettes' (1937)	GP.127	£2.50	£90.00

Size	Printing	Number in set	BRITISH TOBACCO ISSUERS	Handbook reference	Price per card	Complete set
			UNITED SERVICES MANUFACTURING CO. LTD, London			
A1	C	50	Ancient Warriors (1938)		£2.60	£130.00
A	C	25	Ancient Warriors (1954)		£5.00	—
A1	BW	50	Bathing Belles (1939)	H.592	£1.00	£50.00
D	U	100	Interesting Personalities (1935)		£3.50	—
D	U	50	Popular Footballers (1936)		£6.50	—
D	U	50	Popular Screen Stars (1937)		£4.00	—
			UNITED TOBACCONISTS' ASSOCIATION LTD			
A	C	10	*Actresses — 'MUTA' (c1900)	H.265	£250.00	—
A2	C	12	*Pretty Girl Series 'RASH' (c1900)	H.8	£550.00	—
			WALKER'S TOBACCO CO. LTD, Liverpool			
C	P	60	*British Beauty Spots (c1925)	H.553	£20.00	—
A	BW	28	*Dominoes 'Old Monk' issue (1908)		£65.00	—
D2	U	28	*Dominoes 'W.T.C.' Monogram back (c1925)	H.535-2	£6.00	—
A2	P	32	Film Stars — 'Tatley's Cigarettes' (1936)	H.623	—	£100.00
			31 Different (minus Lombard)		£1.80	£55.00
A2	P	48	*Film Stars — Walker's name at base (1937)	H.623	£5.00	—
			WALTERS TOBACCO CO. LTD, London			
B	U	6	Angling Information (wording only) (1939)	H.624	£1.50	£9.00
			E.T. WATERMAN, Coventry			
D	C	30	*Army Pictures, Cartoons, etc. (1916)	H.12	£160.00	—
			WEBB & RASSELL, Reigate			
A	U	50	War Portraits (1916)	H.86	£120.00	—
			H.C. WEBSTER (Q.V. Cigars)			
—	BW	? 7	*Barnum and Bailey's Circus (60 x 42mm) (c1900)	H.428	£400.00	—
			HENRY WELFARE & CO., London			
D	P	? 22	Prominent Politicians (c1911)	H.429	£80.00	—

WESTMINSTER TOBACCO CO. LTD, London

Inscribed 'Issued by the Successors in the United Kingdom to the Westminster Tobacco Co., Ltd.' For other issues without the above see Overseas Issues.

Size	Printing	Number in set			Price	Complete
A2	P	36	Australia — 'First Series' (1932)		27p	£10.00
A2	P	36	Australia, Second Series, plain back, unissued. (1933)	H.680	27p	£10.00
A2	P	48	British Royal and Ancient Buildings (1925):			
			A Unnumbered, without descriptive text		90p	£45.00
			B Numbered, with descriptive text		£1.20	£60.00
A2	P	48	British Royal and Ancient Buildings — 'A Second Series ...' (1926)		50p	£25.00
A2	P	36	Canada — 'First Series' (1927)		70p	£25.00
A2	P	36	Canada — 'Second Series' (1928)		70p	£25.00
A2	P	48	Indian Empire — 'First Series' (1926)		50p	£25.00
A2	P	48	Indian Empire — 'Second Series' (1927)		50p	£25.00
A2	P	36	New Zealand — 'First Series' (1929)		50p	£18.00
A2	P	36	New Zealand — 'Second Series' (1930)		27p	£10.00
A2	P	36	South Africa — 'First Series' (1930)		75p	£27.00
A2	P	36	South Africa — 'Second Series' (1931)		75p	£27.00

Size	Print-ing	Number in set	BRITISH TOBACCO ISSUERS	Handbook reference	Price per card	Complete set

WESTMINSTER TOBACCO CO. LTD, London (continued)

OVERSEAS ISSUES

Size	Printing	Number in set	Title	Ref	Price per card	Complete set
—	BW	332	Adamsons Oplevelser (68 x 50mm) (1930)		£20.00	—
—	P	50	Beauties (63 x 48mm) (1924)		£3.20	—
—	P	100	Beautiful Women (65 x 49mm) (1915)		£3.20	—
—	C	50	Birds, Beasts and Fishes (cut-outs) (63 x 48mm) (1923)		£3.50	—
			British Beauties (1915):			
—	CP	102	A Coloured (60 x 41mm)		£4.00	—
—	P	86	B Uncoloured (57 x 41mm)		£4.00	—
A2	P	48	British Royal and Ancient Buildings (1925)		£1.20	£60.00
—	C	50	Butterflies and Moths (70 x 42mm) (1920)		£4.00	—
A2	P	36	Canada 1st series (1926)		£1.10	£40.00
A2	P	36	Canada 2nd series (1928)		£1.10	£40.00
D2	U	30	Celebrated Actresses (1921)		£6.00	—
—	C	25	Champion Dogs (anonymous back) (95 x 67mm) (1934)		£5.00	—
A	BW	100	Cinema Artistes green back (1929-33)		£3.50	—
A	BW	50	Cinema Artistes grey back (1929-33)		£3.50	—
A	C	48	Cinema Celebrities (1935)		£3.50	—
A	P	50	Cinema Stars (1926)		£3.50	—
—	P	50	Cinema Stars (63 x 48mm) (1930)		£3.50	—
—	CP	50	Cinema Stars (63 x 48mm) (1930)		£3.50	—
—	C	27	Dancing Girls (63 x 44mm) (1917)		£6.50	—
A	C	50	Do You Know (1922)		£2.50	—
D2	C	24	Fairy Tale (booklets) (1926)		£10.00	—
—	C	100	Famous Beauties (64 x 48mm) (1916):			
			A Captions in brown		£2.50	—
			B Captions in blue		£2.80	—
—	U	35	Famous Fighting Ships of Various Nations (138 x 92mm) (c1910)		£60.00	—
		52	Film Favourites (64 x 48mm) (1927):			
—	P		A Uncoloured		£4.00	—
—	CP		B Coloured		£4.00	—
—	U	50	Film Personalities (64 x 48mm) (1931)		£5.00	—
—	C	50	Garden Flowers of the World (70 x 50mm) (1917)		£3.50	—
A1	U	40	The Great War Celebrities (1914)		£11.00	—
A2	P	48	Indian Empire 1st series (1925)		£1.10	£55.00
A2	P	48	Indian Empire 2nd series (1926)		£1.10	£55.00
—	P	50	Islenzkar Eimskipamyndir (Trawlers) (77 x 52mm) (1931)		£3.50	—
—	P	50	Islenzkar Landslagmyndir (Views) (77 x 52mm) (1928)		£2.50	—
—	P	50	Islenzkar Landslagmyndir 2nd series (Views) (77 x 52mm) (1929)		£2.50	—
A1	C	40	Merrie England Studies (1914)		£9.00	—
A	BW	36	Modern Beauties (1938)		£3.50	—
—	CP	52	Movie Stars (63 x 48mm) (1925)		£4.00	—
A2	P	36	New Zealand 1st series (1928)		£1.25	£42.00
A2	P	36	New Zealand 2nd series (1929)		£1.25	£42.00
—	C	53	Playing Cards (63 x 41mm) (1934):			
			A With Exchange Scheme		£3.00	—
			B Without Exchange Scheme		£3.00	—
—	C	55	Playing Cards (72 x 49mm) (1934):			
			A Blue back		£2.00	—
			B Red back		£2.00	—
A	P	50	Popular Film Stars (1926)		£3.50	—
A2	P	36	South Africa 1st series (1928)		£1.10	£40.00
A2	P	36	South Africa 2nd series (1928)		£1.10	£40.00

Size	Printing	Number in set	BRITISH TOBACCO ISSUERS	Handbook reference	Price per card	Complete set

WESTMINSTER TOBACCO CO. LTD, London (Overseas Issues continued)

Size	Printing	Number in set	Description	Handbook ref	Price per card	Complete set
—	C	49	South African Succulents (72 x 50mm) (1936)		35p	£17.50
—	C	100	Stage and Cinema Stars, captions in grey (63 x 47mm) (1921)		£2.50	—
—	C	100	Stage and Cinema Stars, captions in black (63 x 47mm) (1921)		£3.25	—
—	CP	50	Stars of Filmland (63 x 48mm) (1927):			
			A 'Westminster' lettering brown on white		£4.00	—
			B 'Westminster' lettering white on brown		£4.00	—
C2	C	50	Steamships of the World (1920)		£13.00	—
—	C	50	Uniforms of All Ages (69 x 47mm) (1917)		£14.00	—
A	P	50	Views of Malaya (1930)		£7.00	—
D	C	25	Wireless (1923)		£5.00	—
—	C	50	Women of Nations (70 x 49mm) (1922)		£6.00	—
A	BW	50	The World of Tomorrow (1938)		£1.50	£75.00

SILK ISSUES

—	C	50	Garden Flowers of the World (82 x 51mm) (c1914)		£6.00	—
—	C	24	Miniature Rugs (93 x 52mm) (1924)		£20.00	—

WHALE & CO.

A	C	? 12	Conundrums (c1900)	H.232	£450.00	—

M. WHITE & CO., London

—	BW	20	*Actresses — 'BLARM' (c1900)	H.23	£220.00	—

WHITFIELD'S, Walsall

D	C	30	*Army Pictures, Cartoons etc. (c1916)	H.12	£160.00	—

WHITFORD & SONS, Evesham

C2	C	20	*Inventors series (c1924)	H.213	£45.00	—

WHOLESALE TOBACCO SUPPLY CO., London ('Hawser' Cigarettes)

A	C	25	Armies of the World (c1902)	H.43	£80.00	—
A	C	40	Army Pictures (c1902)	H.69	£110.00	—

P. WHYTE, England

D	C	30	*Army Pictures, Cartoons, etc. (1916)	H.12	£160.00	—

W. WILLIAMS & CO., Chester

A	U	30	Aristocrats of the Turf (c1925)	H.554	£11.00	£330.00
A	U	36	Aristocrats of the Turf 2nd series (c1925)	H.554	£16.00	—
A	BW	25	*Boer War Celebrities 'STEW' (c1901)	H.105	£90.00	—
A	C	25	Boxing (c1924)	H.311	£13.00	£325.00
A	C	50	Interesting Buildings (c1910)	H.70	£16.00	£800.00
A	BW	12	Views of Chester (c1910)	H.430	£40.00	£480.00
A	BW	12	Views of Chester — As It Was (c1910):	H.430		
			A Toned card		£40.00	£480.00
			B Bleuté card		£40.00	—

W.D. & H.O. WILLS, Bristol

212 page reference book The Card Issues of W.D. & H.O. Wills (2011 Edition)— £25.00

NOTE: The Imperial Tobacco Co. clause (I.T.C. clause) appears on Home issues dated between 1902 and 1940, excluding those issued in the Channel Islands. For series without I.T.C. clause, see the Overseas section.

A	U		*Actresses — collotype (c1894):			
		25	A 'Wills' Cigarettes'	W.2-1	£100.00	—
		43	B 'Wills's Cigarettes'	W.2-2	£100.00	—
A	C	20	*Actresses, brown type-set back (c1895)	W.3-A	£1400.00	—
A	C	52	*Actresses, brown scroll back, with PC inset (c1898)	W.3-C	£20.00	—

Size	Print-ing	Number in set	BRITISH TOBACCO ISSUERS	Handbook reference	Price per card	Complete set
			W.D. & H.O. WILLS, Bristol (continued)			
A	C	52	*Actresses, grey scroll back (c1897):	W.3-D		
			A Without PC inset		£20.00	—
			B With PC inset		£20.00	—
A	U		*Actresses and Beauties — collotype, 'Three Castles' and 'Firefly' front (c1895):	W.2-4		
		? 125	Actresses		£100.00	—
		? 33	Beauties		£100.00	—
A	C		*Advertisement Cards:	W.1		
		? 4	1888 issue (cigarette packets)		£2500.00	—
		? 1	1889-90 issue (serving maid)		£900.00	—
		? 11	1890-93 issues (tobacco packings)		£1200.00	—
		? 3	1893 issue (showcards):			
			A 'Autumn Gold Cigarettes' back		£350.00	—
			B 'Best Bird's Eye Cigarettes' back		£350.00	—
			C 'Eothen Cigarettes' back		£350.00	—
			D 'Passing Clouds' back		£350.00	—
			E 'Pole Star Cigarettes' back		£350.00	—
			F 'Sahara Cigarettes' back		£350.00	—
			G 'The Three Castles Cigarettes' back		£350.00	—
		? 6	1893-94 issue (posters)		£350.00	—
B	BW	1	Advertisement Card — Wants List (1935)		—	75p
—	C	4	*Advertisement Postcards of Wills Packings (139 x 88mm) (1902)	W.398	£150.00	—
A	C		Air Raid Precautions (1938):	W.123		
		50	A Home issue — adhesive back, with I.T.C. clause		90p	£45.00
			Album (with price)		—	£25.00
		40	B Irish issue — non-adhesive back		£1.80	—
		50	C Channel Islands issue – adhesive back, without I.T.C. clause		£1.30	£65.00
A	C	50	Allied Army Leaders (1917)	W.35	£1.80	£90.00
A	C	50	Alpine Flowers (1913)		90p	£45.00
A	C	48	Animalloys (sectional) (1934)	W.124	40p	£20.00
A	C	50	*Animals and Birds in Fancy Costumes (c1896)	W.4	£50.00	—
B	C	25	Animals and Their Furs (1929)		£2.00	£50.00
A	C	50	Arms of the Bishopric (1907)		£1.00	£50.00
A	C	50	Arms of the British Empire (1910)	W.40	80p	£40.00
B	C	25	Arms of the British Empire — 'First Series' (1931)		£1.80	£45.00
B	C	25	Arms of the British Empire — 'Second Series' (1932)		£1.80	£45.00
A	C	50	Arms of Companies (1913)		90p	£45.00
A	C	50	Arms of Foreign Cities (1912):	W.42		
			A White card		80p	£40.00
			B Cream card		90p	—
			C As A, with 'Mark'		£1.00	—
B	C	42	Arms of Oxford and Cambridge Colleges (1922)		£1.40	£60.00
B	C	25	Arms of Public Schools — '1st Series' (1933)		£2.20	£55.00
B	C	25	Arms of Public Schools — '2nd Series' (1934)		£2.20	£55.00
B	C	25	Arms of Universities (1923)		£1.60	£40.00
A	C	50	Association Footballers 'Frameline' back (1935):	W.134		
			A Home issue – with I.T.C. clause		£1.30	£65.00
			Album		—	£25.00
			B Channel Islands issue – without I.T.C. clause		£3.00	£150.00
A	C	50	Association Footballers — 'No frameline' back (1939):	W.135		
			A Home issue — adhesive back		£1.30	£65.00
			B Irish issue — non-adhesive back		£2.50	£125.00
B	C	25	Auction Bridge (1926)		£2.40	£60.00
A	C	50	Aviation (1910)	W.46	£2.60	£130.00

Size	Print-ing	Number in set	BRITISH TOBACCO ISSUERS	Handbook reference	Price per card	Complete set
			W.D. & H.O. WILLS, Bristol (continued)			
A	U	? 20	*Beauties — collotype (c1894):	W.2-3		
			A 'W.D. & H.O. Wills' Cigarettes'		£190.00	—
			B 'Firefly' Cigarettes		£190.00	—
A1	C	? 10	*Beauties ('Girl Studies'), type-set back (c1895)	W.3-B	£1400.00	—
A	C		*Beauties, brown backs (c1897):	W.3-E		
		52	A With PC inset — scroll back		£25.00	—
		10	B As A, 10 additional pictures		£75.00	—
		? 53	C 'Wills' Cigarettes' front, scroll back		£200.00	—
		? 29	D 'Wills' Cigarettes' front, type-set back		£300.00	—
K	C	52	*Beauties, miniature cards, PC inset, grey scroll back (c1896)	W.3-F	£30.00	—
B	C	25	Beautiful Homes (1930)		£2.60	£65.00
A	C	50	Billiards (1909)		£2.20	£110.00
—	—	10	Boer War Medallions (c1901) (16mm Diameter)	W.18	£120.00	—
A	C	50	*Borough Arms (1-50):			
			A Scroll back, unnumbered (1904)	W.19	£1.20	£60.00
			B Scroll back, numbered on front (1904)		£10.00	—
			C Descriptive back, numbered on back (1905)		£1.20	£60.00
			D 2nd Edition — 1-50 (1906)		£1.10	£55.00
A	C	50	*Borough Arms (51-100):	W.19		
			A 2nd Series (1905)		80p	£40.00
			B 2nd Edition, 51-100 (1906)		80p	£40.00
A	C	50	*Borough Arms (101-150):	W.19		
			A 3rd Series, Album clause in grey (1905)		£1.00	£50.00
			B 3rd Series, Album clause in red (1905)		80p	£40.00
			C 2nd Edition, 101-150 (1906)		80p	£40.00
A	C	50	*Borough Arms (151-200), 4th series (1905)	W.19	80p	£40.00
A	C	24	*Britain's Part in the War (1917)		£1.20	£30.00
A	C	50	British Birds (1917)		£1.50	£75.00
A	C	50	British Butterflies (1927)	W.156	£1.10	£55.00
B	C	25	British Castles (1925)		£3.00	£75.00
—	BW	1	British Commanders in the Transvaal War 1899-1900 (booklet) (206 x 114mm) (1900):	W.511		
			A With 'Bristol & London' on front		—	£120.00
			B Without 'Bristol & London' on front		—	£120.00
—	C	12	The British Empire (133 x 101mm) (c1930)		£10.00	—
B	C	25	British School of Painting (1927)		£1.40	£35.00
—	BW	48	British Sporting Personalities (76 x 52mm) (1937)		£1.00	£50.00
A	C	50	Builders of the Empire (1898):	W.20		
			A White card		£8.50	£425.00
			B Cream card		£8.50	£425.00
B	C	40	Butterflies and Moths (1938)		90p	£36.00
A	C	1	*Calendar for 1911 (1910)		—	£15.00
A	C	1	*Calendar for 1912 (1911)		—	£10.00
B	C	25	Cathedrals (1933)		£5.00	£125.00
A	C	? 12	Celebrated Painters (c1917) (Unissued Plain Backs)	W.389	£250.00	—
B	U	25	Celebrated Pictures (1916):	W.165		
			A Deep brown back		£2.00	£50.00
			B Yellow-brown back		£1.80	£45.00
B	U	25	Celebrated Pictures, 2nd Series (1916)	W.166	£2.20	£55.00
A	C	50	Celebrated Ships (1911)		£1.30	£65.00
A	C	25	Cinema Stars — 'First Series' (1928)		£1.60	£40.00
A	C	25	Cinema Stars — 'Second Series' (1928)		£1.60	£40.00
A	U	50	Cinema Stars — 'Third Series' (1931)		£2.20	£110.00
—	C	12	Cities of Britain (133 x 101mm) (c1930)		£12.00	—
A	C	60	Coronation Series (1902):	W.6		
			A 2mm wide arrow at side of text, back		£7.00	£420.00
			B 1mm narrow arrow at side of text, back		£7.00	£420.00

Size	Print-ing	Number in set	BRITISH TOBACCO ISSUERS	Handbook reference	Price per card	Complete set
			W.D. & H.O. WILLS, Bristol (continued)			
A	C	50	The Coronation Series (1911)		£1.10	£55.00
A	C	50	*Cricketers (1896)	W.7	£120.00	—
A	C		Cricketers Series, 1901:	W.8		
		50	A With Vignette		£26.00	—
		25	B Without Vignette		£26.00	—
A	C		Cricketers (1908):	W.58		
		25	A Numbered 1-25 'Wills' S' at top front		£10.00	£250.00
		50	B Numbered 1-50 'Wills's' at top front:			
			1 Numbers 1 to 25		£10.00	£250.00
			2 Numbers 26 to 50		£8.00	£200.00
A	C	50	Cricketers, 1928 (1928)	W.178	£1.80	£90.00
A	C	50	Cricketers — '2nd Series' (1929)		£1.80	£90.00
B	C	25	Dogs (1914)		£3.60	£90.00
B	C	25	Dogs, 2nd Series (1915)		£3.60	£90.00
A	C	50	Dogs — Light backgrounds (1937):	W.187		
			A Home issue — adhesive back, with I.T.C. clause		60p	£30.00
			Album		—	£25.00
			B Irish issue — non-adhesive back		£1.50	£75.00
			C Channel Islands issue – adhesive back, without I.T.C. clause		£1.40	£70.00
A	C		*Double Meaning (1898):	W.5		
		50	A Without PC inset		£10.00	£500.00
		52	B With PC inset		£10.00	£520.00
A	C	50	Do You Know 'A Series of 50' (1922)	W.188	50p	£25.00
A	C	50	Do You Know '2nd Series of 50' (1924)	W.189	50p	£25.00
A	C	50	Do You Know '3rd Series of 50' (1926)	W.190	50p	£25.00
A	C	50	Do You Know '4th Series of 50' (1933)	W.191	60p	£30.00
A	C	50	Engineering Wonders (1927)	W.193	£1.00	£50.00
A	C	50	English Period Costumes (1929)		£1.00	£50.00
B	C	25	English Period Costumes (1927)	W.195	£2.60	£65.00
B	C	40	Famous British Authors (1937)		£1.75	£70.00
B	C	30	Famous British Liners — 'First Series' (1934)		£5.50	—
B	C	30	Famous British Liners — 'Second Series' (1935) ...		£4.00	£120.00
B	C	25	Famous Golfers (1930)		£20.00	—
A	C	50	Famous Inventions (1915)	W.60	£1.00	£50.00
A	C		A Famous Picture — (sectional):			
		48	Series No. 1 — 'Between Two Fires' (1930) ...	W.207	40p	£20.00
		48	Series No. 2 — 'The Boyhood of Raleigh' (1930)	W.208	40p	£20.00
		48	Series No. 3 — 'Mother and Son' (1931)	W.209	40p	£20.00
		48	'The Toast' (1931):	W.210		
			A Home issue — Series No. 4		50p	£24.00
			B Irish issue — Series No. 1		£2.00	—
		48	'The Laughing Cavalier' (1931):	W.211		
			A Home issue — Series No. 5:			
			1 No stop after numeral		50p	£24.00
			2 Full stop after numeral		50p	£24.00
			B Irish issue — Series No. 2		£2.00	—
		49	Series No. 6 — 'And When did you Last See Your Father?' (1932)	W.212	£1.10	£55.00
A	C	50	First Aid:			
			A Without Album Clause (1913)		£1.50	£75.00
			B With Album Clause (1915)		£1.50	£75.00
A	C	50	Fish & Bait (1910)	W.62	£3.00	£150.00
—	C	6	Flags of the Allies (shaped) (1915)	W.67	£16.00	—
A	C	25	Flags of the Empire (1926)	W.215	£1.60	£40.00
A	C	25	Flags of the Empire — '2nd Series' (1929)		£1.20	£30.00

Size	Print-ing	Number in set	BRITISH TOBACCO ISSUERS	Handbook reference	Price per card	Complete set
			W.D. & H.O. WILLS, Bristol (continued)			
A	C	50	Flower Culture in Pots (1925)	W.217	50p	£25.00
B	C	30	Flowering Shrubs (1935)		£1.20	£36.00
A	C	50	Flowering Trees and Shrubs (1924)		80p	£40.00
A	U	66	*Football Series (1902)	W.22	£13.00	—
A	C	50	Garden Flowers (1933)	W.225	70p	£35.00
A	C	50	Garden Flowers by Richard Sudell (1939):	W.222		
			A Home issue – Album offer with price		25p	£12.50
			B Irish issue – Album offer without price		60p	£30.00
			C Channel Islands issue – no Album offer		60p	£30.00
B	C	40	Garden Flowers — New Varieties — 'A Series' (1938)		60p	£24.00
B	C	40	Garden Flowers — New Varieties — '2nd Series' (1939)		50p	£20.00
A	C	50	Garden Hints (1938):	W.226		
			A Home issue — Album offer with price		25p	£12.50
			B Irish issue — Album offer without price		60p	£30.00
			C Channel Islands issue – no Album offer		60p	£30.00
A	C	50	Garden Life (1914)	W.69	70p	£35.00
A	C	50	Gardening Hints (1923)	W.227	40p	£20.00
A	C	50	Gems of Belgian Architecture (1915)		70p	£35.00
A	C	50	Gems of French Architecture (1917):			
			A White card		£1.40	£70.00
			B Bleuté card		£1.60	—
			C Rough brown card		£1.60	—
A	P	50	Gems of Italian Architecture (1917 unissued). See Reprint section	W.388		
A	C	50	Gems of Russian Architecture (1916)		70p	£35.00
B	C	25	Golfing (1924)		£9.00	—
—	C	32	Happy Families (non-insert) (91 x 63mm) (c1935)		£5.00	—
B	C	25	Heraldic Signs and Their Origin (1925)	W.230	£2.00	£50.00
A	C	50	Historic Events (1912)	W.74	£1.20	£60.00
A2	P	54	Homeland Events (1932)	W.232	70p	£38.00
A	C	50	Household Hints (1927)	W.234	60p	£30.00
A	C	50	Household Hints — '2nd Series' (1930)		60p	£30.00
A	C	50	Household Hints (1936):	W.236		
			A Home issue — Album offer with price		25p	£12.50
			B Irish issue — Album offer without price		60p	£30.00
			C Channel Islands issue – no Album offer		60p	£30.00
A	BW	50	Hurlers (1927)		£1.80	£90.00
—	C	12	Industries of Britain (133 x 101mm) (c1930)		£12.00	—
A	C	25	Irish Beauty Spots (1929)		£5.00	—
A	C	25	Irish Holiday Resorts (1930)		£5.00	—
A	C	50	Irish Industries (1937):			
			A Back 'This surface is adhesive ...'		£3.20	—
			B Back 'Ask your retailer ...'		£1.20	£60.00
A	U	25	Irish Rugby Internationals (1928)		£14.00	—
A	C	50	Irish Sportsmen (1935)		£6.00	—
			Album		—	£40.00
A	C	50	Japanese Series (c1900)	W.23	£40.00	—
B	C	40	The King's Art Treasures (1938)		35p	£14.00
	C		*Kings and Queens:	W.9		
A1		50	A Short card (1897):			
			i Grey back, thin card		£7.00	£350.00
			ii Grey back, thick card		£7.00	£350.00
			iii Brown back		£10.00	—

Size	Print-ing	Number in set	BRITISH TOBACCO ISSUERS	Handbook reference	Price per card	Complete set
			W.D. & H.O. WILLS, Bristol (continued)			
			*Kings and Queens (continued)			
A			B Standard size card (1902):			
		51	i Blue-grey back with 5 substitute titles:			
			50 different ...		£7.00	£350.00
			Edward The Martyr ...		—	£50.00
		50	ii Grey back, different design, thinner card		£14.00	—
B	C	25	Lawn Tennis, 1931 (1931) ...		£10.00	—
A	C	50	Life in the Hedgerow (c1950) (unissued) ...		50p	£25.00
A	C	50	Life in the Royal Navy (1939):	W.253		
			A Home issue – with Album offer ...		40p	£20.00
			Album ...		—	£25.00
			B Channel Islands issue – without Album offer ...		50p	£25.00
A	C	50	Life in the Tree Tops (1925) ...	W.254	50p	£25.00
A	C	50	Life of King Edward VIII (1936) (unissued) ...		—	£1200.00
A	C		*Locomotive Engines and Rolling Stock:	W.24		
		50	A Without I.T.C. clause (1901) ...		£9.00	£450.00
		7	B As A, 7 additional cards (1901) ...		£30.00	—
		50	C With I.T.C. clause (1902) ...		£9.00	£450.00
A	C	50	Lucky Charms (1923) ...	W.256	60p	£30.00
A	C	50	*Medals (1902):	W.25		
			A White card ...		£3.20	£160.00
			B Toned card ...		£3.20	£160.00
A	C	50	Merchant Ships of the World (1924) ...	W.257	£1.40	£70.00
A	C	50	Military Motors (1916):			
			A Without 'Passed for ... Press Bureau' ...		£1.80	£90.00
			B With 'Passed for ... Press Bureau' ...		£1.80	£90.00
K2	C	53	*Miniature Playing Cards (1932-34):	W.260		
			A Home issue, blue back — 'narrow 52'			
			(2 printings) ...		50p	£25.00
			B Home issue, blue back — 'wide 52' (4 printings)		50p	£25.00
			C Home issue, pink back (3 printings) ...		60p	—
			D Irish issue, blue back (7 printings) ...		£1.00	—
A	C	50	Mining (1916) ...	W.81	£1.50	£75.00
B	C	25	Modern Architecture (1931) ...		£1.60	£40.00
B	U	30	Modern British Sculpture (1928) ...		£1.30	£40.00
A	C	50	Musical Celebrities (1911) ...	W.83	£2.50	£125.00
A	C	50	Musical Celebrities — Second Series (1916):	W.83		
			Set of 50 with 8 substituted cards ...		£3.50	£175.00
			8 original cards (later substituted) ...		£350.00	—
A	C	25	*National Costumes (c1895) ...	W.26	£250.00	—
A	C	? 8	*National Types (c1893) ...	W.396	£1500.00	—
A	C	50	Naval Dress & Badges (1909) ...	W.84	£3.50	£175.00
A	C	50	Nelson Series (1905) ...	W.85	£5.50	£275.00
A	C	50	Old English Garden Flowers (1911) ...		£1.50	£75.00
A	C	50	Old English Garden Flowers, 2nd Series (1913) ...		£1.00	£50.00
B	C	25	Old Furniture — '1st Series' (1923) ...		£2.80	£70.00
B	C	25	Old Furniture — '2nd Series' (1924) ...		£2.80	£70.00
B	C	40	Old Inns — 'A Series of 40' (1936) ...		£3.00	£120.00
B	C	40	Old Inns — 'Second Series of 40' (1939) ...		£1.75	£70.00
B	C	25	Old London (1929) ...		£4.00	£100.00
B	C	30	Old Pottery and Porcelain (1934) ...		£1.20	£36.00
B	C	25	Old Silver (1924) ...		£2.40	£60.00
B	C	25	Old Sundials (1928) ...		£3.00	£75.00
A	C	20	Our Gallant Grenadiers (c1901):	W.27		
			A Deep grey on toned card ...		£42.00	—
			B Blue-grey on bluish card ...		£42.00	—

Size	Printing	Number in set	BRITISH TOBACCO ISSUERS	Handbook reference	Price per card	Complete set
			W.D. & H.O. WILLS, Bristol (continued)			
A	BW	50	Our King and Queen (1937):	W.286		
			A　Home issue – with Album offer		30p	£15.00
			Album		—	£25.00
			B　Channel Islands issue – without Album offer ...		60p	£30.00
A	C	50	Overseas Dominions (Australia) (1915)	W.87	80p	£40.00
A	C	50	Overseas Dominions (Canada) (1914)		60p	£30.00
A	C	50	Physical Culture (1914)		£1.10	£55.00
A	C	25	Pond and Aquarium 1st Series (c1950) (unissued) ...		32p	£8.00
A	C	25	Pond and Aquarium 2nd Series (c1950) (unissued)		32p	£8.00
A	U	100	*Portraits of European Royalty (1908):			
			Nos. 1-50		£1.60	£80.00
			Nos. 51-100		£1.60	£80.00
B	C	25	Public Schools (1927)		£2.40	£60.00
B	U	25	Punch Cartoons (1916):			
			A　Toned card		£4.00	£100.00
			B　Glossy white card		£6.00	
B	U	25	Punch Cartoons — Second Series (1917)		£20.00	—
B	C	40	Puppies (c1950) (unissued)			
B	C	40	Racehorses and Jockeys, 1938 (1939)		£2.25	£90.00
A	C	50	Radio Celebrities — 'A Series ...' (1934):	W.301		
			A　Home issue — back 'This surface ...'		£1.00	£50.00
			Album		—	£25.00
			B　Irish issue — back 'Note. This surface ...'		£1.80	—
A	C	50	Radio Celebrities — 'Second Series — (1935):	W.302		
			A　Home issue — back 'This surface ...'		50p	£25.00
			Album		—	£25.00
			B　Irish issue — back 'Note. This surface ...' ...		£1.60	—
A	C	50	Railway Engines (1924)	W.303	£1.30	£65.00
A	C	50	Railway Engines (1936):	W.304		
			A　Home issue — back 'This surface ...'		£1.00	£50.00
			Album (with price) :			
			A　Cream Cover		—	£25.00
			B　Grey Cover		—	£25.00
			B　Irish issue — back 'Note. This surface ...' ...		£1.60	£80.00
			Album (without price)		—	£45.00
A	C	50	Railway Equipment (1939):	W.305		
			A　Home issue – with Album offer		40p	£20.00
			B　Channel Islands issue – without Album offer ...		80p	£40.00
A	C	50	Railway Locomotives (1930)		£1.80	£90.00
A	C	12	Recruiting Posters (1915)	W.92	£7.50	£90.00
A	C	50	The Reign of H.M. King George V (1935)		80p	£40.00
			Album		—	£25.00
B	C	25	Rigs of Ships (1929)		£4.00	£100.00
A	C	50	Romance of the Heavens (1928):	W.313		
			A　Thin card		£1.20	£60.00
			B　Thick card		£1.20	£60.00
A	C	50	Roses (1912)	W.94	£1.60	£80.00
A	C	50	Roses, 2nd Series (1914)	W.94	£1.60	£80.00
A	C	50	Roses (1926)	W.94	£1.10	£55.00
B	C	40	Roses (1936)		£1.60	£65.00
—	BW	48	Round Europe (66 x 52mm) (1937)		50p	£25.00
A	C	50	Rugby Internationals (1929)		£2.00	£100.00
A	C	50	Safety First (1934):	W.321		
			A　Home issue — 'This surface ...'		£1.20	£60.00
			Album (with price)		—	£25.00
			B　Irish issue — 'Note. This surface ...'		£2.50	—

Size	Print-ing	Number in set	BRITISH TOBACCO ISSUERS	Handbook reference	Price per card	Complete set
			W.D. & H.O. WILLS, Bristol (continued)			
A	C	50	School Arms (1906)	W.96	80p	£40.00
A	C	50	The Sea-Shore (1938):	W.322		
			A Home issue — adhesive with Album offer		30p	£15.00
			Album		—	£25.00
			B Irish issue — non-adhesive		80p	£40.00
			C Channel Islands issue – adhesive without Album offer		80p	£40.00
A	C	50	Seaside Resorts (1899):	W.10		
			A 'Best Bird's Eye' back		£16.00	—
			B 'Capstan Navy Cut' back		£16.00	—
			C 'Gold Flake' back		£16.00	—
			D 'The Three Castles' back		£16.00	—
			E 'Traveller' back		£16.00	—
			F 'Westward Ho!' back		£16.00	—
A	U	40	Shannon Electric Power Scheme (1931)		£2.25	£90.00
A	C		*Ships:	W.11		
		25	A Without 'Wills' on front (1895):			
			a 'Three Castles' back		£34.00	£850.00
			b Grey scroll back		£34.00	£850.00
		50	B With 'Wills' on front, dark grey back (1896)		£24.00	—
		100	C Green scroll back on brown card (1898-1902):			
			i 1898-25, Group 1		£24.00	—
			ii 1898-50, Group 2		£24.00	—
			iii 1902-25 additional subjects, Group 3		£24.00	—
A	U	50	Ships' Badges (1925)	W.328	80p	£40.00
A	C	50	Signalling Series (1911)	W.97	£1.80	£90.00
A	C	50	*Soldiers and Sailors (c1894):	W.13		
			A Grey back		£55.00	—
			B Blue back		£55.00	—
A	C		*Soldiers of the World (1895-7):	W.12		
			A Without PC inset:			
		100	a With 'Ld.' back, thick card		£10.00	£1000.00
		100	b With 'Ld.' back, thin card		£10.00	—
		100	c Without 'Ld.' back, thin card		£10.00	£1000.00
		1	Additional card (as c) 'England, Drummer'		—	£175.00
		52	B With PC inset		£25.00	£1300.00
A	C	50	Speed (1930)		£1.60	£80.00
A	C	50	Speed (1938):	W.330		
			A Home issue — Album offer with price		40p	£20.00
			B Irish issue — Album offer without price		90p	£45.00
			C Channel Islands issue – no Album offer		80p	£40.00
A	C	50	Sports of All Nations, multi-backed (1900)	W.14	£13.00	£650.00
A	C	50	Strange Craft (1931)		£1.10	£55.00
A	C	50	Time and Money in Different Countries (1906)	W.104	£2.00	£100.00
A	BW		Transvaal Series:	W.30		
		50	A With black border (1899)		£10.00	—
		66	Bi Without black border (1900-01)		£2.25	£150.00
		258	Bii Intermediate cards — additions and alternatives (1900-01)		£2.25	—
		66	C Final 66 subjects, as issued with 'Capstan' back (1902)		£6.50	—
B	C	40	Trees (1937)		£1.60	£65.00
B	C	25	University Hoods and Gowns (1926)		£3.20	£80.00
A	C		'Vanity Fair' Series (1902):	W.31		
		50	1st series		£7.50	£375.00
		50	2nd series		£7.50	£375.00
		50	Unnumbered — 43 subjects as in 1st and 2nd, 7 new subjects		£7.50	£375.00

Size	Print-ing	Number in set	BRITISH TOBACCO ISSUERS	Handbook reference	Price per card	Complete set
			W.D. & H.O. WILLS, Bristol (continued)			
A	C	50	Waterloo (c1916) (unissued)		£160.00	—
A	C		Wild Animals of the World (c1900):	W.15		
		50	A Green scroll back		£7.00	£350.00
		52	B Grey back, PC inset		£12.00	£600.00
		? 16	C Text back		£35.00	—
A	C	50	Wild Flowers (1923):	W.345		
			A With dots in side panels		80p	£40.00
			B Without dots in side panels		70p	£35.00
A	C	50	Wild Flowers — 'Series of 50' (1936):	W.346		
			A Home issue — back 'This surface ...'		50p	£25.00
			Album (with price)		—	£25.00
			B Irish issue — back 'Note. This surface ...'		£1.00	
			C Channel Islands issue – without Album offer or I.T.C. clause		70p	£35.00
A	C	50	Wild Flowers — '2nd Series.' (1937):	W.37		
			A Home issue — adhesive back, with Album offer		30p	£15.00
			Album (with price)		—	£25.00
			B Irish issue — non-adhesive back		80p	£40.00
			C Channel Islands issue – adhesive back without Album offer		80p	£40.00
A	C	50	Wonders of the Past (1926)	W.348	70p	£35.00
A	C	50	Wonders of the Sea (1928)	W.349	50p	£25.00
A	C	25	The World's Dreadnoughts (1910)	W.115	£3.00	£75.00
POST-1965 ISSUES						
H2	C	30	Britain's Motoring History (1991)	W.416	£1.40	£42.00
			Album		—	£15.00
—	C	6	Britain's Motoring History (149 x 104mm) (1991)	W.416	£1.25	£7.50
H2	C	30	Britain's Steam Railways (1998)		£1.20	£36.00
			Album		—	£15.00
G2	C	30	British Aviation (1994)	W.418	£1.20	£36.00
			Album		—	£15.00
—	C	6	British Aviation (1994) Beer Mats	W418	60p	£3.50
—	C	56	Caribbean Treasure Cruise (1985):	W.419		
—			A Size 75 x 35mm		£1.00	—
—			B Size 80 x 47mm		£1.00	—
G2	C	30	Classic Sports Cars (1996)		£1.20	£36.00
			Album		—	£10.00
G2	C	30	Donington Collection (1993)	W.422	£1.20	£36.00
			Album		—	£15.00
—	C	6	Donington Collection (1993) Beer Mats	W.422	£1.25	—
—	C	12	Embassy World Snooker Championship 17 April-3 May (80 x 47mm) (2004)	W.443	£4.00	—
	C	12	Embassy World Snooker Championship 16 April-2 May (2005):	W.444		
—			A Size 75 x 32mm		£4.00	—
—			B Size 80 x 47mm		£4.00	—
G2	BW	48	Familiar Phrases (1986)		£1.20	£60.00
	C	26	Focus on What's What (1989):	W.425		
—			A Size 75 x 32mm		£1.00	—
—			B Size 80 x 47mm		£1.00	—
G2	C	10	Golden Era (1999)	W.426	£2.00	£20.00
			Album		—	£15.00
H2	C	30	History of Britain's Railways (1987)	W.428	£1.20	£36.00
			Album		—	£15.00
H2	C	30	History of Motor Racing (1987)	W.429	£1.50	—
			Album		—	£15.00

Size	Print-ing	Number in set	BRITISH TOBACCO ISSUERS	Handbook reference	Price per card	Complete set
			W.D. & H.O. WILLS, Bristol (Post-1965 Issues continued)			
G2	C	30	In Search of Steam (1992)	W.430	£1.20	£36.00
			Album		—	£15.00
—	C	6	In Search of Steam (1992) Beer Mats	W.430	£1.25	—
G2	BW	5	Pica Punchline (1984)		£1.20	£6.00
H2	U	144	Punch Lines (1983)	W.433	80p	—
G2	U	288	Punch Lines (1983)	W.433	80p	—
G2	U	48	Ring the Changes (1985):	W.434		
			A With 'Wills' name:			
			i Picture and text black		£4.00	—
			ii Picture and text red		£1.20	£60.00
			B Without 'Wills' Name		£1.60	—
—	C	12	Russ Abbot Advertising Cards (80 x 47mm) (1993)		£1.50	£18.00
	C	56	Showhouse (1988):	W.435		
—			A Size 60 x 43mm		70p	—
—			B Size 80 x 35mm		70p	—
—			C Size 68 x 47mm		70p	—
—			D Size 80 x 47mm		70p	—
G2			E Size 90 x 47mm		70p	—
G2	C	30	Soldiers of Waterloo (1995)		£1.20	£36.00
			Album		—	£15.00
G2	BW	10	Spot the Shot (1986)		£3.00	£30.00
G2	C	30	The Tank Story (1997)		£1.20	£36.00
			Album		—	£15.00
			Three Castles Sailing Ship Model advertisement cards (1965):			
A	C	1	A View from Stern:			
			Three Castles Filter:			
			I. Three Castles Cigarettes		—	£4.00
			II. In the eighteenth century		—	£1.50
A	C	1	B Views from Bows:			
			I. Three Castles Filter		—	£1.50
			II. Three Castles Filter magnum		—	£1.50
A	BW	1	C Sailing Ship Black Line Drawing		—	£5.00
A	BW	1	D Three Castles Shield Black Line Drawing		—	£5.00
—	C	110	200th Anniversary Presentation Pack (2 sets of Playing Cards) (1986)	W.661	—	£100.00
	C	?	Wheel of Fortune (1985):	W.439		
—			A Size 75 x 35mm		70p	—
—			B Size 80 x 47mm		70p	—
—	C	56	Wonders of the World (1986):	W.440		
			A Size 90 x 47mm		60p	£33.00
			B Size 80 x 47mm		80p	£45.00
			C Size 80 x 35mm		90p	—
C1	C	36	World of Firearms (1982)		25p	£9.00
			Album		—	£10.00
C1	C	36	World of Speed (1981)		25p	£9.00
			Album		—	£20.00

OVERSEAS ISSUES

D2	U	50	Actors and Actresses, scroll backs in green (1905):	W.32		
			A Portraits in black and white		£4.00	—
			B Portraits flesh tinted		£3.50	—
D	U	30	Actresses — brown and green (1905) Scissors issue	W.116	£3.50	£100.00
D2	U	50	Actresses — four colours surround (c1904):	W.117		
			A Scissors issue		£9.00	—
			B Green scroll back issue		£3.50	—

Size	Print-ing	Number in set	BRITISH TOBACCO ISSUERS	Handbook reference	Price per card	Complete set
			W.D. & H.O. WILLS, Bristol (Overseas Issues continued)			
D	U	30	Actresses — orange/mauve surround (c1916) Scissors issue:	W.118		
			A Surround in Orange		£2.50	£75.00
			B Surround in mauve		£2.35	£70.00
D2	U	100	Actresses (c1903):	W.34		
			A Capstan issue		£3.50	—
			B Vice Regal issue		£3.50	
D	U		Actresses ('ALWICS') (c1903):	W.33		
		250	A Front portrait in black, border in red		£3.20	—
		50	B Front portrait in red, border in red		£3.50	—
D	BW	25	Actresses — Tabs type numbered (1902)	W.16	£24.00	—
D2	BW	50	Actresses — Tabs type unnumbered, Scissors issue (c1905)	W.119	£13.00	—
D	U	30	Actresses unicoloured I (1908):	W.120		
			A Scissors issue, back in red		£2.20	£66.00
			B Scissors issue, back in purple brown		£2.50	£75.00
A	U	30	Actresses — unicoloured II (c1908) Scissors issue	W.121	£2.20	£66.00
A	C	1	*Advertisement Card 'Capstan' (1902)	W.402	—	£300.00
A	C	50	Aeroplanes (1926)		£3.50	—
A	C	60	Animals (cut-outs) (1913):	W.37		
			A Havelock issue		£2.00	—
			B Wills' Specialities issue		£1.20	£72.00
	C	50	Animals and Birds:	W.17		
A			A With text, without title (c1902)		£15.00	—
D2			B Without text, with title (1912)		£6.00	—
D2			C Without text or title (1909)		£6.00	—
A	C	50	Arms and Armour (1910):	W.38		
			A Capstan issue		£2.50	—
			B Havelock issue		£4.00	—
			C Vice Regal issue		£2.50	—
			D United Service issue		£4.00	£200.00
A	C	50	Arms of the British Empire (1910):	W.40		
			A Backs in black		£1.30	£65.00
			B Wills' Specialities issue		£1.30	—
			C Havelock issue		£7.00	—
A	C	25	Army Life (1914) Scissors issue	W.133	£3.60	£90.00
—	U	50	Art Photogravures 1st series (1912):	W.43		
			A Size 67 x 33mm		£1.20	—
			B Size 67 x 44mm		£1.20	—
A	U	50	Art Photogravures 2nd series (1914)	W.44	£1.20	—
A	C		Australian Club Cricketers (1905):	W.59-1		
		40	A Dark blue back, front blue frameline with state		£22.00	—
		40	B Dark blue back, front blue frameline without state		£22.00	—
		40	C Green back		£22.00	—
		46	D Pale blue back, front brown frameline:			
			i Numbers 1-40 (minus Nos 28 & 33)		£28.00	—
			ii Numbers 41-48		£50.00	—
A	C	25	Australian and English Cricketers (1903)	W.59-2	£28.00	—
D2	U	25	Australian and English Cricketers (1909):	W.59-3		
			A Capstan issue:			
			i Framework in scarlet		£28.00	—
			ii Framework in blue		£28.00	—
			B Vice Regal issue:			
			i Framework in scarlet		£28.00	—
			ii Framework in blue		£28.00	—

Size	Print-ing	Number in set	BRITISH TOBACCO ISSUERS	Handbook reference	Price per card	Complete set
			W.D. & H.O. WILLS, Bristol (Overseas Issues continued)			
D2	U	60	Australian and South African Cricketers (1910):	W.59-4		
			A Capstan issue:			
			i Framework in scarlet		£22.00	—
			ii Framework in blue		£22.00	—
			B Havelock issue:			
			i Framework in scarlet		£45.00	—
			ii Framework in blue		£45.00	—
			C Vice Regal issue:			
			i Framework in scarlet		£22.00	—
			ii Framework in blue		£22.00	—
—	P	100	Australian Scenic Series (69 x 52mm) (1928)	W.138	£1.20	
A	C	50	Australian Wild Flowers (1913):			
			A Wills' Specialities issue, grey-brown back		£1.50	£75.00
			B Wills' Specialities issue, green back		£2.20	—
			C Havelock issue		£3.50	—
A	C		Aviation (1910):	W.46		
		85	A Black backs 'Series of 85':			
			i Capstan issue		£3.00	—
			ii Vice Regal issue		£3.00	—
		75	B Black backs 'Series of 75':			
			i Capstan issue		£3.00	—
			ii Havelock issue		£3.20	—
			iii Vice Regal issue		£3.00	—
		75	C Green back 'Series of 75':			
			i Capstan issue		£3.00	—
			ii Havelock issue		£4.00	—
			iii Vice Regal issue		£3.00	—
D2	C	50	Aviation Series (1911):	W.47		
			A W.D. and H.O. Wills back		£4.00	—
			B Anonymous backs with album clause		£4.00	—
			C Anonymous backs without album clause		£4.00	—
A	C	? 95	Baseball Series (1912) Pirate issue	W.353	£600.00	—
A	U	40	Beauties — brown tinted (1913):	W.139		
			A Scissors issue		£2.25	£90.00
			B Star circle and leaves issue		£3.50	—
D2	U	30	Beauties — 'Celebrated Actresses' Scissors issue (c1912)	W.140	£5.50	—
A2	C	52	Beauties — Heads and shoulders set in background (1911) PC inset:	W.141		
			A Scissors issue:			
			i Background to packets plain		£7.50	—
			ii Background to packets latticework design		£4.00	£210.00
			iii No packet back		£45.00	—
			B Star circle and leaves issue		£6.00	—
—	CP	50	Beauties 1st series (63 x 45mm) (1925)	W.142	£4.00	—
—	P	25	Beauties 1st Series (64 x 40mm) (1925)	W.142	£4.00	—
—	P	50	Beauties 2nd series (64 x 40mm) (1925)	W.143	£4.00	—
A2	C	32	Beauties — Picture Hats (1914):	W.144		
			A Scissors issue		£4.00	—
			B Star circle and leaves issue		£6.00	—
—	CP	72	Beauties — red star and circle back (70 x 47mm) (1923)	W.145	£13.00	—
D2	U	50	Beauties — red tinted (1905)	W.146	£3.50	£175.00
D	C	30	Beauties and Children (c1910) Scissors issue	W.147	£3.30	£100.00
A	P	50	Beautiful New Zealand (1928)		50p	£25.00

Size	Print-ing	Number in set	BRITISH TOBACCO ISSUERS	Handbook reference	Price per card	Complete set
			W.D. & H.O. WILLS, Bristol (Overseas Issues continued)			
D2	C	50	Best Dogs of Their Breed (1914):	W.48		
			A Havelock issue		£8.00	—
			B Wills' Specialities issue		£5.00	—
			C Anonymous back, Wills' on front		£9.00	—
D2	C	30	Birds and Animals (1911) Ruby Queen issue	W.354	£4.50	—
D1	C	50	Birds, Beasts and Fishes (cut-outs) (1924)	W.151	60p	£30.00
A	C	100	Birds of Australasia:			
			A Green backs (1912):			
			i Capstan issue		£1.75	£175.00
			ii Havelock issue		£2.75	—
			iii Vice Regal issue		£1.75	£175.00
			B Yellow backs (1915):			
			i Havelock issue		£2.75	—
			ii Wills' Specialities issue		£1.75	—
D	C	52	Birds of Brilliant Plumage:	W.152		
			A Four Aces issue (1924)		£3.50	—
			B Pirate Issue:			
			i With border on front (1916)		£4.00	—
			ii Without border on front (1916)		£4.00	—
			C Red star, circle and leaves issue (1914)		£5.00	—
D2	C	25	Birds of the East 1st series Ruby Queen issue (1912)	W.355	£1.80	£45.00
D2	C	25	Birds of the East 2nd series Ruby Queen issue (1927)	W.356	£1.80	£45.00
D2	C	36	Boxers (1911):	W.153		
			A Scissors issue		£12.00	—
			B Green star and circle issue		£12.00	—
D2	U		Britain's Defenders (1915):	W.51		
			A Wills' Specialities issue:			
		50	i Inscribed 'A Series of 50'		£1.60	£80.00
		8	ii Without inscription 'A Series of 50'		£11.00	—
		50	B Havelock issue		£3.00	—
		50	C Scissors issue:			
			i Red upright 'Scissors' packet		£3.00	£150.00
			ii Green upright 'Scissors' packet		£3.00	£150.00
			iii Red slanting 'Scissors' packet		£3.00	£150.00
		50	D Green star and circle issue		£3.00	—
D2	C	43	British Army Boxers (1913) Scissors issue		£7.50	—
D2	C	50	British Army Uniforms (c1910):	W.106		
			A Wild Woodbine issue		£7.50	£375.00
			B Flag issue		£7.50	—
			C Scissors issue		£7.50	£375.00
—	C	101	British Beauties (59 x 41mm) (c1915)	W.155	£2.75	—
A	C	50	British Costumes from 100 BC to 1904 (1905) (Unissued Plain Backs)	W.384	£75.00	—
A	C	50	British Empire Series (1912):			
			A Capstan issue		£1.30	£65.00
			B Havelock issue		£2.00	—
			C Vice Regal issue		£1.30	£65.00
A	P	48	British Royal and Ancient Buildings (1925)		60p	£30.00
A	BW	45	British Rugby Players (1930)		£3.00	—
A	U	50	Chateaux (1925)	W.167	£6.00	—
A	C	50	Children of All Nations (1925)		£1.10	£55.00
D2	C	100	China's Famous Warriors (1911) Pirate issue:			
			A First 25 subjects	W.357	£3.20	—
			B Second 25 subjects	W.358	£3.20	—
			C Third 25 subjects	W.359	£3.20	—
			D Fourth 25 subjects	W.360	£3.20	—

Size	Print-ing	Number in set	BRITISH TOBACCO ISSUERS	Handbook reference	Price per card	Complete set
			W.D. & H.O. WILLS, Bristol (Overseas Issues continued)			
D2	C	28	Chinese Actors and Actresses (1907) Pirate issue ...	W.361	£3.25	—
D2	C	25	Chinese Beauties 1st Series (1907) Pirate issue:	W.362		
			A Vertical back		£2.20	£55.00
			B Horizontal back		£2.40	£60.00
D2	C	25	Chinese Beauties 2nd series (1909) Pirate issue:	W.363		
			A With framelines on front		£2.20	£55.00
			B Without framelines on front		£2.20	£55.00
D2	C	30	Chinese Children's Games (1911) Ruby Queen issue	W.364	£3.00	—
D2	C	50	Chinese Costumes Pirate issue (1928)	W.365	£5.00	—
—	C	25	Chinese Pagodas (1911) Pirate issue (138 x 88mm)	W.366	£50.00	—
D2	U	50	Chinese Proverbs brown (138 x 88mm) (1928):	W.367		
			A Pirate issue		£2.00	—
			B Ruby Queen issue		£6.00	—
D2	C	50	Chinese Proverbs coloured (1914-16) Pirate issue:	W.368		
			A Back in blue:			
			i Without overprint		£2.00	—
			ii With overprint		£2.00	—
			B Back in olive green		£2.00	—
D2	C	40	Chinese Trades (c1905) Autocar issue	W.369	£10.00	—
D2	C	50	Chinese Transport (1914) Ruby Queen issue	W.370	£5.00	—
D2	U	50	Cinema Stars Four Aces issue (1926):	W.172		
			A Numbered		£2.50	£125.00
			B Unnumbered		£2.50	£125.00
D2	U	25	Cinema Stars (1916) Scissors issue	W.173	£2.80	£70.00
A1	P	50	Cinema Stars (1926)	W.382	£5.00	—
A	C	50	Coaches and Coaching Days (1925)		£2.40	£120.00
A	C		Conundrums (c1900):	W.21		
		25	A With album clause		£15.00	—
		25	B Without album clause		£15.00	—
		25	C Without album clause redrawn		£15.00	—
		50	D Without album clause inscribed '50 Different'		£15.00	—
—	C	68	Crests and Colours of Australian Universities, Colleges and Schools (70 x 48mm) (1929)	W.176	80p	£55.00
A	P	63	Cricketers (c1925)	W.59-5	£11.00	—
A	U	25	Cricketer Series (1902)	W.59-6	£180.00	—
A	U	50	Cricketer Series (1901)	W.59-7	£180.00	—
A	P	48	Cricket Season 1928-29	W.177	£5.00	—
D2	C	27	Dancing Girls (1915) Scissors issue:	W.180		
			A Inscribed '28 Subjects' (No. 3 not issued)		£3.20	
			B Inscribed '27 Subjects'		£3.20	
D2	C	25	Derby Day Series (1914):	W.181		
			A Scissors issue:			
			i With title		£10.00	—
			ii Without title		£11.00	—
			B Star and circle issue		£11.00	—
A	C	50	Dogs — Scenic backgrounds (1925)		£1.20	£60.00
—	C	20	Dogs — Heads 1st series (70 x 63mm) (1927):			
			A Wills' World Renown Cigarettes issue:			
			i With album clause		£3.50	
			ii Without album clause		£3.50	
			B Three Castles and Vice Regal Cigarettes issue		£3.50	—
—	C	20	Dogs — Heads 2nd series (70 x 63mm) (1927)		£3.50	—
D2	C	32	Drum Horses (1909):	W.192		
			A Scissors issue:			
			i Vertical format, open Scissors packet ...		£9.00	—
			ii Horizontal format, closed Scissors packet		£7.50	—
			B United Service issue		£7.00	—
			C Green star, circle and leaves issue		£7.50	—

Size	Printing	Number in set	BRITISH TOBACCO ISSUERS	Handbook reference	Price per card	Complete set

W.D. & H.O. WILLS, Bristol (Overseas Issues continued)

Size	Printing	Number in set	Description	Handbook reference	Price per card	Complete set
A	P	25	English Cricketers (1926)		£4.00	£100.00
—	C	25	English Period Costumes (70 x 55mm) (1928):	W.195		
			A White card		£2.00	—
			B Cream card		£2.00	£50.00
—	P	10	English Views & Buildings (145 x 108mm) (c1928)	W.407	£14.00	—
	BW		Etchings (of Dogs) (1925):			
A		26	A Small size English language issues:			
			i With 'Gold Flake Cigarettes'		£8.00	—
			ii Without 'Gold Flake Cigarettes'		£3.00	—
A		26	B Small size Dutch language issues:			
			i With framelines to back		£8.00	—
			ii Without framelines to back		£8.00	—
—		26	C Medium size (78 x 54mm)		£5.00	—
D	C	25	The Evolution of the British Navy (1915)		£4.00	£100.00
		10	Famous Castles (c1928):	W.408		
—	P		A Size 145 x 108mm		£13.00	—
—	U		B Size 140 x 75mm		£13.00	—
	U		Famous Film Stars (1934):			
A		100	A Small size		£1.60	—
—		100	B Medium size (67 x 53mm):			
			i White card		£2.50	—
			ii Cream card		£2.50	—
—	P	100	Famous Film Stars (68 x 51mm) (c1936)		£3.50	—
A2	U	50	Famous Footballers (1914):			
			A Scissors issue		£13.00	—
			B Star and circle issue		£13.00	—
A	C	50	Famous Inventions (without ITC clause) (1926)	W.60	£1.20	£60.00
D2	U	75	Film Favourites Four Aces issue (1928)		£2.25	—
A	C	50	Fish of Australasia (1912):			
			A Capstan issue		£1.80	£90.00
			B Havelock issue		£2.50	—
			C Vice Regal issue		£1.80	£90.00
D2	C		Flag Girls of All Nations (1908):	W.64		
		50	A Capstan issue		£2.50	—
		50	B Vice Regal issue		£2.50	—
		25	C United Service issue		£3.60	£90.00
		25	D Scissors issue:			
			i Numbered		£12.00	—
			ii Unnumbered		£12.00	—
		25	E Green star, circle and leaves issue		£3.60	£90.00
—	C	8	Flags, shaped metal (1915)	W.65	£10.00	—
D2	C	126	Flags and Ensigns (1903)	W.66	£1.70	—
A	C	25	Flags of the Empire (no ITC clause) (1926)	W.215	£7.00	—
D2	C		Flowers Purple Mountain issue (1914):			
		20	A Numbered	W.371	£18.00	—
		100	B Unnumbered	W.372	£18.00	—
D2	C	50	Football Club Colours Scissors/Special Army Quality issue (1907)	W.220	£11.00	—
A	C	28	Football Club Colours and Flags (1913):	W.68		
			A Capstan issue		£6.00	—
			B Havelock issue		£7.50	—
	U	200	Footballers (1933):			
A			A Small size		£2.20	—
—			B Medium size (67 x 52mm)		£4.20	—
—	C	? 5	Footballers Shaped Die Cut (59 x 30mm) (1910)	W.404	£150.00	—

Size	Print-ing	Number in set	BRITISH TOBACCO ISSUERS	Handbook reference	Price per card	Complete set
			W.D. & H.O. WILLS, Bristol (Overseas Issues continued)			
D2	C	50	Girls of All Nations (1908):	W.73		
			A Capstan issue		£3.00	—
			B Vice Regal issue		£3.00	—
			C Green star, circle and leaves issue		£3.00	—
D2	C	25	Governor-General of India Scissors issue (1912) ...	W.229	£8.00	—
—	C	25	Heraldic Signs and Their Origins (77 x 59mm) (1925)	W.230	£1.80	£45.00
D2	C	30	Heroic Deeds (1913) Scissors issue		£6.50	—
A	C	50	Historic Events (1913):	W.74		
			A Wills' Specialities issue		£1.50	£75.00
			B Havelock issue		£2.50	—
—	C	25	History of Naval Dress (75 x 55mm) (1930)		£35.00	—
A2	P	50	Homeland Events (1927)	W.233	£1.00	£50.00
A2	C	50	Horses of Today (1906):	W.75		
			A Capstan issue		£3.50	—
			B Havelock issue		£5.00	—
			C Vice Regal issue		£3.50	—
A	C	50	Household Hints (1927):	W.236		
			A With 'Wills' Cigarettes' at top back		60p	—
			B Without 'Wills' Cigarettes' at top back		£1.50	—
D2	C		Houses of Parliament (c1912):	W.237		
		33	A Pirate issue		£1.50	£50.00
		32	B Star and circle issue		£2.50	£80.00
D2	C	50	Indian Regiments (1912):	W.239		
			A Scissors issue		£11.00	—
			B Star and circle issue		£11.00	—
A	C	2	Indian Series – see Bukhsh Ellallie & Co.			
A	C	50	Interesting Buildings (1905)	W.76	£3.00	£150.00
D2	BW	67	International Footballers Season 1909-1910:	W.242		
			A Scissors issue (1910)		£12.00	—
			B United Services issue (1910)		£12.00	—
			C Flag issue (1911)		£12.00	—
A	U	5	Islands of the Pacific (c1916)	W.375	£250.00	—
D2	C	50	Jiu-Jitsu (c1910):			
			A Scissors issue		£7.00	—
			B Flag issue		£6.50	—
D1	C	53	Jockeys and Owners Colours with PC inset Scissors issue (1914)		£8.00	—
A	C	50	Lighthouses (1926)		£2.00	£100.00
A	U		Maori Series (c1900):	W.77		
		100	A White border		£90.00	—
		? 44	B Green border. Numbered bottom left		£90.00	—
		? 3	C Green border. Numbered top left		£200.00	—
		? 4	D Green border. Unnumbered		£200.00	—
		? 100	E White border. Plain back (anonymous)		£75.00	—
A	C	45	Melbourne Cup Winners (1906)	W.78	£11.00	—
A	C	50	Merchant Ships of the World (1925) (without I.T.C. clause)	W.257	£1.50	£75.00
A1	C	40	Merrie England Studies (Male) (1916)	W.79	£9.00	—
A	U	24	Merveilles du Monde (1927)	W.258	£7.00	—
A	BW	25	Military Portraits (1917) Scissors issue		£6.00	—
—	C	25	Miniatures — oval medallions (62 x 45mm) (1914)	W.261	£65.00	—
K2	C	52	Miniature Playing Cards Scissors issue (1906)		£11.00	—
A	U	50	Modern War Weapons (1915):	W.82		
			A Wills' Specialities issue		£2.20	—
			B Havelock issue		£3.00	—
A	C	25	Modes of Conveyance (1928) Four Aces issue		£2.00	£50.00
A	C	48	Motor Cars (1923)		£2.50	£125.00

Size	Printing	Number in set	BRITISH TOBACCO ISSUERS	Handbook reference	Price per card	Complete set
			W.D. & H.O. WILLS, Bristol (Overseas Issues continued)			
A	P	50	Motor Cars (1927)		£2.00	£100.00
A	C	50	Motor Cycles (1926)		£3.20	£160.00
A1	P	48	Movie Stars (1927)		£3.50	—
D2	BW	50	Music Hall Celebrities (1911) Scissors issue	W.269	£7.00	—
A	C	50	National Flags and Arms (1938)		£1.50	—
—	C	25	The Nation's Shrines (71 x 55mm) (1928)		£1.60	£40.00
A	P	50	Nature Studies (1928)		£1.60	—
A	C	50	New Zealand Birds (1925)		£1.40	£70.00
A	P	50	New Zealand — Early Scenes and Maori Life (1926)		50p	£25.00
A	P	50	New Zealand Footballers (1927)		£1.80	£90.00
A	U	50	New Zealand Race Horses (1928):			
			A Cream card		£1.20	£60.00
			B White card		£1.20	—
A	C	50	N.Z. Butterflies, Moths and Beetles (1925)		£1.30	£65.00
A	C	25	Past and Present (1929)		£1.40	£35.00
A1	C	50	Past and Present Champions (1908):	W.89		
			A Capstan Cigarette issue		£14.00	—
			B Capstan Tobacco issue		£14.00	—
A	C	25	Picturesque People of the Empire (1928)		£1.40	£35.00
A	C	25	Pirates and Highwaymen (1925)		£1.60	£40.00
A	C	25	Police of the World (1910)	W.290	£11.00	—
—	C	70	Practical Wireless (69 x 62mm) (1923)		£8.00	—
D2	C		Products of the World — Maps and Scenes (1913):	W.293		
		50	A Pirate issue		£1.50	—
		25	B Green star, circle and leaves issue		£2.00	—
A	C	50	Products of the World — Scenes only (1929)		50p	£25.00
A	C	50	Prominent Australian and English Cricketers (1907)	W.59-8	£18.00	—
D2	C	23	Prominent Australian and English Cricketers (1907)	W.59-9	£22.00	—
D2	BW	59	Prominent Australian and English Cricketers (1911):	W.59-10		
			A Capstan issue:			
			i 'A Series of 50'		£20.00	—
			ii 'A Series of .../A Series of 59'		£22.00	—
			B Vice Regal issue:			
			i 'A Series of 50'		£20.00	—
			ii 'A Series of .../A Series of 59'		£22.00	—
			C Havelock issue		£45.00	—
D2	C	25	Puzzle Series (1910) Scissors/United Service issue:	W.298		
			A Background blue-green		£8.00	—
			B Background light yellow		£8.00	—
D	C	50	Races of Mankind (1911)		£14.00	—
A	C	50	Railway Engines (1924)	W.303	£1.30	£65.00
A	C	50	Railway Working (1927)		£2.50	—
A	C	50	Regimental Colours and Cap Badges (1907):			
			A Scissors issue		£2.00	£100.00
			B United Service issue:			
			i Red back		£2.00	£100.00
			ii Blue back		£2.00	£100.00
D2	C	33	Regimental Pets (1911) Scissors issue	W.309	£6.50	—
A	C	50	Regimental Standards and Cap Badges (1928)		90p	£45.00
A	C	50	Riders of the World:	W.93		
			A Capstan/Vice Regal/Pennant/Wills' Specialities issue (1913)		£1.80	—
			B Havelock issue (1913)		£3.50	—
			C Back in red-brown (1931)		£1.30	£65.00
A	C	50	Romance of the Heavens (1928) (No ITC clause) ...		£1.50	—

Size	Printing	Number in set	BRITISH TOBACCO ISSUERS	Handbook reference	Price per card	Complete set
			W.D. & H.O. WILLS, Bristol (Overseas Issues continued)			
D2	C	25	Roses (1912):	W.373		
			A Purple Mountain issues:			
			i With Wills' Cigarettes on front		£10.00	—
			ii Without Wills' Cigarettes on front		£10.00	—
			B Plain backs with Wills' Cigarettes on front		£10.00	—
A	P	50	The Royal Family at Home and Abroad (1927)		£1.70	—
A	C	50	Royal Mail (with Wills' Cigarettes on fronts) (1913):	W.95		
			A Capstan issue		£5.00	£250.00
			B Havelock issue (without Wills' Cigarettes on fronts)		£6.00	—
			C Vice Regal issue		£5.00	£250.00
			D With anonymous backs		£7.50	—
			E With plain back		£7.50	—
A	P	50	The Royal Navy (1929)		£1.80	£90.00
A	BW	100	Royalty, Notabilities and Events 1900-1902 (1902)	W.28	£3.00	—
D1	U	27	Rulers of the World (1911)	W.320	£8.00	—
D2			Russo-Japanese Series (1905):	W.29		
	BW	100	A Fronts in black		£3.00	—
	U	50	B Fronts in red		£9.00	—
A	C	50	Safety First (1937)	W.321	90p	£45.00
B	CP	48	Scenes from the Empire (1939)		£2.00	£100.00
D2	C	30	Semaphore Signalling (1910)		£3.50	£105.00
A	P	50	Ships and Shipping (1928)		£1.00	£50.00
D2	C	36	Ships and Their Pennants (1913)		£6.00	—
A	C	50	Ships' Badges (1925)		£1.00	£50.00
A	C	50	Signalling Series (1912):	W.97		
			A Capstan issue		£1.70	£85.00
			B Havelock issue		£2.50	—
			C Vice Regal issue		£1.70	£85.00
D2	BW	40	Sketches in black and white (1905)	W.98	£2.75	—
	C		Soldiers of the World (1903):	W.12		
A		50	A Numbered		£12.00	—
D2		75	B Unnumbered		£12.00	—
A	BW	100	South African Personalities (1894)	W.99	£150.00	—
—	P	10	Splendours of New Zealand (140 x 75mm) (c1928)		£13.00	—
D2	C	30	Sporting Girls (1913) Scissors issue	W.331	£10.00	—
	P	50	A Sporting Holiday in New Zealand (1928):	W.332		
A			A Small size		90p	£45.00
—			B Medium size (70 x 57mm)		£1.00	£50.00
D2	C	25	Sporting Terms (1905):	W.100		
			A Capstan issue		£16.00	—
			B Vice Regal issue		£16.00	—
D	C	50	Sports of the World (1917)		£5.00	—
D2		50	Stage and Music Hall Celebrities (1904) (Portrait in oval frame):	W.102		
	BW		A Capstan issue		£3.50	—
	BW		B Vice Regal issue		£3.50	—
	U		C Havelock issue		£4.50	—
D2	BW	50	Stage and Music Hall Celebrities (1908) (Portrait in oblong frame)	W.103	£3.50	—
D1	P	52	Stars of the Cinema (1926):			
			A Text back		£6.50	—
			B Four Aces issue		£6.50	—
A	C	50	Time and Money in Different Countries (1908):	W.104		
			A Capstan issue		£1.80	—

Size	Print-ing	Number in set	BRITISH TOBACCO ISSUERS	Handbook reference	Price per card	Complete set
			W.D. & H.O. WILLS, Bristol (Overseas Issues continued)			
			Time and Money in Different Countries (1908) (continued)			
			B Havelock issue		£3.00	—
			C Vice Regal issue:			
			i With album clause		£1.80	£90.00
			ii Without album clause		£1.80	£90.00
A	C	50	A Tour Round the World (1907)	W.105	£3.20	—
D2	C	50	Types of the British Army (1912):	W.106		
			A Capstan issue		£3.00	—
			B Vice Regal issue		£3.00	—
A	C	50	Types of the Commonwealth Forces (1910):	W.107		
			A Capstan issue		£2.80	—
			B Vice Regal issue		£2.80	—
			C Havelock issue		£5.00	—
A	C	25	United States Warships (1911):	W.108		
			A Capstan issue		£4.00	—
			B Havelock issue		£6.00	—
			C Vice Regal issue		£4.00	—
A	P	50	Units of the British Army and RAF (1928)		60p	£30.00
A	C	50	USS Co's Steamers (1930)		£3.00	—
A	C	50	VCs (1926)		£2.80	—
D2	C	25	Victoria Cross Heroes (1915):			
			A Havelock issue		£6.00	—
			B Wills' Specialities issue		£4.00	£100.00
			C Scissors issue		£5.00	£125.00
A	C	10	Victorian Football Association (1908):	W.110		
			A Capstan on front		£6.00	—
			B Havelock on front		£8.00	—
A	C	19	Victorian Football League (1908):	W.111		
			A Capstan on front		£6.00	—
			B Havelock on front		£8.00	—
—	P	215	Views of the World (66 x 28mm) (1908):	W.112		
			A Numbers 1-50 plain backs (anonymous)		£1.00	—
			B Numbers 51-215 blue back Capstan issue ...		£1.00	—
			C Numbers 51-215 green back Vice Regal issue		£1.00	—
A	C	25	Village Models Series (1925):			
			A Small size		£1.40	£35.00
			B Medium size		£6.00	—
D2	C	50	War Incidents 1st series (1915):	W.113		
			A Wills' Specialities issue		£4.00	—
			B Havelock issue		£5.00	—
			C Scissors issue		£4.00	£200.00
D2	C	50	War Incidents 2nd series (1915):	W.113		
			A Wills' Specialities issue		£4.00	£200.00
			B Havelock issue		£5.00	—
A	BW	50	War Pictures (1915):	W.114		
			A Wills' Specialities issue		£2.20	£110.00
			B Havelock issue		£3.20	—
A	C	50	Warships (1926)		£2.20	£110.00
D2	C	30	What It Means (1916) Scissors issue		£1.50	£45.00
	C		Wild Animals (1934):			
A		50	A Small size titled 'Wild Animals' Heads		80p	£40.00
—		25	B Medium size titled 'Wild Animals' (69 x 55mm) ...		£1.40	£35.00
A	C	50	Wild Animals of the World (1906):	W.15		
			A Bristol and London issue		£12.00	—
			B Celebrated Cigarettes issue		£6.00	£300.00
			C Star, circle and leaves issue		£10.00	—
A	C	25	Wonders of the World (1926)		£1.20	£30.00

Size	Print-ing	Number in set	BRITISH TOBACCO ISSUERS	Handbook reference	Price per card	Complete set

W.D. & H.O. WILLS, Bristol (Overseas Issues continued)

Size	Print	Num	Title	Ref	Price	Set
A	C	25	The World's Dreadnoughts (1910):	W.115		
			A Capstan issue ...		£2.80	—
			B Vice Regal issue ...		£2.80	—
			C No ITC clause ...		£3.00	£75.00
A	P	50	Zoo (1927):			
			A Scissors issue without descriptive back ...		£5.00	—
			B Wills' issue with descriptive back ...		40p	£20.00
—	P	50	Zoological Series (70 x 60mm) (1922) ...		£2.00	—

SILK ISSUES 1911-17

Size	Print	Num	Title	Ref	Price	Set
—	C	50	Arms of the British Empire (70 x 48mm) ...	W.126	£3.50	—
—	C	50	Australian Butterflies (70 x 51mm) ...		£3.20	—
—	C	50	Birds and Animals of Australia (70 x 48mm) ...		£4.00	—
			Crests and Colours of Australian Universities, Colleges and Schools (70 x 48mm):			
—	C	50	A Numbered ...		£3.00	—
—	C	1	B Unnumbered ...		£25.00	—
—	C	1	Flag (Union Jack) (162 x 112mm) ...		£30.00	—
—	C	28	Flags of 1914-18 Allies (64 x 42mm):	W.214		
			A Backs with letterpress in capitals ...		£2.75	—
			B Backs with letterpress in small lettering ...		£2.75	—
—	C	13	*Flags on Lace* (71 x 50mm) ...	W.405	£6.50	—
A	C	38	Kings and Queens of England ...	W.251	£6.00	—
—	C	50	Popular Flowers (72 x 51mm):			
			A Backs inscribed 'Now being inserted in the large packets' ...		£5.00	—
			B Backs inscribed 'Now being inserted in the 1/- packets' ...		£5.00	—
—	C	67	War Medals (82 x 53mm) ...	W.341	£5.00	—

WILSON & CO., Ely

Size	Print	Num	Title	Ref	Price	Set
A	U	50	War Portraits (1916) ...	H.86	£120.00	—

W. WILSON, Birmingham

Size	Print	Num	Title	Ref	Price	Set
D	C	30	*Army Pictures. Cartoons, etc (1916) ...	H.12	£160.00	—
A	U	50	War Portraits (1916) ...	H.86	£130.00	—

HENRI WINTERMANS (UK) LTD

Size	Print	Num	Title	Ref	Price	Set
G	C	30	Disappearing Rain Forest (1991) ...		50p	£15.00
			Album ...		—	£15.00
G	C	30	Wonders of Nature (1992) ...		60p	£18.00
			Album ...		—	£15.00

A. & M. WIX, London and Johannesburg

Size	Print	Num	Title	Ref	Price	Set
—	—		Cinema Cavalcade (50 coloured, 200 black and white; sizes — 70 small, 110 large, 70 extra-large):			
		250	'A Series of 250 ...' ('Max Cigarettes') (1939) ...		£1.80	—
		250	'2nd Series of 250 ...' ('Max Cigarettes') (1940)		£1.80	—
A2	C	100	Film Favourites — 'Series of 100 ...' (c1937) ...	H.581-1	£3.00	—
A2	C	100	Film Favourites — '2nd Series of 100 ...' (1939) ...	H.581-2	£3.00	—
A2	C	100	Film Favourites — '3rd Series of 100 ...' (c1939) ...	H.581-3	£2.00	£200.00
J1	C	100	*Men of Destiny (folders) (P.O. Box 5764, Johannesburg) (c1935) ...		£2.50	—
—	C	250	Speed Through the Ages (171 small, 79 large) (1938):	H.583		
			A Back in English and Afrikaans ...		32p	£80.00
			B Back in English ...		40p	£100.00
—	C	250	This Age of Power and Wonder (170 small, 80 large) ('Max Cigarettes') (c1935) ...		30p	£75.00

Size	Print-ing	Number in set		BRITISH TOBACCO ISSUERS	Handbook reference	Price per card	Complete set
				J. WIX & SONS LTD, London			
—	C	80		Bridge Favours and Place Cards (diecut) (1937) ...	H.681	£20.00	—
—	C	50		Bridge Hands (140 x 105mm) (1930)	H.682	£32.00	—
C	C	50		Builders of Empire — 'Kensitas' (1937)		60p	£30.00
—	U	42		Card Tricks by Jasper Maskelyne (c1935):	H.535-3		
				A Size 70 x 34mm		£6.00	—
				B Size 70 x 47mm		£6.00	—
A2	C	50		Coronation (1937):			
			A	J. Wix and 'Kensitas' back:			
				1 Linen finish		35p	£17.50
				2 Varnished front		60p	£30.00
			B	'Kensitas' back		35p	£17.50
	C			Henry:	H.625		
				'A Series of ...' (1935):			
B1		50		A Large size		£1.00	£50.00
				Album		—	£35.00
—		25		B Extra-large size		£4.00	£100.00
				'2nd Series ...' (1935):			
B1		50		A Large size:			
				i With album price		£1.20	£60.00
				ii Without album price		£4.00	—
				Album		—	£35.00
—		25		B Extra-large size:			
				i Last line of text 'Throat'		£4.00	£100.00
				ii Last line of text 'Your Throat'		£7.00	—
B1		50		3rd Series, nothing after 'copyright reserved' (1936)		£1.00	£50.00
B1		50		4th Series, with full stop after 'copyright reserved' (1936)		£1.00	£50.00
B1		50		5th Series, with dash after 'copyright reserved' (1936)		60p	£30.00
	U			Jenkynisms:			
			A	'The K4's' Series (c1932):			
B2		102		I Known as 1st Series:	H.636-1		
				A Two cigarettes level from packet ...		£1.00	—
				B One cigarette protruding above the others		£1.00	—
B2		50		II Known as 2nd Series	H.636-2	80p	£40.00
B2		30		III Known as 3rd Series:	H.636-3		
				A Size 78 x 65mm clear 'Kensitas' ...		£1.00	—
				B Size 76 x 65mm illegible 'Kensitas'		£1.00	—
B2		1		IV Known as 4th Series:	H.636-4		
				A Clear 'Kensitas'		—	£2.50
				B Illegible 'Kensitas'		—	£2.50
			B	The Red Bordered series (c1932):			
	U	50		I Series of Quotations:	H.637-1		
A2				A Size 65 x 38mm		£4.50	—
—				B Size 69 x 54mm		£4.50	—
	U			II 'Today's Jenkynisms':	H.637-2		
A2				A Size 65 x 38mm			
		? 44		i Without letter		£4.50	—
		? 30		ii Series B		£4.50	—
		? 19		iii Series C		£4.50	—
		? 34		iv Series D		£4.50	—
				B Size 69 x 54mm:			
		? 44		i Without letter		£4.50	—
		? 30		ii Series B		£4.50	—
		? 19		iii Series C		£4.50	—
—		? 34		iv Series D		£4.50	—

Size	Printing	Number in set	BRITISH TOBACCO ISSUERS	Handbook reference	Price per card	Complete set

J. WIX & SONS LTD, London (continued)

Size	Printing	Number in set	Description	Handbook ref	Price per card	Complete set
—	C		Ken-cards (102 x 118mm):			
		12	Series 1 Starters/Snacks (1969)		—	£7.50
		12	Series 2 Main Courses (1969)		—	£7.50
		12	Series 3 Desserts (1969)		—	£7.50
		12	Series 4 Motoring (1969)		—	£7.50
		12	Series 5 Gardening (1969)		—	£7.50
		12	Series 6 Do It Yourself (1969)		—	£7.50
		12	Series 7 Home Hints (1969)		—	£7.50
		12	Series 8 Fishing (1969)		—	£7.50
	U	25	Love Scenes from Famous Films — 'First Series' (1932):			
C2			A Small size		£3.00	£75.00
B1			B Large size		£3.00	£75.00
—			C Extra-large size (127 x 88mm)		£6.50	—
	U	19	Love Scenes from Famous Films — 'Second Series' (1932) (Nos. 5, 9, 13, 20, 23, 24 withdrawn):			
C2			A Small size		£3.00	£60.00
B1			B Large size		£4.00	£76.00
—			C Extra-large size (127 x 88mm)		£9.00	—
K2	C	53	*Miniature Playing Cards (anonymous) (c1935):	H.535-3		
			A Scroll design:			
			1 Red back		25p	£12.50
			2 Blue back		30p	£15.00
			B Ship design:			
			1 Red border — Nelson's 'Victory'		40p	£20.00
			2 Black border — Drake's 'Revenge'		40p	£20.00
	U	25	Scenes from Famous Films — 'Third Series' (1933):			
C2			A Small size		£3.00	£75.00
—			B Extra-large size (127 x 88mm)		£8.00	—

SILKS

Size	Printing	Number in set	Description	Handbook ref	Price per card	Complete set
—	C	48	British Empire Flags — 'Kensitas' (78 x 54mm) (1933)	H.496-4		
			A Inscribed 'Printed in U.S.A.'		£1.00	£50.00
			B Without 'Printed in U.S.A.'		£1.00	£50.00
			Album		—	£35.00
—	C	60	Kensitas Flowers — 'First Series', small (68 x 40mm) (1934):	H.496-1		
			A Back of folder plain		£3.00	—
			B Back of folder printed in green:			
			i Centre oval 19mm deep		£3.00	—
			ii Centre oval 22mm deep		£3.00	—
			iii As ii, inscribed 'washable ...'		£3.00	—
			Album		—	£35.00
—	C	60	Kensitas Flowers — 'First Series', medium (76 x55mm) (1934):	H.496-1		
			A Back of folder plain		£4.50	—
			B Back of folder printed in green:			
			i Line commencing 'Kensitas' 46mm long		£4.50	—
			ii Line commencing 'Kensitas' 50mm long		£4.50	—
			iii As ii, inscribed 'Washable'		£4.50	—
			Album		—	£35.00
	C	30	Kensitas Flowers — 'First Series' Extra-large (138 x96mm) (1934):	H.496-1		
			A Back of folder plain		£50.00	—
			B Back of folder printed in green:			
			i Word 'More' half in oval		£50.00	—
			ii Word 'More' outside oval		£50.00	—
			iii As ii, inscribed 'Washable'		£50.00	—

Size	Print-ing	Number in set	BRITISH TOBACCO ISSUERS	Handbook reference	Price per card	Complete set

J. WIX & SONS LTD, London (Silks continued)

Size	Print-ing	Number in set		Handbook reference	Price per card	Complete set
—	C	40	Kensitas Flowers — 'Second Series' (1935): A Small size, 68 x 40mm	H.496-2		
			1 Nos 1-30		£6.00	—
			2 Nos. 31 to 40		£25.00	—
			Album		—	£35.00
			B Medium size, 76 x 55mm			
			1 Nos 1-30		£6.00	—
			2 Nos. 31 to 40		£26.00	—
			Album		—	£35.00
	C	60	National Flags — 'Kensitas' (78 x 54mm) (1934) ...	H.496-3	£1.25	£75.00
			Album		—	£35.00

OVERSEAS ISSUE

A2	P	24	Royal Tour in New Zealand (1928)		£13.00	—

WOOD BROS., England

—	BW	28	Dominoes (63 x 29mm) (c1910)		£70.00	—

T. WOOD, Cleckheaton

D	C	30	*Army Pictures, Cartoons, etc (1916)	H.12	£160.00	—

JOHN J. WOODS, London

A	BW	? 23	*Views of London (c1905)	H.395	£300.00	—

W.H. & J. WOODS LTD, Preston

—	C	1	Advertisement Card 'Perfection Flake' (86 x 35mm) (c1900)	H.773	—	£1000.00
A2	U	25	Aesop's Fables (c1932)	H.518	£2.00	£50.00
A2	P	50	Modern Motor Cars (c1936)		£8.00	£400.00
D	C	25	Romance of the Royal Mail (c1935)		£1.40	£35.00
A	C	25	*Types of Volunteers and Yeomanry (c1902)	H.455	£40.00	—

J. & E. WOOLF

A	U	? 5	*Beauties 'KEWA' (c1900)	H.139	£1200.00	—

M.H. WOOLLER, London

A	—	25	Beauties 'BOCCA' (c1900)		£1500.00	—

T.E. YEOMANS & SONS LTD, Derby

—	C	72	Beautiful Women (75 x 55mm) (c1900)	H.284	£260.00	—
A	U	50	War Portraits (1916)	H.86	£120.00	—

JOHN YOUNG & SONS LTD, Bolton

A2	C	12	Naval Skits (c1904)	H.457	£150.00	—
A2	C	12	*Russo-Japanese Series (1904)	H.456	£100.00	—

A. ZICALIOTTI

A	C	1	Advertisement Card 'Milly Totty' (c1900)	H.774	—	£2000.00

ANONYMOUS SERIES

A WITH LETTERPRESS ON BACK OF CARD

A2	C	20	Animal Series — see Hill:
			  A 'The cigarettes with which ...' back ....
			  B Space at back			

A	U	? 35	*Beauties — 'KEWA' England Expects ...' back c1900	H.139	£150.00	
D	BW	25	*Boxers, green back — see Cohen Weenen			

142

Size	Print-ing	Number in set	BRITISH TOBACCO ISSUERS	Handbook reference	Price per card	Complete set
			ANONYMOUS SERIES (With Letterpress Back continued)			
A1	C	? 2	*Celebrities — Coloured. 1902 Calendar back — see Cohen Weenen			
D	C	? 2	*Celebrities — 'GAINSBOROUGH I', 1902 Calendar back, gilt border to front — see Cohen Weenen	H.90		
	C	25	Cinema Stars — see Teofani:	H.530		
C2			A Small size			
—			B Extra-large size (109 x 67mm)			
A2	U	50	Cinema Stars — Set 7 — see United Kingdom Tobacco Co.	GP.703		
D2	C	25	Cinema Stars — Set 8 — see Moustafa	GP.542		
A2	C	50	Evolution of the British Navy — see Godfrey Phillips			
A2	BW	40	Famous Film Stars, text in Arabic (two series) — see Hill			
A2	C	50	Famous Footballers — see Godfrey Phillips			
A2	C	35	Famous Stars — see Reliance Tobacco Mfg. Co. ...	H.572		
C2	C	20	Great Inventors — see Teofani	H.213		
A2	C	20	*Interesting Buildings and Views, 1902, Calendar back — see Cohen Weenen	H.96		
—	—	33	Ministry of Information Cards — see Ardath	H.193		
D2	U	48	Modern Movie Stars and Cinema Celebrities — see Teofani	H.569		
D2	C	? 1	*Nations, 1902 Calendar back — see Cohen Weenen	H.97		
D2	C	25	Pictures of World Interest — see Moustafa			
A	C	25	*Types of British Soldiers, 'General Favourite Onyx' back — see E. Robinson	H.144		
D	C	25	V.C. Heroes (Nos. 51-75 — see Cohen Weenen) ...			
A	C	41	V.C. Heroes — 'Pure Virginia Cigarettes' — Dobson Molle & Co. Ltd — Printers — see Thomson and Porteous	H.427		
D	U	50	*War Series (Cohen Weenen — Nos. 1-50)	H.103		
C2	U	24	Well-Known Racehorses — see Teofani	H.609		
B	**WITH PLAIN BACK**					
A	U	25	*Actors and Actresses — 'FROGA C' (c1900)	H.20	£20.00	—
D2	U	? 9	*Actresses — 'ANGLO' (c1896)	H.185	£90.00	—
	U		*Actresses — 'ANGOOD' (c1898):	H.187		
			A Brown tinted:			
		? 22	i Thick board		£40.00	—
		? 14	ii Thin board		£40.00	—
		? 10	B Green tinted		£60.00	—
		? 30	C Black tinted		£40.00	—
A1	BW	20	*Actresses — 'BLARM' (c1900)	H.23	£17.00	—
D	U	20	*Actresses — Chocolate tinted — see Hill	H.207		
A	C	? 50	*Actresses — 'DAVAN' (c1902):	H.124		
			A Portrait in red only		£50.00	—
			B Portrait in colour		£50.00	—
D	BW	12	*Actresses — 'FRAN' — see Drapkin	H.175		
A		26	*Actresses — 'FROGA A' (c1900):	H.20		
	C		i Coloured		£16.00	—
			ii Unicoloured		£16.00	—
A1	BW	10	*Actresses — 'HAGG A' (c1900)	H.24	£16.00	—
A1	BW	? 13	*Actresses — 'HAGG B' (c1900)	H.24	£16.00	—
A	BW	15	*Actresses — 'RUTAN' — see Rutter	H.381		
—	C	50	*Actresses Oval Card — see Phillips	H.324		
A1	U		*Actresses and Beauties — Collotype — see Ogden	H.306		
C	C	20	*Animal Series — see Hill			

Size	Printing	Number in set	BRITISH TOBACCO ISSUERS	Handbook reference	Price per card	Complete set
			ANONYMOUS SERIES (With Plain Back continued)			
—	C	? 12	*Arms of Cambridge Colleges (17 x 25mm) — see Kuit	H.458		
—	C	? 12	*Arms of Companies (30 x 33mm) — see Kuit	H.459		
A2	P	36	Australia. Second Series — see Westminster			
A2	BW	? 13	*Battleships — see Hill	H.208		
A	C	25	*Beauties — 'BOCCA' (c1900)	H.39	£20.00	—
A		50	*Beauties — 'CHOAB' (c1900):	H.21		
	U		A Unicoloured		£16.00	—
	C		B Coloured		£16.00	—
A			*Beauties — 'FECKSA' (c1901):	H.58		
	U	50	A Plum-coloured front		£16.00	—
	C	? 6	B Coloured front		£55.00	—
D2	U	? 23	*Beauties — 'FENA' (c1900)	H.148	£55.00	—
A2	C	25	*Beauties — 'GRACC' (c1900)	H.59	£20.00	—
A	C	26	*Beauties — 'HOL' (c1900)	H.192	£16.00	—
A	U	? 14	*Beauties 'KEWA' (c1900)	H.139	£50.00	—
A	U	? 7	Beauties — 'NANA' (c1895)	H.377	£150.00	—
D	BW	50	*Beauties — 'PLUMS' (c1900)	H.186	£50.00	—
—	C	30	*Beauties — Oval card (36 x 60mm) — see Phillips	H.244		
A2	P	18	*Beauties — see Marcovitch	GP.490		
D1	U		*Bewlay's War Series (c1915):	H.477		
		12	1 Front without captions		£20.00	—
		? 1	2 Front with captions		£30.00	—
A2	BW	20	*Boer War Cartoons (c1901)	H.42	£20.00	—
A	C		*Boer War and General Interest (c1901):	H.13		
		? 20	A Plain cream back		£40.00	—
		? 22	B Brown Leaf Design back		£40.00	—
		? 12	C Green Leaf Design back		£40.00	—
		? 6	D Green Daisy Design back		£60.00	—
A2	BW	? 16	*Boer War Celebrities — 'CAG' (1901)	H.79	£25.00	—
A1	BW	25	Boer War Celebrities 'PAM'- See Drapkin & Millhoff ...	H.140		
A		? 7	Boer War Celebrities 'RUTTER' (1901):	H.382		
	BW		A Front in black and white		£45.00	—
	U		B Front in light orange brown		£45.00	—
D2	BW	20	*Boer War Generals — 'CLAM' (1901)	H.61	£18.00	—
A1	BW	? 10	*Boer War Generals — 'FLAC' (1901)	H.47	£18.00	—
D	C	25	*Boxer Rebellion — Sketches (1904)	H.46	£16.00	—
A	C	54	*British Beauties (Phillips) (1-54)	H.328		
A	C	54	*British Beauties (Phillips) (55-108) Matt	H.328		
A1	P	60	*British Beauty Spots — see Coudens	H.553		
B1	P	50	*British Castles, Nd. S.J.51-S.J.100 — see Pattreiouex			
—	C	108	*British Naval Crests (74 x 52mm) (c1915)	H.504-4/GP.207	£4.00	
A	C	12	British Queens (c1897)	H.480	£32.00	—
A	BW	16	*British Royal Family (1902)	H.28	£16.00	—
D2	CP	50	*Camera Studies — see Moustafa			
B1	P	50	*Cathedrals and Abbeys. Nd. S.J.1-S.J.50 — see Pattreiouex			
A	C	45	*Celebrities — Coloured — see Cohen Weenen ...	GP.357		
D2	C	39	*Celebrities — 'GAINSBOROUGH I' — see Cohen Weenen	GP.358		
D2	BW	? 147	*Celebrities — 'GAINSBOROUGH II' — see Cohen Weenen	GP.359		
A1	P	36	*Celebrities of the Great War (1916) — see Major Drapkin & Co			
A	BW	? 12	Celebrities of the Great War (c1916)	H.236	£90.00	—
A	C	25	*Charming Portraits — see Continental Cigarette Factory	H.549		

Size	Print-ing	Number in set	BRITISH TOBACCO ISSUERS	Handbook reference	Price per card	Complete set
			ANONYMOUS SERIES (With Plain Back continued)			
A2	U	30	*Cinema Stars — Set 3 (1931)	GP.52	£2.00	—
A2	U	30	*Cinema Stars — Set 6 (1935)	GP.55	£1.00	£30.00
A	C		*Colonial Troops (c1901):	H.40		
		30	A Cream card		£17.00	—
		50	B White card		£17.00	—
—	C	110	*Crests and Badges of the British Army (74 x 52mm):	GP.245		
			A Numbered (c1915)		£4.00	—
			B Unnumbered (c1915)		£3.00	—
A	BW	20	Cricketers Series (1901)	H.29	£320.00	—
A	C	50	Dogs (as Taddy) (c1900):	H.487		
			A Borders in green		£34.00	—
			B Borders in white		£34.00	—
A	C	25	*England's Military Heroes — see Player:	H.352		
			A Wide card			
			B Narrow card			
A	C	25	*England's Naval Heroes — see Player:	H.353		
			A Wide card			
			B Narrow card			
A	C	20	*The European War Series (c1915)	H.129	£14.00	—
—	BW	12	*Film Actors and Actresses (56 x 31mm) — see Teofani	H.618		
A	C		*Flags, Arms and Types of Nations (c1910):	H.115		
		24	A Numbered		£15.00	—
		? 2	B Unnumbered		£50.00	—
A	C		*Flags and Flags with Soldiers (c1902):	H.41		
		30	A Flagstaff draped		£15.00	—
		15	B Flagstaff not draped (flags only)		£15.00	—
A1	C	30	*Flags of Nations — see Cope	H.114		
A1	C	24	*Girls, Flags and Arms of Countries — see Rutter	H.383		
A	C	20	*Head Dresses of Various Nations — see Teofani			
A	C	40	*Home and Colonial Regiments (c1901)	H.69	£13.00	—
—	C	17	Industrial Propaganda Cards — see Ardath	H.914		
A	—	20	*Inventors and Their Inventions — see Hill	H.213		
—	C	? 9	*Irish Views (68 x 67mm) — see Lambkin	H.585		
A	C	52	*Japanese Series, P.C. Inset — see Muratti			
A1	P	? 2	*King Edward and Queen Alexandra (c1902)	H.460	£20.00	
—	BW	12	*London Views (57 x 31mm) — see Teofani	H.620		
C	C	20	*National Flag Series — see Hill			
D	C	20	*Nations, gilt border — see Cohen Weenen	GP.369		
A	C	50	*Natives in Costume — see Teofani			
D	C	40	*Naval and Military Phrases (c1904):	H.14		
			A Plain front (no border)		£15.00	—
			B Front with gilt border		£65.00	—
—	P	30	*Photographs (Animal Studies) (64 x 41mm) (c1925)	GP.337	£2.00	—
—	U	? 2	*Portraits — see Drapkin & Millhoff (48 x 36mm)	H.461		
A	U	? 42	*Pretty Girl Series — 'BAGG' (c1900)	H.45	£20.00	
A2	C	12	*Pretty Girl Series 'RASH' (c1897)	H.8	£20.00	—
A1	C	20	*Prince of Wales Series (c1911)	H.22	£15.00	—
D	C	30	*Proverbs (c1903)	H.15	£16.00	—
—	C	? 48	*Regimental Colours II (76 x 70mm) (c1915)	GP.245	£13.00	—
A	BW	19	Russo-Japanese Series (1904)	H.184	£22.00	—
A	C	20	Russo-Japanese War Series (1904)	H.100	£22.00	—
A	C	10	Scenes from San Toy — see Richard Lloyd	H.462		
A	C	25	Sports and Pastimes Series No. 1 (c1912)	H.225	£16.00	—
D	U	? 100	Stage and Variety Celebrities (Collotype) (c1888	H.182	£90.00	—
A	C	25	*Star Girls (c1900)	H.30	£20.00	—
A1	BW	? 28	*Statuary A-D — see Hill	H.218		

Size	Print-ing	Number in set	BRITISH TOBACCO ISSUERS	Handbook reference	Price per card	Complete set
			ANONYMOUS SERIES (continued)			
—	P	22	*Teofani Gems I — Series of 22 (53 x 35mm) — see Teofani			
—	P	28	*Teofani Gems II — Series of 28 (53 x 35mm) see Teofani			
—	P	36	*Teofani Gems III — Series of 36 (53 x 35mm) — see Teofani			
A	C	25	*Types of British and Colonial Troops (c1900)	H.76	£22.00	—
A2	C	25	*Types of British Soldiers (c1914)	H.144	£16.00	—
—	U	? 24	Views and Yachts (narrow, about 63 x 30mm) (c1900)	H.262-2	£50.00	—
D	BW	12	*Views of the World — see Drapkin	H.176		
D	BW	8	*Warships — see Drapkin	GP.426		
D			*War Series (c1915):	H.103		
	U	? 3	A Front in brown		£30.00	—
	BW	? 4	B Front in black and white		£30.00	—
A	C	50	*World's Smokers — see Teofani			

C   WITH DESIGNS ON BACK

A	BW	25	Careless Moments (1922)		£1.00	£25.00
D2	U	28	*Dominoes ('W.T.C.' monogram back) — see Walker's Tobacco Co.	H.535-2		
—	C	53	*Miniature Playing Cards (68 x 42mm) (red back, black cat trade mark in centre) — see Carreras ...	H.535-1		
K2	C	53	*Miniature Playing Cards (blue scroll back) — see Godfrey Phillips			
K2	C	53	*Miniature Playing Cards — see J. Wix: A Scroll design: 1 Red back ... ... 2 Blue back ... ... B Ship design: 2 Black border — Drake's 'Revenge'	H.535-3		
C			*Playing Cards and Dominoes — see Carreras:	H.535-1		
C		52	A Small size: 1 Numbered ... ... 2 Unnumbered			
—		26	B Large size (77 x 69mm): 1 Numbered ... ... 2 Unnumbered			

D   ANONYMOUS SERIES SILKS AND OTHER NOVELTY ISSUES

For Anonymous Metal Plaques — see International Tobacco Co.
For Anonymous Metal Charms — see Rothman's.
For Anonymous Miniature Rugs — see Godfrey Phillips.
For Anonymous Lace Motifs — see Carreras.
For Anonymous Woven Silks — see Anstie and J. Wix.
For Anonymous Printed Silks with Blue Borders — see Themans.

SECTION 2
FOREIGN TOBACCO ISSUERS

Prices are for **Very Good** condition; post-1955 issues are priced as **Finest Collectable Condition** to Mint

Size	Number in set	FOREIGN TOBACCO ISSUERS	Price per card	Complete set
		AFRICAN CIGARETTE CO. LTD, Egypt		
	50	Actresses ALWICS (c1905)	£9.00	—
L	25	Auction Bridge (c1925)	£8.00	—
		AFRICAN TOBACCO MANUFACTURERS, South Africa		
A	**CARD ISSUES**			
L	29	All Blacks South African Tour (1928)	£24.00	—
	60	Animals (c1920):		
		A Cut Outs	£5.00	—
		B Not Cut Out	£5.00	—
	25	The Arcadia Fair (1924)	£12.00	—
MP	48	British Aircraft (1932)	£6.00	—
	50	Chinese Transport (1930)	£6.00	—
MP	48	Cinema Artistes (1930)	£4.50	—
	50	Cinema Stars 'OMBI' Officers Mess Issue 1st Series (1921)	£2.40	£120.00
	50	Cinema Stars 'OMBI' Officers Mess Issue 2nd Series (1921)	£2.60	£130.00
M	50	Famous and Beautiful Women (1938)	£4.00	—
L	50	Famous and Beautiful Women (1938)	£4.00	—
	33	Houses of Parliament (c1920)	£6.50	—
	58	Miniatures (c1925)	£7.50	—
MP	48	National Costume (1930)	£4.00	—
K	53	Playing Cards MP-SA Virginia Cigarettes (c1930)	£3.00	—
K	53	Playing Cards, OK Cigarettes (c1930)	£2.00	—
K	53	Playing Cards, Scotts Cigarettes (c1930)	£2.00	—
MP	48	Popular Dogs (1930)	£6.00	—
M	100	Postage Stamps, Rarest Varieties (1929)	£2.20	—
M	80	Prominent NZ and Australian Rugby Players and Springbok 1937 Touring Team (1937)	£6.00	—
L	80	Prominent NZ and Australian Rugby Players and Springbok 1937 Touring Team (1937)	£4.50	—
	25	The Racecourse (1924) W.181	£12.00	—
M	132	S. African Members of the Legislative Assembly (1921)	£40.00	—
M	100	The World of Sport (1938)	£5.50	—
L	100	The World of Sport (1938)	£4.50	—
B	**SILK ISSUES**			
M	30	Some Beautiful Roses (c1925)	£11.00	—
M	25	Types of British Birds (c1925)	£11.00	—
M	20	Types of British Butterflies (c1925)	£13.00	—
M	25	Types of Railway Engines (c1925)	£34.00	—
M	25	Types of Sea Shells (c1925)	£17.00	—

Size	Number in set	FOREIGN TOBACCO ISSUERS	Price per card	Complete set

M.V. ALBERT (Ram Cigarettes), Martinique

	K12	Film Actors and Actresses (1936) H.618	£5.00	—

ALLEN & GINTER, USA

ALL SERIES ISSUED 1885-95

Size	Number	Title	Price	Set
	?	Actors and Actresses (sepia photographic)	£8.00	—
	?	Actresses and Beauties (coloured)	£12.00	—
	50	American Editors	£38.00	—
L	50	American Editors	£45.00	—
L	50	The American Indian	£65.00	—
	50	Arms of All Nations	£28.00	—
	50	Birds of America	£20.00	—
L	50	Birds of America	£34.00	—
	50	Birds of the Tropics	£22.00	—
L	50	Birds of the Tropics	£38.00	—
	50	Celebrated American Indian Chiefs	£60.00	—
	50	City Flags	£18.00	—
	50	Fans of the Period	£30.00	—
	50	Fish from American Waters	£22.00	—
L	50	Fish from American Waters	£32.00	—
	50	Flags of All Nations (series title curved)	£13.00	—
	48	Flags of All Nations (series title in straight line)	£13.00	—
	50	Flags of All Nations, 2nd series	£15.00	—
	47	Flags of the States and Territories	£15.00	—
	50	Fruits	£32.00	—
	50	Game Birds	£20.00	—
L	50	Game Birds	£36.00	—
	50	General Government and State Capitol Buildings	£20.00	—
	50	Great Generals	£45.00	—
	50	Natives in Costume	£40.00	—
	50	Naval Flags	£22.00	—
	50	Parasol Drill	£30.00	—
	50	Pirates of the Spanish Main	£75.00	—
	50	Prize and Game Chickens	£34.00	—
	50	Quadrupeds	£20.00	—
L	50	Quadrupeds	£34.00	—
	50	Racing Colors of the World:		
		A Front with white frame	£34.00	—
		B Front without white frame	£34.00	—
	50	Song Birds of the World	£20.00	—
L	50	Song Birds of the World	£35.00	—
	50	Types of All Nations	£30.00	—
	50	Wild Animals of the World	£22.00	—
	50	The World's Beauties, 1st series	£25.00	—
	50	The World's Beauties, 2nd series	£25.00	—
	50	The World's Champions, 1st series	£60.00	—
	50	The World's Champions, 2nd series	£70.00	—
L	50	The World's Champions, 2nd series	£110.00	—
	50	The World's Decorations	£20.00	—
L	50	The World's Decorations	£30.00	—
	50	World's Dudes	£30.00	—
	50	The World's Racers	£30.00	—
	50	World's Smokers	£24.00	—
	50	World's Sovereigns	£34.00	—

ALLEN TOBACCO CO., USA

L	?	Views and Art Studies (c1910)	£5.00	—

Size	Number in set	FOREIGN TOBACCO ISSUERS	Price per card	Complete set
		THE AMERICAN CIGARETTE CO. LTD, China		
	10	Admirals and Generals Ref RB.118/155 (c1900)	£75.00	—
	25	Beauties Group 1 Ref RB.118/8 (c1900)	£28.00	—
	? 15	Beauties Group 2 Ref RB.118/21-2 (c1900)	£40.00	—
	53	Beauties with Playing Card inset Ref RB.118/23 (c1900)	£50.00	—
	50	Flowers Ref RB.118/161 (c1900)	£22.00	—
		AMERICAN EAGLE TOBACCO CO., USA		
	20	Actresses blue border (c1890):		
		A With firm's name	£85.00	—
		B 'Double 5' back	£80.00	—
	15	Actresses sepia (c1890)	£85.00	—
	15	Beauties 'PAC' (c1895)	£100.00	—
	36	Flags of Nations (c1890):		
		A Size 70 x 39mm	£45.00	—
		B Size 64 x 39mm	£45.00	—
	36	Flags of States (c1890):		
		A Size 70 x 39mm	£45.00	—
		B Size 64 x 39mm	£45.00	—
	50	Occupations for Women (c1895)	£80.00	—
		Photographic Cards Actresses (c1890):		
	? 33	A Size 69 x 37mm	£30.00	—
L	6	B Size 102 x 52mm	£32.00	—
	23	Presidents of the U.S. (c1890)	£65.00	—

THE AMERICAN TOBACCO COMPANY, USA

ALL SERIES ISSUED 1890-1902

A   *TYPESET BACK IN BLACK (see RB.118 index Fig C-1 for design on back)*

	28	Beauties Domino Girls RB.118/66	£24.00	—
	25	Beauties Group 1 RB.118/4	£5.00	—
	? 1	Beauties Group 2 RB.118/20	—	—
	25	Beauties Group 3 RB.118/25	£5.00	—
	25	Beauties Group 3 RB.118/26	£5.00	£125.00
	25	Beauties Group 3 RB.118/27	£5.00	—
	25	Beauties Group 3 RB.118/29	£5.00	—
		Beauties Group 4 RB.118/36:		
	50	a Coloured	£5.00	£250.00
	? 50	b Sepia	£15.00	—
	? 41	Beauties Photographic Ref RB.118/93 (c1894)	£20.00	—
	52	Beauties PC Inset	£15.00	—
	25	Beauties — Star Girls RB.118/76	£20.00	—
	25	Dancers RB.118/52	£18.00	—
	50	Dancing Women RB.118/135	£25.00	—
	50	Fancy Bathers RB.118/136	£25.00	—
	36	Japanese Girls RB.118/139	£80.00	—
	60	Jokes RB118/175	£25.00	—
	25	Military Uniforms RB.118/101	£22.00	—
	25	Military Uniforms RB.118/102	£18.00	—
	27	Military Uniforms RB.118/103	£13.00	—
	50	Musical Instruments RB.118/140	£20.00	—
	50	National Flag and Arms RB.118/141	£13.00	—
	25	National Flag and Flowers — Girls RB.118/142	£25.00	—
	50	Savage Chiefs and Rulers RB.118/144	£32.00	—

B   *NET DESIGN BACK IN GREEN (see RB.118 index Fig C-2 for design on back)*

	25	Beauties Black background RB.118/62	£16.00	—
	25	Beauties Curtain background RB.118/65	£16.00	£400.00
	25	Beauties Flower Girls RB.118/67	£15.00	—

Size	Number in set	FOREIGN TOBACCO ISSUERS	Price per card	Complete set

THE AMERICAN TOBACCO COMPANY, USA (1890-1902 continued)

B NET DESIGN BACK IN GREEN (continued)

	25	Beauties Group 1 RB.118/1	£4.00	—
	27	Beauties Group 1 RB.118/2	£4.00	—
	25	Beauties Group 1 RB.118/3	£4.00	—
	24	Beauties Group 1 RB.118/4	£4.00	—
	25	Beauties Group 1 RB.118/5	£4.00	—
	25	Beauties Group 1 RB.118/6	£4.00	—
	50	Beauties Group 1 RB.118/10	£4.00	—
	25	Beauties Group 2 RB.118/16	£4.00	—
	25	Beauties Group 2 RB.118/17	£4.00	—
	? 24	Beauties Group 2 RB.118/18	£4.00	—
	25	Beauties Group 2 RB.118/19	£4.00	—
	25	Beauties Group 2 RB.118/20	£4.00	—
	25	Beauties Group 2 RB.118/21	£5.00	—
	36	Beauties Group 2 RB.118/22	£6.00	—
	25	Beauties Group 3 RB.118/25	£4.00	—
	? 10	Beauties Group 3 RB.118/28	—	—
	25	Beauties Group 3 RB.118/30	£4.00	—
	25	Beauties Group 3 RB.118/31	£8.00	—
	25	Beauties Group 3 RB.118/32	£4.00	—
	50	Beauties Marine and Universe Girls RB.118/71	£34.00	—
	25	Beauties Palette Girls RB.118/74	£16.00	—
	25	Beauties Star Girls RB.118/76	£22.00	—
	25	Beauties — Stippled background RB.118/78	£15.00	—
	20	Beauties — thick border RB.118/79	£38.00	—
	52	Beauties with Playing Card inset Set 1 RB.118/85 (Head & Shoulder)	£15.00	—
	52	Beauties with Playing Card inset Set 2 RB.118/86 (Half Length)	£15.00	—
	25	Boer War Series II — Series A RB.118/100:		
		a) numbered	£10.00	£250.00
		b) unnumbered	£10.00	—
		c) unnumbered and untitled 'series A'	£10.00	—
	22	Boer War Series II — Series B RB.118/100	£12.00	—
	25	Chinese Girls RB.118/111	£15.00	—
	25	Fish from American Waters RB.118/137	£15.00	—
	25	International Code Signals RB.118/43	£15.00	—
	27	Military Uniforms numbered RB.118/103	£13.00	—
	25	Military Uniforms unnumbered RB.118/104	£18.00	—
	50	National Flags and Arms RB.118/141	£13.00	—
	25	Old and Ancient Ships 1st Series RB.118/143	£8.00	£200.00
	25	Old and Ancient Ships 2nd Series RB.118/143	£14.00	£350.00
	25	Star Series — Beauties RB.118/77	£22.00	—

C NET DESIGN BACK IN BLUE (see RB.118 index Fig C-2 for design on back)

Actresses RB.118-90:

P	? 300	A Large Letter Back (word 'Brands' 29mm)	£5.50	—
P	? 300	B Small Letter Back (word 'Brands' 25mm)	£6.50	—
	25	Beauties blue frameline RB.118/64:		
		A Matt	£26.00	—
		B Varnished	£26.00	—
	28	Beauties — Domino Girls RB.118/66	£24.00	—
	25	Beauties Group 1 dull backgrounds RB.118/7.2	£18.00	—
	25	Beauties Group 1 vivid coloured backgrounds set 1 RB.118/7.3	£18.00	—
	25	Beauties Group 1 vivid coloured backgrounds set 2 RB.118/9	£18.00	—
	25	Beauties numbered RB.118/72:		
		A Front in black and white	£20.00	—
		B Front in mauve	£20.00	—
	24	Beauties — orange framelines RB.118/73	£38.00	—
		Beauties — playing cards RB.118/87:		
	52	A Inscribed 52 subjects	£15.00	—
	53	B Inscribed 53 subjects	£15.00	—

Size	Number in set		Price per card	Complete set
		FOREIGN TOBACCO ISSUERS		

THE AMERICAN TOBACCO COMPANY, USA (1890-1902 continued)

C *NET DESIGN BACK IN BLUE* (continued)

	32	Celebrities RB.118/94	£10.00	—
	25	Comic Scenes RB.118/113	£12.00	—
P	? 149	Views RB.118/96	£4.00	—

D *'OLD GOLD' BACK (see RB.118 index Fig C-3 for design on back)*

	25	Beauties Group 1 RB.118/1	£4.00	—
	27	Beauties Group 1 RB.118/2	£4.00	—
	25	Beauties Group 1 RB.118/3	£4.00	—
	24	Beauties Group 1 RB.118/4	£4.00	—
	25	Beauties Group 1 RB.118/5	£4.00	—
	25	Beauties Group 1 RB.118/6	£4.00	—
	? 47	Beauties Group 2 RB.118/16, 17, 18	£4.00	—
	25	Beauties Group 2 RB.118/22	£4.00	—
	27	Beauties Group 3 RB.118/25	£4.00	—
	25	Beauties Group 3 RB.118/26	£4.00	—
	25	Beauties Group 3 RB.118/27	£4.00	—
	25	Beauties Group 3 RB.118/28	£4.00	—
	25	Beauties Group 3 RB.118/30	£4.00	—
	25	Flowers Inset on Beauties RB.118/41	£14.00	£350.00
	25	International Code Signals:		
		A With series title RB.118/42	£14.00	£350.00
		B Without series title RB.118/43	£14.00	£350.00

E *LABELS BACK (see RB.118 index Fig C-4/6 for design on back)*

	35	Beauties Group 1 RB.118/2-3	£5.00	—
	25	Beauties Group 2 1st Set RB.118/15	£5.00	—
	25	Beauties Group 2 2nd Set RB.118/16	£5.00	—
		Beauties Group 3 RB.118/25:		
	27	A Old Gold Label	£5.00	—
	26	B Brands Label	£5.00	—

F *OTHER BACKS*

P	126	Actresses RB.118/91	£5.50	—
	44	Australian Parliament RB.118/92	£6.50	—
	25	Battle Scenes RB.118/130	£17.00	—
	24	Beauties RB.118/10 (Packet Issue)	£9.00	—
L	10	Boer War Series 1 Old Gold back	£50.00	—
L	47	Boer War Series 2 Kimball's Old Gold with brown net design back	£50.00	—
	1	Columbian and Other Postage Stamps (1892)	—	£14.00
	50	Congress of Beauty World's Fair 1893 RB.118/134	£25.00	—
	25	Constellation Girls (plain back)	£26.00	—
	50	Fish from American Waters RB.118/137	£16.00	—
	50	Flags of All Nations RB.118/138	£13.00	—
	25	Flower Inset on Beauties RB.118/41	£14.00	£350.00
	50	Heroes of the Spanish War RB.26/A54-112 (Packet Issue) (1900)	£15.00	—
	25	International Code Signals RB.118/42	£14.00	£350.00
	25	Songs A RB.118/46 (1896):		
		A Thicker board size 70 x 39mm	£18.00	—
		B Thinner board size 67 x 39mm	£18.00	—
	25	Songs B RB.118/47 (1898):		
		A Size 70 x 39mm	£18.00	—
		B Size 67 x 39mm	£18.00	—
	25	Songs C 1st series RB.118/48 (1900)	£13.00	—
	25	Songs C 2nd series RB.118/48 (1900)	£15.00	—
	25	Songs D RB.118/49 (1899)	£14.00	—
	27	Songs E RB.118/50 (1901)	£20.00	—
	25	Songs F RB.118/51 (1897):		
		A Size 70 x 36mm, with scroll at base	£15.00	—
		B Size 67 x 38mm, without scroll at base	£15.00	—

Size	Number in set	FOREIGN TOBACCO ISSUERS	Price per card	Complete set

THE AMERICAN TOBACCO COMPANY, USA (1890-1902 continued)

F OTHER BACKS (continued)

	25	Songs G RB.118/53 (1899)	£15.00	—
	25	Songs H RB.118/54 (1901)	£22.00	—
	25	Songs I RB.118/55 (1899)	£28.00	—

ISSUES 1903-1940 *(most series are multi-backed)*

L	50	Actors	£8.00	—
	85	Actress Series	£8.00	—
L	50	Actresses	£12.00	—
		Animals:		
L	40	A Descriptive back	£3.50	—
L	40	B Non descriptive back	£3.50	—
L	25	Arctic Scenes	£6.50	—
M	15	Art Gallery Pictures	£5.00	—
M	50	Art Reproductions	£5.00	—
	21	Art Series (1903)	£17.00	—
	18	Ask Dad	£14.00	—
L	50	Assorted Standard Bearers of Different Countries	£8.00	—
	25	Auto-drivers	£16.00	—
M	50	Automobile Series	£16.00	—
L	50	Baseball Folder series (T201) (1911)	£35.00	—
M	121	Baseball series (T204)	£60.00	—
	208	Baseball series (T205) (1911)	£26.00	—
	522	Baseball series (T206)	£26.00	—
	200	Baseball series (T207) (1910)	£36.00	—
	565	Baseball series (T210)	£40.00	—
	75	Baseball series (T211)	£40.00	—
	426	Baseball series (T212)	£40.00	—
	180	Baseball series (T213)	£40.00	—
	90	Baseball series (T214)	£120.00	—
	100	Baseball series (T215)	£40.00	—
L	76	Baseball Triple Folders (T202) (1912)	£50.00	—
		Bird series:		
	50	A With white borders	£5.00	—
	50	B With gold borders	£5.00	—
	30	Bird Series with Fancy Gold Frame	£5.00	—
M	360	Birthday Horoscopes	£2.75	—
M	24	British Buildings 'Tareyton' issue	£3.50	—
M	42	British Sovereigns 'Tareyton' issue	£3.50	—
M	50	Butterfly Series	£5.50	—
L	153	Champion Athlete and Prize Fighter series (size 73 x 64mm) (1911)	£12.00	—
L	50	Champion Athlete and Prize Fighter series (size 83 x 63 mm)	£22.00	—
L	50	Champion Pugilists	£28.00	—
EL	100	Champion Women Swimmers	£11.00	—
M	150	College series	£3.00	—
M	50	Costumes and Scenery for All Countries of the World	£4.00	—
L	49	Cowboy series	£10.00	—
M	38	Cross Stitch	£10.00	—
M	17	Embarrassing Moments or Emotional Moments	£35.00	—
M	50	Emblem Series	£4.50	—
L	100	Fable Series	£3.50	—
LP	53	Famous Baseball Players, American Athletic Champions and Photoplay Stars	£80.00	—
	50	Fish Series inscribed '1 to 50' — 1st 50 subjects	£5.00	—
	50	Fish Series inscribed '1 to 100' — 2nd 50 subjects	£5.00	—
	200	Flags of All Nations	£3.00	—
M	100	Flags of All Nations	£16.00	—

Size	Number in set	FOREIGN TOBACCO ISSUERS	Price per card	Complete set
		THE AMERICAN TOBACCO COMPANY, USA (1903-1940 continued)		
	50	Foreign Stamp Series	£7.00	—
L	505	Fortune Series	£3.00	—
M	79	Henry 'Tareyton' issue	£3.00	—
L	50	Heroes of History	£12.00	—
M	50	Historic Homes	£6.00	—
L	25	Historical Events Series	£8.50	—
M	25	Hudson — Fulton Series	£7.00	—
L	50	Indian Life in the 60s (1910)	£9.00	—
L	221	Jig Saw Puzzle Pictures	£12.00	—
L	50	Light House Series	£8.00	—
L	50	Men of History 2nd Series	£12.00	—
M	100	Military Series white borders	£6.00	—
	50	Military Series gilt borders	£7.00	—
	50	Military Series 'Recruit' issue:		
		A Uncut cards	£7.00	—
		B Die-cut cards	£7.00	—
	50	Movie Stars	£6.00	—
L	100	Movie Stars	£6.00	—
	33	Moving Picture Stars	£24.00	—
EL	50	Murad Post Card Series	£10.00	—
	100	Mutt & Jeff Series (black and white)	£5.00	—
	100	Mutt & Jeff Series (coloured)	£5.00	—
EL	16	National League and American League Teams	£70.00	—
	50	Pugilistic Subjects	£35.00	—
EL	18	Puzzle Picture Cards	£18.00	—
M	200	Riddle Series	£3.00	—
EL	60	Royal Bengal Souvenir Cards	£10.00	—
M	150	Seals of the United States and Coats of Arms of the World	£2.00	—
L	25	Series of Champions	£45.00	—
L	50	Sights and Scenes of the World	£4.00	—
L	50	Silhouettes	£9.00	—
L	25	Song Bird Series	£40.00	—
	39	Sports Champions	£50.00	—
	45	Stage Stars	£9.00	—
	25	State Girl Series	£9.00	—
L	50	Theatres Old and New Series	£9.00	—
M	50	Toast Series	£9.00	—
M	550	Toast Series	£3.00	—
L	25	Toasts	£16.00	—
	50	Types of Nations:		
		A Without series title	£3.50	—
		B With series title	£3.50	—
		C Anonymous back	£3.50	—
L	25	Up to Date Baseball Comics	£40.00	—
L	25	Up to Date Comics	£10.00	—
P	340	World Scenes and Portraits	£4.00	—
	250	World War I Scenes	£3.50	—
L	50	World's Champion Athletes	£20.00	—
L	25	The World's Greatest Explorers	£8.00	—
		THE AMERICAN TOBACCO CO. OF NEW SOUTH WALES LTD, Australia		
	25	Beauties Group 1 RB.118/8 (c1900)	£16.00	—
	25	Beauties Group 2 (c1900)	£16.00	—
		THE AMERICAN TOBACCO CO. OF VICTORIA LTD, Australia		
?	98	Beauties Group 2 RB.118/16 to 21 (c1900)	£16.00	—

Size	Number in set		Price per card	Complete set
		ASHEVILLE TOBACCO WORKS AND CIGARETTE CO., USA		
	39	Actresses (c1890)	£80.00	—
		ATLAM CIGARETTE FACTORY, Malta		
M	65	Beauties back in blue (c1925)	£3.00	—
	150	Beauties back in brown (c1925)	£8.00	—
M	519	Celebrities (c1925)	£1.50	—
L	50	Views of Malta (c1925)	£7.00	—
M	128	Views of the World (c1925)	£6.50	—
		BANNER TOBACCO CO., USA		
L	? 41	Actors and Actresses (c1890)	£90.00	—
EL	25	Girls (c1890) RB.22/X2-453	£50.00	—
		THOMAS BEAR & SONS LTD		
	50	Aeroplanes (1926)	£5.00	—
	50	Cinema Artistes Set 2 (c1935)	£5.00	—
	50	Cinema Artistes Set 4 (c1935)	£5.00	—
	50	Cinema Stars coloured (1930)	£4.00	—
	50	Do You Know (1923)	£2.00	—
	270	Javanese series 1 blue background (c1925)	£2.00	—
	100	Javanese series 4 yellow background (c1925)	£8.00	—
	50	Stage and Film Stars (1926)	£5.00	—
		AUG BECK & CO. USA		
	? 44	Picture Cards (c1890)	£75.00	—
	23	Presidents of U.S. (coloured) (c1890)	£80.00	—
	23	Presidents of U.S. (sepia) (c1890)	£80.00	—
	? 14	State Seals (c1890)	£85.00	—
		BRITISH AMERICAN TOBACCO CO. LTD		
A		*WITH MAKER'S NAME NET DESIGN IN GREEN (ISSUES 1902-05)*		
	25	Beauties Art series RB.118/61	£16.00	—
	25	Beauties — Black background RB.118/62	£14.00	—
	25	Beauties — Blossom Girls RB.118/63	£45.00	—
	25	Beauties — Flower Girls RB.118/67	£13.00	—
	25	Beauties — Fruit Girls RB.118/68	£16.00	—
	25	Beauties — Girls in Costumes RB.118/69	£16.00	—
	20	Beauties Group 1 RB.118/9	£13.00	—
	25	Beauties — Lantern Girls RB.118/70	£14.00	—
	50	Beauties — Marine and Universe Girls RB.118/71	£15.00	—
	25	Beauties — Palette Girls RB.118/74:		
		A Plain border to front	£14.00	—
		B Red border to front	£20.00	—
	24	Beauties — Smoke Girls RB.118/75	£20.00	—
	25	Beauties — Star Girls RB.118/76	£20.00	—
	25	Beauties — Stippled background RB.118/78	£15.00	£375.00
	25	Beauties — Water Girls RB.118/80	£15.00	£375.00
	50	Buildings RB.118/131	£15.00	—
	25	Chinese Girls 'A' RB.118/111	£15.00	—
	25	Chinese Girls 'B' RB.118/112:		
		A Background plain	£15.00	—
		B Background with Chinese letters	£15.00	—
	25	Chinese Girls 'C' RB.118/113	£15.00	—
		Chinese Girls 'D' RB.118/114:		
	20	A Back design 53mm long	£15.00	—
	25	B Back design 60mm long	£15.00	—

Size	Number in set	FOREIGN TOBACCO ISSUERS	Price per card	Complete set

BRITISH AMERICAN TOBACCO CO. LTD (continued)

A   WITH MAKER'S NAME NET DESIGN IN GREEN (ISSUES 1902-05) (continued)

	25	Chinese Girls 'E' RB.118/115	£15.00	—
	25	Chinese Girls 'F' Set 1 RB.118/116:		
		A Fronts reddish background	£15.00	—
		B Fronts sepia background	£15.00	—
	25	Chinese Girls 'F' Set 2 RB.118/116:		
		A Yellow border	£15.00	—
		B Gold border	£16.00	—
	50	Chinese Girls 'F' Set 3 RB.118/116:		
		A Plain background	£15.00	—
		B Chinese characters background	£16.00	—
	40	Chinese Trades RB.118/108	£9.00	—

B   WITH MAKER'S NAME NET DESIGN IN BLUE (ISSUES 1902-05)

	25	Beauties — numbered RB.118/72	£22.00	—
	53	Beauties — Playing Cards RB.118/87	£15.00	—

C   WITH MAKER'S NAME OTHER BACKS

MP	50	Beauties (1925)	£2.50	—
MP	40	Beauties (1926)	£2.50	—
M	50	Birds, Beasts and Fishes (cut-outs) (1925)	£2.80	£140.00
	50	Danish Athletes (1905)	£15.00	—
	28	Dominoes (1905)	£7.00	—
	48	Fairy Tales (1926)	£6.00	—
	48	A Famous Picture — The Toast (c1930)	£4.00	—
	25	New York Views (c1908)	£20.00	—
	53	Playing Cards (1905)	£12.00	—
M	50	Wild Animals (c1930)	£4.50	—

D   SERIES WITH BRAND NAMES

ALBERT CIGARETTES

M	50	Aeroplanes (Civils) (1935)	£14.00	—
	50	Artistes de Cinema Nd 1-50 (1932)	£4.00	—
	50	Artistes de Cinema Nd 51-100 (1933)	£4.00	—
	50	Artistes de Cinema Nd 101-150 (1934)	£4.00	—
MP	? 67	Beauties (c1928)	£5.00	—
M	75	Belles Vues de Belgique (c1930)	£3.00	—
M	50	Birds, Beasts & Fishes (cut-outs) (c1930)	£5.00	—
M	50	Butterflies (Girls) (1926)	£10.00	—
M	50	Cinema Stars (brown photogravure) (c1927)	£3.50	—
M	100	Cinema Stars (numbered, coloured) (c1928)	£3.50	—
M	208	Cinema Stars (unnumbered, coloured) (c1929)	£3.50	—
M	100	Circus Scenes (c1930)	£3.50	—
M	100	Famous Beauties (1916)	£3.50	—
M	50	L'Afrique Equitoriale de l'Est a l'Ouest (c1930)	£3.00	—
M	100	La Faune Congolaise (c1910)	£1.50	—
M	50	Les Grandes Paquebots du Monde (1924)	£8.00	—
M	50	Merveilles du Monde (1927)	£4.00	—
M	50	Women of Nations (Flag Girls) (1922)	£5.50	—

ATLAS CIGARETTES

	50	Buildings (1907)	£10.00	—
	25	Chinese Beauties (1912)	£7.00	—
	50	Chinese Trades Set IV (1908)	£6.00	—
	85	Chinese Trades Set VI (1912)	£6.00	—

BATTLE AX CIGARETTES

M	100	Famous Beauties (1916)	£7.50	—
M	50	Women of Nations (Flag Girls) (1917)	£7.50	—

COPAIN CIGARETTES

	52	Birds of Brilliant Plumage (1927)	£8.00	—

Size Number in set		FOREIGN TOBACCO ISSUERS	Price per card	Complete set

BRITISH AMERICAN TOBACCO CO. LTD (continued)

D SERIES WITH BRAND NAMES (continued)

DOMINO CIGARETTES

	25	Animaux et Reptiles (1961)	36p	£9.00
	25	Corsaires et Boucaniers (1960)	20p	£5.00
	25	Figures Historiques 1st series (1961)	50p	£12.50
	25	Figures Historiques 2nd series (1961)	80p	£20.00
	25	Fleurs de Culture (1960)	20p	£4.00
	25	Les Oiseaux et l'Art Japonais (1961)	£1.00	—
	25	Les Produits du Monde (1960)	20p	£3.50
	50	Voitures Antiques (1961)	£1.50	—

EAGLE BIRD CIGARETTES

	50	Animals and Birds (1909)	£3.50	—
	50	Aviation series (1912)	£5.50	—
	25	Birds of the East (1912)	£3.60	£90.00
	25	China's Famous Warriors (1911)	£5.00	—
	25	Chinese Beauties 1st series (1908):		
		A Vertical back	£4.00	—
		B Horizontal back	£4.00	—
	25	Chinese Beauties 2nd series (1909):		
		A Front without framelines	£4.00	—
		B Front with framelines	£4.00	—
	50	Chinese Trades (1908)	£3.60	—
	25	Cock Fighting (1911)	£18.00	—
	60	Flags and Pennons (1926)	£2.25	£135.00
	50	Romance of the Heavens (1929)	£4.00	—
	50	Siamese Alphabet (1922)	£1.80	£90.00
	50	Siamese Dreams and Their Meanings (1923)	£1.50	£75.00
	50	Siamese Horoscopes (c1915)	£1.50	£75.00
	50	Siamese Play-Inao (c1915)	£1.50	£75.00
	50	Siamese Play-Khun Chang Khun Phaen 1st series (c1915)	£1.50	£75.00
	50	Siamese Play-Khun Chang Khun Phaen 2nd series (c1915)	£1.50	£75.00
	36	Siamese Play-Phra Aphaiu 1st series (c1918)	£1.50	£55.00
	36	Siamese Play-Phra Aphaiu 2nd series (1919)	£1.50	£55.00
	150	Siamese Play — Ramakien I (c1913)	£1.50	—
	50	Siamese Play — Ramakien II (1914)	£1.50	£75.00
	50	Siamese Uniforms (1915)	£3.00	£150.00
	50	Views of Siam (1928)	£3.00	£150.00
	50	Views of Siam (Bangkok) (1928)	£4.00	£200.00
	30	War Weapons (1914)	£4.00	—

KONG BENG CIGARETTES

	60	Animals (cut-outs) (1912)	£10.00	—

MASCOT CIGARETTES

	100	Cinema Stars (Nd 201-300) (1931)	£3.50	—
M	208	Cinema Stars unnumbered (1924)	£3.00	—

MILLBANK CIGARETTES

	60	Animals (cut-outs):		
		A '1516' at base of back (1922)	£1.50	—
		B '3971' at base of back (1923)	£1.50	—

NASSA CIGARETTES

M	50	Birds, Beasts and Fishes (cut-outs) (1924)	£5.00	—

PEDRO CIGARETTES *(see also Imperial Tobacco Co. of India)*

	50	Actors and Actresses (c1905)	£4.50	—
	40	Nautch Girls. Coloured (1905)	£3.00	—
	37	Nautch Girls. Red border (c1905)	£3.00	—

PINHEAD CIGARETTES

	50	Chinese Modern Beauties (1912)	£5.00	—

Size	Number in set		Price per card	Complete set
		FOREIGN TOBACCO ISSUERS		

BRITISH AMERICAN TOBACCO CO. LTD (continued)

D SERIES WITH BRAND NAMES: PINHEAD CIGARETTES (continued)

	33	Chinese Heroes Set 1 (1912)	£5.00	—
	50	Chinese Heroes Set 2 (1913)	£5.00	—
	50	Chinese Trades Set III (1908)	£5.00	£250.00
	50	Chinese Trades Set IV (1909)	£5.00	£250.00
	50	Chinese Trades Set V (1910)	£5.00	£250.00
	50	Types of the British Army (1909)	£6.50	—

RAILWAY CIGARETTES (see also Imperial Tobacco Co. of India)

	37	Nautch Girls series (1907)	£3.00	—

TEAL CIGARETTES

	30	Chinese Beauties (c1915)	£6.00	—
	50	Cinema Stars (1930):		
		A Back in blue	£3.00	—
		B Back in red brown	£3.00	—
	30	Fish series (1916)	£4.50	—
	50	War Incidents (1916)	£4.50	£225.00

TIGER CIGARETTES

	52	Nautch Girls series (1911):		
		A Without frameline to front	£3.00	—
		B With frameline to front:		
		i With crossed cigarettes on back	£3.00	—
		ii Without crossed cigarettes on back	£3.00	—

NO BRAND NAME BLUE FLAG PACKET WITH SIAMESE TEXT

	50	Puzzle Sectional Series (c1915) RB.21/492-1	£2.00	—
	50	Siamese Dancers (c1915) RB.21/492-2	£1.60	£80.00
	50	Siamese Life (c1915) RB.21/492-3	£1.60	£80.00
	50	Siamese Proverbs (c1915) RB.21/492-4	£1.60	£80.00
	50	Types of the British Army (c1916)	£4.00	—

E PRINTED ON BACK NO MAKER'S NAME OR BRAND
(See also Imperial Tobacco Co. of Canada Ltd and United Tobacco Companies (South) Ltd)

		Actresses 'ALWICS' (c1905):		
	175	A Portrait in black	£4.00	—
	50	B Portrait in red	£4.50	—
	50	Aeroplanes (1926)	£4.00	£200.00
	50	Aeroplanes of Today (1936)	£1.60	£80.00
	25	Angling (1930)	£7.00	—
	50	Arms and Armour (1910)	£7.00	—
	25	Army Life (c1910)	£7.50	—
	50	Art Photogravures (1913)	£1.25	—
	1	Australia Day (1915)	—	£16.00
	22	Automobielen (c1925)	£8.50	—
	75	Aviation (1910)	£5.00	—
	50	Aviation series (1911):		
		A With album clause	£4.50	—
		B Without album clause	£4.50	—
		Beauties Set I (1925):		
P	50	A Black and white	£2.50	£125.00
MP	50	B Coloured	£2.00	—
P	50	Beauties 2nd series (1925):		
		A Black and white	£2.30	£115.00
		B Coloured	£2.00	—
P	50	Beauties 3rd series (1926)	£1.50	£75.00
	50	Beauties red tinted (c1906)	£3.50	—
		Beauties tobacco leaf back (c1908):		
	52	A With PC inset	£3.50	£175.00
	50	B Without PC inset	£4.50	£225.00

Size	Number in set	FOREIGN TOBACCO ISSUERS	Price per card	Complete set

BRITISH AMERICAN TOBACCO CO. LTD (continued)

E   PRINTED ON BACK NO MAKER'S NAME OR BRAND (continued)

Size	Number in set		Price per card	Complete set
P	50	Beauties of Great Britain (1930):		
		A Non-stereoscopic	80p	£40.00
		B Stereoscopic	£2.50	—
P	50	Beautiful England (1928)	60p	£30.00
MP	60	La Belgique Monumentale et Pittoresque (c1925)	£3.25	—
	50	Best Dogs of Their Breed (1916)	£5.00	—
	50	Billiards (1929)	£2.20	—
	50	Birds, Beasts and Fishes (cut-outs) (1937)	£1.00	£50.00
M	50	Birds, Beasts and Fishes (cut-outs) (1929)	£1.50	£75.00
	24	Birds of England (1924)	£3.00	£75.00
	50	Boy Scouts (1930) — without album clause	£3.00	£150.00
	50	Britain's Defenders (1915):		
		A Blue grey fronts	£2.50	—
		B Mauve fronts	£2.20	£110.00
	50	British Butterflies (1930)	£1.20	£60.00
	50	British Empire series (1913)	£3.00	—
	25	British Trees and Their Uses (1930)	£3.00	£75.00
	50	British Warships and Admirals (1915)	£5.50	—
	50	Butterflies and Moths (1911):		
		A With album clause	£3.00	—
		B Without album clause	£2.50	—
	50	Butterflies (Girls) (1928)	£6.00	£300.00
M	50	Butterflies (Girls) (1928)	£8.00	£400.00
M	50	Celebrities of Film and Stage (1930):		
		A Title on back in box	£2.00	£100.00
		B Title on back not in box	£2.00	£100.00
LP	48	Channel Islands Past and Present (1939):		
		A Without '3rd Series'	£1.20	—
		B With '3rd Series'	40p	£20.00
	40	Characters from the Works of Charles Dickens (1919):		
		A Complete set	—	£50.00
		B 38 different (— Nos 33, 39)	80p	£30.00
	50	Cinema Artistes, black and white set 1 (Nd 1-50) (c1928)	£2.00	£100.00
	50	Cinema Artistes black and white set 4 (Nd 101-150) (c1928)	£2.00	£100.00
		Cinema Artistes brown set 1 (c1930):		
	60	A With 'Metro Golden Mayer'	£2.50	—
	50	B Without 'Metro Golden Mayer'	£2.50	—
	50	Cinema Artistes brown set 2 (c1931):		
		A Oblong panel at top back	£2.00	£100.00
		B Oval panel at top back	£2.00	£100.00
L	48	Cinema Artistes set 3 (c1931)	£2.00	£100.00
	48	Cinema Celebrities (C) (1935)	£1.30	£65.00
L	48	Cinema Celebrities (C) (1935)	£1.60	£80.00
L	56	Cinema Celebrities (D) (1936)	£2.80	—
	50	Cinema Favourites (1929)	£2.20	£110.00
	50	Cinema Stars Set 2 (Nd 1-50) (1928) RB.21/253-2	£1.20	£60.00
	50	Cinema Stars Set 3 (Nd 51-100) (1929) RB.21/253-3	£3.00	—
	50	Cinema Stars Set 4 (Nd 101-150) (1930) RB.21/253-4	£1.20	—
	100	Cinema Stars 'BAMT' (coloured) (1931) RB.21/260-4	£2.50	—
P	50	Cinema Stars Set 1 (c1928) RB.21/235-1	£1.50	—
P	50	Cinema Stars Set 2 (c1928) RB.21/235-2	£1.20	£60.00
P	50	Cinema Stars Set 3 (c1928) RB.21/235-3	£1.50	—
MP	52	Cinema Stars Set 4 (c1928) RB.21/236-1	£1.80	—
MP	52	Cinema Stars Set 5 (c1928) RB.21/236-2	£1.80	—
MP	52	Cinema Stars Set 6 (c1928) RB.21/236-3	£2.50	—
LP	48	Cinema Stars Set 7 (c1928) RB.21/236-4	£3.00	—

Size	Number in set	FOREIGN TOBACCO ISSUERS	Price per card	Complete set

BRITISH AMERICAN TOBACCO CO. LTD (continued)

E PRINTED ON BACK NO MAKER'S NAME OR BRAND (continued)

Size	Number	Title	Price	Set
P	50	Cinema Stars Set 8 (Nd 1-50) (c1928) RB.21/237-1	£1.20	£60.00
P	50	Cinema Stars Set 9 (Nd 51-100) (c1928)) RB.21/237-2	£2.50	—
P	50	Cinema Stars Set 10 (Nd 101-150) (c1928)) RB.21/237-3	£2.50	—
P	50	Cinema Stars Set 11 (Nd 151-200) (c1928)) RB.21/237-4	£2.50	—
	25	Derby Day series (1914)	£10.00	—
	50	Do You Know? (1923)	60p	£30.00
	50	Do You Know? 2nd series (1931)	60p	£30.00
	25	Dracones Posthistorici (c1930)	£10.00	—
	25	Dutch Scenes (1928)	£3.20	£80.00
	50	Engineering Wonders (1930)	80p	£40.00
	40	English Costumes of Ten Centuries (1919)	£1.50	£60.00
P	25	English Cricketers (1926)	£4.00	£100.00
	26	Etchings (of Dogs) (1926)	£3.00	£80.00
P	50	Famous Bridges (1935)	£1.00	£50.00
	50	Famous Footballers Set 1 (1923)) RB.21/458-1	£6.00	—
	50	Famous Footballers Set 2 (1924) RB.21/458-2	£6.00	—
	50	Famous Footballers Set 3 (1925) RB.21/458-3	£6.00	—
	25	Famous Racehorses (1926)	£3.00	£75.00
	25	Famous Railway Trains (1929)	£2.60	£65.00
	50	Favourite Flowers (c1925)	£1.10	£55.00
	50	Film and Stage Favourites (c1925)	£2.00	£100.00
	75	Film Favourites (1928)	£1.50	£115.00
	50	Flags of the Empire (1928)	90p	£45.00
	50	Foreign Birds (1930)	90p	£45.00
	50	Game Birds and Wild Fowl (1929)	£1.50	£75.00
LP	45	Grace and Beauty (Nos 1-45) (1938)	50p	£22.50
LP	45	Grace and Beauty (Nos 46-90) (1939)	40p	£18.00
LP	48	Guernsey, Alderney and Sark Past and Present 1st series (1937)	50p	£25.00
LP	48	Guernsey, Alderney and Sark Past and Present 2nd series (1938)	40p	£20.00
L	80	Guernsey Footballers Priaulx League (1938)	80p	£65.00
P	52	Here There and Everywhere:		
		A Non stereoscopic (1929)	50p	£25.00
		B Stereoscopic (1930)	80p	£40.00
	25	Hints and Tips for Motorists (1929)	£2.60	£65.00
P	50	Homeland Events (1928)	90p	£45.00
	50	Horses of Today (1906)	£6.00	—
	32	Houses of Parliament (red back) (1912)	£2.00	—
	32	Houses of Parliament (brown backs with verse) (1912)	£10.00	—
	50	Indian Chiefs (1930)	£13.00	—
	50	Indian Regiments series (1912)	£13.00	—
	50	International Air Liners (1937)	£1.00	£50.00
	25	Java Scenes (1929)	£10.00	—
LP	48	Jersey Then and Now 1st series (1935)	£1.10	£55.00
LP	48	Jersey Then and Now 2nd series (1937)	£1.00	£50.00
	50	Jiu Jitsu (1911)	£4.00	—
	50	Keep Fit (1939)	£1.00	£50.00
	50	Leaders of Men (1929)	£3.50	—
	50	Life in the Tree Tops (1931)	50p	£25.00
	50	Lighthouses (1926)	£2.40	£120.00
	40	London Ceremonials (1929)	£1.50	£60.00
P	50	London Zoo (1927)	90p	£45.00
	50	Lucky Charms (1930)	£1.50	£75.00
	25	Marvels of the Universe series (c1925)	£3.00	£75.00
	45	Melbourne Cup Winners (1906)	£10.00	—
	50	Merchant Ships of the World (1925)	£5.50	—
	25	Merchant Ships of the World (1925)	£4.40	—

Size	Number in set	FOREIGN TOBACCO ISSUERS	Price per card	Complete set

BRITISH AMERICAN TOBACCO CO. LTD (continued)

E PRINTED ON BACK NO MAKER'S NAME OR BRAND (continued)

Size	Number in set	Title	Price per card	Complete set
	25	Military Portraits (1917)	£3.60	—
	36	Modern Beauties 1st series (1938)	£1.25	£45.00
	36	Modern Beauties 2nd series (1939)	90p	£33.00
MP	54	Modern Beauties 1st series (1937)	£1.00	£55.00
MP	54	Modern Beauties 2nd series (1938)	£1.00	£55.00
MP	36	Modern Beauties 3rd series (1938)	£1.50	£55.00
MP	36	Modern Beauties 4th series (1939)	£1.00	£36.00
ELP	36	Modern Beauties 1st series (1936)	£1.25	£45.00
ELP	36	Modern Beauties 2nd series (1936)	£1.00	£36.00
ELP	36	Modern Beauties 3rd series (1937)	£1.00	£36.00
ELP	36	Modern Beauties 4th series (1937)	£1.50	£55.00
ELP	36	Modern Beauties 5th series (1938)	£1.25	£45.00
ELP	36	Modern Beauties 6th series (1938)	£1.00	£36.00
ELP	36	Modern Beauties 7th series (1938)	£1.25	£45.00
LP	36	Modern Beauties 8th series (1939)	£1.50	£55.00
LP	36	Modern Beauties 9th Series (1939)	£1.50	£55.00
LP	36	Modern Beauties (1939)	£1.25	£45.00
	50	Modern Warfare (1936)	£1.50	£75.00
M	48	Modern Wonders (1938)	£3.00	—
	25	Modes of Conveyance (1928)	£2.20	£55.00
	48	Motor Cars green back (1926)	£6.00	—
	36	Motor Cars brown back (1929)	£9.00	—
	50	Motorcycles (1927)	£4.50	—
P	50	Native Life in Many Lands (1932)	£1.60	£80.00
P	50	Natural and Man Made Wonders of the World (1937)	60p	£30.00
P	50	Nature Studies stereoscopic (1928)	70p	£35.00
P	48	Nature Studies stereoscopic (1930)	£1.00	£50.00
	50	Naval Portraits (1917)	£4.00	—
	25	Notabilities (1917)	£3.00	£75.00
	25	Past and Present (1929)	£1.80	£45.00
P	48	Pictures of the East (1930):		
		A 'A Series of 48' 17mm long	£1.50	£75.00
		B 'A Series of 48' 14mm long	£1.50	£75.00
M	48	Picturesque China (c1925):		
		A With 'P' at left of base	£1.60	£80.00
		B Without 'P' at left of base	£1.60	£80.00
M	53	Playing Cards Ace of Hearts Back (c1935)	40p	£20.00
K	53	Playing Cards designed back (c1935):		
		A Blue back	£1.00	—
		B Red back	£1.00	—
	36	Popular Stage, Cinema and Society Celebrities (c1928)	£3.50	—
	25	Prehistoric Animals (1931)	£4.00	£100.00
	50	Prominent Australian and English Cricketers (1911)	£55.00	—
	25	Puzzle series (1916)	£6.00	—
	50	Railway Working (1927)	£2.00	£100.00
	10	Recruiting Posters (1915)	£8.50	—
	33	Regimental Pets (1911)	£8.50	—
	50	Regimental Uniforms (1936)	£1.60	£80.00
	50	Romance of the Heavens (1929)	£1.10	£55.00
P	50	Round the World in Pictures stereoscopic (1931)	£1.20	£60.00
	50	Royal Mail (1912)	£4.50	—
P	50	Royal Navy (1930)	£2.00	—
	27	Rulers of the World (1911)	£8.00	—
	40	Safety First (1931)	£2.00	£80.00
	25	Ships' Flags and Cap Badges 1st series (1930)	£3.40	£85.00
	25	Ships' Flags and Cap Badges 2nd series (1930)	£3.40	£85.00

Size	Number in set	FOREIGN TOBACCO ISSUERS	Price per card	Complete set

BRITISH AMERICAN TOBACCO CO. LTD (continued)

E   PRINTED ON BACK NO MAKER'S NAME OR BRAND (continued)

P	50	Ships and Shipping (1928)	£1.50	£75.00
	50	Signalling series (1913)	£5.00	—
	100	Soldiers of the World (tobacco leaf back) (c1902)	£14.00	—
	50	Speed (1938)	70p	£35.00
	25	Sports and Games in Many Lands (1930):		
		A 24 Different minus No. 25	£5.00	£120.00
		B Number 25 (Babe Ruth)	—	£50.00
	50	Stage and Film Stars (1926)	£1.60	—
M	50	Stars of Filmland (1927)	£2.50	—
	100	Transfers (Spanish wording headed 'Moje la calcomania') RB.21/587 c1930:		
		A Size 55 x 35mm	£4.00	—
		B Size 62 x 40mm wording 37mm deep	£3.00	—
		C Size 62 x 40mm wording 44mm deep	£4.00	—
	48	Transport Then and Now (1940)	50p	£25.00
	32	Transport of the World (1917)	£9.00	—
	20	Types of North American Indians (c1930)	£25.00	—
P	50	Types of the World (1936)	£1.00	£50.00
P	270	Views of the World stereoscopic (1908)	£3.00	—
	50	War Incidents (brown back) (1915)	£2.80	£140.00
	50	War Incidents (blue back) (1916)	£2.80	£140.00
	25	Warriors of All Nations (gold panel) (1937)	£2.00	£50.00
	50	Warships (1926)	£8.00	—
	25	Whaling (1930)	£2.40	£60.00
P	50	Who's Who in Sport (1926)	£3.20	£160.00
	50	Wild Animals of the World (tobacco leaf back) (1902)	£9.00	—
	25	Wireless (1923)	£4.60	—
	50	Wonders of the Past (1930)	80p	£40.00
	50	Wonders of the Sea (1929)	80p	£40.00
	25	Wonders of the World (c1928)	80p	£20.00
	40	World Famous Cinema Artistes (1933)	£1.65	£65.00
M	40	World Famous Cinema Artistes (1933)	£1.65	£65.00
	50	World's Products (1929)	50p	£25.00
P	50	The World of Sport (1927)	£3.00	—
P	50	Zoo (1935)	80p	£40.00
	50	Zoological Studies (1928):		
		A Brown back	60p	£30.00
		B Black back	£1.50	—

F   PLAIN BACKS

	50	Actors and Actresses 'WALP' (c1905):		
		A Portraits in black and white, glossy	£3.00	£150.00
		B Portraits flesh tinted, matt	£3.00	£150.00
	50	Actresses 'ALWICS' (c1905)	£3.00	—
	50	Actresses, four colours surround (c1905) W.117:		
		A Dotted frameline glossy front	£3.00	—
		B Dotted frameline matt front	£3.00	—
		C Curved frameline brown surround	£12.00	—
		D Curved frameline mauve surround	£12.00	—
	30	Actresses unicoloured (c1910):		
		A Fronts in purple brown	£1.10	£33.00
		B Fronts in light brown	£1.10	£33.00
	50	Animals and Birds (1912)	£2.00	—
	60	Animals — cut-outs (1912)	£1.20	—
	50	Art Photogravures (1912)	£2.00	—
	50	Aviation series (1911)	£4.00	—
M	50	Beauties 1st series Coloured (1925) RB.21/231-1A	£5.00	—

Size	Number in set	FOREIGN TOBACCO ISSUERS	Price per card	Complete set

BRITISH AMERICAN TOBACCO CO. LTD (continued)

F *PLAIN BACKS* (continued)

Size	Number in set		Price per card	Complete set
	40	Beauties — brown tinted (1913)	£2.50	—
	50	Beauties with backgrounds (1911) W.141	£3.00	—
	50	Beauties 'LAWHA' (c1906) W.146:		
		A Black with red border	£3.50	—
		B Light Green with red border	£5.00	—
		C Dark Purple picture and border	£3.50	—
		D Light Purple/Mauve picture and border	£3.50	—
		E Red with black border	£3.50	—
	32	Beauties Picture Hats I with borders (1914)	£3.20	—
	45	Beauties Picture Hats II without borders (1914)	£3.20	—
	30	Beauties and Children (c1910)	£5.00	—
	30	Beauties 'Celebrated Actresses' (c1910)	£3.00	—
	52	Birds of Brilliant Plumage — PC inset (1914)	£3.00	—
	25	Bonzo series (1923):		
		A With series title	£4.00	—
		B Without series title	£4.00	—
	30	Boy Scouts Signalling (c1920):		
		A Captions in English	£4.00	£120.00
		B Captions in Siamese	£4.00	£120.00
	50	British Man of War series (1910)	£12.00	—
	50	Butterflies and Moths (1910)	£2.50	—
	50	Cinema Artistes (c1928)	£3.00	—
	50	Cinema Stars RB.21/259 (c1930):		
		A Front matt	£1.50	£75.00
		B Front glossy	£1.50	—
	50	Cinema Stars RB.21/260 (Nd 1-50) (c1930)	£1.50	—
	50	Cinema Stars RB.21/260 (Nd 51-100) (c1930)	£1.50	—
	50	Cinema Stars RB.21/260 (Nd 101-150) (c1930)	£1.50	—
	100	Cinema Stars RB.21/260 (Nd 201-300) (c1930)	£1.50	£150.00
	50	Cinema Stars 'FLAG' (c1930)	£1.50	—
	27	Dancing Girls (1913)	£2.00	—
	32	Drum Horses (1910)	£6.00	—
	50	English Period Costumes	£1.00	£50.00
	50	Flag Girls of All Nations (1911)	£2.00	—
		Flags, Pennons and Signals (c1910):		
	70	A Numbered 1-70	£1.50	—
	70	B Unnumbered	£1.50	—
	50	C Numbered 71-120	£1.50	—
	45	D Numbered 121-165	£1.50	—
	20	Flowers (1915)	£2.00	£40.00
	50	Girls of All Nations (1908)	£2.20	—
	30	Heroic Deeds (1913)	£3.50	—
	25	Hindoo Gods (1909)	£11.00	—
	32	Houses of Parliament (1914)	£3.25	—
	25	Indian Mogul Paintings (1909)	£11.00	—
LP	48	Jersey Then and Now 3rd series (coloured) (c1940)	£2.00	—
	53	Jockeys and Owners Colours — PC inset (c1914)	£4.00	—
	30	Merrie England Female Studies (1922)	£5.00	—
K	36	Modern Beauties 1st series (1938)	£3.00	—
	36	Modern Beauties 2nd series (1939)	£3.00	—
P	48	Movie Stars (c1930)	£1.80	—
	50	Music Hall Celebrities (1911):		
		A Blue border	£3.00	—
		B Gilt border	£3.00	—
		C Red border	£3.00	—
		D Yellow border	£4.50	—

Size	Number in set	FOREIGN TOBACCO ISSUERS	Price per card	Complete set

BRITISH AMERICAN TOBACCO CO. LTD (continued)

F *PLAIN BACKS* (continued)

Size	Number	Title	Price	Complete
P	50	New Zealand, Early Scenes and Maori Life (c1928)	£1.60	—
	50	Poultry and Pidgeons (c1926)	£9.00	—
	25	Products of the World (1914)	£1.00	£25.00
	25	Roses (1912) W.373	£8.00	—
	50	Royal Mail (1912)	£7.00	—
	36	Ships and Their Pennants (1913)	£3.00	—
	75	Soldiers of the World (c1902)	£10.00	—
	30	Sporting Girls (1913) W.331	£8.00	—
	50	Sports of the World (1917):		
		A Brown front	£5.00	—
		B Coloured front	£5.00	—
M	50	Stars of Filmland (1927)	£2.00	—
	32	Transport of the World (1917)	£1.50	—
	50	Types of the British Army (1908):		
		A Numbered	£5.00	—
		B Unnumbered	£5.00	—
P	50	Types of the World (1936)	£2.50	—
P	50	Units of the British Army and RAF (c1930)	£2.50	—
M	50	Women of Nations (Flag Girls) (1922)	£4.00	—

G *PAPER BACKED SILKS ISSUED 1910-1917*

Size	Number	Title	Price	Complete
M	25	Arabic Proverbs	£14.00	—
M	50	Arms of the British Empire:		
		A Back in blue	£3.00	—
		B Back in brown	£4.00	—
M	50	Australian Wild Flowers	£4.50	—
M	50	Best Dogs of Their Breed	£6.00	—
	110	Crests and Badges of the British Army	£3.50	—
	108	Crests and Badges of the British Army	£3.50	—
M	50	Crests and Colours of Australian Universities, Colleges and Schools	£3.00	—

BRITISH AMERICAN TOBACCO COMPANY (CHINA) LTD

	32	Sectional Picture — 'Beauties of Old China' (1934)	£5.00	—

BRITISH AMERICAN TOBACCO CO. LTD, Switzerland

	30	Series Actrices (1921) RB.21/200-140	£6.00	—

BRITISH AUSTRALASIAN TOBACCO CO., Australia

Size	Number	Title	Price	Complete
		Flags of all Nations (c1903):		
	?126	A Yankee Doodle and Pilot	£10.00	—
		B Yankee Doodle and Champion:		
	126	i Subjects as Wills Reference W.66	£10.00	—
	?22	ii Other Flags	£12.00	—
	?106	iii Steamship Company Flags	£12.00	—

BRITISH CIGARETTE CO. LTD, China

	25	British and Foreign Actresses and Beauties (c1900)	£90.00	—
	25	South African War Scenes (c1900)	£45.00	—

BROWN & WILLIAMSON TOBACCO CORP, USA (Wings Cigarettes)

Size	Number	Title	Price	Complete
M	50	Modern American Airplanes (c1938):		
		A Inscribed 'Series A'	£5.00	—
		B Without 'Series A'	£4.50	—
M	50	Modern American Airplanes 'Series B' (c1938)	£4.50	—
M	50	Modern American Airplanes 'Series C' (c1938)	£4.50	—
	50	Movie Stars (1940) (Golden Grain Tobacco)	£7.00	—

Size	Number in set	FOREIGN TOBACCO ISSUERS	Price per card	Complete set

D. BUCHNER & CO., USA

Size	Number in set		Price	Complete
	48	Actors (1887)	£45.00	—
L	50	Actresses (1891)	£45.00	—
L	? 61	American Scenes with a Policeman (c1890)	£85.00	—
	144	Baseball Players (c1890)	£220.00	—
L	28	Butterflies and Bugs (c1890)	£90.00	—
L	51	Morning Glory Maidens (c1890)	£75.00	—
L	23	Musical Instruments (c1890)	£75.00	—
L	21	Yacht Club Colours (c1890)	£85.00	—

BUCKTROUT & CO. LTD, Guernsey, Channel Islands

Size	Number in set		Price	Complete
M	416	Around the World (1926):		
		A Inscribed 'Places of Interest' Nd. 1-104	50p	£52.00
		B Inscribed 'Around the World' Nd. 105-208	50p	£52.00
		C Inscribed 'Around the World' Nd. 209-312	50p	£52.00
		D Inscribed 'Around the World' Nd. 313-416	50p	£52.00
	24	Birds of England (1923)	£3.60	£90.00
	50	Cinema Stars, 1st series (1921)	£2.00	£100.00
	50	Cinema Stars, 2nd series (1922)	£2.20	£110.00
M	50	Football Teams (1924)	£4.50	—
M	22	Football Teams of the Bailiwick (1924)	£1.50	£33.00
	123	Guernsey Footballers (multi-backed) (c1925)	£5.00	—
	20	Inventors Series (1924)	£1.50	£30.00
	25	Marvels of the Universe Series (1923)	£3.00	£75.00
M	54	Playing Cards (1928)	80p	£42.00
	25	Sports and Pastimes (1925)	£6.00	—

BUKHSH ELLAHIE & CO., India

Size	Number in set		Price	Complete
	53	Indian Girl Playing Card inset (c1898):		
		A Full length girl seated	£25.00	—
		B Full length girl standing	£25.00	—
		C Bust length	£25.00	—
	2	Indian Series (c1898) W.240	£350.00	—

CALCUTTA CIGARETTE CO., India

Size	Number in set		Price	Complete
	25	Actresses — 'ALWICS' (c1905):		
		A Fronts in blue	£34.00	—
		B Fronts in chocolate	£34.00	—

A. G. CAMERON & SIZER, USA (including Cameron & Cameron)

Size	Number in set		Price	Complete
	25	The New Discovery (1889):		
		A Without overprint	£34.00	—
		B With overprint	£34.00	—
	24	Occupations for Women (1895)	£60.00	—
		Photographic Cards (c1895) RB.29/C7-6:		
	? 230	Actresses	£18.00	—
L	? 6	Actresses	£22.00	—
	75	Framed Paintings	£15.00	—

V. CAMILLERI, Malta

Size	Number in set		Price	Complete
MP	104	Popes of Rome (1922):		
		A Nd. 1-52	£2.00	£100.00
		B Nd. 53-104	£2.00	£100.00

Size	Number in set	FOREIGN TOBACCO ISSUERS	Price per card	Complete set

CAMLER TOBACCO COY, Malta

P	250	Footballers (c1925)	£12.00	—
M	96	Maltese Families Coats of Arms:		
		A Thick board (c1925)	£1.30	—
		B Thin board (1958)	£1.30	—

CARROL'S TRIUMPH, Scandinavia

	?160	Actors and Actresses – Collotypes (c1895)	£100.00	—

CHING & CO., Jersey, Channel Islands

L	24	Around and About in Jersey, 1st series (1963)	32p	£8.00
		Album	—	£15.00
L	24	Around and About in Jersey, 2nd series (1964)	80p	£20.00
		Album	—	£20.00
	25	Do You Know? (1962)	20p	£4.00
		Album	—	£12.00
	48	Flowers (1962)	£1.00	£50.00
L	24	Jersey Past and Present, 1st series (1960)	25p	£6.00
L	24	Jersey Past and Present, 2nd series (1961)	70p	£17.50
		Album (1st & 2nd Series combined)	—	£15.00
L	24	Jersey Past and Present, 3rd series (1961)	25p	£6.00
		Album	—	£12.00
	25	Ships and Their Workings (1961)	20p	£4.00
	50	Veteran and Vintage Cars (1960)	60p	£30.00
		Album	—	£15.00

THE CIGARETTE COMPANY, Jersey, Channel Islands

	72	Jersey Footballers (c1910)	£9.00	—

LA CIGARETTE ORIENTAL DE BELGIQUE, Belgium

L	100	Famous Men Throughout the Ages (c1940)	50p	£50.00

C. COLOMBOS, Malta

MP	200	Actresses (c1900)	£4.50	—
MP	59	Actresses (c1900)	£17.00	—
	50	Actresses (coloured) (c1900)	£17.00	—
MP	57	Celebrities (c1900)	£24.00	—
P	136	Dante's Divine Comedy (c1914)	£2.50	—
		Famous Oil Paintings (c1910):		
MP	72	1 Series A	£1.00	—
MP	108	2 Series B	£1.00	—
MP	240	3 Series C	£1.00	—
MP	100	4 Series D	£1.00	—
LP	91	5 Large size	£7.50	—
MP	100	Life of Napoleon Bonaparte (c1914)	£3.50	—
MP	70	Life of Nelson (c1914)	£3.50	—
MP	70	Life of Wellington (c1914)	£3.50	—
MP	100	National Types and Costumes (c1910)	£3.00	—
MP	30	Opera Singers (c1900)	£34.00	—
	120	Paintings and Statues (c1912)	£1.00	—
M	112	Royalty and Celebrities (c1910)	£3.50	—

COLONIAL TOBACCOS (PTY) LTD, South Africa

EL	150	World's Fairy Tales (c1930)	£4.00	—

D. CONDACHI & SON, Malta

?	15	Artistes & Beauties (c1905)	£25.00	—

Size	Number in set	FOREIGN TOBACCO ISSUERS	Price per card	Complete set

CONSOLIDATED CIGARETTE CO., USA

Ladies of the White House (c1895):
	14	A	Size 73 x 43mm, white borders	£40.00	—
	25	B	Size 70 x 38mm, no borders	£35.00	—

A.G. COUSIS & CO., Malta

Actors and Actresses (c1910):
P	100	A	Back with framework	£2.50	—
KP	100	B	Back without framework	£2.50	—
K	254		Actors and Actresses (c1925)	£1.50	—
KP	100		Actresses Series I (c1910)	£2.50	—
KP	80		Actresses Series II (c1910)	£2.50	—
P	100		Actresses (c1910):		
		A	Series I	£2.50	—
		B	Series II	£2.50	—
		C	Series III	£2.50	—
		D	Series IV	£2.50	—
		E	Series V	£2.50	—
		F	Series VI	£2.50	—
		G	Series VII	£2.50	—
		H	Series VIII	£2.50	—
		I	Series IX	£2.50	—
		J	Series X	£2.50	—
		K	Series XI	£2.50	—
		L	Series XII	£2.50	—
		M	Series XIII	£2.50	—
		N	Series XIV	£2.50	—
		O	Series XV	£2.50	—
		P	Series XVI	£2.50	—
		Q	Series XVII	£2.50	—
		R	Series XVIII	£2.50	—
		S	Series XIX	£2.50	—
			Actresses (c1910):		
KP	2281	A	Miniature size 50 x 30mm	£1.50	—
P	1283	B	Small size 58 x 39mm	£1.50	—
MP	325		Actresses, Celebrities and Warships (c1910)	£10.00	—
			Actresses, Partners and National Costumes (c1910):		
KP	200	A	Miniature size 50 x 30mm	£2.50	—
P	100	B	Small size 60 x 39mm	£3.00	—
MP	50		Beauties, Couples and Children (c1908):		
		A	Back inscribed 'Collection No. 1'	£3.50	—
		B	Back inscribed 'Collection No. 2'	£3.50	—
		C	Back inscribed 'Collection No. 3'	£3.50	—
K	50		Beauties, Couples and Children (red back) (c1925)	£2.50	—
P	402		Celebrities numbered matt (c1910):		
		A	Front inscribed 'Dubec Cigarettes', Nd. 1-300	£2.00	—
		B	Front inscribed 'Cousis' Cigarettes', Nd. 301-402	£2.00	—
P	2162		Celebrities unnumbered (c1910):		
		A	Miniature size 50 x 30mm	£1.50	—
		B	Small size 59 x 39mm	£1.50	—
MP	72		Grand Masters of the Order of Jerusalem (c1910)	£3.50	—
P	100		National Costumes (c1910)	£3.00	—
MP	? 57		Paris Exhibition 1900 (c1901)	£32.00	—
MP	102		Paris Series (1902)	£32.00	—
			Popes of Rome (c1910):		
MP	182	A	Back inscribed 'A.G. Cousis & Co'	£2.00	—
MP	81	B	Back inscribed 'Cousis' Dubec Cigarettes'	£3.20	—
P	100		Statues and Monuments (c1910):		
		A	Numbered	£2.00	—
		B	Unnumbered	£2.00	—

Size	Number in set		FOREIGN TOBACCO ISSUERS	Price per card	Complete set
			A.G. COUSIS & CO., Malta (continued)		
KP	127		Views of Malta (c1910)	£2.50	—
P	115		Views of Malta numbered (c1910)	£1.50	—
MP	127		Views of Malta numbered (c1910)	£1.50	—
MP	? 65		Views of Malta unnumbered (c1910)	£1.50	—
P	559		Views of the World (c1910):		
		A	Small size 59 x 39mm	£1.50	—
		B	Medium size 65 x 45mm	£1.50	—
P	99		Warships, white border (c1910)	£4.00	—
			Warships, Liners and Other Vessels (c1904):		
MP	105	A	'Cousis' Dubec Cigarettes'	£8.00	—
MP	22	B	'Cousis' Excelsior Cigarettes'	£8.00	—
MP	40	C	'Cousis' Superior Cigarettes'	£8.00	—
MP	851	D	'Cousis' Cigarettes'	£3.50	—
KP	851	E	'Cousis' Cigarettes'	£3.50	—
			CROWN TOBACCO CO., India		
			National Types, Costumes and Flags (c1900):		
	? 19	A	Size 70 x 40mm. Back 'These Pictures are used'	£40.00	—
	? 14	B	Size 88 x 49mm. Back 'Smoke Crown's High-Class'	£45.00	—
			CHARLES C DAVIS & CO., USA		
K	15		Actresses (c1890)	£90.00	—
			DIXSON, Australia		
	50		Australian MPs and Celebrities (c1900)	£24.00	—
			DOMINION TOBACCO CO., Canada		
	50		The Smokers of the World (c1905)	£75.00	—
			DOMINION TOBACCO CO. LTD, New Zealand		
	50		Coaches and Coaching Days (c1928)	£4.00	—
	50		People and Places Famous in New Zealand History (c1928)	£2.00	—
	50		Products of the World (c1928)	£1.30	£65.00
	50		USS Co's Steamers (c1928)	£4.00	—
			DUDGEON & ARNELL, Australia		
K	16		1934 Australian Test Team (1934)	£12.00	—
K	55		Famous Ships (1933)	£4.50	—
			W. DUKE, SONS & CO., USA		
ALL SERIES ISSUED 1885-95					
	50		Actors and Actresses Series No. 1	£22.00	—
M	50		Actors and Actresses Series No. 1	£45.00	—
	50		Actors and Actresses Series No. 2	£22.00	—
M	50		Actors and Actresses Series No. 2	£45.00	—
EL	30		Actors and Actresses (3 subjects per card)	£45.00	—
	25		Actresses RB.118/27	£13.00	—
EL	25		Actresses (black border)	£40.00	—
EL	25		Actresses (Folders)	£55.00	—
EL	25		Albums of American Stars:		
		A	Folder with card	£70.00	—
		B	Card only without folder	£60.00	—
EL	25		Battle Scenes	£50.00	—
EL	25		Bicycle and Trick Riders	£42.00	—
EL	25		Breeds of Horses	£42.00	—
EL	25		Bridges	£32.00	—

Size	Number in set	FOREIGN TOBACCO ISSUERS	Price per card	Complete set
		W. DUKE, SONS & CO., USA (continued)		
EL	25	Burlesque Scenes	£40.00	—
	50	Coins of All Nations:		
		A White background	£20.00	—
		B Shaded background	£20.00	—
EL	25	Comic Characters	£30.00	—
EL	25	Cowboys Scenes	£55.00	—
EL	50	Fairest Flowers in the World	£36.00	—
	50	Fancy Dress Ball Costumes	£20.00	—
M	50	Fancy Dress Ball Costumes	£36.00	—
EL	50	Fancy Dress Ball Costumes	£30.00	—
	50	Fishers and Fish	£24.00	—
EL	25	Fishes and Fishing (2 subjects per card)	£40.00	—
EL	25	Flags and Costumes	£40.00	—
	50	Floral Beauties and Language of Flowers	£20.00	—
EL	25	French Novelties	£34.00	—
EL	25	Gems of Beauty:		
		A Back 'Fair Play Long Cut'	£34.00	—
		B Back 'Honest Long Cut'	£34.00	—
	50	Great Americans	£34.00	—
EL	16	Great Americans (3 subjects per card)	£50.00	—
	25	Gymnastic Exercises	£30.00	—
EL	25	Habitations of Man	£30.00	—
	50	Histories of Generals (Booklets) (1888)	£50.00	—
EL	50	Histories of Generals (Cards)	£50.00	—
	50	Histories of Poor Boys who have become rich and other famous people (Booklets)	£36.00	—
	50	Holidays	£22.00	—
EL	25	Illustrated Songs	£30.00	—
EL	25	Industries of the States	£38.00	—
	50	Jokes:		
		A With A.T.C. name	£20.00	—
		B Without A.T.C. name	£20.00	—
EL	25	Jokes (2 subjects per card)	£36.00	—
EL	25	Lighthouses (die cut)	£38.00	—
EL	25	Miniature Novelties	£34.00	—
	50	Musical Instruments	£25.00	—
EL	25	Musical Instruments of the World (2 subjects per card)	£36.00	—
	36	Ocean and River Steamers	£30.00	—
M	240	Photographs from Life RB.23/D76-84	£6.00	—
	53	Playing Cards	£12.00	—
	50	Popular Songs and Dancers	£25.00	—
	50	Postage Stamps	£18.00	—
EL	25	Presidential Possibilities	£36.00	—
		Rulers, Flags and Coats of Arms (1888):		
EL	50	A Thick card type	£26.00	—
EL	50	B Thin folders (titled Rulers, Coats of Arms & Flag)	£20.00	—
	50	Scenes of Perilous Occupations	£28.00	—
EL	25	Sea Captains	£50.00	—
	50	Shadows	£24.00	—
EL	25	Snap Shots from Puck	£30.00	—
EL	25	Stars of the Stage, 1st series (bust poses, white edge) RB.22/X2-129:		
		A With 'Duke'	£32.00	£800.00
		B Inscribed 'Third Series'	£32.00	—
EL	25	Stars of the Stage, 2nd series (full length poses) RB.22/X2-130	£32.00	—
EL	25	Stars of the Stage, 3rd series (bust poses, black edge) RB.22/X2-131	£32.00	£800.00
EL	25	Stars of the Stage, 4th series (die cut) RB.22/X2-132	£32.00	—
EL	48	State Governors' Coats of Arms	£30.00	—

Size	Number in set		FOREIGN TOBACCO ISSUERS	Price per card	Complete set
		W. DUKE, SONS & CO., USA (continued)		
EL	48		State Governors' Coats of Arms (Folders)	£20.00	—
EL	25		Talk of the Diamond	£100.00	—
	50		The Terrors of America and Their Doings	£24.00	—
M	50		The Terrors of America and Their Doings	£36.00	—
EL	50		The Terrors of America and Their Doings	£32.00	—
	50		Tinted Photos RB.22/X2-89:		
		A	Standard size	£24.00	—
		B	Die cut to shape	£18.00	—
EL	24		Tricks With Cards	£55.00	—
EL	25		Types of Vessels (die cut)	£40.00	—
	50		Vehicles of the World	£30.00	—
	50		Yacht Colors of the World	£22.00	—
M	50		Yacht Colors of the World	£38.00	—
EL	50		Yacht Colors of the World	£38.00	—
PHOTOGRAPHIC CARDS					
			Actors and Actresses Plain Back (c1890):		
	?340		Group 1 'Cross-Cut Cigarettes', number and caption in design	£6.00	—
	?259		Group 2 'Cross-Cut Cigarettes are the Best' in design. Number and caption at base	£6.00	—
	?148		Group 3 'Duke's Cameo Cigarettes' in design. Number and caption at base	£6.00	—
	?192		Group 4 'Duke Cigarettes are the Best' in design. Number and caption at base	£6.00	—
			Group 5 All wording at base:		
	?218	A	'Cross-Cut Cigarettes are Best'	£6.00	—
	?204	B	'Duke's Cameo Cigarettes are the Best'	£6.00	—
	?567	C	'Duke Cigarettes Are the Best'	£6.00	—
	?		Actors, Actresses and Celebrities, printed back:		
		1	Horizontal 'Dukes Cameo Cigarettes' back	£6.00	—
		2	Vertical 'Sales 1858' back	£6.00	—
		3	Horizontal 'Dukes Cigarettes' back	£6.00	—
EL	?		Actors, Actresses, Celebrities etc	£9.00	—
		E A TOBACCO, East Africa		
M	50		Aeroplanes and Steamships c1936	£6.00	—
		H. ELLIS & CO., USA		
	25		Breeds of Dogs (c1890):		
		A	'Bengal Cheroots'	£50.00	—
		B	'Tiger Cigarettes'	£50.00	—
		C	'Triplex Cigarettes'	£50.00	—
	25		Costumes of Women (c1890)	£65.00	—
	25		Generals of the Late Civil War (c1890)	£100.00	—
	25		Photographic Cards — Actresses (c1887)	£18.00	—
		JOHN FINZER & BROS., USA		
L	10		Inventors and Inventions (c1891)	£60.00	—
		FOH CHONG, China		
M	10		Chinese Series (c1930)	—	£20.00
		G.W. GAIL & AX., USA		
EL	25		Battle Scenes (c1890)	£65.00	—
EL	25		Bicycle and Trick Riders (c1890)	£65.00	—
EL	25		French Novelties (c1890)	£48.00	—
EL	25		Industries of the States (c1890)	£48.00	—

Size	Number in set	FOREIGN TOBACCO ISSUERS	Price per card	Complete set
		G.W. GAIL & AX., USA (continued)		
EL	25	Lighthouses (die cut) (c1890)	£40.00	—
EL	25	Novelties (die cut) (c1890)	£38.00	—
EL	?	Photographic Cards (c1890)	£7.00	—
EL	25	Stars of the Stage (c1890)	£38.00	—
		GALA CIGARETTES, Australia		
	? 1	Stamp Card (see British Tobacco Handbook Ref H.589) (c1910)	—	£170.00
		GENERAL CIGAR COMPANY, Montreal, Canada		
		Northern Birds:		
EL	24	A With series title Nd. 1-24 (1968)	£1.40	—
EL	12	B Without series title, Nd. 25-36 (1977)	£1.60	—
EL	1	C The White Owl Trophy Conservation Award (c1977)	—	£5.00
		G.G. GOODE LTD, Australia		
	17	Prominent Cricketers Series 1924	£130.00	—
		GOODWIN & CO., USA		
	15	Beauties — 'PAC' (c1888)	£75.00	—
	50	Champions (c1888)	£75.00	—
	50	Dogs of the World (c1888):		
		A Captions front and back	£36.00	—
		B Captions front only	£36.00	—
		C Captions back only	£36.00	—
	50	Flowers (c1888)	£36.00	—
	50	Games and Sports Series (c1888)	£55.00	—
	50	Holidays (c1888)	£34.00	—
	50	Occupations for Women (c1888)	£60.00	—
	10	Old Judge Actresses (thick card) (c1888)	£95.00	—
		Photographic Cards (c1888):		
	?	Actors and Actresses	£7.00	—
	?	Baseball Players	£60.00	—
	?	Celebrities and Prizefighters	£35.00	—
	50	Vehicles of the World (c1888)	£36.00	—
	50	Wild Animals of the World (c1888)	£30.00	—
		GUERNSEY TOBACCO CO., Channel Islands		
		A Famous Picture:		
	49	A And When Did You Last See Your Father? (1934)	£2.50	—
	48	B The Laughing Cavalier (1935)	£2.50	—
	48	C The Toast (1936)	£2.50	—
K	52	Miniature Playing Cards (1933)	£1.20	—
		THOS. H. HALL, USA		
	4	Actresses RB.23/H6-1 (1880)	£85.00	—
	14	Actresses RB.23/H6-2, multi-backed (c1885)	£20.00	—
	140	Actors and Actresses RB.23/H6-3. Front 'Between the Acts & Bravo Cigarettes', multi-backed (c1885)	£20.00	—
	112	Actresses and Actors RB.23/H6-4. Black background in oval, multi-backed (c1885)	£20.00	—
	? 196	Actresses and Actors RB.23/H6-5. Fancy triangular corners to oval, multi-backed (c1885)	£20.00	—
	? 158	Actresses and Actors RB.23/H6-6. Sun rays around oval, multi-backed (c1885)	£20.00	—
	52	Actresses RB.23/H6-7. Tiled wall around oval (c1885)	£25.00	—
	12	Actresses RB.23/H6-8. 'Hall's Between the Acts All Tobacco Cigarettes' at base (c1885)	£45.00	—
	25	Actresses RB.23/H6-9. Portraits without firm's name on front (c1885)	£40.00	—

Size	Number in set	FOREIGN TOBACCO ISSUERS	Price per card	Complete set

THOS. H. HALL, USA (continued)

	11	Actresses RB.23/H6-10. 'Ours All Tobacco Cigarettes' on back and front (c1885)	£90.00	—
	12	Athletes RB.23/H6-3 (1881)	£85.00	—
	4	Presidential Candidates RB.23/H6-1 (1880)	£85.00	—
	22	Presidents of the United States RB.23/H6-11 (c1888)	£45.00	—
	25	Theatrical Types RB.23/H6-12 (c1890)	£38.00	—

HARTLEY'S TOBACCO CO., South Africa

L	19	South African English Cricket Tour 1929	£90.00	—

THE HILSON CO., USA

L	25	National Types (1900)	£30.00	—

IMPERIAL CIGARETTE & TOBACCO CO., Canada

?	24	Actresses (c1900)	£65.00	—

IMPERIAL TOBACCO COMPANY OF CANADA LTD, Canada

A   WITH FIRM'S NAME

	30	Beauties Art Series, 'Bouquet Cigarettes' back (c1902)	£70.00	—
	25	Beauties — Girls in Costume (c1903) RB.118/69	£60.00	—
	24	Beauties — Smoke Girls (c1903) RB.118/75	£60.00	—
M	50	Birds, Beasts and Fishes (cut-outs) (1923)	£2.00	—
L	100	Birds of Canada (1924)	£5.00	—
L	100	Birds of Canada (Western Canada) (1925)	£9.00	—
	50	British Birds (cut-outs) (1923)	£1.10	£55.00
	48	Canadian History Series (1926)	£2.00	—
	50	Children of All Nations (1924)	£1.00	£50.00
	23	Dogs Series (1924)	£2.00	£45.00
	50	Dogs, 2nd series (1925)	£2.00	£100.00
	50	Famous English Actresses (1924)	£1.30	£65.00
	50	Film Favourites (1925):		
		A English Issue:		
		i Numbered	£3.00	—
		ii Unnumbered	£3.20	—
		B French Issue:		
		i Numbered	£6.00	—
		ii Unnumbered	£6.00	—
	50	Fish and Bait (1924)	£2.80	£140.00
	50	Fishes of the World (1924)	£3.20	£160.00
	50	Flower Culture in Pots (1925)	80p	£40.00
	30	Game Bird Series (1925)	£3.00	£90.00
	50	Gardening Hints (1923)	80p	£40.00
M	25	Heraldic Signs and Their Origins (1925)	£1.60	£40.00
	50	How to Play Golf (1925)	£12.00	—
	50	Infantry Training (1915):		
		A Front caption all capital letters glossy fronts. Soldier with shoulder straps		
		i Back letter N of No with serif	£3.50	—
		ii Back letter N of No san serif	£3.25	—
		B Front caption in capitals and small case letters. Soldier without shoulder straps		
		i Glossy fronts	£3.25	—
		ii Matt fronts	£3.00	—
L	48	Mail Carriers and Stamps (1903)	£32.00	—
	50	Merchant Ships of the World (1924)	£1.50	£75.00
	25	Military Portraits (1914)	£3.00	—

Size	Number in set		FOREIGN TOBACCO ISSUERS	Price per card	Complete set

IMPERIAL TOBACCO COMPANY OF CANADA LTD (continued)

A   WITH FIRM'S NAME (continued)

	50	Modern War Weapons, 'Sweet Caporal' issue (1914)		£5.00	—
	56	Motor Cars (1924)		£2.50	—
	50	Naval Portraits (1914)		£3.00	—
	25	Notabilities (1914)		£3.00	—
	53	Poker Hands (1924)		£1.50	—
	53	Poker Hands, New Series (1925)		£1.50	—
	25	Poultry Alphabet (1924)		£3.60	—
	50	Railway Engines (1924):			
		A With 'Wills' blanked out		£1.50	—
		B Without 'Wills'		£1.50	£75.00
	50	The Reason Why (1924)		£1.20	£60.00
	127	Smokers Golf Cards (1925)		£6.50	—

B   WITHOUT FIRM'S NAME

	50	Actresses — Framed Border (plain back) RB.21/321 (c1910)		£4.00	—
	50	Arms of the British Empire (1911)		£2.80	—
	50	Around the World (c1910):			
		A Numbered		£4.00	—
		B Unnumbered		£6.50	—
	90	Baseball Series (1912)		£60.00	—
	30	Beauties Art Series (plain back) (c1902)		£16.00	—
	30	Bird Series (c1910)		£3.00	—
	50	Boy Scouts (1911) — with album clause		£6.50	—
	50	British Man of War Series (plain back) c1905		£12.00	—
	50	Canadian Historical Portraits (1913)		£6.00	—
	50	Canadian History Series (1914)		£2.00	—
M	45	Canadian Views (plain back) (c1910)		£7.00	—
	50	Fish Series (c1910)		£3.00	—
	50	Fowls, Pigeons and Dogs (1911)		£4.00	—
	45	Hockey Players (1912)		£40.00	—
	36	Hockey Series (coloured) (1911)		£40.00	—
	50	How To Do It (c1910)		£3.50	—
	100	Lacrosse Series (coloured), Leading Players (c1910)		£15.00	—
	100	Lacrosse Series (coloured) (c1910)		£15.00	—
	50	Lacrosse Series (black and white) (c1910)		£15.00	—
	50	L'Historie du Canada (1926)		£1.50	—
	50	Movie Stars (c1930)		£2.50	—
L	50	Pictures of Canadian Life (c1910):			
		A Brown front		£7.00	—
		B Green front		£7.00	—
	50	Prominent Men of Canada (c1910)		£4.00	—
	50	Tricks and Puzzles (c1910)		£7.00	—
	50	Types of Nations (c1910)		£3.00	—
	25	Victoria Cross Heroes (blue back) (1915)		£5.60	£140.00
L	45	Views of the World (c1910)		£6.00	—
L	25	Wild Animals of Canada (c1910)		£12.00	—
		World War I Scenes and Portraits (plain back) (1916):			
M	144	A Text in italics		£4.50	—
M	32	B Text in standard upright print (Nos 1 to 32 only)		£6.50	—
	25	The World's Dreadnoughts (1910)		£4.00	—

C   SILKS ISSUED 1910-25

M	55	Animals with Flags		£4.00	—
EL	50	Canadian History Series		£12.00	—
M	121	Canadian Miscellany		£5.00	—
M	55	Garden Flowers of the World		£3.50	—
M	55	Orders and Military Medals		£5.00	—

Size	Number in set	FOREIGN TOBACCO ISSUERS	Price per card	Complete set

IMPERIAL TOBACCO COMPANY OF CANADA LTD (continued)

C SILKS ISSUED 1910-25 (continued)

M	55	Regimental Uniforms of Canada	£4.00	—
L	50	Yachts, Pennants and Views	£8.00	—

THE IMPERIAL TOBACCO CO. OF INDIA LTD, India

	25	Indian Historical Views (1915):		
		A Set 1, First Arrangement	£3.60	—
		B Set 2, Second Arrangement	£3.60	—
	40	Nautch Girl Series:		
		A 'Pedro Cigarettes' (c1905)	£3.25	—
		B 'Railway Cigarettes' (c1907)	£3.00	—
	52	Nautch Girl Series, PC inset:		
		A 'Pedro Cigarettes' (c1905)	£3.25	—
		B 'Railway Cigarettes' (c1907)	£3.00	—
K	53	Playing Cards, red back (1919)	£1.50	—
K	52	Playing Cards, blue back (1933)	£1.50	—

THE JERSEY TOBACCO CO. LTD, Channel Islands

K	53	Miniature Playing Cards (1933)	£1.20	—

JUST SO, USA

EL	?	Actresses (c1890)	£13.00	—

KENTUCKY TOBACCO PTY. LTD, South Africa

L	120	The March of Mankind (1940)	£3.00	—

KHEDIVIAL CO., USA

M	10	Aeroplane Series (c1910):		
		A Back 'Duke of York Cigarettes'	£28.00	—
		B Back 'Oxford Cigarettes'	£28.00	—
M	10	Prize Dog Series (c1910):		
		A Back 'Duke of York Cigarettes'	£28.00	—
		B Back 'Oxford Cigarettes'	£28.00	—
M	25	Prize Fight Series No. 101 (c1910):		
		A Back with Fight Details	£35.00	—
		B Back without Fight Details	£35.00	—
M	25	Prize Fight Series No. 102 (c1910)	£35.00	—

WM. S. KIMBALL & CO., USA

ALL SERIES ISSUED 1885-95

	? 46	Actresses collotypes c1888	£150.00	—
	72	Ancient Coins:		
		A Title Ancient Coins	£38.00	—
		B Title Facsimile of Ancient Coins	£38.00	—
	48	Arms of Dominions	£30.00	—
	50	Ballet Queens	£30.00	—
	52	Beauties with Playing Card Insets	£30.00	—
EL	20	Beautiful Bathers	£60.00	—
	50	Butterflies	£30.00	—
		Champions of Games and Sports:		
	25	A Front with Firm's name	£80.00	—
	50	B Front without Firm's name	£80.00	—
	50	Dancing Girls of the World	£30.00	—
	50	Dancing Women	£30.00	—
	50	Fancy Bathers	£30.00	—

Size	Number in set	FOREIGN TOBACCO ISSUERS	Price per card	Complete set

WM. S. KIMBALL & CO., USA (continued)

ALL SERIES ISSUED 1885-95 (continued)

Size	Number		Price	Complete
EL	25	French Novelties	£50.00	—
EL	25	Gems of Beauty	£45.00	—
	50	Goddesses of the Greeks & Romans	£32.00	—
EL	25	Household Pets	£45.00	—
	? 469	Photographic Actresses RB.23/K26-15-2	£8.50	—
EL	20	Pretty Athletes	£50.00	—
	50	Savage and Semi Barbarous Chiefs and Rulers	£36.00	—

KINNEY BROS., USA

ALL SERIES ISSUED 1885-95

Size	Number		Price	Complete
	25	Actresses Group 1 Set 1 RB.118/1	£12.00	—
	25	Actresses Group 1 Set 2 RB.118/2	£13.00	—
	25	Actresses Group 1 Set 3 RB.118/3	£13.00	—
	25	Actresses Group 1 Set 4 RB.118/4	£15.00	—
	25	Actresses Group 1 Set 5 RB.118/5	£15.00	—
	25	Actresses Group 2 RB.118/15	£9.00	—
	25	Actresses Group 2 RB.118/16:		
		A Subjects named	£9.00	—
		B Subjects unnamed	£9.00	—
	25	Actresses Group 3 RB.118/26	£9.00	—
	25	Actresses Group 3 RB.118/29	£9.00	—
	50	Actresses Group 4 RB.118/36 (black text back)	£9.00	—
	129	Actresses Group 4 RB.118/36-37 (plain back)	£7.00	—
	25	Animals	£22.00	—
	10	Butterflies of the World. Light background	£22.00	—
	50	Butterflies of the World. Gold background	£22.00	—
	25	Famous Gems of the World	£24.00	—
	52	Harlequin Cards 1st series	£30.00	—
	53	Harlequin Cards 2nd series (1889)	£30.00	—
L	50	International Cards	£50.00	—
K	24	Jocular Oculars	£40.00	—
	25	Leaders:		
		A Standard size	£28.00	—
		B Narrow card — officially cut	£28.00	—
	50	Magic Changing Cards (1881)	£30.00	—
	622	Military Series:		
		A Coloured background:		
	50	1 Inscribed '7' on front	£11.00	—
	50	2 Inscribed '8' on front	£11.00	—
	30	3 Inscribed '9' on front	£11.00	—
	50	4 Without numeral	£11.00	—
	50	5 Foreign 1886 Types	£11.00	—
		6 Other coloured background:		
	18	A U.S. Continental	£11.00	—
	3	B Vatican	£85.00	—
	5	C Decorations	£65.00	—
		B Plain white or lightly coloured background:		
	51	1 U.S Army and Navy	£11.00	—
	85	2 U.S. State Types	£11.00	—
	60	3 U.S and Foreign Types	£12.00	—
	50	4 England and N.G.S.N.Y.	£18.00	—
	50	5 Foreign 1853 Types	£12.00	—
	50	6 Foreign Types 1886	£11.00	—
	15	7 French Army and Navy	£11.00	—
	5	8 State Seals	£60.00	—

Size	Number in set		FOREIGN TOBACCO ISSUERS	Price per card	Complete set

KINNEY BROS., USA (continued)

National Dances:
	50	A	Front with white border	£22.00	—
	26	B	Front without border	£26.00	—
	25		Naval Vessels of the World	£26.00	—
	50		New Year 1890 (1889)	£28.00	—
	25		Novelties Type 1. Thick circular, no border RB.26/Fig K32-17	£34.00	—
	50		Novelties Type 2. Thin circular with border RB.26/Fig K32-18	£22.00	—

Novelties Type 3. Die cut RB.26/Fig K32-19-1 and 2:
	25	A	Inscribed '25 Styles'	£13.00	—
	50	B	Inscribed '50 Styles'	£13.00	—
	75	C	Inscribed '75 Styles'	£13.00	—
	50		Novelties Type 5. Standard size cards	£16.00	—
	14		Novelties Type 6. Oval RB.26/XA2-120	£34.00	—

Photographic Cards:
	?	A	Actors and Actresses. Horizontal back with Kinney's name	£4.50	
	?	B	Actors and Actresses. Vertical, Sweet Caporal backs	£4.50	—
	45	C	Famous Ships	£16.00	—

Racehorses (1889):
	25	1	American Horses:		
			A Back with series title 'Famous Running Horses'	£34.00	—
			B Back 'Return 25 of these small cards' 11 lines of text	£30.00	—
	25	2	English Horses 'Return 25 of these cards' with 6 lines of text	£30.00	—
	25	3	Great American Trotters	£32.00	—
	50		Surf Beauties	£28.00	—
	52		Transparent Playing Cards	£16.00	—
	25		Types of Nationalities (folders)	£30.00	—

KRAMERS TOBACCO CO. (PTY) LTD, South Africa

	50	Badges of South African Rugby Football Clubs (1933)	£10.00	—

LEWIS & ALLEN CO. USA

L	? 120	Views and Art Studies (c1910)	£6.00	—

LONE JACK CIGARETTE CO., USA

	25	Inventors and Inventions (c1888)	£85.00	—
	50	Language of Flowers (1888):		
		A Front 'Lone Jack Cigarettes'	£35.00	—
		B Front 'Ruby Cigarettes'	£35.00	—
		C Front 'Unknown Cigarettes'	£35.00	—

P. LORILLARD CO., USA

For issues after 1900 see American Tobacco Co.

ALL SERIES ISSUED 1885-98

M	25	Actresses RB.23/L70-4-3	£32.00	—
M	25	Actresses RB.23/L70-5	£32.00	—
EL	25	Actresses RB.23/L70-6:		
		A 'Red Cross' long cut	£32.00	—
		B 'Sensation Cut Plug' front and back	£32.00	—
		C 'Sensation Cut Plug' front only	£32.00	—
EL	25	Actresses RB.23/L70-8	£32.00	—
EL	25	Actresses in Opera Roles RB.23/L70-9	£55.00	—
M	25	Ancient Mythology Burlesqued RB.23/L70-10	£32.00	—
M	50	Beautiful Women RB.23/L70-11:		
		A '5c Ante' front and back	£32.00	—
		B 'Lorillard's Snuff' front and back	£32.00	—
		C 'Tiger' front and back	£32.00	—

Size	Number in set	FOREIGN TOBACCO ISSUERS	Price per card	Complete set

P. LORILLARD CO., USA (continued)

ALL SERIES ISSUED 1885-98 (continued)

Size	Number	Title	Price	Set
EL	25	Circus Scenes	£90.00	—
	25	National Flags	£32.00	—
EL	50	Prizefighters	£160.00	—
M	25	Types of the Stage	£32.00	—

W.C. MACDONALD INC., Canada

Size	Number	Title	Price	Set
	?	Aeroplanes and Warships (c1940)	£2.00	—
M	53	Playing Cards (different designs) (1926-47)	75p	—

B. & J.B. MACHADO, Jamaica

Size	Number	Title	Price	Set
	25	British Naval series (1916)	£30.00	—
	50	The Great War — Victoria Cross Heroes (1916)	£45.00	—
P	50	Popular Film Stars (1926)	£10.00	—
P	50	The Royal Family at Home and Abroad (1927)	£7.00	—
P	52	Stars of the Cinema (1926)	£10.00	—
P	50	The World of Sport (1928)	£15.00	—

MACLIN-ZIMMER-MCGILL TOB. CO., USA

Size	Number	Title	Price	Set
EL	53	Playing Cards — Actresses (c1890)	£24.00	—

MALTA CIGARETTE CO., Malta

Size	Number	Title	Price	Set
	135	Dante's Divine Comedy (c1905)	£15.00	—
	M40	Maltese Families Arms & Letters (c1905)	£8.00	—
?	44	Prominent People (c1905)	£15.00	—

H. MANDELBAUM, USA

Size	Number	Title	Price	Set
	36	Flags of Nations (c1890)	£45.00	—
	20	Types of People (c1890)	£70.00	—

MARBURG BROS., USA

Size	Number	Title	Price	Set
	50	National Costume Cards (c1890):		
		A Front 'Greenback Smoking Mixture'	£70.00	—
		B Front 'Seal of Virginia Smoking Mixture'	£70.00	—
	50	Typical Ships (c1890)	£70.00	—

MASPERO FRERES LTD, Palestine

Size	Number	Title	Price	Set
	50	Birds, Beasts and Fishes (cut-outs) (1925)	£4.50	—

P.H. MAYO & BROTHER, USA

Size	Number	Title	Price	Set
	25	Actresses RB.23/M80-1 (c1890)	£40.00	—
M	25	Actresses RB.23/M80-3 (c1890)	£40.00	—
L	12	Actresses RB.23/M80-4 (c1890)	£90.00	—
?	39	Actresses RB.23/M80-5 (c1890)	£40.00	—
	40	Baseball Players (c1890)	£180.00	—
	20	Costumes and Flowers (c1890)	£34.00	—
	25	Head Dresses of Various Nations (c1890)	£40.00	—
M	25	National Flowers (Girl and Scene) (c1890)	£40.00	—
	20	Naval Uniforms (c1890)	£40.00	—
	35	Prizefighters (c1890)	£90.00	—
	20	Shakespeare Characters (c1890)	£45.00	—

M. MELACHRINO & CO., Switzerland

Size	Number	Title	Price	Set
	52	Peuples Exotiques 1st series (c1925)	£1.00	—
	52	Peuples Exotiques 2nd series (c1925)	£1.00	—
	52	Peuples Exotiques 3rd series (c1925)	£1.00	—

Size	Number in set	FOREIGN TOBACCO ISSUERS	Price per card	Complete set

MEXICAN PUFFS, USA
	20	Actresses (c1890)	£100.00	—

MIFSUD & AZZOPARDI, Malta
KP	59	First Maltese Parliament (1922)	£8.50	—

L. MILLER & SONS, USA
M	25	Battleships (c1900)	£40.00	—
M	25	Generals and Admirals (Spanish War) (c1900)	£40.00	—
M	24	Presidents of US (c1900)	£32.00	—
M	50	Rulers of the World (c1900)	£30.00	—

CHAS. J. MITCHELL & CO., Canada
	26	Actresses — 'FROGA A' (1900):		
		A Backs in brown	£40.00	—
		B Backs in green	£40.00	—
	26	Actresses – 'FROGA B' with Playing Card inset (1900)	£60.00	—

MITSUI & CO., Japan
	?	Japanese Women (c1908)	£12.00	—

MOORE & CALVI, USA
EL	53	Playing Cards — Actresses (c1890):		
		A 'Trumps Long Cut' back	£30.00	—
		B 'Hard-A-Port' with maker's name	£30.00	—
		C 'Hard-A-Port' without maker's name	£30.00	—

MURAI BROS. & CO., Japan
	150	Actresses — 'ALWICS' (c1905) W.33	£14.00	—
	100	Beauties — 'THIBS' (c1900)	£40.00	—
	50	Beauties Group 1 (c1902)	£18.00	—
	25	Chinese Beauties 1st series Peacock issue (c1910)	£5.00	£125.00
	25	Chinese Beauties 3rd series Peacock issue (c1910)	£6.00	—
	50	Chinese Beauties, back in red (c1908)	£7.50	—
	50	Chinese Children's Games without border Peacock issue (c1910)	£4.50	—
	20	Chinese Children's Games with border Peacock issue (c1910)	£4.50	—
	54	Chinese Girls Set 3 (c1905)	£8.00	—
	50	Chinese Pagodas Peacock issue (c1910)	£5.00	—
	30	Chinese Series Peacock issue (c1910)	£5.00	—
	40	Chinese Trades I, back in black (c1905)	£28.00	—
	40	Chinese Trades II, back in olive, Peacock issue (c1910)	£5.00	—
	50	Dancing Girls of the World (c1900)	£45.00	—

NATIONAL CIGARETTE CO., Australia
	13	English Cricket Team 1897-8:		
		A Front black and white	£600.00	—
		B Front yellow-brown	£600.00	—

NATIONAL CIGARETTE AND TOBACCO CO., USA
National Types (Sailor Girls) (c1890):
	25	A Back 'Julius Bien & Co'	£30.00	—
	25	B Back 'The Girsch Lithographing Co.'	£30.00	—
	25	C Back without printer's credit	£30.00	—
	26	D Back 'Sackett Wilhelms Litho Co.'	£30.00	—

Size	Number in set	FOREIGN TOBACCO ISSUERS	Price per card	Complete set

NATIONAL CIGARETTE AND TOBACCO CO., USA (continued)

PHOTOGRAPHIC CARDS

	?	Actresses (c1888):		
		A Plain back	£8.00	—
		B Printed back	£9.00	—

NATIONAL TOBACCO WORKS, USA

EL	13	Art Miniatures (1892)	£28.00	—
EL	?	Cabinet Pictures (c1890)	£28.00	—

OLD FASHION, USA

L	? 200	Photographic Cards — Actresses (c1890)	£16.00	—

PENINSULAR TOBACCO CO. LTD, India

	50	Animals and Birds (1910)	£3.00	—
	52	Birds of Brilliant Plumage (1916):		
		A Back with single large packings	£3.20	—
		B Back with two small packings	£3.20	—
	25	Birds of the East, 1st series (1912)	£3.00	—
	25	Birds of the East, 2nd series (1912)	£3.00	£75.00
	25	China's Famous Warriors:		
		A Back 'Monchyr India'	£4.00	£100.00
		B Back 'India' only	£4.00	£100.00
	25	Chinese Heroes (1913)	£4.00	£90.00
	50	Chinese Modern Beauties (1912)	£8.00	—
	50	Chinese Trades (1908):		
		A Back with 'Monchyr'	£3.20	—
		B Back without 'Monchyr'	£3.20	—
	30	Fish series (1916)	£4.00	—
	25	Hindoo Gods (1909)	£4.00	£100.00
	37	Nautch Girl series (1910)	£7.00	—
	25	Products of the World (1915)	£2.60	£65.00

PIZZUTO, Malta

	50	Milton's Paradise Lost (c1910)	£18.00	—

PLANTERS' STORES & AGENCY CO. LTD, India

	? 47	Actresses — 'FROGA' (1900)	£45.00	—
	25	Beauties 'FECKSA' (1900)	£45.00	—

POLICANSKY BROS., South Africa

	50	Beautiful Illustrations of South African Fauna (1925):		
		A Back 'Mast Cigarettes'	£10.00	—
		B Back 'Mignon Cigarettes'	£10.00	—

R.J. REYNOLDS (Doral), USA

		America's Backyard (plants) (2006):		
	23	A Set of 23	£1.25	—
	1	B Limited Edition Holographic Card	—	£6.00
		America On The Road (2004):		
	25	A Set of 24 plus List Card	£1.25	—
	1	B Limited Edition Card	—	£6.00
		American Treasures (2005):		
	25	A Set of 24 plus List Card	£1.25	—
	1	B Limited Edition Card	—	£6.00

Size	Number in set			FOREIGN TOBACCO ISSUERS	Price per card	Complete set
				R.J. REYNOLDS (Doral), USA (continued)		
	8			Celebrate America Road Trip Series (1999)	£2.00	—
	4			Doral's Employees (2006)	£1.25	£5.00
				The 50 States (2000):		
	52	A		Set of 50 plus 2 List Cards	£1.25	—
	2	B		Limited Edition Cards (Washington and Lady Liberty)	£5.00	—
	1	C		Limited Edition Card We The People	£10.00	—
				Great American Festivals (2003):		
	31	A		Set of 30 plus List Card	£1.25	—
	1	B		Limited Edition Card	—	£6.00
	1	C		Special Edition Card	—	£6.00
				Smoking Moments (2007):		
	24	A		Set of 24	£1.25	—
	1	B		Limited Edition Card — At The Drive In	—	£6.00
				Snapshots of The Century (2001):		
	36	A		Set of 35 plus Title Card	£1.25	—
	1	B		Limited Edition Card	—	£4.00
	1	C		Special Edition Card	—	£8.00
				D. RITCHIE & CO., Canada		
	52			Beauties Playing Card inset, multi-backed (c1890)	£40.00	—
	52			Playing Cards, mutli-backed (c1890)	£40.00	—
				RUGGIER BROS., Malta		
M	50			Story of the Knights of Malta (c1925)	£7.00	—
				SANTA FE NATURAL TOBACCO CO., USA		
	36			A Tribute To The Endangered Set 1 (2001)	£1.25	—
	36			A Tribute To The Endangered Set 2 (2001)	£1.25	—
	36			Century of The Great American Spirit Set 1 (2000)	£1.25	—
	36			Century of The Great American Spirit Set 2 (2000)	£1.25	—
	25			Music of America (2003)	£1.25	—
	36			Spirit of The Old West Series 1 (1999)	£1.25	—
	36			Spirit of The Old West Series 2 (1999)	£1.25	—
				SCERRI, Malta		
				Beauties and Children (c1930):		
	150	A		Black and white, no borders	£1.80	—
	? 86	B		Black and white, white border	£17.00	—
	45	C		Coloured	£2.00	—
MP	50			Beautiful Women (c1935)	£3.50	£175.00
MP	480			Cinema Artists (c1935)	£2.75	—
MP	180			Cinema Stars (c1935)	£3.00	—
MP	50			Famous London Buildings (c1935)	£5.00	—
MP	60			Film Stars 1st series Nos 1-60 (c1935)	£3.50	—
MP	60			Film Stars 2nd series Nos 61-120 (c1935)	£3.50	—
	52			Interesting Places of the World (c1936)	60p	£32.00
P	25			International Footballers (c1935)	£40.00	—
M	401			Malta Views (c1930)	80p	—
M	51			Members of Parliament — Malta (c1930)	50p	£25.00
	146			Prominent People (c1930)	£2.00	—
MP	100			Scenes from Films (c1935)	£3.50	—
LP	100			Talkie Stars (c1930)	£3.50	—
M	100			World's Famous Buildings (c1930)	60p	£60.00

Size	Number in set	FOREIGN TOBACCO ISSUERS	Price per card	Complete set
		J.J. SCHUH TOBACCO CO. PTY LTD, Australia		
		ALL SERIES ISSUED 1920-25		
	60	Australian Footballers series A (half-full length)	£18.00	—
	40	Australian Footballers series B (Rays)	£18.00	—
	59	Australian Footballers series C (oval frame)	£30.00	—
		Australian Jockeys:		
	30	A Numbered	£10.00	—
	30	B Unnumbered	£10.00	—
P	72	Cinema Stars	£3.00	—
	60	Cinema Stars	£3.50	—
L	12	Maxims of Success	£40.00	—
P	72	Official War Photographs	£5.00	—
P	96	Portraits of Our Leading Footballers	£10.00	—
		G. SCLIVAGNOTI, Malta		
	50	Actresses and Cinema Stars (1923)	£4.00	—
MP	71	Grand Masters of the Orders of Jerusalem (1897)	£12.00	—
P	102	Opera Singers (1897)	£15.00	—
M	100	Opera Singers (1897)	£15.00	—
		SIMONETS LTD, Jersey, Channel Islands		
MP	36	Beautiful Women (c1925) GP.417	£6.00	—
P	24	Cinema Scenes series (c1925)	£7.50	—
P	27	Famous Actors and Actresses (c1925)	£6.50	—
	50	Local Footballers (c1914)	£7.00	—
	25	Picture Series (c1920)	£5.00	—
P	27	Sporting Celebrities (c1930)	£13.00	—
LP	50	Views of Jersey (black and white, glossy front, numbered, plain back) (c1940)	£2.50	—
LP	100	Views of Jersey (black and white, matt front, unnumbered, plain back) (c1940)	£2.50	—
		THE SINSOCK & CO., Korea		
	20	Korean Girls (c1905)	£20.00	—
		SNIDERS & ABRAHAMS PTY LTD, Australia		
		Actresses (c1905):		
	30	A Gold background	£10.00	—
	14	B White Borders	£10.00	—
	20	Admirals and Warships of USA (1908)	£13.00	—
	60	Animals (c1912)	£5.00	—
	60	Animals and Birds (c1912):		
		A 'Advertising Gifts' issue	£4.00	—
		B 'Peter Pan' issue	£4.50	—
	15	Australian Cricket Team (1905)	£65.00	—
	16	Australian Football Incidents in Play (c1906)	£24.00	—
	24	Australian Footballers (full length) series AI, back with 'O & A' (1905)	£30.00	—
	50	Australian Footballers (full length) series AII, back without 'O & A' (1905)	£30.00	—
	76	Australian Footballers (½ length) series B (1906)	£30.00	—
	76	Australian Footballers (½ length) series C (1907)	£30.00	—
	140	Australian Footballers (head and shoulders) series D (1908)	£26.00	—
	60	Australian Footballers (head in oval) series E (1910)	£26.00	—
	60	Australian Footballers (head in rays) series F (1911)	£26.00	—
	60	Australian Footballers (with pennant) series G (1912)	£26.00	—
	60	Australian Footballers (head in star) series H (1913)	£26.00	—
	60	Australian Footballers (head in shield) series I (1914)	£26.00	—

Size	Number in set	FOREIGN TOBACCO ISSUERS	Price per card	Complete set
		SNIDERS & ABRAHAMS PTY LTD, Australia (continued)		
	56	Australian Footballers (½-¾ length) series J (1910)	£26.00	—
	48	Australian Jockeys, back in blue (1907)	£7.00	—
	60	Australian Jockeys, back in brown (1908):		
		52 Back with 'O & A' at base	£7.00	—
		31 Back with 'O & Co' at base	£7.00	—
	56	Australian Racehorses, horizontal back (1906)	£7.00	—
	56	Australian Racehorses, vertical back (1907)	£7.00	—
	40	Australian Racing Scenes (1911)	£7.00	—
	? 133	Australian VCs and Officers (1917)	£8.00	—
	12	Billiard Tricks (c1910)	£26.00	—
	60	Butterflies and Moths, captions in small letters (c1912)	£2.75	—
	60	Butterflies and Moths, captions in block letters (c1912)	£2.75	—
	60	Cartoons and Caricatures (c1908):		
		A Front with border	£7.00	—
		B Front without border	£7.00	—
	12	Coin Tricks (c1910)	£20.00	—
	64	Crests of British Warships (1915):		
		A Back in blue	£8.00	—
		B Back in green	£8.00	—
	40	Cricketers in Action (1906)	£80.00	—
	12	Cricket Terms (c1906)	£50.00	—
	32	Dickens series (c1910)	£6.50	—
	16	Dogs (c1910):		
		A 'Standard' issue	£13.00	—
		B 'Peter Pan' issue:		
		1 White panel	£13.00	—
		2 Gilt panel	£13.00	—
		C 'Coronet' issue	£13.00	—
	6	Flags (shaped metal) (c1910)	£8.00	—
	6	Flags (shaped card) (c1910)	£8.00	—
	60	Great War Leaders and Warships (c1915):		
		A Front in green (Peter Pan issue)	£8.00	—
		B Front in sepia brown (Peter Pan issue)	£8.00	—
	30	How to Keep Fit (c1908)	£8.00	—
	60	Jokes (c1906):		
		A 'Aristocratica' back in brown	£5.00	—
		B 'Standard' back in blue	£5.00	—
		C 'Milo' back in green	£5.00	—
	12	Match Puzzles (c1910)	£20.00	—
	48	Medals and Decorations (c1915)	£9.00	—
M	48	Melbourne Buildings (c1915)	£9.00	—
	25	Natives of the World (c1906)	£22.00	—
	12	Naval Terms (c1906)	£12.00	—
	29	Oscar Ashe, Lily Brayton and Lady Smokers (1911)	£7.00	—
	40	Shakespeare Characters (c1908)	£6.00	—
	30	Signalling — Semaphore and Morse (c1916)	£8.00	—
	14	Statuary (c1906)	£10.00	—
	60	Street Criers in London, 1707 (c1916)	£10.00	—
	32	Views of Victoria in 1857 (c1908):		
		A Green back	£10.00	—
		B Brown back	£10.00	—
P	250	Views of the World 1908	£4.00	—

STAR TOBACCO CO., India

| | 52 | Beauties (PC inset), multi-backed (c1898) | £32.00 | — |
| | 52 | Indian Native Types (PC inset) (c1898) | £32.00 | — |

Size	Number in set	FOREIGN TOBACCO ISSUERS	Price per card	Complete set

SUM MUYE & CO., Siam

	50	Siamese Royalty (c1912)	£8.00	—
	220	Movie Stars (1915)	£4.00	—
	100	Movie Stars (sepia) (c1915)	£4.50	—
	120	Movie Stars (portrait in oval) (c1915)	£4.50	—

TOBACCO PRODUCTS CORPORATION OF CANADA LTD

	? 45	Canadian Sports Champions (c1920)	£20.00	—
	60	Do You Know (1924)	£7.00	—
	60	Hockey Players (1926)	£45.00	—
	120	Movie Stars (c1920)	£4.00	—
	100	Movie Stars (sepia) (c1920)	£4.00	—
	L20	Movie Stars Series 3 (Mack Sennett Girls)	£5.00	—
	? 120	Movie Stars Set 4 (c1920)	£4.00	—
	? L67	Movie Stars Series 5 (c1920)	£5.00	—
	L100	Movie Stars (sepia) (c1920)	£5.00	—

TUCKETT LIMITED, Canada

	25	Autograph Series (c1913)	£35.00	—
	? 210	Beauties and Scenes (c1910)	£8.00	—
	25	Boy Scout Series (c1915)	£36.00	—
P	100	British Views without Tucketts on front (plain back) (c1912)	£2.50	—
P	? 224	British Views with Tucketts on front (c1912):		
		A Back 'Karnak Cigarettes'	£2.50	—
		B Back 'T & B' trade mark	£2.50	—
		C Back 'Tuckett's Special Turkish Cigarettes'	£2.50	—
P	80	British Warships (c1915):		
		A Back 'T & B' trade mark	£13.00	—
		B Back 'Tuckett's Special Turkish Cigarettes'	£13.00	—
P	50	Canadian Scenes (plain back) (c1912)	£2.75	—
	53	Playing Card Premium Certificates (c1930)	£7.50	—
	52	Tucketts Aeroplane Series (1930)	£6.50	—
	52	Tucketts Aviation Series (1929)	£6.50	—
	52	Tucketts Auction Bridge Series (1930)	£7.50	—

TURKISH-MACEDONIAN TOBACCO CO., Holland (TURMAC)

The illustration numbers are taken from Reference Book No. 138, Handbook of Worldwide Tobacco & Trade Silk issues. The first reference number is from the 2005 hardback edition and the second number is from the revised 2016 paperback edition.

ANONYMOUS SILK ISSUES:

M	20	Arms of Cities and Dutch Provinces Ref 611/435 c1930	£4.00	—
EL	18	Arms of Dutch Cities and Towns Ref 617/438 c1930	£5.00	—
M	18	Arms of Dutch East and West Indies Ref 613/437 c1930	£5.00	—
M	74	By Towns and Villages Ref 614/441 c1930	£4.00	—
M	20	Decorations and Medals Ref 619/443 c1930	£7.00	—
	100	Dutch Celebrities Ref 620/444 c1930	£5.00	—
	57	Flowers Ref 636/452 c1930	£7.00	—
M	25	Flower and Leaf Design Series A Ref 626/450 c1930	£5.00	—
M	16	Flower and Leaf Design Series B Ref 626/450 c1930	£5.00	—
M	16	Flower and Leaf Design Series C Ref 626/450 c1930	£5.00	—
M	16	Flower and Leaf Design Series D Ref 626/450 c1930	£5.00	—
M	16	Flower and Leaf Design Series E Ref 626/450 c1930	£5.00	—
M	20	Flowers (Europa/Afrika) Ref 627/451 c1930	£6.00	—
M	3	Girls of Many Lands (black silk) Ref 628/453 c1930	£8.00	—
M	50	Girls of Many Lands (white silk) Ref 629/454 c1930	£5.00	—

Size	Number in set	FOREIGN TOBACCO ISSUERS	Price per card	Complete set

TURKISH-MACEDONIAN TOBACCO CO., Holland (TURMAC) (continued)

ANONYMOUS SILK ISSUES (continued)

Illustrated Initials c1930:

M	26	A Single letters Ref 630/455	£4.00	—
M	28	B Double letters Ref 631/456	£4.00	—
M	35	Japanese Subjects Ref 638/460 c1930	£8.00	—
M	46	Javanese Figures Ref 633/461 c1930	£6.00	—
M	34	National and Provincial Costumes Ref 635/464 c1930	£4.00	—
M	67	National Flags (white silk) Ref 642/467 c1930	£4.00	—

National Flags, Standards and Arms c1930:

A   Size 75 x 50mm:

M	83	i National Flags Ref 643/468	£2.50	—
M	83	ii National Standards Ref 643/468	£2.50	—
M	83	iii National Arms Ref 643/468	£2.50	—
M	76	B Size 65 x 50mm National Arms Ref 643/468	£3.00	—

C   Size 65 x 36mm:

	81	i National Flags with caption Ref 643/468	£3.00	—
	79	ii National Flags without caption Ref 643/468	£3.00	—
M	144	National Flags (paper backed) Ref 644/469 c1930	£4.00	—
M	16	Nature Calendar Ref 645/470 c1930	£5.00	—
M	20	Ships of All Ages Ref 650/477 c1930	£10.00	—

Sport and Nature Series c1930:

M	55	A Sports Subjects Ref 657/478	£6.00	—
M	27	B Animals and Birds Ref 657/478	£5.00	—
M	10	C Butterflies Ref 657/478	£5.00	—
M	34	D Flowers Ref 657/478	£5.00	—

Sporting and Other Figures (size 45 x 30mm) c1930:

K	16	Series A Sport (No. 16 size 75 x 55mm) Ref 652/479	£7.00	—
K	15	Series B Music Ref 652/479	£7.00	—
K	17	Series C Transport Ref 652/479	£7.00	—
K	14	Series D Flying (No. 4 size 75 x 55mm) Ref 652/479	£7.00	—
K	24	Series E Miscellaneous Ref 652/479	£7.00	—
M	25	Sporting Figures (Numbered CA1 to CA25) Ref 653/480 c1930	£7.00	—
M	47	World Celebrities and Film Stars Ref 655/483 c1930	£8.00	—

UNITED TOBACCO COMPANIES (SOUTH) LTD, South Africa

A   WITH FIRM'S NAME

	50	Aeroplanes of Today (1936):		
		A 'Box 78 Capetown'	£2.50	£125.00
		B 'Box 1006 Capetown'	£2.50	£125.00
	50	Animals and Birds Koodoo issue (1923)	£7.00	—
L	24	Arms and Crests of Universities and Schools of South Africa (1930)	£1.60	£40.00
L	52	Boy Scout, Girl Guide and Voortrekker Badges (1932)	£2.50	—
L	62	British Rugby Tour of South Africa (1938)	£2.50	—
	50	Children of All Nations (1928)	£1.10	—
	50	Cinema Stars 'Flag Cigarettes' (1924)	£2.50	£125.00
	60	Do You Know? (1929)	70p	£42.00
	50	Do You Know 2nd series (1930)	70p	£35.00
	50	Do You Know 3rd series (1931)	70p	£35.00
K	28	Dominoes 'Ruger Cigarettes' (1934)	£6.00	—
L	50	Exercises for Men and Women (1932)	£1.60	£80.00
	48	Fairy Tales 1st series Flag issue (1928)	£3.00	—
	48	Fairy Tales 2nd series Flag issue (1928)	£3.00	—
	24	Fairy Tales (1926) (booklets)	£10.00	—
L	120	Farmyards of South Africa (1934)	£1.70	—
M	50	Household Hints (1926)	£2.00	—
	25	Interesting Experiments (1930)	£1.40	£35.00

Size	Number in set	FOREIGN TOBACCO ISSUERS	Price per card	Complete set

UNITED TOBACCO COMPANIES (SOUTH) LTD (continued)

A WITH FIRM'S NAME (continued)

Size	Number in set		Price per card	Complete set
L	100	Medals and Decorations of the British Commonwealth of Nations (1941)	£1.00	—
	50	Merchant Ships of the World (1925)	£1.30	£65.00
	50	Motor Cars (1923)	£5.00	—
L	100	Our Land (1938)	30p	£30.00
L	200	Our South Africa Past and Present (1938)	35p	£70.00
L	24	Pastel Plates (1938)	£1.40	£35.00
L	88	Philosophical Sayings (1938)	£1.20	—
	25	Picturesque People of the Empire (1929)	£1.80	£45.00
K	53	Playing Cards 'Flag' Cigarettes	£2.00	—
K	53	Playing Cards 'Lifeboat' Cigarettes (1934)	£2.00	—
M	53	Playing Cards 'Lotus Cigarettes' (1934)	£2.50	—
L	53	Playing Cards 'Loyalist Cigarettes' (1934)	£2.00	—
K	53	Playing Cards 'MP Cigarettes' (1934)	£2.00	—
K	53	Playing Cards 'Rugger Cigarettes' (1934)	£3.00	—
L	50	Racehorses South Africa Set 1 (1929)	£3.00	—
L	52	Racehorses South Africa Set 2 (1930):		
		A Inscribed 'a series of 50'	£3.00	—
		B Inscribed 'a series of 52'	£3.00	—
	50	Regimental Uniforms (1937)	£2.50	£125.00
	50	Riders of the World (1931)	£1.60	£80.00
L	52	S. A. Flora (1935):		
		A With 'CT Ltd'	70p	—
		B Without 'CT Ltd'	60p	£32.00
	25	South African Birds 1st series (1927)	£2.40	—
	25	South African Birds 2nd series (1927)	£2.40	—
L	52	South African Butterflies (1937)	£1.50	£78.00
L	52	South African Coats of Arms (1931)	50p	£26.00
L	65	South African Rugby Football Clubs (1933)	£3.50	—
L	52	Sports and Pastimes in South Africa (1936)	£4.50	—
L	47	Springbok Rugby and Cricket Teams (1931)	£4.50	—
L	28	1912-13 Springboks (1913)	£85.00	—
	25	Studdy Dogs (1925)	£6.00	—
?	98	Transfers (c1925)	£6.00	—
L	40	Views of South African Scenery 1st series (1918):		
		A Text back	£4.50	—
		B Anonymous plain back	£4.50	—
L	36	Views of South African Scenery 2nd series (1920)	£4.50	—
	25	Wild Flowers of South Africa 1st series (1925)	£2.00	—
	25	Wild Flowers of South Africa 2nd series (1926)	£2.00	—
	50	The World of Tomorrow (1938)	£1.20	£60.00

B WITHOUT FIRM'S NAME

	50	African Fish (1937)	£2.20	£110.00
	50	British Aeroplanes (1933)	£2.75	—
EL	25	Champion Dogs (1934)	£5.00	—
	30	Do You Know (1933)	£2.00	£60.00
	50	Eminent Film Personalities (1930)	£2.75	—
	50	English Period Costumes (1932)	£1.20	£60.00
	25	Famous Figures from South African History (1932)	£2.80	—
L	100	Famous Works of Art (1939)	40p	£40.00
	25	Flowers of South Africa (1932)	£2.00	—
M	50	Humour in Sport (1929)	£5.50	—
L	100	Our Land (1938)	30p	—
M	150	Our South African Birds (1942)	60p	£90.00
L	150	Our South African Birds (1942)	60p	£90.00
M	100	Our South African Flora (1940)	35p	£35.00

Size	Number in set	FOREIGN TOBACCO ISSUERS	Price per card	Complete set
		UNITED TOBACCO COMPANIES (SOUTH) LTD, South Africa (continued)		
B	*WITHOUT FIRM'S NAME* (continued)			
L	100	Our South African Flora (1940)	32p	£32.00
M	100	Our South African National Parks (1941)	35p	£35.00
L	100	Our South African National Parks (1941)	32p	£32.00
L	50	Pictures of South Africa's War Effort (1942)	60p	£30.00
	50	Riders of the World (1931)	£1.60	£80.00
	50	Safety First (1936)	£1.20	£60.00
	40	Ships of All Times (1931)	£2.00	—
	25	South African Birds 2nd series	£3.00	—
L	17	South African Cricket Touring Team British Isles 1929 (1929):		
		A Fronts with autographs	£35.00	—
		B Fronts without autographs	£35.00	—
M	100	South African Defence (1939)	40p	£40.00
L	50	South African Places of Interest (1934)	40p	£20.00
P	50	Stereoscopic Photographs Assorted Subjects (1928)	£1.30	—
P	50	Stereoscopic Photographs of South Africa (1929)	£1.30	—
	50	The Story of Sand (1934)	£1.00	£50.00
M	50	Tavern of the Seas (1939)	60p	£30.00
	25	Warriors of All Nations (crossed swords at base) (1937)	£2.60	£65.00
	25	What's This (1929)	£2.00	£50.00
	50	Wild Animals of the World (1932)	£1.50	£75.00
M	40	Wonders of the World (1931)	£1.25	—
M	100	World Famous Boxers (c1935)	£11.00	—
C	*SILK ISSUES*			
M	20	British Butterflies (c1920)	£14.00	—
M	30	British Roses (c1920)	£14.00	—
M	65	Flags of All Nations (c1920)	£3.00	—
M	25	Old Masters (c1920)	£8.00	—
M	50	Pottery Types (c1920)	£7.00	—
M	50	South African Flowers Nd 1-50 (c1920)	£4.00	—
M	50	South African Flowers Nd 51-100 (c1920)	£4.00	—
		UNIVERSAL TOBACCO CO. PTY LTD, South Africa		
	835	Flags of All Nations (1935)	£1.30	—
		S.W. VENABLE TOBACCO CO., USA		
EL	? 56	Actresses, multi-backed (c1890)	£50.00	—
		GEO. F. YOUNG & BRO., USA		
L	?	Actresses (c1890)	£36.00	—
		ANONYMOUS SERIES — Chinese Language		
M	10	Chinese Beauties (Ref ZE2-11) (c1930)	—	£20.00
M	10	Chinese Series (Ref ZE9-31) (c1930)	—	£20.00
	10	Chinese Views & Scenes (Ref ZE9-49) (c1930) (San Shing)	—	£20.00
	48	Hints on Association Football (Ref ZE3-2) (c1930)	—	£10.00
	30	Safety First (Ref ZE9-41) (c1930) (Hwa Ching)	—	£45.00

SECTION 3
REPRINT SERIES

Prices are for **Finest Collectable Condition** to **Mint**.

During the past twenty years or so, around 400 classic cigarette and trade card series have been reprinted. Many of the originals are extremely rare and do not often turn up in collections, so reprints provide an opportunity to enjoy cards rarely seen. At such low prices, reprints have established a following in their own right, and have also become popular for framing to make an interesting decorative feature. The quality of reproduction is very good, and they are clearly marked as reprints to avoid confusion.

NOTE: C.C.S. = Card Collectors Society

Size	Print-ing	Number in set	REPRINT SERIES	Complete set
			REPRINT MIXTURE	
A	C	100	Randomly mixed reprinted cards, mainly from Card Promotions issues from 1995/2003. May be small amount of duplication. Very few Poor and good otherwise Mint	£4.25
			ADKIN & SONS	
—	C	4	Games by Tom Browne (135 x 83mm) c1900 (reprinted 2001)	£4.00
			A.W. ALLEN LTD (Australia)	
D2	U	18	Bradman's Records (Cricketer) 1932 (reprinted 2002)	£7.00
			ALLEN & GINTER/GOODWIN/KIMBALL (USA)	
A	C	28	Baseball Greats of 1890 (reprinted 1991)	£12.50
			ALLEN & GINTER (USA)	
A	C	50	Celebrated American Indian Chiefs 1888 (reprinted 1989)	£15.00
A	C	50	Fans of The Period 1890 (reprinted 2005)	£8.50
A	C	50	Fruits (Children) 1891 (reprinted 1989)	£8.50
A	C	50	Pirates of the Spanish Main 1888 (reprinted 1996)	£15.00
A	C	50	Prize and Game Chickens c1890 (reprinted 2000)	£10.00
D2	U	9	Women Baseball Players c1888 (reprinted 2001)	£3.00
—	C	50	The World's Champions 2nd Series (82 x 73mm) c1890 (reprinted 2001) ...	£17.50
			AMERICAN TOBACCO CO. (USA)	
B	C	50	Lighthouse Series 1912 (reprinted 2000)	£12.00
A	C	25	Military Uniforms — numbered (green net design back) 1900 (reprinted 2003)	£6.50
			ARDATH TOBACCO CO. LTD	
A2	C	35	Hand Shadows c1930 (reprinted 2001)	£7.50
			A. BAKER & CO. LTD	
A	C	25	Star Girls c1898 (reprinted 2001)	£6.00
			BARBERS TEA LTD	
A.	C	24	Cinema & Television Stars 1955 (reprinted 1993)	£6.50

Size	Print-ing	Number in set	REPRINT SERIES	Complete set
			BENSDORP COCOA (Holland)	
—	C	3	Deep Sea Divers (99 x 70mm) c1900 (reprinted c1995)	£3.00
			FELIX BERLYN	
A	C	25	Golfing Series Humorous 1910 (reprinted 1989)	£6.00
			ALEXANDER BOGUSLAVSKY LTD	
—	C	12	Big Events on the Turf (133 x 70mm) 1924 (reprinted 1995)	£12.00
A	C	25	Conan Doyle Characters 1923 (reprinted 1996)	£6.50
A	C	25	Winners on the Turf 1925 (reprinted 1995)	£6.50
			BOWMAN GUM INC. (USA)	
—	C	108	Jets-Rockets-Spacemen (80 x 54mm) 1951 (reprinted 1985)	£9.00
			WM BRADFORD	
D2	U	20	Boer War Cartoons c1901 (reprinted 2001)	£5.00
			BRIGHAM & CO	
B2	BW	16	Down The Thames From Henley to Windsor c1912 (reprinted 2001)	£6.50
			BRITISH AMERICAN TOBACCO CO. LTD	
A	C	50	Aeroplanes 1926 (reprinted 2001)	£8.50
D	C	25	Beauties — Blossom Girls c1904 (reprinted 2001)	£6.00
A	C	32	Drum Horses 1910 (reprinted 2001)	£6.50
A	C	50	Indian Regiments 1912 (reprinted 2001)	£8.50
A	C	50	Lighthouses 1926 (reprinted 2000)	£8.50
A	C	45	Melbourne Cup Winners 1906 (reprinted 1992)	£8.50
A	C	50	Motorcycles 1927 (reprinted 1991)	£15.00
A	C	33	Regimental Pets 1911 (reprinted 1998)	£6.50
			CADBURY BROS. LTD	
—	C	6	Sports Series (109 x 35mm) c1905 (reprinted 2001)	£3.00
			CARRERAS LTD	
A	C	50	Famous Airmen & Airwomen 1936 (reprinted 1996)	£8.50
A	C	75	Footballers 1934 (reprinted 1997)	£13.50
			H. CHAPPEL & CO.	
A2	C	10	British Celebrities 1905 (reprinted 2001)	£3.00
			W.A. & A.C. CHURCHMAN	
A	U	50	Boxing Personalities 1938 (reprinted 1990)	£8.50
A	C	50	Cricketers 1936 (C.C.S. reprinted 1999)	£10.00
A	C	25	Eastern Proverbs 1st Series 1931 (C.C.S. reprinted 2001)	£8.00
A	C	52	Frisky 1935 (reprinted 1994)	£8.50
A	C	50	In Town To-Night 1938 (C.C.S. reprinted 1999)	£10.00
A	C	25	Interesting Door Knockers 1928 (C.C.S reprinted 2000)	£6.50
A	C	50	The King's Coronation 1937 (C.C.S. reprinted 2001)	£12.50
A	C	50	Landmarks in Railway Progress 1931 (reprinted 1994)	£8.50
A	C	50	Pioneers 1956 (reprinted 2000)	£9.50
A	C	25	Pipes of The World 1927 (C.C.S. reprinted 2000)	£6.50
A	C	50	Prominent Golfers 1931 (reprinted 1989)	£8.50
B	C	12	Prominent Golfers 1931 (reprinted 1989)	£6.00

Size	Print-ing	Number in set	REPRINT SERIES	Complete set
			W.A. & A.C. CHURCHMAN (continued)	
A	C	50	Racing Greyhounds 1934 (reprinted 1989)	£8.50
—	C	48	The RAF at Work (68 x 53mm) 1938 (reprinted 1995)	£16.00
A	C	50	The Story of Navigation 1936 (C.C.S. reprinted 1999)	£10.00
			WM. CLARKE & SON	
A	BW	30	Cricketer Series 1901 (reprinted 2001)	£7.50
			COHEN WEENEN & CO. LTD	
A	C	60	Football Captains 1907-8 (reprinted 1998)	£10.00
A	C	40	Home & Colonial Regiments 1901 (reprinted 1998)	£8.50
A	C	50	Star Artistes 1905 (reprinted 1998)	£8.50
A	C	50	V.C. Heroes (of World War I) 1915 (reprinted 1998)	£8.50
			COOPERATIVE WHOLESALE SOCIETY LTD (C.W.S.)	
A	C	25	Parrot Series 1910 (reprinted 1996)	£6.00
A	C	48	Poultry 1927 (reprinted 1996)	£8.50
			COPE BROS. & CO. LTD	
A	C	50	British Warriors 1912 (reprinted 1996)	£8.50
A	C	50	Cope's Golfers 1900 (reprinted 1983)	£15.00
A	C	50	Dickens Gallery 1900 (reprinted 1989)	£15.00
—	C	7	The Seven Ages of Man (114 x 78mm) c1885 (reprinted 2001)	£6.00
A	C	50	Shakespeare Gallery 1900 (reprinted 1989)	£15.00
A	C	25	Uniforms of Soldiers and Sailors 1898 (reprinted 1996)	£6.50
A	C	25	The World's Police 1935 (reprinted 2005)	£6.00
			DAH TUNG NAN (China)	
—	C	18	Golf Girl Series (65 x 50mm) c1920 (reprinted 1997)	£6.00
			W. DUKE, SONS & CO (USA)	
A	C	25	Fishers c1890 (reprinted 2002)	£6.00
A	C	30	Generals of American Civil War (Histories of Generals) 1888 (reprinted 1995)	£6.50
			J. DUNCAN & CO. LTD	
D1	C	50	Evolution of The Steamship 1925 (reprinted 2002)	£8.50
			EDWARDS RINGER & BIGG	
A	C	25	Prehistoric Animals 1924 (C.C.S. reprinted 2000)	£10.00
			H. ELLIS & CO. (USA)	
A	C	25	Generals of the Late Civil War 1890 (reprinted 1991)	£6.00
			EMPIRE TOBACCO CO.	
D	C	6	Franco-British Exhibition 1908 (reprinted 2001)	£3.00
			W. & F. FAULKNER	
C	C	25	Beauties (coloured) c1898 (reprinted 2001)	£6.00
D	C	12	Cricket Terms 1899 (reprinted 1999)	£3.00
D	C	12	Football Terms 1st Series 1900 (reprinted 1999)	£3.00
D	C	12	Football Terms 2nd Series 1900 (reprinted 1999)	£3.00
D	C	12	Golf Terms (with "Faulkners" on front) 1901 (reprinted 1999)	£5.00
D2	C	12	Golf Terms (without "Faulkners" titled Golf Humour) 1901 (reprinted 1998)	£3.00
D	C	12	Grenadier Guards 1899 (reprinted 1999)	£3.00
D	C	12	Military Terms 1st Series 1899 (reprinted 1999)	£3.00
D	C	12	Military Terms 2nd Series 1899 (reprinted 1999)	£3.00

Size	Print-ing	Number in set	REPRINT SERIES	Complete set

W. & F. FAULKNER (continued)

Size	Printing	Number in set	Title	Complete set
D	C	12	Nautical Terms 1st Series 1900 (reprinted 1999)	£3.00
D	C	12	Nautical Terms 2nd Series 1900 (reprinted 1999)	£3.00
A	C	25	Optical Illusions 1935 (C.C.S. reprinted 2002)	£8.00
D	C	12	Police Terms (with "Faulkners" on front) 1899 (reprinted 1999)	£3.00
D2	C	12	Police Terms (without "Faulkners" titled Police Humour) 1899 (reprinted 1998)	£3.00
D	C	12	Policemen of the World 1899 (reprinted 1999)	£3.00
A	C	25	Prominent Racehorses of the Present day 1923 (reprinted 1993)	£6.00
D	C	12	Puzzle Series 1897 (reprinted 1999)	£3.00
D	C	12	Sporting Terms 1900 (reprinted 1999)	£3.00
D	C	12	Street Cries 1902 (reprinted 1999)	£3.00

FRANKLYN, DAVEY & CO.

Size	Printing	Number in set	Title	Complete set
A	C	25	Boxing 1924 (reprinted 2002)	£6.00
A	C	50	Modern Dance Steps 1st Series 1929 (reprinted 2002)	£12.50

J.S. FRY & SONS LTD

Size	Printing	Number in set	Title	Complete set
A	C	25	Days of Nelson 1906 (reprinted 2003)	£6.50
A	C	25	Days of Wellington 1906 (reprinted 2003)	£6.50

J. GABRIEL

Size	Printing	Number in set	Title	Complete set
A	BW	20	Cricketers Series 1901 (reprinted 1992)	£5.00

GALLAHER LTD

Size	Printing	Number in set	Title	Complete set
A	C	48	Army Badges 1939 (reprinted 2001)	£8.50
A	C	50	The Great War Nos. 1-50 1915 (reprinted 2001)	£8.50
A	C	50	The Great War Nos. 51-100 1915 (reprinted 2003)	£8.50
A	C	25	The Great War Victoria Cross Heroes 1st Series 1915 (reprinted 2001)	£6.50
A	C	25	The Great War Victoria Cross Heroes 2nd Series 1915 (reprinted 2001)	£6.50
A	C	25	The Great War Victoria Cross Heroes 3rd Series 1915 (reprinted 2001)	£6.50
A	C	25	The Great War Victoria Cross Heroes 4th Series 1915 (reprinted 2001)	£6.50
A	C	25	The Great War Victoria Cross Heroes 5th Series 1915 (reprinted 2003)	£6.50
A	C	25	The Great War Victoria Cross Heroes 6th Series 1915 (reprinted 2017)	£6.50
A	C	25	The Great War Victoria Cross Heroes 7th Series 1915 (reprinted 2003)	£6.50
A	C	25	The Great War Victoria Cross Heroes 8th Series 1915 (reprinted 2003)	£6.50
A	C	50	Lawn Tennis Celebrities 1928 (reprinted 1997)	£8.50
A	C	25	Motor Cars 1934 (reprinted 1995)	£6.50
A	C	50	Regimental Colours and Standards 1899 (reprinted 1995)	£8.50
A	C	48	Signed Portraits of Famous Stars 1935 (reprinted 1997)	£8.50
A	C	50	South African Series No. 101-150 (Boer War Uniforms) (reprinted 2000)	£8.50
A	C	50	South African Series No. 151-200 (Boer War Uniforms) (reprinted 2000)	£8.50
A	C	50	Types of the British Army No. 1-50 1900 (reprinted 1995)	£8.50
A	C	50	Types of the British Army No. 51-100 1900 (reprinted 1996)	£8.50

GLOBE CIGARETTE CO.

Size	Printing	Number in set	Title	Complete set
D	BW	25	Actresses — French c1900 (reprinted 2001)	£6.00

GLOBE INSURANCE

Size	Printing	Number in set	Title	Complete set
—	U	11	Famous Golfers (75 x 60mm) 1929 (reprinted 1996)	£6.00

G.G. GOODE LTD (Australia)

Size	Printing	Number in set	Title	Complete set
D2	U	17	Prominent Cricketer Series 1924 (reprinted 2001)	£5.00

THOS. H. HALL (USA)

Size	Printing	Number in set	Title	Complete set
C1	C	8	Presidential Candidates & Actresses 1880 (reprinted 2001)	£3.00

Size	Print-ing	Number in set	REPRINT SERIES	Complete set

HIGNETT BROS. & CO.

| A | C | 25 | Greetings of The World 1907 (C.C.S. reprinted 2000) | £6.50 |
| A | C | 50 | Prominent Racehorses of 1933 (C.C.S. reprinted 2000) | £10.00 |

R. & J. HILL LTD

| A | C | 25 | Battleships and Crests 1901 (reprinted 1995) | £6.50 |
| A | C | 20 | Types of The British Army 1914 (reprinted 2001) | £6.50 |

HUDDEN & CO. LTD

| A | C | 25 | Famous Boxers 1927 (reprinted 1992) | £6.50 |

HUNTLEY & PALMER (France)

| — | C | 12 | Aviation (114 x 85mm) c1908 (reprinted 2001) | £7.50 |

IMPERIAL TOBACCO COMPANY OF CANADA LTD

| A | C | 45 | Hockey Players 1912 (reprinted 1987) | £15.00 |
| A | C | 36 | Hockey Series 1911 (reprinted 1987) | £15.00 |

INTERNATIONAL CHEWING GUM (USA)

| — | C | 24 | Don't Let It Happen Over Here (80 x 64mm) 1938 (reprinted 1984) | £10.00 |

JAMES & CO.

| — | C | 20 | Arms of Countries (70 x 52mm) c1915 (reprinted 2001) | £7.50 |

JONES BROS., Tottenham

| A | BW | 18 | Spurs Footballers 1912 (reprinted 1986) | £3.00 |

WM. S. KIMBALL & CO. (USA)

| A1 | C | 50 | Champions of Games & Sports c1890 (reprinted 2001) | £10.00 |

KINNEAR LTD

| D1 | BW | 15 | Australian Cricketers 1897 (reprinted 2001) | £4.00 |

KINNEY BROS. (USA)

| A | C | 25 | Famous English Running Horses 1889 (reprinted 1996) | £6.50 |
| A | C | 25 | Leaders 1889 (reprinted 1990) | £6.50 |

J. KNIGHT (HUSTLER SOAP)

| A | C | 30 | Regimental Nicknames 1924 (reprinted 1996) | £6.50 |

B. KRIEGSFELD & CO.

| A | C | 50 | Phrases and Advertisements c1900 (reprinted 2001) | £10.00 |

A. KUIT LTD

| A | U | 25 | Principal Streets of British Cities and Towns 1916 (reprinted 2001) | £6.00 |

LACY'S CHEWING GUM

| A | BW | 50 | Footballers c1925 (reprinted 2001) | £10.00 |

LAMBERT & BUTLER

A	C	25	Aviation 1915 (reprinted 1997)	£6.00
A	C	25	Dance Band Leaders 1936 (reprinted 1992)	£6.00
A	C	50	Empire Air Routes 1936 (C.C.S. reprinted 2000)	£15.00
A	C	25	Hints and Tips for Motorists 1929 (reprinted 1994)	£6.00

Size	Print-ing	Number in set	REPRINT SERIES	Complete set
			LAMBERT & BUTLER (continued)	
A	C	50	Horsemanship 1938 (reprinted 1994)	£8.50
A	C	50	Interesting Sidelights On The Work of The GPO 1939 (C.C.S. reprinted 1999)	£10.00
A	C	20	International Yachts 1902 (reprinted 2001)	£5.00
A	C	25	London Characters 1934 (reprinted 1992)	£6.00
A	C	25	Motor Cars 1st series 1922 (reprinted 1988)	£8.00
A	C	25	Motor Cars 2nd series 1923 (reprinted 1988)	£6.50
A	C	25	Motor Cars 1934 (reprinted 1992)	£6.50
A	C	50	Motor Cycles 1923 (reprinted 1990)	£8.50
A	C	25	Motors 1908 (reprinted 1992)	£6.00
A	C	25	Winter Sports 1914 (reprinted 1998)	£10.00
A	C	50	World's Locomotives 1912 (reprinted 1988)	£8.50
			R. J. LEA LTD	
A	C	50	Flowers to Grow 1913 (reprinted 1997):	
			A Complete set of 50	£15.00
			B Numbers 1 to 25 only	£6.50
			LEAF GUM CO. (USA)	
—	BW	72	Star Trek (87 x 61mm) 1967 (reprinted 1981)	£12.50
			J. LEES	
A	C	20	Northampton Town Football Club c1912 (reprinted 2001)	£5.00
			LIEBIG (France)	
J2	C	6	Famous Explorers (F1088) 1914 (reprinted 2001)	£5.00
			LUSBY LTD	
D	C	25	Scenes From Circus Life c1900 (reprinted 2001)	£6.00
			MARBURG BROS. (USA)	
A	C	15	Beauties "PAC" c1890 (reprinted 2001)	£4.00
			P.H. MAYO & BROTHER (USA)	
C	U	35	Prizefighters c1890 (reprinted 2001)	£7.50
			STEPHEN MITCHELL & SON	
A	C	25	Angling 1928 (reprinted 1993)	£6.00
A	C	50	Famous Scots 1933 (C.C.S. reprinted 1999)	£10.00
A	U	50	First Aid 1938 (C.C.S. reprinted 2001)	£10.00
A	C	50	A Gallery of 1935 (C.C.S. reprinted 1999)	£10.00
A	C	50	Humorous Drawings 1924 (C.C.S. reprinted 1999)	£10.00
A	C	25	Money 1913 (C.C.S. reprinted 2000)	£6.50
A	C	25	Regimental Crests, Nicknames and Collar Badges 1900 (reprinted 1993) ...	£10.00
A	C	50	Scotland's Story 1929 (C.C.S. reprinted 2000)	£10.00
			MURRAY, SONS & CO. LTD	
A	BW	20	Cricketers 1912 (reprinted 1991)	£7.50
A	C	20	War Series K — Uniforms 1915 (reprinted 2000)	£6.50
A	C	15	War Series K — World War I Leaders & Generals 1915 (reprinted 2000) ...	£12.50
			NATIONAL CIGARETTE CO. (Australia)	
A	BW	13	English Cricket Team 1897-8 (reprinted 2001)	£4.00
			NATIONAL EXCHANGE BANK, USA	
—	C	9	Seven Ages of Golf (85 x 57mm) c1885 (reprinted 1995)	£4.50

Size	Printing	Number in set	REPRINT SERIES	Complete set
			OGDENS LTD	
A	C	25	ABC of Sport 1927 (C.C.S. reprinted 2002)	£12.50
A	C	50	A.F.C. Nicknames 1933 (reprinted 1996)	£8.50
A	C	50	Air Raid Precautions 1938 (C.C.S. reprinted 1999)	£10.00
A	C	50	British Birds 1905 (C.C.S. reprinted 2000)	£12.50
A	C	50	By The Roadside 1932 (C.C.S. reprinted 2000)	£10.00
A	C	50	Champions of 1936 (C.C.S. reprinted 2000)	£10.00
A	C	50	Construction of Railway Trains 1930 (C.C.S. reprinted 1999)	£15.00
D2	U	50	Cricketers and Sportsmen c1898 (reprinted 2001)	£10.00
A	C	50	Flags and Funnels of Leading Steamship Lines 1906 (reprinted 1997)	£8.50
A	C	50	Jockeys 1930 (reprinted 1990)	£15.00
A	C	50	Modern British Pottery 1925 (C.C.S. reprinted 1999)	£15.00
A	C	50	Modern Railways 1936 (reprinted 1996)	£15.00
A	C	50	Motor Races 1931 (reprinted 1993)	£12.50
A	C	25	Poultry 1st Series 1915 (reprinted 1998)	£6.50
A	C	25	Poultry 2nd Series 1916 (reprinted 2000)	£10.00
A	C	50	Shakespeare Series 1903 (C.C.S. reprinted 2000)	£15.00
A	C	50	Smugglers & Smuggling 1931 (C.C.S. reprinted 1999)	£15.00
A	C	50	Soldiers of the King 1909 (reprinted 1993)	£8.50
A	C	50	The Story of the Life Boat c1950 (reprinted 1989)	£15.00
A	C	50	The Story of The Lifeboat c1950 (without "Ogdens") (reprinted 2001)	£8.50
A	C	50	The Story of Sand 1934 (C.C.S. reprinted 2001)	£12.50
A	C	50	Swimming, Diving and Life-Saving 1931 (C.C.S. reprinted 2000)	£10.00
A	C	50	Trick Billiards 1934 (C.C.S. reprinted 2001)	£12.50
			OLD CALABAR BISCUIT CO. LTD	
J2	C	16	Sports and Games c1900 (reprinted 2001)	£7.50
			THE ORLANDO CIGARETTE & CIGAR CO.	
A	C	40	Home & Colonial Regiments c1901 (reprinted 2001)	£8.50
			PALMER MANN & CO (Sifta Sam)	
—	C	25	Famous Cricketers (set 24 plus 1 variety) 1950 (reprinted 2001):	
			A Size 74 x 36mm	£6.00
			B Size 69 x 38mm	£6.00
			J.A. PATTREIOUEX, Manchester	
A	C	75	Cricketers Series 1926 (reprinted 1997)	£13.50
			GODFREY PHILLIPS LTD	
A	C	30	Beauties "Nymphs" c1896 (reprinted 2001)	£7.50
A	C	25	Railway Engines 1924 (reprinted 1997)	£12.50
A	C	20	Russo-Japanese War Series 1904 (reprinted 2001)	£5.00
A	C	25	Territorial Series 1908 (reprinted 2001)	£6.50
A	C	25	Types of British Soldiers 1900 (reprinted 1997)	£6.50
			JOHN PLAYER & SONS	
A	C	50	Aeroplanes (Civil) 1935 (reprinted 1990)	£8.50
A	C	50	Aircraft of The Royal Air Force 1938 (reprinted 1990)	£8.50
A	C	50	Animals of The Countryside 1939 (C.C.S. reprinted 1999)	£10.00
A	C	50	Aviary & Cage Birds 1933 (reprinted 1989)	£12.50
B	C	25	Aviary and Cage Birds 1935 (reprinted 1987)	£8.50
A	C	50	Boy Scout and Girl Guide Patrol Signs and Emblems 1933 (C.C.S reprinted 2001)	£12.50
A	C	50	British Empire Series 1904 (C.C.S. reprinted 1999)	£10.00

Size	Print-ing	Number in set	REPRINT SERIES	Complete set
			JOHN PLAYER & SONS (continued)	
A	C	50	Butterflies & Moths 1904 (C.C.S. reprinted 2000)	£12.50
B	C	24	Cats 1936 (reprinted 1986)	£8.50
A	C	25	Characters from Dickens 1912 (reprinted 1990)	£6.00
A	C	25	Characters from Dickens 2nd series 1914 (reprinted 1990)	£6.00
A	C	50	Cities of The World 1900 (C.C.S. reprinted 1999)	£10.00
A	C	50	Countries Arms and Flags 1905 (C.C.S. reprinted 2001)	£12.50
B	C	25	Country Sports 1930 (reprinted 2000)	£8.50
A	C	50	Cricketers 1930 (reprinted 2000)	£8.50
A	C	50	Cricketers 1934 (reprinted 1990)	£8.50
A	C	50	Cricketers 1938 (C.C.S. reprinted 2000)	£10.00
A	C	50	Cricketers Caricatures by "Rip" 1926 (reprinted 1993)	£8.50
A	C	50	Derby and Grand National Winners 1933 (reprinted 1988)	£8.50
A	C	50	Dogs – Full Length 1931 (C.C.S. reprinted 2000)	£10.00
A	C	50	Dogs – Scenic Backgrounds 1924 (C.C.S. reprinted 1997)	£12.50
A	C	50	Dogs' Heads (silver-grey backgrounds) 1940 (reprinted 1994)	£8.50
A2	C	25	England's Naval Heroes 1898 descriptive (reprinted 1987)	£15.00
A	C	50	Famous Irish-Bred Horses 1936 (C.C.S. reprinted 2001)	£15.00
A	C	50	Film Stars 1st Series 1934 (C.C.S. reprinted 2000)	£15.00
A	C	50	Film Stars 2nd Series 1934 (C.C.S. reprinted 2001)	£15.00
A	C	50	Film Stars 3rd series 1938 (reprinted 1989)	£8.50
A	C	50	Fire-Fighting Appliances 1930 (reprinted 1991)	£8.50
A	C	50	Game Birds and Wild Fowl 1927 (C.C.S. reprinted 1999)	£10.00
B	C	25	Game Birds and Wild Fowl 1928 (reprinted 1987)	£8.50
A	C	50	Gilbert & Sullivan 2nd series 1927 (reprinted 1990)	£8.50
B	C	25	Golf 1939 (reprinted 1986)	£8.50
A	C	25	Highland Clans 1908 (reprinted 1997)	£10.00
A	C	50	History of Naval Dress 1930 (C.C.S. reprinted 2001)	£12.50
A	C	50	International Air Liners 1936 (C.C.S. reprinted 2001)	£10.00
A	C	50	Kings & Queens 1935 (reprinted 1990)	£10.00
A	C	50	Military Head-Dress 1931 (C.C.S. reprinted 1999)	£10.00
A	C	50	Military Series 1900 (reprinted 1983)	£8.50
A	C	50	Motor Cars 1st series 1936 (reprinted 1990)	£8.50
A	C	50	Motor Cars 2nd series 1937 (C.C.S. reprinted 2000)	£10.00
A	C	25	Napoleon 1916 (reprinted 1989)	£6.00
A	C	50	Nature Series 1908 (C.C.S. reprinted 2000)	£10.00
A	C	50	Old England's Defenders 1898 (reprinted 1987)	£15.00
B	C	25	Old Hunting Prints 1938 (reprinted 1989)	£8.50
B	C	25	Old Naval Prints 1936 (reprinted 1989)	£8.50
B	C	25	Picturesque London 1931 (reprinted 1997)	£8.50
A	C	50	Poultry 1931 (reprinted 1993)	£8.50
A	C	50	Products of The World 1928 (C.C.S. reprinted 1999)	£10.00
B	C	25	Racing Yachts 1938 (reprinted 1987)	£8.50
A	C	50	Regimental Standards & Cap Badges 1930 (reprinted 1993)	£8.50
A	C	50	Regimental Uniforms Nd. 51-100 1914 (reprinted 1995)	£8.50
A	C	50	Speedway Riders 1937 (C.C.S. reprinted 2000)	£15.00
A	C	50	Tennis 1936 (C.C.S. reprinted 1999).	£10.00
B	C	24	Treasures of Britain 1931 (reprinted 1996)	£8.50
B	C	25	Types of Horses 1939 (reprinted 1998)	£8.50
A	C	50	Uniforms of the Territorial Army 1939 (reprinted 1990)	£8.50
B	C	25	Wild Birds 1934 (reprinted 1997)	£8.50
			JOHN PLAYER & SONS (OVERSEAS)	
A	C	50	Ships, Flags and Cap Badges 1930 (reprinted 1997)	£15.00
			REEVES LTD	
D	C	25	Cricketers 1912 (reprinted 1993)	£8.00

Size	Printing	Number in set	REPRINT SERIES	Complete set
			RICHMOND CAVENDISH CO. LTD	
A	C	20	Yachts c1900 (reprinted 2001)	£5.00
			E. ROBINSON & SONS LTD	
A	C	6	Medals & Decorations of Great Britain c1905 (reprinted 2001)	£3.00
A2	C	25	Regimental Mascots 1916 (reprinted 2001)	£6.00
			S.D.V. TOBACCO CO. LTD	
A1	BW	16	British Royal Family c1901 (reprinted 2001)	£4.00
			SALMON & GLUCKSTEIN LTD	
A	C	15	Billiard Terms 1905 (reprinted 1997)	£5.00
A	C	25	Coronation Series 1911 (C.C.S. reprinted 2000)	£6.50
C2	C	30	Music Hall Celebrities c1902 (reprinted 2001)	£7.50
			JOHN SINCLAIR LTD	
A	C	50	British Sea Dogs 1926 (reprinted 1997)	£8.50
			SINGLETON & COLE LTD	
A	BW	35	Famous Boxers 1930 (reprinted 1992)	£10.00
D	BW	50	Footballers c1905 (reprinted 2001)	£10.00
			F. & J. SMITH	
A	C	25	Advertisement Cards 1899 (reprinted 2001)	£6.00
D	BW	50	Champions of Sport (unnumbered) 1902 (reprinted 2001)	£10.00
A	C	25	Cinema Stars 1920 (reprinted 1987)	£6.50
A	C	50	Fowls, Pigeons and Dogs 1908 (C.C.S. reprinted 2000)	£15.00
A	C	25	Holiday Resorts 1925 (C.C.S. reprinted 2000)	£6.50
A	C	25	Prominent Rugby Players 1924 (reprinted 1992)	£8.00
			SPIRO VALLERI & CO.	
A1	U	10	Noted Footballers c1905 (reprinted 2001)	£3.00
			SPRATTS PATENT LTD	
C2	C	12	Prize Dogs c1910 (reprinted 2001)	£3.50
			TADDY & CO.	
A	C	20	Clowns & Circus Artists 1920 (reprinted 1991)	£6.00
A	BW	238	County Cricketers 1907 (reprinted 1987)	£48.00
			Individual Counties of the above set:	
		15	Derbyshire	£3.00
		15	Essex	£3.00
		16	Gloucestershire	£3.00
		15	Hampshire	£3.00
		15	Kent	£3.00
		15	Lancashire	£3.00
		14	Leicestershire	£3.00
		15	Middlesex	£3.00
		15	Northamptonshire	£3.00
		14	Nottinghamshire	£3.00
		15	Somersetshire	£3.00
		15	Surrey	£3.00
		15	Sussex	£3.00
		15	Warwickshire	£3.00
		14	Worcestershire	£3.00
		15	Yorkshire	£3.00

Size	Print-ing	Number in set	REPRINT SERIES	Complete set
			TADDY & CO. (continued)	
A	U	5	English Royalty c1898 (reprinted 2001)	£3.00
A	C	25	Famous Jockeys 1910 (reprinted 1996)	£6.50
A	C	25	Natives of the World c1900 (reprinted 1999)	£6.00
A	BW	15	Prominent Footballers Aston Villa 1907 (reprinted 1992)	£3.00
A	BW	15	Prominent Footballers Chelsea 1907 (reprinted 1998)	£3.00
A	BW	15	Prominent Footballers Everton 1907 (reprinted 1998)	£3.00
A	BW	15	Prominent Footballers Leeds 1907 (reprinted 1992)	£3.00
A	BW	15	Prominent Footballers Liverpool 1907 (reprinted 1992)	£3.00
A	BW	15	Prominent Footballers Manchester Utd 1907 (reprinted 1992)	£3.00
A	BW	15	Prominent Footballers Middlesbrough 1907 (reprinted 1998)	£3.00
A	BW	15	Prominent Footballers Newcastle Utd 1907 (reprinted 1992)	£3.00
A	BW	15	Prominent Footballers Queens Park Rangers 1907 (reprinted 1992)	£7.50
A	BW	15	Prominent Footballers Sunderland 1907 (reprinted 1998)	£3.00
A	BW	15	Prominent Footballers Tottenham Hotspur 1907 (reprinted 1998)	£3.00
A	BW	15	Prominent Footballers West Ham Utd 1907 (reprinted 1998)	£3.00
A	BW	15	Prominent Footballers Woolwich Arsenal 1907 (reprinted 1992)	£3.00
A2	C	20	Royalty, Actresses, Soldiers c1898 (reprinted 2001)	£5.00
A	C	25	Royalty Series 1908 (reprinted 1998)	£6.50
A	BW	15	South African Cricket Team 1907 (reprinted 1992)	£7.50
A	C	25	Territorial Regiments 1908 (reprinted 1996)	£6.50
A	C	25	Thames Series 1903 (reprinted 1996)	£6.50
A	C	20	Victoria Cross Heroes (Nos 1-20) 1900 (reprinted 1996)	£6.50
A	C	20	Victoria Cross Heroes (Nos 21-40) 1900 (reprinted 1996)	£6.50
A	C	20	VC Heroes — Boer War (Nos 41-60) 1901 (reprinted 1997)	£6.50
A	C	20	VC Heroes — Boer War (Nos 61-80) 1901 (reprinted 1997)	£6.50
A	C	20	VC Heroes — Boer War (Nos 81-100) 1902 (reprinted 1997)	£6.50
A	C	25	Victoria Cross Heroes (Nos 101-125) 1905 (reprinted 1996)	£6.50
			TEOFANI & CO. LTD	
A	C	24	Past and Present The Army 1938 (reprinted 2001)	£6.50
A	C	24	Past and Present Weapons of War 1938 (reprinted 2001)	£6.50
			D. C. THOMSON	
A	C	24	Motor Bike Cards 1929 (reprinted 1993)	£6.00
A	C	20	Motor Cycles 1923 (Wizard Series) (reprinted 1993)	£6.00
			TOPPS CHEWING GUM INC. (USA)	
—	C	56	Mars Attacks (90 x 64mm) 1962 (reprinted 1987)	£12.50
—	C	51	Outer Limits (90 x 64mm) 1964 (reprinted 1995)	£12.50
			UNION JACK	
—	C	8	Police of All Nations (70 x 45mm) 1922 (reprinted 2005)	£4.00
			UNITED TOBACCONISTS' ASSOCIATION LTD	
A	C	10	Actresses "MUTA" c1900 (reprinted 2001)	£3.00
			HENRY WELFARE & CO.	
D	BW	22	Prominent Politicians c1911 (reprinted 2001)	£6.00
			W.D. & H.O. WILLS	
—	C	4	Advert Postcards of Packings (140 x 90mm) 1902 (reprinted 1988)	£5.00
A	C	50	Allied Army Leaders 1917 (C.C.S reprinted 2000)	£10.00
A	C	50	Arms of Companies 1913 (C.C.S reprinted 1999)	£10.00
A	C	50	Builders of The Empire 1898 (C.C.S. reprinted 1999)	£12.50
B	C	7	Cathedrals 1933 (from set of 25) (reprinted 2000)	£3.00

Size	Print-ing	Number in set	REPRINT SERIES	Complete set
			W.D. & H.O. WILLS (continued)	
A	C	50	Cricketers 1896 (reprinted 1982)	£8.50
A	C	50	Cricketers 1901 (reprinted 1983)	£15.00
A	C	50	Do You Know 2nd Series 1924 (C.C.S. reprinted 2003)	£10.00
B	C	25	Dogs 1914 (reprinted 1987)	£8.50
A	C	50	Dogs 1937 (C.C.S. reprinted 2001)	£12.50
A	C	50	Double Meaning 1898 (C.C.S. reprinted 1999)	£10.00
A	C	50	Engineering Wonders 1927 (C.C.S. reprinted 1999)	£10.00
B	C	25	Famous Golfers 1930 (reprinted 1987)	£8.50
A	C	50	First Aid 1915 (C.C.S. reprinted 1999)	£12.50
A	C	50	Fish & Bait 1910 (reprinted 1990)	£8.50
A	C	50	Flower Culture In Pots 1925 (C.C.S. reprinted 2000)	£10.00
A	C	50	Gardening Hints 1923 (C.C.S. reprinted 2003)	£10.00
A	C	50	Gems of Belgian Architecture 1915 (C.C.S. reprinted 2001)	£10.00
A	C	50	Gems of French Architecture 1917 (C.C.S. reprinted 2003)	£12.50
A	BW	50	Gems of Italian Architecture 1917 (black & white reprinted 1960)	£35.00
A	C	50	Household Hints 1st Series 1927 (C.C.S. reprinted 1999)	£10.00
B	C	25	Lawn Tennis 1931 (reprinted 1988)	£8.50
A	C	50	Life in the Hedgerow 1950 (reprinted 1991, Swan Vestas)	£12.50
A	C	50	Life In The Royal Navy 1939 (C.C.S. reprinted 1999)	£10.00
A	C	50	Military Aircraft (unissued c1967) (reprinted 1991)	£8.50
A	C	50	Military Motors 1916 (reprinted 1994)	£8.50
A	C	58	Musical Celebrities 2nd series including 8 substituted cards 1914 (reprinted 1987)	£9.50
A	C	25	National Costumes c1895 (reprinted 1999)	£6.00
A	C	50	Naval Dress & Badges 1909 (reprinted 1997)	£8.50
A	C	25	Naval Dress & Badges 1909 (Nos. 1 to 25 Naval Dress only reprinted) Inscribed 'Commissioned by Sydney Cigarette Card Company, Australia' (reprinted 1993)	£6.50
A	C	50	Old English Garden Flowers 2nd Series 1913 (reprinted 1994)	£8.50
A	C	50	Overseas Dominions (Australia) 1915 (C.C.S. reprinted 2003)	£10.00
A	C	50	Overseas Dominions (Canada) 1914 (C.C.S. reprinted 2002)	£10.00
B	C	40	Puppies by Lucy Dawson (unissued) (reprinted 1990)	£15.00
A	C	50	Railway Engines 1924 (reprinted 1995)	£8.50
A	C	50	Railway Engines 1936 (reprinted 1992)	£12.50
A	C	50	Railway Equipment 1939 (reprinted 1993)	£8.50
A	C	50	Railway Locomotives 1930 (reprinted 1993)	£8.50
A	C	12	Recruiting Posters 1915 (reprinted 1987)	£3.00
B	C	25	Rigs of Ships 1929 (reprinted 1987)	£8.50
A	C	50	Roses 1st series 1912 (reprinted 1994)	£8.50
A	C	50	Rugby Internationals 1929 (reprinted 1996)	£8.50
A	C	50	Safety First 1934 (C.C.S. reprinted 2000)	£10.00
A	C	50	School Arms 1906 (C.C.S. reprinted 2000)	£10.00
A	C	50	Ships Badges 1925 (C.C.S. reprinted 2000)	£10.00
A	C	50	Speed 1930 (C.C.S. reprinted 2001)	£12.50
A	C	50	Waterloo 1915 (reprinted 1987)	£20.00
A	C	50	Wild Flowers 1923 (C.C.S. reprinted 1999)	£10.00
A	C	50	Wild Flowers 1st series 1936 (reprinted 1993)	£15.00
A	C	50	Wonders of The Sea 1928 (C.C.S. reprinted 2000)	£10.00
A	C	25	World's Dreadnoughts 1910 (reprinted 1994)	£6.00
			W.D. & H.O. WILLS (Overseas)	
A	C	50	Types of the British Army 1912 (reprinted 1995)	£12.50
A	C	50	War Incidents 2nd Series 1917 (reprinted 1995)	£8.50
			W.H. & J. WOODS LTD	
A	C	25	Types of Volunteers & Yeomanry 1902 (reprinted 1996)	£8.50

1

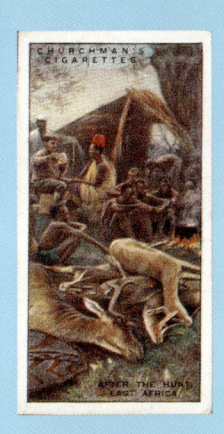

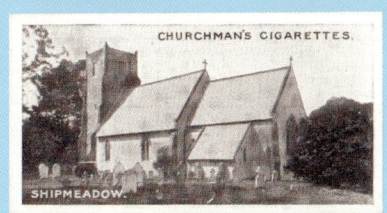

2

3

4

5

6

7

8

9

10

11

12

13. WILLS'S CIGARETTES — "PATH OF PEACE" JOCKEY: M. BEARY

14. Player's Cigarettes — The "Terra Nova"

15. Ceylon

16. FAMOUS CROWNS — NAPOLEON I

17. CHURCHMAN'S CIGARETTES — THE HOLY HEAD OF HALIFAX

18. OGDEN'S CIGARETTES — J. MARSHALL, MRS. G. DRUMMOND'S COLOURS

19. VICTORY SIGNS SERIES — 267TH S.B.A.C. — British Army Distinguishing Mark

20. CARRERAS CIGARETTES — OXEYE DAISY

21. CINEMA STARS — No. 30. MAURICE CHEVALIER. — LLOYD'S CIGARETTES

22    23    24    25

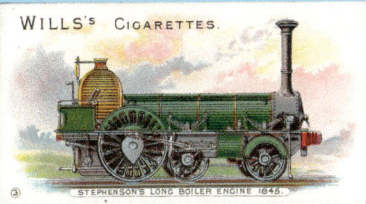

26 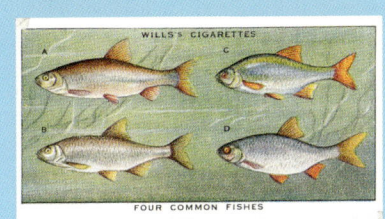   27

28    29

30    31    32    33

34
35
36
37
38
39
40
41
42
43
44
45

46
47
48
49
50
51
52
53
54
55

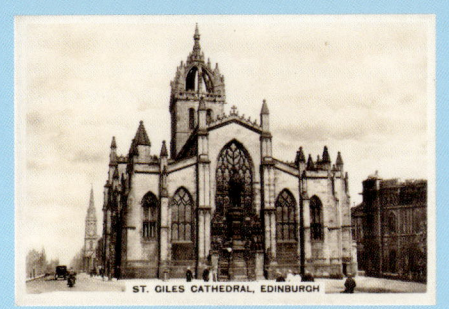

56  57  58  59

60  61

62  63

64  65  66  67

68

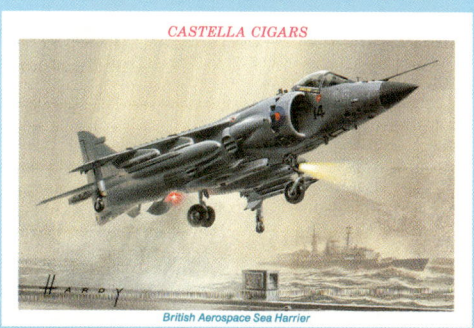

69

70

71

73

72

74

75

76

77  78  79  80

81  82

83  84

85  86  87  88

89

90

MULTI-STAGE LIQUID-PROPELLANT ROCKET

91

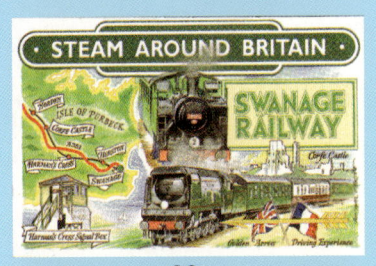

92

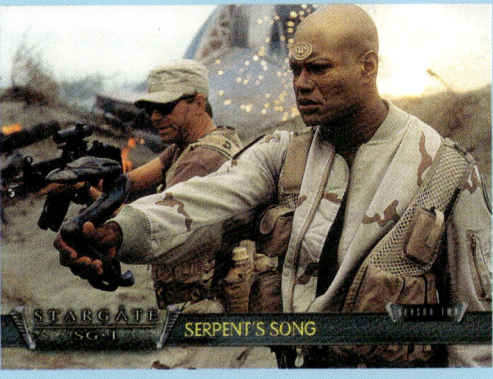

93

94

95

96  97 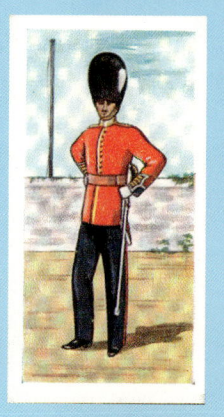 98  99

100  101

102  103

104  105  106  107

108

109

110

111

112

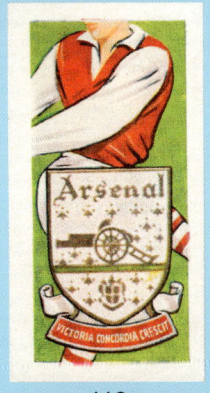

113

114

115

116

117

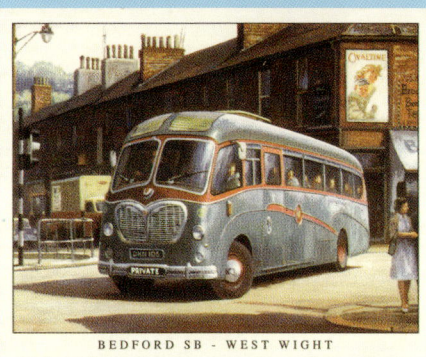

118
BEDFORD SB – WEST WIGHT

119
L.N.E.R. CLASS A4 PACIFIC EXPRESS LOCO. NO. 4468 "MALLARD". 1937

120

121

122

123

124  125  126  127

128  129

130  131

132 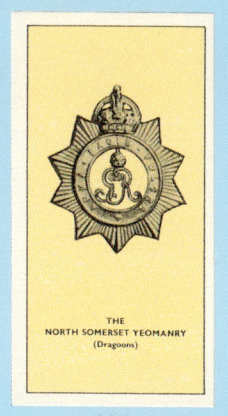 133  134  135

136

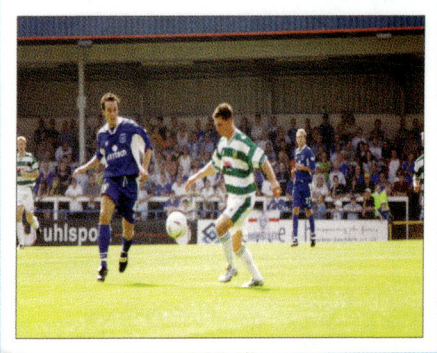

137

138

139

140

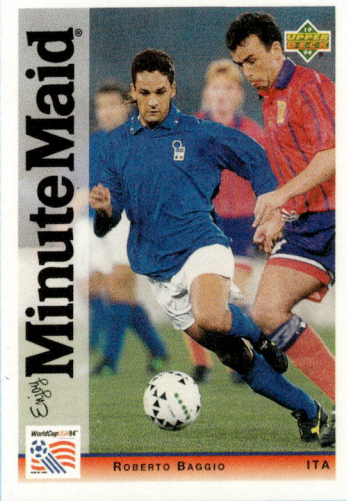

141

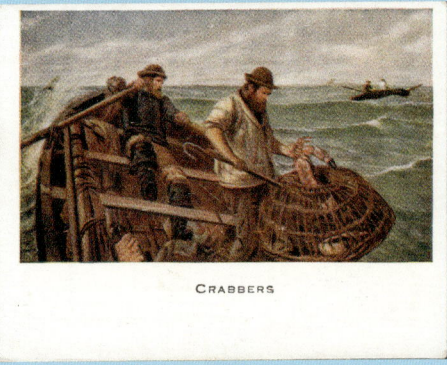

142

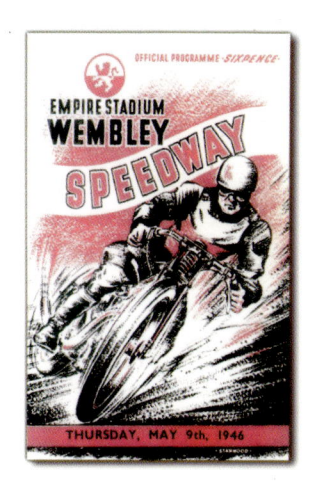

143

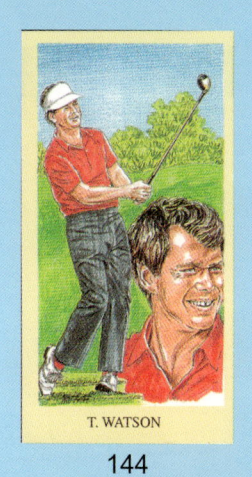

144

145

146

147

148

149

150

151

152

153

154

155

156

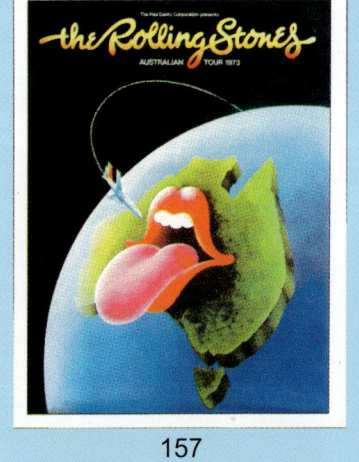

157

158

159

160

ILLUSTRATIONS OF CIGARETTE CARDS

1. Churchman Sports & Games in Many Lands 1929
2. R.J. Lea Old Pottery & Porcelain 5th Series 1913
3. Pattreiouex Builders of The British Empire c1929
4. Carreras Film Favourites 1938
5. Churchman East Suffolk Churches 1912
6. Players Game Birds and Wild Fowl 1927
7. British American Tobacco Britain's Defenders 1915
8. Ogdens Sea Adventure 1939
9. Taddy Famous Jockeys c1905
10. Gallaher Sporting Personalities 1936
11. Adcock Ancient Norwich 1928
12. J. Wix Coronation 1937
13. Wills Racehorses and Jockeys 1938
14. Players Ships Figureheads 1931
15. Drapkin Girls of Many Lands 1929
16. G Phillips Famous Crowns 1938
17. Churchman Legends of Britain 1936
18. Ogdens Jockeys and Owners Colours 1927
19. Morris Victory Signs 1928
20. Carreras Wild Flower Art Series 1923
21. R. Lloyd Cinema Stars 2nd Series c1934
22. Brumfit The Public Schools Ties Series (Old Boys) 1925
23. Gallaher Wild Animals 1937
24. G. Phillips Popular Superstitions 1930
25. Wills Ships Badges 1925
26. Wills Locomotive Engines and Rolling Stock 1901
27. Wills Pond and Aquarium 1st Series c1950
28. G. Phillips Bird Painting 1938
29. Lambert & Butler A History of Aviation 1932
30. Wills Borough Arms Second Edition (51-100) 1906
31. Carreras Film Stars by Florence Desmond 1936
32. Ardath Life in the Services 1938
33. G. Phillips Soldiers of the King 1939
34. Players Coronation Series Ceremonial Dress 1937
35. Churchman Kings of Speed 1939
36. Gallaher Army Badges 1939
37. Wills The Coronation Series 1911
38. Gallaher Butterflies and Moths 1938
39. Players Aircraft of the Royal Air Force 1938
40. Players Life on Board a Man of War in 1805 and 1905 (1905)
41. Ogdens A.B.C. of Sport 1927
42. Wills Flags of the Empire 1st Series 1926
43. Carreras School Emblems 1929
44. Wills Railway Equipment 1939
45. Pattreiouex Cricketers Series 1926
46. Pattreiouex Sights of Britain 3rd Series 1937
47. Players Golf 1939
48. Amalgamated Tobacco Famous British Ships 2nd Series 1952
49. Pattreiouex Natives and Scenes Series CB1 to CB96 c1925
50. Wills Donington Collection 1993
51. Ogdens Modes of Conveyance 1927
52. Mitchell Stars of Screen and History 1939
53. Players Military Series 1900
54. Wills Cinema Stars 1st Series 1928
55. Teofani Past and Present Series A The Army 1938
56. Ogdens Modern British Pottery 1925
57. Rothmans Landmarks in Empire History c1936
58. Gallaher The Reason Why 1924
59. Carreras Glamour Girls of Stage and Films 1939
60. Ardath Stamps Rare and Interesting 1939
61. Players Fire-Fighting Appliances 1930
62. Players Regimental Standards and Cap Badges 1930
63. Taddy Motor Cars 1980
64. Carreras Military Uniforms 1976
65. Abdulla Screen Stars 1939
66. Wills Overseas Horses of Today 1906
67. Gallaher My Favourite Part 1939
68. Players Uniforms of the Territorial Army 1939
69. Mitchell Clan Tartans 2nd Series 1927
70. Carreras Amusing Tricks and How to Do Them 1937
71. Carreras British Costume 1927
72. Players Racehorses 1926
73. Cope Dickens Character Series 1939
74. Players British Naval Craft 1939
75. Wills Old Furniture 1st Series 1923
76. Wills British Aviation 1994
77. Players Wild Animals Heads 1931
78. Carreras Orchids 1925
79. Wills Roses 2nd Series 1914
80. American Tobacco Co Beauties Playing Card Inset c1900
81. Players Country Seats and Arms 2nd Series 1907
82. Ogdens Cathedrals & Abbeys 1936
83. Amalgamated Tobacco Butterflies and Moths 1957
84. Ogdens British Birds 1905
85. Moustafa Leo Chambers Dogs Heads 1924
86. Players Aviary and Cage Birds 1933
87. Wills Cricketers 1908
88. Drapkin Puzzle Pictures 1926

ILLUSTRATIONS OF TRADE CARDS

89 Rittenhouse The Umbrella Academy 2020
90 Weetabix Conquest of Space Series B 1959
91 Cadbury Strange But True 1969
92 Reflections of a Bygone Age Steam Around Britain 2nd Series 2001
93 Rittenhouse Stargate SG1 Seasons 1 to 3 2001
94 Inkworks The Phantom the Movie 1996
95 Golden Era Classic British Motor Cycles of the 1950s and 1960s 1993
96 Musgrave Brothers Wild Flowers 1961
97 A.T. Marks Post Box 2021
98 Properts British Uniforms 1955
99 Musical Collectables Gilbert & Sullivan 2nd Series 1995
100 Lifeguard British Butterflies 1955
101 Beaulah Modern British Aircraft 1953
102 Tonibell Did You Know 1963
103 Daily Ice Cream Modern British Locomotives 1954
104 Brooke Bond Tropical Birds 1961
105 Glengettie Medals of the World 1961
106 A.T. Marks Yorkshire Cricketers 1903 (1990)
107 Welsh Rugby Union Great Welsh Rugby Players 1980
108 Rolls Royce Motors Rolls Royce Motor Cars 2nd Series 1987
109 Starline USA Hollywood Walk of Fame (nos. 1 to 125) 1991
110 Inkworks Firefly the Complete Collection 2006
111 Golden Era Aston Martin Cars 1993
112 Coopers Tea Do You Know 1962
113 Kane Football Clubs and Colours 1957
114 Brindley Hampshire County Cricket Club 1991
115 Duttons Bears Team of Sporting Heroes 1980
116 Merlin Star Wars Trilogy 1997
117 Cryptozoic The Vampire Diaries Season 1 2011
118 Golden Era Bygone Buses (1950s & 1960s) 2010
119 Prescott Pickup Railway Locomotives 1978
120 Typhoo Tea Interesting Events in British History 1938
121 Sweetule Historic Cars & Cycles 1957
122 Skybox Star Trek Insurrection 1998
123 Redsky Grace Kelly 2012
124 Mister Softee Top 20 1963
125 Polydor Polydor Guitar 1975

126 Paramint Cards Arthur Askey Comedy Heroes 2012
127 Primrose Popeye 3rd Series 1961
128 Brooke Bond History of the Motor Car 1968
129 Brooke Bond Wild Birds in Britain 1965
130 Brooke Bond Transport Through the Ages 1966
131 Walls Moon Fleet 1966
132 Brooke Bond The Magical World of Disney 1989
133 Walters Palm Toffee Some Cap Badges of Territorial Regiments 1938
134 Phillips Tea Army Badges Past & Present 1964
135 England's Glory England 66 (Football World Cup) 2004
136 J. Lyons Catweazle Magic Cards 1971
137 Sheldon Collectibles Match of the Day Rochdale v Yeovil Town 2003
138 Moseley Historical Buildings 1956
139 G.D.S Cards Great Racehorses of Our Time 1994
140 Halpin's Willow Tea Aircraft of the World 1958
141 Minute Maid/Upper Deck USA World Cup Stars (Football) 1994
142 MacFisheries Gallery Pictures 1924
143 Aston Cards Speedway Programme Covers The Fabulous 40s 4th Series 2004
144 Gallery of Legends The British Open Golf Collection 1999
145 Bassett World Heroes (Footballers) 1999
146 Golden Grain Tea Passenger Liners 1966
147 Kellogg A History of British Military Aircraft 1963
148 Brooke Bond Queen Elizabeth I-Queen Elizabeth II 1983
149 Halpin's Willow Tea Nature Studies 1957
150 Rittenhouse James Bond 007 The Complete Series 2007
151 Empson Tea Tropical Birds 1966
152 Rockwell Heath Robinson On Golf 2020
153 Teacards Solar System 2021
154 Clover Dairies Prehistoric Animals 1966
155 Sanitarium New Zealand Kiwi Heroes 1994
156 Bassett Disney Health & Safety 1977
157 Sporting Profiles The Rolling Stones Concert Posters 2006
158 Sporting Profiles The Who Concert Posters 2009
159 Bishops Stortford Dairy Pond Life 1966
160 Walls Magicards Prehistoric Animals 1971

SECTION 4
TRADE CARD ISSUES

Prices are for **Finest Collectable Condition to Mint**, pre-1955 issues are priced as **Very Good**.

Size & quantity	TRADE CARD ISSUES	Date	Handbook reference	Price per card	Complete set
	A-1 DAIRIES LTD				
25	Birds and Their Eggs	1964	HX-1	£2.00	£50.00
25	Butterflies and Moths	1965	HX-2	32p	£8.00
25	The Story of Milk	1967	HX-3	£1.40	—
	A-1 DOLLISDALE TEA				
25	Do You Know about Shipping and Trees?	1962	HX-4	20p	£3.50
	AAA SPORTS (USA)				
LT100	Decision 92 (United States Presidential Election)	1992		—	£9.50
	ABC (Cinema)				
10	An Adventure in Space (Set 3)	1950		£5.00	—
10	Animals (Set 5)	1952		£2.50	—
10	Birds (Set 19)	1958		£1.60	—
10	Birds and Bird Watching (Set 7)	1953		£4.00	—
10	British Athletes (Set 11)	1955		£2.50	£25.00
20	British Soldiers (Set 2):				
	A Brown Back				
	i 17 different (minus numbers 14, 15 and 18)	1950		50p	£8.50
	ii Numbers 14, 15 and 18	1950		£3.00	—
	B Black Back				
	i 19 different (minus number 5)	1950		£1.00	£19.00
	ii Number 5	1950		£6.00	—
10	Colorstars 1st Series	1961		£1.20	£12.00
10	Colorstars 2nd Series	1962		£5.00	—
10	Colorstars 3rd Series	1962		£4.00	—
10	Dogs (Set 17)	1957		£3.00	£30.00
10	Film Stars (Set 1)	1950		£4.00	—
10	Horses (Set 21)	1959		£2.00	—
10	Interesting Buildings (Set 10)	1955		£1.00	£10.00
10	Journey by Land (Set 8)	1954		£4.00	—
10	Journey by Water (Set 9)	1954		£4.00	—
10	Journey to the Moon (Set 12)	1956		£4.00	—
10	Parliament Buildings (Set 18)	1958		£1.20	£12.00
10	Railway Engines (Set 4)	1951		£5.00	—
10	Scenes from the Films (Set 6)	1953		£5.00	—
10	Sea Exploration (Set 16)	1958		£2.00	£20.00
10	Sea Scenes (Set 20)	1958		£1.00	£10.00
10	Sports on Land (Set 15)	1956		£1.00	£10.00
10	Travel of the Future (Set 14)	1957		£1.50	£15.00
10	Water Sports (Set 13)	1957		£1.00	£10.00

Size & quantity	TRADE CARD ISSUES	Date	Handbook reference	Price per card	Complete set
	ABC (Monogram)				
L16	Film Stars	1935	HX-43	£7.00	—
12	Star Series (Film Stars)	1936		£7.00	—

A & BC
(AMERICAN & BRITISH CHEWING GUM LTD)
(44-page Illustrated Reference Book, revised 2004 edition — £4.50)

Size & quantity		Date	Handbook reference	Price per card	Complete set
M120	All Sports	1954		£5.50	—
EL17	Banknotes	1971	HA-1	£4.00	—
L55	Batman (pink back):				
	A With 'Batman Fan Club'	1966		£3.50	—
	B Without 'Batman Fan Club'	1966		£2.75	£150.00
L55	Batman (number on front) (back 'Bat Laffs')	1966		£3.25	—
L44	Batman (Nd 1A to 44A)	1966		£4.00	—
L44	Batman (Nd 1B to 44B)	1966		£6.00	—
L38	Batman (black back):				
	A English text	1966		£5.00	—
	B Dutch text	1966		£6.00	—
M1	Batman Secret Decoder (for Series of 38) (3 lines of code)	1966		—	£20.00
	Battle:				
L73	A Complete set	1966		—	£180.00
L69/73	B (Minus Nos 32, 39, 42, 44)	1966		£2.00	£140.00
LT66	Battle of Britain	1970		£1.70	—
LT60	Bazooka Joe and His Gang	1968		£5.00	—
L60	Beatles (black and white)	1964		£5.00	—
L45	Beatles (black and white) 2nd Series	1965		£12.00	—
L40	Beatles (coloured)	1965		£15.00	—
K114	Car Stamps (Set of 21 sheets each holding 5 or 6 stamps with 21 albums, price per sheet and album)	1971	HA-2	£8.00	—
L45	The Champions (TV Series)	1969		£5.00	—
M1	The Champions Secret Decoder (4 lines of code)	1969		—	£20.00
M56	Christian Name Stickers	1967	HA-7	£5.00	—
EL15	Civil War Banknotes	1965	HA-4	£4.00	—
L88	Civil War News	1965		£4.00	—
EL43	Comic Book Folders (No. 7 not issued)	1968		£4.50	—
EL24	Crazy Disguises	1970		£12.00	—
L66	Creature Feature (purple backs)	1974		£2.00	£135.00
L48	Cricketers	1959		£3.00	—
L48	Cricketers 1961 Test Series:				
	A Size 90 × 64mm	1961		£3.50	—
	B Size 94 × 68mm	1961		£3.50	—
L66	Elvis Presley Series	1959		£20.00	—
L36	Exploits of William Tell	1960		£3.25	—
M22	Famous Indian Chiefs	1968		£9.00	—
EL54	Fantastic Twisters	1972		£9.00	—
M48	Film and TV Stars 1st Series	1953		£4.00	—
M48	Film and TV Stars 2nd Series	1953		£4.00	—
M48	Film and TV Stars 3rd Series	1954		£4.00	—
L48	Film Stars:		HX-30.1		
	A Set of 48 (grey back)	1955		£3.00	—
	B Set of 48 (white back)	1955		£3.20	—
	C Set of 24 (white back with stand)	1955		£3.20	—
40	Flag Stickers	1966		£7.00	—
L73	Flags	1971	HA-8	£3.00	—

Size & quantity	TRADE CARD ISSUES	Date	Handbook reference	Price per card	Complete set
	A & BC (continued)				
L80	Flags of the World:				
	A Size 95 × 67mm	1959		£1.60	£130.00
	B Size 82 × 57mm:				
	i English Text	1963		£1.60	£130.00
	ii German Text Title 'Flaggen Der Welt'	1963		£6.50	—
L46	Footballers 1st Series:				
	A Front without 'Planet Ltd'	1958		£4.25	—
	B Front inscribed 'Planet Ltd'	1958		£4.00	—
L46	Footballers 2nd Series:				
	A Front without 'Planet Ltd'	1958		£11.00	—
	B Front with 'Planet Ltd'	1958		£9.00	—
L49	Footballers (in Action) 1st Series (red)	1959		£4.50	—
L49	Footballers (in Action) 2nd Series (red)	1959		£7.50	—
LT42	Football 1st Series (black)	1960		£4.50	—
LT42	Football 2nd Series (black)	1960		£8.50	—
LT64	Footballers	1961		£7.00	—
LT44	Footballers — Scottish	1961		£18.00	—
L82	Footballers (Bazooka)	1962		£10.00	—
L55	Footballers 1st Series (blue)	1963		£5.50	—
L55	Footballers 2nd Series (blue)	1963		£5.50	—
L81	Footballers — Scottish (green)	1963		£18.00	—
L58	Footballers 1st Series (red)	1964		£5.00	—
L45	Footballers 2nd Series (red)	1964		£12.00	—
L46	Footballers 3rd Series (red)	1964		£15.00	—
L81	Footballers — Scottish (green)	1964		£16.00	—
M110	Footballers (black and white, issued in pairs) 1st Series	1966	HA-12.1	£6.00	—
M110	Footballers (black and white, issued in pairs) 2nd Series	1966	HA-12.2	£10.00	—
M54	Footballers — Scottish (coloured, Nos 1 to 42, issued in pairs)	1966	HA-12.3	£16.00	—
L55	Football Star Players	1967		£4.00	—
EL12	Footballers (Posters)	1967	HA-13	£10.00	—
L54	Footballers 1st Series (yellow)	1968	HA-14	£4.75	—
L47	Footballers 2nd Series (yellow)	1968		£4.25	—
L45	Footballers — Scottish (yellow)	1968		£13.00	—
EL26	Football Team Pennants — English	1968	HA-11	£12.00	—
M20	Football Team Emblems	1968	HA-10	£10.00	—
L65	Footballers 1st Series (green)	1969		£3.00	—
L54	Footballers 2nd Series (green)	1969		£3.00	—
L55	Footballers 3rd Series (green)	1969		£3.00	—
MP36	Footballers	1969	HA-15.1	£3.50	—
L42	Footballers — Scottish 1st Series (blue)	1969		£11.00	—
L35	Footballers — Scottish 2nd Series (blue)	1969		£12.00	—
MP15	Football Photos — Scottish	1969	HA-15.2	£9.00	—
LT84	Footballers 1st Series (orange)	1970		£1.50	£125.00
LT85	Footballers 2nd Series (orange)	1970		£1.25	£105.00
LT86	Footballers 3rd Series (orange)	1970		£4.50	—
EL14	Footballers Pin Ups	1970	HA-17.1	£8.50	—
M72	Football Colour Transparencies	1970	HA-16	£13.00	—
LT85	Footballers — Scottish 1st Series (green)	1970		£6.00	—
LT86	Footballers — Scottish 2nd Series (green)	1970		£6.00	—
EL28	Footballers Pin Ups — Scottish	1970	HA-17.2	£12.00	—
L109	Footballers 1st Series (purple)	1971	HA-18	£3.25	—
L110	Footballers 2nd Series (purple)	1971	HA-18	£3.25	—
L71	Footballers 3rd Series (purple)	1971		£6.50	—
M23	Football Club Crests	1971	HA-9A	£3.00	—
M23	Football Superstars	1971	HA-19	£10.00	—

Size & quantity	TRADE CARD ISSUES	Date	Handbook reference	Price per card	Complete set
	A & BC (continued)				
L73	Footballers — Scottish 1st Series (purple)	1971		£1.40	£100.00
L71	Footballers — Scottish 2nd Series (purple)	1971		£10.00	—
M16	Football Club Crests — Scottish	1971	HA-9B	£3.50	£55.00
L109	Footballers 1st Series (orange/red)	1972	HA-20	£3.50	£380.00
L110	Footballers 2nd Series (orange/red)	1972	HA-20	£4.50	£500.00
M22	Football Card Game	1972		£1.60	—
L89	Footballers — Scottish 1st Series (blue)	1972		£7.50	—
L88	Footballers — Scottish 2nd Series (orange/red) (No. 164 not issued)	1972		£10.00	—
L131	Footballers 1st Series (blue)	1973		£5.50	—
L130	Footballers 2nd Series (blue) (Nos 235 and 262 not issued)	1973		£5.50	—
M32	Football Photos	1973		£3.75	—
EL16	Football Giant Team Posters	1973		£15.00	—
L90	Footballers — Scottish 1st Series (red)	1973		£8.00	—
L88	Footballers — Scottish 2nd Series (red)	1973		£8.00	—
L132	Footballers (red)	1974		£2.50	£330.00
L132	Footballers — Scottish (green)	1974		£5.00	—
L40	Fotostars	1961	HA-21	£4.50	—
LT66	Funny Greetings	1961		£2.25	—
LT66	Funny Valentines	1961		£5.00	—
L25	Girl from Uncle	1967	HA-22	£5.00	—
	Golden Boys:		HA-23		
L36	A Size 96 × 67mm	1960		£6.50	—
LT40	B Size 89 × 64mm	1960		£7.50	—
M27	Grand Prix (sectional)	1970	HA-24	£1.00	£27.00
L36	The High Chaparral	1969		£3.25	£120.00
L55	Huck Finn:				
	A Inscribed 'Hanna-Barbera Production Inc.'	1968		£3.60	£200.00
	B Inscribed ILAMI 1968'	1968		£3.60	—
L60	Kung Fu	1974		£3.00	—
L55	Land of the Giants	1969		£6.50	—
L54	The Legend of Custer	1968		£3.00	—
L55	Lotsa Laffs (various back colours, not purple)	1970	HA-25	£5.00	—
L84	Love Initials	1970	HA-26	£3.20	—
L36	Magic	1967		£5.00	£180.00
L55	Man from UNCLE	1965		£1.80	£100.00
	Man on the Moon:		HA-27		
LT55	Space Ship Back	1970		£5.00	—
LT19	Text Back	1970		£5.00	—
L52	Mickey Takers	1970	HA-28	£6.00	—
M24	Military Emblem Stickers	1966	HA-29	£5.50	—
L55	Monkees (black and white)	1967		£2.00	£110.00
L55	Monkees (coloured)	1967		£4.00	—
L30	Monkees Hit Songs	1967		£5.00	—
EL16	Monster Tattoos	1970		£7.00	—
EL16	Olympic Posters	1972		£6.00	—
L36	Olympics	1972		£6.00	—
L55	Partridge Family	1972		£3.00	—
L120	Planes:				
	A Size 94 × 67mm	1958		£3.00	—
	B Size 88 × 64mm	1958		£3.00	—
L44	Planet of the Apes	1968		£6.00	—
L33	Put-on Stickers	1969	HA-32	£4.50	—
LT48	Railway Quiz	1958		£2.00	£100.00
L72	Railway Quiz	1959		£3.00	—
L40	The Rolling Stones	1965		£18.00	—

Size & quantity	TRADE CARD ISSUES	Date	Handbook reference	Price per card	Complete set
	A & BC (continued)				
M24	Royal Portraits	1953		£4.00	£100.00
L25	Sir Francis Drake	1961		£6.00	—
LT88	Space Cards	1958		£8.00	—
L44	Stacks of Stickers	1971	HA-34	£6.00	—
L55	Star Trek	1969		£13.00	—
L66	Superman in the Jungle	1968		£4.00	—
L16	Superman in the Jungle (jig-saw)	1968		£8.00	—
L50	Top Stars	1964		£5.50	—
L40	Top Stars	1964		£7.00	—
EL15	TV Cartoon Tattoos	1972		£10.00	—
L44	Ugly Stickers	1967		£4.50	—
EL88	Wacky Plaks	1965		£5.00	—
EL15	Walt Disney Characters Tattoos	1973		£14.00	—
EL16	Wanted Posters	1968	HA-39	£7.00	—
L56	Western Series	1959	HA-36	£4.00	—
LT70	Who-Z-At Star?	1961		£4.00	—
L55	Winston Churchill	1965		90p	£50.00
L37	World Cup Footballers	1970	HA-41	£8.00	—
EL16	World Cup Posters	1970		£7.50	—
L48	You'll Die Laughing (purple backs)	1967	HA-25	£2.00	—
	AMA GROUP (USA)				
LT60	Desert Storm Operation Yellow Ribbon	1991		—	£10.00
	A & P PUBLICATIONS				
24	Post-war British Classic Cars	1992		24p	£6.00
	A.W. SPORTS (USA)				
LT100	All World Racing (Motor Racing)	1991		—	£10.00
LT100	All World Racing (Motor Racing)	1992		—	£10.00
	ABBEY GRANGE HOTEL				
15	Fighting Vessels	1986		—	£6.00
	ACE CARD ENTERPRISES				
EL16	Brighton Music Walk of Fame	2016		—	£10.00
EL1	Brighton Music Walk of Fame Promo Card	2016		—	50p
EL12	Klinger Card Collection	2017		—	£7.00
EL1	Klinger Card Collection Promo Card	2017		—	50p
	ACTION STARS				
20	Action Stars (1950s Footballers) 1st Series	2010		—	£7.50
20	Action Stars (1950s Footballers) 2nd Series	2010		—	£7.50
20	Action Stars (1950s Footballers) 3rd Series	2011		—	£7.50
	P.A. ADOLPH (Subbuteo Table Soccer)				
24	Famous Footballers 1st Series of 24	1954		£1.25	£30.00
24	Famous Footballers 2nd Series of 24	1954		£1.25	£30.00
50	Famous Footballers 'A Series of 50'	1954		£16.00	—
	AHC (Ace High Confectionery)				
25	Wonders of the Universe	1955	HX-14	80p	£20.00
	ALICE'S ATTIC				
EL16	Fry's Chocolate Advertising Postcards from the Early 1900s	2012		—	£10.00

Size & quantity	TRADE CARD ISSUES	Date	Handbook reference	Price per card	Complete set
	ALL INC.				
L20	Actors (and Actresses) (Caricatures by Bob Hoare)	2003		50p	£10.00
L25	Films (Caricatures by Bob Hoare)	2003		50p	£12.50
L20	Musicians (Caricatures by Bob Hoare)	2003		50p	£10.00
L30	Politicians (Caricatures by Bob Hoare)	2003		50p	£15.00
L13	Sports (Caricatures by Bob Hoare)	2003		50p	£7.00
	ALL SPORTS INC. (USA)				
LT100	Exotic Dreams — Cars	1992		—	£10.00
	A.W. ALLEN LTD (Australia)				
32	Bradman's Records	1931		£50.00	—
72	Butterflies and Moths	c1920		£3.00	—
36	Cricketers (brown fronts)	1932		£17.00	—
36	Cricketers (dark brown fronts)	1933		£17.00	—
36	Cricketers (flesh tinted, frameline back)	1934		£15.00	—
36	Cricketers (flesh tinted, no frameline back)	1936		£15.00	—
36	Cricketers (coloured)	1938		£15.00	—
36	Defence 1st Series	1939		£6.00	—
36	Defence 2nd Series	1939		£6.00	—
144	Footballers (striped background)	1933		£7.50	—
72	Footballers (Club flag)	1934		£7.50	—
48	Footballers (players in action)	1939		£12.00	—
49	Kings and Queens of England	1937/53		£2.00	—
36	Medals	1938		£3.00	—
36	Royalty Series	1937		£5.00	—
36	Soldiers of The Empire	1938		£3.00	—
36	Sports and Flags of Nations	1936		£4.00	—
	J. ALLEN SPORTS				
25	Sportsmen	1997		—	£10.00
	ALMA CONFECTIONERY				
48	James Bond 007 Moonraker	1980		£6.00	—
	JAMES ALMOND				
25	Sports and Pastimes	c1925	HX-225	£11.00	—
	AMABILINO PHOTOGRAPHIC				
M30	Display Fireworks	1988		—	£8.00
	AMALGAMATED PRESS LTD				
24	Aeroplanes (plain back)	1933	HA-56	£5.00	—
M12	Catchy Tricks and Teasers	1933	HA-58	£5.00	—
M22	English League (Div. 1) Footer Captains	1926		£5.00	—
M16	Exploits of the Great War	1929		£4.00	—
16	Famous Aircraft	1927		£4.00	—
M24	Famous Footer Internationals	1926		£5.00	—
M22	Famous Shipping Lines	1926		£6.00	—
M32	Famous Test Match Cricketers	1926		£9.00	—
24	Famous Trains & Engines	1932	HA-62	£5.00	—
M16	Great War Deeds	1927		£4.00	—
M32	Great War Deeds	1928		£4.00	—
M24	The Great War — 1914-1918	1928		£4.00	—
M16	The Great War — 1914-1918 — New Series	1929		£4.00	—
M16	Heroic Deeds of the Great War	1927		£4.00	—

Size & quantity	TRADE CARD ISSUES	Date	Handbook reference	Price per card	Complete set
	AMALGAMATED PRESS LTD (continued)				
32	Makes of Motor Cars and Index Marks (without date at base)	1923		£3.00	—
24	Motors (plain black)	1933	HA-65	£5.00	—
M16	RAF at War (plain black)	1940	HA-66	£7.00	—
24	Ships of the World	1924		£3.00	—
33	Ships of the World	c1935	HA-67	£4.00	—
M12	Sports 'Queeriosities'	1933		£5.00	—
MP66	Sportsmen	1922-3		£2.25	—
32	Sportsmen of the World	1934	HA-68	£5.00	—
M32	Thrilling Scenes from the Great War	1927		£4.00	—
M16	Thrills of the Dirt Track	1929		£12.00	—
M16	Tip-Top Tricks and Teasers	1927		£4.00	—
M14	VCs and Their Glorious Deeds of Valour (plain back)	c1930	HA-70	£6.00	—
	AUSTRALIAN ISSUES				
M32	Australian and English Cricket Stars	1932		£16.00	—
M16	England Test Match Cricketers	1928		£15.00	—
M16	Famous Australian Cricketers	1928		£16.00	—
16	Famous Film Stars	1927		£7.00	—
32	Makes of Motor Cars and Index Marks (with date at base)	1924		£4.00	—
16	Modern Motor Cars	1926		£7.50	—
M24	Wonderful London	1926		£6.00	—
	AMANDA'S FLOWERS				
L12	Flower Children	1990		40p	£5.00
	AMARAN TEA				
25	The Circus	1968	HX-79	50p	£12.50
25	Coins of the World	1965	HX-6	60p	£15.00
25	Do You Know	1969	HX-166.4	£1.00	£25.00
25	Dogs' Heads	1965	HX-16	50p	£12.50
25	Flags and Emblems	1964	HX-17	60p	£15.00
25	Naval Battles	1971	HX-21	£1.20	—
25	Old England	1969		20p	£4.00
25	Science in the 20th Century	1966	HX-18	20p	£4.00
25	Veteran Racing Cars	1966	HX-19	£1.00	£25.00
	AMBER TIPS TEA (New Zealand)				
M20	The Living Seashore	1975		20p	£3.50
	AMBERVILLE CARDS				
15	Jayne Mansfield	2014		—	£6.50
	THE ANGLERS MAIL				
EL3	Terminal Tackle Tips	1976		—	£6.00
	ANGLING TIMES				
M15	Series 1 Floats	1980		40p	£6.00
M15	Series 2 Species	1980		40p	£6.00
M15	Series 3 Baits	1980		40p	£6.00
M15	Series 4 Sea Fish	1980		40p	£6.00
M24	Fish	1987		30p	£7.50
M24	Fishing Floats	1986		25p	£6.00
	ANGLO-AMERICAN CHEWING GUM LTD				
LTC6	The Horse	1966		40p	£25.00
L36	Kidnapped	c1955		£8.00	—

Size & quantity	TRADE CARD ISSUES	Date	Handbook reference	Price per card	Complete set
	ANGLO-AMERICAN CHEWING GUM LTD (continued)				
M12	M.G.M. Film Stars	1935	HA-74	£12.00	—
40	Underwater Adventure	1966		20p	£6.00
50	Zoo Stamps of the World	1966		90p	£45.00
	WAXED PAPER ISSUES:				
M72	Animal World (2 pictures per card)	c1965		£2.50	—
M72	Coaching Secrets	1964		£2.25	—
M32	Famous International Teams (inscribed 'Series of 72')	1960		£3.00	—
M128	Famous Soccer Clubs	1960		£3.00	—
M36	Flags of The Nations	c1965		£3.00	—
M36	Men of Courage	1958		£4.00	—
M48	Men of Progress	1958		£3.25	—
M72	Noted Football Clubs	1961		£3.50	—
M48	Race Around The World	1959		£4.00	—
M72	Soccer Hints	1961		£3.00	—
M48	Sports Gallery	c1960		£4.00	—
M48	Sports Parade	1957		£4.00	—
M48	Strange But True	1957		£3.00	—
M72	Strange World	1964		£3.00	—
M72	Swimming Know-How	1962		£2.25	—
M36	Transport Through the Ages	c1960		£3.00	—
M36	World Airlines	1960		£4.50	—
M72	World Famous Football Clubs	1969		£6.00	—
M48	World of Wonders (anonymous)	1957		£3.00	—
	ALBUMS OR FOLDERS WITH CARDS PRINTED THEREIN:				
72	Strange World	1965		—	£14.00
	ANGLO CONFECTIONERY LTD				
LT66	The Beatles — Yellow Submarine	1968		£18.00	—
LT66	Captain Scarlet and the Mysterons	1968		£4.00	—
L12	Football Hints (Booklet Folders)	1970		£2.00	—
L84	Football Quiz	1969		£1.60	—
LT66	The Horse	1966		£2.50	—
LT66	Joe 90	1968		£5.00	—
L56	The New James Bond 007 On Her Majesty's Secret Service	1970		£13.00	—
L84	Railway Trains and Crests	1974		£1.30	—
LT66	Space	1967		£1.50	£100.00
LT66	Tarzan	1967		£1.50	£100.00
L64	UFO	1970		£3.25	£210.00
M24	Vintage Car Series (Paper wrappers)	1970		£5.00	—
L78	Walt Disney Characters	1971		£6.00	—
L66	Wild West	1970		£3.25	—
L48	World Cup 1970 (Football)	1970		£4.00	—
	APLIN & BARRETT				
L25	Whipsnade (Zoo)	1937		£1.60	£40.00
	ARDMONA (Australia)				
L50	International Cricket Series III	1980		—	£15.00
	ARMITAGE BROS. LTD				
25	Animals of the Countryside	1965	HX-9	20p	£4.00
25	Country Life	1968	HX-11	20p	£4.00
	ARMY RECRUITING OFFICE				
M24	British Regiments 1st Series (without text)	1992		35p	£8.00
M24	British Regiments 2nd Series (with text)	1992		35p	£8.00

Size & quantity	TRADE CARD ISSUES	Date	Handbook reference	Price per card	Complete set
	THE ARROW CONFECTIONERY CO.				
13	Conundrums	c1905	HX-232	£45.00	—
12	Shadowgraphs	c1905		£45.00	—
	ARTBOX (USA)				
LT90	Charlie and The Chocolate Factory — The Film	2005		—	£9.50
LT72	Dexter's Laboratory	2001		—	£9.50
LT72	Doom The Movie	2005		—	£9.50
LT72	Finding Nemo — Film Cardz (Disney Film)	2003		—	£12.00
LT54	Harry Potter and the Deathly Hallows Part 2	2011		—	£12.00
LT90	Harry Potter & The Goblet of Fire 1st Series	2005		—	£12.00
LT90	Harry Potter & The Goblet of Fire 2nd Series	2006		—	£12.00
LT90	Harry Potter & The Half-Blood Prince 1st Series	2009		—	£12.00
LT90	Harry Potter & The Half-Blood Prince 2nd Series	2009		—	£12.00
LT90	Harry Potter & The Order of The Phoenix 1st Series	2008		—	—
LT90	Harry Potter & The Order of The Phoenix 2nd Series	2008		—	£12.00
LT90	Harry Potter & The Prisoner of Azkaban 1st Series	2004		—	£15.00
LT90	Harry Potter & The Prisoner of Azkaban 2nd Series	2004		—	£9.50
LT72	Harry Potter & The Prisoner of Azkaban Film Cardz	2004		—	£12.00
LT90	Harry Potter & The Sorcerer's Stone	2005		—	£12.00
LT72	Harry Potter Memorable Moments 1st Series	2006		—	£12.00
LT72	Harry Potter Memorable Moments 2nd Series	2009		—	£12.00
M18	Pokemon Chrome Series	1999		—	£8.00
M80	Pokemon 3-D Action Cards	1999		25p	£16.00
M40	Pokemon Premier Edition (3-D Action Cards)	1999		—	£12.00
LT72	The Powerpuff Girls 1st Series	2000		—	£9.50
LT12	The Powerpuff Girls 1st Series Foil Series	2000		—	£4.00
M40	Sailor Moon — 3D	2000		—	£12.00
LT45	The Simpsons (Film Cells)	2000		—	£16.00
LT72	Terminator 2 Judgment Day — Film Cardz	2003		20p	£9.50
LT24	Terminator 2 Judgment Day — Film Cardz Cyberetch Series	2003		40p	£9.50
LT90	24 Season 4	2006		—	£9.50
LT90	24 Season 4 Expansion Series	2007		—	£12.00
LT40	World Wrestling Federation Lenticular Series 2	2001		—	£12.00
	ASKEYS				
25	People and Places	1968	HX-26	20p	£4.00
25	Then and Now	1968	HX-27	20p	£4.50
	THE ASSEMBLY ROOMS (Briggate)				
50	War Portraits	1916	HX-86	£120.00	—
	ASTON & ERDINGTON POLICE				
L24	Cop Card-Toons	1989		—	£5.00
	Album			—	£5.00
	ASTON CARDS				
LT24	Speedway Programme Covers 1st Series Inaugural Season 1928	2002		—	£16.00
LT24	Speedway Programme Covers ,2nd Series The Early Years 1920/30s	2003		—	£16.00
LT24	Speedway Programme Covers 3rd Series More Early Years 1920/30s	2003		—	£16.00
LT24	Speedway Programme Covers 4th Series The Fabulous '40s	2004		—	£16.00
LT24	Speedway Programme Covers 5th Series More Early Years 1900s	2005		—	£16.00

Size & quantity	TRADE CARD ISSUES	Date	Handbook reference	Price per card	Complete set
	ASTON CARDS (continued)				
LT24	Speedway Programme Covers 6th Series More Early Years 1920/40s	2006		—	£16.00
LT24	Speedway Programme Covers 7th Series More Fabulous '40s	2008		—	£16.00
LT24	Wimbledon Speedway Stars 1929-1939	2002		—	£16.00
	ATLANTIC SERVICE STATIONS (Australia)				
M32	Australia in the 20th Century 1st Series	1959		£1.50	£50.00
M32	Australia in the 20th Century 2nd Series	1960		£1.25	£40.00
M32	English Historical Series	c1961		£1.50	—
M32	Queensland's Centenary	1959		£1.50	—
	AUSTIN MOTOR CO. LTD				
L13	Famous Austin Cars	1953		£13.00	—
	AUSTRALIAN BUTTER				
L54	Cricketers	1982		—	£15.00
L50	Cricketers	1983		30p	£15.00
	AUSTRALIAN DAIRY CORPORATION				
L63	Kanga Cards (Cricket)	1985		—	£15.00
	AUTHENTIX (USA)				
LT50	Beetle Bailey	1995		—	£10.00
LT50	Blondie (Comic Strip)	1995		—	£10.00
LT50	Hagar The Horrible	1995		—	£10.00
	AUTOBRITE (Car Polish)				
25	Vintage Cars	1965	HX-33	70p	£17.50
	AUTOGRAPH ADICTS				
L16	England Rugby World Cup Winners	2003		—	£16.00
	AUTOMATIC MACHINE CO. LTD				
25	Modern Aircraft	1958	HX-219	36p	£9.00
	AUTOMATIC MERCHANDISING CO. LTD				
L25	Adventure Twins and the Treasure Ship:				
	A Coloured	1959		£1.80	£45.00
	B Black, White and Pink only	1959		£1.80	£45.00
	AVON & SOMERSET POLICE				
L37	British Stamps	1985		£1.20	—
	AVON RUBBER CO. LTD				
30	Leading Riders of 1963 (Motor Cyclists)	1963		£2.30	£70.00
	Folder			—	£5.00
	B.B.B. PIPES				
25	Pipe History	c1925		£12.00	—
	B.J.B. CARDS (Canada)				
L25	Famous Golfers of the 40s and 50s	1992		—	£15.00
	B.N.A. (Canada)				
LT49	Canadian Winter Olympic Winners	1992		—	£10.00

Size & quantity	TRADE CARD ISSUES	Date	Handbook reference	Price per card	Complete set
	B.P. PETROL				
25	Team England (Football World Cup)	1998		32p	£8.00
	Album			—	£4.00
	B.T. LTD				
25	Aircraft	1964	HX-36	£1.40	—
25	British Locomotives	1961		£1.60	£40.00
25	Do You Know?	1967	HX-166.2	40p	£10.00
25	Holiday Resorts	1963	HX-38	20p	£4.50
25	Modern Motor Cars	1962	HX-39	£1.60	—
25	Occupations	1962		50p	£12.50
25	Pirates and Buccaneers	1961	HX-40	£1.80	£45.00
25	The West	1966	HX-42	36p	£9.00
	BAD AXE STUDIOS (USA)				
LT52	Dungeon Dolls — Adult Fantasy Art	2011		—	£9.50
	BADSHAH TEA CO.				
25	British Cavalry Uniforms of the 19th Century	1963	HX-43	70p	£17.50
25	Butterflies and Moths	1967	HX-2	20p	£3.50
25	Fish and Bait	1965	HX-44	24p	£6.00
25	Fruits of Trees and Shrubs	1965	HX-45	36p	£9.00
25	Garden Flowers	1963	HX-46	60p	£15.00
24	The Island of Ceylon	1962	HX-47	£6.00	—
25	Naval Battles	1968	HX-21	£1.20	—
25	People and Places	1968	HX-26	20p	£3.50
25	Regimental Uniforms of the Past	1971		20p	£3.50
25	Romance of the Heavens	1968	HX-48	£1.60	—
25	Wonders of the World	1967	HX-49	40p	£10.00
	J. BAINES & SON				
L?	Cricket and Football Cards, etc. (Shapes)	c1905		£45.00	—
	BAKE-A-CAKE LTD				
56	Motor Cars	1952		£6.50	—
	BAKER, WARDELL & CO. LTD				
25	Animals in the Service of Man	c1964	HX-51	£3.50	—
36	Capital Tea Circus Act	c1960		£5.00	—
25	Do You Know 1st Series	c1962	HX-166.3	£4.00	—
25	Do You Know 2nd Series	c1962	HX-166.3	£4.00	—
25	History of Flight 1st Series	c1966		£10.00	—
25	History of Flight 2nd Series	c1966		£10.00	—
25	Irish Patriots	c1960		£12.00	—
25	They Gave Their Names	c1963	HX-52	£3.50	—
25	Transport — Present and Future	c1956		£6.50	—
25	World Butterflies	c1960		£6.50	—
	BARBERS TEA LTD				
1	Advertisement Card — Cinema & TV Stars	1955		—	£5.00
1	Advertisement Card — Dogs	1960		—	£2.50
1	Advertisement Card — Railway Equipment	1958		—	£4.00
25	Aeroplanes	1954		£1.20	—
24	Cinema and Television Stars	1955		£3.00	—
24	Dogs	1960		25p	£6.00

Size & quantity	TRADE CARD ISSUES	Date	Handbook reference	Price per card	Complete set
	BARBERS TEA LTD (continued)				
25	Locomotives	1953		£1.60	£40.00
	Album			—	£30.00
24	Railway Equipment	1958		50p	£12.00
	JOHN O. BARKER (Ireland) LTD (Gum)				
EL24	Circus Scenes	1960		£2.00	£50.00
EL24	Famous People	1960	HX-53	£2.00	£50.00
25	The Wild West	1960	HX-55.3	£4.50	—
	BARRATT & CO. LTD				
	(AFTER 1973 SEE GEO. BASSETT)				
M30	Aircraft	1941	HB-6	£7.00	—
M30	Aircraft	1943	HB-7	£7.00	—
25	Animals in the Service of Man	1964	HX-51	30p	£7.50
16	Australian Cricketers Action Series	1926		£20.00	—
15	Australian Test Players	1930	HB-10	£40.00	—
45	Beauties Picture Hats	c1910		£25.00	—
25	Birds	1960	HX-71	£1.20	—
50	Botany Quest	1966		£2.00	—
25	British Butterflies	1965		£3.00	—
25	Butterflies and Moths	1960	HX-2	30p	£7.50
25	Cage and Aviary Birds	1960		50p	£12.50
50	Captain Scarlet and The Mysterons	1967		£4.00	—
50	Cars of the World	1965		£2.00	£100.00
	Characters From Fairy Stories and Fiction (plain back):				
M53	Characters From Fairy Stories	c1940	HB-16	£13.00	—
M12	Gulliver's Travels	c1940	HB-51	£13.00	—
M12	Pinocchio	c1940	HB-65	£13.00	—
M36	Snow White and the Seven Dwarfs	c1940	HB-75	£13.00	—
M12	The Wizard of Oz	1939	HB-82	£13.00	—
	Cricketers, Footballers and Football Teams:		HB-25		
81	Cricketers	c1925		£30.00	—
201	Footballers	c1925		£20.00	—
3	Football Teams	c1925		£50.00	—
M20	Cricket Team Folders	1933		£28.00	—
M60	Disneyland 'True Life'	1956		£2.00	—
M50	FA Cup Winners 1883-1935	1935		£30.00	—
25	Fairy Stories	c1925		£4.00	—
12	Famous British Constructions, Aircraft Series	c1930		£20.00	—
M25	Famous Cricketers — 1930	1930	HB-29	£17.00	—
M50	Famous Cricketers — 1932	1932	HB-30	£17.00	—
M9	Famous Cricketers — 1932	1932	HB-31	£32.00	—
M34	Famous Cricketers — 1934	1934	HB-32	£25.00	—
M7	Famous Cricketers — 1936	1936	HB-33	£25.00	—
M60	Famous Cricketers — 1937, unnumbered	1937	HB-34	£16.00	—
M40	Famous Cricketers — 1938, numbered	1938		£16.00	—
35	Famous Film Stars	1960		£3.50	—
M100	Famous Footballers — 1935-36, unnumbered (black back)	1935	HB-35A	£18.00	—
M98	Famous Footballers — 1936-37, unnumbered (sepia back)	1936	HB-35B	£18.00	—
M100	Famous Footballers — 1937-38, numbered	1937	HB-35C	£18.00	—
M20	Famous Footballers — 1938-39, numbered	1938	HB-35D	£18.00	—
M110	Famous Footballers — 1939-40, numbered	1939	HB-35E	£18.00	—
M50	Famous Footballers — 1947-48	1947	HB-37A	£16.00	—
M50	Famous Footballers — 1948-49	1948	HB-37B	£16.00	—
M50	Famous Footballers — 1949-50	1949	HB-37C	£16.00	—
M50	Famous Footballers New Series — 1950-51	1950	HB-38	£11.00	—

Size & quantity	TRADE CARD ISSUES	Date	Handbook reference	Price per card	Complete set
	BARRATT & CO. LTD (continued)				
M50	Famous Footballers New Series — 1951-52	1951	HB-38	£11.00	—
M50	Famous Footballers New Series — 1952-53	1952	HB-38	£11.00	—
M50	Famous Footballers, Series A.1	1953	HX-57	£7.50	—
M50	Famous Footballers, Series A.2	1954	HX-58	£7.50	—
M50	Famous Footballers, Series A.3	1955	HX-59	£7.50	—
60	Famous Footballers, Series A.4	1956		£7.00	—
60	Famous Footballers, Series A.5	1957		£7.00	—
60	Famous Footballers, Series A.6	1958		£7.00	—
60	Famous Footballers, Series A.7	1959		£7.00	—
50	Famous Footballers, Series A.8	1960		£7.00	—
50	Famous Footballers, Series A.9:		HB-39		
	A Back Series A.8 Error printing	1961		£7.00	—
	B Back Series A.9	1961		£7.00	—
50	Famous Footballers, Series A.10	1962		£2.50	—
50	Famous Footballers, Series A.11	1963	HB-40	£6.00	—
50	Famous Footballers, Series A.12	1964		£6.00	—
50	Famous Footballers, Series A.13	1965		£6.00	—
50	Famous Footballers, Series A.14	1966		£6.00	—
50	Famous Footballers, Series A.15	1967		£1.50	£75.00
50	Famous Sportsmen:		HB-41		
	A Without Printed in England	1971		£4.00	—
	B With Printed in England:				
	i 27 Scarce cards	1971		£4.00	—
	ii 23 Common cards (Nos 2, 3, 5, 9, 10, 15, 22, 23, 26, 27, 29, 31, 32, 35, 36, 38, 42, 43, 44, 46, 47, 48, 49)	1971		£1.20	£27.50
M45	Fastest on Earth	1953	HX-60	£2.20	—
32	Felix Pictures	c1930	HX-56	£50.00	—
50	Film Stars (without name of film company)	c1940	HB-42	£8.00	—
50	Film Stars (with name of film company)	c1940	HB-43	£8.00	—
25	Fish and Bait	1962	HX-44	£1.20	£30.00
12	Footballers Action Caricatures	c1930	HB-49	£40.00	—
100	Football 'Stars'	c1930	HB-47	£40.00	—
50	Football 'Stars'	1973		£11.00	—
M66	Football Teams — 1st Division	c1930	HB-48	£22.00	—
M22	Football Team Folders, English League Division I	1932	HB-28.1	£40.00	—
M22	Football Team Folders, English League Division I	1933	HB-28.1	£40.00	—
M22	Football Team Folders, English League Division I	1934	HB-28.1	£40.00	—
M22	Football Team Folders, English League Division II	1932	HB-28.2	£40.00	—
M22	Football Team Folders, English League Division II	1933	HB-28.2	£40.00	—
M22	Football Team Folders, English League Division II	1934	HB-28.2	£40.00	—
M1	Football Team Folder, English League Division III	c1933	HB-28.3	£40.00	—
M20	Football Team Folders, Scottish League Divison I	1934	HB-28.4	£40.00	—
M3	Football Team Folders, Irish League	c1933	HB-28.5	£65.00	—
M1	Football Team Folder, Rugby Union	1934		£65.00	—
48	Giants in Sport	1959		£11.00	—
EL12	Gold Rush (Package Issue)	c1960	HB-50	£9.00	—
25	Head-Dresses of the World	1962	HX-197	40p	£10.00
25	Historical Buildings	1960	HX-72	40p	£10.00
25	History of the Air	1960	HX-180	50p	£12.50
32	History of the Air	1959		£5.00	—
48	History of the Air:				
	A Cream card	1959		£1.50	—
	B White card	1959		£1.50	—
25	Interpol — back with chain frameline	1964		£4.00	—
25	Interpol — back without chain frameline (different subjects)	1964		£8.00	—
48	Leaders of Sport	c1930		£20.00	—

Size & quantity	TRADE CARD ISSUES	Date	Handbook reference	Price per card	Complete set
	BARRATT & CO. LTD (continued)				
35	Magic Roundabout	1968		£2.50	—
25	Merchant Ships of the World:		HX-63		
	A Black back	1962		80p	£20.00
	B Blue back	1962		60p	£15.00
M40	Modern Aircraft	1955		£3.50	—
M45	Modern British Aircraft	1949	HB-56	£4.00	—
13	National Flags	c1915	HB-57	£25.00	—
64	Natural History Series	c1935	HB-62	£9.00	—
M24	Naval Ships	c1940	HB-63	£11.00	—
M6	Our King and Queen	c1940	HB-64	£11.00	—
25	People and Places	1965	HX-26	20p	£5.00
25	Pirates and Buccaneers	1960	HX-40	£1.20	£30.00
12	Prominent London Buildings	c1920	HB-67	£26.00	—
M5	Regimental Uniforms	c1930	HB-70	£13.00	—
36	Robin Hood	1957		£2.50	—
30	Robin Hood	1961		£3.00	£90.00
36	Sailing Into Space	1959	HX-123	£4.00	—
35	Sea Hunt	1961		£2.80	—
50	The Secret Service	1970		£2.50	—
50	Soccer Stars	1972		£4.00	—
50	Soldiers of the World	1966		50p	£25.00
16	South African Cricketers Series	c1930	HB-76	£27.00	—
25	Space Mysteries	1966		70p	£17.50
L20	Speed Series	c1930		£12.00	—
50	Tarzan	1967		50p	£25.00
35	Test Cricketers by E.W. Swanton, Series A	1956		£8.00	—
48	Test Cricketers, Series B	1957		£9.00	—
50	Thunderbirds 1st Series	1966		£4.00	—
50	Thunderbirds 2nd Series	1967		£1.00	£50.00
50	Tom and Jerry	1971		60p	£30.00
50	Trains	1970		60p	£30.00
50	Trains of the World	1964		40p	£20.00
35	TV's Huckleberry Hound and Friends	1961		£2.00	£70.00
35	TV's Yogi Bear	1963		£7.00	—
35	TV's Yogi Bear and Friends	1964		£1.20	—
70	UFO	1971	HX-179	£1.20	—
M35	Walt Disney Characters	1955	HX-65	£5.50	—
50	Walt Disney Characters 2nd Series	1957		£5.50	£275.00
35	Walt Disney's True Life	1962		£1.50	—
25	Warriors Through the Ages	1962		£1.20	£30.00
25	What Do You Know?	1964	HX-67	20p	£5.00
L72	Wild Animals	1970		£1.00	—
M50	Wild Animals by George Cansdale:		HX-68		
	A With 'printed in England'	1954		£2.00	—
	B Without 'printed in England'	1954		£2.00	—
36	Wild West Series No.1	1959		£2.50	—
24	The Wild West	1961		80p	£20.00
25	The Wild West	1963	HX-55.2	50p	£12.50
50	The Wild Wild West	1968		£2.00	—
25	Willum	1961		£8.00	—
50	Wisecracks 1st Series	1969		20p	£7.50
50	Wisecracks 2nd Series	1970		50p	£25.00
50	Wisecracks 3rd Series	1971		50p	£25.00
50	Wonders of the World	1962	HX-49	20p	£10.00
25	World Locomotives	1963	HX-70	£1.20	—
50	Wunders der Welt	1968		20p	£9.00
25	The Young Adventurer	1964		£3.00	£75.00
50	Zoo Pets	1964		£1.20	£60.00

Size & quantity	TRADE CARD ISSUES	Date	Handbook reference	Price per card	Complete set
	GEO. BASSETT & CO. LTD				
30	Adventures With Ben and Barkley	2001		25p	£7.50
50	Age of the Dinosaurs:				
	A Complete set	1979		£1.20	—
	B 35 Different	1979		—	£25.00
	Album			—	£25.00
40	Ali-Cat Magicards	1978		£3.00	—
50	Asterix in Europe	1977		50p	£25.00
	Album			—	£25.00
M20	The A Team	1986		80p	—
50	Athletes of the World	1980		50p	—
48	Bananaman	1985		20p	£4.50
	Album			—	£6.00
M20	Battle (Package Issue)	1985		£3.00	—
50	The Conquest of Space — 1980-81	1980		50p	£25.00
	Album			—	£25.00
50	Cricket 1st Series	1978		£9.00	—
50	Cricket 2nd Series	1979		£5.00	—
	Album			—	£25.00
48	Dandy Beano Collection (black back)	1989		30p	£15.00
48	Dandy/Beano 2nd Series (blue back)	1990		20p	£8.00
48	Dinosaurs and Prehistoric Creatures	1994		£2.50	—
8	Dinosaurs and Prehistoric Creatures	1997		£3.50	—
50	Disney/Health and Safety	1977		25p	£12.50
EL6	Europe's Best (Footballers)	1992		£1.50	—
EL6	Europe's Best — Captains (Footballers)	1996		—	£6.00
EL6	Europe's Best — Defenders (Footballers)	1996		£1.50	—
EL6	Europe's Best — Goalkeepers (Footballers)	1996		—	£6.00
EL6	Europe's Best — Midfielders (Footballers)	1996		—	£6.00
EL6	Europe's Best — Strikers Series 1 (Footballers)	1996		—	£6.00
EL6	Europe's Best — Strikers Series 2 (Footballers)	1996		—	£9.00
50	Football Action	1976		£6.00	—
50	Football Action	1977		£6.00	—
EL6	Football Action	1991		£1.50	—
50	Football 1978-79:				
	A Complete set	1978		—	£200.00
	B 42 Different (Minus Nos 26, 31, 33, 43, 44, 45, 49, 50)	1978		£1.50	£65.00
	Album			—	£25.00
50	Football 1979-80	1979		70p	£35.00
	Album			—	£25.00
50	Football 1980-81	1980		70p	£35.00
	Album			—	£25.00
50	Football 1981-82	1981		£5.00	£250.00
	Album			—	£25.00
50	Football 1982-83 (Blue back left margin 5mm)	1982		£3.00	—
	Album			—	£25.00
50	Football 1983-84 (Blue back left margin 7mm)	1983		25p	£12.50
	Album			—	£8.00
50	Football 1984-85 (Black back without Candy Sticks)	1984		£1.80	£90.00
	Album			—	£25.00
48	Football 1985-86 (Black back with Candy Sticks and Large letter)	1985		25p	£12.50
	Album			—	£25.00
48	Football 1986-87 (Black back with Candy Sticks without Large letter)	1986		35p	£17.50
	Album			—	£8.00

Size & quantity	TRADE CARD ISSUES	Date	Handbook reference	Price per card	Complete set
	GEO. BASSETT & CO. LTD (continued)				
48	Football 1987-88 (Back Compiled up to March 31st 1987)	1987		£1.30	£65.00
48	Football 1988-89 (Back Compiled up to April 30th 1988)	1988		25p	£12.50
48	Football 1989-90 (Back Compiled up to May 31st 1989):				
	A Red back	1989		25p	£12.50
	B Purple-red back	1989		20p	£10.00
48	Football 1990-91 (Back Compiled up to May 31st 1990)	1990		60p	£30.00
48	Football 1991-92 (Back Compiled up to June 30th 1991)	1991		£1.00	£50.00
48	Football 1992-93 (Back Compiled up to June 30th 1992)	1992		60p	£30.00
48	Football 1995-96 (Back Compiled up to June 30th 1995)	1995		60p	£30.00
50	Football Stars	1974		£3.50	—
50	Football Stars — 1975-76	1975		£5.00	—
EL6	Great Defenders (Footballers)	1992		—	£6.00
EL6	Great Goalkeepers (Footballers)	1991		£1.50	—
EL6	Great Grounds (Football)	1991		£1.50	—
EL6	Great Managers 1st Series (Football)	1991		£1.50	—
EL6	Great Managers 2nd Series (Football)	1992		—	£6.00
M50	Guinness Book of Records	1990		50p	—
48	Hanna Barbera's Cartoon Capers	1983		£2.00	£100.00
	Album			—	£10.00
24	Holograms:				
	A Red back	1986		36p	£9.00
	B Plain back	1986		60p	£15.00
	Album			—	£12.00
50	House of Horror	1982		£2.00	—
20	Jurassic Park (package issue)	1993		—	£15.00
40	Knight Rider	1987		40p	£16.00
	Album			—	£12.00
50	Living Creatures of Our World	1979		20p	£10.00
	Album			—	£25.00
45	Looney Tunes (blue border & blue back)	1995		25p	£11.00
30	Looney Tunes Cartoons (yellow border)	1997		30p	£9.00
25	Looney Tunes Cartoons (blue border, purple back)	1999		50p	£12.50
32	Lord of The Rings	2003		80p	£25.00
12	The Magic Sword Quest for Camelot	1998		30p	£3.50
EL6	Midfield Dynamos (Footballers)	1992		—	£6.00
25	Motor Cars — Vintage and Modern	1968		£1.00	£25.00
	Album			—	£25.00
25	Nursery Rhymes	1967		£1.00	£25.00
	Album			—	£25.00
50	Play Cricket	1980		40p	£20.00
	Album			—	£20.00
25	Pop Stars	1974		60p	£15.00
EL25	Pop Stars	1984		£1.50	—
25	Popular Dogs	1966		60p	£15.00
	Album			—	£25.00
48	Premier Players (Footballers)	1994		30p	£15.00
EL6	Premier Players — Goalkeepers (Footballers)	1994		£1.50	—
EL6	Premier Players — Midfielders (Footballers)	1994		£1.50	—
35	Secret Island 1st Series	1976		£1.50	—
40	Secret Island 2nd Series	1976		20p	£3.50
20	Sky Fighters (Package Issue)	1986		£2.50	—
48	Sonic the Hedgehog	1994		20p	£9.00
50	Space 1999:				
	A Complete set	1976		—	£90.00
	B 49 different (minus No. 42)	1976		60p	£30.00

Size & quantity	TRADE CARD ISSUES	Date	Handbook reference	Price per card	Complete set
	GEO. BASSETT & CO. LTD (continued)				
50	Super Heroes	1984		£1.50	—
	Album			—	£12.00
50	Survival on Star Colony 9	1979		50p	£25.00
	Album			—	£25.00
40	Swim and Survive	1982		40p	£16.00
50	Tom and Jerry	1974		£3.00	—
EL6	Top Strikers 1st Series (Footballers)	1991		£1.50	—
EL6	Top Strikers 2nd Series (Footballers)	1992		£1.50	—
70	UFO	1974		35p	£25.00
25	Victoria Cross Heroes in Action:				
	A Title black print on white	1970		70p	£17.50
	B Title white print on black	1970		£4.00	—
	Album			—	£25.00
EL6	Winners in 1992 (Football Teams)	1992		—	£6.00
48	World Beaters (Footballers)	1993		50p	£25.00
EL6	World Beaters (Footballers)	1993		—	£6.00
50	World Cup Stars/World Cup '74	1974		40p	£20.00
40	World Heroes (Footballers):				
	A 'Bassett's & Beyond' at top	1999		£1.25	£50.00
	B 'Barratt' at top	1999		£1.50	—
40	World of The Vorgans	1978		£2.50	—
50	World Record Breakers	1983		£1.50	£75.00
48	World Stars (Football)	1997		£1.30	—
EL6	World's Greatest Teams (Football)	1991		£1.50	—
50	Yogi's Gang	1976		£2.20	—
	BATGER & CO.				
20	Batgers Sweet Advertisement Series	c1905		£50.00	—
	J.I. BATTEN & CO. LTD ('Jibco' Tea)				
28	Dominoes	c1955		£3.50	—
K25	Screen Stars 1st Series	1955		£5.50	—
K25	Screen Stars 2nd Series	1956		£1.20	£30.00
	S.P. BATTEN				
50	War Portraits	1916	HX-8C	£120.00	—
	BATTLE PICTURE WEEKLY				
16	Weapons of World War II — Germany	c1975		£1.75	—
16	Weapons of World War II — Great Britain	c1975		£1.75	—
16	Weapons of World War II — Japan	c1975		£1.75	—
16	Weapons of World War II — USA	c1975		£1.75	—
16	Weapons of World War II — USSR	c1975		£1.75	—
	BATTLEAXE TOFFEE				
24	British and Empire Uniforms	1915		£35.00	—
	J.C. BATTOCK				
?M78	Cricket and Football Cards	c1920	HB-85/6	£70.00	—
	BAYTCH BROS LTD				
64	Fighting Favourites	1951	HX-8	£16.00	—
	BEANO LTD				
50	Conquest of Space	1956	HX-73	25p	£12.50
25	Fascinating Hobbies	1950	HX-74	£4.00	—
50	Modern Aircraft	1953	HX-35	£1.50	—

Size & quantity	TRADE CARD ISSUES	Date	Handbook reference	Price per card	Complete set
	BEANO LTD (continued)				
50	Ships of the Royal Navy	1955	HX-76	50p	£25.00
50	This Age of Speed — No.1 Aeroplanes	1954		80p	£40.00
50	This Age of Speed — No. 2 Buses and Trams	1954		£2.50	—
50	Wonders of Modern Transport	c1955	HX-35	£1.20	£60.00
	BEANSTALK CARDS				
15	Saturday Afternoon Heroes (Footballers)	2003		—	£6.50
15	Vintage Football Stars	2003		—	£6.50
	BEATALLS				
?22	Beauties	c1920	HB-88	£32.00	—
	S.N. BEATTIE & CO. LTD				
24	Safety Signs	1955		£6.00	—
12	Southgate Series (Prize scheme with letters):				
	A Titled Southgate Series in box at top	1955		£6.00	—
	B Text back without series title	1955		£7.00	—
	C Plain back	1955		£7.00	—
	J.J. BEAULAH LTD				
1	Boston Stump Advertisement Card				
	A 'Boston Stump' in black	1953		—	60p
	B 'Boston Stump' in blue	1954		—	60p
25	Coronation Series	1953		£1.80	£45.00
24	Marvels of the World	1954	HX-234	20p	£4.00
24	Modern British Aircraft	1953		30p	£7.50
	BEAUTIFUL GAME LTD				
LT50	Football Greats	1999		—	£25.00
LT4	Football Greats Sir Tom Finney	1999		—	£4.00
	BEAVERBROOK NEWSPAPERS (Daily Express)				
L59	Car Cards '71	1971	HD-2	20p	£6.00
L53	Star Cards (pop stars)	1972		£1.00	—
	T.W. BECKETT & CO. LTD (South Africa)				
M50	Animals of South Africa, Series 3	1966		20p	£10.00
	Album			—	£20.00
M50	Birds of South Africa 1st Series	1965		20p	£10.00
	Album			—	£20.00
M50	Birds of South Africa 2nd Series	1966		20p	£10.00
	Album			—	£20.00
	THE BEEHIVE				
25	British Uniforms of the 19th Century	1959	HX-78	£1.20	£30.00
	BEL UK (Laughing Cow)				
M12	Animal Antics	1997		£1.50	—
L8	Chicken Run	2000		£1.50	—
	BELL TEA (New Zealand)				
EL20	Historic New Zealand	1991		75p	—
	BELL'S WHISKY				
42	Other Famous Bells (shaped)	1975		60p	£25.00
	Album			—	£20.00
1	The Queen's Silver Jubilee 1952-1977 (shaped)	1977		—	£5.00

Size & quantity	TRADE CARD ISSUES	Date	Handbook reference	Price per card	Complete set
	J. BELLAMY & SONS LTD				
25	Vintage and Modern Trains of the World 1st Series	1968		50p	£12.50
	BENSEL WORKFORCE LTD				
20	Occupations	1991		—	£7.00
	BETTER PUBS LTD				
EL20	East Devon Inn Signs + 2 varieties	1976		£1.25	£25.00
	J. BIBBY & SONS LTD (Trex)				
L25	Don't You Believe It	1956		£1.00	—
	Album			—	£20.00
L25	Good Dogs	1956		£2.60	—
	Album			—	£20.00
L25	How, What and Why?	1956		£1.00	—
	Album			—	£18.00
L25	Isn't It Strange?	1956		£1.00	—
	Album			—	£20.00
L25	They Gave it a Name	1956		£2.20	—
	Album			—	£20.00
L25	This Wonderful World	1956		£1.00	—
	Album			—	£18.00
	BIRCHGREY LTD				
L25	Panasonic European Open (Golf)	1989		—	£15.00
	ALFRED BIRD & SONS				
K49	Happy Families	1938		£2.00	—
	BIRD'S EYE				
EL12	Recipe Cards	c1965	HB-104	50p	£6.00
30	Wonders of the Seven Seas	c1975		£1.50	—
	BIRKUM (Denmark)				
25	Motor Cars	1956		£1.80	—
	BISHOPS STORTFORD DAIRY FARMERS LTD (Tea)				
25	Dogs' Heads	1965	HX-16	£1.20	£30.00
25	Freshwater Fish	1964	HX-80	£2.00	—
25	Historical Buildings	1964	HX-72	60p	£15.00
25	History of Aviation	1964	HX-36	60p	£15.00
25	Passenger Liners	1965	HX-82	20p	£4.00
25	Pond Life	1966	HX-81	20p	£3.50
25	Science in the 20th Century	1966	HX-18	20p	£4.50
25	The Story of Milk	1966	HX-3	32p	£8.00
	BLACK ROOK PRESS				
10	Classic Football Stars (1960s) Series 1	2010		—	£5.00
10	Classic Football Stars (1960/70s) 2nd Series	2010		—	£5.00
	BLACKCAT CARDS				
15	Sunderland F.C. Cup Kings of '73	2003		—	£6.00
	BLACKPOOL PROGRAMME & MEMORABILIA COLLECTORS CLUB (BPMCC)				
13	Blackpool FC Legends	2004		—	£13.00

Size & quantity		TRADE CARD ISSUES	Date	Handbook reference	Price per card	Complete set
		BLAKEY'S BOOT PROTECTORS LTD				
72		War Pictures	c1916	HX-200	£10.00	—
		BLUE BAND				
24		History of London's Transport:				
	A	Black printing	1954		£2.00	—
	B	Blue printing	1954		£2.00	—
	C	Red printing	1954		£2.00	—
24		History of London's Transport 2nd Series	1955		£3.50	—
16		See Britain by Coach:		HX-84		
	A	Black back	1954		35p	£6.00
	B	Blue back	1954		£1.00	—
		THE BLUE BIRD				
M10		Famous Beauties of the Day	1922	HB-112	£10.00	—
		BLUE BIRD STOCKINGS				
EL12		Exciting Film Stars 3rd Series	1954		—	£36.00
		BLUE CAP LTD				
		Flixies Coloured Film Transparencies:				
K12	i	Ancient Monuments	1959		£1.25	—
K12	ii	Aviation Series	1959		£1.25	—
K12	iii	British Bird Series	1959		£1.25	£15.00
K12	iv	Butterflies	1959		£1.25	—
K12	v	Dog Series	1959		£1.25	£15.00
K12	vi	Flowers	1959		£1.25	—
K12	vii	Football Teams	1959		£1.25	—
K12	viii	Military Uniforms	1959		£1.25	—
K12	ix	Robin Hood	1959		£1.25	—
K12	x	Ships	1959		£1.25	—
K12	xi	Sport Series	1959		£1.25	—
K12	xii	Tropical Fish	1959		£1.25	—
		Album for Series ii, iii, v, xi			—	£12.00
		Album number 2 for Series i, viii, ix, xii			—	£12.00
		Album number 3 for Series iv, vi, vii, x			—	£12.00
		BLUEBELL COLLECTION				
10		W. C. Fields A Tribute to a Comedy Legend	2015		—	£5.00
		BON AIR (USA)				
LT50		Birds and Flowers of the States	1991		—	£12.00
LT20		Civil War The Heritage Collection 1st Series	1991		—	£15.00
LT12		Civil War The Heritage Collection 2nd Series	1992		—	£9.00
LT100		18 Wheelers 1st Series (Lorries)	1994		—	£9.50
LT100		18 Wheelers 2nd Series (Lorries)	1995		—	£9.50
LT62		Federal Duck Stamps (ducks featured on stamps)	1992		—	£12.00
LT100		Fire Engines 1st Series	1993		—	£15.00
LT100		Fire Engines 2nd Series	1993		—	£15.00
LT100		Fire Engines 3rd Series	1994		—	£15.00
LT100		Fire Engines 4th Series	1994		—	£15.00
LT100		Fire Engines 5th Series	1998		—	£15.00
LT90		Native Americans	1995		—	£12.00
LT63		On Guard The Heritage Collection	1992		—	£9.50
LT50		Wildlife America	1991		—	£10.00

Size & quantity	TRADE CARD ISSUES	Date	Handbook reference	Price per card	Complete set
	E.H. BOOTH & CO. LTD (Tea)				
25	Badges and Uniforms of Famous British Regiments and Corps	1964		30p	£7.50
24	The Island of Ceylon	c1955	HX-47	£6.00	—
25	Ships and Their Workings	1963	HX-85	£1.40	—
	BOW BELLS				
MP6	Handsome Men of the British Screen	1922		£8.00	—
	BOWATER-SCOTT				
EL9	Scotties Famous Football Teams	1969		£8.00	—
EL3	Scotties Grand Prix Series I	1968		£8.00	—
EL4	Scotties Grand Prix Series II	1969		£8.00	—
	BOWMAN GUM INC. (USA)				
M108	Jets-Rockets-Spacemen	1951		—	—
	BOYS' CINEMA				
M24	Boys' Cinema Famous Heroes	1922		£5.00	—
MP6	Cinema Stars (plain back)	1932	HB-129	£5.00	—
EL10	Cinema Stars (plain back)	1934	HB-128	£10.00	—
MP6	Famous Film Heroes	1922		£5.00	—
EL8	Favourite Film Stars	1940	HB-131	£5.00	—
7	Film Stars	c1930	HB-133	£4.00	—
MP8	Film Stars, brown glossy photos	1930		£5.00	—
MP8	Film Stars, black glossy photos	1931		£5.00	—
	BOYS' COMIC LIBRARY				
4	Characters from Boys' Fiction	c1910	HB-137	£22.00	—
4	Heroes of the Wild West	c1910		£22.00	—
6	One and All Flowers	c1910	HB-138	£22.00	—
	BOYS' FRIEND				
3	Famous Boxers Series	1911		£18.00	—
3	Famous Flags Series	1911		£10.00	—
3	Famous Footballers Series	1911		£20.00	—
3	Famous Regiments Series	1911		£10.00	—
MP4	Footballers, half length studies	1923		£6.00	—
MP5	Footballers, two players on each card	1922		£6.00	—
MP15	Rising Boxing Stars	1922		£5.00	—
	BOYS' MAGAZINE				
M8	Coloured Studies of Famous Internationals	1922	HB-140	£7.00	—
P10	Famous Cricketers Series	1928		£9.00	—
P12	Famous Footballers Series	c1930		£7.00	—
MP10	Football Series	c1923		£5.00	—
EL9	Football Teams	c1925	HB-145	£13.00	—
	Sportsmen:				
M8	Boxers	c1926	HB-139	£10.00	—
M10	Cricketers	c1926	HB-142	£12.00	—
M30	Footballers (picture 49 × 39mm)	c1926	HB-147	£6.00	—
M64	Footballers and Miscellaneous (picture 56 × 35mm)	c1926	HB-148	£6.00	—
12	'Zat' Cards, Cricketers	c1930	HB-154	£12.00	—
M11	'Zat' Cards, Cricketers	1932		£12.00	£135.00

Size & quantity	TRADE CARD ISSUES	Date	Handbook reference	Price per card	Complete set
	BOYS' REALM				
MP15	Famous Cricketers	1922		£4.00	—
MP9	Famous Footballers	1922		£5.00	—
	BRAINTREE TOWN F.C.				
M12	Braintree Town F.C. 1st Series (Nos 1 to 12)	2012		—	£5.00
M12	Braintree Town F.C 2nd Series (Nos 13 to 24)	2014		—	£5.00
	BREWER'S				
24	Nursery Rhymes	c1920	HX-25A	£12.00	—
	BREYGENT (USA)				
LT72	American Horror Story Season 1	2014		—	£9.50
LT72	Bates Motel Season 1	2016		—	£9.50
LT72	Classic Vintage Poster Collection Movie Posters (black back)	2007		—	£12.00
LT72	Classic Vintage Posters Stars – Monsters – Comedy (yellow orange back)	2009		—	£12.00
LT72	Dawn New Horizon (Adult Fantasy Art)	2013		—	£12.00
LT72	Dexter Seasons 1 and 2	2009		—	£9.50
LT72	Dexter Season 3	2011		—	£9.50
LT72	Dexter Season 4	2012		—	£9.50
LT72	Dexter Season 5 and 6	2014		—	£9.50
LT72	Dexter Season 7 and 8	2016		—	£9.50
LT72	Ghost Whisperer Seasons 1 and 2	2009		—	£9.50
LT72	Ghost Whisperer Seasons 3 and 4	2010		—	£9.50
LT72	Grimm Season 1	2013		—	£9.50
LT72	Grimm Season 2	2015		—	£9.50
LT12	Jurassic Domination (Sketch Art)	2016		—	£9.50
LT72	Marilyn Monroe (Photos by Shaw Family Archives)	2007		—	£12.00
LT72	The Three Stooges	2005		—	£9.50
LT72	Transformers Optimum Collection (First Three Movies)	2013		—	£9.50
LT72	The Tudors Seasons I, II & III	2011		—	£9.50
LT72	Vampirella — Adult Fantasy Art	2011		—	£9.50
LT72	Warlord of Mars	2012		—	£12.00
LT72	Witchblade	2014		—	£10.00
LT72	The Wizard of Oz	2006		—	£9.50
LT12	Women of Dynamite (Sketch Art)	2016		—	£9.50
	C. & T. BRIDGEWATER LTD				
KP48	Coronation Series	1937		20p	£7.50
KP96	Film Stars (CE over No.) (No. 54 without CE)	1932		75p	£75.00
KP96	Film Stars (E below No.)	1933		£1.00	£100.00
KP96	Film Stars (number only)	1934		£1.00	£100.00
KP48	Film Stars 4th Series	1935	HB-163	40p	£20.00
KP48	Film Stars 5th Series	1937	HB-163	£1.80	£90.00
KP48	Film Stars 6th Series (F before No.)	1938		£2.25	—
P48	Film Stars 7th Series	1939		£2.00	£100.00
KP48	Film Stars 8th Series	1940	HB-164	60p	£30.00
KP48	Radio Stars 1st Series	1935		£1.50	£75.00
KP48	Radio Stars 2nd Series	1936	HB-165	40p	£20.00
	BRIMSTONE PRODUCTIONS				
10	Hollywood Beauties (of the 40s & 50s)	2009		—	£5.00
	J.M. BRINDLEY				
30	The Artist Impression Series Opera Stars	c1993		—	£15.00
30	Australian Cricketers	1986		—	£15.00

Size & quantity	TRADE CARD ISSUES	Date	Handbook reference	Price per card	Complete set
	J.M. BRINDLEY (continued)				
30	Bentley Cars	1993		40p	£12.00
M20	Birds of Britain 1st Series Nos 1-20	1991		50p	£10.00
M20	Birds of Britain 2nd Series Nos 21-40	1992		50p	£10.00
M20	Birds of Britain 3rd Series Nos 41-60	1993		50p	£10.00
M20	Birds of Britain 4th Series Nos 61-80	1993		50p	£10.00
M20	Birds of Britain 5th Series Nos 81-100	1993		50p	£10.00
M12	British Birds of Prey	1995		—	£9.00
20	Car Badges and Emblems	1987		30p	£6.00
30	Cricketers 1st Series	1984		—	£20.00
30	Cricketers 2nd Series	1985		—	£20.00
L16	Cricketers 3rd Series	1985		—	£15.00
30	Cricketers 4th Series	1985		40p	£12.00
L20	Cricket (cartoons) 5th Series	1985		—	£10.00
12	Cricket Caricatures 1st Series Nos 1-12	1992		60p	—
18	Cricket Caricatures 2nd Series Nos 13-30	1993		60p	—
30	Cricket — The Old School	1987		—	£12.00
20	Cricket Old Timers	1993		—	£10.00
30	Cricket — Surrey v Yorkshire	1988		—	£9.00
20	Cricketers of the 1880s	1992		50p	£10.00
25	Cricketing Greats	1987		40p	£10.00
EL1	Cricketing Greats — W.G. Grace	1987		—	50p
18	Famous Operatic Roles	1992		50p	£9.00
18	Fish	1989		50p	£9.00
EL3	Fish	1989		50p	£1.50
EL35	Full Dress Uniforms of the British Army c1914 1st Series	1990		35p	£12.00
EL35	Full Dress Uniforms of the British Army c1914 2nd Series	1990		35p	£12.00
EL35	Full Dress Uniforms of the British Army c1914 3rd Series	1990		35p	£12.00
EL35	Full Dress Uniforms of the British Army c1914 4th Series	1990		35p	£12.00
EL35	Full Dress Uniforms of the British Army c1914 5th Series	1990		35p	£12.00
20	Golf	1987		60p	£12.00
38	Hampshire County Cricket Club	1991		50p	—
24	Hampshire Cricket Sunday League Era	1987		—	£6.00
20	Horse Racing	1987		30p	£6.00
20	Loco's	1987		40p	£8.00
30	London, Brighton and South Coast Railway	1986		33p	£10.00
20	Military	1987		30p	£6.00
EL1	Motor Car The Bentley	1993		—	50p
25	Old Golfing Greats	1987		80p	£20.00
EL1	Old Golfing Greats — H. Vardon	1987		—	50p
12	Old Motor Cycles	1993		50p	£6.00
30	Opera Stars	1988		40p	£12.00
16	Players of the Past — 1930s Football	1992		65p	£10.00
8	Pop Stars (Series of 15, but only 8 cards issued)	c1993		50p	£4.00
EL6	Regimental Drum Majors	1992		—	£3.50
EL7	The Royal Hussars Bandsmen 1979-1989	1989		60p	£4.00
20	S.E.C.R. Locos	1995		60p	£12.00
16	Sea Fish	1992		50p	£8.00
20	South African Test Cricket 1888-1988	1989		70p	£14.00
20	Trains — London & S.W. Railways	1992		—	£8.00
	Victorian and Edwardian Soldiers in Full Dress:				
30	A Back with black background	1988		50p	—
30	B Back with olive/green background	1988		40p	£12.00
30	C Back with white background	1988		40p	£12.00

Size & quantity		TRADE CARD ISSUES	Date	Handbook reference	Price per card	Complete set
		J.M. BRINDLEY (continued)				
M6		World Boxers 1st Series Nos 1-6	1992		—	£4.50
M6		World Boxers 2nd Series Nos 7-12	1993		—	£4.50
		BRISTOL–MYERS CO. LTD				
25		Speed 1st Series	1966	HX-153	£5.00	—
25		Speed 2nd Series	1966	HX-153	£5.00	—
		THE BRITISH AUTOMATIC CO. LTD (Weight Cards)				
K24		British Aircraft	1950		£2.50	£60.00
K24		British Birds	1949		£2.50	—
K24		British Locomotives	1948		£1.40	£35.00
K36		British Motor Cars	1950		£8.00	—
K44		Coronation Information	1952		£1.75	—
K32		Dogs 1st Series:				
	A	Front with 'Weigh Daily' across picture	1953		£1.00	£32.00
	B	Front without 'Weigh Daily' across picture	1953		£1.50	—
K32		Dogs 2nd Series	1953		£1.25	—
K24		Famous Trains of the World 1st Series	1951		£2.00	—
K24		Famous Trains of the World 2nd Series	1952		£1.25	£30.00
K37		Fortunes, Horoscopes, Quotations numbered	1953		£3.00	—
		Fortunes, Horoscopes, Quotations unnumbered:				
K37	A	With frame lines, no Serifs, horizontal	1948	HB-166.1	£3.00	—
K33	B	Without frame line, no Serifs, horizontal	1953	HB-166.2	£3.00	—
K32	C	Without frame line, or Serif, vertical	1952	HB-166.3	£3.00	—
K33	D	Without frame line, with Serifs, horizontal	c1953	HB-166.4	£3.00	—
K32		Fortunes 2nd Series	1953		£3.00	—
K24		Fresh Water Fish	1950		£2.00	—
K24		History of Transport	1948		60p	£15.00
K44		Jokes	1951		£1.25	—
K24		Olympic Games	1949		£8.00	—
K24		Racing and Sports Cars	1957		£4.00	—
K24		Space Travel	1956		£3.00	—
K24		Speed	1948		60p	£15.00
K24		Sportsman	1955		£3.50	—
K20		Twenty Questions	1951		£3.50	—
K24		Warships of the World	1952		£1.20	£30.00
		BRITISH EDUCATIONAL SERIES				
50		Modern Aircraft	1953	HX-35	40p	£20.00
		BRITISH TOURIST AUTHORITY				
25		Industrial Heritage Year	1993		—	£15.00
		C. BRITTON				
L24		Golf Courses of the British Isles	1993		30p	£7.50
		BROOK MOTORS LTD (Motor Engineers)				
EL12		Motor Cars 1910-1931	1961		£2.50	£30.00
EL12		Railway Engines (size 120 × 83mm)	1962		£3.00	£36.00
EL12		Railway Engines (size 125 × 105mm)	c1970		£1.25	£15.00
EL12		Traction Engines	1968		£2.00	£24.00

Size & quantity	TRADE CARD ISSUES	Date	Handbook reference	Price per card	Complete set

BROOKE BOND & CO. LTD
BRAND NEW 'Brooke Bond Tea Cards' Reference book, to be published 2021

50	Adventurers and Explorers	1973	B-26	20p	£4.00
	Album		—		£5.00
50	African Wild Life:		B-8		
	A Blue back	1961		25p	£12.50
	Album (original matt cover with price). Small print on front black			—	£40.00
	Album (original matt cover with price). Small print on front bluish grey			—	£30.00
	B Black back	1973		20p	£5.00
	Album (re-issue glossy cover with price)			—	£25.00
	Album (re-issue glossy cover without price)			—	£20.00
50	Asian Wild Life	1962	B-10	20p	£10.00
	Album (price sixpence)			—	£35.00
50	Bird Portraits:		B-4		
	A With address	1957		£1.30	£65.00
	B Without address	1957		£2.50	—
	Album (solid border to card space)			—	£90.00
	Album (dotted border to card space)			—	£75.00
50	British Butterflies:		B-11		
	A Blue back	1963		80p	£40.00
	Album (original matt cover)			—	£30.00
	B Black back	1973		25p	£12.50
	Album (re-issue glossy cover with price)			—	£25.00
	Album (re-issue glossy cover without price)			—	£20.00
50	British Costume:		B-19		
	A Blue back	1967		20p	£5.00
	Error and Corrected Cards of Nos 3, 4, 23, 24			—	£30.00
	Album (original matt cover with price and printer's credit)			—	£25.00
	B Black back	1973		20p	£5.00
	Album (re-issue glossy cover with price, without printer's credit)			—	£20.00
	Album (re-issue glossy cover without price, with printer's credit)			—	£25.00
	Album (re-issue glossy cover with price with printer's credit)			—	£25.00
50	British Wild Life:		B-5		
	A Brooke Bond (Great Britain) Ltd	1958		£2.00	—
	B Brooke Bond Tea Ltd	1958		£1.20	£60.00
	C Brooke Bond & Co. Ltd	1958		£2.00	—
	Album			—	£65.00
50	Butterflies of the World	1964	B-14	20p	£7.50
	Album (price sixpence)			—	£30.00
	Creatures of Legend:		B-49		
M24	A Standard set	1994		32p	£8.00
EL12	B Two pictures per card	1994		£1.00	£12.00
	Album			—	£9.00
	Wallchart	1994		—	£7.00
	The Dinosaur Trail:		B-48		
20	A Standard set:				
	i Postcode BB1 1PG	1993		90p	£18.00
	ii Postcode BB11 1PG	1993		20p	£4.00
L10	B Two pictures per card:				
	i Postcode BB1 1PG	1993		£1.80	—
	ii Postcode BB11 1PG	1993		60p	£6.00
	Album (with © Marshall on back cover)			—	£40.00
	Album (without © Marshall on back cover)			—	£5.00

Size & quantity	TRADE CARD ISSUES	Date	Handbook reference	Price per card	Complete set
	BROOKE BOND & CO. LTD (continued)				
	Discovering Our Coast:		B-42		
50	A Standard set Blue back	1989		20p	£4.50
50	B Standard set Black back	1992		20p	£7.00
L25	C Two pictures per card	1989		40p	£10.00
	Album			—	£5.00
	Wallchart	1989		—	£8.00
50	Famous People:		B-21		
	A Blue back	1969		20p	£4.00
	Album (original with printer's credit and price)			—	£18.00
	B Black back	1973		20p	£5.00
	Album (re-issue with price, without printer's credit)			—	£25.00
	Album (re-issue without price, with printer's credit)			—	£25.00
	Album (re-issue without price and printer's credit)			—	£12.00
	Features of the World:		B-37		
50	A Standard set	1984		20p	£5.00
L25	B Two pictures per card	1984		£1.00	£25.00
	Album			—	£5.00
50	Flags and Emblems of the World:		B-18		
	A Blue back	1967		20p	£5.00
	Album (original, matt cover with printer's credit)			—	£8.00
	B Black back	1973		30p	£15.00
	Album (re-issue, glossy cover without printer's credit)			—	£10.00
48	40 Years of Cards:		BM-13		
	A Dark Blue back	1994		20p	£9.00
	B Light Blue back	1994		20p	£7.50
	C Black back	1994		20p	£7.50
LT40	40 Years of the Chimps Television Advertising	1995	B-52	30p	£12.00
	Album with '17 Roadworks' printed in red underneath No. 26			—	£40.00
	Album without '17 Roadworks' printed in red underneath No. 26			—	£10.00
20	Frances Pitt — British Birds:		B-1		
	A Cream Card	1954		£4.00	£80.00
	B White Card	1954		£3.00	£60.00
	Album (price 3d)			—	£150.00
50	Freshwater Fish:		B-7		
	A Blue back	1960		£1.00	£50.00
	Album (original matt cover with price)			—	£35.00
	B Black back	1973		50p	£25.00
	Album (re-issue glossy cover with price)			—	£25.00
	Album (re-issue glossy cover without price)			—	£25.00
	Going Wild — Wildlife Survival:		B-50		
M40	A Standard set	1994		20p	£6.00
EL20	B Two pictures per card	1994		50p	£10.00
	Album			—	£5.00
50	History of Aviation	1972	B-25	20p	£5.00
	Album (original matt inside cover)			—	£9.00
	Album (re-issue glossy inside cover)			—	£8.00
50	History of the Motor Car:		B-20		
	A Blue back	1968		25p	£12.50
	Album (original with price, inside cover cream)			—	£9.00
	B Black back	1974		25p	£12.50
	Album (re-issue without price, inside cover white)			—	£25.00
	Album (re-issue with price, inside cover white)			—	£25.00

Size & quantity	TRADE CARD ISSUES	Date	Handbook reference	Price per card	Complete set
	BROOKE BOND & CO. LTD (continued)				
	Incredible Creatures:		B-38		
40	A Standard set:				
	i 'Sheen Lane' address	1985		30p	£12.00
	ii 'Walton' address with Dept. I.C.	1986		20p	£5.00
	iii 'Walton' address without Dept. I.C.	1986		50p	£20.00
L20	B Two pictures per card:				
	i 'Sheen Lane' address	1985		£2.50	—
	ii 'Walton' address with Dept. I.C.	1986		£1.75	—
	iii 'Walton' address without Dept. I.C.	1986		£3.00	—
	Set of 4 Wallcharts			—	£10.00
LT20	International Soccer Stars	1998	B-55	75p	£15.00
	Album			—	£12.00
50	Inventors and Inventions	1975	B-28	20p	£5.00
	Album			—	£16.00
	A Journey Downstream:		B-44		
25	A Standard set	1990		20p	£3.50
L25	B Two pictures per card	1990		60p	£15.00
	Album			—	£5.00
12	The Language of Tea (flags)	1988	B-41	30p	£3.50
	Wallchart			—	£16.00
LT45	The Magical, Mystical World of Pyramids:		B-53		
	A Red & black back	1996		40p	£18.00
	B Black back	1998		40p	£18.00
	Album			—	£5.00
	The Magical World of Disney:		B-43		
25	A Standard set	1989		30p	£7.50
	B Two pictures per card:				
L13	i Two pictures per card all 25 pictures			£1.00	£13.00
L25	ii Two pictures per card all varieties			—	£25.00
	Album			—	£5.00
	Natural Neighbours:		B-47		
40	A Standard set	1992		25p	£10.00
L20	B Two pictures per card	1992		50p	£10.00
	Album			—	£5.00
	Olympic Challenge 1992:		B-46		
40	A Standard set	1992		25p	£10.00
L20	B Two pictures per card	1992		75p	£15.00
	Album			—	£5.00
40	Olympic Greats:		B-33		
	A Green back	1979		40p	£16.00
	B Black back	1988		£2.50	—
	Album			—	£5.00
50	Out Into Space:		B-3		
	A 'Issued with Brooke Bond ...'	1956		£11.00	—
	Album (back cover without 'P.G. Tips')	1956		—	£40.00
	B 'Issued in packets ...'	1958		£1.20	£60.00
	Album (back cover with 'P.G. Tips')	1958		—	£60.00
40	Play Better Soccer	1976	B-30	20p	£4.00
	Album (original, inside pages white)			—	£15.00
	Album (re-issue, inside pages cream)			—	£5.00
40	Police File	1977	B-31	20p	£4.00
	Album			—	£5.00
EL10	Polyfilla Modelling Cards	1974	BM-6	£14.00	—
50	Prehistoric Animals	1972	B-24	20p	£7.50
	Album			—	£20.00

Size & quantity	TRADE CARD ISSUES	Date	Handbook reference	Price per card	Complete set
	BROOKE BOND & CO. LTD (continued)				
	Queen Elizabeth I - Queen Elizabeth II:		B-36		
50	A Blue/purple back	1983		20p	£7.50
50	B Black back	1988		20p	£9.00
L25	C Two pictures per card	1983		£1.40	£35.00
	Album			—	£5.00
50	The Race Into Space:		B-23		
	A Blue back	1971		20p	£6.00
	Album (original, printer's credit 45mm)			—	£25.00
	B Black back	1974		20p	£5.00
	Album (re-issue, printer's credit 39mm)			—	£30.00
50	Saga of Ships:		B-22		
	A Blue back	1970		20p	£4.00
	Album (original, cover light blue sky)			—	£20.00
	B Black back	1973		20p	£5.00
	Album (re-issue, cover dark blue sky).........			—	£8.00
50	The Sea — Our Other World	1974	B-27	20p	£4.00
	Album (original, with printer's credit)			—	£10.00
	Album (re-issue, without printer's credit)			—	£20.00
LT50	The Secret Diary of Kevin Tipps.........	1995	B-51	20p	£10.00
	Album			—	£5.00
40	Small Wonders:		B-35		
	A Blue back	1981		20p	£5.00
	B Black back	1988		20p	£5.00
	Album			—	£5.00
LT19	Tea Leaf Oracle	1999	BM-16	£4.00	—
	Teenage Mutant Hero Turtles:		B-45		
12	A Standard set	1991		30p	£3.50
L6	B Two pictures per card	1991		80p	£5.00
	Album			—	£5.00
12	30 Years of The Chimps:		B-39		
	A Thin Card plain back.....................	1986		£7.00	—
	B Thick Card plain back	1986		85p	£10.00
	C Thin Card Tak Tik back	1986		£5.00	—
	Album			—	£25.00
50	Transport Through the Ages:		B-16		
	A Blue back	1966		20p	£5.00
	Album			—	£25.00
	B Black back	1973		£4.00	—
50	Trees in Britain:		B-17		
	A Blue back	1966		20p	£4.00
	Album (original matt cover with letter 'T')			—	£12.00
	Album (original matt cover without letter 'T') ...			—	£35.00
	B Black back	1973		20p	£5.00
	Album (re-issue glossy cover with price and printer's credit)			—	£25.00
	Album (re-issue glossy cover with price, without printer's credit)			—	£20.00
	Album (re-issue glossy cover without price)			—	£20.00
50	Tropical Birds:		B-9		
	A Blue back	1961		40p	£20.00
	Album (original matt cover with price)			—	£25.00
	B Black back	1974		20p	£5.00
	Album (re-issue glossy cover with price)			—	£20.00
	Album (re-issue glossy cover without price or printer's credit)			—	£6.00
	Album (re-issue glossy cover without price with printer's credit)			—	£20.00

Size & quantity	TRADE CARD ISSUES	Date	Handbook reference	Price per card	Complete set
	BROOKE BOND & CO. LTD (continued)				
	Unexplained Mysteries of the World:		B-40		
40	A Standard set	1987		20p	£4.00
L20	B Two pictures per card	1987		50p	£10.00
	Album...			—	£5.00
40	Vanishing Wildlife:		B-32		
	A Brown back	1978		20p	£4.00
	Album (original matt inside cover)			—	£6.00
	B Black back.................................	1988		20p	£5.00
	Album (re-issue glossy inside cover)			—	£5.00
50	Wild Birds in Britain:		B-15		
	A Blue back	1965		20p	£5.00
	Album (original matt cover with price)			—	£30.00
	B Black back.................................	1973		20p	£6.00
	Album (re-issue glossy cover with price)			—	£25.00
	Album (re-issue glossy cover without price)			—	£25.00
50	Wild Flowers, Series 1:		B-2		
	A Thick Card.................................	1955		£3.00	£150.00
	B Paper Thin Card	1955		£10.00	—
	Album (cover with price)			—	£45.00
	Album (cover without price)			—	£85.00
50	Wild Flowers, Series 2:		B-6		
	A Blue back with 'issued by ...'	1959		25p	£12.50
	B Blue back without 'issued by ...'	1959		£2.50	—
	Album (original matt cover with price)			—	£30.00
	C Black back.................................	1973		20p	£6.00
	Album (re-issue glossy cover with price)			—	£25.00
	Album (re-issue glossy cover without price)			—	£10.00
50	Wild Flowers, Series 3	1964	B-13	20p	£6.00
	Album			—	£25.00
50	Wild Life in Danger:		B-12		
	A Blue back	1963		20p	£4.00
	Album (original matt cover with price sixpence)			—	£25.00
	B Black back.................................	1973		20p	£5.00
	Album (re-issue glossy cover with price)			—	£20.00
	Album (re-issue glossy cover without price)			—	£20.00
LT30	The Wonderful World of Kevin Tipps	1997	B-51	50p	£15.00
	Album...			—	£5.00
50	Wonders of Wildlife	1976	B-29	20p	£4.00
	Error and corrected card of No. 37			—	£18.00
	Album...			—	£5.00
40	Woodland Wildlife:		B-34		
	A Green back	1980		30p	£12.00
	B Black back.................................	1988		20p	£7.50
	Album			—	£5.00
L50	Zena Skinner International Cookery Cards	1974	BM-7	£28.00	—
	BROOKE BOND OVERSEAS ISSUES				
	IRELAND				
40	Incredible Creatures.............................	1986	IR-1	£3.00	£120.00
	CANADA				
48	Songbirds of North America:		CU-1		
	A Back 'Red Rose Tea & Coffee' Album clause reading:				
	i 'Mount Your Collection, Send 25c'	1959		£7.00	—
	ii 'Album available at your grocer's or from us 25c'	1959		£4.00	—

Size & quantity	TRADE CARD ISSUES	Date	Handbook reference	Price per card	Complete set
	BROOKE BOND & CO. LTD (Overseas Issues, Canada continued)				
48	Songbirds of North America continued:		CU-1		
	B Back 'Red Rose and Blue Ribbon Tea and Coffee'	1959		£1.80	£90.00
	Album (back cover 'Red Rose' only)			—	£75.00
	Album (back cover 'Red Rose & Blue Ribbon')			—	£60.00
48	Animals of North America:		CU-2		
	A 'Rolland' back	1960		£3.50	£175.00
	B 'Roland' back:				
	i Text between lines 47mm	1960		£3.00	£150.00
	ii Text between lines 49mm	1960		£15.00	—
	Album			—	£40.00
48	Wild Flowers of North America	1961	CU-3	£1.00	£50.00
	Album			—	£40.00
48	Birds of North America	1962	CU-4	£1.20	£60.00
	Album			—	£40.00
48	Dinosaurs	1963	CU-5	£3.00	£150.00
	Album			—	£90.00
48	Tropical Birds:		CU-6		
	A Top line in red	1964		£12.00	—
	B Top line in black	1964		£1.00	£50.00
	Album			—	£20.00
48	African Animals	1964	CU-7	20p	£6.00
	Album			—	£20.00
48	Butterflies of North America	1965	CU-8	90p	£45.00
	Album			—	£30.00
48	Canadian/American Songbirds	1966	CU-9	£2.50	£125.00
	Album			—	£25.00
48	Transportation Through the Ages:		CU-10		
	A Top line in red	1967		£12.00	—
	B Top line in black	1967		40p	£20.00
	Album			—	£25.00
48	Trees of North America	1968	CU-11	40p	£20.00
	Album (pages 3, 8, 9 etc. green)			—	£30.00
	Album (pages 3, 6, 7 etc. green)			—	£25.00
48	The Space Age	1969	CU-12	35p	£17.50
	Album			—	£15.00
48	North American Wildlife in Danger	1970	CU-13	30p	£15.00
	Album			—	£15.00
48	Exploring the Ocean	1971	CU-14	20p	£7.50
	Album			—	£6.00
48	Animals and Their Young:		CU-15		
	A Text ends 'Products'	1972		40p	£20.00
	B Text ends 'Tea/Coffee'	1972		£11.00	—
	Album			—	£16.00
	Note: Without Brooke Bond name — see Liptons Tea				
48	The Arctic	1973	CU-16	25p	£12.00
	Album			—	£5.00
48	Indians of Canada	1974	CU-17	£1.20	£60.00
	Album			—	£6.00
	USA				
48	Animals of North America:		CU-2		
	A Blue text on back	1960		£10.00	—
	B Black text on back	1960		£12.00	—
48	Wild Flowers of North America:		CU-3		
	A Dark Blue back	1961		£6.00	—
	B Light Blue back	1961		£20.00	—

Size & quantity	TRADE CARD ISSUES	Date	Handbook reference	Price per card	Complete set

BROOKE BOND & CO. LTD (Overseas Issues USA continued)

48	Birds of North America	1962	CU-4	£8.00	—
48	Dinosaurs	1963	CU-5	£10.00	—
48	Tropical Birds	1964	CU-6	£6.00	—
48	Butterflies of North America	1965	CU-8	£6.00	—
48	Canadian/American Songbirds	1966	CU-9	£3.00	—

SOUTHERN RHODESIA AND EAST AFRICA

50	African Wild Life	1961	SR-2	£7.00	—
	Album (no price with red line under C.F. Tunnicliffe)			—	£150.00
50	Tropical Birds	1962	SR-3	£6.00	—
	Album (no price with red line under C.F. Tunnicliffe)			—	£150.00
50	Asian Wild Life..	1963	SR-4	£7.00	—
	Album (50 cents East Africa 6d Rhodesia)			—	£150.00
50	Wild Life in Danger	1964	SR-5	£7.00	—
	Album (East Africa issue price 50 cents)			—	£150.00
	Album (Rhodesia issue price nine pence)			—	£150.00
50	African Birds	1965	SR-6	£6.00	—
	Album (East Africa issue price 50 cents)			—	£100.00
	Album (Rhodesia issue price 9d)			—	£150.00
50	Butterflies of the World....................................	1966	SR-7	£6.00	£300.00
	Album (price 9d)			—	£150.00

SOUTH AFRICA

50	Wild van Africa (alternate cards English and Afrikaans)	1965	SA-1	£20.00	—
50	Wild van Africa (bilingual)	1965	SA-2	£6.00	£300.00
	Album			—	£60.00
50	Out Into Space	1966	SA-3	£6.00	£300.00
	Album			—	£60.00
50	Our Pets:		SA-4		
	A Printing A	1967		£6.00	£300.00
	B Printing B (revised numbering)	1967		£20.00	—
	Album			—	£60.00

MUSGRAVE-BROOKE BOND (Eire)

20	British Birds..	1964	MBB-1	£14.00	—
	Album (price 6d)			—	£200.00
50	British Wild Life	1964	MBB-2	£12.00	—
	Album (Musgrave Brothers on back)			—	£200.00
50	Butterflies of the World....................................	1965	MBB-3	£12.00	—
	Album (Musgrave Brooke Bond address)			—	£200.00
50	Transport Through the Ages	1966	MBB-4	£6.00	£300.00
	Album (Musgrave Brooke Bond on front cover) ...			—	£150.00

BROOKE BOND-LIEBIG (Italy)

EL6	F.1845 The Nativity	1971		—	£25.00
EL6	F.1850 Self-Portraits of Famous Artists	1972		—	£8.00
EL6	F.1851 Journey to the Moon (II).......................	1972		—	£10.00
EL6	F.1852 Historical Fights	1972		—	£8.00
EL6	F.1853 The Resurrection	1972		—	£18.00
EL6	F.1854 History of the Typewriter......................	1972		—	£12.00
EL6	F.1855 How Animals See (I)	1973		—	£8.00
EL6	F.1856 Ludwig van Beethoven	1973		—	£8.00
EL6	F.1857 The Fight Against Microbes (I)	1973		—	£8.00
EL6	F.1858 How Animals See (II)	1973		—	£8.00
EL6	F.1859 The Story of the Circus (I)	1973		—	£14.00
EL6	F.1860 The Fight Against Microbes (II)	1973		—	£16.00
EL6	F.1861 The Story of the Circus (II)	1974		—	£16.00
EL6	F.1862 War at Sea	1974		—	£40.00

Size & quantity	TRADE CARD ISSUES	Date	Handbook reference	Price per card	Complete set
	BROOKE BOND & CO. LTD (continued)				
	BROOKE BOND-LIEBIG (Italy)Continued..				
EL6	F.1863 Animals	1974		—	£16.00
EL6	F.1867 Journey to the Moon (I)	1975		—	£13.00
EL6	F.1868 Protected Birds	1975		—	£12.00
EL6	F.1869 Old Military Dress (I)	1975		—	£12.00
EL6	F.1871 Old Military Dress (II)	1975		—	£45.00
	BROOKE BOND NOVELTY INSERTS				
	ADVERTISEMENT CARD INSERTS (Great Britain)				
1	Why is Crown Cup 'Medium Roasted'?	1963	BA-2	—	£6.00
1	3 Crown Cups and Saucers	1963	BA-3	—	£15.00
2	Danish Designed Tableware	1964	BA-4	£16.00	—
2	Radio London	1965	BA-5	£16.00	—
2	Six-Piece Cutlery Set	1966	BA-6	£16.00	—
1	Free Opal Glass Jar:		BA-7		
	A Original card plain back	1967		—	£60.00
	B Reprint card printed back	2004		—	£4.00
	Place The Face Bingo:		BM-5		
15	A Single Face with PG Tips	1972		£35.00	—
15	B Single Face without PG Tips	1972		£35.00	—
15	C Three Faces	1972		£35.00	—
K15	D Flap of Packet	1972		£45.00	—
1	Play Better Soccer set and album offer	1976	BA-8	—	£6.00
1	Play Better Soccer 'Great New Series!'	1976	BA-9	—	£12.00
1	Police File 'New picture Card Series'	1977	BA-10	—	£45.00
LT11	PG Tips Phonecards:		BM-15		
	A 8 Different 3 Minutes	1998		£6.00	—
	B 3 Different 21, 42, 84 Minutes	1998		£11.00	—
LT1	P.G. Tips Tipps Family 1997 Calendar	1996	BA-21	—	£10.00
LT3	Farewell to Picture Cards	1999	BA-24	£1.50	£4.50
LT1	P.G. Tips Need Your Help	1999	BA-22	—	£1.50
LT1	Thank You	1999	BA-23	—	£1.50
LT1	PG Tips Bean Chimp:		BA-25		
	A With Multi Coloured Circle	2001		—	£5.00
	B With Dark Brown Circle	2001		—	£10.00
EL1	World Cup 1966 Souvenir (booklet)	1966	BM-2	—	£75.00
	ADVERTISEMENT CARDS (Eire)				
	Match-Maker Cards:		MBBM-1		
	A Blue & black printing:				
39	a 'Musgrave Brooke Bond' on front	1967		£45.00	—
39	b 'PG Tips' on front	1967		£45.00	—
9	B Red & black printing	1967		£45.00	—
	CARD GAMES				
L36	British Costume	1974	BP-2	—	£25.00
L36	Flags and Emblems	1974	BP-3	—	£25.00
L36	Motor History	1974	BP-4	—	£25.00
L55	P.G. Tips Card Game — Get Out	1995	BP-5	—	£7.00
L54	P.G. Tips Card Game — Playing Cards	1995	BP-6	—	£4.00
L36	P.G. Tips Card Game — Snap	1995	BP-7	—	£4.00
L54	P.G. Tips Card Game — Trick Cards	1995	BP-8	—	£4.00
	BROOKFIELD SWEETS (Ireland)				
50	Animals of the World	c1956	HX-93	£5.00	—
25	Aquarium Fish 1st Series	c1959	HX-87	£5.00	—
25	Aquarium Fish 2nd Series	c1959	HX-87	£5.00	—
25	Conquest of Space	c1956	HX-73	£5.00	—
25	Motor Cars	c1954	HX-15	£5.00	—

Size & quantity	TRADE CARD ISSUES	Date	Handbook reference	Price per card	Complete set
	BROOKS DYE WORKS LTD				
EL4	Interesting Shots of Old Bristol	c1950		£1.50	£6.00
	BROWN & POLSON				
L25	Brown & Polson Picture Cards (Recipe)	1925		£4.00	—
	DAVID BROWN (Tractors)				
EL3	Is Your Slip Showing?	1954		£3.50	—
	BROWNE BROS. LTD (Tea)				
25	Birds	1963	HX-71	£2.00	—
25	British Cavalry Uniforms of the 19th Century	1964	HX-73	£1.20	—
25	Garden Flowers	1965	HX-46	£2.00	—
25	History of the Railway 1st Series	1964	HX-88	50p	£12.50
25	History of the Railway 2nd Series	1964	HX-88	50p	£12.50
24	The Island of Ceylon	1961	HX-47	£6.00	—
25	Passenger Liners	1966	HX-82	£2.00	—
25	People and Places	1967	HX-26	20p	£4.00
25	Tropical Birds	1966	HX-13.2	20p	£4.00
25	Wonders of the Deep	1965	HX-89	20p	£4.00
25	Wonders of the World	1967	HX-49	20p	£5.00
	BRYANT & MAY				
L12	The Thirties	1992		—	£12.00
	BUBBLES INC. (Chewing Gum)				
L55	Mars Attacks	1964		£30.00	—
L50	Outer Limits	1966		£6.50	—
	BUCHANAN'S (Jam)				
24	Birds and Their Eggs	1923	HX-164	£12.00	—
	BUITONI				
L6	National Costume Dolls	c1980		£4.00	—
L6	Performance Cars	c1980		£4.00	—
	JOHNNY BUNNY				
25	Football Clubs and Badges	c1960	HX-137	£4.00	—
	BUNSEN CONFECTIONERY CO.				
200	Famous Figures Series	c1925	HB-186	£20.00	—
	BURDALL & BURDALL				
30	Wild Animals	c1920		£10.00	—
	BURLINGTON SLATE				
L20	Processing and Use of Slate	1992		—	£15.00
	BURTONS (Wagon Wheels)				
EL12	Football Skills Cards (Size 230 x 110mm)	1996		£2.50	—
25	Indian Chiefs	1972		£1.00	£25.00
EL8	NFL Heroes (American Football)	1987		—	£24.00
L7	Pictures of the Wild West	1983		£7.00	—
EL12	Super Strikers	1998		£2.50	—
25	The West	1972		36p	£9.00
25	Wild West Action	1972		36p	£9.00
EL12	World Cup Dream Team	1998		£2.50	£30.00

Size & quantity	TRADE CARD ISSUES	Date	Handbook reference	Price per card	Complete set
	BUTTAPAT DAIRIES				
25	People of the World	1915	HB-188	£24.00	—
	BUTTERCUP BREAD (Australia)				
M24	Allan Border Tribute (Cricketers)	1994		—	£18.00
M24	Border's Ashes Heroes (Cricketers)	1993		—	£18.00
M24	1993-94 World Series All Stars (Cricketers)	1993		—	£18.00
	BUTTERWORTH & SON				
EL25	Airborne Over East Anglia Series A	2015		£1.00	—
EL25	Airborne Over East Anglia Series B	2016		£1.00	—
EL25	America Airborne Over East Anglia	2017		£1.25	—
EL12	Animals Gone But Not Forgotten	2016		£1.50	—
EL24	Anthropomorphic Menagerie	2017		£1.25	—
M5	The Butterworth Ladies (Nos. 1, 2, 3 & 2 different No. 4)	2013		£2.00	—
EL12	Careless Moments	2017		£1.50	—
EL12	The Childhood Year	2017		£1.50	—
EL25	Delhi Durbar 1903 Series A	2013		£1.20	—
EL25	Delhi Durbar 1903 Series B	2014		£1.20	—
EL25	Delhi Durbar 1903 Series C	2016		£1.20	—
EL25	Delhi Durbar 1903 Series D	2017		£1.20	—
EL12	Delhi Durbar 1903 Series E	2018		£1.25	—
EL20	Dinosaurs and Prehistoric Life	2015		£1.50	—
EL1	East of England CO-OP Celebrating 150 Years	2018		—	£3.00
EL25	East Suffolk Churches Series 1	2012		£1.00	—
EL25	East Suffolk Churches Series 2	2013		£1.00	—
M15	The Endless Landscape or Myriorama Blue Back	2018		£1.25	—
M15	The Endless Landscape or Myriorama Red Back	2018		£1.25	—
M21	Fine Flavours & Classic Adverts	2012		£1.25	—
M12	Fine Flavours & Classic Adverts (Tea & Biscuits)	2009		£1.50	—
EL12	Flight into Danger	2018		£1.25	—
EL20	Goals & Winners	2016		£1.25	—
L12	Historic Bury St. Edmunds	1993		£1.00	—
M18	History of the Suffolk Regiment	1999		£1.50	—
EL20	Images of the Great War	2014		£1.50	—
EL20	Legacy of The Great War	2018		£1.25	—
EL18	Mandalas	2018		£1.25	—
EL20	Military Tanks	2017		£1.50	—
EL12	Modern Ethnic Beauties 1st Series Numbers 1 to 12	2019		£1.25	—
EL12	Modern Ethnic Beauties 2nd Series Numbers 13 to 24	2020		£1.25	—
EL20	Notables in East Anglia	2018		£1.25	—
EL20	Our Christian Heritage	2015		£1.25	—
EL20	The Romance of Kenya Tea & Coffee	2015		£1.20	—
EL25	Scenes of Historic Bury St. Edmunds Series A	2013		£1.20	—
EL25	Scenes of Historic Bury St. Edmunds Series B	2014		£1.20	—
EL12	Sleepy Goes Missing	2015		£1.25	—
EL20	Sporting Ladies	2016		£1.50	—
EL20	Submarines of WWII	2014		£1.50	—
EL12	Suffolk Maids	2017		£1.50	—
EL6	Suffolk Regiment Land Rover Series 1	2010		£2.00	—
M12	Suffolk Steam Railways 1st Series	2002		£1.50	—
M6	Suffolk Steam Railways 2nd Series	2002		£1.50	—
EL20	Up for the Cup	2017		£1.25	—
EL28	Vignettes of World War Two 1st Series Nd 1 to 28	2019		£1.25	—
EL28	Vignettes of World War Two 2nd Series Nd 29 to 56	2019		£1.25	—
EL28	Vignettes of World War Two 3rd Series Nd 57 to 84	2019		£1.25	—
EL28	Vignettes of World War Two 4th Series Nd 85 to 112	2019		£1.25	—
EL25	West Suffolk Churches Series 1	2016		£1.40	—
EL25	West Suffolk Churches Series 2	2016		£1.40	—

Size & quantity	TRADE CARD ISSUES	Date	Handbook reference	Price per card	Complete set
	BYRNES ENT. (USA)				
LT22	Firemen in Action	1981		—	£12.00
LT22	Firemen in Action	1982		—	£12.00
	C.B.S. LTD				
30	Glamorgan Cricketers	1984		—	£20.00
	CCC LTD				
L15	Arsenal FC Cup Winners 1992/1993	1993		—	£7.50
L20	Doctor Who (TV Series)	1993		—	£15.00
L6	Wild Cats by Joel Kirk	1994		—	£3.50
	C & G CONFECTIONERY CO.				
25	Box of Tricks 1st Series	1963		£6.00	—
25	Box of Tricks 2nd Series	1963		£6.00	—
	C.H. PUBLICATIONS				
L6	MG World 1st Series Nos 1-6 (Cars)	1999		—	£3.50
L6	MG World 2nd Series Nos 7-12 (Cars)	1999		—	£3.50
L6	Triumph World 1st Series Nos 1-6 (Cars)	1999		—	£3.50
L6	Triumph World 3rd Series Nos 13-18 (Cars)	2000		—	£3.50
	CMA (UK)				
LT82	Hammer Horror Series 2	1996		20p	£16.00
LT74	Hammer Horror Entombed	2000		—	£20.00
	C.N.G. (New Zealand)				
M10	Trees of New Zealand	1992		—	£9.00
	C.S. LTD (Comet Sweets)				
50	Footballers and Club Colours	1963		£1.80	—
25	Record Holders of the World 1st Series	1962		60p	£15.00
25	Ships Through the Ages 1st Series	1963	HX-94	£1.40	—
25	Ships Through the Ages 2nd Series	1963	HX-94	£1.40	—
	CADBURY BROS. LTD				
EL12	Antarctic Series	c1915	HC-11	£34.00	—
EL6	Bay City Rollers	1975		£2.00	£12.00
L12	Birds in Springtime	1983		—	£3.50
6	Bourneville Series B	c1905		£22.00	—
6	Bourneville Village Series	c1905		£22.00	—
EL25	British Birds (Reward Cards)	c1910	HC-12	£12.00	—
12	British Birds and Eggs	c1910	HC-13	£16.00	—
EL12	British Birds and Their Eggs (Reward Cards)	c1910	HC-14	£15.00	—
EL32	British Butterflies and Moths (Reward Cards)	c1910	HC-15	£9.00	—
6	British Colonies, Maps and Industries	c1910		£25.00	—
120	British Marvels Vol. I	1936		£2.25	—
120	British Marvels Vol. II	1936		£2.25	—
12	British Trees Series	1911		£8.00	—
80	Cadbury's Picture Making	c1935		£2.25	—
	Cathedral Series:				
12	A Standard size (size 65 x 37mm)	1913		£8.00	—
EL6	B Strip of two (size 165 x 37mm)	1913		£20.00	—
EL6	C Strip of two (size 150 x 37mm)	1913		£20.00	—
6	Colonial Premiers Series	c1910		£25.00	—
	Constellations Series:				
12	A Standard size (size 65 x 37mm)	1912		£10.00	—
EL6	B Strip of two (size 152 x 36mm)	1912		£16.00	—
24	Copyright (Inventors) Series	c1915		£16.00	—
	Coronation:				
1	A Size 73 x 34mm	1911		—	£30.00
EL1	B Size 149 x 38mm	1911		—	£40.00

Size & quantity	TRADE CARD ISSUES	Date	Handbook reference	Price per card	Complete set
	CADBURY BROS. LTD (continued)				
48	Dangerous Animals	1970		45p	£22.50
6	Dogs Series	c1910		£40.00	—
EL12	English Industries	c1910	HC-19	£32.00	—
25	Fairy Tales	1924		£4.60	—
27	Famous Steamships	1923		£4.60	—
12	Fish	c1910	HC-20	£16.00	—
EL6	Fish and Bait Series	c1910		£38.00	—
	Flag Series (horizontal):				
12	A Standard size (size 65 × 36mm)	1912		£4.00	—
EL6	B Strips of Two (size 150 × 36mm)	1912		£8.00	—
	Flag Series (vertical):				
EL12	A Size 107 × 35mm	1912		£30.00	—
EL12	B Size 146 × 50mm	1912		£30.00	—
EL12	Flight, The World's Most Spectacular Birds	1983		—	£6.00
1	Largest Steamers in the World	c1905		—	£100.00
6	Locomotive Series	c1910		£40.00	—
12	Match Puzzles	c1905		£38.00	—
6	Old Ballad Series	c1905		£26.00	—
EL6	Panama Series	1914		£30.00	—
EL5	Pop Stars	1975		£1.50	—
EL8	Prehistoric Monsters	1975		£1.50	£12.00
EL6	Rivers of the British Isles	c1910	HC-26	£17.00	—
24	Shadow Series	c1915		£17.00	—
6	Shipping Series:				
	A Size 84 × 40mm	c1910		£16.00	—
	B Size 134 × 58mm	c1910		£16.00	—
	C Size 153 × 39mm	c1910		£16.00	—
	D Size 164 × 81mm	c1910		£16.00	—
EL6	Sports Series	c1905		£55.00	—
24	Strange But True	1969		20p	£3.50
	Album			—	£20.00
25	Transport	1925		50p	£12.50
M6	Wildlife Stickers	1986		75p	—
	CADBURY-SCHWEPPES FOODS LTD				
12	The Age of the Dinosaur	1971		60p	£7.00
	Folder/Album			—	£10.00
	CADET (Sweets)				
48	Adventures of Rin Tin Tin:				
	A Size 60 × 32mm	1960		£1.20	—
	B Size 65 × 37mm:				
	i 'Cadet Sweets' in two lines	1960		60p	£30.00
	ii 'Cadet Sweets' in one line	1960		£1.50	—
25	Arms and Armour	1960		20p	£3.50
50	Buccaneers:		HC-29A		
	A Size 58 × 30mm	1959		£1.00	—
	B Size 63 × 33mm	1959		50p	£25.00
50	Buccaneers (different Series) (size 65 × 35mm)	1959	HC-29B	60p	£30.00
50	Conquest of Space:		HX-73		
	A Size 64 × 35mm	1957		70p	—
	B Size 69 × 37mm	1957		40p	£20.00
25	Daktari	1968		40p	£10.00
50	Doctor Who and The Daleks	1965		£4.00	£200.00
25	Dogs 1st Series:				
	A Size 60 × 32mm	1958		50p	£12.50
	B Size 65 × 35mm	1958		£3.50	—
25	Dogs 2nd Series:				
	A Size 60 × 32mm	1958		50p	£12.50
	B Size 65 × 35mm	1958		£3.50	—

234

Size & quantity	TRADE CARD ISSUES	Date	Handbook reference	Price per card	Complete set
	CADET (Sweets) (continued)				
25	Evolution of the Royal Navy	1960	HX-90	20p	£5.00
22	Famous Explorers (Package Issue)	c1960		£10.00	—
50	Fifty Years of Flying	1954		£1.40	£70.00
50	Footballers Size 66 x 35mm	1957		70p	£35.00
50	Footballers Size 61 x 31mm. Title 28mm, large text print inverted backs	1958		50p	£25.00
50	Footballers Size 61 x 31mm. Title 19mm, small text print	1959		50p	£25.00
50	Footballers Size 61 x 31mm. Title 28mm, small text print, standard backs	c1960		£5.00	—
25	How?	1968		36p	£9.00
50	Motor Cars	1954		£2.00	—
25	Prehistoric Animals	1961	HX-92	£1.20	—
50	Railways of the World	1955		30p	£15.00
50	Record Holders of the World	1956		35p	£17.50
50	Stingray	1965		£1.00	£50.00
K48	Transfers All Sports	1959		£7.00	—
K48	Transfers Footballers	1959		£7.00	—
25	Treasure Hunt	1964		20p	£4.50
50	UNCLE (TV Series):				
	A Photos	1966		£1.50	£75.00
	B Drawings	1966		£2.50	—
25	What Do You Know?	1965	HX-67	60p	£15.00
	A.J. CALEY & SON				
K24	Film Stars	c1930	HC-34	£10.00	—
48	Mickey Mouse Wisequacks	1939		£14.00	—
L50	Tricks & Puzzles	c1930		£7.50	—
	CALFUN INC (Canada)				
LT100	Fantazy Cards (Pin Up Girls)	1992		—	£15.00
	CALICO GRAPHICS (USA)				
LT54	League of Nations 2nd Series	1990		—	£10.00
EL1	League of Nations 2nd Series advert card	1990		—	£1.00
	CALRAB (USA)				
LT24	The California Raisins World Tour	1988		—	£6.00
	CALTEX OIL (Australia)				
EL6	Stargazer (Haley's Comet)	1986		75p	£4.50
	F.C. CALVERT & CO. LTD (Tooth Powder)				
K25	Dan Dare	1954		£5.00	£125.00
	Album			—	£50.00
	CANDY GUM				
M50	Auto Sprint 1st Series	1975		30p	—
M30	Auto Sprint 2nd Series	1975		25p	£7.50
	CANDY NOVELTY CO.				
25	Animals of the Countryside	1960	HX-9	£6.00	—
50	Animals of the World	c1960	HX-93	£5.00	—
M50	Dog Series A.1:				
	A Complete set	c1955		£1.50	—
	B 25 different	c1955		20p	£4.00
	Album			—	£25.00

Size & quantity		TRADE CARD ISSUES	Date	Handbook reference	Price per card	Complete set
		CANDY NOVELTY CO. (continued)				
32		Motor Car Series:				
	A	Blue green	c1953		£7.50	—
	B	Orange	c1953		£7.50	—
25		Ships through the Ages 2nd Series...................	c1960	HX-94	£6.50	—
32		Western Series:				
	A	Black on blue green	c1953		£7.50	—
	B	Green on blue green	c1953		£7.50	—
		CANNING'S				
25		Types of British Soldiers	c1914	HX-144	£22.00	—
		CANNON PRESS				
10		Screen Gems David Niven	2010		—	£5.00
20		Screen Gems Lana Turner	2009		—	£9.00
20		Screen Gems Natalie Wood...............................	2009		—	£9.00
10		Screen Gems Rock Hudson	2010		—	£5.00
10		Screen Gems Will Hay	2009		—	£5.00
10		Treasure Island	2009		—	£5.00
		CAPERN (Bird Food)				
7		Cage Birds (blue backgrounds)	c1920	HC-43B	£14.00	—
7		Cage Birds (white backgrounds).........................	c1920	HC-43A	£14.00	—
		Cage Birds:		HC-44		
EL51	A	Plain back	c1925		£5.50	—
	B	Postcard back:				
EL11		i With bird sketches on left of back	c1925		£6.00	—
EL7		ii Without bird sketches on back..................	c1925		£6.00	—
EL1	C	Text back	c1925		£9.00	—
24		Capern Picture Aviary	1964		£1.25	—
		Album			—	£20.00
1		Capern Picture Aviary Introductory Card	1964			25p
		CAR AND DRIVER (USA)				
EL100		Cadillac Collection	1993		—	£15.00
		CARAMAC				
M42		Railway Locomotives	1976		50p	£21.00
		CARD CRAZY (New Zealand)				
LT90		High Velocity New Zealand Cricketers................	1996		20p	£15.00
LT90		New Zealand Rugby League Superstars	1995		20p	£12.00
LT110		New Zealand Rugby Union Superstars	1995		20p	£12.00
LT10		Rugby Superstars Express Delivery Chase Set (Rugby Union)	1996		—	£15.00
LT5		Rugby Superstars Super 12 Logos Chase Set (Rugby Union)	1996		—	£10.00
LT3		Rugby Superstars Factor J Jonah Lomu Chase Set (Rugby Union)	1996		—	£15.00
LT8		Rugby Superstars Terminators Chase Set (Rugby Union)	1996		—	£12.00
LT55		Shortland Street (TV Series)	1995		—	£8.00

CARD COLLECTORS SOCIETY – See Section 3 Reprint Series

		CARD CREATIONS (USA)				
LT100		Popeye	1994		—	£12.00

Size & quantity	TRADE CARD ISSUES	Date	Handbook reference	Price per card	Complete set
	CARD INSERT LTD				
1	Famous Footballers (only No.12 issued)	c1955		—	£9.00
	CARDLYNX				
EL6	Bookmarks High Grade Series	2008		—	£4.50
L6	Butterflies	2007		—	£3.00
L6	Eagles	2007		—	£3.00
L6	Gangsters	2005		—	£3.00
L6	Golfers	2006		—	£3.00
L6	Horses	2007		—	£3.00
L6	Jazz Greats	2005		—	£3.00
L6	Lighthouses	2008		—	£3.00
L6	Owls	2004		—	£3.00
L6	Parrots	2004		—	£3.00
L6	Poultry	2005		—	£3.00
L6	Poultry Breeds	2007		—	£3.00
L6	Sea Shells	2008		—	£3.00
L6	Space Firsts	2004		—	£3.00
EL6	UFOs & Aliens From Space	2010		—	£4.50
L6	Victorian Poultry	2007		—	£3.00
EL6	Wild West Outlaws	2013		—	£4.50
EL6	Wizards Past, Present & Future/ World's Most Valuable Baseball Cards	2010		—	£4.50
	CARDS INC				
LT72	Beyblade	2000		—	£9.50
LT72	Captain Scarlet	2002		20p	£9.50
LT72	Harry Potter and The Prisoner of Azkaban	2004		20p	£9.50
LT17	Harry Potter and The Prisoner of Azkaban Foil Series	2004		25p	£5.00
LT72	The Prisoner Volume 1 (1960/70s TV Series)	2002		—	£12.00
LT30	Scarface The Film	2003		—	£9.50
LT72	Shrek 2 The Film:				
	A Standard Series	2004		20p	£12.00
	B Foil Parallel Series	2004		40p	£30.00
LT72	Thunderbirds	2001		20p	£9.50
LT72	Thunderbirds The Movie	2004		—	£11.00
LT100	U.F.O. (TV Series)	2004		—	£12.00
LT100	The Very Best of The Saint	2003		—	£12.00
	CARDTOON CREATIONS				
24	Championship Champions 2005-2006 (Reading F.C.)	2006		—	£8.00
	CARDTOONS (USA)				
LT95	Baseball Parodies	1993		—	£8.00
LT9	Baseball Parodies Field of Greed Puzzle	1993		—	£3.00
LT11	Baseball Parodies Politics in Baseball	1993		—	£3.00
	CARDZ (USA)				
LT100	Hitchhiker's Guide to the Galaxy (Cartoon)	1994		—	£14.00
LT50	Lee MacLeod — Fantasy Art	1994		—	£8.50
LT10	Lee MacLeod Tekchrome Nos T1 to T10 — Fantasy Art	1994		—	£8.50
LT100	The Mask — The Film	1994		—	£9.50
LT60	Maverick — The Movie	1994		—	£9.50
LT60	The Muppets	1993		—	£12.00
LT80	Muppets Take The Ice	1994		—	£9.50

Size & quantity	TRADE CARD ISSUES	Date	Handbook reference	Price per card	Complete set
	CARDZ (USA) (continued)				
LT60	Return of The Flintstones	1994		—	£9.50
LT110	San Diego Zoo	1993		—	£12.00
LT60	Tiny Toons Adventures	1994		—	£9.50
LT60	Tom & Jerry	1993		—	£12.00
LT100	WCW Main Event (Wrestling)	1995		—	£12.00
LT100	William Shatner's Tek World	1993		—	£10.00
LT100	World War II	1994		—	£10.00
LT10	World War II Tekchrome Nos T1-T10	1994		—	£4.00
	CARNATION (Tinned Milk)				
EL12	Recipe Service	1971		35p	£4.50
	CARR'S BISCUITS				
EL20	Cricketers	1968		£9.00	—
EL48	Sporting Champions	1966		£9.00	—
EL20	Sports — Soccer Card Series	c1967		£13.00	—
	CARSON'S CHOCOLATE				
72	Celebrities	1901	HC-48	£20.00	—
	CARTER'S LITTLE LIVER PILLS				
28	Dominoes	c1910		£2.25	—
	F.C. CARTLEDGE				
L96	Epigrams (Rheuma Salts)	c1939		21p	£20.00
L48	Epigrams (Knock-out Razor Blades)	1939	HC-52	20p	£10.00
L12	Epigrams (without maker's name)	c1939	HC-53	—	£10.00
L64	Epigrams (without product)	1942	HC-54	20p	£12.00
50	Famous Prize Fighters:				
	A Complete set (matt)	1938		—	£160.00
	B 49/50 (—No. 23) (matt)	1938		£2.50	£125.00
	C 2 variety cards (matt) (Nos 13 & 19)	1939		—	£8.00
	D Complete set (glossy)	1938		£3.50	—
	CASEY CARDS				
10	The Casey (Football Stars of the 1960s)	2010		—	£5.00
	CASH & CO.				
20	War Pictures	c1910	HX-122	£22.00	—
	CASSELL'S				
M6	British Engines	c1925		£13.00	—
M12	Butterflies and Moths Series	c1925		£8.50	—
	CASTROL OIL				
L18	Famous Riders (motorcyclists)	1956	HC-59	£5.00	£90.00
L24	Racing Cars	1955		£4.00	—
	CAVE, AUSTIN & CO. LTD				
20	Inventors Series	1928	HX-213	£13.00	—
	C.E.D.E. LTD				
25	Coins of the World	1956	HX-6	20p	£4.50

Size & quantity	TRADE CARD ISSUES	Date	Handbook reference	Price per card	Complete set
	CENTRAL ELECTRICITY AUTHORITY				
M10	Careers in the Central Electricity Board	1957	HC-61	35p	£3.50
	CEREAL PARTNERS				
L44	Digital Digimon Monsters (Numbered CP1 TO CP44)	1999		60p	—
EL6	Disney Hercules (3-D)	1997		£2.00	—
	CEREBOS				
100	Sea Shells:				
	A Brown back:				
	i 'Bisto the Gravy Maker' back	1925		£3.00	—
	ii 'Cerebos Blanc Mange' back	1925		£3.00	—
	iii 'Cerebos Custard' back	1925		£3.00	—
	iv 'Cerebos Health Saline' back	1925		£3.00	—
	v 'Cerebos Jelly Crystals' back	1925		£3.00	—
	vi 'Cerebos Jelly Tablets' back	1925		£3.00	—
	vii 'Cerebos Salt' back	1925		£3.00	—
	viii 'Saxa Salt' back	1925		£3.00	—
	ix 'To Collectors' back	1925		£3.00	—
	B Grey back	1925		£4.50	—
	CEYLON TEA CENTRE				
24	Island of Ceylon	1955	HX-47	20p	£3.50
	Album			—	£20.00
	CHAMPS (USA)				
LT100	American Vintage Cycles Series 1	1992		—	£12.00
LT100	American Vintage Cycles Series 2	1993		—	£12.00
	CHANNEL 4/CHEERLEADER				
L20	All Time Great Quarterbacks	1989		£1.25	£25.00
	H. CHAPPEL & CO.				
?10	British Celebrities...................................	1905	HC-65	£38.00	—
? 8	Characters from Nursery Rhymes	1905	HB-17	£48.00	—
	CHARTER TEA & COFFEE CO LTD				
25	Prehistoric Animals 1st Series	c1965	HX-151	£1.40	—
25	Prehistoric Animals 2nd Series	c1965	HX-151	£1.40	—
25	Strange but True 1st Series	1961	HX-96	£1.00	£25.00
25	Strange but True 2nd Series	1961	HX-96	80p	£20.00
25	Transport Through the Ages 1st Series	c1965	HX-97	90p	£22.50
25	Transport Through the Ages 2nd Series	c1965	HX-97	70p	£17.50
	Album for 1st and 2nd Series combined			—	£20.00
	CHEF & BREWER				
L20	Historic Pub Signs	1984		£1.00	—
	CHESDALE (New Zealand)				
M6	Action Sports	1983		75p	£4.50
	CHIVERS & SONS LTD				
M10	Firm Favourites 1st Series.............................	c1930		£4.00	—
M10	Firm Favourites 2nd Series	c1930		£4.00	—
M10	Firm Favourites 3rd Series	c1930		£4.00	—
M95	Firm Favourites (Nos 31 to 125).....................	c1930		£3.00	—
K53	Miniature Playing Cards	c1965		£3.00	—

Size & quantity	TRADE CARD ISSUES	Date	Handbook reference	Price per card	Complete set
	CHIVERS & SONS LTD (continued)				
EL6	Studies of English Fruits (Series 1)	c1930		£6.00	—
EL6	Studies of English Fruits (Series 2)	c1930		£6.00	—
24	Wild Wisdom	c1960		£5.00	—
48	Wild Wisdom in Africa	c1960		£5.00	—
48	Wild Wisdom, River and Marsh	c1960		£5.00	—
	PACKAGE ISSUES:				
L15	Children of Other Lands	c1955		£1.50	—
L15	Chivers British Birds	c1955		£1.50	—
	Album			—	£20.00
L20	On Chivers Farms	c1955		£1.50	—
	Album			—	£20.00
	CHIX CONFECTIONERY CO. LTD				
M12	Batman P.C. inset (Package issue)	1989		50p	£6.00
M48	Facts & Feats (Waxed Paper issue)	c1960		£5.50	—
	Famous Footballers No.1 Series:				
L24	A Inscribed 'Set of 48' (Nos 1-24 only issued)	1955		£5.00	—
L24	B Inscribed 'Numbers 1 to 24'	1955		£5.00	—
L24	C Inscribed 'Numbers 25 to 48'	1955		£5.00	—
L48	D Inscribed 'Numbers 1 to 48'	1955		£5.00	—
L48	Famous Footballers 2nd Series	1957		£6.00	—
L48	Famous Footballers 3rd Series	1958		£7.00	—
L50	Famous Footballers	1961		£7.00	—
L50	Famous Last Words	1969		£2.00	—
L48	Footballers (double picture):				
	A 'Ask for Chix' back	1960		£2.00	—
	B Anonymous Back:				
	i Caricature on left Black & White	1960		£1.00	£50.00
	ii Caricature on left Pink tinted	1960		£3.00	—
L50	Funny Old Folk	1970		90p	£45.00
L50	Happy Howlers	1969		£1.20	—
L6	Joker P.C. inset (Double Package issue)	1990		£1.50	£9.00
L50	Krazy Kreatures from Outer Space	1968		£2.50	£125.00
L50	Military Uniforms	1969		£1.00	—
L50	Moon Shot	1966		£3.50	—
L50	Popeye	1959		£5.50	—
L24	Scottish Footballers (SFBL 1 back)	c1960		£11.00	—
L50	Ships of the Seven Seas	1964		£2.50	—
L50	Soldiers of the World	1960		£1.80	—
L50	Sports Through the Ages	1963		£4.00	—
96	TV and Radio Stars	1955		£4.25	£425.00
L50	Wild Animals	c1960		£2.00	—
	CHOCOLAT DE VILLARS				
24	British Birds and Their Eggs	1926	HX-164	£6.00	£150.00
	CHUMS				
MP23	'Chums' Cricketers	1923		£6.00	—
MP20	'Chums' Football Teams	1922		£4.50	—
P8	'Chums' Football Teams, New Series	c1925		£4.50	—
LP10	'Chums' Real Colour Photos	c1925		£8.00	—
	CHURCH & DWIGHT (USA)				
M60	Beautiful Flowers, New Series	c1888		£4.50	—
EL10	Birds of Prey	1975		—	£25.00
M30	Fish Series	1900		£4.50	—

Size & quantity	TRADE CARD ISSUES	Date	Handbook reference	Price per card	Complete set
	CHURCH & DWIGHT (USA) (continued)				
M30	New Series of Birds	1908		£4.00	—
M30	Useful Birds of America (no series number)	1915		£4.00	—
M30	Useful Birds of America 1st Series	1915		£3.25	—
M30	Useful Birds of America 2nd Series	1918		£3.25	—
M30	Useful Birds of America 3rd Series	1922		£3.25	—
M30	Useful Birds of America 4th Series	1924		£3.25	—
M15	Useful Birds of America 5th Series	1928		£3.25	—
M15	Useful Birds of America 6th Series	1931		£3.25	—
M15	Useful Birds of America 7th Series	1933		£3.25	—
M15	Useful Birds of America 8th Series	1936		£3.25	—
M15	Useful Birds of America 9th Series	1938		£1.20	£18.00
M15	Useful Birds of America 10th Series	1938		£1.20	£18.00
	THE CITY BAKERIES LTD				
8	The European War Series	1916	HX-129	£55.00	—
4	Shadow Series	1916		£50.00	—
	CLARNICO (CLARKE, NICKHOLLS & COOMBS)				
30	Colonial Troops	c1910	HX-100	£34.00	—
25	Great War Leaders	c1915	HC-101	£28.00	—
29	Wolf Cubs	c1910		£55.00	—
	CLASSIC COLLECTIONS				
50	Newcastle United FC (Football)	1993		50p	—
	CLASSIC GAMES INC. (USA)				
LT100	Deathwatch 2000	1993		—	£9.50
LT50	McDonalds History	1996		—	£9.50
LT150	WWF The History of Wrestle Mania Series 2	1990		—	£15.00
LT150	World Wrestling Federation Superstars	1991		—	£15.00
	CLEARY'S (Australia)				
50	Flags & Funnels of Australian Registered Shipping Companies 1st Series	2014		—	£8.50
	CLEVEDON CONFECTIONERY LTD				
K50	British Aircraft:				
	A Title in one line	1956		£4.00	—
	B Title in two lines	1956		£4.00	—
K25	British Orders of Chivalry and Valour:				
	A Black back	1960		£7.50	—
	B Blue back	1960		£7.50	—
K50	British Ships	1956		£4.20	—
M50	British Trains and Engines	1958		£10.00	—
K25	Dan Dare:				
	A Back in black	1960		£10.00	—
	B Back in dark/violet blue	1960		£10.00	—
	C Back in light blue	1960		£10.00	—
K40	Did You Know?	1957		£6.00	—
K40	Famous Cricketers	c1960		£16.00	—
K25	Famous Cricketers	c1960		£16.00	—
K50	Famous Football Clubs	1961		£7.00	—
K50	Famous Footballers	1961		£10.00	—
K50	Famous International Aircraft	1963	HX-98	£2.00	—
M50	Famous Screen Stars, Series A.1	1959		£5.00	—
K40	Film Stars	1958		£5.00	—

Size & quantity	TRADE CARD ISSUES	Date	Handbook reference	Price per card	Complete set
	CLEVEDON CONFECTIONERY LTD (continued)				
K50	Football Club Managers:				
	A Background in blue	1961		£20.00	—
	B Background in mauve	1961		£20.00	—
K50	Hints on Association Football:				
	A Black back & front	1957		£5.00	—
	B Blue back, coloured front	1957		£5.00	—
	C Blue back & front	1957		£10.00	—
K50	Hints on Road Safety	1958		£4.00	—
K50	International Sporting Stars	1960		£6.50	—
M50	Regimental Badges	1956		£4.50	—
EL25	Sporting Memories	1960		£18.00	—
K50	The Story of the Olympics	1960		£4.00	—
K50	Trains of the World:				
	A Back in blue	1962		£4.00	—
	B Back in violet	1962		£4.00	—
	CLEVELAND PETROL				
K16	Campaign Medals (Metal Coins) (19mm diiameter)	1972		£2.00	—
EL20	Golden Goals (numbered 1-41)	1972		£1.50	—
	Album			—	£20.00
	CLIFFORD				
50	Footballers	c1950		£27.00	—
	CLOVER DAIRIES LTD				
25	Animals and Reptiles	1965	HX-99	20p	£4.00
25	British Rail	1973	HX-107	20p	£3.50
25	People and Places	1970	HX-26	20p	£3.50
25	Prehistoric Animals	1966	HX-92	36p	£9.00
25	Science in the 20th Century	1965	HX-18	20p	£4.50
25	Ships and Their Workings	1966	HX-85	20p	£4.50
25	The Story of Milk	1964	HX-3	50p	£12.50
25	Transport Through the Ages	1967	HX-101	20p	£4.00
	COACH HOUSE STUDIOS				
50	Railway Locomotives	1987		50p	—
	COCA-COLA (UK)				
LT10	Football Match World Cup USA (scratch cards)	1994		—	£4.00
LT49	Football World Cup (yellow back)	2002		—	£15.00
	COCA-COLA (South Africa)				
M100	Our Flower Paradise	1964		55p	£55.00
	COCA-COLA (USA)				
	The World of Nature:				
EL12	Series I — Earth and Air and Sky	c1960		£2.00	—
EL12	Series II — Man's Closest Friends and Most Inveterate Enemies	c1960		£2.00	—
EL12	Series III — Trees and Other Plants Useful to Man	c1960		£2.00	—
EL12	Series IV — Some Common Wild Flowers	c1960		£2.00	—
EL12	Series V — Among Our Feathered Friends	c1960		£2.00	—
EL12	Series VI — Native Wild Animals	c1960		£2.00	—
EL12	Series VII — Life In and Around the Water	c1960		£2.00	—
EL12	Series VIII — Insects, Helpful and Harmful	c1960		£2.00	—

Size & quantity	TRADE CARD ISSUES	Date	Handbook reference	Price per card	Complete set
	COFTON COLLECTIONS				
L7	Alice in Wonderland	2002	—		£3.50
15	Birmingham City F.C. Stars of The 1970s	2007	—		£6.00
25	Dogs 1st Series	1988		30p	—
25	Dogs 2nd Series	1988		30p	£7.50
25	Dogs 3rd Series	1988		30p	—
L25	Nursery Rhymes	1992	—		£7.50
15	West Brom. Heroes & Legends (Footballers)	2012	—		£6.00
L20	Worcestershire County Cricketers	1989	—		£7.50
	CECIL COLEMAN LTD				
24	Film Stars	c1935		£10.00	—
	COLGATE-PALMOLIVE				
EL4	Coronation Souvenir	1953		£2.50	£10.00
M24	Famous Sporting Trophies	1979		27p	£6.50
	Album			—	£6.00
	COLINVILLE LTD				
L28	Fantasy of Space 1st Series	1956		£14.00	—
L28	Fantasy of Space 2nd Series	1956		£14.00	—
K48	Football Internationals British (size 28 x 20mm)	1958	HC-111	£10.00	—
L25	Prairie Pioneers	1960		£8.00	—
K36	TV 6 5 Special Stars and Guests (size 28 x 20mm)	1958	HC-112	£7.00	—
	COLLECT-A-CARD (USA)				
LT50	Adventures of Ronald McDonald — McDonald Land 500	1996	—		£7.50
LT100	American Bandstand (T.V. Music Show)	1993	—		£12.00
LT72	The Campbell's (Soup) Collection	1995	—		£9.50
LT120	Centennial Olympic Games	1996	—		£9.50
LT100	The Coca Cola Collection 2nd Series	1994	—		£15.00
K8	The Coca Cola Collection 2nd Series Coke Caps	1994	—		£4.00
LT100	The Coca Cola Collection 3rd Series	1994	—		£12.50
LT100	The Coca Cola Collection 4th Series	1995	—		£12.50
LT50	The Coca Cola Polar Bears South Pole Vacation	1996	—		£9.50
LT60	Coca Cola Super Premium Series	1995	—		£12.00
LT100	Country (Music) Classics	1992	—		£9.50
LT72	Dinotopia — Fantasy Art Dinosaurs	1995	—		£9.50
LT100	Harley Davidson Series 2	1992	—		£9.50
LT100	Harley Davidson Series 3	1993	—		£9.50
LT100	King Pins (Ten Pin Bowling)	1990	—		£10.00
LT50	Norfin Trolls	1992	—		£6.00
LT72	Power Rangers 1st Series	1994	—		£9.50
LT72	Power Rangers 2nd Series	1994	—		£9.50
LT72	Power Rangers New Season	1994	—		£9.50
LT100	Stargate Plus Set LT12 Puzzle	1994	—		£9.50
LT100	Vette Set (Corvette Cars)	1991	—		£9.50
LT10	Vette Set (Corvette Cars) Bonus Series	1991	—		£4.00
	COLLECTABLE PICTURES				
L13	England Win The Ashes 2005 (Cricket)	2005	—		£8.50
L15	England Win Cricket World Cup	2019	—		£10.00
L20	Liverpool F.C. European Champions 2005	2005	—		£12.00
L20	Liverpool F.C. European Champions 2019	2019	—		£12.00
L20	Liverpool F.C League Champions 2020	2021	—		£15.00
L8	Star Trek (The Original Series)	2019	—		£7.50
L7	Views of Bath	2005	—		£5.00

Size & quantity	TRADE CARD ISSUES	Date	Handbook reference	Price per card	Complete set
	COLLECTABLES OF SPALDING				
25	British Cavalry Uniforms	1987		30p	—
25	Military Maids	1987		30p	—
25	Warriors Through the Ages	1987		30p	£7.50
	THE COLLECTOR AND DEALER MAGAZINE				
6	Animal Series	1953		£3.00	—
	THE COLLECTOR & HOBBYIST				
25	Fascinating Hobbies:		HX-74		
	A Cream Card	1950		60p	£15.00
	B White Card	1950		20p	£3.50
	COLLECTORS' CORNER				
L20	Halifax As It Was	1989		30p	£6.00
	COLLECTORS FARE				
16	Reading Football Club Simod Cup Winners	1990		—	£9.00
EL16	Reading Football Club Simod Cup Winners	1990		—	£6.00
	COLLECTORS SHOP				
25	Bandsmen of the British Army	1960	HX-62	£1.40	—
	COLONIAL BREAD (USA)				
LT33	Star Trek The Motion Picture	1979		—	£12.00
	COMET (Sweets)				
25	Armand & Michaela Denis on Safari 1st Series	1961		40p	£10.00
25	Armand & Michaela Denis on Safari 2nd Series	1961		40p	£10.00
25	Modern Wonders:		HX-130		
	A Black back	1961		20p	£4.50
	B Blue back	1961		80p	—
25	Olympic Achievements 1st Series	1959		70p	£17.50
25	Olympic Achievements 2nd Series	1959		70p	£17.50
	COMIC ENTERPRISES				
L15	Superman Action Comics	2005		—	£6.50
	COMIC IMAGES (USA)				
LT70	The Art of Coca Cola	1999		—	£9.50
LT90	The Beast Within — Ken Barr Fantasy Art	1994		—	£9.50
LT72	The Beatles — Yellow Submarine	1999		—	£16.00
LT90	Beyond Bizarre — Jim Warren Surrealism Fantasy Art	1993		—	£12.00
LT90	Bill Ward (Saucy Cartoons)	1994		—	£14.00
LT90	Blueprints of The Future - Vincent Di Fate Fantasy Art	1994		—	£9.50
LT90	Bone	1994		—	£9.50
LT90	The Brothers Hildebrandt — Fantasy Art	1994		—	£9.50
LT72	The Cat In The Hat — The Film	2003		—	£9.50
LT72	Coca Cola — The Art of Haddon Sundblom	2001		—	£12.00
LT90	Colossal Conflicts (Marvel Heroes & Villains) Series 2	1987		—	£12.00
LT72	Comic Greats 98	1998		—	£9.50
LT90	Conan The Marvel Years	1996		—	£12.00
LT72	Crimson Embrace — Adult Fantasy Art	1998		—	£9.50
LT72	Dark Horse Presents Ghost	1997		—	£9.50
LT72	Elvira Mistress of Omnichrome	1997		—	£14.00
LT72	Final Fantasy — The Spirits Within	2001		—	£9.50
LT90	Frazetta II The Legend Continues — Fantasy Art	1993		—	£9.50
LT90	Greg Hildebrandt II — 30 Years of Magic	1993		—	£9.50

Size & quantity	TRADE CARD ISSUES	Date	Handbook reference	Price per card	Complete set

COMIC IMAGES (USA) (continued)

Size & quantity	Title	Date		Price	Complete set
LT90	Harlem Globetrotters	1992		—	£9.50
LT90	Hildebrandt (Fantasy Art)	1992		—	£12.00
LT90	Jack Kirby The Unpublished Archives — Fantasy Art	1994		—	£9.50
LT72	Judgment Day (cartoon)	1997		—	£9.50
LT72	Julie Strain Queen of the 'B' Movies	1996		—	£12.00
LT72	Madagascar The Film	2005		—	£9.50
LT90	Magnificent Myths — Boris 4 Fantasy Art	1994		—	£9.50
LT90	Maxfield Parrish Portrait of America — Fantasy Art	1994		—	£9.50
LT61	Meanie Babies	1998		—	£9.50
LT90	Moebius — Fantasy Art	1993		—	£9.50
LT90	More Than Battlefield Earth - Ron Hubbard Fantasy Art	1994		—	£9.50
LT72	The New American Pin Up (Pin Up Girls)	1997		—	£12.00
LT90	Olivia (Adult Fantasy Art)	1992		—	£15.00
LT72	Olivia 98 (Adult Fantasy Art)	1998		—	£12.00
LT72	Olivia Obsessions in Omnichrome (Adult Fantasy Art)	1997		—	£12.00
LT72	Olivia 2 All Prism (Adult Fantasy Art)	1993		—	£20.00
LT90	Other Worlds — Michael Whelan Fantasy Art	1995		—	£12.00
LT90	Other Worlds — Michael Whelan II Fantasy Art	1995		—	£9.50
LT72	The Painted Cow	1997		—	£9.50
LT90	The Phantom	1995		—	£9.50
LT90	Prince Valiant	1995		—	£9.50
LT90	Richard Corben Fantasy Art	1993		—	£12.00
LT72	The Rock's Greatest Matches — WWF	2000		—	£15.00
LT90	Ron Miller's Firebrands Heroines of Science Fiction & Fantasy	1994		—	£12.00
LT90	Sachs & Violens	1993		—	£9.50
LT90	The Savage Dragon	1992		—	£9.50
LT90	Shadow Hawk (Comic Book Art by Jim Valentino)	1992		—	£9.50
LT90	Shi Visions of The Golden Empire	1996		—	£9.50
LT72	Shrek 2 The Film	2004		—	£9.50
LT70	South Park	1998		—	£9.50
LT90	Species — The Movie	1995		—	£9.50
LT90	Spiderman The McFarlane Era	1992		—	£9.50
LT90	Spiderman II 30th Anniversary	1992		—	£9.50
LT90	Strangers in Paradise	1996		—	£9.50
LT90	Supreme — Adult Fantasy Art	1996		—	£9.50
LT72	Terminator 3 Rise of The Machines — The Movie	2003		—	£9.50
LT90	30th Salute G.I. Joe	1994		—	£9.50
LT90	24 — TV Series	2003		—	£12.00
LT90	Ujena Swimwear Illustrated	1993		—	£9.50
LT90	Ujena Swimwear Illustrated	1994		—	£9.50
LT90	Unity Time Is Not Absolute	1992		—	£9.50
LT72	Van Helsing — The Film	2004		—	£9.50
LT90	William Stout 2 (Fantasy Art etc)	1994		—	£9.50
LT90	Wolverine From Then Till Now II	1992		—	£9.50
LT81	World Wrestling Federation No Mercy	2000		—	£12.00
LT90	Young Blood (Super Heroes)	1992		—	£9.50

COMIC LIFE

MP4	Sports Champions	1922		£8.00	—

COMMODEX (Gum)

M88	Operation Moon	1969		£2.50	—
L120	Super Cars	1970		£2.50	—

COMMONWEALTH SHOE & LEATHER CO. (USA)

M12	Makes of Planes	c1930		£4.00	—

Size & quantity	TRADE CARD ISSUES	Date	Handbook reference	Price per card	Complete set
	COMO CONFECTIONERY PRODUCTS LTD				
K25	Adventures of Fireball XL5	c1970		£22.00	—
M25	History of the Wild West 1st Series	1960		£6.00	—
M25	History of the Wild West 2nd Series	1963		£1.40	£35.00
50	Lenny's Adventures	1960		£1.00	£50.00
50	Noddy and His Playmates	1962		£2.50	—
	Noddy's Adventures 1st Series:				
M25	A Size 63 × 63mm	1961		£4.00	—
K25	B Size 46 × 46mm	c1970		£7.00	—
M25	Noddy's Adventures 2nd Series	1961		£4.00	—
25	Noddy's Budgie and Feathered Friends 1st Series	1959		£4.00	—
25	Noddy's Budgie and Feathered Friends 2nd Series	1959		£4.00	—
	Noddy's Friends Abroad:				
M50	A Size 62 × 62mm	1959		£3.50	—
K25	B Size 46 × 46mm	c1970		£7.00	—
	Noddy's Nursery Rhyme Friends:				
M50	A Size 63 × 60mm	1959		£3.00	—
K25	B Size 46 × 46mm	c1970		£7.00	—
M50	Sooty's Adventures	1961		£3.00	—
25	Sooty's Latest Adventures 3rd Series, No.1-25				
	A Black back	c1960		£3.00	—
	B Blue back	c1960		£3.00	—
	C Navy blue back	c1960		£3.00	—
	D Red back	c1960		£3.00	—
25	Sooty's Latest Adventures 3rd Series, No. 26-50				
	A Black back	c1960		£3.00	—
	B Blue back	c1960		£3.00	—
	C Navy blue back	c1960		£3.00	—
	D Red back	c1960		£3.00	—
M50	Sooty's New Adventures 2nd Series	1961		£3.00	—
25	Speed 1st Series	1962	HX-153	£1.60	£40.00
25	Speed 2nd Series	1962	HX-153	80p	£20.00
	Album for 1st and 2nd Series combined			—	£30.00
25	Supercar 1st Series	1962		£10.00	—
25	Supercar 2nd Series	1962		£8.00	—
25	Top Secret 1st Series	1965		£3.40	—
25	Top Secret 2nd Series	1965		£3.40	—
M26	XL5 1st Series	1965		£26.00	—
M26	XL5 2nd Series	1966		£26.00	—
	COMPTONS				
22	Footballers Series A (coloured)	1925		£30.00	—
22	Footballers Series A (black and white)	1925		£30.00	—
22	Footballers Series B (coloured)	1925		£30.00	—
22	Footballers Series B (black and white)	1925		£30.00	—
22	Footballers Series C (coloured)	1925		£30.00	—
22	Footballers Series D (coloured)	1925		£30.00	—
	CONNOISSEUR POLICIES				
M25	The Dorking Collection (Antiques)	2004		—	£9.00
	CONTINENTAL CANDY CO. (UK)				
LT81	Snoots Nosy Bodies	1989		—	£9.50
	COOPER & CO. STORES LTD				
50	Do You Know?	1962	HX-166.1	20p	£8.00
25	Inventions and Discoveries 1st Series	1962	HX-131	£1.80	—
25	Inventions and Discoveries 2nd Series	1962	HX-131	£1.80	—

Size & quantity	TRADE CARD ISSUES	Date	Handbook reference	Price per card	Complete set
	COOPER & CO. STORES LTD (continued)				
25	Island of Ceylon	1958	HX-47	£6.00	—
25	Mysteries & Wonders of the World 1st Series	1960		60p	£15.00
25	Mysteries & Wonders of the World 2nd Series	1960		40p	£10.00
	Album for 1st and 2nd Series combined			—	£25.00
25	Prehistoric Animals 1st Series	1962	HX-151	£1.80	£45.00
25	Prehistoric Animals 2nd Series	1962	HX-151	£1.80	£45.00
25	Strange but True 1st Series	1960	HX-96	20p	£4.50
25	Strange but True 2nd Series	1960	HX-96	20p	£4.50
25	Transport Through the Ages 1st Series	1961	HX-97	36p	£9.00
25	Transport Through the Ages 2nd Series	1961	HX-97	40p	£10.00
	Album for 1st and 2nd Series combined			—	£25.00
	COORS BREWING CO. (USA)				
LT100	Coors	1995		—	£9.50
	CORNERSTONE MARKETING LTD				
LT8	Bestie 75 A Tribute to a Football Genius (George Best) Preview Set	2021		—	£10.00
LT75	Bestie 75 A Tribute to a Football Genius (George Best) Limited Edition	2021		—	£45.00
	CORNERSTONE (USA)				
LT72	Austin Powers The Spy Who Shagged Me — The Movie	1999		—	£9.50
LT90	The Avengers in Colour Series 2	1993		—	£15.00
LT81	The Avengers Return Series 3	1995		—	£15.00
LT110	Doctor Who 1st Series (TV Series)	1994		—	£25.00
LT110	Doctor Who 2nd Series (TV Series)	1995		—	£20.00
LT110	Doctor Who 3rd Series (TV Series)	1996		—	£15.00
LT90	Doctor Who 4th Series (TV Series)	1996		—	£17.50
LT90	Kiss Series 2, silver foil fronts (Pop Group)	1998		—	£12.00
LT81	Robot Carnival Masters of Japanese Animation	1994		—	£9.50
	COUNTY PRINT SERVICES				
M25	Australian Test Cricketers	1993		60p	£15.00
25	Australiian Test Cricketers 1876-1896	c1992		—	£40.00
EL48	County Cricket Teams 1900-1914	1992		—	£12.00
50	County Cricketers 1990	1990		50p	£25.00
LT72	County Cricketers Autograph Series Nos. 1 to 72	1993		20p	£12.50
LT72	County Cricketers Autograph Series Nos. 73 to 144	1993		20p	£12.50
LT72	County Cricketers Autograph Series Nos. 145 to 216	1993		20p	£12.50
M25	Cricket Caricatures	1991		£1.60	£40.00
20	Cricket Pavilions	1991		75p	£15.00
EL24	Cricket Teams 1884-1900	1990		—	£7.00
M25	Cricket's Golden Age	1991		40p	£10.00
EL12	Cricket's Pace Partners	1996		70p	£8.00
EL12	Cricket's Spin Twins	1996		—	£8.00
50	Cricketers 1890	1989		20p	£8.00
50	Cricketers 1896	1989		20p	£10.00
50	Cricketers 1900	1990		20p	£8.00
50	Cricketers 1906	1992		25p	£12.50
EL5	Cricketing Knights	1994		—	£15.00
L25	Derbyshire Test Cricketers	1994		—	£12.50
EL7	Durham County Cricket Club Pavilions (postcards)	1992		—	£7.00
14	England Cricket Team 1901-02	1991		90p	£12.00
14	England Cricket Team 1903-04	1991		35p	£4.50
15	England Cricket Team 1907-08	1992		£1.00	£15.00
17	England Cricket Team 1932-33	1995		30p	£6.00
16	England Cricket Team 1990-91	1990		40p	£6.00

Size & quantity	TRADE CARD ISSUES	Date	Handbook reference	Price per card	Complete set
	COUNTY PRINT SERVICES (continued)				
L25	Essex Test Cricketers	1993		—	£15.00
M27	Famous Cricket Crests	1992		60p	£15.00
M25	Famous Cricket Ties	1992		50p	£12.00
EL12	First Knock Cricket's Opening Pairs	1994		—	£9.00
L25	Glamorgan Test Cricketers	1993		50p	£12.50
L25	Gloucestershire Test Cricketers	1994		50p	£12.50
L25	Hampshire Test Cricketers	1995		50p	£12.50
L25	Kent Test Cricketers	1993		—	£12.50
L25	Lancashire Test Cricketers	1993		50p	£12.50
L25	Leicestershire Test Cricketers	1995		50p	£12.50
L25	Middlesex Test Cricketers	1994		80p	£20.00
50	1912 Triangular Tournament Cricket	1992		20p	£9.00
M24	1920s Test Cricketers 1st Series	1994		40p	£10.00
M24	1920s Test Cricketers 2nd Series	1996		40p	£10.00
25	1950s England Cricket Characters	1995		—	£20.00
50	1950s Test Cricketers	1992		50p	£25.00
M50	1960s Test Cricketers	1992		—	£25.00
25	1995 England Cricket Characters	1996		40p	£10.00
L25	Northamptonshire Test Cricketers	1993		50p	£12.50
L25	Nottinghamshire Test Cricketers	1994		50p	£12.50
25	Prominent Cricketers of 1894	1990		—	£40.00
50	Somerset County Championship Cricket Series 1	1990		20p	£10.00
50	Somerset County Championship Cricket Series 2	1990		20p	£10.00
L25	Somerset Test Cricketers	1994		50p	£12.50
16	The South African Cricket Team 1894	1990		50p	£8.00
M15	The South African Cricket Team 1965	1994		40p	£6.00
L25	Surrey Test Cricketers	1994		50p	£12.50
L25	Sussex Test Cricketers	1994		50p	£12.50
EL16	The 13th Australian Cricket Team to England 1909 (Limited Edition of 200 postcards)	c1995		—	£16.00
L25	Warwickshire Test Cricketers	1994		50p	£12.50
L25	Worcestershire Test Cricketers	1995		50p	£12.50
M30	World Stars of Cricket & Showbusiness	1992		—	£9.00
L25	Yorkshire Test Cricketers	1993		—	£20.00
	CECIL COURT				
L20	Christopher Columbus	1992		—	£7.00
L12	Class of 66 (England World Cup Team)	2002		—	£9.00
L20	Famous Film Directors	1992		—	£7.00
	COW & GATE				
L12	Advertisement Series 1st Series	1928	HC-137.1	£2.50	£30.00
L12	Advertisement Series 2nd Series	1928	HC-137.2	£2.00	£24.00
L48	Happy Families	1928	HC-138	£1.50	—
	COWAN CO. LTD (Canada)				
EL24	Animal Cards	1923		£8.00	—
EL24	Birds Series	c1925		£8.00	—
EL6	Boy Scouts 1st Series	c1925		£20.00	—
15	Boy Scouts 2nd Series	c1925		£20.00	—
EL24	Canadian Birds	1922		£8.00	—
EL24	Canadian Fish	c1924		£8.00	—
EL24	Chicken Cards	c1924		£8.00	—
M24	Dog Pictures	c1925		£8.00	—
M24	Learn To Swim	1929		£8.00	—
24	Noted Cats	c1927		£8.00	—
EL12	Scenic Canada	c1925		£12.00	—
EL24	Wild Flowers of Canada	c1925		£8.00	—

Size & quantity	TRADE CARD ISSUES	Date	Handbook reference	Price per card	Complete set
	CRAIG & HALES (Australia)				
30	Footballers	c1930		£25.00	—
	CRAWLEY CAKE & BISCUIT CO.				
24	World's Most Beautiful Birds	c1925	HX-22	£10.00	—
	CREATURE FEATURES				
10	Spooky TV (The Addams Family)	2011		—	£5.00
	CREEPY CARD COLLECTABLES				
10	Zorita Queen of Burlesque	2015		—	£5.00
	CRESCENT CONFECTIONERY CO. LTD				
85	Footballers	c1925	HC-139	£55.00	—
97	Sportsmen	c1925		£55.00	—
	CRICKET MEMORABILIA SOCIETY				
L50	Memorabilia Through the Ages (Cricket)	2000		20p	£10.00
	CROMWELL STORES				
1	Advertisement Card — Girl Bugler	c1963		—	£5.00
25	Do You Know?	1963	HX-166.2	40p	£10.00
25	Racing Colours	1963		70p	£17.50
	CROSBIE				
K54	Miniature Playing Cards	c1930		£1.50	—
	J. CROSFIELD				
36	Film Stars	1924		£11.00	—
	CROWN SPORTS CARDS (USA)				
LT10	Landforce Series 2 (Military)	1991		—	£5.00
LT9	Seaforce Series 3 (Naval)	1991		—	£5.00
LT9	Skyforce Series 1 (Aircraft)	1991		—	£5.00
	CROXLEY CARD CO.				
L20	British Lions Series 1 (Rugby Union)	1999		—	£10.00
LT20	Leicester Tigers Series 3 (Rugby Union)	2001		—	£10.00
LT21	Leicester Tigers Series 5 (Rugby Union)	2001		—	£10.00
LT20	Saracens Series 2 (Rugby Union)	2000		—	£10.00
LT21	Saracens Series 4 (Rugby Union)	2001		—	£10.00
	CRYPTOZOIC				
LT95	Arrow Season 1	2015		—	£11.00
LT72	Arrow Season 2	2015		—	£9.50
LT81	Arrow Season 3	2016		—	£20.00
LT68	The Big Bang Theory Seasons 3 & 4	2012		—	£12.00
LT68	The Big Bang Theory Season 5	2013		—	£9.50
LT72	The Big Bang Theory Seasons 6 & 7	2016		—	£9.50
LT72	Castle Seasons 1 & 2	2012		—	£9.50
LT72	Castle Seasons 3 and 4	2014		—	£9.50
LT69	Ender's Game The Movie	2014		—	£10.00
LT72	The Flash Season 2	2017		—	£10.00
LT9	The Flash Season 2 Location (Nd L01 to L09)	2017		—	£5.50
LT9	The Flash Season 2 Metas (Nd MT01 to MT09)	2017		—	£5.50
LT9	The Flash Season 2 Quotables Cisco (Nd Q01 to Q09)	2017		—	£5.50
LT72	Fringe — Imagine The Impossibilities Seasons 1 & 2	2012		—	£8.50
LT73	Fringe — Imagine The Impossibilities Seasons 3 & 4	2013		—	£8.50
LT72	Gotham Before the Legend Season 1	2016		—	£16.00
LT72	Gotham Before the Legend Season 2	2017		—	£16.00

Size & quantity	TRADE CARD ISSUES	Date	Handbook reference	Price per card	Complete set
	CRYPTOZOIC (continued)				
LT101	The Hobbit An Unexpected Journey	2014		—	£12.00
LT90	The Hobbit The Battle of the Five Armies	2016		—	£12.00
LT72	Outlander Season 1	2016		—	£12.00
LT72	Penny Dreadful Season 1	2015		—	£9.50
LT100	Sons of Anarchy Season 1 to 3	2014		—	£16.00
LT71	Sons of Anarchy Season 4 & 5	2015		—	£16.00
LT63	Sons of Anarchy Season 6 & 7	2015		—	£16.00
LT72	Supernatural Join The Hunt Season 1 to 3	2014		—	£16.00
LT72	Supernatural Seasons 4 to 6	2016		—	£20.00
LT63	The Vampire Diaries Season 1	2011		—	£10.00
LT69	The Vampire Diaries Season 2	2012		—	£10.00
LT72	The Vampire Diaries Season 3	2014		—	£10.00
LT72	The Walking Dead Season 3 Part 1	2014		—	£12.00
LT72	The Walking Dead Season 3 Part 2	2014		—	£12.00
LT72	The Walking Dead Season 4 Part 1	2016		—	£16.00
LT72	The Walking Dead Season 4 Part 2	2016		—	£16.00
	CRYSELCO				
EL25	Beautiful Waterways	1939		£1.20	£30.00
EL25	Buildings of Beauty	1938		£1.40	£35.00
EL12	Interesting Events of 60 Years Ago	1955		£2.50	£30.00
	CRYSTAL CAT CARDS				
LT6	Attitude Cats by Louis Wain Series LW5	2005		—	£3.00
LT6	Cats in Black by Louis Wain Series LW6	2005		—	£3.00
LT6	Cats Prize Winners by Louis Wain Series LW1	2005		—	£3.00
LT6	Cats Sports & Leisure by Louis Wain Series LW2	2005		—	£3.00
LT6	Diabolo Cats by Louis Wain Series LW7	2005		—	£3.00
EL6	First World War Cats by Louis Wain Series LW12	2009		—	£3.00
LT6	Happy Days Cats by Louis Wain Series LW4	2005		—	£3.00
EL6	Mascots Cats by Louis Wain Series LW10	2009		—	£3.00
EL6	Mikado Cats by Louis Wain Series LW13	2010		—	£3.00
EL6	Out In All Weathers Cats by Louis Wain Series LW8	2009		—	£3.00
EL6	Persians 1st Series Cats by Louis Wain Series LW9	2009		—	£3.00
EL6	Persians 2nd Series Cats by Louis Wain Series LW11	2009		—	£3.00
LT6	Purr-Fect Reaction Cats by Louis Wain Series LW3	2005		—	£3.00
	CULT-STUFF				
LT28	Adventures Into the Unknown	2016		—	£15.00
LT27	Adventures of Sherlock Holmes	2013		—	£10.00
LT10	The Art of Burlesque Headline Honeys (Chase Set)	2013		—	£8.00
LT27	The Art of Burlesque 'Kiss' Limited Edition	2013		—	£15.00
LT18	Beyond Stoker's Dracula	2013		—	£12.00
LT10	Beyond Stoker's Dracula Nosferatu (Chase Set)	2013		—	£7.50
LT27	Bram Stoker's Dracula	2012		—	£10.00
LT36	Civil War Chronicles Volume 1	2013		—	£15.00
LT36	Civil War Chronicles Volume 2	2015		—	£15.00
LT18	Civil War Chronicles Portraits (Chase Sets Volume 1 & 2 combined)	2015		—	£10.00
LT18	Dixon's Vixens 1st Series (Numbered 1 to 18 LCC issue)	2015		—	£10.00
LT18	Dixon's Vixens 2nd Series (Numbered 19 to 36)	2015		—	£10.00
1	Largest Steamers in the World (Olympic & Titanic) (reprint)	2013		—	£1.50
LT27	Memoirs of Sherlock Holmes 2nd Series	2014		—	£15.00
LT6	1914 Preview (World War I)	2014		—	£4.00
LT36	Propaganda and Poster Series 1 (World War 1 & 2)	2013		—	£12.00

Size & quantity	TRADE CARD ISSUES	Date	Handbook reference	Price per card	Complete set
	CULT-STUFF (continued)				
LT9	Pulp Detectives (Pulp Dicks) (Ultra Limited Edition) ...	2012		—	£18.00
LT27	RMS Titanic	2012		—	£15.00
LT18	Sherlock Holmes and Victorian Crime	2013		—	£9.00
LT4	Sherlock Holmes Terror by Night (Limited Edition of 600)	2015		—	£5.00
LT18	Sherlock Holmes The Long Stories Volume 1 The Sign Of Four	2015		—	£12.00
LT18	Sherlock Holmes The Long Stories Volume 1 A Study In Scarlet.....................................	2015		—	£12.00
LT10	Sherlock Holmes The Long Stories The Hound of the Baskervilles (Chase Set)	2015		—	£8.00
LT36	Vintage Erotica (postcard back)	2013		—	£13.00
LT6	Vintage Erotica Sectional Chase Set	2013		—	£6.00
LT21	The War Illustrated (World War I)	2015		—	£10.00
LT27	War of the Worlds – H.G. Wells	2013		—	£10.00
LT10	War of the Worlds – H.G. Wells (Chase Set)	2013		—	£7.00
LT10	War of the Worlds – H.G. Wells Hack Puzzle	2014		—	£8.00
LT28	War of the Worlds Earth Under the Martians	2014		—	£12.00
	CULT TV CLASSICS				
M10	Heroes and Heroines of Classic Cult TV	2019		—	£7.00
	D. CUMMINGS & SON				
64	Famous Fighters (Boxers)............................	1948		£5.00	£320.00
	THE CUNNING ARTIFICER				
6	Advertising Cards Discworld Emporium	2009		—	£3.00
20	Bernard Pearson's Clare Craft Pottery	2009		—	£6.00
	Album			—	£5.00
20	Discworld Advertisements and Labels...............	2009		—	£6.00
	Album			—	£5.00
25	Discworld Scout Insignia Collection (Terry Pratchett's Scouting For Trolls)	2009		—	£10.00
	Album			—	£5.00
M25	The Discworld Stamp Collection (based on Terry Pratchett's Discworld Books)	2009		—	£10.00
	Album			—	£5.00
M10	Discworld Toy Shop Collection (Props from The Hogfather film)	2009		—	£5.00
	Album			—	£5.00
22	Famous Footballers of Ankh-Morpork (Terry Pratchett's Discworld)	2010		—	£10.00
	Album			—	£6.00
	D.S.I. (USA)				
LT50	Desert Storm	1991		—	£9.50
	DAILY HERALD				
32	Cricketers	1954		£5.00	—
32	Footballers	1954	HD-7	£5.00	—
32	Turf Personalities...................................	1955		£1.10	£35.00
	DAILY ICE CREAM CO.				
24	Modern British Locomotives	1954		£1.50	£36.00
	DAILY MIRROR				
M100	Star Soccer Sides	1971		75p	—
EL60	Star Soccer Sides 'My Club' Premium Issue	1971	HD-15	£8.00	—

Size & quantity	TRADE CARD ISSUES	Date	Handbook reference	Price per card	Complete set

DAILY SKETCH

| 40 | World Cup Souvenir | 1970 | | £3.25 | — |
| | Album | | | — | £25.00 |

DAILY TELEGRAPH

26	England Rugby World Cup	1995		30p	£7.50
26	Ireland Rugby World Cup	1995		30p	£7.50
26	Scotland Rugby World Cup	1995		30p	£7.50
26	Wales Rugby World Cup	1995		30p	£7.50

DAINTY NOVELS

| 10 | World's Famous Liners | 1915 | HD-20 | £14.00 | — |

DANDY GUM

M200	Animal Fables (Nd. K1 to K200):				
	A Black back	1971		50p	—
	B Red back	1971		50p	—
M100	Captains Tattoos - Tattoo-Ole (black and white)				
	(Nd A1 to A100)	c1985		£1.50	—
M160	Cars and Bikes (Nd. A1 to A160):				
	A Black back with 'Dandy'	1977		90p	—
	B Blue back, anonymous	1977		90p	—
M116	Flag Parade (Nd. U1 to U116)	1965		50p	—
M160	Flag Parade (Nd. F1 to F160)	1978		50p	—
M210	Football Clubs and Colours of the World				
	(Nd. X1 to X200)	c1970		60p	—
M54	Football — European Cup (without firm's name)	1988		60p	—
M55	Football World Cup (with firm's name)	1986		60p	—
M80	Hippy Happy Tattoos (black and white) (Nd A1 to A80)	c1965		£1.50	—
M72	Motor Cars	c1960		£1.75	—
M53	Our Modern Army (with PC inset)	1956		£1.30	—
M53	Pin-up Girls (Original Set) (with PC inset)	1955		£2.20	—
M53	Pin-up Girls (with 'Substitute' cards) (with PC inset)	1955	HD-30	£2.20	—
M54	Pin-up Girls	1977		75p	—
M80	Pirate Tattoos (coloured)	c1965		£1.50	—
M70	Pop Stars (Nd P1 to P70)	1977		£1.20	—
M56	Rock 'N' Bubble Pop Stars (with PC inset)	1987		50p	—
M100	Soldier Parade (Nd P1 to P100)	1969		90p	—
	Album			—	£15.00
M200	Struggle for the Universe (black back) (Nd A1 to A200)	1970		50p	—
M72	Veteran and Vintage Cars (Nd V1 to V72):				
	A Numbers 1 to 48 British Issue	1966		£1.60	—
	B Numbers 49 to 72 Overseas Issue	1966		£1.60	—
M100	Wild Animals (Nd H1 to H100):				
	A Danish/English text	1969		40p	£40.00
	B Arabic/English text	1978		45p	£45.00
M200	Wonderful World (Nd Y1 to Y200)	c1975		40p	—

DART FLIPCARDS (USA)

LT72	Battlestar Galactica	1996		—	£12.00
LT72	Betty Boop	2001		—	£25.00
LT100	Fern Gully The Last Rainforest	1992		—	£9.50
LT72	The Frighteners — The Film	1996		—	£12.00
LT72	I Love Lucy 50th Anniversary	2001		—	£9.50
LT4	I Love Lucy 50th Anniversary Silver Foil Sub Set	2001		—	£10.00
LT6	I Love Lucy 50th Anniversary Classic Memories Sub Set	2001		—	£15.00
LT72	The Lone Ranger	1997		—	£15.00
LT72	Mr Bean (Rowan Atkinson)	1998		—	£9.50
LT72	The Munsters All New Series	1998		—	£14.00

Size & quantity	TRADE CARD ISSUES	Date	Handbook reference	Price per card	Complete set
	DART FLIPCARDS (USA) (continued)				
LT100	100 Years of Hersheys	1995	—		£9.50
LT72	Pepsi Around the Globe	2000	—		£12.00
LT100	Pepsi Cola 1st Series	1994	—		£13.00
LT100	Pepsi Cola 2nd Series	1995	—		£9.50
LT72	Sabrina The Teenage Witch	1999	—		£9.50
LT72	Sailor Moon	1997	—		£9.50
LT72	Shrek The Film	2001	—		£8.00
LT72	Titanic (The Liner)	1998	—		£20.00
LT100	Vietnam Series 2	1991	—		£9.50
	DE BEUKELAER BISCUITS				
KP100	All Sports	1932		85p	£85.00
M125	Dumbo	c1940		£1.50	—
KP100	Film Stars 1st Series (Nd 1-100)	c1930	HB-199	£6.00	—
KP100	Film Stars 2nd Series (Nd 101-200)	c1930		£1.40	—
KP100	Film Stars 3rd Series (Nd 201-300)	c1930		£1.40	—
KP100	Film Stars 4th Series (Nd 301-400)	1932		£1.40	£140.00
KP100	Film Stars 5th Series (Nd 401-500)	c1935	HB-97	£1.40	—
KP100	Film Stars 6th Series (Nd 501-600)	c1935		£1.40	—
KP100	Film Stars 7th Series (Nd 601-700)	c1935		£1.40	—
KP100	Film Stars 8th Series (Nd 701-800)	c1935		£1.40	—
KP100	Film Stars 9th Series (Nd 801-900)	c1935		£1.40	—
KP100	Film Stars 10th Series (Nd 901-1,000)	c1935		£1.40	—
KP100	Film Stars 11th Series (Nd 1,001-1,100)	1940		£1.40	—
KP100	Film Stars (A) (B1-B100) small figure	c1935		£1.40	—
KP100	Film Stars (B) (B1-B100) large figure	c1935		£1.40	—
K160	Film Stars (gold background)	1938		£2.00	—
132	Film Stars (gold background)	1939	HB-98	£1.80	£240.00
M125	Gulliver's Travels	c1940		£1.25	—
	Album	—		—	£30.00
M125	Pinocchio Series	c1940		£1.50	—
M60	Sixty Glorious Years	c1940		£2.00	—
	Album	—		—	£40.00
M100	Snow White Series	c1940		£1.80	—
	DE COUBERTIN BOOKS				
6	Famous Toffeemen (Everton F.C.) Limited Edition	2017	—		£6.00
5	Red Men (Liverpool F.C.) Limited Edition	2017	—		£5.00
	DERBY EVENING TELEGRAPH				
EL8	150 Years of British Railways (Derby)	1980	—		£5.00
	DESIGN AT LONDON COLOUR LTD				
EL4	Advert Cards (Paintings and Artwork)	2018	—		£2.00
10	Bizarre Imagination	2013	—		£4.00
M8	Calendar Girls	2017	—		£5.00
10	More Bizarre Imagination Series	2013	—		£4.00
10	The Story of Barratt's Sweets Factory — The Early Years	2013	—		£5.50
EL20	Underwater Predators	2018	—		£20.00
	DESIGNS ON SPORT				
25	Test Cricketers	1992	—		£8.00
	LIAM DEVLIN & SONS LTD				
M36	Coaching Gaelic Football	c1960		£13.00	—
48	Corgi Toys	1971		£3.00	—
50	Do You Know?	1964	HX-166.2	20p	£7.50
M50	Famous Footballers New Series	1952	HX-102	£22.00	—

Size & quantity	TRADE CARD ISSUES	Date	Handbook reference	Price per card	Complete set
	LIAM DEVLIN & SONS LTD (continued)				
M50	Famous Footballers, Series A1	1953	HX-57	£22.00	—
M50	Famous Footballers, Series A2	1954	HX-58	£22.00	—
50	Famous Footballers, Series A3	1955	HX-59	£22.00	—
M45	Famous Speedway Stars	c1960	HD-38	£22.00	—
M45	Fastest on Earth	c1953	HX-60	£6.00	—
36	Flags of All Nations	1958		£6.00	—
48	Gaelic Sportstars	c1960		£12.00	—
48	Irish Fishing	1962		70p	£35.00
50	Modern Transport	1966	HX-125	25p	£12.50
48	Our Dogs	c1960		£12.00	—
48	Right or Wrong	c1960		£8.00	—
M35	Walt Disney Characters	c1955	HX-65	£8.00	—
M50	Wild Animals by George Cansdale	1954	HX-68	£8.00	—
48	Wild Wisdom	c1965		£5.00	—
50	Wonders of the World	1968	HX-49	20p	£10.00
100	World Flag Series	c1965	HD-40	£7.00	—
	DIAMOND COLLECTION (UK)				
L20	Rock 'n' Roll	1998		—	£7.50
	DICKSON, ORDE & CO. LTD				
50	Footballers	1960		45p	£22.50
25	Ships Through the Ages	1960	HX-94	£4.00	—
25	Sports of the Countries	1962		£1.40	£35.00
	DIGIT CARDS				
LT40	Happy Puppy Your Best Friends (Game Cards)	c1995		—	£6.00
	DIGITAL IMPACT				
L20	Caricatures From The Movies	2002		—	£8.00
30	Victorian & Edwardian Soldiers in Full Dress	2001		—	£12.00
	DINERS CLUB				
EL8	Reminders	1976		45p	£3.50
	DINKIE PRODUCTS LTD (Hair Grips)				
M24	Stars and Starlets	1947		£3.00	—
M20	Stars and Starlets 2nd Series	1947		£3.00	—
M20	MGM Films 3rd Series	1948		£4.00	—
M24	Warner Bros. Artists 4th Series	1948		£5.00	—
M20	Gone With the Wind 5th Series	1948		£7.00	—
M24	Warner Bros. Films 6th Series	1949		£4.00	—
M24	MGM Stars 7th Series	1949		£5.00	—
M24	Paramount Pictures 8th Series	1950		£5.00	—
M24	M.G.M. Films 9th Series	1950		£7.00	—
M24	M.G.M. Films 10th Series	1951		£8.00	—
M24	United Artists Releases 11th Series	1951		£8.00	—

(N.B. these prices are for complete cards with space for grips.
If cards have grip holder cut off these will be 80% of prices shown.)

	DINOCARDZ (USA)				
LT80	Dinosaurs Series 1	1992		—	£10.00
	DIRECT ACCESS				
L8	Atlanticard (British Sports Stars)	1992		£1.25	£10.00
	DIRECT TEA SUPPLY CO.				
25	British Uniforms of the 19th Century	c1960	HX-78	£1.00	£25.00

Size & quantity	TRADE CARD ISSUES	Date	Handbook reference	Price per card	Complete set
	J. ARTHUR DIXON				
	Collectacard Series:				
EL15	Vintage Steam (GWR), Set 6	1978	—		£5.00
EL15	Vintage Steam (SR), Set 7	1978	—		£5.00
EL15	Vintage Steam (LMS), Set 8	1978	—		£5.00
EL15	Vintage Steam (LNER), Set 9	1978	—		£5.00
EL15	Vintage Steam (Scottish), Set 10	1978	—		£5.00
	F. & M. DOBSON (SOUTHERN) LTD				
L72	Flags of the World, Nos 1-72	1978	—		£10.00
L72	Flags of the World, Nos 73-144	1978	—		£10.00
100	Newcastle and Sunderland's Greatest Footballers	1981		25p	—
	A. & J. DONALDSON LTD				
534	Sports Favourites	c1950	HD-48	£12.00	—
64	Sports Favourites Golden Series (Footballers)	c1950		£26.00	—
	DONRUSS (USA)				
LT56	Dallas	1981	—		£15.00
LT78	The Dark Crystal — The Film	1982	—		£12.00
LT66	Elvis	1978	—		£40.00
LT55	Knight Rider	1982	—		£20.00
LT66	Magnum P.I.	1983	—		£16.00
EL60	Major League All-Stars Baseball	1986	—		£12.00
LT66	Sgt Pepper's Lonely Hearts Club Band	1978	—		£15.00
LT66	Tron (including set 8 stickers)	1981	—		£15.00
LT92	Twister The Film	1996	—		£12.00
	DORMY COLLECTION				
25	Golf — The Modern Era	1994		£1.20	£30.00
	DOUBLE Z ENTERPRISE (USA)				
LT66	Zig & Zag	1994	—		£9.50
	DRIFTER				
M24	Pop Stars	1983		£1.00	—
	DRYFOOD LTD				
50	Animals of the World	1955	HX-93	20p	£4.50
K50	Zoo Animals	1955		20p	£4.50
	DUCHESS OF DEVONSHIRE DAIRY CO. LTD				
L25	Devon Beauty Spots	1936		£5.00	£125.00
	DUNHILLS				
25	Ships and Their Workings	1962	HX-85	60p	£15.00
	DUNKIN (Malta)				
L88	Martial Arts	c1975		£1.00	—
M50	Motor Cycles of the World	1976		£2.20	—
	DUNN'S LONDON				
60	Animals	1924	HX-140	£11.00	—
48	Birds	1924	HX-141	£11.00	—
	J.A. DUNN & CO.				
26	Actresses 'FROGA A'	1902	HX-155	£50.00	—

Size & quantity	TRADE CARD ISSUES	Date	Handbook reference	Price per card	Complete set

DUO (USA)

LT72	Abbott & Costello ...	1996		20p	£12.00
EL72	The Beatles — Yellow Submarine (152 × 102mm) ...	1999		—	£16.00
LT90	Gone with the Wind — The Film...	1996		—	£9.50
LT72	Happy Days (1970s TV Series) ...	1998		—	£12.00
LT72	It's A Wonderful Life (The 1946 Film) ...	1996		—	£9.50
LT72	Lionel Greatest Trains ...	1998		—	£20.00
LT72	Lionel Legendary Trains ...	1997		20p	£12.00
LT72	Lionel Legendary Trains 1900-2000 Centennial ...	2000		—	£20.00
LT81	The Outer Limits ...	1997		—	£12.00
LT72	The Wizard of Oz...	1996		—	£15.00
LT72	WWF Smack Down (Wrestling) ...	1999		—	£12.00
LT72	Zorro — The Film...	1998		—	£9.50

MICKEY DURLING (Sunday Empire)

(Cards issued with staple holes.)

48	Footballers of Today...	c1950		£6.50	—

DUTTON'S BEERS

12	Team of Sporting Heroes ...	1980		30p	£3.50
	Folder/Album ...			—	£8.00

DYNAMIC (Australia)

LT100	Disney's Aladdin ...	1995		20p	£9.50
LT60	Escape of the Dinosaurs ...	1997		—	£9.50
LT55	New Zealand All Blacks ...	1995		20p	£9.50

DYNAMIC FORCES (USA)

LT72	Lexx Premiere Series (TV, Sci-Fi Series)...	2002		—	£9.50

THE EAGLE

16	Soccer Stars ...	1965		£4.00	—

EAST KENT NATIONAL BUS CO.

L8	British Airways Holidays ...	1984		—	£4.00

EBRO

EL69	Pop Singers ...	c1963	HE-4	£6.50	—

ECLIPSE ENTERPRISES (USA)

LT110	The Beverly Hillbillies ...	1993		—	£12.00
LT110	National Lampoon Loaded Weapon I ...	1993		—	£9.50

EDGE ENTERTAINMENT (USA)

LT82	Judge Dredd — Movie & Comic...	1995		—	£9.50

J. EDMONDSON & CO. LTD

26	Actresses 'FROGA' ...	c1901	HE-6	£70.00	—
4	Aeroplane Models ...	1939	HE-7	£20.00	—
?72	Art Pictures...	c1914	HE-8	£16.00	—
14	Birds and Eggs ...	c1925	HE-9	£16.00	—
?22	Boy Scout Proficiency Badges ...	c1925	HE-10	£50.00	—
25	British Army Series ...	c1915	HX-144	£45.00	—
20	British Ships ...	1925		£5.00	—
20	Dogs ...	c1930	HE-11	£10.00	—
20	Famous Castles ...	1925		£9.00	—
30	Flags & Flags With Soldiers (Flags only) ...	c1905		£24.00	—
42	Flags of All Nations (3 printings)...	c1930	HE-12	£12.00	—

Size & quantity	TRADE CARD ISSUES	Date	Handbook reference	Price per card	Complete set
	J. EDMONDSON & CO. LTD (continued)				
24	Pictures from the Fairy Stories	c1930	HE-15	£7.00	—
?13	Playtime Series	c1915		£30.00	—
24	Popular Sports	c1925	HE-17	£16.00	—
25	Sports and Pastimes	c1910	HX-225	£20.00	—
12	Throwing Shadows on the Wall:				
	A Light blue background	1937		£5.50	
	B Dark blue background	1937		£5.50	
25	War Series	c1916	HX-290	£18.00	—
12	Woodbine Village	c1930	HE-18	£5.50	—
26	Zoo Alphabet	c1930		£10.00	—
	EDWARDS & SONS (Confectionery)				
27	Popular Dogs	1954		£5.00	—
12	Products of the World	1957		30p	£3.50
25	Transport — Present and Future:				
	A Descriptive back	1955		20p	£4.00
	B Album offer back	1955		40p	£10.00
25	Wonders of the Universe:		HX-14		
	A With title	1956		20p	£4.00
	B Without title	1956		£1.00	£25.00
	THE 'ELITE' PICTURE HOUSE				
50	War Portraits	1916	HX-86	£120.00	—
	ELKES BISCUITS LTD				
25	Do You Know? (Mechanical)	1964	HX-166.1	20p	£3.50
	ELY BREWERY CO. LTD				
M24	Royal Portraits	1953	HX-10	£2.50	£60.00
	EMERALD COLLECTABLES				
M72	Birds & their Eggs	1996		—	£15.00
	EMPIRE COLLECTIONS				
10	Football Elite	2018		—	£5.00
10	Star Footballers (1940s and '50s) 1st Series	2017		—	£5.00
10	Star Footballers (1940s and '50s) 2nd Series	2017		—	£5.00
	EMPIRE MARKETING BOARD				
12	Empire Shopping	c1925		£6.00	£75.00
	H.E. EMPSON & SON LTD				
25	Birds	1962	HX-71	80p	—
25	British Cavalry Uniforms of the 19th Century	1963	HX-43	80p	—
25	Garden Flowers	1966	HX-46	£1.00	£25.00
25	History of the Railways 1st Series	1966	HX-88	£1.80	—
25	History of the Railways 2nd Series	1966	HX-88	£1.80	—
24	The Island of Ceylon	1962	HX-47	£6.00	—
25	Passenger Liners	1964	HX-82	£1.60	—
25	Tropical Birds	1966	HX-13	50p	£12.50
25	Wonders of the Deep	1965	HX-89	20p	£4.00
	ENESCO (USA)				
LT16	Precious Moments	1993		—	£8.00
	ENGLAND'S GLORY				
15	England '66 (Football World Cup)	2004		—	£6.00

Size & quantity	TRADE CARD ISSUES	Date	Handbook reference	Price per card	Complete set
	ENGLISH AND SCOTTISH CWS				
?23	British Sports Series	c1910	HE-24	£60.00	—
25	Humorous Peeps into History (Nd 1-25)	1927		£4.00	£100.00
25	Humorous Peeps into History (Nd 26-50)	1928		£5.00	—
25	In Victoria's Days	1930		£4.00	£100.00
L12	The Rose of the Orient, Film Series	1925	HE-29.1	60p	£7.50
L12	The Rose of the Orient 2nd Film Series	1925	HE-29.2	75p	£9.00
L12	The Story of Tea (brown back)	1925	HE-31	£1.00	£12.00
L12	The Story of Tea (blue back)	1925		£1.50	£18.00
	ENSIGN FISHING TACKLE				
L6	Advertising Blotters	2002		—	£3.00
L6	Advertising Cards	2002		—	£3.00
L6	The Art of Angling 1st Series	1997		—	£3.00
L6	The Art of Angling 2nd Series	1997		—	£3.00
L6	The Art of Angling 3rd Series	2002		—	£3.00
L6	Birds of Prey	1997		—	£3.00
L6	Fisherman's Lore	2002		—	£3.00
L6	Fishing Tackle Advertisements	1995		—	£3.00
L20	Freshwater Fish	1995		—	£7.50
L6	Game Birds (By Graham Payne)	1996		—	£3.00
L6	Garden Birds	1997		—	£3.00
L6	It's A Dog's Life	2002		—	£3.00
L6	Lifeboats	2002		—	£3.00
L6	Lighthouses	2002		—	£3.00
L6	Norman Neasom's Rural Studies Series 1	2002		—	£3.00
L6	Norman Neasom's Rural Studies Series 2	2002		—	£3.00
L6	Owls	1997		—	£3.00
L25	Salmon Flies	1995		—	£7.50
L6	Sea Fish	2002		—	£3.00
L6	Sharks	2002		—	£3.00
L6	Water Loving Birds	2002		—	£3.00
	EPIC CARDS				
10	European Footballers 1st Series (from the 1940s onwards)	2019		—	£7.50
10	Grand Prix Drivers 1st Series	2019		—	£7.50
10	Grand Prix Drivers 2nd Series	2019		—	£7.50
	EPOL (South Africa)				
M30	Dogs	1974		70p	£20.00
	JOHN E. ESSLEMONT LTD (Tea)				
25	Before Our Time	1966	HX-103	60p	£15.00
25	Into Space	1966	HX-147	£1.00	£25.00
24	The Island of Ceylon	c1960	HX-47	£6.00	—
	ESSO				
K30	England World Cup Squad Mexico 1970 (Metal Coins) (27mm diameter)	1970		£2.00	—
	FA Cup Centenary 1872 to 1972 (metal coins):				
K30	A Football Club Aluminium Coins (27mm diameter)	1972		£2.00	—
K1	B 1972 Winners Leeds United (v Arsenal) brass coin (32mm diameter)	1972		£4.00	—
K76	Football Club Badges (shaped card)	1971		£1.00	—
EL20	Olympics (Nd 1-40)	1972		£2.00	—
K22	Soccer Superstars (metal coins) (38mm diameter)	c1970		£2.50	—
M16	Squelchers Booklets (Football)	1970		£2.00	—

Size & quantity	TRADE CARD ISSUES	Date	Handbook reference	Price per card	Complete set
	ESSO (Australia)				
L18	Australia's Great Mineral Discoveries	1971		£1.00	£18.00
	EUROSTAR				
LT125	Tour de France (Cycling)	1997		20p	—
	EVERSHED AND SON LTD				
25	Sports and Pastimes	c1910	HX-225	£20.00	—
	EVERY GIRLS PAPER				
MP17	Film Stars	c1924	HE-42	£7.50	—
	EWBANKS LTD				
25	Animals of the Farmyard	1960		36p	£9.00
25	British Uniforms	1957	HX-108	24p	£6.00
25	Miniature Cars and Scooters	1959		24p	£6.00
50	Ports and Resorts of the World	1958	HX-38	20p	£10.00
25	Ships Around Britain	1961		20p	£4.50
25	Sports and Games	1958	HX-154	60p	£15.00
25	Transport Through the Ages:		HX-101		
	A Black back	1957		20p	£4.00
	B Blue back	1957		50p	£12.50
	EXPRESS WEEKLY				
	The Wild West:				
25	A No overprint	1958	HX-55.5	40p	£10.00
25	B Red overprint	1958		24p	£6.00
L25	C 2 Pictures per card	1958		£1.00	—
	EXTRAS				
24	Prehistoric Monsters and the Present	1979		£4.00	—
	F1 SPORTS CARD MARKETING INC. (Canada)				
LT200	Grid Formula 1 Racing	1992		—	£20.00
	F.P.G. (USA)				
LT90	Barclay Shaw — Fantasy Art	1995		—	£9.50
LT44	Bernie Wrightson Frankenstein Nd. F1 to F44	1993		—	£10.00
LT90	Bernie Wrightson More Macabre Series 2 — Fantasy Art	1994		—	£10.00
LT90	Bob Eggleton — Fantasy Art	1995		—	£10.00
LT90	Chris Foss — Fantasy Art	1995		—	£12.00
LT90	Christos Achilleos — Fantasy Art	1992		—	£12.00
LT90	Darrell Sweet — Fantasy Art	1994		—	£9.50
LT90	David Cherry — Fantasy Art	1995		—	£9.50
LT90	David Mattingly — Fantasy Art	1995		—	£9.50
LT90	Everway Vision Cards — Fantasy Art	1995		—	£12.00
LT90	J.K. Potter – Fantasy Art	1995		—	£12.00
LT90	James Warhola — Fantasy Art	1995		—	£9.50
LT60	Janny Wurts — Fantasy Art	1996		—	£9.50
LT90	Jeffrey Jones Series 1 — Fantasy Art	1993		—	£9.50
LT90	Jeffrey Jones Series 2 — Fantasy Art	1995		—	£9.50
LT90	Joe Devito — Fantasy Art	1995		—	£12.00
LT60	Joe Jusko's Edgar Rice-Burroughs Collection 1 (Tarzan)	1994		—	£12.00
LT60	Joe Jusko's Edgar Rice-Burroughs Collection 2	1995		—	£15.00
LT90	John Berkey Series 2 — Fantasy Art	1996		—	£12.00

Size & quantity	TRADE CARD ISSUES	Date	Handbook reference	Price per card	Complete set
	F.P.G. (USA) (continued)				
LT90	Michael Kaluta 1st Series — Fantasy Art...............	1994		—	£9.50
LT90	Michael Kaluta 2nd Series — Fantasy Art	1995		—	£9.50
LT90	Mike Ploog — Fantasy Art...................................	1994		—	£9.50
LT90	Paul Chadwick — Fantasy Art	1995		—	£9.50
LT90	Robh Ruppel — Fantasy Art	1996		—	£9.50
LT90	Thomas Canty — Fantasy Art	1996		—	£9.50
	FACCHINO				
	Cinema Stars:				
K50	A Inscribed Series of 50	1936		£7.00	—
K100	B Inscribed Series of 100	1936	HF-2	75p	£75.00
	Album			—	£25.00
K50	How or Why	1937		60p	£30.00
	Album			—	£25.00
K50	People of All Lands	c1935		£2.70	—
K50	Pioneers	c1935		£2.70	—
	FACTORY ENTERTAINMENT				
LT50	The Prisoner Volume 2	2010		—	£12.00
	FAIRLEY'S RESTAURANT				
20	The European War Series	1916	HX-129	£32.00	—
	FAITH PRESS				
10	Boy Scouts L.C.C I	1928		£10.00	—
10	Girl Guides L.C.C. II	1928		£10.00	—
12	Religious Subjects Series L.C.C. III	c1928		£10.00	—
12	Religious Subjects Series L.C.C. IV	c1928		£10.00	—
8	Religious Subjects Series L.C.C. V	c1928		£10.00	—
	FAMILY STAR				
EL8	Good Luck Song Cards.......................................	c1930		£4.00	—
K52	Miniature Playing Cards	c1955		£1.00	—
M4	Film Stars	c1955	HF-3	£6.50	—
	FANTASY (USA)				
LT50	Rocketship X-M	1979		—	£10.00
	FANTASY TRADE CARD CO. (USA)				
LT60	Alien Nation	1990		—	£20.00
	FARM-TO-DOOR SUPPLIES				
25	Castles of Great Britain.......................................	1965	HX-161	£5.60	—
25	Cathedrals of Great Britain	1965	HX-162	£5.60	—
	FARROW'S				
50	Animals in the Zoo	1925		£11.00	—
	FASCINATING CARDS (USA)				
LT535	116th United States Congress (American Politicians) 2020 (Limited Edition)	2020		—	£120.00
	FAULDERS CHOCOLATE				
10	Ancient v Modern Sports	1924		£10.00	—
10	Birds and Nests	1924		£8.00	—
10	Fruits	1924		£8.00	—
10	Game..	1924		£8.00	—
10	Zoology	1924		£8.00	—

Size & quantity	TRADE CARD ISSUES	Date	Handbook reference	Price per card	Complete set
	FAX PAX				
L36	ABC and Numbers (Early Learning Cards)	1988		—	£4.00
L40	The American West (19th Century)	1992		—	£10.00
L40	Birds of the British Isles	1991		—	£6.00
L40	Britain's Royal Heritage	1991		—	£6.00
LT50	Butterflies of the British Isles	1996		—	£6.00
L40	Castles	1990		—	£6.00
L40	Cathedrals and Minsters	1989		—	£6.00
L39	Dinosaurs	1993		—	£6.00
L36	Equestrianism	1986		—	£6.00
L36	Fables	1988		—	£4.00
LT40	Famous Golfers	1993		—	£7.50
L42	First Ladies of the United States	1997		—	£6.00
L36	Football Greats	1989		—	£6.00
L36	Football Stars	1989		—	£6.00
L40	Forty Great Britons	1992		—	£6.00
L36	Golf	1986		—	£15.00
L40	Historic Houses	1990		—	£6.00
L40	Kings and Queens	1985		—	£6.00
L40	The Lake District	1993		—	£6.00
L40	London	1985		—	£5.00
L40	Modern Rhymes	c1990		—	£6.00
L36	Nursery Rhymes	1988		—	£4.00
	Presidents of the United States 1993:				
L41	A Complete set	1993		—	—
L40	B Different (minus George Bush 1989-93)	1993		—	£5.00
L40	Scotland's Heritage	1990		—	£6.00
L38	Tennis	1986		—	£8.00
LT50	Wild Flowers of the British Isles	1996		—	£6.00
L40	Wildlife of the British Isles	1991		—	£6.00
LT40	World of Sport	1993		—	£7.50
	FEATHERED WORLD				
EL?	Poultry, Pigeons, Cage Birds, etc. postcards	c1910	HF-6.8	£2.50	—
	ALEX FERGUSON				
20	The European War Series	1917	HX-129	£32.00	—
41	VC Heroes	1917	HX-220	£32.00	—
	FESTIVAL OF 1000 BIKES				
L24	The Vintage Motor Cycle Club	1993		—	£6.00
	FIELD GALLERIES				
L7	Racehorses & Jockeys 1st Series	1997		—	£3.00
L7	Racehorses & Jockeys 2nd Series	1997		—	£3.00
	FIFE POLICE				
L36	British Stamps	1987		20p	£6.00
EL20	Intercity British Rail	1990		50p	£10.00
	FILM PICTORIAL				
EL2	Film Stars (paper-backed silks)	c1930		£35.00	—
	FILSHILL				
24	Birds and Their Eggs	c1920	HX-164	£11.00	—
25	Footballers	1922	HF-18	£30.00	—
25	Types of British Soldiers	c1920	HX-144	£32.00	—

Size & quantity	TRADE CARD ISSUES	Date	Handbook reference	Price per card	Complete set
	FINDUS (Frozen Foods)				
20	All About Pirates	1967		40p	£8.00
	FINE FARE TEA				
25	Inventions and Discoveries 1st Series...	1962	HX-131	80p	£20.00
25	Inventions and Discoveries 2nd Series	1962	HX-131	80p	£20.00
	Album for 1st and 2nd Series combined			—	£20.00
12	Your Fortune in a Teacup	1965		30p	£3.50
	FISH MARKETING BOARD				
18	Eat More Fish	c1930		£4.50	—
	FIZZY FRUIT				
25	Buses and Trams...	c1960	HX-109	£1.20	£30.00
	FLEER				
LT84	Believe It or Not	c1970		50p	—
LT192	Mad	1985		50p	—
	FLEER (USA)				
LT90	Aaahh! Real Monsters	1995		—	£9.50
LT10	Aaahh! Real Monsters Colouring Cards	1995		—	£3.00
LT120	Batman Forever:				
	A Fleer 1995 on front	1995		—	£12.00
	B Fleer 95 Ultra on front	1995		—	£12.00
LT100	Batman Forever Metal	1995		—	£12.00
LT119	Casper — The Movie (Nos 13 & 77 unissued, 2 different Nos 12 & 69)	1995		—	£9.50
LT42	Christmas Series	1995		—	£12.00
LT66	Grossville High	1986		—	£9.50
LT72	Here's Bo Derek	1981		20p	£10.00
LT146	MTV Animation	1995		—	£12.00
LT42	Nursery Rhymes	1995		—	£12.00
LT150	Power Rangers The Movie	1995		—	£12.00
LT24	Power Rangers The Movie Power Pop Up	1995		—	£5.00
LT150	Reboot (TV Series)	1995		—	£12.00
LT100	Skeleton Warriors	1995		—	£9.50
LT50	Spiderman '97 with Fleer on front	1997		—	£9.50
LT50	Spiderman '97 without Fleer on front	1997		—	£15.00
LT80	World Wrestling Federation Clash	2001		—	£10.00
LT100	WWF Wrestlemania	2001		—	£10.00
LT100	X-Men (Non-Chromium Walmart Edition)	1996		—	£12.00
	FLEETWAY PUBLICATIONS LTD				
L72	Adventures of Sexton Blake	1968		£6.50	£470.00
EL1	The Bobby Moore Book of The F.A. Cup (booklet) ...	1968		—	£16.00
EL28	Football Teams 1958-59 (issued with 'Lion/Tiger') ...	1958	HF-27	£4.00	—
EL28	Football Teams 1959-60 (issued with 'Lion/Tiger') ...	1959	HF-27	£4.00	—
EL2	Pop Stars (Roxy)	1961		£1.75	£3.50
50	Star Footballers of 1963 (issued with 'Tiger')	1963		£2.20	
	FLORENCE CARDS				
24	Luton Corporation Tramways...	1983		—	£3.50
M20	Tramway Scenes	1984		—	£6.00
	FOOTBALL AND SPORTS FAVOURITE				
M10	Sportsmen (Anonymous plain back)	c1925	HF-39	£10.00	

Size & quantity	TRADE CARD ISSUES	Date	Handbook reference	Price per card	Complete set
	FOOTBALL ASSOCIATION OF WALES				
LT17	The Dragons Dream Team (Welsh International Footballers)	2000		—	£6.00
	FOOTBALL CARD COLLECTOR				
10	Association Footballers (of the 1960s) 1st Series	2012		—	£5.00
10	Association Footballers (of the 1960s) 2nd Series	2012		—	£5.00
10	Association Footballers (of the 1950/60s) 3rd Series	2012		—	£5.00
10	Football Action (1940s to 1960s)	2019		—	£5.00
10	Footballers 1960s 1st Series	2011		—	£5.00
10	Footballers 1960s 2nd Series	2011		—	£5.00
10	Footballers 1960s 3rd Series	2011		—	£5.00
10	Footballers 1960s 4th Series	2011		—	£5.00
10	Soccer Heroes (1945-66) 1st Series	2014		—	£5.00
10	Soccer Heroes (1950-60s) 2nd Series	2014		—	£5.00
	FOOTBALL COLLECTOR CARDS				
20	Football (1950s Footballers) blue fronts 1st Series	2011		—	£7.50
20	Football (1950s Footballers) yellow fronts 2nd Series	2011		—	£7.50
20	Football (1950s Footballers) green fronts 3rd Series	2011		—	£7.50
10	Top Star Football Cards 1st Series (Footballers of the 50s)	2010		—	£5.00
10	Top Star Football Cards 2nd Series (Footballers of the 50s)	2010		—	£5.00
10	Top Star Football Cards 3rd Series (Footballers of the '50s & '60s)	2017		—	£5.00
10	Top Star Football Cards 4th Series (Footballers of the '50s & '60s)	2018		—	£5.00
10	Top Star Football Cards 5th Series (Footballers of the '50s & '60s)	2019		—	£5.00
10	Top Star Football Cards 6th Series (Footballers of the '50s & '60s)	2020		—	£5.00
10	Top Star Football Cards 7th Series (Footballers of the '50s & '60s)	2020		—	£5.00
	FOOTBALL FANFARE				
20	Football Fanfare (1950s Footballers) 1st Series	2010		—	£7.50
20	Football Fanfare (1950s Footballers) 2nd Series	2010		—	£7.50
20	Football Fanfare (1950/60s Footballers) 3rd Series	2010		—	£7.50
20	Football Fanfare (1950/60s Footballers) 4th Series	2010		—	£7.50
	FOOTBALL STAR COLLECTOR CARDS				
20	Football Star	2010		—	£7.50
	FOOTBALL TRADER				
16	Legends of The Orient (Leyton Orient F.C.)	2011		—	£7.00
	FOOTBALLER MAGAZINE				
24	Hall of Fame (Footballers)	1994		50p	£12.00
	Album			—	£15.00
	FORD MOTOR CO. LTD				
L50	Major Farming	c1955		£10.00	—
	FOSSE COLLECTION				
11	F.A. Cup Winners 1950 (Arsenal F.C.)	1998		—	£6.75
22	F.A. Cup Final 1951 Blackpool v Newcastle United	1998		—	£13.50
22	League Champions 1949-50 Portsmouth & Tottenham Hotspur	2005		—	£13.50

Size & quantity	TRADE CARD ISSUES	Date	Handbook reference	Price per card	Complete set
	FOSTER CLARK (Malta)				
50	The Sea Our Other World	1974		80p	£40.00
	FOSTER'S LAGER				
30	Sporting Greats	1992		£2.00	—
	FOTO BUBBLE GUM				
25	Wonders of the Universe	1957	HX-14	20p	£4.50
	FRAME SET & MATCH				
25	Wembley Magpies (Newcastle Utd Footballers)	1995		24p	£6.00
	FRAMEABILITY				
L17	British Steam Locomotives	2002		—	£6.00
L16	Fire Engines 1st Series	1996		—	£6.00
L16	Fire Engines 2nd Series	1998		—	£6.00
L10	Highwaymen	2003		—	£6.00
L17	Police — British Police Vehicles	2002		—	£6.00
L6	Traction Engines	1999		—	£4.00
L10	World Cup Winners 1966 England	2002		—	£6.00
	FRAMES OF MIND				
L11	World Cup Winners 1966 (Football)	1997		—	£11.00
	A.C.W. FRANCIS (West Indies)				
25	British Uniforms of the 19th Century	c1965		£1.00	—
25	Castles of Britain	c1965		£1.00	—
25	The Circus	1966		£1.00	—
25	Football Clubs and Badges	c1965		£1.00	—
25	Pond Life	1967		40p	£10.00
25	Sports of the Countries:				
	A Black back	1967		£1.20	
	B Blue back	1967		£1.20	
	FRANK'S SWEETS				
32	Felix Pictures	c1922	HX-56	£65.00	—
	FREEDOM PRESS (USA)				
LT40	The JFK Assassination	1991		—	£9.00
LT16	Official Currier and Ives Civil War	1994		—	£7.00
	LES FRERES				
25	Aircraft of World War II:		HX-7		
	A Black back	1966		£2.00	£50.00
	B Blue black	1966		£1.20	£30.00
	FRESHMAID LTD (Jubbly)				
50	Adventurous Lives	1966		20p	£4.50
	J.S. FRY & SONS LTD (Chocolate)				
4	Advertisement Cards:				
	A G.H. Elliott (size 63 × 38mm), dark brown	c1910		—	£40.00
	B G.H. Elliott (size 66 × 38mm), light brown	c1910		—	£40.00
	C Hello Daddy (size 66 × 38mm)	c1910		—	£40.00
	D Vinello (size 80 × 62mm)	c1920		—	£50.00
50	Ancient Sundials:				
	A With series title, text back	1924		£3.20	—
	B Without series title, plain back	1924		£7.50	—

Size & quantity	TRADE CARD ISSUES	Date	Handbook reference	Price per card	Complete set
	J.S. FRY & SONS LTD (Chocolate) (continued)				
50	Birds and Poultry	1912		£5.00	£250.00
24	Birds and Their Eggs	1912		£6.00	£150.00
15	China and Porcelain	1907		£15.00	—
25	Days of Nelson	1906		£14.00	—
25	Days of Wellington	1906		£14.00	—
25	Empire Industries	1924		£8.00	—
	Exercises for Men and Women:				
13	A Exercises for Men	1926		£7.00	—
12	B Exercises for Men and Boys	1926		£7.00	—
13	C Exercises for Women	1926		£7.00	—
12	D Exercises for Women and Girls	1926		£7.00	—
K48	Film Stars	1934		£3.50	—
50	Fowls, Pigeons and Dogs:				
	A Size 65 x 36mm	1908		£6.00	£300.00
	B Size 67 x 36mm	1908		£6.00	£300.00
EL12	Fun Cards	1972		30p	£3.50
25	Match Tricks	c1921		£38.00	—
15	National Flags	1908		£8.00	—
50	Nursery Rhymes	1917		£5.00	£250.00
50	Phil May Sketches	1905		£5.00	—
25	Red Indians	1927		£10.00	—
25	Rule Britannia	1915		£6.00	—
50	Scout Series	1912		£12.00	—
48	Screen Stars	1928		£4.50	—
120	This Wonderful World	1935		£3.00	—
50	Time and Money in Different Countries	1908		£4.00	£200.00
50	Tricks and Puzzles (blue back)	1918		£4.50	£225.00
50	Tricks and Puzzles (black back)	1924		£4.50	£225.00
6	War Leaders — Package Issue	1915	HF-58	£40.00	—
25	With Captain Scott at the South Pole	1912		£15.00	£375.00
	J.S. FRY & SONS LTD (Canada)				
50	Children's Pictures	c1915		£15.00	—
25	Hunting Series	c1915		£22.00	—
25	Radio Series	c1930		£13.00	—
50	Scout Series 2nd Series	c1930		£20.00	—
50	Treasure Island Map	c1915		£11.00	—
	FUTERA (Australia)				
LT60	Cricket Elite	1996		25p	£15.00
LT110	Cricketers	1994		—	£16.00
LT9	Rugby Union 1996 No Barriers	1996		—	£18.00
LT3	Rugby Union 1996 Predictors	1996		—	£15.00
LT15	Rugby Union 1996 World Cup XV 1991	1996		—	£30.00
	FUTERA				
	(SEE ALSO TRADE CARDS (EUROPE) LTD)				
LT18	Aston Villa F.C.	2000		—	£18.00
LT18	Aston Villa F.C. (silver foil fronts)	2000		—	£27.00
LT14	Aston Villa F.C. (gold edging)	2000		—	£35.00
LT14	Celtic F.C. (gold edging)	2000		—	£35.00
M180	Chicken Run (Aardman/Dreamworks film) Stickers	2000		—	£9.50
LT18	Derby County F.C.	2000		—	£18.00
LT18	Derby County F.C. (silver foil fronts)	2000		—	£27.00
LT14	Leeds United F.C. (gold edging)	2000		—	£35.00

Size & quantity	TRADE CARD ISSUES	Date	Handbook reference	Price per card	Complete set
	FUTERA (continued)				
LT18	Manchester City F.C.	2000		—	£18.00
LT18	Manchester City F.C. (silver foil fronts)	2000		—	£27.00
LT14	Manchester City F.C. (gold edging)	2000		—	£35.00
LT18	Middlesbrough F.C.	2000		—	£18.00
LT18	Middlesbrough F.C. (silver foil fronts)	2000		—	£27.00
LT14	Middlesbrough F.C. (gold edging)	2000		—	£35.00
LT64	Red Dwarf (TV Series)	2002		—	£15.00
LT18	West Ham United F.C.	2000		—	£18.00
LT18	West Ham United F.C. (silver foil fronts)	2000		—	£27.00
LT50	World Stars Platinum Series (Footballers)	2001		—	£16.00
M24	World Stars 3D Footballers	2002		—	£10.00
	G.B. & T.W.				
L20	Golfing Greats	1989		—	£12.00
	G. D. S. CARDS				
L25	American Civil War Battles	2006		—	£15.00
L25	Birds by C.R. Bree	2007		—	£9.50
L25	Birds by Cassell 1860	2007		—	£9.50
L20	Birds of North America by John Cassin	2007		—	£8.50
L20	Birds of The United States	2007		—	£8.50
L20	British Birds of Prey Series 1	2006		—	£8.50
L20	British Birds of Prey Series 2	2008		—	£8.50
L20	British Butterflies (1841) Series 1	2008		—	£8.50
L20	British Butterflies (1841) Series 2	2008		—	£8.50
L20	British Fresh-Water Fish	2006		—	£8.50
EL4	Cattle Breeds	2007		—	£4.50
L20	Champion Hurdle — Winners 1976-1995	1997		—	£12.00
L20	Cheltenham Gold Cup — Winners 1976-1995	1997		—	£12.00
L20	Clippers and Yachts	2007		—	£8.50
L16	Derby Winners 1953-1968	1994		—	£10.00
L20	Dogs	2006		—	£8.50
L20	Earl of Derby Collection of Racehorse Paintings	2004		—	£13.00
L20	European Birds	2007		—	£9.50
L20	Famous Jockeys	2001		—	£9.50
L20	Famous Jockeys of Yesterday, Series 1	2003		—	£12.00
L20	Famous Titled Owners and Their Racing Colours, Series 1	2003		—	£12.00
L20	Famous Trainers (Horse Racing)	2001		—	£9.50
L20	Finches by Butler and Frohawk (1899)	2010		—	£7.00
EL4	Fusiliers by Richard Simkin (1890-1905)	2008		—	£4.50
L20	Grand National — Winners 1976-1995	1997		—	£12.00
L20	Great Racehorses	2003		—	£12.00
L16	Great Racehorses of Our Time	1994		—	£14.00
L25	Hawks and Owls of The America	2007		—	£9.50
L20	Heads of Famous Winners (Racehorses)	2001		—	£12.00
L20	Horses	2008		—	£8.50
L20	Hummingbirds by M.E. Mulsant & J.B.E. Verreaux (1876-77)	2010		—	£7.00
L25	Indian Chiefs of North America Series 1	2006		—	£12.00
L25	Indian Chiefs of North America Series 2	2007		—	£12.00
L20	Indian Tribes of North America	2007		—	£12.00
L16	Lester Piggott's Classic Winners	1994		—	£10.00
L25	Light Infantries and Regiments by Richard Simkin (1890-1905)	2008		—	£9.50
EL4	Military (1890-1905) by Richard Simkin	2008		—	£4.50
L25	Monkeys by J.G. Keulemans	2007		—	£9.50

Size & quantity	TRADE CARD ISSUES	Date	Handbook reference	Price per card	Complete set
	G. D. S. CARDS (continued)				
L25	1950's Racehorse Winners	2008		—	£10.50
L20	1960's Racehorse Winners	2007		—	£10.50
L25	1970's Racehorse Winners	2007		—	£10.50
L20	One Thousand Guineas Winners 1981-2000	2005		—	£10.50
L20	Orchids by Robert Warner & Thomas Moore (1882)	2010		—	£7.00
L20	Parakeets and Parrots (1903) by David Seth-Smith	2008		—	£8.50
L25	Parrots	2007		—	£9.50
L25	Pigeons	2006		—	£12.50
L20	Poultry	2006		—	£8.50
L25	Poultry by Harrison Weir 1904	2008		—	£9.50
L20	St Leger 1776-1815 Winning Owners Colours	2005		—	£10.50
EL6	Soldiers and Cavalry by Richard Simkin (1890-1905)	2008		—	£7.00
L20	Tropical Birds	2007		—	£8.50
L20	Trotters (American Style Horse Racing)	2006		—	£8.50
L20	Two Thousand Guineas Winners 1981-2000	2005		—	£10.50
L25	World's Birds of Prey (1876) Series 1	2008		—	£12.50
L25	World's Birds of Prey (1876) Series 2	2008		—	£9.50
	GALBRAITH'S TEA				
25	Types of British Soldiers	c1916	HX-144	£30.00	—
	GALBRAITH'S STORES				
25	Animals in the Service of Man	c1964	HX-51	£6.00	—
50	Strange Creatures	c1963	HX-120	£5.00	—
	GALLERY OF LEGENDS				
72	The British Open Golf Collection	1999		—	£15.00
	GAMEPLAN LTD				
L25	Open Champions (Golf)	1993		—	£10.00
L25	Vauxhall Motor Sport	1993		—	£10.00
	GANONG BROS. LTD (Canada)				
50	Big Chief	c1925		£8.50	—
	GARDEN RAILWAYS MAGAZINE (USA)				
20	Daventry Garden Railway	1991		—	£6.00
20	Garden Railway Structures Set E	1991		—	£6.00
20	Trains in the Garden: USA Set C	1991		—	£6.00
20	Trains in the Garden: Britain Set D	1991		—	£6.00
	GAUMONT CHOCOLATE				
K50	Film Stars	1936		£5.00	—
	GAYCON PRODUCTS LTD (Confectionery)				
25	Adventures of Pinky and Perky 1st Series:				
	A Blue back	1961		£5.00	—
	B Black back	1961		£5.00	—
25	Adventures of Pinky and Perky 2nd Series:				
	A Blue back	1961		£5.00	—
	B Black back	1961		£5.00	—
50	British Birds and Their Eggs	1961	HX-105	60p	£30.00
25	British Butterflies 1st Series	1963		80p	£20.00
25	Do You Know? 1st Series	1962	HX-166.3	£1.80	£45.00
25	Do You Know? 2nd Series	1962	HX-166.3	£1.80	£45.00
50	Flags of All Nations	1963	HX-112	£3.50	—
25	History of the Blue Lamp 1st Series	1961		80p	£20.00
25	History of the Blue Lamp 2nd Series	1961		80p	£20.00
30	Kings and Queens	1961	HX-116	20p	£5.00

Size & quantity	TRADE CARD ISSUES	Date	Handbook reference	Price per card	Complete set
	GAYCON PRODUCTS LTD (Confectionery) (continued)				
25	Modern Motor Cars	1959	HX-39	£6.40	—
25	Modern Motor Cars of the World 1st Series	1962		£6.40	—
25	Modern Motor Cars of the World 2nd Series	1962		£6.40	—
25	Red Indians 1st Series	1960	HX-118	£1.20	£30.00
25	Red Indians 2nd Series	1960	HX-118	£1.20	£30.00
25	Top Secret 1st Series	1967	HX-156	£5.40	—
25	Top Secret 2nd Series	1967	HX-156	£5.40	—
	GEE'S FOOD PRODUCTS				
30	Kings and Queens	1961	HX-116	80p	£24.00
16	See Britain by Coach	1955	HX-84	30p	£5.00
	THE GEM LIBRARY				
MP15	Footballers Special Action Photo	1922		£5.50	—
MP6	Footballers Autographed Real Action Photo Series	1922		£5.50	—
MP4	Footballers Autographed Action Series	1923		£5.50	—
L16	Marvels of the Future	1929		£4.50	—
	GENERAL FOODS (South Africa)				
L50	Animals and Birds	1973		20p	£10.00
	Album			—	£15.00
	GENERAL MILLS (Canada)				
LT6	Baseball Players (10 players per card)	1989		—	£5.00
	THE GIRLS FRIEND				
M6	Actresses (Silk)	1912	HG-12	£12.00	—
	GIRLS MIRROR				
MP10	Actors and Actresses	c1922	HG-14	£6.00	—
	GIRLS WEEKLY				
12	Flower Fortune Cards	1912		£16.00	—
	GLENGETTIE TEA				
25	Animals of the World	1964	HX-61	20p	£4.00
25	Birds and Their Eggs	1970	HX-1.3	40p	£10.00
25	The British Army, 1815:				
	A Black back	1976		50p	£12.50
	B Blue back	1976		50p	£12.50
25	British Locomotives	1959	HX-157	24p	£6.00
25	Do You Know?	1970	HX-166.4	20p	£3.50
25	Historical Scenes	1968	HX-143	20p	£3.50
25	History of the Railway 1st Series	1974		30p	£7.50
25	History of the Railway 2nd Series	1974		30p	£7.50
25	International Air Liners	1963	HX-125.1	70p	—
25	Medals of the World:		HX-110		
	A Black back	1961		20p	£4.00
	B Blue back	1961		70p	£17.50
25	Modern Transport:		HX-125.1		
	A Black back	1963		70p	£17.50
	B Blue back	1963		70p	£17.50
25	Naval Battles	1971	HX-21	24p	£6.00
25	Rare British Birds	1967		30p	£7.50
25	Sovereigns, Consorts and Rulers of Great Britain, 1st Series	1970	HX-201	£1.60	—
25	Sovereigns, Consorts and Rulers of Great Britain, 2nd Series	1970	HX-201	£1.60	£40.00

Size & quantity	TRADE CARD ISSUES	Date	Handbook reference	Price per card	Complete set
	GLENGETTIE TEA (continued)				
25	Trains of the World	1966	HX-121.2	32p	£8.00
25	Veteran and Vintage Cars	1966	HX-159	£1.00	£25.00
25	Wild Flowers	1961	HX-124	50p	£12.50
	GLENTONS LTD				
24	World's Most Beautiful Butterflies	c1920	HX-23	£10.00	—
	GLOUCESTERSHIRE C.C.C.				
M12	Gloucestershire Cricketers of 1990	1990		30p	£3.50
	J. GODDARD & SONS LTD				
	BACK 'Eighty'				
M3	Four Generations	c1925	HG-24	£2.00	£6.00
M12	London Views	c1925	HG-25	£2.50	£30.00
M12	Old Silver	c1925	HG-26	£1.75	£21.00
M2	Use and Cleaning of Silverware I	c1925		£1.25	£2.50
	BACK 'Eighty-five'				
M4	Cleaning a Silver Teapot	c1930	HG-23	£4.00	£16.00
M12	Ports of the World	c1930	HG-28	£2.50	—
M4	Silverware and Flowers I	c1930	HG-29	£2.50	£10.00
M12	Views of Old Leicester	c1930		£5.00	—
	BACK 'Ninety'				
M9	Old Silver at the Victoria and Albert Museum	c1935	HG-27	£2.25	£20.00
M8	Silverware and Flowers II	c1935	HG-30	£3.50	—
M8	Views of Leicester	c1935		£5.00	—
	BACK '95'				
M12	Present Day Silverware	c1940		£2.00	£24.00
M6	Use and Cleaning of Silverware II	c1940	HG-31	£4.00	
	GOLDEN CHICK				
24	World's Most Beautiful Birds	c1920	HX-22	£10.00	—
	GOLDEN ERA				
L7	A.J.S. Motor Cycles	1995		—	£3.00
L25	Aircraft of the First World War	1994		—	£7.50
L7	Alfa Romeo (Cars)	1998		—	£3.00
LT10	American Automobiles of the 1950s	2003		—	£4.50
LT7	Anglia, Prefect, Popular Small Fords 1953-1967	2005		—	£3.75
L7	Antique Dolls	1996		—	£3.00
L7	Ariel Motor Cycles	1995		—	£3.00
L7	Aston Martin (Cars)	1993		—	£3.00
L7	Aston Martin Post-War Competition Cars	2001		—	£3.00
L10	Austin Cars	1996		—	£3.75
L7	Austin Healey Motor Cars	1995		—	£3.00
L9	BMW (Cars)	1999		—	£3.75
L7	BSA 1st Series (Motor Cycles)	1993		—	£5.00
L7	BSA 2nd Series (Motor Cycles)	1999		—	£3.00
L10	British Buses of the 1950s	1999		—	£3.75
L10	British Buses of the 1960s	1999		—	£3.75
L10	British Lorries of the 1950s	2000		—	£3.75
EL4	British Lorries of the 1950s (numbered 081-084)	1999		—	£2.25
L10	British Lorries of the 1950s & 1960s	1999		—	£3.75
L10	British Lorries of the 1960s	2000		—	£3.75
L10	British Military Vehicles of WWII	2000		—	£3.75
L25	British Motor Cycles of the Fifties	1993		—	£7.50

Size & quantity	TRADE CARD ISSUES	Date	Handbook reference	Price per card	Complete set
	GOLDEN ERA (continued)				
L7	British Tanks of WWII	2000		—	£3.00
L10	British Trucks (1950s and 1960s)	2010		—	£3.75
L7	British Vans of The 1950s	2002		—	£3.00
L7	British Vans of The 1960s	2002		—	£3.00
LT10	Buses in Britain 1950s	2005		—	£4.50
LT10	Buses in Britain 1960s	2005		—	£4.50
L10	Bygone Buses (1950s and 1960s)	2010		—	£3.75
L7	Capri Mk1 1969-74	2007		—	£3.00
L7	Capri Mk3 1978-86	2007		—	£3.00
LT7	Capri Mk I Performance Models (1969-74)	2004		—	£3.75
LT7	Capri Mk II Performance Models (1974-78)	2004		—	£3.75
LT7	Capri Mk III Performance Models (1978-86)	2004		—	£3.75
L25	Cats (Full Length)	1994		—	£7.50
L26	Cats (Heads)	1995		—	£7.50
LT7	Chevrolet Camaro 1967-69	2004		—	£3.75
L7	Citroen (Cars)	2001		—	£3.00
L10	Classic American Motor Cycles	1998		—	£3.75
L7	Classic Bentley (Cars)	1997		—	£3.00
L26	Classic British Motor Cars	1992		—	£7.50
L25	Classic British Motor Cycles of the '50s & '60s	1993		—	£7.50
L7	Classic Citroen 2CV	2001		—	£3.00
LT10	Classic Corvette (Cars)	1994		—	£4.50
L7	Classic Ferrari (Cars)	1993		—	£7.00
L7	Classic Ferrari F1 1961-2000	2002		—	£3.00
L7	Classic Fiat	2002		—	£3.00
L7	Classic Honda (Motor Cycles)	1999		—	£3.00
EL4	Classic Jaguar Series 1 (numbered 153-156)	2010		—	£2.25
L10	Classic Jeep	2002		—	£3.75
L7	Classic Kawasaki (Motor Cycles)	1999		—	£3.00
EL6	Classic Lambretta — The Golden Era of Scootering	2008		—	£3.00
L10	Classic Lorries (1950s and 1960s)	2010		—	£3.75
L7	Classic Lotus (Cars) 1st Series	1995		—	£3.00
L7	Classic Lotus (Cars) 2nd Series	1997		—	£3.00
L7	Classic MG (Cars) 1st Series	1992		—	£3.00
L7	Classic MG (Cars) 2nd Series	1994		—	£3.00
L7	Classic MG Sports Cars	1996		—	£3.00
L10	Classic Mercedes	2000		—	£3.75
LT10	Classic Mini	2005		—	£4.50
L7	Classic Morgan Sports Cars	1997		—	£3.00
LT10	Classic Mustang (Cars)	1994		—	£7.50
L13	Classic Porsche Cars	1996		—	£4.50
L7	Classic Rally Cars of the 1970s	2001		—	£3.00
L7	Classic Rally Cars of the 1980s	2001		—	£3.00
EL6	Classic Riley	2008		—	£3.00
L7	Classic Rolls-Royce (Cars)	1997		—	£3.00
L7	Classic Rover (Cars)	1995		—	£3.00
L10	Classic Scooters	2000		—	£3.75
L7	Classic Suzuki	1999		—	£3.00
L10	Classic Tractors	1998		—	£3.75
L7	Classic T.V.R. (Cars)	1997		—	£3.00
L7	Classic Vauxhalls of the 1950s & 1960s	2002		—	£3.00
L7	Classic Volkswagen Karmann Ghia 1955-74	2002		—	£3.00
L7	Classic Volkswagen Transporter 1950-79	1999		—	£5.00
L7	Classic Volkswagen VW Beetle 1949-66	1999		—	£3.00
L7	Classic Volkswagen VW Beetle 1967-80	1999		—	£3.00
L7	Classic Volkswagen VW Golf GTI 1975-92	2002		—	£3.00

Size & quantity	TRADE CARD ISSUES	Date	Handbook reference	Price per card	Complete set
	GOLDEN ERA (continued)				
L7	Classic Volvo (Cars)	2003		—	£3.00
L13	Classic VW (Cars)	1993		—	£4.50
EL6	Classic VW Transporter	2008		—	£3.00
EL6	Classic Wolseley	2008		—	£3.00
L7	Classic Yamaha	1999		—	£3.00
L7	Cobra The Sports Car 1962-1969	1996		—	£3.00
LT7	Consul, Zephyr, Zodiac Big Fords 1951-1971	2005		—	£3.75
L7	Cortina Mk1 1962-1966	2007		—	£3.00
L7	Daimler Classics	2004		—	£3.00
L7	Dolls	1996		—	£3.00
L7	Ducati (Motor Cycles)	1999		—	£3.00
L7	E-Type Jaguar (Cars)	1993		—	£3.00
L10	Eight Wheelers Classic British Lorries	2007		—	£3.75
L7	Escort Mk1 R S Models	2007		—	£3.00
L7	Escort Mk2 1975-80	2007		—	£3.00
L7	Escort Twin-cam, RS & Mexico 1969-80	1999		—	£3.00
L7	Escort Works Rally Mk I, MK II	1999		—	£3.00
LT7	Escort Mk I The Performers	2004		—	£3.75
LT7	Escort Mk II The Performers	2004		—	£3.75
LT10	Famous Bombers (Aircraft)	1997		—	£4.50
LT10	Famous Fighters (Aircraft)	1997		—	£4.50
M20	Famous Footballers by Stubbs — Arsenal	2001		—	£5.00
M20	Famous Footballers by Stubbs — Aston Villa	2002		—	£5.00
M20	Famous Footballers by Stubbs — Chelsea	2001		—	£5.00
M20	Famous Footballers by Stubbs — Leeds	2001		—	£5.00
M20	Famous Footballers by Stubbs — Liverpool	2001		—	£5.00
M20	Famous Footballers by Stubbs — Manchester United	2001		—	£5.00
M20	Famous Footballers by Stubbs — Newcastle United	2002		—	£5.00
M20	Famous Footballers by Stubbs — Spurs	2001		—	£5.00
M20	Famous Footballers by Stubbs — West Ham United	2002		—	£5.00
L7	Famous Fords — Capri Mk2 1974-78	2008		—	£3.00
L7	Famous Fords — Cortina Mk2 1966-70	2008		—	£3.00
L10	Famous T.T. Riders (Motorcyclists)	1998		—	£3.75
L7	Ferrari 1950s & 1960s	2003		—	£3.00
L7	Ferrari 1970s & 1980s	2003		—	£3.00
L7	Ford and Fordson Tractors 1945-1970	2010		—	£3.00
L10	The Ford Capri (Cars)	1995		—	£7.50
L7	Ford Cortina Story 1962-82	2002		—	£3.00
L7	Ford Executive (Cars)	1994		—	£3.00
L10	Ford in the Sixties (Cars)	1996		—	£3.75
L7	Ford RS Models 1983-92	2001		—	£3.00
LT7	Ford Sierra — The Performers	2005		—	£3.75
L7	Ford XR Performance Models 1980-89	2001		—	£3.00
L10	Formula 1 (Grand Prix)	1996		—	£3.75
L10	F1 Champions 1991-2000	2001		—	£3.75
L7	German Military Vehicles of WWII	2001		—	£3.00
L7	Graham & Damon Hill (Grand Prix Drivers)	2000		—	£3.00
LT7	Granada-Consul and Granada MkI and MkII	2005		—	£3.75
L10	Grand Prix Greats	1996		—	£3.75
L26	Grand Prix The Early Years (Cars)	1992		—	£7.50
L10	Heavy Haulage (Lorries etc)	2000		—	£3.75
EL4	Jaguar At Le Mans (numbered 029-032)	1995		—	£2.25
L7	Jaguar Classic (Cars) 1st Series	1992		—	£3.00
L7	Jaguar Classic (Cars) 2nd Series	1993		—	£3.00
L7	Jaguar Classic (Cars) 3rd Series	1997		—	£3.00
L7	Jaguar Classics (Cars) 4th Series	2003		—	£3.00
EL4	Jaguar E-Type (numbered 149-152)	2010		—	£2.25
L7	Jaguar Modern Classics (Cars) 5th Series	2003		—	£3.00

Size & quantity	TRADE CARD ISSUES	Date	Handbook reference	Price per card	Complete set

GOLDEN ERA (continued)

Size & quantity	Title	Date			Complete set
L7	Jim Clark (Grand Prix Driver)	2000		—	£3.00
L7	Lambretta (Motor Cycles)	2000		—	£3.00
EL6	Lambretta Innocetti — The Golden Era of Scootering	2008		—	£3.00
L10	Lambretta The World's Finest Scooter	2007		—	£3.75
EL6	Lambrettability — The Golden Era of Scootering	2008		—	£3.00
L7	Lancia (Cars)	1998		—	£3.00
L7	Land Rover Series I models 1948 to 1958	1996		—	£3.00
EL4	Land Rover 1st Series (numbered 049-052)	1997		—	£4.00
L7	Land Rover Series II & IIA models 1958 to 1971	1996		—	£3.00
EL4	Land Rover 2nd Series (numbered 053-056)	1997		—	£4.00
L7	Land Rover Series III models 1971 to 1985	1996		—	£3.00
EL4	Land Rover 3rd Series (numbered 057-060)	1997		—	£4.00
L7	Land Rover Discovery	2001		—	£3.00
L7	Land Rover Legends Series 1	2000		—	£3.00
EL4	Land Rover Legends Series 1 (numbered 093-096)	2000		—	£2.25
L7	Land Rover Legends Series 2	2000		—	£3.00
EL4	Land Rover Legends Series 2 (numbered 097-100)	2000		—	£2.25
L7	Land Rover Legends Series 3	2000		—	£3.00
EL4	Land Rover Legends Series 3 (numbered 101-104)	2000		—	£2.25
L7	Land Rover, Ninety, One Ten & Defender	2000		—	£3.00
EL4	Land Rover Ninety, One Ten & Defender (numbered 105-108)	2000		—	£2.25
L7	The Legend Lives On, Ayrton Senna (Grand Prix Driver)	2000		—	£3.00
L10	London Buses of the Post-War Years	1997		—	£3.75
EL4	London Buses Post-War (numbered 069-072)	1999		—	£2.25
L10	London Buses of the Pre-War Years	1997		—	£3.75
EL4	London Buses Pre-War (numbered 065-068)	1999		—	£2.25
L7	The London Taxi	2001		—	£3.00
L10	London's Country Buses	2000		—	£3.75
EL4	London's Country Buses (numbered 061-064)	2000		—	£2.25
L7	Mansell (by Wayne Vickery)	1994		—	£3.00
L7	Matchless Motor Cycles	1995		—	£3.00
L7	Mercedes SL (Cars)	1994		—	£3.00
EL4	M.G. Greats (Cars) (numbered 033-036)	1995		—	£2.25
EL4	M.G.B. (Cars) (numbered 037-040)	1995		—	£2.25
L10	Micro & Bubble Cars	2000		—	£3.75
EL4	Midland Red Buses (numbered 117-120)	2000		—	£2.25
L7	Mini Cooper (Cars)	1994		—	£3.00
EL4	Mini Cooper (Cars) (numbered 001-004)	1994		—	£2.25
EL4	Mini Cooper (numbered 161-164)	2010		—	£2.25
L10	Mini Cooper The 1960's	2007		—	£3.75
L10	The Mini Legend (Cars)	1995		—	£3.75
L7	Mini Moke 1961-89	2007		—	£3.00
L10	Mini (Cars) — Special Edition	1999		—	£3.75
EL4	Mini Vans (numbered 025-028)	1995		—	£2.25
EL4	Monte Carlo Minis (Cars) (numbered 009-012)	1994		—	£4.00
L9	Morris Minor (Cars)	1993		—	£3.75
EL4	Morris Minor (Cars) (numbered 045-048)	1995		—	£2.25
L9	Morris Minor — Fifty Years (Cars)	1998		—	£3.75
EL4	Morris Minor (Vans) (numbered 005-008)	1994		—	£2.25
L10	Motorcycling Greats	1997		—	£3.75
L10	Municipal Buses of The 1950s and 1960s	2007		—	£3.75
L7	Norton (Motor Cycles) 1st Series	1993		—	£3.00
L7	Norton (Motor Cycles) 2nd Series	1998		—	£3.00
L7	Old Teddy Bears	1995		—	£3.00
L10	On The Move Classic British Lorries	2004		—	£3.75

Size & quantity	TRADE CARD ISSUES	Date	Handbook reference	Price per card	Complete set
	GOLDEN ERA (continued)				
EL6	Original Vespa — The Golden Age of Scootering	2009		—	£3.00
EL4	Police Vehicles (numbered 013-016)	1994		—	£2.25
LT7	Pontiac GTO 1964-74	2004		—	£3.75
L7	Porsche 356 (1950-65)	2003		—	£3.00
L7	Porsche 911 (1963-77)	2003		—	£3.00
L7	Porsche 911 (1978-98)	2003		—	£3.00
L7	Racing & Rallying Mini Coopers of the 60's	2000		—	£3.00
LT7	Racing Legends (Formula 1 Drivers)	2004		—	£3.75
L7	Range Rover (Cars)	1996		—	£3.00
L7	The Ringmaster — Michael Schumacher	2002		—	£3.00
L10	Road Haulage Classic British Lorries	2004		—	£3.75
LT10	Rootes Sixties Classics (Cars)	2005		—	£4.50
EL4	Southdown Buses (numbered 121-124)	2000		—	£2.25
L7	Spitfire (Cars)	1994		—	£3.00
L7	Sporting Ford (Cars)	1992		—	£3.00
EL4	Sporting Mini Cooper (numbered 157-160)	2010		—	£2.25
L7	Spridget — Austin Healey Sprite & MG Midget 1958-79	2002		—	£3.00
L13	Superbikes of the 70s	2000		—	£4.50
L7	Tanks of WWII	2000		—	£3.00
L7	Teddies	1997		—	£3.00
L7	Teddy Bears	1994		—	£3.00
EL4	Teddy Bears (numbered 021-024)	1995		—	£2.25
EL4	Teddy Bear Families (numbered 017-020)	1995		—	£2.25
L10	35 Years of the Mini 1959-1994	1994		—	£3.75
LT7	Thunderbird American Classics 1955-63 (Cars)	2003		—	£4.00
L10	Traction Engines	1999		—	£3.75
EL4	Traction Engines (numbered 109-112)	2000		—	£4.00
EL4	Tractors 1st Series (numbered 073-076)	1999		—	£4.00
EL4	Tractors 2nd Series (numbered 077-080)	1999		—	£4.00
L7	Tractors of the Fifties	1999		—	£5.00
L7	Tractors of the Sixties	1999		—	£3.00
L7	TR Collection (Triumph Cars)	1992		—	£3.00
L7	Triumph (Motor Cycles) 1st Series	1993		—	£3.00
L7	Triumph (Motor Cycles) 2nd Series	1998		—	£3.00
L10	Triumph Herald 1959-71	2007		—	£3.75
L7	Triumph Saloon Cars 1960s & 1970s	2002		—	£3.00
L7	Triumph Spitfire 1962-80	2007		—	£3.00
L7	Triumph Stag Motor Cars	1995		—	£3.00
L7	Triumph TR2 and TR3 1953-61	2007		—	£3.00
L7	Triumph TR4, TR5 and TR6 1961-76	2007		—	£3.00
L7	Triumph Vitesse 1962-71	2007		—	£3.00
L7	U.S. Military Vehicles of WWII	2001		—	£3.00
L7	Velocette (Motor Cycles)	1993		—	£3.00
L7	Vespa (Motor Cycles)	2000		—	£3.00
L7	Vincent Motor Cycles	1995		—	£3.00
L7	Vintage Vespa 1958-1966	2005		—	£5.00
EL4	Volkswagen Beetle (numbered 085-088)	1999		—	£4.00
EL4	Volkswagen Transporter (numbered 089-092)	1999		—	£4.00
L7	VW Transporter 1956-1961	2005		—	£3.00
EL6	VW Transporter Bus 1950-67	2008		—	£3.00
L7	VW Transporter 1968-80 Bay Window Models	2007		—	£3.00
EL6	VW Transporter Type 2	2008		—	£3.00
LT7	World Champions (Formula 1 Drivers)	2004		—	£3.75
	GOLDEN FLEECE (Australia)				
L36	Dogs	1967		55p	£20.00

Size & quantity	TRADE CARD ISSUES	Date	Handbook reference	Price per card	Complete set
	GOLDEN GRAIN TEA				
25	Birds	1963	HX-71	£1.60	—
25	British Cavalry Uniforms of the 19th Century	1965	HX-43	£1.00	£25.00
25	Garden Flowers	1965	HX-46	20p	£4.50
25	Passenger Liners	1966	HX-82	60p	£15.00
	GOLDEN WONDER				
24	Soccer All Stars	1978		60p	£15.00
	Album			—	£10.00
14	Space Cards (yellow background)	1978		25p	£3.50
14	Space Cards (coloured):				
	A Rounded corners	1979		25p	£3.50
	B Square corners	1979		£2.00	—
24	Sporting All Stars	1979		20p	£4.00
	Album			—	£8.00
24	TV All Stars	1979		20p	£3.50
	Album			—	£15.00
36	World Cup Soccer All Stars	1978		70p	£25.00
	Album			—	£10.00
	GOLF GIFTS LTD				
M24	Ryder Cup 1989	1991		—	£17.50
	GOOD TIMES CREATIONS				
21	Blades Legends (Sheffield United F.C. from 1889 to 2014	2014		—	£12.00
34	Colours of Brazil (2014 Football World Cup)	2014		—	£12.00
13	Golf Legends	2012		—	£8.50
23	Great Britons (Olympic Athletes Post War Gold Medalists)	2012		—	£12.00
13	Ladies of Rock	2013		—	£8.50
13	Legends of Rock	2012		—	£8.50
20	Lendas Brasileiras (Brazilian Football Legends)	2013		—	£12.00
13	Silkmen Legends (Macclesfield Town F.C.)	2012		—	£8.50
13	Twelve Days of Christmas	2012		—	£8.50
25	24 Lions in Brazil (English World Cup Footballers)	2014		—	£12.00
	GOODIES LTD				
50	Doctor Who and the Daleks	1969		£11.00	—
25	Flags and Emblems	1961		20p	£4.50
25	Indian Tribes	1969		£7.00	—
25	Mini Monsters	1970		£2.00	£50.00
25	The Monkees 1st Series	1967		£1.20	£30.00
25	The Monkees 2nd Series	1968		£7.00	—
24	Olympics	1972		£3.00	—
25	Pirates	1970		£3.40	—
25	Prehistoric Animals	1969		£4.00	—
25	Robbers and Thieves	1971		£3.00	—
25	Vanishing Animals	1971		£2.60	—
25	Weapons Through the Ages	1970		£2.60	—
25	Wicked Monarchs	1973		£2.00	£50.00
25	Wide World/People of Other Lands	1968		£1.40	£35.00
25	Wild Life	1969		£2.60	—
25	World Cup	1974		£4.00	£100.00
	D.W. GOODWIN & CO.				
36	Careers for Boys and Girls	c1930		£11.00	—
24	Extra Rhymes 2nd Series	c1930		£15.00	—

Size & quantity	TRADE CARD ISSUES	Date	Handbook reference	Price per card	Complete set
	D.W. GOODWIN & CO.(continued)				
	Flags of All Nations (12 different backs):				
36	Series A Home Nursing	c1930		£7.00	—
36	Series B Common Ailments and Their Cures	c1930		£7.00	—
36	Series C Tenants' Rights	c1930		£7.00	—
36	Series D Gardening Hints	c1930		£7.00	—
36	Series E Household Hints	c1930		£7.00	—
36	Series F Poultry Keeping	c1930		£7.00	—
36	Series G Beauty Aids	c1930		£7.00	—
36	Series H The World's Great Women	c1930		£7.00	—
36	Series I First Aid	c1930		£7.00	—
36	Series J Cookery Recipes	c1930		£7.00	—
36	Series K Cookery Recipes	c1930		£7.00	—
36	Series L General Knowledge	c1930		£7.00	—
36	Jokes Series (multi-backed)	c1930	HG-34	£13.00	—
36	Optical Illusions (multi-backed)	c1930	HG-35	£14.00	—
36	Ships Series (multi-backed)	c1930	HG-37	£14.00	—
24	Wireless Series	c1930		£15.00	—
36	World Interest Series (multi-backed)	c1930	HG-38	£9.00	—
24	World's Most Beautiful Birds	c1930	HX-22	£10.00	—
24	World's Most Beautiful Fishes	c1930	HX-24	£10.00	—
	W. GOSSAGE & SONS LTD				
48	British Birds and their Eggs	1924	HX-141	£4.00	—
48	Butterflies and Moths	1925		£3.50	—
	GOWERS & BURGONS				
25	British Birds and Their Nests	1967	HX-104	40p	£10.00
25	The Circus	1966	HX-79	£2.80	—
25	Family Pets	1967	HX-136	20p	£4.50
25	People and Places	1966	HX-26	20p	£3.50
25	Prehistoric Animals	1967	HX-92	£1.60	£40.00
25	Sailing Ships Through the Ages	1963	HX-119	£1.60	£40.00
25	Veteran and Vintage Cars	1965	HX-159	£1.60	£40.00
25	Veteran Racing Cars	1963	HX-19	£1.60	£40.00
	GRAFFITI INC. (USA)				
LT90	Goldeneye, James Bond 007	1997		—	£9.50
	GRAIN PRODUCTS (New Zealand)				
M20	Adventuring in New Zealand	1982		—	£12.00
M20	American Holiday	1986		—	£12.00
M20	Amusement Parks	1987		—	£12.00
M20	Cats	1983		—	£15.00
M20	European Holiday	1980		—	£12.00
M20	Farming in N.Z.	1986		—	£15.00
M20	Fire Engines	1988		—	£15.00
M20	Fish of the New Zealand Seas	1981		—	£15.00
M20	Hong Kong Highlights	1991		—	£15.00
M20	Horse and Pony World	1978		—	£15.00
EL9	How to Cartoon	1989		—	£9.00
M20	Kennel Companions	1976		—	£20.00
M25	National Costumes of the Old World	1977		—	£25.00
M20	New Zealand Police	1984		—	£15.00
M20	Our Heritage on Parade	1980		—	£15.00
M20	Our Mighty Forests	1979		—	£15.00
M20	Passport Los Angeles	1990		—	£12.00
M20	Space Exploration	1986		—	£15.00
M20	Television in New Zealand	1983		—	£12.00
EL10	Vintage and Veteran Cars	1985		—	£12.00
M20	World of Bridges	1981		—	£15.00

Size & quantity	TRADE CARD ISSUES	Date	Handbook reference	Price per card	Complete set
	GRAMPUS PHOTOS				
M20	Film Favourites (of 1920s)	1993		—	£10.00
M20	Modern Beauties (topless pin-up girls)	1992		—	£15.00
	GRANDSTAND				
LT100	Scottish Footballers Nos 1-100	1993		20p	£12.00
LT102	Scottish Footballers Nos 101-202	1993		20p	£12.00
	GRANGER'S				
12	Dr. Mabuse	c1920		£12.00	—
	GRANOSE FOODS LTD				
M48	Adventures of Billy the Buck	1952		20p	£4.50
M16	Air Transport	1957	HG-40.1	40p	£6.00
M16	Animal Life	1957	HG-40.2	30p	£5.00
25	Animals in the Service of Man	c1965	HX-51	£3.00	
M16	Aquatic and Reptile Life	1957	HG-40.3	40p	£6.00
M48	King of the Air	1956		70p	—
M48	Life Story of Blower the Whale	1956		70p	—
M48	Lone Leo the Cougar	1955		70p	—
M20	150 Years of British Locomotives	1980		75p	£15.00
M16	Our Winged Friends	1957	HG-40.4	75p	—
M16	Plant Life	1957	HG-40.5	75p	—
M48	Silver Mane, The Timber Wolf	1955		40p	—
M16	Space Travel	1957	HG-40.6	60p	£10.00
M48	Tippytail the Grizzly Bear	1956		20p	£8.00
M16	Water Transport	1957	HG-40.7	30p	£5.00
M16	World Wide Visits	1957	HG-40.8	25p	£4.00
	W. GRANT & SONS LTD				
25	Clan Tartans	1992		—	£15.00
	GREATER MANCHESTER POLICE				
L24	British Lions (Rugby League)	1992		—	£7.50
EL16	British Stamps	1986		30p	£4.50
L24	Riversiders Wigan R.L.F.C.	1990		30p	£7.50
L12	Rugby 13 Hall of Fame	1992		—	£7.50
L24	Wigan R.L.F.C. Simply the Best	1996		—	£12.00
L24	Wigan Rugby League F.C. (As Safe As ...)	2001		—	£6.00
	D. GREEN				
15	Alexandra The Greats (Crewe Alexandra F.C. Footballers)	2006		—	£6.00
	GREGG (New Zealand)				
M48	Aquatic Birds	1965		50p	£25.00
	Album			—	£20.00
M40	Birds (Land Birds)	1963		60p	—
	Album			—	£20.00
M40	Introduced Birds	1967		60p	£24.00
	Album			—	£20.00
M40	Native Birds of New Zealand	1971		30p	£12.00
	Album			—	£20.00
M35	Rare and Endangered Birds	1977		60p	—
	Album			—	£25.00
M40	Remarkable Birds	1969		60p	£24.00
	Album			—	£20.00
M35	Unusual Birds of the World	1981		60p	—
	Album			—	£25.00

Size & quantity	TRADE CARD ISSUES	Date	Handbook reference	Price per card	Complete set
	GUINNESS				
EL6	Famous Guinness Alice Posters............	1951		£15.00	£90.00
EL6	Famous Guinness for Strength Posters	1951		£15.00	£90.00
EL6	Guinness Advertisements, Set A	1932		£20.00	—
EL6	Guinness Advertisements, Set B	1932		£20.00	—
EL6	Guinness Advertisements, Set C	1932		£20.00	—
	H B ICE CREAM				
24	Do You Know	1968		£7.00	—
	H.M.A.F. TOYS				
EL9	H.M. Armed Forces	2009		—	£9.00
	HADDEN'S				
24	World's Most Beautiful Butterflies	c1920	HX-23	£10.00	—
	NICHOLAS HALL				
25	War Series	1915	HX-290	£28.00	—
	B. HALLS				
M35	Cricket Sudocards	2006		—	£5.00
M25	Rowing Sudocards	2006		—	£4.00
	HALPIN'S WILLOW TEA				
	Aircraft of the World:				
25	A Standard Set	1958	HX-180	20p	£4.50
M20	B Two Pictures per Card, 25 Subjects	1958		£1.25	£25.00
25	Nature Studies...	1957	HX-9	30p	£7.50
	T. P. K. HANNAH (Confectionery)				
25	Top Flight Stars (Sport)...	1960		£4.00	—
	THE HAPPY HOME				
M8	Child Studies (silks) (multi-backed)	c1915	HH-5	£22.00	—
M9	Flags (silks)...	c1915	HH-6	£11.00	—
K14	The Happy Home Silk Button (silks)	c1915		£13.00	—
M9	Our Lucky Flowers (silks) (multi-backed)	c1915	HH-8	£16.00	—
M12	Women on War Work (silks)	c1915	HH-9	£16.00	—
	HARBOUR DIGITAL				
M12	Birds in Flight	1997		—	£9.00
30	Cars At the Turn of the Century	1996		—	£9.00
M18	Cricket Teams of the 1890s	1997		—	£12.00
12	England & South Africa Cricketers	1996		—	£9.00
12	European Locomotives	1996		—	£7.50
L38	Famous Cricketers 1895	2000		—	£15.00
24	Golden Oldies Extracts from Famous Cricketer 1890	1996		—	£15.00
M20	Harry Vardon's Golf Clinic	1997		—	£10.00
24	Historic Hampshire	1996		—	£6.00
24	Jaguar Cars	1996		—	£9.00
20	More Golden Oldies — Cricketers	1995		60p	£12.00
30	The Old Fruit Garden	1995		40p	£12.00
20	The Operatic Stage	1996		60p	£12.00
L18	The Romance of India	2000		—	£6.00
M10	The Sea Mens Dress	1997		—	£8.00
18	Ships That Battle the Seas	1996		—	£9.00
M12	World Boxers 3rd Series	1996		—	£8.00

Size & quantity	TRADE CARD ISSUES	Date	Handbook reference	Price per card	Complete set
	HARDEN BROTHERS & LINDSAY LTD				
50	Animals of the World	1959	HX-93	40p	£20.00
	Album (titled Wild Animals of the World)			—	£10.00
50	British Birds and Their Eggs	1960	HX-105	£1.60	—
	Album			—	£40.00
50	National Pets	1961	HX-145	20p	£4.50
	Album			—	£8.00
	HAROLD HARE				
L16	Animals and Pets plus album	1960		—	£10.00
	HARRISON				
25	Beauties	c1910	HH-10	£30.00	—
25	Types of British Soldiers	c1910	HX-144	£45.00	—
	HARTLEPOOL UNITED F.C.				
EL32	Hartlepool United Legends	2011		—	£16.00
	HAT-TRICK CARDS				
15	Burnley (Footballers of the 1960s)	2011		—	£6.00
10	Everton Heroes (Footballers of the 1960s)	2011		—	£5.00
10	Hat-Trick Football Cards 1960/70s (black and white)	2011		—	£5.00
10	Hat-Trick Football Cards 1st Series (1970s footballers) coloured	2011		—	£5.00
10	Hat-Trick Football Cards 2nd Series (1970s footballers) coloured	2011		—	£5.00
10	Hat-Trick Football Cards 3rd Series (1970s footballers) coloured	2011		—	£5.00
10	Hat-Trick Football Cards 4th Series (1970s footballers) coloured	2011		—	£5.00
10	Hat-Trick Football Cards 5th Series (1970s footballers) coloured	2011		—	£5.00
10	Hat-Trick Football Cards 6th Series (1970s footballers) coloured	2011		—	£5.00
10	Hat-Trick Football Cards 7th Series (1970s footballers) coloured	2011		—	£5.00
10	Hat-Trick Football Cards 8th Series (1970s footballers) coloured	2013		—	£5.00
10	Hat-Trick Football Cards 9th Series (1970s footballers) coloured	2013		—	£5.00
10	Kick Off 1st Series (Footballers of the 1960/70s)	2012		—	£5.00
10	Kick Off 2nd Series (Footballers of the 1960/70s)	2012		—	£5.00
	J. HAWKINS & SONS LTD				
M30	The Story of Cotton	c1920		£6.50	—
	HAYMAN				
24	World's Most Beautiful Butterflies	c1920	HX-23	£10.00	—
	S. HENDERSON & SONS LTD				
	General Interest Series:		HH-17		
L6	Egypt Nos 79 to 84	c1908		£12.00	—
L6	Fairy Tales Nos 67 to 72	c1908		£12.00	—
L6	Home Life in Various Countries Nos 73 to 78	c1908		£12.00	—
L48	International Series Flags and Costumes of all Nations Nos 85 to 132	c1908		£12.00	—

Size & quantity	TRADE CARD ISSUES	Date	Handbook reference	Price per card	Complete set
	S. HENDERSON & SONS LTD (continued)				
	Natural History Series:				
L6	Big Game Nos 7 to 12	c1908		£12.00	—
L6	Birds Nos 1 to 6	c1908		£12.00	—
L6	Carniverous Animals Nos 13 to 18	c1908		£12.00	—
L6	Butterflies Nos 61 to 66	c1908		£12.00	—
L6	Cat Tribe Nos 37 to 42	c1908		£12.00	—
L6	Dogs Nos 43 to 48	c1908		£12.00	—
L6	Farmyard Fowls Nos 49 to 54	c1908		£12.00	—
L6	Fishes Nos 55 to 60	c1908		£12.00	—
L6	Herbivorous Animals Nos 19 to 24	c1908		£12.00	—
L6	Reptiles Nos 25 to 30	c1908		£12.00	—
L6	Serpents Nos 31 to 36	c1908		£12.00	—
	HEDNESFORD TOWN FOOTBALL CLUB				
24	Hednesford Town Football Stars (including Information Sheets)	1986		25p	£6.00
	HEINZ				
EL1	Australian Cricket Team England	1964		—	£18.00
	HERALD ALARMS				
10	Feudal Lords	1986		—	£20.00
EL10	Feudal Lords	1986		£1.20	£12.00
	HERTFORDSHIRE POLICE				
L12	Stamp Out Crime	1983		—	£6.00
	HITCHMAN'S DAIRIES LTD				
25	Aircraft of World War II:		HX-7		
	A Black back	1966		50p	£12.50
	B Blue back	1966		£1.20	£30.00
25	Animals of the World	1965	HX-61	80p	£20.00
25	British Birds and their Nests	1966	HX-104	£1.60	—
25	British Railways	1964	HX-107	20p	£4.50
25	Buses & Trams:		HX-109		
	A White card	1966		24p	£6.00
	B Cream card	1966		24p	£6.00
25	Merchant Ships of the World	1962	HX-63	£1.00	—
25	Modern Wonders	1965	HX-130	50p	£12.50
25	Naval Battles	1971	HX-21	30p	£7.50
25	People and Places	1971	HX-26	24p	£6.00
25	Regimental Uniforms of the Past	1973		20p	£4.50
25	Science in the 20th Century	1966	HX-18	36p	£9.00
25	The Story of Milk	1965	HX-3	70p	£17.50
25	Trains of the World	1970	HX-121	£1.00	—
	F. HOADLEY LTD				
24	World's Most Beautiful Birds	c1920	HX-22	£12.00	—
	HOADLEY'S CHOCOLATES LTD (Australia)				
50	The Birth of a Nation	c1940		£2.50	—
50	British Empire Kings and Queens	c1940		£2.50	—
?33	Cricketers (black and white)	1928		£22.00	—
K36	Cricketers (brown)	1933		£18.00	—
50	Early Australian Series	c1940		£2.20	—
50	Empire Games and Test Teams	1934		£12.00	—

Size & quantity	TRADE CARD ISSUES	Date	Handbook reference	Price per card	Complete set
	HOADLEY'S CHOCOLATES LTD (Australia) (continued)				
32	Gulliver's Travels	1939		£6.50	—
50	National Safety Council	c1937		£5.50	—
40	Test Cricketers	1936		£17.00	—
M36	Test Cricketers	1938		£17.00	—
50	Victorian Footballers 1st Series nd 1-50	c1940		£8.00	—
50	Victorian Footballers 2nd Series nd 51-100	c1940		£8.00	—
50	Victorian Footballers (action studies)	c1940		£8.00	—
50	Wild West Series	c1940		£4.00	—
	HOBBYPRESS GUIDES				
20	Preserved Railway Locomotives	1983		20p	£3.50
20	Preserved Steam Railways 1st Series	1983		20p	£3.50
20	Preserved Steam Railways 2nd Series	1984		20p	£4.00
20	The Worlds Great Cricketers	1984		35p	£7.00
	THOMAS HOLLOWAY LTD				
EL60	Natural History Series — Animals (full length)	c1900		£11.00	—
EL39	Natural History Series — Animals' Heads	c1900		£10.00	—
EL39	Natural History Series — Birds	c1900		£10.00	—
EL50	Pictorial History of the Sports and Pastimes of All Nations	c1900		£13.00	—
	HOME AND COLONIAL STORES LTD				
26	Advertising Alphabet (boxed letters)	1913	HH-27.1	£9.00	—
26	Advertising Alphabet different series (unboxed letters)	1913	HH-27.2	£16.00	—
M100	Flag Pictures	1915	HH-28	£5.00	—
100	War Pictures	1915		£7.00	—
M40	War Pictures (Personalities)	c1915	HH-29.1	£10.00	—
M40	War Pictures (Scenes)	c1915	HH-29.2	£10.00	—
	HOME COUNTIES DAIRIES TEA				
25	Country Life	1964	HX-11	20p	£5.00
25	International Air Liners	1968	HX-125	20p	£4.00
25	The Story of Milk	1965	HX-3	24p	£6.00
	THE HOME MIRROR				
M4	Cinema Star Pictures (silks)	1919	HH-31	£20.00	—
	HOME PUBLICITY LTD				
	Merry Miniatures:				
16	Adventures of the Arkubs	c1950	HH-32.1	£13.00	—
14	Adventures of The Bruin Boys	c1950	HH-32.2	£13.00	—
11	The Adventures of Golly	c1950	HH-32.3	£13.00	—
8	The Further Adventures of Golly	c1950	HH-32.4	£13.00	—
15	Adventures of the Nipper	c1950	HH-32.5	£13.00	—
19	Adventures of Pip, Squeak and Wilfred	c1950	HH-32.6	£13.00	—
15	The Adventures of Popeye	c1950	HH-32.7	£13.00	—
	HOME WEEKLY				
12	Little Charlie Cards	c1915		£18.00	—
	HORNIMAN TEA				
EL10	Boating Ways	c1910	HH-38	£26.00	—
EL12	British Birds and Eggs	c1910	HH-37	£26.00	—

Size & quantity	TRADE CARD ISSUES	Date	Handbook reference	Price per card	Complete set
	HORNIMAN TEA (continued)				
48	Dogs	1961		20p	£5.00
	Album			—	£25.00
EL10	Naval Heroes	c1910	HH-39	£26.00	—
48	Pets	1960		20p	£5.00
	Album			—	£16.00
48	Wild Animals	1958		20p	£5.00
	Album (titled 'On Safari')			—	£25.00
	HORSLEY'S STORES				
25	British Uniforms of the 19th Century	1968	HX-79	50p	£12.50
25	Castles of Britain	1968	HX-134	£1.80	—
25	Family Pets	1968	HX-136	60p	£15.00
	HUDDERSFIELD TOWN F.C.				
M37	Huddersfield Town Players and Officials Season 1935-36	1936		£17.00	—
	HULL CITY FOOTBALL CLUB				
L20	Footballers	1950		£16.00	—
	HULL DAILY MAIL				
EL8	100 Years of Hull Public Transport	1980		—	£5.00
	HUMBERSIDE POLICE				
EL36	East Yorkshire Scenes of Natural Beauty	1987		35p	£12.00
	HUNT, CROP AND SONS				
15	Characters from Dickens	1912		£16.00	—
	D.J. HUNTER				
	Infantry Regimental Colours:				
L7	The Argyll & Sutherland Highlanders 1st Series:				
	A Error Set with light yellow border	2008		—	£3.00
	B Corrected Set with orange border	2008		—	£3.00
L7	The Argyll & Sutherland Highlanders 2nd Series ...	2011		—	£3.00
L7	The Bedfordshire & Herefordshire Regiment	2009		—	£3.00
L7	The Black Watch 1st Series	2006		—	£3.00
L7	The Black Watch 2nd Series	2011		—	£3.00
L7	The Border Regiment	2005		—	£3.00
L7	The Buffs (Royal East Kent Regiment)	2005		—	£3.00
L7	The Cameronians (Scottish Rifles)	2009		—	£3.00
L7	The Cheshire Regiment	2006		—	£3.00
L7	The Coldstream Guards 1st Series	2009		—	£3.00
L7	The Coldstream Guards 2nd Series	2009		—	£3.00
L7	The Coldstream Guards 3rd Series	2009		—	£3.00
L7	The Connaught Rangers	2010		—	£3.00
L7	The Devonshire Regiment 1st Series	2006		—	£3.00
L7	The Devonshire Regiment 2nd Series	2012		—	£3.00
L7	The Dorset Regiment 1st Series	2010		—	£3.00
L7	The Dorset Regiment 2nd Series	2012		—	£3.00
L7	The Duke of Cornwall's Light Infantry	2007		—	£3.00
L7	The Duke of Wellington's Regiment 1st Series	2006		—	£3.00
L7	The Duke of Wellington's Regiment 2nd Series ...	2011		—	£3.00
L7	The Durham Light Infantry 1st Series	2009		—	£3.00
L7	The Durham Light Infantry 2nd Series	2012		—	£3.00

Size & quantity	TRADE CARD ISSUES	Date	Handbook reference	Price per card	Complete set
	D.J. HUNTER (continued)				
	Infantry Regimental Colours (continued):				
L7	The East Lancashire Regiment 1st Series	2007		—	£3.00
L7	The East Lancashire Regiment 2nd Series	2012		—	£3.00
L7	The East Surrey Regiment	2004		—	£3.00
L7	The East Yorkshire Regiment 1st Series	2010		—	£3.00
L7	The East Yorkshire Regiment 2nd Series	2011		—	£3.00
L7	The Essex Regiment	2007		—	£3.00
L7	The Gloucestershire Regiment 1st Series	2006		—	£3.00
L7	The Gloucestershire Regiment 2nd Series	2013		—	£3.00
L7	The Gordon Highlanders 1st Series	2004		—	£3.00
L7	The Gordon Highlanders 2nd Series	2013		—	£3.00
L7	The Green Howards	2010		—	£3.00
L7	The Grenadier Guards 1st Series	2009		—	£3.00
L7	The Grenadier Guards 2nd Series	2009		—	£3.00
L7	The Grenadier Guards 3rd Series	2009		—	£3.00
L7	The Highland Light Infantry	2007		—	£3.00
L7	The Irish Guards 1st Series	2009		—	£3.00
L7	The Irish Guards 2nd Series	2009		—	£3.00
L7	The King's Own Royal Regiment (Lancaster) 1st Series	2005		—	£3.00
L7	The King's Own Royal Regiment (Lancaster) 2nd Series	2012		—	£3.00
L7	The King's Own Scottish Borderers 1st Series	2004		—	£3.00
L7	The King's Own Scottish Borderers 2nd Series (includes errors and two number 3s but no number 4)	2013		—	£3.00
L7	The King's Own Yorkshire Light Infantry	2009		—	£3.00
L7	The King's Regiment (Liverpool)	2005		—	£3.00
L7	The King's Shropshire Light Infantry 1st Series	2004		—	£3.00
L7	The King's Shropshire Light Infantry 2nd Series	2008		—	£3.00
L7	The Lancashire Fusiliers 1st Series:				
	A Error Set with 'Royal' in title	2005		—	£3.00
	B Corrected Set without 'Royal' in title	2006		—	£3.00
L7	The Lancashire Fusiliers 2nd Series	2011		—	£3.00
L7	The London Regiment 1st Series	2008		—	£3.00
L7	The London Regiment 2nd Series	2008		—	£3.00
L7	The Loyal Regiment (North Lancashire)	2009		—	£3.00
L7	The Manchester Regiment 1st Series	2005		—	£3.00
L7	The Manchester Regiment 2nd Series	2012		—	£3.00
L7	The Middlesex Regiment (Duke of Cambridge Own)	2007		—	£3.00
L9	Miscellaneous Colours	2013		—	£3.00
L7	The North Staffordshire Regiment 1st Series	2004		—	£3.00
L7	The North Staffordshire Regiment 2nd Series	2008		—	£3.00
L7	The Northamptonshire Regiment 1st Series	2007		—	£3.00
L7	The Northamptonshire Regiment 2nd Series	2013		—	£3.00
L7	The Oxfordshire & Buckinghamshire Light Infantry 1st Series	2007		—	£3.00
L7	The Oxfordshire & Buckinghamshire Light Infantry 2nd Series	2011		—	£3.00
L7	The Prince of Wales's Leinster Regiment	2010		—	£3.00
L7	The Queen's Own Cameron Highlanders 1st Series	2006		—	£3.00
L7	The Queen's Own Cameron Highlanders 2nd Series	2012		—	£3.00
L7	The Queen's Own Royal West Kent Regiment	2005		—	£3.00
L7	The Queen's Royal Regiment (West Surrey) 1st Series	2004		—	£3.00
L7	The Queen's Royal Regiment (West Surrey) 2nd Series	2012		—	£3.00

Size & quantity	TRADE CARD ISSUES	Date	Handbook reference	Price per card	Complete set

D.J. HUNTER (continued)

Infantry Regimental Colours (continued):

Size & quantity	Title	Date	Handbook reference	Price per card	Complete set
L7	The Royal Berkshire Regiment	2010	—		£3.00
L7	The Royal Dublin Fusiliers	2010	—		£3.00
L7	The Royal Fusiliers (City of London Regiment)	2005	—		£3.00
L7	The Royal Hampshire Regiment	2008	—		£3.00
L7	The Royal Inniskilling Fusiliers 1st Series	2005	—		£3.00
L7	The Royal Inniskilling Fusiliers 2nd Series	2011	—		£3.00
L7	The Royal Irish Fusiliers	2008	—		£3.00
L7	The Royal Irish Regiment (18th Foot) 1st Series	2006	—		£3.00
L7	The Royal Irish Regiment (18th Foot) 2nd Series	2012	—		£3.00
L7	The Royal Irish Rifles	2010	—		£3.00
L7	The Royal Leicestershire Regiment 1st Series	2006	—		£3.00
L7	The Royal Leicestershire Regiment 2nd Series	2013	—		£3.00
L7	The Royal Lincolnshire Regiment	2006	—		£3.00
L7	The Royal Marines 1st Series	2008	—		£3.00
L7	The Royal Marines 2nd Series	2008	—		£3.00
L7	The Royal Munster Fusiliers	2010	—		£3.00
L7	The Royal Norfolk Regiment	2004	—		£3.00
L7	The Royal Northumberland Fusiliers	2005	—		£3.00
L7	The Royal Scots 1st Series	2004	—		£3.00
L7	The Royal Scots 2nd Series	2007	—		£3.00
L7	The Royal Scots Fusiliers 1st Series	2006	—		£3.00
L7	The Royal Scots Fusiliers 2nd Series	2012	—		£3.00
L7	The Royal Sussex Regiment	2007	—		£3.00
L7	The Royal Warwickshire Fusiliers	2005	—		£3.00
L7	The Royal Welch Fusiliers 1st Series	2008	—		£3.00
L7	The Royal Welch Fusiliers 2nd Series	2011	—		£3.00
L7	The Scots Guards 1st Series	2009	—		£3.00
L7	The Scots Guards 2nd Series	2009	—		£3.00
L7	The Scots Guards 3rd Series	2009	—		£3.00
L7	The Seaforth Highlanders 1st Series	2006	—		£3.00
L7	The Seaforth Highlanders 2nd Series	2012	—		£3.00
L7	The Seaforth Highlanders 3rd Series	2012	—		£3.00
L7	The Sherwood Foresters 1st Series	2004	—		£3.00
L7	The Sherwood Foresters 2nd Series	2007	—		£3.00
L7	The Somerset Light Infantry 1st Series	2010	—		£3.00
L7	The Somerset Light Infantry 2nd Series	2011	—		£3.00
L7	The South Lancashire Regiment	2007	—		£3.00
L7	The South Staffordshire Regiment 1st Series	2004	—		£3.00
L7	The South Staffordshire Regiment 2nd Series	2008	—		£3.00
L7	The South Wales Borderers 1st Series	2006	—		£3.00
L7	The South Wales Borderers 2nd Series	2011	—		£3.00
L7	The Suffolk Regiment 1st Series	2004	—		£3.00
L7	The Suffolk Regiment 2nd Series:				
	A Error Set with light yellow border	2008	—		£3.00
	B Corrected Set with orange border	2008	—		£3.00
L7	The Welch Regiment	2005	—		£3.00
L7	The Welsh Guards	2009	—		£3.00
L7	The West Yorkshire Regiment	2010	—		£3.00
L7	The Wiltshire Regiment 1st Series	2010	—		£3.00
L7	The Wiltshire Regiment 2nd Series	2011	—		£3.00
L7	The Worcestershire Regiment 1st Series	2004	—		£3.00
L7	The Worcestershire Regiment 2nd Series (Error on No. 6 marked 1st Series)	2007	—		£3.00
L7	The York and Lancaster Regiment 1st Series	2009	—		£3.00
L7	The York and Lancaster Regiment 2nd Series	2011	—		£3.00

Size & quantity	TRADE CARD ISSUES	Date	Handbook reference	Price per card	Complete set
	HUNTLEY & PALMERS				
EL12	Animals and Birds	c1900	HH-95	£10.00	—
EL12	Aviation	c1908		£50.00	—
EL12	Biscuits in Various Countries	c1900	HH-96	£10.00	—
EL6	Biscuits with Travellers	c1900	HH-97	£10.00	—
EL12	Children of Nations (Gold Border)	c1900	HH-98	£10.00	—
EL12	Children of Nations (White Border)	c1900	HH-99	£10.00	—
EL12	Children at Leisure and Play (No Captions)	c1900	HH-100	£10.00	—
EL12	Harvests of the World	c1900	HH-101	£20.00	—
EL12	Hunting	c1900	HH-102	£12.50	—
EL8	Inventors	c1900	HH-103	£25.00	—
EL11	Rhondes Enfantines (Children's Rhymes)	c1900	HH-104	£30.00	—
EL12	Scenes with Biscuits	c1900	HH-105	£10.00	—
EL12	The Seasons	c1900		£15.00	—
EL8	Shakespearian Subjects	c1900	HH-106	£12.50	—
EL12	Soldiers of Various Countries	c1900	HH-107	£15.00	—
EL12	Sports (With Semi-Circular Effect)	c1900	HH-108	£20.00	—
EL12	Sports (Without Semi-Circular Effect)	c1900	HH-108	£20.00	—
EL12	Travelling During the 19th Century	1900	HH-109	£25.00	—
EL12	Views of Italy and the French Riviera	c1900	HH-110	£12.50	—
EL12	Warships	c1900	HH-111	£15.00	—
EL8	Watteau	c1900	HH-112	£10.00	—
EL8	Wonders of the World	c1900	HH-113	£25.00	—
	R. HYDE & CO. LTD				
80	British Birds	1929		£3.00	—
80	Cage Birds	1930		£2.25	—
80	Canary Culture	1930		£1.50	—
?M63	Hyde's Cartoons (multi-backed)	1908	HH-114	£17.00	—
	IDEAL ALBUMS				
L25	Boxing Greats	1991		—	£12.50
	IKON (Australia)				
LT81	Buffy The Story Continues	2003		—	£16.00
LT81	Buffy The Story So Far	2000		—	£16.00
LT81	Cricketer Australia 2003	2003		—	£20.00
	IMPEL (USA)				
LT150	An American Tail — Fievel Goes West	1991		—	£12.00
LT80	Laffs	1991		—	£9.50
LT160	Minnie 'N' Me	1991		—	£12.00
LT120	Star Trek The Next Generation	1992		—	£14.00
LT5	Star Trek The Next Generation Bonus Foreign Language	1992		—	£5.00
LT160	Star Trek 25th Anniversary 1st Series	1991		—	£12.00
LT150	Star Trek 25th Anniversary 2nd Series	1991		—	£12.00
LT140	Terminator 2 — The Film	1991		—	£9.50
LT36	Trading Card Treats (Cartoon Characters)	1991		—	£9.50
LT90	U.S. Olympic Hall of Fame	1991		20p	£9.50
LT162	WCW Wrestling	1991		—	£12.00
	IMPERIAL PUBLISHING				
L20	American Golfers	1990		43p	£8.50
L24	Birds of Britain	2000		35p	£8.50
L6	Breeds of Cats	2000		—	£3.00

Size & quantity	TRADE CARD ISSUES	Date	Handbook reference	Price per card	Complete set
	IMPERIAL PUBLISHING (continued)				
L6	Dogs — Airedale Terriers	1999		—	£3.00
L6	Dogs — Border Collies	1999		—	£3.00
L6	Dogs — Boxers	1999		—	£3.00
L6	Dogs — Bulldogs	1999		—	£3.00
L6	Dogs — Cocker Spaniels	1999		—	£3.00
L6	Dogs — Dachshunds	1999		—	£3.00
L6	Dogs — Dalmatians	1999		—	£3.00
L6	Dogs — Dobermann	1999		—	£3.00
L6	Dogs — German Shepherds	1999		—	£3.00
L6	Dogs — Golden Retrievers	1999		—	£3.00
L6	Dogs — Greyhounds	2000		—	£3.00
L6	Dogs — Jack Russell Terriers	1999		—	£3.00
L6	Dogs — Labrador Retrievers	1999		—	£3.00
L6	Dogs — Pekingese	1999		—	£3.00
L6	Dogs — Poodles	1999		—	£3.00
L6	Dogs — Scottish Terriers	1999		—	£3.00
L6	Dogs — Staffordshire Bull Terriers	2000		—	£3.00
L6	Dogs — West Highland White Terriers	2000		—	£3.00
L6	Dogs — Yorkshire Terriers	1999		—	£6.00
L24	The History of The Olympic Games	1996		—	£12.00
L20	Native North Americans	1995		—	£10.00
L48	Olympic Champions	1996		—	£15.00
L18	Snooker Celebrities	1993		—	£12.00
	IN LINE (USA)				
LT56	Motor Cycles	1993		—	£10.00
	INDIA & CEYLON TEA CO LTD				
24	The Island of Ceylon	c1955	HX-47	£6.00	—
	INDIAN MOTOCYCLE CO (USA)				
LT10	Indian Motorcycles	1993		—	£10.00
	INEDA (New Zealand)				
LT11	New Zealand All Blacks Elite Rookies (Rugby Union)	1997		—	£36.00
LT9	New Zealand All Blacks Tempered Steel (Rugby Union)	1997		—	£22.00
	INKWORKS (USA)				
LT90	The Adventures of Pinocchio	1996		—	£9.50
LT81	Alias Season 1	2002		—	£11.00
LT81	Alias Season 2	2003		—	£10.00
LT81	Alias Season 3	2004		—	£9.50
LT81	Alias Season 4	2006		—	£9.50
LT90	Alien Legacy (The Four Films)	1998		—	£12.00
LT90	Alien vs Predator — The Film	2004		—	£12.00
LT81	Aliens vs Predator Requiem	2007		—	£8.50
LT45	American Pride	2000		—	£5.00
LT90	Andromeda Season 1	2001		—	£9.50
LT90	Andromeda Reign of The Commonwealth	2004		—	£8.00
LT90	Angel Season 1	2000		—	£9.50
LT90	Angel Season 2	2001		—	£9.50
LT90	Angel Season 3	2002		—	£9.50
LT90	Angel Season 4	2003		—	£9.50
LT90	Angel Season 5	2004		—	£9.50
LT90	Buffy The Vampire Slayer Season 3	1999		—	£16.00
LT90	Buffy The Vampire Slayer Season 4	2000		—	£12.00

Size & quantity	TRADE CARD ISSUES	Date	Handbook reference	Price per card	Complete set
	INKWORKS (USA) (continued)				
LT90	Buffy The Vampire Slayer Season 5	2001		—	£12.00
LT90	Buffy The Vampire Slayer Season 6	2002		—	£12.00
LT90	Buffy The Vampire Slayer Season 7	2003		—	£9.50
LT72	Buffy The Vampire Slayer Big Bads	2004		—	£12.00
LT72	Buffy The Vampire Slayer Connections	2003		—	£18.00
LT50	Buffy The Vampire Slayer Evolution	2002		—	£15.00
LT90	Buffy The Vampire Slayer Memories	2006		—	£9.50
LT81	Buffy The Vampire Slayer Men of Sunnydale	2005		—	£9.50
LT72	Buffy The Vampire Slayer Reflections	2000		—	£15.00
LT90	Buffy The Vampire Slayer 10th Anniversary	2007		—	£9.50
LT90	Buffy The Vampire Slayer Women of Sunnydale	2004		—	£9.50
LT72	Catwoman — The Movie	2004		—	£12.00
LT72	Charmed Season 1	2000		—	£9.50
LT72	Charmed Connections	2004		—	£11.00
LT72	Charmed Conversations	2005		—	£9.50
LT72	Charmed Destiny	2006		—	£9.50
LT72	Charmed Forever	2007		—	£9.50
LT72	Charmed The Power of Three	2003		—	£12.00
LT72	Family Guy Season 1	2005		—	£9.50
LT72	Family Guy Season 2	2006		—	£9.50
LT3/4	Family Guy Season 2 Box Loader Sub Set (minus BL4)	2006		—	£3.00
LT72	Firefly The Complete Collection	2006		—	£10.00
LT72	The 4400 Season 1	2006		—	£9.50
LT81	The 4400 Season 2	2007		—	£9.50
EL72	Godzilla — The Film	1998		—	£9.50
LT72	The Golden Compass — The Film	2007		—	£9.50
LT72	Hell Boy — The Film	2004		—	£12.00
LT72	Hellboy Animated Sword of Storms	2006		—	£9.50
LT90	James Bond 007 3rd Series	1997		—	£20.00
LT72	Jericho Season 1	2007		—	£9.50
LT72	Jurassic Park III — The Movie	2001		—	£10.00
LT72	Looney Tunes Back in Action	2003		—	£9.50
LT90	Lost Season 1	2005		—	£9.50
LT90	Lost Season 2	2006		—	£9.50
LT90	Lost Season 3	2007		—	£9.50
LT81	Lost Revelations	2006		—	£9.50
LT90	Lost in Space — The Film	1998		—	£9.50
LT72	Lost in Space Archives	1997		—	£12.00
LT9	Lost in Space Archives Movie Preview	1997		—	£4.00
LT90	Men in Black — The Film	1997		—	£9.50
LT81	Men In Black II — The Film	2002		—	£12.00
LT81	Mummy Returns — The Movie	2001		—	£9.50
LT72	The Osbournes	2002		—	£9.50
LT90	The Phantom — The Movie	1996		—	£9.50
LT90	Robots — The Movie	2005		—	£9.50
LT90	Roswell Season 1	2000		—	£9.50
LT72	Scooby Doo — The Movie	2002		—	£9.50
LT72	Scooby Doo 2 Monsters Unleashed	2004		—	£11.00
LT72	The Scorpion King — The Movie	2002		—	£12.00
LT72	Serenity — The Film	2005		—	£9.50
LT81	The Simpsons Anniversary Celebration	2000		—	£16.00
LT72	Simpsons Mania	2001		—	£12.00
LT90	Sleepy Hollow — The Movie	1999		—	£9.50
LT72	Sliders (TV Sci-Fi Series)	1997		—	£9.50
LT90	Small Soldiers — The Film	1998		—	£9.50
LT90	Smallville Season 1	2002		—	£9.50
LT90	Smallville Season 2	2003		—	£14.00

Size & quantity	TRADE CARD ISSUES	Date	Handbook reference	Price per card	Complete set
	INKWORKS (USA) (continued)				
LT90	Smallville Season 3	2004		—	£12.00
LT90	Smallville Season 4	2005		—	£9.50
LT90	Smallville Season 5	2007		—	£9.50
LT90	Smallville Season 6	2008		—	£9.50
LT72	The Sopranos Season 1	2005		—	£9.50
LT81	Spawn The Movie	1997		—	£9.50
LT90	Spawn The Toy Files	1999		—	£9.50
LT72	Spike The Complete Story (Buffy & Angel)	2005		—	£11.00
LT72	The Spirit — The Film	2008		—	£9.50
LT81	Starship Troopers — The Movie	1997		—	£9.50
LT90	Supernatural Season 1	2006		—	£9.50
LT90	Supernatural Season 2	2007		—	£9.50
LT81	Supernatural Season 3	2008		—	£9.50
LT72	Supernatural Connections	2008		—	£9.50
LT90	Titan A.E.	2000		—	£9.50
LT90	Tomb Raider — The Movie	2001		—	£9.50
LT81	Tomb Raider 2 — The Cradle of Life	2003		—	£9.50
LT90	Tomorrow Never Dies — James Bond 007	1997		—	£12.00
LT90	TV's Coolest Classics Volume One	1998		—	£9.50
LT72	Veronica Mars Season 1	2006		—	£9.50
LT81	Veronica Mars Season 2	2007		—	£9.50
LT81	Witchblade	2002		—	£9.50
LT90	The World Is Not Enough James Bond 007 the Movie	1999		20p	£12.00
LT90	The X Files Season 4 & 5	2001		20p	£9.50
LT90	The X Files Season 6 & 7	2001		—	£12.00
LT90	The X Files Season 8	2002		20p	£12.00
LT90	The X Files Season 9	2003		20p	£12.00
LT72	The X Files Connections	2005		—	£9.50
LT72	The X Files I Want to Believe — The Film	2008		—	£9.50
	INTERNATIONAL HERITAGE				
L20	Squadrons and Aircraft of the RAF	1993		—	£15.00
	INTREPID (Australia)				
LT100	Tennis — A.T.P. Tour	1996		—	£15.00
LT90	X-Files	1996		—	£9.50
	IPC MAGAZINES LTD				
M25	Lindy's Cards of Fortune	1975		24p	£6.00
	My Favourite Soccer Stars (blue back):				
M32	Issued with 'Buster' including album	1970		£1.50	—
M32	Issued with 'Lion' including album	1970		£1.50	—
M32	Issued with 'Scorcher' including album	1970		£1.50	—
M32	Issued with 'Smash' including album	1970		£1.50	—
M32	Issued with 'Tiger' including album	1970		£1.50	—
	My Favourite Soccer Stars — (red back):				
M32	Issued with 'Buster and Jet' including album	1971		£1.25	£40.00
M32	Issued with 'Lion and Thunder' including album	1971		£1.25	£40.00
M32	Issued with 'Scorcher and Score' including album	1971		£1.25	£40.00
M32	Issued with 'Tiger' including album	1971		£1.25	£40.00
M32	Issued with 'Valiant and TV21' including album	1971		£1.25	£40.00
	JOHN IRWIN & SON				
12	Characters from Dickens' Works	1912	HX-172	£20.00	—
6	Characters from Shakespeare	c1910	HI-6	£20.00	—

287

Size & quantity	TRADE CARD ISSUES	Date	Handbook reference	Price per card	Complete set
	J. F. SPORTING COLLECTIBLES				
LT24	Abbeys, Monasteries & Priorys in The 20th Century ...	2011		—	£16.00
LT24	Academy Award Winners 1st Series (Film Stars)	2010		—	£16.00
LT24	Academy Award Winners 2nd Series (Film Stars)	2013		—	£16.00
LT24	Ali — His Fights, His Opponents	2004		—	£16.00
LT24	The Armies of India	2010		—	£16.00
LT36	Association Footballers 1920/30s 1st Series	2013		—	£27.00
LT36	Association Footballers 1920/30s 2nd Series	2014		—	£27.00
LT36	Association Footballers 1920/30s 3rd Series	2014		—	£27.00
LT36	Association Footballers 1920/30s 4th Series	2014		—	£27.00
LT36	Association Footballers 1920/30s 5th Series	2015		—	£27.00
LT24	Association Footballers 1950s 1st Series...	2013		—	£16.00
LT24	Association Footballers in Action 1920/30s 1st Series	2014		—	£16.00
LT24	Australian Cricket Tourists to England Through the Ages	2017		—	£16.00
LT15	Australian Cricketers 1930...	1999		—	£10.00
LT30	Australian Rugby League Tourists 1948	2002		—	£21.00
LT36	Battle of The Roses Pre War Personalities (Cricketers)	2003		—	£27.00
LT24	Belle Vue Speedway Aces	2001		—	£16.00
LT24	Birds in Britain and Their Eggs 1st Series	2013		—	£16.00
LT24	Boer War Officers	2008		—	£16.00
LT24	Boston United Celebrities	1999		—	£16.00
LT24	Boston United 1st League Season 2002-2003	2002		—	£16.00
LT25	Boxers World Champions	2000		—	£16.00
L24	British Yeomanry Uniforms	2004		—	£16.00
LT24	Bygone Railway Stations and Architecture	2012		—	£16.00
LT24	Castles in Britain in the 20th Century 1st Series	2009		—	£16.00
LT24	Castles in Britain in the 20th Century 2nd Series	2010		—	£16.00
LT25	Centenarians Cricket's 100 100s Club...	2008		—	£18.00
LT24	Classic Movies of the 1930s 1st Series	2013		—	£16.00
LT24	Classic Movies of the 1930s 2nd Series	2015		—	£16.00
LT24	Classic Steam Locos 1st Series	2007		—	£16.00
LT24	Classic Steam Locos 2nd Series	2008		—	£16.00
LT24	Country Seats in the 19th Century in Great Britain & Ireland	2013		—	£16.00
LT24	County Cricketers 1940/50s 1st Series	2014		—	£16.00
LT24	County Cricketers 1940/50s 2nd Series	2016		—	£16.00
LT24	Cowboy Film & TV Stars	2011		—	£16.00
LT24	Cricket England One Cap Winners	2011		—	£16.00
LT24	Cricket Parade 1940/50s	2001		—	£24.00
LT24	Cricket Personalities 1940/50s 1st Series	2000		—	£16.00
LT24	Cricket Personalities 1940/50s 2nd Series	2003		—	£16.00
LT24	Cricket Personalities 1940/50s 3rd Series	2004		—	£16.00
LT24	Cricket Personalities 1940/50s 4th Series	2005		—	£16.00
LT24	Cricket Personalities 1940/50s 5th Series	2006		—	£16.00
LT24	Cricket Personalities 1940/50s 6th Series	2007		—	£16.00
LT24	Cricket Personalities 1940/50s 7th Series	2009		—	£16.00
LT24	Cricket Personalities 1940/50s 8th Series	2013		—	£16.00
LT24	Cricket Personalities 1940/50s 9th Series	2014		—	£16.00
LT24	Cricket Personalities 1940/50s 10th Series	2015		—	£16.00
LT24	Cricket Personalities 1960s 1st Series	2007		—	£16.00
LT24	Cricket Personalities 1960s 2nd Series	2007		—	£16.00
LT24	Cricket Personalities 1960s 3rd Series	2008		—	£16.00
LT24	Cricket Personalities 1960s 4th Series	2010		—	£16.00
LT24	Cricket Personalities 1970s 1st Series	2014		—	£16.00
LT24	Cricket Personalities 1970s 2nd Series	2014		—	£16.00
LT24	Cricketers From Overseas 1919-1939 1st Series	2009		—	£16.00
LT36	Cricketers From Overseas 1940/50s 1st Series	2005		—	£27.00

Size & quantity	TRADE CARD ISSUES	Date	Handbook reference	Price per card	Complete set

J. F. SPORTING COLLECTIBLES (continued)

Size & quantity	Title	Date	Handbook reference	Price per card	Complete set
LT36	Cricketers From Overseas 1960s	2007	—		£27.00
LT24	Cricketers in Action 1940/50s 1st Series	2004	—		£16.00
LT24	Cricketers in Action 1940/50s 2nd Series	2005	—		£16.00
LT24	Cricketers In Action 1940/50s 3rd Series	2005	—		£16.00
LT24	Cricketers In Action 1940/50s 4th Series	2006	—		£16.00
LT24	Cricketers in Action 1960s 1st Series	2007	—		£16.00
LT24	Cricketers in Action 1960s 2nd Series	2007	—		£16.00
LT24	Cricketers in Action 1960s 3rd Series	2008	—		£16.00
LT24	Cricketers The Golden Age Pre Great War 1st Series	2009	—		£16.00
LT24	Cricketers The Golden Age Pre Great War 2nd Series	2010	—		£16.00
LT24	Cricketers The Golden Age Pre Great War 3rd Series	2010	—		£16.00
LT24	Cricketers The Golden Age Pre Great War 4th Series	2011	—		£16.00
LT24	Cricketers The Golden Age Pre Great War 5th Series	2011	—		£16.00
LT24	Cricketers The Golden Age Pre Great War 6th Series	2012	—		£16.00
LT24	Cricketers The Golden Age Pre Great War 7th Series	2014	—		£16.00
LT24	Cricketers The Golden Age Pre Great War 8th Series	2017	—		£16.00
LT24	Cricketers 1919-1939 1st Series	2008	—		£16.00
LT24	Cricketers 1919-1939 2nd Series	2008	—		£16.00
LT24	Cricketers 1919-1939 3rd Series	2008	—		£16.00
LT24	Cricketers 1919-1939 4th Series	2009	—		£16.00
LT24	Cricketers 1919-1939 5th Series	2009	—		£16.00
LT24	Cricketers 1919-1939 6th Series	2010	—		£16.00
LT24	Cricketers 1919-1939 7th Series	2011	—		£16.00
LT24	Cricketers 1919-1939 8th Series	2013	—		£16.00
LT24	Cricketers 1919-1939 9th Series	2013	—		£16.00
LT24	Cricketers 1919-1939 10th Series	2015	—		£16.00
LT24	The Empire's Air Power World War II	2007	—		£16.00
LT36	England Footballers One Cap Winners 1st Series	2013	—		£27.00
LT36	England Footballers One Cap Winners 2nd Series	2013	—		£27.00
LT24	English International Footballers 1872 to 1939	2018	—		£16.00
LT24	F.A. Cup Winners Through the Years	2015	—		£16.00
LT24	Families in First Class Cricket	2011	—		£16.00
LT24	Famous British Film & Stage Stars 1920-40s 1st Series	2009	—		£16.00
LT24	Famous Film Stars 1940/50s 1st Series	2008	—		£16.00
LT24	Famous Film Stars 1940/50s 2nd Series	2009	—		£16.00
LT24	Famous Film Stars 1940/50s 3rd Series	2009	—		£16.00
LT24	Famous Film Stars 1940/50s 4th Series	2015	—		£16.00
M40	Famous Footballers 1896-97 1st Series	1998	—		£30.00
LT36	Famous Footballers Pre-Great War 1st Series	2003	—		£27.00
LT36	Famous Footballers Pre-Great War 2nd Series	2005	—		£27.00
LT20	Famous Heavyweight Fights	2007	—		£12.50
LT24	Favourite Films of the 50s 1st Series	2016	—		£16.00
LT24	50s Glamour Girls	2015	—		£16.00
LT24	Film Stars of The World 1930s 1st Series	2009	—		£16.00
LT24	Film Stars of The World 1930s 2nd Series	2013	—		£16.00
LT24	Films and Their Stars 1940/50s 1st Series	2012	—		£16.00
LT24	Films and Their Stars 1940/50s 2nd Series	2013	—		£16.00
LT36	Football Club Managers 1940/50s 1st Series	2001	—		£27.00
LT24	Football Fallen Heroes of WWI	2014	—		£16.00
LT24	Football Forgotten Caps of WWII (World War 2)	2014	—		£16.00
LT24	Football Personalities Pre-Great War 1st Series	2015	—		£16.00
LT24	Football Personalities Pre-Great War 2nd Series	2015	—		£16.00
LT24	Football Personalities Pre-Great War 3rd Series	2016	—		£16.00
LT24	Football Personalities Pre-Great War 4th Series	2017	—		£16.00
LT36	Football Personalities 1940/50s 1st Series	2007	—		£27.00
LT36	Football Personalities 1940/50s 2nd Series	2007	—		£27.00

Size & quantity	TRADE CARD ISSUES	Date	Handbook reference	Price per card	Complete set
	J. F. SPORTING COLLECTIBLES (continued)				
LT36	Football Personalities 1940/50s 3rd Series	2008		—	£27.00
LT36	Football Stars 1950s 1st Series	2003		—	£27.00
LT24	Football Stars 1950s 2nd Series	2003		—	£16.00
LT36	Football Stars of the Seventies 1st Series	2000		—	£27.00
LT36	Football Stars of the Seventies 2nd Series	2002		—	£27.00
LT36	Football Wartime Guests 1st Series	2011		—	£27.00
LT36	Football Wartime Guests 2nd Series	2011		—	£27.00
LT36	Football Wartime Guests 3rd Series	2012		—	£27.00
LT36	Football Wartime Guests 4th Series	2013		—	£27.00
LT48	Footballers 1950s 1st Series	1999		—	£36.00
LT48	Footballers 1950s 2nd Series	2000		—	£36.00
LT36	Footballers 1960s 1st Series	2000		—	£27.00
LT36	Footballers 1960s 2nd Series	2000		—	£27.00
LT36	Footballers 1960s 3rd Series	2001		—	£27.00
LT36	Footballers 1960s 4th Series	2001		—	£27.00
LT36	Footballers 1960s 5th Series	2002		—	£27.00
LT36	Footballers 1960s 6th Series	2002		—	£27.00
LT36	Footballers 1960s 7th Series	2003		—	£27.00
LT36	Footballers 1960s 8th Series	2003		—	£27.00
LT36	Footballers 1960s 9th Series	2004		—	£27.00
LT36	Footballers 1960s 10th Series	2005		—	£27.00
LT36	Footballers 1960s 11th Series	2006		—	£27.00
LT36	Footballers 1960s 12th Series	2006		—	£27.00
LT36	Footballers 1960s 13th Series	2007		—	£27.00
LT36	Footballers 1960s 14th Series	2008		—	£27.00
LT36	Footballers 1960s 15th Series	2010		—	£27.00
LT36	Footballers 1960s 16th Series	2011		—	£27.00
LT36	Footballers 1970s 1st Series	2002		—	£27.00
LT36	Footballers 1970s 2nd Series	2005		—	£27.00
LT36	Footballers 1970s 3rd Series	2007		—	£27.00
LT36	Footballers 1970s 4th Series	2008		—	£27.00
LT36	Footballers 1970s 5th Series	2009		—	£27.00
LT36	Footballers 1980s 1st Series	2010		—	£27.00
LT36	Footballers 1980s 2nd Series	2011		—	£27.00
LT36	Footballers in Action 1919-1939 1st Series	2010		—	£27.00
LT36	Footballers in Action 1919-1939 2nd Series	2010		—	£27.00
LT24	Footballers In Action 1940/50s 1st Series	1999		—	£16.00
LT24	Footballers in Action 1940/50s 2nd Series	1999		—	£16.00
LT24	Footballers in Action 1940/50s 3rd Series	2000		—	£16.00
LT24	Footballers in Action 1940/50s 4th Series	2003		—	£16.00
LT36	Footballers in Action 1950s 1st Series	2008		—	£27.00
LT36	Footballers in Action 1950s 2nd Series	2009		—	£27.00
LT36	Footballers in Action 1950s 3rd Series	2010		—	£27.00
LT36	Footballers in Action 1950s 4th Series	2011		—	£27.00
LT36	Footballers in Action 1950s 5th Series	2012		—	£27.00
LT36	Footballers in Action 1950s 6th Series	2013		—	£27.00
LT36	Footballers in Action 1950s 7th Series	2013		—	£27.00
LT36	Footballers in Action 1960s 1st Series	2002		—	£27.00
LT36	Footballers in Action 1960s 2nd Series	2004		—	£27.00
LT36	Footballers in Action 1960s 3rd Series	2005		—	£27.00
LT36	Footballers in Action 1960s 4th Series	2006		—	£27.00
LT36	Footballers in Action 1960s 5th Series	2007		—	£27.00
LT36	Footballers in Action 1960s 6th Series	2008		—	£27.00
LT36	Footballers in Action 1960s 7th Series	2012		—	£27.00
LT36	Footballers in Action 1970s 1st Series	2007		—	£27.00
LT36	Footballers in Action 1970s 2nd Series	.2009		—	£27.00
LT36	Footballers of the 1920/30s 1st Series	2013		—	£27.00

Size & quantity	TRADE CARD ISSUES	Date	Handbook reference	Price per card	Complete set
	J. F. SPORTING COLLECTIBLES (continued)				
LT36	Footballers of the 1920/30s 2nd Series	2013		—	£27.00
LT36	Footballers of the 50s 1st Series	2012		—	£27.00
LT36	Footballers of the 50s 2nd Series	2012		—	£27.00
LT36	Footballers of the 50s 3rd Series	2012		—	£27.00
LT36	Forties Favourites in Action (Footballers) 1st Series	2004		—	£27.00
LT36	Forties Favourites in Action (Footballers) 2nd Series	2005		—	£27.00
LT36	Forties Favourites in Action (Footballers) 3rd Series	2005		—	£27.00
LT36	Forties Favourites in Action (Footballers) 4th Series	2006		—	£27.00
LT36	Forties Favourites in Action (Footballers) 5th Series	2007		—	£27.00
LT24	Gentlemen v Players Pre-War Personalities (Cricketers) 1st Series	2003		—	£16.00
LT24	Gentlemen v Players Pre-War Personalities (Cricketers) 2nd Series	2004		—	£16.00
LT24	Gentlemen v Players Pre-War Personalities (Cricketers) 3rd Series	2007		—	£16.00
LT24	George Formby Tribute	2011		—	£16.00
LT24	Golf Personalities 1940/50s	2005		—	£16.00
LT24	Great Goalies 1920-30s 1st Series	2015		—	£16.00
LT24	Great Goalscorers 1920-30s 1st Series	2015		—	£16.00
LT16	Huddersfield Town 1952/53 Team Squad	2018		—	£12.00
LT40	International Footballers in Action 1940/50s 1st Series	2011		—	£30.00
LT40	International Footballers in Action 1940/50s 2nd Series	2012		—	£30.00
LT40	Leeds Road Legends (Huddersfield Town F.C.)	2010		—	£30.00
LT25	Manchester United 1951/52 Team Squad	2016		—	£18.00
LT27	Middlesbrough 1929/30 Team Squad	2016		—	£20.00
LT24	Music Hall Artistes	2013		—	£16.00
LT24	Ocean Steamers Through The Ages	2010		—	£16.00
LT24	Personalities on the TV and Radio 1950/60s 1st Series	2015		—	£16.00
LT24	Personalities on the TV and Radio 1950/60s 2nd Series	2015		—	£16.00
LT24	Pop Stars of the 60s 1st Series	2016		—	£16.00
LT24	Popular Footballers 1919-1939 1st Series	2002		—	£16.00
LT24	Popular Footballers 1919-1939 2nd Series	2002		—	£16.00
LT24	Popular Footballers 1919-1939 3rd Series	2002		—	£16.00
LT36	Popular Footballers 1919-1939 4th Series	2002		—	£27.00
LT36	Popular Footballers 1919-1939 5th Series	2003		—	£27.00
LT36	Popular Footballers 1919-1939 6th Series	2006		—	£27.00
LT36	Popular Footballers 1919-1939 7th Series	2007		—	£27.00
LT36	Popular Footballers 1919-1939 8th Series	2007		—	£27.00
LT36	Popular Footballers 1919-1939 9th Series	2008		—	£27.00
LT36	Popular Footballers 1919-1939 10th Series	2009		—	£27.00
LT36	Popular Footballers 1919-1939 11th Series	2012		—	£27.00
LT24	Popular Footballers Pre 1940 1st Series	2019		—	£16.00
LT36	Popular Footballers 1950s 1st Series	1998		—	£27.00
LT36	Popular Footballers 1950s 2nd Series	1999		—	£27.00
LT36	Popular Footballers 1950s 3rd Series	1999		—	£27.00
LT36	Popular Footballers 1950s 4th Series	1999		—	£27.00
LT36	Popular Footballers 1950s 5th Series	1999		—	£27.00
LT36	Popular Footballers 1950s 6th Series	2003		—	£27.00
LT36	Popular Footballers 1950s 7th Series	2008		—	£27.00
LT36	Popular Footballers 1950s 8th Series	2010		—	£27.00
LT36	Popular Footballers 1960s 1st Series	1999		—	£27.00
LT36	Popular Footballers 1960s 2nd Series	2000		—	£27.00
LT36	Popular Footballers 1960s 3rd Series	2000		—	£27.00
LT36	Popular Footballers 1960s 4th Series	2000		—	£27.00
LT36	Popular Footballers 1960s 5th Series	2000		—	£27.00
LT36	Popular Footballers 1960s 6th Series	2005		—	£27.00

Size & quantity	TRADE CARD ISSUES	Date	Handbook reference	Price per card	Complete set

J. F. SPORTING COLLECTIBLES (continued)

Size & quantity	Title	Date	Handbook ref	Price per card	Complete set
LT36	Popular Footballers 1970s 1st Series	2001		—	£27.00
LT36	Popular Footballers 1970s 2nd Series	2001		—	£27.00
LT36	Popular Footballers 1970s 3rd Series	2002		—	£27.00
LT36	Popular Footballers 1970s 4th Series	2004		—	£27.00
LT36	Popular Footballers 1970s 5th Series	2004		—	£27.00
LT36	Popular Footballers 1970s 6th Series	2005		—	£27.00
LT36	Popular Footballers 1970s 7th Series	2006		—	£27.00
LT36	Popular Footballers 1970s 8th Series	2007		—	£27.00
LT36	Popular Footballers 1970s 9th Series	2008		—	£27.00
LT36	Popular Footballers in Action 1970s 1st Series	2006		—	£27.00
LT36	Popular Footballers in Action 1970s 2nd Series	2006		—	£27.00
LT36	Popular Footballers in Action 1970s 3rd Series	2007		—	£27.00
LT36	Popular Footballers in Action 1970s 4th Series	2008		—	£27.00
LT36	Popular Footballers in Action 1970s 5th Series	2008		—	£27.00
LT36	Popular Footballers in Action 1970s 6th Series	2010		—	£27.00
LT16	Premier League Top Guns 2002 (Speedway)	2002		—	£12.00
LT24	Rugby League Stars 1940/50s 1st Series	2002		—	£16.00
LT24	Rugby League Stars Pre 1950	2016		—	£16.00
LT24	Rugby League Stars In Action 1940/50s	2007		—	£16.00
	Scottish Clan Tartans 1st Series:				
L24	A Titled Scottish Clan Tartans	2002		—	—
LT24	B Titled Scottish Tartans	2012		—	£16.00
L24	Scottish Clan Tartans 2nd Series	2003		—	£16.00
LT24	Seaside Piers in England and Wales in The 20th Century 1st Series	2009		—	£16.00
LT24	Seaside Piers in England and Wales in The 20th Century 2nd Series	2010		—	£16.00
LT24	Sheffield Tigers Speedway Post-War Legends	2001		—	£16.00
LT24	Sherlock Holmes Film Stars	2011		—	£16.00
LT24	Silent Movie Stars 1st Series	2009		—	£16.00
LT24	Silver Screen Actors 1930s	2012		—	£16.00
LT24	Silver Screen Actresses 1930s	2009		—	£16.00
L24	Soldiers of Queen Victoria's Army 1837-1901 1st Series	2004		—	£16.00
L24	Soldiers of Queen Victoria's Army 1837-1901 2nd Series	2007		—	£16.00
LT24	Soldiers of Queen Victoria's Army 1837-1901 3rd Series	2015		—	£16.00
LT24	South Africa & The Transvaal War – British Regiments	2016		—	£16.00
LT24	Southern League Footballers 1894-1920 1st Series	2018		—	£16.00
LT24	Southern League Footballers 1894-1920 2nd Series	2019		—	£16.00
LT24	Speedway All-Time Greats 1st Series	1999		—	£16.00
LT24	Speedway All-Time Greats 2nd Series	1999		—	£16.00
LT24	Speedway All-Time Greats 3rd Series	2000		—	£16.00
LT24	Speedway Personalities In Action 1st Series	2000		—	£16.00
LT24	Speedway Personalities In Action 2nd Series	2000		—	£16.00
LT24	Speedway Riders From Overseas 1st Series	2006		—	£16.00
LT24	Stars of Bradford Speedway	2004		—	£16.00
LT30	Stars of Football 1940s	2002		—	£21.00
LT24	Stars of London Speedway	2002		—	£16.00
LT24	Stars of Midland Speedway 1st Series	2006		—	£16.00
LT36	Stars of Scottish Football Pre-Great War 1st Series	2004		—	£27.00
LT25	Stars of Scottish Speedway	2002		—	£17.50
LT24	Stars of the Radio Shows 1940/50s 1st Series	2013		—	£16.00
LT20	Tennis Stars 1950/60s	2007		—	£13.00
LT24	Test Cricketers 1950s/60s 1st Series	2013		—	£16.00
LT24	Top Pop Groups of the 60s 1st Series	2016		—	£16.00
LT18	Tottenham Hotspur 1960/61 Team Squad	2016		—	£13.50

Size & quantity	TRADE CARD ISSUES	Date	Handbook reference	Price per card	Complete set
	J. F. SPORTING COLLECTIBLES (continued)				
L24	Uniforms of The Royal Regiment of Artillery............	2003		—	£16.00
LT24	University Cricket Blues Pre WWII	2019		—	£16.00
LT28	Victorian Cricket Personalities	2000		—	£20.00
LT24	Victorian Cricketers	2012		—	£16.00
LT24	Victorian Railway Stations	2011		—	£16.00
LT15	Wembley Speedway Stars 1st Series	1999		—	£10.00
LT21	Wembley Speedway Stars 2nd Series.................	2000		—	£16.00
LT22	West Bromwich Albion Team Squad 1953/54	2019		—	£15.00
LT24	Western Films and Their Stars 1st Series	2013		—	£16.00
LT24	Western Films and Their Stars 2nd Series	2016		—	£16.00
L24	World Heavyweight Boxing Champions	1999		—	£16.00
LT20	World Heavyweight Championship Contenders	2000		—	£12.00
LT24	World War II Films and Their Stars.....................	2013		—	£16.00
	JACOB & CO.				
EL24	Banknotes that Made History...........................	1975		20p	£3.50
	Album			—	£4.00
EL6	Build Your Own Prize	1972		£3.50	—
EL16	Circus..	c1970		£3.50	—
EL8	Doodles	1970		£3.50	—
32	Famous Picture Cards from History	1978		20p	£3.50
EL18	Happy Families	1967	HJ-2	£3.50	—
EL6	Nursery Rhymes	1969		£3.50	—
M30	School of Dinosaurs	1994		30p	£9.00
	Album			—	£16.00
EL10	Through the Looking Glass	1971		£3.50	—
25	Vehicles of All Ages	1924	HX-111	£3.60	£90.00
25	Zoo Series:		HX-186		
	A (brown back)	1924		£2.40	£60.00
	B (green back)	1924		£2.00	£50.00
	M.V. JASINSKI (USA)				
LT36	Flash Gordon 1st Series	1990		—	£15.00
LT36	Flash Gordon's Trip to Mars 2nd Series	1991		—	£15.00
LT36	Flash Gordon Conquers the Universe 3rd Series	1992		—	£15.00
	JENSEN PRINT				
10	Soccer Stars (1960s Footballers) 1st Series	1998		—	£5.00
10	Soccer Stars (1960s Footballers) 2nd Series	1998		—	£5.00
	JERMYN'S				
25	National Heroes	c1975		£3.40	—
	JESK CONFECTIONERY				
25	Buses and Trams.......................................	1959	HX-109	£1.20	£30.00
	JET PETROL				
M10	Motor Car Series — Grand Prix Contest	c1975		£4.00	—
	JIFFI				
M64	Kama Sutra..	1989		80p	£50.00
	JONDER (UK)				
L53	Doctor Who — Playing Cards	1996		—	£20.00
	R.L. JONES & CO. LTD				
24	Jet Aircraft of the World	1957		25p	£6.00

Size & quantity	TRADE CARD ISSUES	Date	Handbook reference	Price per card	Complete set
	JUNIOR EXPRESS WEEKLY				
25	Jeff Hawke & Space Gen.	1956		£6.00	—
	JUNIOR PASTIMES				
	(Cards issued with staple holes)				
52	Popular English Players:				
	A 51 different (minus No. 21)	c1960		£5.00	—
	B Number 21	c1960		£25.00	—
52	Popular Players (Footballers):				
	A 51 different (minus No. 42)	c1960		£9.00	—
	B Number 42...	c1960		£25.00	—
52	Popular Railway Engines:				
	A 51 different (minus No. 38)	c1960		£3.25	—
	B Number 38	c1960		£25.00	—
M80	Star Pix	c1960	HX-187	£2.25	—
	JUST CARDS				
10	Buster Keaton	2015		—	£5.00
10	Robert Mitchum	2015		—	£5.00
	JUST JAZZ MAGAZINE				
EL12	Jazz on a Sunday	2010		50p	£6.00
	JUST SEVENTEEN (Periodical)				
M17	Advertisement Stickers	1985		—	£3.50
	K.P. FOODS				
K30	Flintstones, Wackey Races, Tom & Jerry	1996		60p	—
20	Wonderful World of Nature	1983		75p	£15.00
	KADLE KARDS				
10	Who (Doctor Who)	2007		—	£5.00
	KANE PRODUCTS LTD				
36	A.T.V. Stars (Package issue, with blue border)	1958	HK-1	£7.00	—
50	British Birds and Their Eggs	1960	HX-105	80p	£40.00
25	Cricket Clubs & Badges	1957		20p	£4.50
L50	Disc Stars	1959		£2.50	£125.00
M50	Disc Stars	1960		£3.50	—
50	Dogs	1955	HX-205	£3.20	—
L72	Film Stars	1955	HX-30-2	£2.40	—
50	Flags of All Nations	1959	HX-112	60p	£30.00
25	Football Clubs and Colours	1957		20p	£4.50
50	Historical Characters	1957		50p	£25.00
25	International Football Stars	1958		£2.00	—
30	Kings and Queens	1959	HX-116	60p	£18.00
L30	Kings and Queens	1959	HX-116	£1.20	£36.00
25	Modern Motor Cars	1959	HX-39	80p	£20.00
50	Modern Racing Cars...	1954		80p	£40.00
25	National Pets Club 1st Series	1958	HX-145	24p	£6.00
25	National Pets Club 2nd Series	1958	HX-145	£2.40	—
25	1956 Cricketers 1st Series	1956		80p	£20.00
25	1956 Cricketers 2nd Series	1956		80p	£20.00
25	Red Indians 1st Series	1957	HX-118	£1.00	£25.00
25	Red Indians 2nd Series...	1958	HX-118	£1.00	£25.00
25	Roy Rogers Colour Series...	1958		£2.40	£60.00
25	Roy Rogers Series	1957		£4.40	—
50	Space Adventure	1955		£1.20	—
50	20th Century Events	1959		£1.60	—
K50	Wild Animals	1954		20p	£5.00

Size & quantity	TRADE CARD ISSUES	Date	Handbook reference	Price per card	Complete set
	KARDOMAH				
K50	Wild Animals	c1920	HX-216	£6.00	—
K50	Wonders of the Deep	c1920	HK-4.2	£6.00	—
	M. & S. KEECH				
15	Australian Cricket Team 1905	1986		—	£4.00
15	English Cricketers 1902	1987		—	£6.00
	KEEPSAKE (USA)				
LT72	The Blue and the Gray — Civil War Art by Kunstler	1997		—	£20.00
LT72	Wild West by Mort Kunstler	1996		—	£15.00
	JAMES KEILLER & SON LTD				
ELP18	Film Favourites	c1925		£12.00	—
25	Scottish Heritage	c1970		60p	£15.00
	KELLOGG COMPANY OF GREAT BRITAIN LTD				
K16	Animals — 3D	c1968	HK-17	£3.50	—
K5	Coco Pops 3D Animals	1988		£2.50	—
M56	Crunchy Nut Corn Flakes Playing Cards	1986		—	£4.00
12	Famous Firsts	1963		30p	£3.50
M20	Gardens to Visit	1987		35p	£7.00
	Album			—	£16.00
16	History of British Military Aircraft	1963		£1.50	£24.00
12	International Soccer Stars	1961		£1.25	£15.00
	Album			—	£30.00
M8	International Soccer Tips	c1978		£6.00	—
M8	Lost in Space	1998		£2.50	—
40	Motor Cars:				
	A Black and white	1949		£4.50	—
	B Coloured	1949		£7.50	—
M20	Olympic Champions	1991		£1.75	—
K8	Prehistoric Monsters and the Present — 3D	1985		£1.50	£12.00
16	Ships of the British Navy	1962		£1.50	£24.00
12	The Story of the Bicycle	1960		£3.50	—
	Story of the Locomotive 1st Series:		HK-25		
16	A Inscribed 'A Series of 16'	1962		£1.50	£24.00
12	B Inscribed 'A Series of 12'	1962		£4.00	—
16	The Story of the Locomotive 2nd Series:				
	A Inscribed 'Series 2'	1965		£1.50	£24.00
	B Without 'Series 2'	1965		£3.50	—
L6	Stumper Puzzles	1987		£2.00	—
K8	Tony Racing Stickers	1988		45p	£3.50
16	Veteran Motor Cars	1962		£1.00	£16.00
	KELLOGG (Canada)				
M32	Dinosaur Stickers	1992		—	£8.00
	General Interest Set 1:				
M15	Aeroplanes	c1937		£2.00	—
M15	Campcraft	c1937		£2.00	—
M15	Firearms	c1937		£2.00	—
M15	People of the World	c1937		£2.00	—
M15	Ships of War	c1937		£2.00	—
M15	Sports Records	c1937		£2.00	—
M30	Sports Tips	c1937		£2.00	—
M15	Strange Animals	c1937		£2.00	—
M15	Vehicles of War	c1937		£2.00	—

Size & quantity	TRADE CARD ISSUES	Date	Handbook reference	Price per card	Complete set
	KELLOGG (Canada) (continued)				
	General Interest Set 2:				
M15	Aeroplanes	c1938		£2.00	—
M15	Denizens of the Deep	c1938		£2.00	—
M15	Dogs	c1938		£2.00	—
M15	Great Deeds in Canada	c1938		£2.00	—
M15	Histories of Flight	c1938		£2.00	—
M30	Sports Tips	c1938		£2.00	—
M15	Things to Make	c1938		£2.00	—
M15	Tricks	c1938		£2.00	—
M15	Uniforms	c1938		£2.00	—
	General Interest Set 3:				
M15	Aeroplanes	c1939		£2.00	—
M15	Boats	c1939		£2.00	—
M15	First Aid Tips	c1939		£2.00	—
M15	Historic Automobiles	c1939		£2.00	—
M15	Picture Puzzles	c1939		£2.00	—
M15	Sports Histories	c1939		£2.00	—
M30	Sports Tips	c1939		£2.00	—
M15	Strange Birds	c1939		£2.00	—
M15	Things to Make	c1939		£2.00	—
	KENT COUNTY CONSTABULARY				
L24	England World Cup Squad	1982		£3.00	—
L30	England World Cup Squad	1986		£2.50	£75.00
L30	Olympic Athletes	1988		£1.50	£45.00
	KENT COUNTY CRICKET CLUB				
50	Cricketers of Kent	1985		—	£9.00
	KENTUCKY FRIED CHICKEN				
M20	Star Wars Episode 1	1999		38p	£7.50
	KICK OFF CARDS				
10	Kick Off (Footballers of the 1970s)	2011		—	£5.00
	KIDDY'S FAVOURITES LTD				
	(Cards issued with staple holes)				
52	New Popular Film Stars	c1950		£4.00	—
50	Popular Boxers:				
	A 49 different (minus No. 46)	c1950		£4.00	—
	B Number 46	c1950		£25.00	—
52	Popular Cricketers:		HX149		
	A 51 different (minus No. 48)	1948		£4.00	—
	B Number 48	1948		£30.00	—
65	Popular Film Stars	c1950		£5.00	—
52	Popular Footballers:				
	A 51 different (minus No. 52)	c1950		£4.00	—
	B Number 52	c1950		£25.00	—
52	Popular Olympics	c1950		£4.00	—
	'Popular' Players (Footballers):				
75	A Five red hearts at top of front	c1950		£7.00	—
52	B Three red shamrocks at top of front:				
	i 51 different (minus No. 44)	1949		£4.00	—
	ii Number 44	1949		£25.00	—
52	'Popular' Speedway Riders:				
	A 51 different (minus No. 23)	c1950		£4.00	—
	B Number 23	c1950		£25.00	—

Size & quantity	TRADE CARD ISSUES	Date	Handbook reference	Price per card	Complete set
	KILPATRICKS BREAD (USA)				
LT33	Star Trek The Motion Picture	1979	—		£12.00
	KIMBALL (USA)				
LT12	The Space Shuttle	1992		—	£6.00
	KINGS, YORK (Laundry)				
K25	Flags of all Nations (silks)	1954		£3.00	—
30	Kings and Queens of England	1954	HX-116	30p	£9.00
	KING'S LAUNDRIES LTD (Walthamstow)				
25	Famous Railway Engines	c1955		£6.40	—
25	Modern British Warplanes	1953		£5.40	—
25	Modern Motor Cycles	c1955		£5.40	—
25	Radio and Television Stars	c1955		£5.40	—
	KING'S SPECIALITIES				
26	Alphabet Rhymes...	c1915		£14.00	—
24	'Don'ts' or Lessons in Etiquette	c1915		£12.00	—
25	Great War Celebrities & Warships	c1915	HK-37	£13.00	—
25	Heroes of Famous Books	1914		£13.00	—
25	King's Discoveries	c1915	HK-38	£12.00	—
25	King's Servants	c1915	HK-39	£13.00	—
24	Proverbs...	c1915		£12.00	—
37	Unrecorded History	c1915		£12.00	—
100	War Pictures	c1915	HX-200	£14.00	—
25	Where King's Supplies Grow	1913	HK-40	£13.00	—
	KITCHEN SINK (USA)				
LT90	The Crow — City of Angels — The Film	1996		—	£9.50
LT90	Universal Monsters of the Silver Screen	1996		—	£12.00
	KLENE (GUM)				
L50	Footballers (Val Footer Gum)...	1936		£45.00	—
L80	Shirley Temple and Film Stars (Nos 1 to 80)	1935		£7.00	—
L70	Shirley Temple (black and white) (Nos 81 to 100 & 161 to 210)	1935		£8.00	—
L80	Shirley Temple (coloured) title in blue (Nos 81 to 160)	1935		£8.00	—
L60	Shirley Temple (coloured) title in black (Nos 101 to 160)	1935		£8.00	—
	J. KNIGHT (Hustler Soap)				
20	Animals of the World (cut outs):				
	A Corner officially cut	1925		£1.25	£25.00
	B Uncut card	1925		£1.50	£30.00
20	Animals of the World 2nd Series (cut outs):				
	A Corner officially cut	1925		£1.25	£25.00
	B Uncut card	1925		£1.50	£30.00
20	Animals of the World 3rd Series (cut outs):				
	A Corner officially cut	1925		£1.25	£25.00
	B Uncut card	1925		£1.50	£30.00
30	Regimental Nicknames:				
	A Corner officially cut	1925		£3.00	—
	B Uncut card	1925		£3.50	—
	KNOCKOUT				
20	Super Planes of Today	c1960		30p	£6.00

Size & quantity	TRADE CARD ISSUES	Date	Handbook reference	Price per card	Complete set
	KNORR				
L6	Great Trains of Europe … … … … … … … … … …	1983		£6.00	—
	KRAFT CHEESE				
12	Historic Military Uniforms … … … … … … … … …	1971		30p	£3.50
	Album … … … … … … … … … … … … …			—	£4.00
	KROME (USA)				
LT50	Betty Boop 1st Series … … … … … … … … … …	1996		—	£25.00
LT45	Betty Boop 2nd Series … … … … … … … … …	1997		—	£25.00
LT100	Bloom County Outland Chromium … … … … … …	1995		—	£12.00
LT50	Creed Chromium From Lightning Comics … … … …	1996		—	£12.00
	LACEY'S CHEWING GUM				
50	Footballers … … … … … … … … … … … … …	c1925		£42.00	—
40	Uniforms … … … … … … … … … … … … …	c1925	HL-1	£32.00	—
	F. LAMBERT & SONS LTD (Tea)				
25	Before our Time … … … … … … … … … …	1961	HX-103	20p	£3.50
25	Birds & Their Eggs … … … … … … … … … …	1960	HX-1.1	£1.20	£30.00
25	Butterflies & Moths … … … … … … … … … …	1966	HX-2	40p	£10.00
25	Cacti … … … … … … … … … … … … … …	1962	HX-133	20p	£3.50
25	Car Registration Numbers 1st Series … … … … … …	1959		60p	£15.00
25	Car Registration Numbers 2nd Series … … … … … …	1960		£1.20	—
25	Football Clubs and Badges … … … … … … … …	1958	HX-137	24p	£6.00
25	Game Birds and Wild Fowl … … … … … … … …	1964		£1.00	—
25	Historic East Anglia … … … … … … … … …	1963		20p	£3.50
25	Interesting Hobbies … … … … … … … … …	1965		60p	£15.00
25	Passenger Liners … … … … … … … … … …	1965	HX-82	60p	£15.00
25	Past and Present … … … … … … … … … …	1964		20p	£3.50
25	People and Places … … … … … … … … … …	1966	HX-26	24p	£6.00
25	Pond Life … … … … … … … … … … … …	1964	HX-81	60p	£15.00
25	Sports and Games … … … … … … … … … …	1964	HX-154	36p	£9.00
	LAMPORT AND HOLT				
L1	TSS Vandyck and TSS Voltaire:				
	A Criss Cross border … … … … … … … … …	1925		—	£12.00
	B Chain border with circles at corners … … … …	1925		—	£25.00
	LANCASHIRE CONSTABULARY				
L12	Austin Rover Motor Cars … … … … … … … …	1987		50p	£6.00
11	History of the Police … … … … … … … … …	1989		35p	£3.50
24	Lancashire Police File … … … … … … … … …	1986		50p	£12.00
	LANCASHIRE COUNTY CRICKET CLUB				
M150	Lancashire Greats (Cricketers) … … … … … … …	2014		—	£15.00
	LANG'S BREAD CO LTD				
25	Holsum Series (Recipe Cards) … … … … … … …	c1920		£12.00	—
	LATARCHE				
L25	Skiing Through the Ages … … … … … … … …	1994		—	£8.50

Size & quantity	TRADE CARD ISSUES	Date	Handbook reference	Price per card	Complete set
	LEAF (USA)				
LT50	Family Guy	2011		—	£9.50
	LEAF GUM CO. (USA)				
L72	Star Trek	1967		—	—
	LEAF SALES CONFECTIONERY LTD				
L50	Cliff Richard	1961		£5.00	—
EL50	Do You Know?	1961		£1.00	£50.00
EL90	Famous Artists	1963		£2.50	—
EL50	Famous Discoveries and Adventures	1961		£3.50	—
EL40	The Flag Game	1960		£1.00	£40.00
EL50	Footballers (Portraits and Caricatures)	1961	HL-7	£3.00	—
EL50	Totem Pole Talking Signs	1960		£1.80	—
	LEEDS POLICE				
L20	Leeds Rugby League F.C....	1992		—	£8.00
L20	Leeds Rugby League F.C....	1993		—	£6.00
L20	Leeds Rugby League F.C....	1994		—	£6.00
L20	Leeds Rugby League F.C....	1995		—	£6.00
	LEESLEY (USA)				
LT100	Big Foot (Trucks)	1988		—	£9.50
	LEGENDS				
L20	British Rock Legends	1993		—	£10.00
	LEICESTER MERCURY				
LT40	Leicester City Footballers	2003		—	£30.00
	LEVER BROS				
20	British Birds and Their Nests ('Sunlight Soap')	1961	HX-104	30p	£6.00
152	Celebrities, white borders large and small	1905	HL-15	£6.00	—
M39	Celebrities, black border	1905	HL-16	£8.00	—
	LIFEGUARD PRODUCTS (Soap etc.)				
25	British Butterflies	1955		24p	£6.00
	LIME ROCK (USA)				
LT40	Dallas Cowboys Cheerleaders	1992		—	£6.00
LT110	Dream Machines Nos 1-110 (Motoring)	1991		—	£15.00
LT55	Dream Machines Nos 111-165 (Motoring & Powerboats)	1992		—	£9.50
LT110	Heroes of the Persian Gulf	1991		—	£9.50
LT49	Los Angeles Raiderettes Cheerleaders	1992		—	£6.00
LT31	Miami Dolphins Cheerleaders	1992		—	£6.00
LT36	New Orleans Saintsations Cheerleaders	1992		—	£6.00
LT44	Pro Cheerleaders (basketball)	1991		—	£8.00
LT55	Space Art	1993		—	£12.00
	JOSEPH LINGFORD & SON LTD (Baking Powder)				
36	British War Leaders	1950		£2.50	£90.00

Size & quantity	TRADE CARD ISSUES	Date	Handbook reference	Price per card	Complete set
	LIPTON LTD (Tea)				
50	Conquest of Space	1962	HX-73	£1.00	—
60	Flags of the World	1966		25p	£15.00
	Album			—	£8.00
	LIPTON TEA (Canada)				
48	Animals and Their Young	1991		£1.00	£50.00
	LIPTON TEA (Overseas)				
EL30	Birds of Prey (Arabic text)	c1970		—	£25.00
	J. LIVINGSTONE				
11	Flags, Arms and Types of Nations	c1905	HL-45	£32.00	—
	LOBO (Portugal)				
L12	David Bowie 1993 Calendar Back	1992		—	£6.00
L12	Iron Maiden (Pop Group) 1990 Calendar Back	1989		—	£6.00
L16	Iron Maiden (Pop Group) 1992 Calendar Back	1991		—	£6.00
L12	Michael Jackson 1992 Calendar Back	1991		—	£6.00
L12	Mick Jagger (Rolling Stones) 1992 Calendar Back	1991		—	£7.00
	LOCAL AUTHORITIES CATERERS ASSOCIATION				
5	British Sporting Personalities	1997		—	£3.50
	LODGE PLUGS LTD				
M20	Vintage Cars	c1950	HL-47	£12.00	—
	LONGLEAT HOUSE				
25	Longleat House	1966		20p	£3.50
	LOS ANGELES POLICE (USA)				
EL30	Dodgers Baseball Players	1988		—	£10.00
	LOT-O-FUN				
MP4	Sports Champions	1922		£7.50	—
	G.F. LOVELL & CO. LTD				
?31	British Royalty Series	1911		£45.00	—
36	Football Series	1910		£85.00	—
25	Photos of Football Stars	1928	HX-188	£40.00	—
	LUAKA TEA				
M12	Wildlife (with token)	c1985		—	£6.00
	B. LUND				
6	Rugby Union Six Nations 2000	2000		—	£1.50
6	Rugby Union Six Nations 2001	2001		—	£1.50
8	Rugby Union World Cup 1999	1999		—	£1.50
	LYCHGATE PRESS				
L25	Abandoned (Buildings in the North West of England)	2018		—	£10.00
10	Amazing World	2004		—	£5.00
10	The Beatles	2002		—	£5.00
12	The Beatles 1963	2005		—	£5.00
L6	The Cramps (Punk Rock Band of the 1970s)	2019		—	£5.00
10	Crystal Palace Legends 1st Series	2014		—	£5.00
10	Crystal Palace Legends 2nd Series	2015		—	£5.00
10	Eloise (Adult Fantasy Art)	2001		—	£5.00
10	Everton Ladies Football in Action	2017		—	£5.00

Size & quantity	TRADE CARD ISSUES	Date	Handbook reference	Price per card	Complete set
	LYCHGATE PRESS (continued)				
10	Flags of Micronations	2014	—		£5.00
10	Football Stars 1st Series (Footballers of the 1980s) ...	2016	—		£5.00
10	Football Stars 2nd Series (Footballers of the 1980s) ...	2016	—		£5.00
10	Football Stars 3rd Series (Footballers of the 1980s) ...	2016	—		£5.00
10	Hendrix (Jimi)	2010	—		£5.00
10	Images of the Great War 1st Series	2013	—		£5.00
10	Images of the Great War 2nd Series	2013	—		£5.00
10	Images of the Great War 3rd Series	2013	—		£5.00
10	Images of the Great War 4th Series	2013	—		£5.00
10	Kings of Comedy	2005	—		£5.00
M10	Manchester Street Art	2019	—		£7.00
10	Premier Stars 1st Series (Premier League Footballers)	2016	—		£5.00
10	Premier Stars 2nd Series (Premier League Footballers)	2017	—		£5.00
10	Premier Stars 3rd Series (Premier League Footballers)	2017	—		£5.00
10	Premier Stars 4th Series (Premier League Footballers)	2018	—		£5.00
10	Punk Icons 1st Series	2014	—		£5.00
10	Punk Icons 2nd Series	2015	—		£5.00
10	Rock Icons 1st Series	2015	—		£5.00
10	Rock'N'Roll Greats	2005	—		£5.00
10	60's Soccer Stars	2006	—		£5.00
L25	Soccer Gallery (Footballers of the 1960s)	2000	—		£10.00
10	Soccer Parade (Footballers of the 1960/70s) 1st Series	2015	—		£5.00
10	Soccer Parade (Footballers of the 1960/70s) 2nd Series (not marked 2nd Series)	2015	—		£5.00
18	Tottenham (Footballers)	2000	—		£6.50
10	The Wonderful World of Inventions	2004	—		£5.00
	J. LYONS				
48	Australia	1959		20p	£8.00
	Album			—	£25.00
L16	Catweazle Magic Cards	1971	HL-80	60p	£10.00
32	HM Ships 1902-1962:		HL-81		
	A Descriptive Back	1962		25p	£8.00
	B Advertisement Back	1962		40p	£12.00
	Album			—	£25.00
	Illustrated Map of the British Isles:				
M35	A Set of 35	1959		£1.20	—
M1	B Key card	1959		—	£2.00
EL6	150th Anniversary of the Postage Stamp	1990		60p	£3.50
EL15	The Story od Indian Tea Series (Package Issue)	c1970	HX-189	£3.00	—
K100	Tricks and Puzzles	1926		£4.00	—
48	What Do You Know?	1957		20p	£4.50
	Album			—	£25.00
24	Wings Across the World:		HL-83		
	A Descriptive Back	1961		30p	£7.50
	B Advertisement Back	1961		60p	£15.00
	Album			—	£20.00
24	Wings of Speed:		HL-84		
	A Descriptive Back	1960		20p	£5.00
	B Advertisement Back	1960		32p	£8.00
	Album			—	£20.00
	LYONS MAID (Ice Cream)				
40	All Systems Go	1967		£2.00	—
M20	Banknotes	1974		50p	£10.00
M12	Beautiful Butterflies	1974		50p	£6.00
25	Birds and Their Eggs	1963		£1.40	—

Size & quantity	TRADE CARD ISSUES	Date	Handbook reference	Price per card	Complete set
	LYONS MAID (Ice Cream) (continued)				
40	British Wildlife	1970		£1.50	£60.00
M20	County Badge Collection	1974		25p	£5.00
EL12	Did You Know?	1975		50p	£6.00
40	European Adventure	1969		£2.00	—
40	Famous Aircraft	1965		50p	£20.00
	Album			—	£6.00
40	Famous Cars	1966		£2.00	—
	Album.			—	£25.00
40	Famous Locomotives	1964		£2.50	—
48	Famous People:		HX-53		
	A Panel at top 29mm	1962		£1.50	£75.00
	B Panel at top 32mm	1962		£1.00	£50.00
M12	Farmyard Stencils	1977		75p	£8.00
M14	Flowers	c1976		—	£28.00
EL12	Horses in the Service of Man	1984		50p	£6.00
40	International Footballers	1971		£6.50	—
40	Into the Unknown	1968		£2.00	—
15	Jubilee Kings and Queens of England	1977		£2.50	—
EL10	Junior Champs	1983		60p	£6.00
50	100 Years of Motoring	1961	HX-117	£1.50	—
40	On Safari	1969		£1.65	—
40	Pop Scene	1970		£4.00	—
40	Pop Stars	1969		£4.00	—
M10	Pop Stars (shaped)	1975		£1.00	—
40	Soccer Stars	1970		£5.00	—
40	Space Age Britain	1968		£2.00	—
40	Space Exploration	1963		£2.50	—
25	Space 1999	1976		£6.00	—
25	Star Trek	1980		£8.00	—
50	Train Spotters	1962	HX-157	90p	£45.00
40	Views of London	1967		£1.00	£40.00
	M AND C CARDS				
15	Gloucester Premiership Heroes (Rugby Union)	2018		—	£6.50
	M.B.T.W.				
10	Footballers 60 (Footballers of the 1960s)	2016		—	£5.00
10	Footballers 70 1st Series (Footballers of the 1970s)	2016		—	£5.00
10	Footballers 70 2nd Series (Footballers of the 1970s)	2016		—	£5.00
10	Footballers 70 3rd Series (Footballers of the 1970s)	2016		—	£5.00
	M.P. CARDS				
L12	The Geisha Collection	1997		—	£12.00
L14	Nishikigoi — Koi Carp	1997		—	£15.00
L6	The Staffordshire Bull Terrier	1996		—	£6.00
	MAC FISHERIES				
L12	Gallery Pictures	1924		£1.50	£18.00
L14	Japanese Colour Prints	1924		£1.50	—
L12	Poster Pointers	1925		£1.50	£18.00
L12	Sporting Prints	1923		£4.50	—
	Wm. McEWAN & CO. LTD				
25	Old Glasgow	1929		£14.00	—
	McVITIE & PRICE				
8	The European War Series	1915	HX-129	£22.00	—

Size & quantity	TRADE CARD ISSUES	Date	Handbook reference	Price per card	Complete set
	MADISON CONFECTIONERY PRODUCTS LTD				
L48	Disc Jockey 1st Series	1957		£2.50	—
L48	Disc Jockey 2nd Series	1958		£2.00	£100.00
L50	Recording Stars	c1960		£2.50	—
	THE MAGNET LIBRARY				
MP6	Football Teams (11.11.22 to 16.12.22)	1922	HM-13.1	£5.00	—
MP4	Football Teams (3.2.23 to 24.2.23)	1923	HM-13.2	£5.00	—
MP15	Footballers	1922		£4.50	—
	MAINSTREAM PUBLISHING				
13	The Story of Newcastle United's No. 9 Heroes	2004		—	£6.00
	MANCHESTER EVENING NEWS				
L30	Manchester City & United Footballers	1976		£3.00	—
	MANDERS-FITZROY ART PRODUCTIONS LTD				
10	British Jazz Greats	1997		—	£8.00
25	Celebrated Band Leaders	2001		—	£20.00
25	Jazz Greats 1st Series	1995		—	£20.00
25	Jazz Greats 2nd Series	1996		—	£20.00
25	Jazz Greats 3rd Series	1998		—	£20.00
	MANOR BREAD (USA)				
LT33	Star Trek The Motion Picture	1979		—	£15.00
	R. MARCANTONIO LTD				
50	Interesting Animals:				
	A Black and white front	1953		20p	£4.50
	B Coloured front	1953	HX-115	£4.00	—
	MARKET-SCENE LTD (New Zealand)				
M21	Super Stars of Wrestling 1st Series	1989		£1.00	—
M21	Super Stars of Wrestling 2nd Series	1989		£1.00	—
M21	Super Stars of Wrestling 3rd Series	1990		£1.00	—
	A.T. MARKS				
20	Buses	2021		—	£4.00
8	Buses in Luton	1991		—	£3.50
20	Lorries 1st Series	2021		—	£4.00
20	Post Box 1st Series	2021		—	£4.00
20	Ships	2021		—	£4.00
20	Trains 1st Series	2021		—	£4.00
	CRICKET SETS				
14	Australian Cricketers 1893	1993		—	£6.00
M35	Cricket (1900 Period) unnumbered	1994		—	£6.00
M16	Cricket (1900 Period) 1st Series nos 1-16	1994		—	£3.50
M16	Cricket (1900 Period) 2nd Series nos 17-32	1995		—	£3.50
M16	Cricket (1900 Period) 3rd Series nos 33-48	1995		—	£3.50
M8	Cricket (1900 Period) 4th Series nos 49-56	1995		—	£3.50
12	Derbyshire Cricketers 1895	1993		—	£3.50
13	Essex Cricketers 1895	1993		—	£3.50
11	Gloucestershire Cricketers 1892	1990		—	£3.50
13	Gloucestershire Cricketers 1894	1993		—	£3.50
13	Hampshire Cricketers 1895	1993		—	£3.50
11	Kent Cricketers 1892	1991		—	£3.50
14	Kent Cricketers 1897	1993		—	£3.50
13	Kent Cricketers 1909	1991		—	£3.50
12	Lancashire Cricketers 1892	1992		—	£3.50
14	Lancashire Cricketers 1895	1993		—	£3.50

Size & quantity	TRADE CARD ISSUES	Date	Handbook reference	Price per card	Complete set
	A.T. MARKS (continued)				
13	Leicestershire Cricketers 1895	1993	—		£3.50
11	Middlesex Cricketers 1892	1990	—		£3.50
12	Middlesex Cricketers 1895	1993	—		£3.50
12	Middlesex Cricketers 1903	1990	—		£3.50
11	Northamptonshire Cricketers 1912	1990	—		£3.50
13	Nottinghamshire Cricketers 1895	1992	—		£3.50
12	Somerset Cricketers 1894	1992	—		£3.50
11	Surrey Cricketers 1892	1990	—		£3.50
13	Surrey Cricketers 1896	1993	—		£3.50
11	Sussex Cricketers 1892	1990	—		£3.50
15	Sussex Cricketers 1895	1993	—		£3.50
12	Warwickshire Cricketers 1895	1992	—		£3.50
12	Yorkshire Cricketers 1892	1991	—		£3.50
17	Yorkshire Cricketers 1898	1993	—		£3.50
12	Yorkshire Cricketers 1903	1990	—		£3.50
	MARLOW CIVIL ENGINEERING				
25	Famous Clowns	1990		—	£30.00
	MARS CONFECTIONS LTD				
25	Ceremonies of the Coronation:				
	A Caption on front in black, back in black	1937		£2.00	—
	B Caption on front in blue, back in black	1937		£1.60	£40.00
	C Caption on front in blue, back in blue	1937		£5.00	—
50	Famous Aeroplanes, Pilots and Airports	1938		£2.00	£100.00
50	Famous Escapes	1937		£1.50	£75.00
50	Famous Film Stars	1939		£1.80	£90.00
25	Wonders of the 'Queen Mary'	1936		£1.80	£45.00
	JAMES MARSHALL (GLASGOW) LTD				
30	Colonial Troops	1900	HX-100	£50.00	—
? 7	Recipes/House Hints (unnumbered)	1926	HM-24	£7.00	—
10	Recipes (coloured) (numbered)	1926		£6.00	—
	MARSTON'S BREWERY				
8	Marston's Victorian Moments (Selection from Wills Famous Inventions 1915)	1994		50p	£4.00
	MASONIC TRADE CARDS CO.				
EL20	Famous Freemasons 1st Series	2017		—	£15.00
EL24	Masonic Tercentenary Celebrating 300 Years of British Freemasonry	2017		—	£15.00
	THE MASTER VENDING CO. LTD (Chewing Gum)				
L25	A Bombshell for the Sheriff	1959		£1.40	£35.00
L16	Cricketer Series, New Zealand	1958		£1.75	£28.00
L50	Did You Know? (Football Cards):				
	A Cream Card	1959		£2.50	—
	B Grey Card	1959		£2.50	—
L50	Football Tips:				
	Printing A Cream Card	1958		£2.50	—
	Printing B Cream Card	1958		£2.50	—
	Printing B Grey Card	1958		£2.50	—
L100	Jet Aircraft of the World:		HM-29		
	A Send 3/6 for 20 page album	1958		£2.25	—
	B Send for details of the Album	1958		£2.25	—
	C German Text	1958		£3.00	—
L25	Taxing the Sheriff	1959		£1.40	£35.00
L36	Tommy Steele	1960		£5.00	—

Size & quantity	TRADE CARD ISSUES	Date	Handbook reference	Price per card	Complete set
	MASTERS				
L12	Food From Britain	1986		30p	£3.50
	MATCH DAY CARDS				
LT14	Papa John's Trophy Final 2020 (Football) Portsmouth vs Salford City	2021		—	£5.00
	MATCH WEEKLY				
M36	Euro Football	1988		—	£3.50
L31	FA Cup Facts File	1986		30p	£9.00
	MATCHBOX INT. LTD				
75	Matchbox Models	1985		90p	£70.00
	Album			—	£30.00
	MATCHDAY CARDS				
EL18	Stockport County F.C. 2010-11	2010		—	£6.00
EL16	Stockport County F.C. 2011-12	2011		—	£6.00
	MAXILIN MARKETING CO. LTD				
25	Motor Cars	1951		40p	£10.00
	MAXX (UK)				
LT76	British Athletics nos 1-76	1992		20p	£10.00
LT74	British Athletics nos 77-150	1992		20p	£10.00
	MAYNARDS LTD				
12	Billy Bunter Series	c1920	HM-31	£30.00	—
8	European War Series	c1915	HX-129	£24.00	—
17	Football Clubs	1932	HM-32	£55.00	—
18	Girl Guides	c1920	HM-33	£20.00	—
50	Girls of All Nations	1924	HM-34	£6.00	—
12	Strange Insects	c1920		£6.00	—
12	Wonders of the Deep	c1920		£7.00	—
	World's Wonder Series:				
12	A Numbered	c1920		£5.50	—
10	B Unnumbered	c1920	HM-35	£6.50	—
	MAYPOLE				
25	War Series	1915		£13.00	—
	MAZAWATTEE (Tea)				
L39	Kings and Queens	c1905	HM-37	£5.50	—
	MEADOW DAIRY CO.				
50	War Series	1914	HX-290	£13.00	—
	MELOX				
L50	Famous Breeds of Dogs	1937		£8.50	—
M32	Happy Families (Dogs)	1937		£8.50	—
	MERCURY HOUSE CONSUMER PUBLICATIONS LTD				
L4	PM Car Starter ('Popular Motoring')	1972		90p	£3.50
	MERLIN				
LT120	Football Premier League	1994		—	£15.00
LT88	Football Premier League	1996		—	£20.00
LT161	Football Premier League Gold	1997		—	£25.00
LT150	Football Premier League Gold	1998		—	£25.00
LT150	Football Premier League Gold	1999		—	£25.00
LT20	Football Premier League Gold Club Badges Nos A1 to A20	1999		—	£15.00

Size & quantity	TRADE CARD ISSUES	Date	Handbook reference	Price per card	Complete set
	MERLIN (continued)				
LT10	Football Premier League Gold World Cup Superstars etc. Nos B1 to B10	1999	—	—	£15.00
LT105	Football Premier League Gold	2000	—	—	£15.00
LT20	Football Premier League Gold — Top Scorers	2000	—	—	£15.00
LT20	Football Premier League Gold — Key Players	2000	—	—	£15.00
LT80	Rugby League Footballers Nos 1-80	1991	—	20p	£9.50
LT80	Rugby League Footballers Nos 81-160	1991	—	20p	£9.50
LT100	Shooting Stars (Footballers) Nos 1-100	1991	—	20p	£15.00
LT100	Shooting Stars (Footballers) Nos 101-200	1991	—	20p	£15.00
LT100	Shooting Stars (Footballers) Nos 201-300	1991	—	20p	£15.00
LT96	Shooting Stars (Footballers) Nos 301-396	1991	—	20p	£15.00
LT125	Star Wars Trilogy	1997	—	20p	£15.00
LT96	World Wrestling Federation Gold Series Part 1	1992	—	20p	—
LT96	World Wrestling Federation Gold Series Part 2	1992	—	20p	—
LT75	World Wrestling Federation Stars Nos 1-75	1991	—	20p	—
LT75	World Wrestling Federation Stars Nos 76-150	1991	—	20p	—
	MERRYSWEETS LTD				
L48	Telegum TV Stars	1958	—	£2.00	—
L48	World Racing Cars	1959	—	£3.40	—
	GEOFFREY MICHAEL PUBLISHERS LTD				
40	Modern Motor Cars (booklets)	1953	—	£2.00	£80.00
48	Mystery Cards -Modern Motor Cars	c1953	—	£15.00	—
	MIDLAND CARTOPHILIC BRANCH				
L24	Silhouettes of Veteran & Vintage Cars	1991	—	—	£7.50
	MIDLAND COUNTIES				
M20	Banknotes of the World	1974	—	—	£12.50
M12	Farmyard Stencils	1977	—	—	£4.00
M24	Kings of the Road	1977	—	—	£10.00
EL10	Steam Power	1978	—	50p	£5.00
	MIDLAND COUNTIES & CADBURY				
12	Action Soldiers	1976	—	35p	£4.00
	MILK MARKETING BOARD				
25	Prehistoric Animals	1964	—	30p	£7.50
	Album		—	—	£15.00
	MILLERS (Tea)				
25	Animals and Reptiles	1962	HX-99	20p	£4.50
	MINUTE MAID/UPPER DECK (USA)				
LT25	World Cup All Stars (Football)	1994	—	—	£10.00
	ROBERT R. MIRANDA LTD				
50	150 Years of Locomotives:		HX-178		
	A White lettering on black panel	1957		20p	£8.00
	B Black lettering on white background	1958		20p	£6.00
50	100 Years of Motoring	1955	HX-117	20p	£6.00
25	Ships Through the Ages	1958	HX-94	40p	£10.00
50	Strange Creatures	1960	HX-120	20p	£8.00
	MIS-SPENT YOUTH				
L55	Toon Traders (Newcastle Utd. Footballers)	1996	—	—	£12.00

Size & quantity	TRADE CARD ISSUES	Date	Handbook reference	Price per card	Complete set
	MISTER SOFTEE LTD (Ice Cream)				
M12	Beautiful Butterflies	1977		75p	£9.00
M20	County Badge Collection	1976		30p	£6.00
L12	Did You Know?	1976		38p	£4.50
25	Do You Know?	1961	HX-166.1	£3.50	—
L20	Famous Sports Trophies (shaped)	1975		—	£12.00
M12	Farmyard Stencils	1977		40p	£5.00
M24	1st Division Football League Club Badges	1972		40p	£10.00
L12	Horses in the Service of Man..........................	1977		£1.25	£15.00
M24	Kings of the Road (car radiator badges)	1977		40p	—
20	Mister Softee's TOP 20....................................	1963		£1.00	£20.00
EL12	Mister Softee TOP 10 ('Record Mirror' blue printed back — no address)	1964	HM-61	£1.00	£12.00
EL12	First 12 Subjects: Mister Softee's Top Ten (black printing on back 'Win a Big Prize')	1965		£2.00	£24.00
EL12	Second 12 Subjects: A Mister Softee's Top Ten — address '350 King Street'	1966		£5.00	—
	B Lord Neilson's Star Cards, address '350 King Street'	1966		£3.00	—
EL12	Third 12 Subjects: Lord Neilson's Star Cards — no address	1967		£2.00	£24.00
EL24	Lord Neilson's Star Cards ('Disc and Music Echo') unnumbered	1968	HM-62	£2.50	£60.00
EL24	Mister Softee's Pop Parade ('Disc and Music Echo') numbered	1969		£1.75	£42.00
EL24	Lord Neilson's Star Cards ('Disc and Music Echo') numbered	1969		£2.50	—
M24	Mister Softee Pop Discs (circular card)	1973	HM-63B	£2.00	—
L24	Lord Neilson Star Discs (circular card)	1970	HM-63A	£2.00	£48.00
15	Moon Mission	1962		£3.50	—
M10	Pop Stars (star shaped)	1975		—	£16.00
M20	Stamp in a Million	1976		—	£10.00
L10	Steam Power	1978		35p	£3.50
M4	Super Human Heroes	1979		—	£3.50
25	TV Personalities	1962		£3.50	—
EL12	Your World	1963		35p	£4.00
	MISTER SOFTEE & CADBURY				
12	Action Soldiers	1976		40p	£5.00
	MITCHAM FOODS LTD				
25	Aircraft of Today: A With "Top Flight Sweet Cigarettes"	1960		30p	£7.50
	B Without "Top Flight Sweet Cigarettes"	1960		£2.00	—
25	Aquarium Fish 1st Series	1957	HX-87	£2.00	£50.00
25	Aquarium Fish 2nd Series	1957	HX-87	20p	£4.00
50	Butterflies and Moths (issued in pairs)............	1959		£2.00	—
25	Footballers	1956	HX-54	£4.00	—
50	Mars Adventure	c1960	HX-138	£7.50	—
25	Motor Racing	1957		£2.40	£60.00
	MOBIL OIL CO. LTD				
M30	Football Club Badges (Canvas)	1977		£3.00	—
EL36	The Story of Grand Prix Motor Racing............	1970		55p	£20.00
25	Veteran and Vintage Cars	1963	HX-159	£2.40	£60.00
24	Vintage Cars	1966		25p	£6.00
	Album			—	£15.00

Size & quantity	TRADE CARD ISSUES	Date	Handbook reference	Price per card	Complete set
	MODERN BOY				
16	Fighting Planes of the World	1936		£5.00	—
32	Mechanical Wonders of 1935	1935		£3.00	—
	MOFFAT BROS				
L100	Cinema Artistes	1914		£15.00	—
	MOFFAT (B. & G. LTD)				
EL102	Money That Made History	1971		20p	£10.00
	MOLASSINE (Vims)				
50	Dogs (full length):		HX-135		
	A Title boxed	1963		£1.50	—
	B Title unboxed	1963		£1.50	—
50	Dogs (head and shoulder):				
	A Back with "Dogs Love Vims"	1964		£2.20	—
	B Back with "Vims - Pet Dog Cards"	1964		£2.20	—
25	Dogs at Work	1971		20p	£4.50
12	Dogs of All Countries	1925		£12.00	—
50	Puppies:				
	A Large print "A Series of 50" 16mm long	1966		£2.50	—
	B Small print "A Series of 50" 12mm long	1966		£2.20	—
	MOMENTS IN HISTORY (New Zealand)				
LT18	The Canterbury Earthquakes	2016		—	£12.00
	MONTAGU MOTOR MUSEUM				
M24	Veteran & Vintage Cars 1st Series	1961		£4.00	—
	Album			—	£30.00
M24	Veteran & Vintage Cars 2nd Series	1961		£6.00	—
	MONTY GUM				
M54	Bay City Rollers (Playing Card inset)	1978		60p	£32.00
L72	Daily Fables	1969		33p	£25.00
M94	Dallas	1981		—	£12.00
LT50	Elvis	1978		—	£100.00
M98	Flags + 2 varieties (nos. 59 and 92 not issued)	c1980		—	£14.00
L56	Footballers (Playing Card inset)	1961	HM-73	£3.25	—
M54	Hitmakers (Playing Card inset)	1978		60p	—
M72	Kojak	1975		—	£36.00
M54	Kojak (Playing Card inset) black back	1976		50p	£27.00
M56	Kojak (Playing Card inset) red back	1976		70p	—
L55	Motor Cars (Playing Card inset) Symbols 36-38mm apart	1960		£2.20	—
L56	Motor Cars (Playing Card inset) Symbols 33-34mm apart	1960		£2.00	—
M64	Space Alpha 1999	1978		50p	£32.00
L56	Vintage Cars	1962		£1.75	—
L52	World Aircraft (Playing Card inset)	c1960		£3.00	—
	MORLEY LTD				
10	The Morley Circus	c1960		£3.00	—
	MORNING FOODS LTD				
1	Advertisement Card	c1955		—	£5.00
P25	British Planes:		HM-78		
	A Unnumbered	1953		60p	£15.00
	B Numbered	1953		£8.00	—
P50	British Trains	1952		£8.00	—

Size & quantity	TRADE CARD ISSUES	Date	Handbook reference	Price per card	Complete set
	MORNING FOODS LTD (continued)				
25	British Uniforms	1954	HX-108	30p	£7.50
12	The Cunard Line:				
	A Black back	1957		30p	£3.50
	B Blue back	1957		40p	£4.50
50	Modern Cars	1954		40p	£20.00
50	Our England	1955		20p	£8.00
25	Test Cricketers	1953		£4.00	£100.00
25	World Locomotives:		HX-70		
	A Black back	1956		20p	£4.00
	B Blue back	1956		£1.00	£25.00
	E.D.L. MOSELEY				
M25	Historical Buildings	1956		20p	£4.00
	MOTOR ART (USA)				
LT110	Iditarod (Sled Dog Race Across Alaska)	1992		—	£9.50
	MOTOR CYCLE NEWS				
M24	Best of British Motor Cycling (including poster)	1988		—	£3.50
L6	Motorcycle Classics	1995		—	£3.50
	MOTOR MAGAZINE				
24	The Great British Sports Car (including album)	1988		25p	£6.00
	MOTOR SPORT CHARITY MEMORABILIA				
50	Formula 1 World Championship	1999		—	£15.00
	MURCO PETROLEUM				
50	Airlines of the World	1978		—	£4.50
	R.S. MURRAY & CO.				
9	Alphabet Cards	c1930		£35.00	—
	MUSEUM OF BRITISH MILITARY UNIFORMS				
25	British Cavalry Uniforms	1987		30p	£7.50
25	Military Maids	1987		30p	£7.50
25	Warriors Through the Ages	1987		30p	£7.50
	MUSGRAVE BROTHERS LTD				
	(SEE ALSO BROOKE BOND & CO LTD)				
25	Birds	1961	HX-71	£1.60	—
25	Into Space	1961	HX-147	70p	£17.50
25	Modern Motor Cars	1963	HX-39	£1.00	£25.00
25	Pond Life	1963	HX-81	60p	£15.00
25	Products of the World	1961	HX-152	24p	£6.00
25	Tropical Birds	1963	HX-13	30p	£7.50
25	Wild Flowers	1961	HX-124	70p	£17.50
	MUSICAL COLLECTABLES				
25	Gilbert & Sullivan 1st Series	1995		—	£6.00
25	Gilbert & Sullivan 2nd Series	1995		24p	£6.00
	MY WEEKLY				
M9	Battle Series (silk)	1916	HM-87	£10.00	—
M12	Floral Beauties (silk)	c1915	HM-82	£10.00	—
M15	Language of Flowers (silk)	c1915	HM-84	£10.00	—

Size & quantity	TRADE CARD ISSUES	Date	Handbook reference	Price per card	Complete set
	MY WEEKLY (continued)				
M54	Lucky Emblems (silk)	c1915	HM-85	£11.00	—
M6	Lucky Flowers (silk)	c1915	HM-86	£14.00	—
M12	Our Soldier Boys (silk)	c1915	HM-88	£10.00	—
M14	Soldiers of the King (silk)	c1915	HM-91	£10.00	—
M6	Sweet Kiss Series (silk)	c1915	HM-94	£10.00	—
M6	War Heroes (silk)	c1915	HM-95	£10.00	—
	MYERS & METREVELI				
K48	Film Stars 1st Series (Numbered 1 to 48, Wow Gum issue)	c1955		£4.50	—
K48	Film Stars 2nd Series (Numbered 49 to 96 Anonymous issue)	c1955		£4.50	—
	Film Stars and Biographies:		HM-97		
L59	A Back Stupendous News	c1953		£8.00	—
L1	B Back Wow News	c1953		£10.00	—
L60	Hollywood Peep Show	c1953		£5.00	—
L50	Spot the Planes (Strato Gum issue)	c1954		£7.00	—
	NABISCO FOODS LTD				
K5	Aces in Action	1980		£4.00	—
M24	Action Shots of Olympic Sports	1980		£2.00	—
L4	Adventure Books	1970		£6.00	—
EL20	Champions of Sport	1961		£3.75	—
EL6	Eagle Eye	1979		—	£3.50
12	ET — The Extra-Terrestrial	1982		50p	£6.00
M24	Footballers	1970		£3.50	—
EL8	Football Tactics (England Soccer Stars)	1977		—	£12.00
EL12	Freshwater Fishes of Britain	1974		—	£18.00
EL6	Henry Cooper's Champions of Sport	1984		£3.00	—
M10	History of Aviation	1970		£2.50	£25.00
K4	Johan Cruyff Demonstrates	1980	HN-3	£5.00	—
EL10	Kevin Keegan's Keep Fit with the Stars	1977		—	£12.00
EL6	Kevin Keegan's Play 'N' Score	1977		—	£7.00
EL6	Kevin Keegan's Quiz Game	1980		£3.00	—
EL10	Motor Show	1960		£4.00	—
EL6	Superman III Action Replay Game	1983		£3.00	—
L6	World Super Stars and Sporting Trophies	1980		£4.00	—
EL6	Worzel Gummidge Play 'n' Wipe	1979		£3.00	—
	NAC (USA)				
LT100	Branson on Stage (TV Music Show)	1992		—	£9.50
	NASSAR (Gold Coast)				
25	Transport — Present and Future	1955		30p	£7.50
	NATIONAL BASEBALL HALL OF FAME (USA)				
EL36	Baseball's Hall of Famers	1995		—	£7.50
	NATIONAL GALLERY				
EL24	Masterpieces	1978		—	£7.50
	NATIONAL SPASTICS SOCIETY				
24	Famous County Cricketers (booklet)	1958		£2.40	£60.00
24	Famous Footballers	1958		£1.00	£25.00
	NECA				
LT24	Beetlejuice The Movie	2001		—	£6.00

Size & quantity	TRADE CARD ISSUES	Date	Handbook reference	Price per card	Complete set
	NEEDLERS				
13	Military Series	1916	HX-128	£38.00	—
	PHILIP NEILL				
15	Aberdeen Kings of Europe 1982/83	2018	—	£6.50	
15	Arsenal Double Legends of 1970/71	2002	—	£6.00	
15	Arsenal 79 (A Tribute To The Classic FA Cup Winners of 1979)	2009	—	£6.00	
15	Aston Villa F.C. European Champions 81/82	2013	—	£6.00	
10	Bizarre Club Shirts (Football)	2001	—	£5.00	
15	Blackburn Rovers Heroes & Legends	2009	—	£6.00	
15	Blades Heroes & Legends (Sheffield United F.C)	2014	—	£6.00	
12	Brazil '70 (Football)	2005	—	£5.00	
10	Brazilliant — The Story of Pele (Footballer)	2001	—	£5.00	
20	British Internationals 1950-2 (Football)	1999	—	£7.00	
15	The Busby Babes 1st Series (Manchester United F.C.)	2002	—	£6.00	
15	The Busby Babes 2nd Series (Manchester United F.C.)	2005	—	£6.00	
L8	Celtic '67 The Lisbon Lions (Footballers)	2003	—	£5.00	
15	Chelsea F.C. 1970 (F.A. Cup Winners)	2008	—	£6.00	
10	Chelsea's Top Ten Goalscorers	2013	—	£5.00	
15	Claret Heroes of The 1970s (Burnley F.C.)	2008	—	£6.00	
15	Classic F.A. Cup Winners Tottenham Hotspur 1981 ...	2013	—	£6.00	
10	Classic Kits (Football Team Colours)	2001	—	£5.00	
15	Classic Soccer Strips	2006	—	£6.00	
10	Crystal Palace Heroes and Legends (Footballers) ...	2012	—	£5.00	
15	Derby County Champions of 1971/72	2007	—	£6.00	
18	Derby County Champions of 1974/75 40th Anniversary Edition	2015	—	£7.50	
L10	Elvis in Pictures	2003	—	£6.00	
15	England World Cup Winners 1966	2006	—	£6.00	
10	England's Top Goal Scorers	2002	—	£5.00	
10	Everton Heroes and Legends	2012	—	£5.00	
20	Favourite Footballers Pre 1st & 2nd World War 1st Series	2009	—	£7.00	
20	Favourite Footballers Pre 1st & 2nd World War 2nd Series	2009	—	£7.00	
20	Favourite Footballers Pre 1st & 2nd World War 3rd Series	2009	—	£7.00	
20	Favourite Footballers Pre 1st & 2nd World War 4th Series	2009	—	£7.00	
25	Fergie's Heroes 2003/04 — Manchester United Footballers	2003	—	£7.50	
10	Football Favourites (Prominent Players of the 1960s)	2015	—	£5.00	
10	Football Heroes (Stars of the 1960s)	2001	—	£5.00	
10	Football Icons 1st Series	2014	—	£5.00	
10	Football Icons 2nd Series	2015	—	£5.00	
10	Football in the Fifties	2001	—	£5.00	
10	Football League Stars	2005	—	£5.00	
25	Football Stars of the '20s and '30s	2004	—	£7.50	
15	Football Stars of The Seventies 1st Series	2002	—	£6.00	
15	Football Stars of The Seventies 2nd Series	2003	—	£6.00	
15	Footballer of the Year (1948-1965)	1999	—	£6.00	
10	Footy Star 1st Series (Soccer Stars of the 1950s) ...	2008	—	£5.00	
10	Footy Star 2nd Series (Soccer Stars of the 1970s) ...	2016	—	£5.00	
12	Forest Kings of Europe 1979 (Nottingham Forest F.C.)	2005	—	£5.00	
10	George Best Football Legend	2016	—	£5.00	
10	George Formby 50th Anniversary Issue	2011	—	£5.50	
10	Greavsie — A Tribute to Jimmy Greaves (Footballer)	2001	—	£5.00	

Size & quantity	TRADE CARD ISSUES	Date	Handbook reference	Price per card	Complete set
	PHILIP NEILL (continued)				
15	Hibernian Scottish F.A. Cup Winners 2016	2017		—	£6.50
10	Hotshot Football (Soccer Stars of the 1960s)	2008		—	£5.00
10	International Stars of Yesteryear 1st Series (Footballers)	2000		—	£5.00
10	International Stars of Yesteryear 2nd Series (Football)	2001		—	£5.00
15	Ipswich Town F.C. (UEFA Cup Winners 1981)	2008		—	£6.00
15	Kings of Europe (Manchester United F.C.)	1999		—	£6.00
15	Leeds United The Revie Era	2002		—	£6.00
12	The Lisbon Lions (Celtic European Cup Winning Legends)...	1999		—	£5.00
15	Liverpool F.C. Champions League 2005	2005		—	£6.00
15	Liverpool F.C. Kings of Europe 1977	2005		—	£6.00
15	Liverpool Legends (Footballers)	2000		—	£6.00
15	Maine Road Heroes (Manchester City Footballers) ...	2003		—	£6.00
15	Manchester City's Euro Kings of '70	2006		—	£6.00
15	Manchester United Classic Kits	2004		—	£6.00
10	Masters of Horror...	2015		—	£5.00
15	Middlesbrough Heroes and Legends (Footballers) ...	2017		—	£6.50
15	Moscow Magic (Manchester United Champions League Winners)	2008		—	£6.00
15	Newcastle Heroes — Post War Toon Legends.........	2004		—	£6.00
10	Nicole Kidman	1999		—	£5.00
10	Post War Footballers	2010		—	£5.00
15	Premiership Burnley Tribute To The Turf Moor Play-off Heroes	2009		—	£6.00
15	Rangers Euro Kings of '72	2006		—	£6.00
20	Red Legends (Manchester United Footballers).........	1998		—	£7.50
10	Scottish Footballers of the 1930s	2000		—	£5.00
10	Scottish Internationals (1960s Footballers)	2002		—	£5.00
15	70's Soccer Stars...	2003		—	£6.00
10	Soccer in the 60s 1st Series	1999		—	£5.00
10	Soccer in the 60s 2nd Series	2000		—	£5.00
15	Soccer Portraits The 1950s Series 1	2008		—	£6.00
15	Soccer Portraits The 1960s Series 1:				
	A Black and White	2008		—	£6.00
	B Red and Blue panel on front	2019		—	£6.00
15	Soccer Portraits The 1970s Series 1	2008		—	£6.00
10	Soccer Selection (Footballing Greats).................	2004		—	£5.00
10	Soccer 70 (1970s Footballers)	2002		—	£5.00
10	Soccer Sketch (Footballers of 50s and 60s)	2010		—	£5.00
10	Soccer Stars of The 50s	2001		—	£5.00
10	Soccer Stars of The 60s	2001		—	£5.00
15	Stamford Bridge Superstars — Chelsea F.C.	2006		—	£6.00
10	Striker Soccer Cards (of the '70s) 1st Series	2009		—	£5.00
10	Striker Soccer Cards (of the '70s) 2nd Series	2009		—	£5.00
15	Sunderland FA Cup Winners of 1973	2008		—	£6.00
L18	Super Reds (Manchester United Footballers)	1998		—	£7.50
10	Ten of the Best — George Best (Footballer)	2000		—	£5.00
10	10 Select Manchester United Footballers.............	2011		—	£5.50
10	Third Lanark Favourites (Footballers)	2009		—	£5.00
15	Tottenham Double Winners 1960-61	2004		—	£6.00
10	Tottenham Heroes & Legends	2012		—	£5.00
25	United Legends (Manchester United Footballers)	2000		—	£7.50
15	United '68 (Manchester United F.C.)	2006		—	£6.00
12	Villa Cup Winners 1957 (Aston Villa F.C.)	2005		—	£5.00
10	Vintage Footballers of the 1900s	2005		—	£5.00
15	Vintage Soccer Heroes...................................	2005		—	£6.00

Size & quantity	TRADE CARD ISSUES	Date	Handbook reference	Price per card	Complete set
	PHILIP NEILL (continued)				
L7	Visions of Marilyn Munroe	2003		—	£5.00
15	West Ham Legends (Footballers)	2015		—	£6.00
15	West Ham United Cup Winning Sides of 1964 and 1965	2007		—	£6.00
15	Wolves Heroes and Legends (Wolverhampton Wanderers F.C.)	2011		—	£6.00
10	World Cup Heroes and Legends 1st Series (Football)	2009		—	£5.00
10	World Cup Heroes and Legends 2nd Series (Football)	2010		—	£5.00
10	World Soccer Heroes 1st Series	2009		—	£5.00
10	World Soccer Heroes 2nd Series	2009		—	£5.00
10	World Soccer Stars (1960s to 1980s)	2013		—	£5.00
	NEILSON'S				
50	Interesting Animals	1954	HX-115	20p	£4.50
	THE NELSON LEE LIBRARY				
MP15	Footballers	1922		£5.00	—
MP6	Modern British Locomotives	1922		£7.50	—
	NESTLE (Chocolate)				
EL12	Animal Bar (wrappers)	1970	HN-23	—	£3.50
49	Happy Families:		HN-31		
	A Without Overprint	1935		£1.30	—
	B With Overprint	1935		£2.00	—
100	Stars of the Silver Screen, Vol I	1936		£2.00	—
50	Stars of the Silver Screen, Vol II	1937		£2.50	—
136	This England	1936		£1.30	—
156	Wonders of the World, Vol I	1932		£1.30	—
144	Wonders of the World, Vol II	1933		£1.30	—
288	Wonders of the World, Vol III	1934		£1.30	—
	NEW ENGLAND CONFECTIONERY (USA)				
M12	Real Airplane Pictures	c1930		£3.00	£36.00
	NEW SOUTH WALES CRICKET ASSOCIATION (Australia)				
L20	The Blues — N.S.W. Cricketers 1998-99 (inscribed 'Toyota')	1998		—	£6.00
L20	The Blues — N.S.W. Cricketers 1999-2000 (without 'Toyota')	1999		—	£6.00
	NEW SOUTH WALES FIRE SERVICE (Australia)				
L10	Fire Appliances and Equipment 1st Series	1980		75p	—
L10	Fire Appliances and Equipment 2nd Series	1981		75p	—
L10	Fire Appliances and Equipment 3rd Series	1982		75p	—
L10	Fire Appliances and Equipment 4th Series	1983		75p	—
L10	Fire Appliances and Equipment 5th Series	1984		75p	—
L10	Fire Appliances and Equipment 7th Series	1986		75p	—
L10	Fire Appliances and Equipment 8th Series	1987		75p	£7.50
L10	Fire Appliances and Equipment 9th Series	1988		75p	£7.50
L10	Fire Appliances and Equipment 10th Series	1989		75p	£7.50
L10	Fire Appliances and Equipment 11th Series	1990		75p	£7.50
	NEW ZEALAND MEAT PRODUCERS BOARD				
EL6	New Zealand Pastoral Scenes	c1930		60p	£3.50
M25	Scenes of New Zealand Lamb	c1930		£4.00	—
	NEWMARKET HARDWARE				
L24	Some of Britain's Finest (Motor) Bikes	1993		—	£6.00

Size & quantity		Date	Handbook reference	Price per card	Complete set
	NEWS CHRONICLE				
L12	Cricketers — England v S Africa 1955	1955	HN-36	£15.00	—
	Football Players:				
L13	Barrow RFC	1955	HN-39.1	£2.50	—
L14	Blackburn Rovers FC	1955	HN-37.5A	£2.50	—
L12	Bradford City FC	1955	HN-37.7A	£2.50	—
L11	Chesterfield FC	1955	HN-37.13	£2.50	—
L12	Everton FC (no stars at base)	1955	HN-37.18A	£2.50	—
L10	Everton FC (two stars at base)	1955	HN-37.18B	£2.50	—
L15	Manchester City FC	1955	HN-37.27	£2.50	—
L12	Newcastle United FC	1955	HN-37.29	£3.50	—
L14	Rochdale Hornets RFC	1955	HN-39.7	£2.50	—
L13	Salford RFC	1955	HN-39.9	£2.50	—
L17	Stockport County FC	1955	HN-37.47	£2.50	—
L13	Sunderland FC	1955	HN-37.49	£2.50	—
L13	Swinton RFC	1955	HN-39.10	£2.50	—
L11	Workington AFC	1955	HN-37.56	£2.50	—
L11	York City FC	1955	HN-37.57	£2.50	—
L12	The Story of Stirling Moss	1955	HN-40	£10.00	—
	NEWTON, CHAMBERS & CO.				
EL18	Izal Nursery Rhymes 1st Series	c1930		£4.50	—
EL18	Izal Nursery Rhymes 2nd Series	c1930		£4.50	—
	NINETY MINUTES				
20	Ninety Minutes Footballers of the 1950s 1st Series	2009		—	£9.00
20	Ninety Minutes Footballers of the 1950s 2nd Series	2009		—	£9.00
20	Ninety Minutes Footballers of the 1950s 3rd Series	2010		—	£7.50
20	Ninety Minutes Footballers of the 1950s 4th Series	2010		—	£7.50
20	Ninety Minutes Footballers of the 1950s 5th Series	2010		—	£7.50
	NORTHAMPTONSHIRE COUNTY CRICKET CLUB				
30	Northamptonshire County Cricket 1905-1985	1985		50p	£15.00
	NORTHERN CONFECTIONS LTD				
48	Aeroplanes	c1955		£5.00	—
	NORTHERN CO-OPERATIVE SOCIETY LTD				
25	Birds	1963	HX-71	£1.60	—
25	History of the Railways 1st Series	1964	HX-88	60p	£15.00
25	History of the Railways 2nd Series	1964	HX-88	80p	£20.00
25	Passenger Liners	1963	HX-82	20p	£4.50
25	Then and Now	1963	HX-27	£1.00	£25.00
25	Tropical Birds	1967	HX-13	50p	£12.50
25	Weapons of World War II	1962		£1.00	—
25	Wonders of the Deep	1966	HX-89	24p	£6.00
	NORTH'S BREAD (New Zealand)				
LT16	Canterbury Crusaders (Rugby Union)	1997		32p	£5.00
	Album			—	£5.00
	NORTHUMBRIA POLICE				
EL21	Sunderland AFC (Footballers)	1991		—	£12.00
	NORTON'S				
25	Evolution of The Royal Navy	c1965	HX-90	£1.60	—

Size & quantity	TRADE CARD ISSUES	Date	Handbook reference	Price per card	Complete set

THE NOSTALGIA SHOP
15	Owls Heroes and Legends (Sheffield Wednesday F.C.)	2018		—	£6.50

NUGGET POLISH CO.
EL30	Allied Series	c1910		£18.00	—
50	Flags of all Nations	c1925	HN-47	£6.50	—
EL40	Mail Carriers and Stamps	c1910	HN-48	£16.00	—

NUMBER ONE MAGAZINE
EL5	Get Fit And Have Fun	1991		—	£3.50

NUNBETTA
25	Motor Cars	1955	HN-49	£14.00	—

NUNEATON F C
L30	Nuneaton Borough Footballers	1995		—	£10.00
L30	Nuneaton Football Greats	1992		—	£15.00

O'CARROLL KENT LTD
50	Railway Engines	c1955		£5.00	—

OCTUS SPORTS (USA)
LT44	Rams NFL Cheerleaders	1994		—	£7.50

ODLING & WILLSON
25	Bygone Locomotives	1999		50p	—

N. OLDHAM
12	Blackpool Legends (Footballers)	2015		—	£7.50
14	The Boys of 66 (England World Cup 1966)	2016		—	£8.50
13	Golf Legends	2005		—	£6.00
EL12	Lisbon Lions The Bhoys of 67 (Celtic F.C.)	2017		—	£8.50

OLDHAM EDUCATIONAL COMMITTEE
M40	Reward Cards	c1915	HO-8	£7.50	—

TONY L. OLIVER
1	Advert Card for German Orders & Decorations	1963		—	£3.00
25	Aircraft of World War II	c1970	HX-7	£5.00	—
50	German Orders and Decorations	1963		£2.50	£125.00
50	German Uniforms	1971		35p	£17.50
M25	Vehicles of the German Wehrmacht	c1970		£1.20	£30.00

ORBIS LTD
EL90	Dinosaurs	1992		20p	£12.00

ORBIT ADVERTISING
15	Engines of the London & North Eastern Railway	1986		—	£6.00
20	Famous Douglas Aeroplanes	1986		—	£10.00
28	Great Rugby Sides New Zealand Tourists 1905	1986		22p	£6.00
16	New Zealand Cricketers of 1958	1988		45p	£7.00

OVALTINE
25	Do You Know?	1968	HX-166.2	36p	£9.00

Size & quantity	TRADE CARD ISSUES	Date	Handbook reference	Price per card	Complete set
	O.V.S. TEA CO.				
K25	Modern Engineering	1955		36p	£9.00
	OXO LTD				
K?	Advertisement Cards	c1925	HL-96/9	£10.00	—
K20	British Cattle	1924		£5.00	£100.00
15	Bull Series	1927		£3.00	£45.00
K24	Feats of Endurance	1926		£3.00	£75.00
K20	Furs and their Story	1924		£3.00	£60.00
K36	Lifeboats and their History	1925		£3.50	—
K30	Mystery Painting Pictures	1928		£3.50	—
EL6	Oxo Cattle Studies	c1920		£40.00	—
25	Oxo Recipes	1936		£3.00	—
	P.C.G.C. (Gum)				
LT88	War Bulletin	1966		£2.50	—
	P.M.R. ASSOCIATES LTD				
25	England The World Cup Spain '82	1982		20p	£3.50
	P.Y.Q.C.C. (USA)				
LT100	Great Guns	1993		—	£15.00
	PACIFIC TRADING (USA)				
LT110	American Soccer Players 1987-88	1987		—	£12.00
LT110	American Soccer Players 1988-89	1989		—	£12.00
LT110	American Soccer Players 1989-90	1990		—	£12.00
LT220	American Soccer Players 1990-91	1990		—	£15.00
LT110	American Soccer Players NPSL 1992/93	1993		20p	£15.00
LT110	Bingo — The Film	1991		—	£9.50
LT110	The College Years Saved By the Bell (TV Show)	1994		—	£9.50
LT110	Eight Men Out — The Film	1998		—	£9.50
LT110	Gunsmoke (1950-60s TV Show)	1993		—	£12.00
LT110	I Love Lucy (TV Series):				
	A Pink Border	1991		—	£16.00
	B Silver Border	1991		—	£12.00
LT110	Operation Desert Shield (Gulf War)	1991		—	£9.50
LT110	Total Recall — The Movie	1990		—	£9.50
LT110	Where Are They	1992		—	£9.50
LT110	The Wizard of Oz	1991		—	£15.00
LT110	World War II	1992		—	£9.50
	H.J. PACKER LTD				
K30	Footballers	c1930		£55.00	—
50	Humorous Drawings	1936		£5.00	—
	PAGE WOODCOCK				
20	Humorous Sketches (multi-backed)	c1905	HP-4	£28.00	—
	PALMER MANN & CO. LTD				
	Sifta Sam Salt Package Issues				
24	Famous Cricketers	c1953		£25.00	—
24	Famous Footballers	c1954		£25.00	—
12	Famous Jets	c1955		£15.00	—
12	Famous Lighthouses	c1956		£15.00	—
	PALS				
M8	Famous Footballers Fineart Supplements	1922	HP-8	£10.00	—
MP12	Football Series	1922		£6.00	—

Size & quantity	TRADE CARD ISSUES	Date	Handbook reference	Price per card	Complete set

PANINI (UK)

CARDS:

LT150	Disney's Aladdin	1994		20p	£16.00
LT45	England Football Stars Gold Collection	1996		—	£15.00
LT100	Footballers 92 Nos 1-100	1991		20p	—
LT100	Footballers 92 Nos 101-200	1991		20p	—
LT100	Footballers 92 Nos 201-300	1991		20p	—
LT122	Footballers 92 Nos 301-422	1991		20p	—

Sticker sets complete with albums:

M180	The Adventures of the Animals of Farthing Wood	1995		—	£22.00
M255	Care Bears News	1987		—	£22.00
M120	ET — The Extra Terrestrial	1982		—	£22.00

PANINI (USA and Canada)

CARDS:

LT100	Antique Cars 1st Series	c1995		—	£9.50
EL72	Austin Powers	1998		—	£12.00
LT198	Barbie and Friends	1992		—	£12.00
LT100	Dream Cars 1st Series	1991		—	£12.00
LT100	Dream Cars 2nd Series	1992		—	£9.50
LT90	The Lion King — Walt Disney Film	1995		—	£9.50
EL108	NSYNC (Pop Group) (Nos 34 & 100 blurred as issued)	1999		—	£12.00
LT100	Wildlife in Danger	1992		—	£10.00
LT100	Wings Of Fire (Military Aircraft etc)	1992		—	£12.00

Sticker Sets complete with albums:

M240	Star Trek — The Next Generation (Factory Set)	1993		—	£12.00

PARAMINT CARDS

10	Arthur Askey — Comedy Heroes	2012		—	£5.00
10	Classic Football Stars 1st Series	2015		—	£5.00
10	Classic Football Stars 2nd Series	2015		—	£5.00
10	Classic Football Stars 3rd Series	2015		—	£5.00
10	Classic Football Stars 4th Series	2016		—	£5.00
20	Football Favourites (1960s/70s Footballers) 1st Series	2014		—	£8.00
20	Football Favourites (1960s/70s Footballers) 2nd Series	2014		—	£8.00
10	Football Stars (of the 1970s) 1st Series	2012		—	£5.00
10	Football Stars (of the 1970s) 2nd Series	2012		—	£5.00
10	Football Stars (of the 1970s) 3rd Series	2012		—	£5.00
10	Football Stars (of the 1970s) 4th Series	2012		—	£5.00
10	Football Stars (of the 1970s) 5th Series	2012		—	£5.00
10	Gracie Fields From Rochdale to Capri	2012		—	£5.00
10	Margaret Rutherford	2012		—	£5.00
10	Norman Wisdom — Comedy Heroes	2012		—	£5.00
10	Scottish Football Stars (1970s footballers)	2011		—	£5.00

PARAMOUNT LABORATORIES LTD

50	Railways of the World:				
	A 'Paramount Sweets':				
	(i) Correct numbering	1955		50p	£25.00
	(ii) Incorrect numbering	1955		£1.00	—
	B 'Paramount Laboratories Ltd'	1955		80p	£40.00

PARRS

L20	Famous Aircraft	1953		£10.00	—

Size & quantity	TRADE CARD ISSUES	Date	Handbook reference	Price per card	Complete set
	JAMES PASCALL LTD				
48	Boy Scouts Series (multi-backed)	c1910	HP-14	£15.00	—
24	British Birds	1925		£4.50	—
30	Devon Ferns	1927		£2.50	—
30	Devon Flowers:				
	A Without Red Overprint	1927		£2.50	—
	B With Red Overprint	1927		£5.00	—
24	Devon Worthies	1927		£2.50	—
18	Dogs	1924		£6.00	—
12	Felix the Film Cat	c1920	HP-15	£50.00	—
15	Flags and Flags with Soldiers (with bow, cord) (multi-backed)	c1910	HX-41	£25.00	—
15	Flags and Flags with Soldiers (without bow, cord) (multi-backed)	c1910	HX-41	£25.00	—
30	Glorious Devon	1929		£2.50	—
36	Glorious Devon 2nd Series:				
	A Marked 2nd Series	1929		£2.50	—
	B Marked Aids for Mothers	1929		£7.50	—
36	Glorious Devon (Ambrosia black back)	c1930		£2.50	—
2	King George V and Queen Mary (multi-backed)	c1915	HP-16	£40.00	—
44	Military Series (multi-backed)	c1910	HP-17	£28.00	—
20	Pascall's Specialities (multi-backed)	c1920	HP-18	£22.00	—
12	Royal Navy Cadet Series (multi-backed)	c1915	HP-19	£26.00	—
8	Rulers of the World	c1910	HP-20	£36.00	—
68	Town and Other Arms (multi-backed)	c1910	HP-21	£15.00	—
50	Tricks and Puzzles	c1920		£14.00	—
13	War Portraits	c1915		£40.00	—
	J. PATERSON & SON LTD				
M48	Balloons	1964		90p	£45.00
	PATRICK GARAGES				
	The Patrick Collection (Motor Cars):				
M24	A Without Coupon	1986		60p	£15.00
EL24	B With Coupon	1986		£1.00	£25.00
	GEORGE PAYNE (Tea)				
25	American Indian Tribes:		HX-28		
	A Cream Card	1962		£1.20	£30.00
	B White Card	1962		£1.20	£30.00
25	British Railways	1962	HX-107	40p	£10.00
	Characters from Dickens' Works:		HX-172		
12	A Numbered	c1912		£17.00	—
6	B Unnumbered	c1912		£17.00	—
25	Dogs' Heads	1963	HX-16	50p	£12.50
25	Mickey Mouse Pleasure Cruise	c1920		£40.00	—
25	Science in the 20th Century	1963	HX-18	20p	£4.50
	Album			—	£30.00
	PENGUIN BISCUITS				
EL10	Home Hints	c1974		£3.00	—
EL10	Making the Most of Your Countryside	1975		£3.00	—
EL10	Pastimes	c1972		£3.00	—
EL12	Penguin Farm Animal Series	c1968		£3.00	—
EL10	Penguin Zoo Animal Series	c1968		£3.00	—
EL10	Playday	c1974		£3.00	—
EL12	Wildlife	1973		£3.00	—
	PENNY MAGAZINE				
M12	Film Stars	c1930		£5.00	—

Size & quantity	TRADE CARD ISSUES	Date	Handbook reference	Price per card	Complete set
	PEPSI (UK)				
L7	Star Wars Episode 1 The Phantom Menace............	1999		—	£6.00
	PEPSI (Thailand)				
LT8	Britney Spears...............................	2002		—	£8.00
LT32	World Football Stars...........................	2002		—	£10.00
	PEPSICO FOODS (Saudi Arabia)				
M22	World Soccer	1998		40p	£8.00
	PEPSINET GUM				
K76	Film Stars (size 28 x 22mm)	c1935		£6.00	—
	PERENNIAL MUSIC				
M45	Forever Gold Entertainment Legends	2000		—	£12.00
	PERFETTI GUM				
40	Famous Trains:				
	A Numbered	1983		£4.00	—
	B Unnumbered	1982		£3.75	—
	PERIKIM				
L7	Dogs — The Boxer	2001		—	£3.00
L7	Dogs — The Bull Terrier	2005		—	£3.00
L7	Dogs — The Bulldog	2005		—	£3.00
L7	Dogs — The Cocker Spaniel	2001		—	£3.00
L7	Dogs — The Dalmatian.........................	2005		—	£3.00
L7	Dogs — The Dobermann	2001		—	£3.00
L7	Dogs — The English Springer Spaniel	2001		—	£3.00
L7	Dogs — The German Shepherd....................	2001		—	£3.00
L7	Dogs — The Golden Retriever	2001		—	£3.00
L7	Dogs — The Irish Setter	2005		—	£3.00
L7	Dogs — The Jack Russell......................	2001		—	£3.00
L7	Dogs — The King Charles Cavalier	2005		—	£3.00
L7	Dogs — The Rottweiler........................	2005		—	£3.00
L7	Dogs — The Rough Collie	2005		—	£3.00
L7	Dogs — The Staffordshire Bull Terrier...............	2005		—	£3.00
L7	Dogs — The West Highland	2005		—	£3.00
L7	Dogs — The Yorkshire Terrier	2005		—	£3.00
L13	Nursery Rhymes	1996		—	£5.00
	PETER MAX (USA)				
LT6	Peter Max Posters	1994		—	£3.50
	PETERKIN				
M8	English Sporting Dogs (multi-backed)	c1930	HP-43	£15.00	—
	PETPRO LTD				
35	Grand Prix Racing Cars (64 × 29mm)	1966		50p	£17.50
	THE PHILATELIC POSTCARD PUBLISHING CO. LTD				
EL10	Philatelic Anniversary Series	1983		—	£5.00
	PHILLIPS TEA				
25	Army Badges, Past and Present...................	1964		20p	£5.00
25	British Birds and Their Nests	1971	HX-104	£2.00	—
25	British Rail	1965	HX-107	50p	£12.50

Size & quantity	TRADE CARD ISSUES	Date	Handbook reference	Price per card	Complete set
	PHILOSOPHY FOOTBALL				
L20	Philosopher Footballers	1998		—	£12.00
	PHOTAL				
EL2	Duncan Edwards (Footballer)	2001		—	£5.00
EL4	Manchester United F.C. 1967 Series 1	2001		—	£8.00
EL10	Manchester United F.C. 1968 Series 2 Nos 1-10	2001		—	£15.00
EL10	Manchester United F.C. 1968 Series 2 Nos 11-20	2001		—	£15.00
EL6	Northern Footballing Knights	2001		—	£12.00
EL10	Sir Tom Finney (Footballer)	2001		—	£16.00
	PHOTO ANSWERS MAGAZINE				
EL12	Holiday Fax	1990		—	£3.50
	PHOTO PRECISION				
EL20	Fighting Aircraft of World War II	1978		—	£5.00
EL10	Flowers	1979		—	£3.50
EL10	Old English Series	1979		—	£3.50
EL10	Traction Engines	1979		—	£3.50
EL12	Vintage Cars	1975		—	£3.50
EL10	Wild Birds	1979		—	£3.50
EL10	Wild Life	1979		—	£3.50
	PICTURETTES LTD				
60	Aeroplanes	c1950		£5.00	—
60	Merchant Ships	c1950		£4.50	—
	PILOT				
32	Aeroplanes and Carriers	1937		£5.00	—
32	Football Fame Series	1935	HP-52	£5.00	—
	GEO. M. PITT				
25	Types of British Soldiers	1914	HX-144	£32.00	—
	PIZZA HUT				
EL12	Football Skill Cards	c1995		—	£6.00
	PLANET LTD				
L50	Racing Cars of the World	1959		£3.00	—
	PLANTERS NUT AND CHOCOLATE CO. (USA)				
M25	Hunted Animals	1933		£3.00	£75.00
	PLAY HOUR				
M24	Zoo plus album	c1960		—	£12.00
	PLAYER PARADE				
20	Player Parade (Footballers of the 50s) 1st Series	2010		—	£7.50
20	Player Parade (Footballers of the 50s) 2nd Series	2011		—	£7.50
	PLAYERS INTERNATIONAL				
LT40	Boxing Personalities — Ringlords	1991		—	£5.00
	PLUCK				
MP27	Famous Football Teams	1922	HP-56	£4.00	—
	PLYMOUTH COUNTY COUNCIL				
EL20	Endangered Species	1985		—	£5.00

Size & quantity	TRADE CARD ISSUES	Date	Handbook reference	Price per card	Complete set
	POLAR PRODUCTS LTD (BARBADOS)				
25	International Air Liners	c1970		60p	£15.00
25	Modern Motor Cars	c1970		80p	£20.00
25	Tropical Birds	c1970		60p	£15.00
25	Wonders of the Deep	c1970		50p	£12.50
	POLYDOR				
16	Polydor Guitar	1975		60p	£10.00
	PONY MAGAZINE				
EL26	Horse & Pony Breeds (Trumps Cards)	2008		—	£6.00
	H. POPPLETON & SONS				
50	Cricketers Series	1926		£50.00	—
16	Film Stars	1928	HP-58	£12.00	—
15	War Series	c1915	HP-59	£36.00	—
12	Wembley Empire Exhibition Series	c1920	HP-60	£36.00	—
	POPULAR GARDENING				
EL6	Colour Schemes With Garden Flowers	1939	HP-61	£2.50	—
	PORTFOLIO INTERNATIONAL (USA)				
LT50	Endless Summer (Pin Up Girls)	1993		—	£9.50
LT50	Portfolio (Pin Up Girls)	1992		—	£9.50
LT50	Portfolio (Pin Up Girls)	1993		—	£9.50
LT36	Portfolio's Secret (Pin Up Girls) (No. 12 unissued, 2 different No. 15s)	1994		—	£9.50
	PoSTA				
25	Modern Transport	1957		24p	£6.00
	PREMIER SPORTS CARD CREATION				
11	F.A Cup Heroes Sheffield Wednesday 1966	2005		—	£6.75
25	Footballing Favourites Arsenal (1930s to 50s)	2004		—	£15.00
25	Footballing Favourites Chelsea (1950s)	2004		—	£15.00
	PRESCOTT CONFECTIONERY				
L36	Speed Kings	1966		75p	£27.00
	PRESCOTT — PICKUP				
EL60	Action Portraits of Famous Footballers	1979		—	£15.00
	Album			—	£15.00
EL60	Interregnum (Military)	1978		—	£20.00
	Album			—	£15.00
EL64	Our Iron Roads (Railways)	1980		—	£12.00
	Album			—	£15.00
EL60	Queen and People	1977		—	£12.00
	Album			—	£15.00
EL60	Railway Locomotives:				
	A Post Card back	1976		—	£12.00
	B Textback	1978		—	£12.00
	Album			—	£15.00
50	Railway Locomotives	1978		25p	£12.50
	Album			—	£12.00
EL12	The Royal Wedding	1981		—	£9.00

Size & quantity	TRADE CARD ISSUES	Date	Handbook reference	Price per card	Complete set
	PRESCOTT — PICKUP (continued)				
EL60	Sovereign Series No. 1 Royal Wedding	1981		—	£20.00
	Album			—	£15.00
EL60	Sovereign Series No. 2 30 Years of Elizabeth II	1982		—	£15.00
	Album			—	£15.00
EL30	Sovereign Series No. 3 — Charles & Diana in the Antipodes	1983		—	£8.00
EL15	Sovereign Series No. 3 — Charles & Diana in Canada	1983		—	£4.00
EL70	Sovereign Series No. 4 — Royal Family	1982		—	£15.00
	Album			—	£15.00
EL63	Sovereign Series No. 6 — Papal Visit	1982		—	£10.00
	Album			—	£15.00
EL63	Sovereign Series No. 7 — Falklands Task Force	1982		—	£25.00
	Album			—	£15.00
EL63	Sovereign Series No. 8 — War in the South Atlantic	1983		—	£20.00
	Album			—	£15.00
EL60	Tramcars & Tramways	1977		—	£15.00
	Album			—	£15.00
EL60	Tramcyclopaedia	1979		—	£18.00
	Album			—	£15.00
	PRESS PASS (USA)				
LT80	Elvis By The Numbers	2008		—	£15.00
LT100	Elvis Is (Elvis Presley)	2008		—	£20.00
LT110	Royal Family	1993		20p	£9.50
LT90	Tribe	1993		—	£9.50
	PRESTON DAIRIES				
25	Country Life	1966	HX-11	20p	£3.50
	PRICE'S PATENT CANDLE CO. LTD				
EL12	Famous Battles	c1910	HP-68	£16.00	—
	W.R. PRIDDY				
80	Famous Boxers	1992		—	£20.00
	PRIMROSE CONFECTIONERY CO. LTD				
24	Action Man	1976		£4.00	—
50	Amos Burke, Secret Agent:				
	A With 'printed in England'	1970		£1.20	£60.00
	B Without 'printed in England'	1966		£1.20	—
50	Andy Pandy	1960		40p	£20.00
50	Bugs Bunny	1964		£1.20	£60.00
50	Burke's Law	1966		£7.00	—
25	Captain Kid	1975		£6.00	—
50	Chitty Chitty Bang Bang:				
	A Thick card	1969		£1.20	£60.00
	B Paper thin card	1969		45p	£22.50
50	Cowboy	1961		30p	£15.00
25	Cup Tie Quiz	1973		20p	£3.50
25	Dad's Army	1973		80p	£20.00
50	Famous Footballers (F.B.S.1) back	1961		60p	£30.00
50	Flintstones:				
	A Back headed Primrose at top	1963		£1.20	—
	B Back Primrose at base				
	i Thick card	c1965		£3.00	—
	ii Paper thin card	c1970		£3.00	—
25	Football Funnies	1974		30p	£7.50
25	Happy Howlers	1975		20p	£4.50

Size & quantity	TRADE CARD ISSUES	Date	Handbook reference	Price per card	Complete set
	PRIMROSE CONFECTIONERY CO. LTD (continued)				
50	Joe 90:				
	A Thick card	1969		£3.00	—
	B Paper thin card	1970		£2.60	—
50	Krazy Kreatures from Outer Space:				
	A Thick card	1970		60p	£30.00
	B Thin card	1972		30p	£7.50
	C Paper thin card	1972		20p	£5.00
50	Laramie	1964		£1.60	£80.00
50	Laurel & Hardy:				
	A Thick card	1968		£3.00	—
	B Thin card	1972		£1.60	£80.00
	C Paper thin card	1972		£1.20	£60.00
22	Mounties (Package Issue)	1960		£8.50	—
50	Popeye 1st Series	1960		£9.00	—
50	Popeye 2nd Series	1960		£6.00	£300.00
50	Popeye 3rd Series	1961		25p	£12.50
50	Popeye 4th Series:				
	A Back headed '4th Series Popeye No. ...'				
	i Address with 'Argyle Avenue' Album clause 'send only 9d ...'	1963		30p	£15.00
	ii Address with 'Argyle Avenue' Album clause 'send only 1/-'	c1965		£3.00	—
	iii Address without 'Argyle Avenue' Album clause 'send only 1/-'	c1965		£3.00	—
	B Back headed 'Popeye ... 4th Series' Address 'Farnham Road'				
	i with album clause 'send only 1/-' thick card...	c1968		40p	£20.00
	ii with album clause 'send only 1/-' thin card ...	c1968		30p	£15.00
	iii with album clause 'send 1/6'	c1970		£3.00	—
	iv without album clause paper thin card	c1972		60p	£30.00
50	Queen Elizabeth 2 (The Cunard Liner):				
	A Cream card	1969		£1.20	£60.00
	B White card	1969		£1.00	£50.00
50	Quick Draw McGraw, Series Q.1	1965		£1.60	£80.00
50	Space Patrol:				
	A Size 65 x 33mm with copright date 1965				
	i Address with Argyle Ave Album clause 'send only 9d'	1965		£3.50	—
	ii Address without Argyle Ave Album clause 'send only 9d'	1965		£3.00	—
	iii Address without Argyle Ave Album clause 'send only 1/-'	c1968		£3.50	—
	B Size 65 x 35mm Address Argyle Ave Album clause 'send only 9d	c1968		£4.00	—
	C Size 64 x 35mm Address Farnham Road Album 'clause 'send only 1/-'				
	i With Wonderama Productions thick card	c1970		£3.00	—
	ii With Wonderama Productions thin card	c1970		25p	£12.50
	iii Without Wonderama Production	c1970		50p	£25.00
50	Space Race	1969		20p	£10.00
12	Star Trek	1971		75p	£9.00
50	Superman:				
	A Size 64 x 33mm	1968		£4.00	—
	B Size 64 x 34mm				
	i Thick card	c1970		£1.00	—
	ii Thin card	c1971		£1.50	—
	iii Paper Thin card	1972		70p	£35.00

Size & quantity	TRADE CARD ISSUES	Date	Handbook reference	Price per card	Complete set
	PRIMROSE CONFECTIONERY CO. LTD (continued)				
50	Yellow Submarine	1968		£9.00	—
50	Z Cars:				
	Size 60 x 33mm				
	i Without album clause	c1964		£4.00	—
	ii With album clause 'send only 9d'	1964		30p	£15.00
	iii With album clause 'send only 1/-'	c1966		£4.00	—
50	Z Cars (different from above series):				
	A Size 64 x 33mm with album clause 'send only 1/-'				
	No underline under Farnham Road	c1966		£4.00	—
	B Size 64 x 34mm with album clause with underline under Farnham Road				
	i Album clause 'send only 1/-'	1968		70p	£35.00
	ii Album clause 'send only 1/6'	c1969		£4.00	—
	A.S. PRIOR (Fish and Chips)				
25	Evolution of the Royal Navy	c1965	HX-90	£1.40	—
	S. PRIOR (Bookshop)				
25	British Uniforms of the 19th Century	c1965	HX-78	£1.40	—
25	Do You Know?	c1965	HX-166.2	£1.20	—
	PRIORY TEA & COFFEE CO. LTD				
1	Advert Card Set Completion Offer	1966		—	£10.00
50	Aircraft	1961		£1.50	—
	Album			—	£6.00
50	Birds	1963		£1.50	—
	Album			—	£25.00
24	Bridges	1959		20p	£4.50
50	Cars	1964		60p	£30.00
	Album			—	£6.00
24	Cars	1958		£5.00	—
50	Cycles and Motorcycles	1960		£2.50	—
	Album			—	£20.00
24	Dogs	1957		20p	£4.50
24	Flowering Trees	1959		20p	£5.00
24	Men at Work	1959		20p	£4.00
24	Out and About	1957		50p	£12.00
24	People in Uniform	1957		£2.00	—
24	Pets	1957		20p	£4.00
50	Wild Flowers	1961		£1.20	£60.00
	Album			—	£20.00
	Album for Bridges and Men at Work combined			—	£20.00
	Album for Cars (24) and Flowering Trees combined			—	£20.00
	Album for Dogs and People in Uniform combined			—	£20.00
	Album for Out and About and Pets combined			—	£20.00
	PRISM LEISURE				
L30	George Formby	1993		60p	£18.00
L12	Patsy Cline (Country Singer)	1993		—	£10.00
	PRO SET (UK)				
	Advertisement Cards:				
L1	A Football League Instant Winner	1992		—	50p
L1	B Football League Points Winner 10 Points	1992		—	50p
L1	C Official Pro Set Binder Offer!	1991		—	50p
L1	D Pro Set Time to Re-Order	1991		—	£1.00

Size & quantity	TRADE CARD ISSUES	Date	Handbook reference	Price per card	Complete set
	PRO SET (UK) (continued)				
LT100	Bill & Ted's Excellent Adventure	1992		20p	£9.50
LT100	Football Fixtures/Footballers	1991		20p	£10.00
LT110	Footballers 1990-91 Nos 1-110	1990		20p	£10.00
LT110	Footballers 1990-91 Nos 111-220	1990		20p	£10.00
LT108	Footballers 1990-91 Nos 221-328	1990		20p	£10.00
LT115	Footballers 1991-92 Nos 1-115	1991		20p	£10.00
LT115	Footballers 1991-92 Nos 116-230	1991		20p	£10.00
LT125	Footballers 1991-92 Nos 231-355	1992		20p	£10.00
LT124	Footballers 1991-92 Nos 356-479	1992		20p	£10.00
LT100	Footballers — Scottish 1991-92	1991		20p	£9.50
LT100	Guinness Book of Records	1992		20p	£8.50
LT75	Super Stars Musicards (Pop Stars) Nos 1-75	1991		20p	£8.00
LT75	Super Stars Musicards (Pop Stars) Nos 76-150	1991		20p	£8.00
LT100	Thunderbirds	1992		20p	£9.50
	PRO SET (USA)				
LT150	American Football World League	1991		—	£12.00
LT95	Beauty and The Beast	1992		—	£9.50
LT90	The Little Mermaid (Disney Film) + 37 Bonus Cards	1991		—	£12.00
LT160	NFL Super Bowl XXV	1991		—	£15.00
LT100	PGA Golf	1990		—	£12.00
LT285	PGA Golf Tour	1991		—	£25.00
LT100	PGA Golf nos E1-E20, 1-80	1992		20p	£10.00
LT100	PGA Golf nos 81-180	1992		20p	£10.00
LT100	PGA Golf nos 181-280	1992		20p	£10.00
LT50	Petty Family Racing (Motor Racing)	1991		—	£7.50
LT260	Super Stars Musicards 1st Series (backs white with yellow blobs):				
	A Nos. 1 to 90	1991		—	£9.00
	B Nos. 91 to 180	1991		—	£9.00
	C Nos. 181 to 260	1991		—	£8.00
LT80	Super Stars Musicards 2nd Series Nos 261 to 340	1992		—	£8.00
LT100	Yo MTV Raps Musicards Nos 1-100	1991		—	£9.50
LT50	Yo MTV Raps Musicards Nos 101-150	1991		—	£7.50
LT95	The Young Indiana Jones Chronicles	1992		20p	£8.50
LT8	The Young Indiana Jones Chronicles Hidden Treasures	1992		35p	£3.00
LT11	The Young Indiana Jones Chronicles 3-D	1992		25p	£3.00
	PRO TRAC'S (USA)				
LT100	Formula One Racing Series 1 Nos 1-100	1991		—	£15.00
LT100	Formula One Racing Series 1 Nos 101-200	1991		—	£15.00
	PROMATCH				
LT200	Premier League Footballers 1st Series	1996		—	£25.00
LT110	Premier League Footballers 2nd Series (10 numbers unissued)	1997		—	£25.00
LT200	Premier League Footballers 3rd Series	1998		—	£25.00
LT198	Premier League Footballers 4th Series (number 163 not issued, 2 different number 162s)	1999		—	£25.00
	PROPERT SHOE POLISH				
25	British Uniforms	1955	HX-108	36p	£9.00
	PUB PUBLICITY				
M45	Inns of East Sussex	1975		22p	£10.00

Size & quantity	TRADE CARD ISSUES	Date	Handbook reference	Price per card	Complete set
	PUBLICATIONS INT (USA)				
M100	Micro Machines 1st Series (Cars, etc)	1989		—	£10.00
M100	Micro Machines 2nd Series (Cars, etc)	1989		—	£10.00
	PUKKA TEA CO. LTD				
50	Aquarium Fish	1960	HX-87	£1.00	£50.00
	PURITY PRETZEL CO. (USA)				
M56	US Air Force Planes, US Navy Planes, Ships of the US Navy	c1930		£1.50	—
	PYREX				
EL16	The Pyrex Guide to Simple Cooking	1975		22p	£3.50
	QUADRIGA				
M126	Snooker Kings	1985		—	£20.00
	Album			—	£12.00
	QUAKER OATS				
EL12	Armour Through the Ages	1963		£1.25	£15.00
M4	Famous Puffers	1978		£5.00	—
M54	Historic Arms of Merry England	c1938	HQ-5	£1.75	—
EL8	Historic Ships	1965		£6.00	—
15	Honey Monster Crazy Games	1982		£1.50	—
M16	Jeremy's Animal Kingdom	1970		£1.50	—
L8	Legends of Batman	1995		£1.50	—
12	Monsters of the Deep	1984		£2.25	—
M6	Nature Trek	1976		60p	£3.50
EL12	Prehistoric Animals	1964		£7.00	—
EL12	Space Cards	1963	HQ-6	£7.00	—
EL12	Vintage Engines	1964		£7.00	—
	Package Issues:				
	Quaker Cards blue border issues:				
L36	British Landmarks	1961		£1.50	—
L36	Great Moments of Sport	1961		£5.00	—
L36	Household Hints	1961		£1.50	—
L36	Phiz Quiz	1961		£3.00	—
L36	Railways of the World	1961		£3.50	—
L36	The Story of Fashion	1961		£2.50	—
	Quaker Quiz Cards yellow border issues:				
M12	British Customs	1961		£2.00	—
M12	Famous Explorers	1961		£2.00	—
M12	Famous Inventors	1961		£2.00	—
M12	Famous Ships	1961		£2.00	—
M12	Famous Women	1961		£2.00	—
M12	Fascinating Costumes	1961		£1.50	—
M12	Great Feats of Building	1961		£1.50	—
M12	History of Flight	1961		£2.00	—
M12	Homes and Houses	1961		£1.50	—
M12	On the Seashore	1961		£1.50	—
M12	The Wild West	1961		£2.00	—
M12	Weapons & Armour	1961		£2.00	—
	Sugar Puffs Series (text back):				
12	Exploration & Adventure	1974		£1.50	—
12	National Maritime Museum	1974		£1.50	—
12	National Motor Museum	1974		£1.50	—
12	Royal Air Force Museum	1974		£1.50	—
12	Science & Invention	1974		£1.50	—

Size & quantity	TRADE CARD ISSUES	Date	Handbook reference	Price per card	Complete set
	QUEENS OF YORK				
30	Kings and Queens of England	1955	HX-116	£1.50	£45.00
	QUESS CARDS				
M20	Renowned Footballers Series 1	1999		—	£10.00
	QUORN SPECIALITIES LTD				
25	Fish and Game	1963		£7.00	—
	RADIO FUN				
20	British Sports Stars	1956		25p	£5.00
	RADIO REVIEW				
L36	Broadcasting Series	1935		£5.00	—
EL20	Broadcasting Stars	c1935	HR-7	£5.00	—
	RAIL ENTHUSIAST				
EL48	British Diesel and Electric Railway Engines	1984		—	£6.00
	RAILWAY TAVERN				
L12	Preserved British Locomotives	2000		—	£7.50
12	Steam Locomotives	1999		—	£10.00
	RAINBO BREAD (USA)				
LT33	Star Trek The Motion Picture	1979		—	£12.00
	RAINBOW PRESS				
L26	Grand Prix The Early Years (Cars)	1992		—	£15.00
	RALEIGH BICYCLES				
M48	Raleigh, The All Steel Bicycle	1957		£1.60	£80.00
	RARE BREEDS SURVIVAL TRUST				
M20	Breeds of Turkeys	2016		40p	£8.00
	RED AND GREEN				
20	Football Heroes (1950s Footballers) 1st Series	2009		—	£9.00
20	Football Heroes (1950s Footballers) 2nd Series	2010		—	£7.50
20	Football Heroes (1950s Footballers) 3rd Series	2010		—	£7.50
	RED HEART				
EL6	Cats	1954	HR-7	—	£40.00
EL6	Dogs 1st Series	1955	HR-8.1	—	£40.00
EL6	Dogs 2nd Series	1955	HR-8.2	—	£40.00
EL6	Dogs 3rd Series	1956		—	£40.00
	RED LETTER, RED STAR WEEKLY				
EL29	Charlie Chaplin	c1915	HR-9	£15.00	—
L104	Fortune Cards	c1930	HR-11	£3.50	—
EL8	Good Luck Song Cards	c1930		£3.00	—
	Midget Message Cards (Gravures):				
L6	A Green – Fragments From France (cartoons)	1915		£4.00	—
L26	B Brown – Rhymes letters of the alphabet	c1930		£3.00	—
L6	C Brown – Pictures of woman, short verse beneath	1915		£3.00	—
L12	D Green – Dark green borders with small picture inset	1915		£3.00	—
L12	E Green – White frameline inside fancy green border	1915		£3.00	—

Size & quantity	TRADE CARD ISSUES	Date	Handbook reference	Price per card	Complete set
	RED LETTER, RED STAR WEEKLY (continued)				
	Midget Message Cards (Gravures) continued:				
L12	F Green – White borders	1915		£3.00	—
L12	G Light brown Set 1	1915	HR-13	£3.00	—
L12	H Light brown Set 2	1915	HR-13	£3.00	—
L12	Red Letter Message Cards	c1920		£3.50	—
	RED ROSE RADIO				
EL6	Disc Jockeys from Gold AM	1992		—	£5.00
EL5	Disc Jockeys from Rock FM	1992		—	£4.00
	RED, WHITE & BLUE PRINT				
15	Aston Villa European Champions 81/82	2010		—	£6.50
	REDDINGS TEA COMPANY				
25	Castles of Great Britain	1965	HX-161	£2.20	£55.00
	Album			—	£25.00
25	Cathedrals of Great Britain	1965	HX-162	£2.20	£55.00
25	Heraldry of Famous Places	1966		£2.20	£55.00
48	Ships of the World	1963		20p	£8.00
25	Strange Customs of the World:				
	A Text back	1969		20p	£3.50
	B Advertisement back	1969		£5.00	—
	Album			—	£25.00
24	Warriors of the World 1st Series	1962		£2.00	£50.00
24	Warriors of the World 2nd Series	1962		£2.00	£50.00
	Album for 1st and 2nd Series combined			—	£20.00
24	Warriors of the World with Ships of the World fronts	1963		£7.00	—
	REDDISH MAID CONFECTIONERY				
K50	Famous International Aircraft	1963	HX-98	£4.50	—
K25	Famous International Athletes	1965		£10.00	—
25	International Footballers of Today	1966		£13.00	—
	REDSKY				
10	Audrey Hepburn	2011		—	£5.00
10	Ava Gardner	2012		—	£5.00
10	Brigitte Bardot	2011		—	£5.00
10	Claudia Cardinale	2011		—	£5.00
10	Doris Day	2011		—	£5.00
10	Elizabeth Taylor	2011		—	£5.00
10	Gene Tierney	2014		—	£5.00
10	Grace Kelly	2012		—	£5.00
10	Hedy Lamarr	2014		—	£5.00
10	Ingrid Bergman	2011		—	£5.00
10	Jane Russell	2012		—	£5.00
10	Jayne Mansfield	2011		—	£5.00
10	Joan Fontaine	2014		—	£5.00
10	Lauren Bacall	2011		—	£5.00
10	Leslie Caron	2014		—	£5.00
10	Olivia De Havilland	2014		—	£5.00
10	Rita Hayworth	2011		—	£5.00
10	Sophia Loren	2011		—	£5.00
10	Susan Hayward	2011		—	£5.00
	REDSTONE (USA)				
LT50	Dinosaurs	1993		20p	£9.50
	REEVES LTD				
25	Cricketers	1912		£45.00	—

Size & quantity	TRADE CARD ISSUES	Date	Handbook reference	Price per card	Complete set
	REFLECTIONS OF A BYGONE AGE				
12	Nottingham Heritage/Poster	1996		—	£3.00
12	Nottingham Trams	2004/07		—	£3.00
4	Nottingham Trams	2008/10		—	£1.50
6	Nottinghamshire Towns 1st Series	1999		—	£1.50
4	Nottinghamshire Towns 2nd Series	2009		—	£1.50
6	Railways Around Nottingham	1996		—	£1.50
4	Rugby Union World Cup 2003	2003		—	£1.50
6	Sporting Occasions	2002		—	£1.50
6	St Pancras International (Railway Station)	2008		—	£1.50
6	Steam Around Britain 1st Series Nos 1-6 (Railways)	1999		—	£1.50
6	Steam Around Britain 2nd Series Nos 7-12 (Railways)	2001		—	£1.50
6	Steam Around Britain 3rd Series Nos 13-18 (Railways)	2003		—	£1.50
6	Steam Around Britain 4th Series Nos 19-24 (Railways)	2005		—	£1.50
6	Steam Around Britain 5th Series Nos 25-30 (Railways)	2008		—	£1.50
6	Steam Around Britain 6th Series Nos 31-36 (Railways)..	2009		—	£1.50
6	Steam Around Britain 7th Series Nos. 37-42 (Railways)	2012		—	£1.50
	REGENT OIL				
L25	Do You Know?	1964		20p	£3.50
	REMLAP WORKS				
50	Keep Fit Games and Exercise Ball Games 1st Series	c1930		£15.00	—
50	Keep Fit Games and Exercise Ball Games 2nd Series	c1930		£12.00	—
	RICHARDS COLLECTION				
25	Soccer Stars of Yesteryear 1st Series	1995		—	£10.00
25	Soccer Stars of Yesteryear 2nd Series	1997		—	£9.00
25	Soccer Stars of Yesteryear 3rd Series	1997		—	£9.00
25	Soccer Stars of Yesteryear 4th Series	1998		—	£5.00
5	Soccer Stars of Yesteryear 5th Series	2002		—	£3.00
20	Sporting Stars by Jos Walker (Cricketers)	1997		—	£6.00
21	Stars of the Past (Football)	1994		—	£9.00
	RINGSIDE TRADING (USA)				
LT80	Ringside Boxing	1996		—	£15.00
	RINGTONS LTD (Tea)				
25	Aircraft of World War II	1962	HX-7	£2.40	—
25	British Cavalry Uniforms of the 19th Century	1971	HX-43	£1.20	£30.00
25	Do You Know?	1964	HX-166.4	20p	£3.50
25	Fruits of Trees and Shrubs	1963	HX-45	20p	£3.50
25	Head Dresses of the World	1973	HX-197	20p	£3.50
25	Historical Scenes	1964	HX-143	20p	£4.50
25	Old England	1964		20p	£3.50
25	People and Places	1964	HX-26	20p	£3.50
25	Regimental Uniforms of the Past	1966		32p	£8.00
25	Sailing Ships Through the Ages	1964	HX-119	32p	£8.00
25	Ships of the Royal Navy	1963		50p	£12.50
25	Sovereigns, Consorts and Rulers of Great Britain, 1st Series	1961	HX-201	50p	£12.50
25	Sovereigns, Consorts and Rulers of Great Britain, 2nd Series	1961	HX-201	50p	£12.50
25	Then and Now	1970	HX-27	£1.40	—
25	Trains of the World	1970	HX-121	20p	£4.50
25	The West	1968	HX-42	36p	£9.00
	RISCA TRAVEL AGENCY				
25	Holiday Resorts	1966	HX-38	£1.20	£30.00

Size & quantity	TRADE CARD ISSUES	Date	Handbook reference	Price per card	Complete set

RITTENHOUSE ARCHIVES (USA)

Size & quantity	Title	Date	Handbook ref	Price per card	Complete set
LT72	Agents of S.H.I.E.L.D Season 1	2015	—		£9.50
LT72	Agents of S.H.I.E.L.D Season 2	2016	—		£9.50
LT81	Art and Images of Star Trek The Original Series...	2005	—		£9.50
LT120	Babylon 5 The Complete Series...	2002	—		£16.00
LT72	Battlestar Galactica	2005	—		£9.50
LT72	Battlestar Galactica Colonial Warriors	2005	—		£10.00
LT72	Battlestar Galactica The Complete Series	2004	—		£11.00
LT81	Battlestar Galactica Season 1	2006	—		£9.50
LT72	Battlestar Galactica Season 2	2007	—		£9.50
LT63	Battlestar Galactica Season 3	2008	—		£9.50
LT63	Battlestar Galactica Season 4	2009	—		£9.50
LT72	The Chronicles of Riddick	2004	—		£9.50
LT81	The Complete Avengers 1963-Present	2007	—		£12.00
LT72	Conan Art of The Hyborian Age	2004	—		£11.00
LT69	Continuum Seasons 1 & 2	2014	—		£9.50
LT60	Continuum Season 3	2015	—		£9.50
LT50	D C Legacy...	2007	—		£10.00
LT100	The Dead Zone	2004	—		£12.00
LT90	Die Another Day James Bond 007	2002	—		£15.00
LT72	Fantastic Four Archives	2008	—		£9.50
LT100	The Fantasy Worlds of Irwin Allen	2003	—		£12.00
LT72	Farscape Season 1	2001	—		£9.50
LT72	Farscape Season 2	2001	—		£9.50
LT72	Farscape Season 3	2002	—		£9.50
LT72	Farscape Season 4	2003	—		£9.50
LT72	Farscape Through The Wormhole	2004	—		£9.50
LT72	Game of Thrones Season 1	2012	—		£15.00
LT88	Game of Thrones Season 2	2013	—		£15.00
LT98	Game of Thrones Season 3	2014	—		£9.50
LT100	Game of Thrones Season 4	2015	—		£9.50
LT100	Game of Thrones Season 5	2016	—		£9.50
LT100	Game of Thrones Season 6	2017	—		£9.50
LT81	Game of Thrones Season 7	2018	—		£9.50
LT60	Game of Thrones Season 8	2020	—		£10.00
LT73	Game of Thrones The Complete Series	2020	—		£12.00
LT72	Hercules and Xena The Animated Adventures	2005	—		£9.50
LT120	Hercules The Legendary Journeys	2001	—		£9.50
LT72	Heroes Archives	2010	—		£9.50
LT126	Highlander The Complete Series	2003	20p		£18.00
LT72	The Hobbit The Desolation of Smaug	2015	—		£9.50
LT70	Iron Man The Film	2008	—		£9.50
LT66	James Bond 007 Archives...	2009	—		£9.50
LT83	James Bond 007 Archives Final Edition Die Another Day	2017	—		£9.50
LT99	James Bond 007 Casino Royale	2014	—		£9.50
LT72	James Bond 007 Classics The World Is Not Enough...	2016	—		£9.50
LT189	James Bond 007 The Complete Series	2007	—		£18.00
LT110	James Bond 007 Dangerous Liaisons	2006	—		£9.50
LT60	James Bond 007 40th Anniversary	2002	—		£18.00
LT19	James Bond 007 40th Anniversary — Bond Extras ...	2002	—		£10.00
LT19	James Bond 007 40th Anniversary — Bond Villains ...	2002	—		£12.00
LT99	James Bond 007 50th Anniversary Series 1 (only odd numbers issued)	2012	—		£12.00
LT99	James Bond 007 50th Anniversary Series 2 (only even numbers issued)	2012	—		£12.00
LT81	James Bond 007 Heroes and Villains	2010	—		£12.00
LT63	James Bond 007 In Motion (3-D)	2008	—		£12.00
LT66	James Bond 007 Mission Logs	2011	—		£9.50

Size & quantity	TRADE CARD ISSUES	Date	Handbook reference	Price per card	Complete set
	RITTENHOUSE ARCHIVES (USA) (continued)				
LT90	James Bond 007 Quantum of Solace	2015		—	£9.50
LT100	James Bond 007 Quotable Series	2004		—	£9.50
LT110	James Bond 007 Skyfall	2013		—	£9.50
LT76	James Bond 007 Spectre	2016		—	£9.50
LT72	Lost Archives	2010		—	£9.50
LT108	Lost Seasons 1 Thru 5	2009		—	£9.50
LT90	Lost In Space (The Complete Series)	2005		—	£12.00
LT72	The Orville Season 1	2019		—	£9.50
LT81	The Outer Limits Sex, Cyborgs & Science Fiction	2003		—	£9.50
LT81	Six Feet Under	2004		20p	£9.50
LT72	Six Million Dollar Man	2004		—	£12.00
LT72	Spiderman Archives	2009		—	£9.50
LT79	Spiderman III — The Film	2007		—	£9.50
LT100	Star Trek Aliens	2014		—	£9.50
LT85	Star Trek Beyond	2017		—	£9.50
LT90	Star Trek Celebrating 40 Years	2006		—	£9.50
LT189	Star Trek Deep Space Nine The Complete Series	2003		—	£18.00
LT108	Star Trek Deep Space Nine Quotable Series	2007		—	£9.50
LT90	Star Trek Discovery Season 1	2019		—	£15.00
LT84	Star Trek Discovery Season 2	2020		—	£12.00
LT81	Star Trek Enterprise Season I	2002		—	£12.00
LT81	Star Trek Enterprise Season 2	2003		—	£12.00
LT72	Star Trek Enterprise Season 3	2004		—	£9.50
LT72	Star Trek Enterprise Season 4	2005		—	£9.50
LT100	Star Trek 50th Anniversary Greatest Moments	2017		—	£9.50
LT110	Star Trek Into Darkness	2014		—	£9.50
LT81	Star Trek Movie	2009		—	£9.50
LT60	Star Trek Movies In Motion (3-D)	2008		—	£15.00
LT90	Star Trek Movies The Complete Series	2007		—	£9.50
LT90	Star Trek Movies Quotable Series	2010		—	£9.50
LT72	Star Trek Nemesis	2002		20p	£9.50
LT90	Star Trek The Next Generation Complete Series 1 (1987-1991) (Nos 1 to 88, 177 & 178)	2011		—	£9.50
LT90	Star Trek The Next Generation Complete Series 2 (1991-1994) (Nos 89 to 176, 179 & 180)	2012		—	£9.50
LT100	Star Trek The Next Generation Heroes and Villains	2013		—	£9.50
LT89	Star Trek The Next Generation Portfolio Prints (front Art by Juan Ortiz) 1st Series (odd numbers only 1 to 177)	2015		—	£9.50
LT89	Star Trek The Next Generation Portfolio Prints (front art By Juan Ortiz) 2nd Series (even numbers only 2 to 178)	2015		—	£9.50
LT110	Star Trek The Next Generation Quotable Series	2005		—	£9.50
LT110	Star Trek The Original Series Archives	2009		—	£9.50
LT80	Star Trek The Original Series Artwork by Juan Ortiz	2014		—	£9.50
LT110	Star Trek The Original Series 40th Anniversary 1st Series	2006		—	£9.50
LT110	Star Trek The Original Series 40th Anniversary 2nd Series	2008		—	£9.50
LT100	Star Trek The Original Series Heroes and Villains	2013		—	£9.50
EL24	Star Trek The Original Series in Motion (3D)	1999		—	£20.00
LT110	Star Trek The Original Series Quotable	2004		—	£12.00
LT60	Star Trek Picard Season 1	2021		—	£12.00
LT81	Star Trek The Remastered Original Series	2010		—	£9.50
LT183	Star Trek Voyager The Complete Series	2002		—	£18.00
LT99	Star Trek Voyager Heroes & Villains	2015		—	£9.50
LT72	Star Trek Voyager Quotable Series	2012		—	£9.50
LT63	Stargate Atlantis Season 1	2005		—	£9.50
LT72	Stargate Atlantis Season 2	2006		—	£9.50

Size & quantity	TRADE CARD ISSUES	Date	Handbook reference	Price per card	Complete set
	RITTENHOUSE ARCHIVES (USA) (continued)				
LT81	Stargate Atlantis Seasons 3 and 4	2008		—	£9.50
LT72	Stargate SG1 Season 1 to 3	2001		—	£9.50
LT72	Stargate SG1 Season 4	2002		—	£9.50
LT72	Stargate SG1 Season 5	2002		20p	£9.50
LT72	Stargate SG1 Season 6	2004		—	£9.50
LT3	Stargate SG1 Season 6 Checklist Corrected Cards ...	2004		—	£3.00
LT72	Stargate SG1 Season 7	2005		—	£9.50
LT81	Stargate SG1 Season 8	2006		—	£9.50
LT72	Stargate SG1 Season 9	2007		—	£9.50
LT72	Stargate SG1 Season 10	2008		—	£9.50
LT90	Stargate SG1 Heroes	2009		—	£9.50
LT72	Stargate Universe SG-U Season 1	2010		—	£9.50
LT98	Trueblood Seasons 1 to 4	2012		—	£9.50
LT72	Trueblood Archives Season 5 (Nos. 99 to 122 plus Character Profiles Nos. 1 to 48)	2013		—	£9.50
LT72	Twilight Zone 1st Series	1999		—	£9.50
LT9/10	Twilight Zone 1st Series Autograph Challenge Game (Minus 'Z')	1999		—	£3.50
LT72	Twilight Zone 2nd Series	2000		—	£9.50
LT8/9	Twilight Zone 2nd Series Challenge Game (Minus 'S')	2000		—	£3.50
LT72	Twilight Zone 3rd Series	2002		—	£9.50
LT72	Twilight Zone 4th Series	2005		—	£9.50
LT64	Twilight Zone Archives	2020		—	£12.00
LT79	Twilight Zone 50th Anniversary	2009		—	£9.50
LT72	Twin Peaks	2019		—	£9.50
LT63	The Umbrella Academy...............	2020		—	£9.50
LT81	Under the Dome Season 1	2014		—	£9.50
LT72	Warehouse 13...............	2010		—	£9.50
LT63	Women of James Bond in Motion (3-D)	2003		—	£20.00
LT81	The Women of Star Trek	2010		—	£9.50
EL32	Women of Star Trek in Motion (3-D)	1999		—	£25.00
LT70	Women of Star Trek Voyager Holofex Series	2001		—	£16.00
LT72	X-Men Origins Wolverine	2009		—	£9.50
LT72	X-Men The Last Stand	2006		—	£9.50
LT72	Xena Warrior Princess Season 4 and 5	2001		—	£9.50
LT72	Xena Warrior Princess Season 6	2001		—	£9.50
LT63	Xena Warrior Princess Art & Images	2004		—	£9.50
LT72	Xena Warrior Princess Beauty & Brawn (No 70 not issued)	2002		20p	£9.50
LT72	Xena Warrior Princess Dangerous Liaisons	2007		—	£9.50
LT135	Xena Warrior Princess Quotable Series	2003		—	£15.00
LT9	Xena Warrior Princess Quotable Series Words from the Bard...............	2003		—	£4.00
	RIVER GROUP (USA)				
LT220	The Beatles Collection	1993		20p	£30.00
LT150	Dark Dominion...............	1993		—	£12.00
LT660	The Elvis Collection	1992		—	£96.00
LT150	Plasm O	1993		—	£12.00
LT31	Splatter Bowl	1993		—	£6.00
	RIVER WYE PRODUCTIONS				
LT81	D-Day Commemorative Series	2005		—	£25.00
LT72	Hammer Horror Behind The Screams	2004		—	£20.00
LT9	Laurel and Hardy Babes At War (Limited Edition)	2006		—	£12.00
LT90	Laurel & Hardy 70th Anniversary	1997		—	£20.00
LT72	Laurel & Hardy Millennium 2000 Celebration	2000		—	£18.00
LT72	Sherlock Holmes	2002		—	£25.00

Size & quantity	TRADE CARD ISSUES	Date	Handbook reference	Price per card	Complete set
	THE 'RK' CONFECTIONERY CO. LTD				
32	Felix	1922	HX-56	£65.00	—
	ROB ROY				
L20	Manchester United Footballers	1995		—	£15.00
	ROBERTSON LTD (Jam)				
1	Advertisement Gollies:				
	A Shaped figure...	c1960		—	£4.00
	B Medium card 60 × 47mm	c1960		—	£4.00
10	Musical Gollies:		HR-26.2		
	A Shaped figure...	c1960		£4.00	—
	B Medium card 60 × 47mm	c1960		£4.00	—
10	Sporting Gollies:		HR-26.3		
	A Shaped figure...	c1960		£4.00	—
	B Medium card 60 × 47mm	c1960		£4.00	—
	ROBERTSON & WOODCOCK LTD				
50	British Aircraft Series	1930		£4.00	—
	C. ROBINSON ARTWORKSHOP				
L16	Plymouth Argyle FA Cup Squad 1983-84	1984		—	£8.00
	ROBINSON'S BARLEY WATER				
EL30	Sporting Records..	1983		20p	£6.00
	ROBINSON BROS. & MASTERS				
25	Tea from the Garden to the House	c1930		£15.00	—
	ROCHE & CO. LTD				
K50	Famous Footballers	1927		—	£950.00
	49/50 (— No. 21)..	1927		£16.00	—
	THE ROCKET				
MP11	Famous Knock-Outs..	1923		£11.00	—
	ROCKWELL				
	Airship The Story of the R101:				
10	A Standard size	2003		—	£5.50
L10	B Large size	2003		—	£7.50
	Arsenal Goalscorers The Modern Era:				
10	A Standard size	2010		—	£5.50
L10	B Large size	2010		—	£7.50
	Battle of Britain (World War II):				
10	A Standard size	2020		—	£5.50
L10	B Large size	2020		—	£7.50
	Bodyline — The Fight For The Ashes 1932-33:				
10	A Standard size	2005		—	£5.50
L10	B Large size	2005		—	£7.50
	Britain's Lost Railway Stations:				
10	A Standard size	2005		—	£5.50
L10	B Large size	2005		—	£7.50
	British Armoured Vehicles of World War II:				
10	A Standard size	2001		—	£5.50
L10	B Large size	2001		—	£7.50
	British Fighting Jets:				
10	A Standard size	2003		—	£5.50
L10	B Large size	2003		—	£7.50
	British Warplanes of the Second World War:				
10	A Standard size	2000		—	£5.50
L10	B Large size	2000		—	£7.50

Size & quantity	TRADE CARD ISSUES	Date	Handbook reference	Price per card	Complete set
	ROCKWELL (continued)				
10	Bygone Chingford	1998		—	£5.50
10	Bygone Highams Park	1998		—	£5.50
	Children's Book Illustrators of The Golden Age:				
10	A Standard size	2005		—	£5.50
L10	B Large size	2005		—	£7.50
L7	Classic Chelsea F.C.	2005		—	£5.50
L7	Classic Everton F.C.	2005		—	£5.50
	Classic Football Teams Before The First World War:				
10	A Standard size	2000		—	£5.50
L10	B Large size	2000		—	£7.50
	Classic Football Teams of the 1960s:				
10	A Standard size	1999		—	£5.50
L10	B Large size	1999		—	£7.50
	Classic Gunners (Arsenal F.C.):				
7	A Standard size	2010		—	£8.50
L7	B Large size	2001		—	£5.50
L7	Classic Hammers (West Ham United F.C.)	2003		—	£5.50
L7	Classic Liverpool F.C.	2005		—	£5.50
L7	Classic Reds (Manchester United F.C.)	2003		—	£5.50
	Classic Sci-Fi 'B' Movies:				
10	A Standard size	2007		—	£5.50
L10	B Large size	2007		—	£7.50
	Classic Spurs (Tottenham Hotspur F.C.):				
7	A Standard size	2010		—	£8.50
L7	B Large size	2002		—	£5.50
	Cunard In The 1950s:				
10	A Standard size	2003		—	£5.50
L10	B Large size	2003		—	£7.50
	Dunkirk (World War II):				
10	A Standard size	2020		—	£5.50
L10	B Large size	2020		—	£7.50
	Early Allied Warplanes:				
10	A Standard size	2000		—	£5.50
L10	B Large size (79 × 62mm)	2000		—	£7.50
LT10	C Large size (89 × 64mm)	2000		—	£8.00
	Early Balloon Flight:				
10	A Standard size	2001		—	£5.50
L10	B Large size	2001		—	£7.50
	Early Locomotives Series One:				
10	A Standard size	2005		—	£5.50
L10	B Large size	2005		—	£7.50
	Early Locomotives Series Two:				
10	A Standard size	2005		—	£5.50
L10	B Large size	2005		—	£7.50
	Family Cars of the 1950s:				
10	A Standard size	2000		—	£5.50
L10	B Large size (79 × 62mm)	2000		—	£7.50
LT10	C Large size (89 × 64mm)	2000		—	£8.00
	Flying So High — West Ham United F.C. 1964-66:				
10	A Standard size	2005		—	£5.50
L10	B Large size	2005		—	£7.50
	German Armoured Vehicles of World War II:				
10	A Standard size	2001		—	£5.50
L10	B Large size (79 × 62mm)	2001		—	£7.50
LT10	C Large size (89 × 64mm)	2001		—	£8.00
	German Warplanes of the Second World War:				
10	A Standard size	2000		—	£5.50
L10	B Large size (79 × 62mm)	2000		—	£7.50
LT10	C Large size (89 × 64mm)	2000		—	£8.00

Size & quantity	TRADE CARD ISSUES	Date	Handbook reference	Price per card	Complete set
	ROCKWELL (continued)				
	The Great Heavyweights (Boxers):				
10	A Standard size	2002		—	£5.50
L10	B Large size	2002		—	£7.50
	The Great Middleweights (Boxers):				
10	A Standard size	2002		—	£5.50
L10	B Large size	2002		—	£7.50
	Heath Robinson At The Seaside:				
10	A Standard size	2010		—	£5.50
L10	B Large size	2010		—	£7.50
	Heath Robinson on Golf:				
10	A Standard size	2020		—	£5.50
L10	B Large size	2020		—	£7.50
	Heath Robinson Sporting Eccentricities:				
10	A Standard size	2010		—	£5.50
L10	B Large size	2005		—	£7.50
	Heath Robinson Urban Life:				
10	A Standard size	2010		—	£5.50
L10	B Large size	2005		—	£7.50
	The Hornby Book of Trains:				
10	A Standard size	2005		—	£5.50
L10	B Large size	2005		—	£7.50
	Hurricane Flying Colours:				
10	A Standard size	2002		—	£5.50
L10	B Large size	2002		—	£7.50
	Images of World War One:				
10	A Standard size	1999		—	£5.50
L10	B Large size (79 × 62mm)	1999		—	£7.50
LT10	C Large size (89 × 64mm)	1999		—	£8.00
	Lost Warships of WWII:				
10	A Standard size	2002		—	£5.50
L10	B Large size	2002		—	£7.50
	Meccano The Aviation Covers:				
10	A Standard size	2006		—	£5.50
L10	B Large size	2006		—	£7.50
	Meccano The Railway Covers:				
10	A Standard size	2006		—	£5.50
L10	B Large size	2006		—	£7.50
	Mighty Atoms The All Time Greats (Boxers):				
10	A Standard size	2004		—	£5.50
L10	B Large size	2004		—	£7.50
	Modern Family Cars:				
15	A Standard size	2001		—	£7.00
L15	B Large size (79 × 62mm)	2001		—	£10.00
LT15	C Large size (89 × 64mm)	2001		—	£11.00
	The 1948 Australians (Cricketers):				
10	A Standard size	2006		—	£5.50
L10	B Large size	2006		—	£7.50
	Officers of the Titanic:				
10	A Standard size	2020		—	£5.50
L10	B Large size	2020		—	£7.50
	Olympic, Titanic, Britannic (Liners):				
25	A Standard size	2001		—	£10.00
L25	B Large size	2001		—	£12.00
	Post War Wimbledon Ladies Champions 1st Series:				
10	A Standard size	2004		—	£5.50
L10	B Large size	2004		—	£7.50
	Post-War Wimbledon Ladies Champions 2nd Series:				
10	A Standard size	2005		—	£5.50
L10	B Large size	2005		—	£7.50

Size & quantity	TRADE CARD ISSUES	Date	Handbook reference	Price per card	Complete set
	ROCKWELL (continued)				
	Post War Wimbledon Men's Champions 1st Series:				
10	A Standard size	2004		—	£5.50
L10	B Large size	2004		—	£7.50
	Post-War Wimbledon Men's Champions 2nd Series:				
10	A Standard size	2005		—	£5.50
L10	B Large size	2005		—	£7.50
	Relegated to History England's Lost Football Grounds:				
10	A Standard size	2004		—	£5.50
L10	B Large size	2004		—	£7.50
	Solar System:				
10	A Standard size	2001		—	£5.50
L10	B Large size	2001		—	£7.50
	Spitfire Flying Colours:				
10	A Standard size	1999		—	£5.50
L10	B Large size (79 × 62mm)	1999		—	£7.50
LT10	C Large size (89 × 64mm)	1999		—	£8.00
	Spurs Great Post-War Goalscorers Series 1 (Tottenham Hotspur F.C.):				
10	A Standard size	2007		—	£5.50
L10	B Large size	2007		—	£7.50
	Spurs Great Post-War Goalscorers Series 2 (Tottenham Hotspur F.C.):				
10	A Standard size	2007		—	£5.50
L10	B Large size	2007		—	£7.50
	Spurs 1960-1963 — The Glory Years (Tottenham Hotspur F.C.):				
10	A Standard size	2005		—	£5.50
LT10	B Large size	2005		—	£8.00
	Suffragettes:				
10	A Standard size	2005		—	£5.50
L10	B Large size	2005		—	£7.50
	The Titanic Series:				
25	A Standard size	1999		—	£10.00
L25	B Large size (79 × 62mm)	1999		—	£12.00
LT25	C Large size (89 × 64mm)	1999		—	£15.00
	Twopenny Tube Edwardian Sketches of The Central Railway:				
10	A Standard size	2010		—	£5.50
L10	B Large size	2010		—	£7.50
L7	World Cup 1966	2005		—	£5.50
	World War I Posters:				
10	A Standard size	2001		—	£5.50
L10	B Large size	2001		—	£7.50
	World War II Posters — The Home Front:				
10	A Standard size	2001		—	£5.50
L10	B Large size	2001		—	£7.50
	World War II Posters — Industry:				
10	A Standard size	2005		—	£5.50
L10	B Large size	2007		—	£7.50
	World War II Posters — Morale:				
10	A Standard size	2005		—	£5.50
L10	B Large size	2007		—	£7.50
	World War II Posters — The Services:				
10	A Standard size	2001		—	£5.50
L10	B Large size	2001		—	£7.50

Size & quantity	TRADE CARD ISSUES	Date	Handbook reference	Price per card	Complete set
	RODEO BUBBLE GUM				
M84	Western Stars	c1953		£12.00	—
	ROGERSTOCK				
LT13	American Cars of the 1950s	2007		—	£6.50
LT13	American Cars of the 1960s	2007		—	£6.50
LT13	Ferrari — Classic Ferrari Models 1958-92	2007		—	£6.50
LT13	Jaguar — Classic Jaguar Models 1950-96	2007		—	£6.50
	ROLLS-ROYCE MOTORS				
L25	Bentley Motor Cars 1st Series:				
	A Original Issue Thin frameline back...	1985		£2.40	£60.00
	B Inscribed 'Second Edition' thin frameline back...	1987		£2.00	£50.00
L25	Bentley Motor Cars 2nd Series thick frameline to two sides	1987		£2.00	£50.00
L25	Rolls Royce Motor Cars 1st Series:				
	A Original Issue Thin frameline back...	1985		£2.40	£60.00
	B Inscribed 'Second Edition' thin frameline back...	1987		£2.00	£50.00
L25	Rolls Royce Motor Cars 2nd Series thick frameline to two sides...	1987		£2.00	£50.00
	ROSEBERRY PRESS				
10	Carmen Miranda A Tribute to a Hollywood Legend ...	2015		—	£5.00
	ROSSI'S ICES				
M48	Flags of the Nations	1975		20p	£10.00
	Album			—	£15.00
25	History of Flight 1st Series...	1966		60p	£15.00
25	History of Flight 2nd Series	1966		60p	£15.00
	Album for 1st and 2nd Series combined			—	£30.00
25	World's Fastest Aircraft...	1966		60p	£15.00
	Album			—	£30.00
	ROUND HOUSE				
10	Sound of the Psychedelic 60s 1st Series	2014		—	£5.00
10	Sound of the 60s 1st Series (Pop Stars)	2013		—	£5.00
10	Sound of the 60s 2nd Series (Pop Stars)	2013		—	£5.00
10	Sound of the 60s 3rd Series (Pop Stars)	2014		—	£5.00
10	Sound of the 60s 4th Series (Pop Stars)	2014		—	£5.00
10	Sound of the 60s 5th Series (Pop Stars)	2014		—	£5.00
10	Sound of the 60s 6th Series (Pop Stars)	2014		—	£5.00
10	Sound of the 60s 7th Series (Pop Stars)	2014		—	£5.00
10	Sound of the 70s 1st Series (Pop Stars)	2014		—	£5.00
10	Sound of the 70s 2nd Series (Pop Stars)...	2014		—	£5.00
	D. ROWLAND				
L20	Arsenal F.C. 2002-03	2004		—	£15.00
25	Association Footballers Series 1	1999		50p	£12.50
25	Association Footballers Series 2	1999		50p	£12.50
25	Association Footballers Series 3	1999		50p	£12.50
25	Association Footballers Series 4	1999		50p	£12.50
25	Association Footballers Series 5	c1999		50p	£12.50
20	Boxers Series 1	1999		50p	£10.00
20	Boxing Legends Series 1	1999		50p	£10.00
L20	Chelsea F.C. 2002-03	2004		—	£12.00
25	Cricketers Series 1	1999		50p	£12.50
25	Cricketers Series 2	1999		50p	£12.50
20	Famous Footballers Series 1	1999		40p	£8.00

Size & quantity	TRADE CARD ISSUES	Date	Handbook reference	Price per card	Complete set
	D. ROWLAND (continued)				
20	Famous Footballers Series 2	1999		40p	£8.00
20	Famous Footballers Series 3	1999		50p	£10.00
20	Famous Footballers Series 4 (Managers)	1999		40p	£8.00
20	Famous Footballers Series 5	1999		—	£10.00
L10	Famous Footballers Series 6 (Teams)	2000		—	£7.00
L10	Famous Footballers Series 7 (Teams)	2000		—	£7.00
L20	Liverpool F.C. 2002-03	2004		—	£12.00
L20	Manchester City F.C. 2002-03	2004		—	£12.00
L20	Manchester United F.C. 2002-03	2004		—	£12.00
L20	Wolverhampton Wanderers F.C. 2002-03	2004		—	£12.00
	ROWNTREE & CO.				
25	Celebrities of 1900 Period	1900	HR-35	£38.00	—
M20	Merry Monarchs	1977		20p	£4.00
	The Old and the New:		HR-40		
25	A i Rowntree's Elect Chocolate (with coupon)	1912		£11.00	
25	A ii Rowntree's Elect Chocolate (without coupon)	1912		£7.00	
48	B i Rowntree's Elect Chocolate Delicious (with coupon)	1912		£11.00	
48	B ii Rowntree's Elect Chocolate Delicious (without coupon)	1912		£7.00	—
M18	Prehistoric Animals	1978		33p	£6.00
M10	Texan Tall Tales of The West	1977		£2.50	—
120	Treasure Trove Pictures	c1930		£2.50	—
24	York Views:		HR-41		
	A Unicoloured	c1920		£16.00	—
	B Coloured	c1920		£16.00	—
	ROYAL ARMY MEDICAL CORPS HISTORICAL MUSEUM				
M16	Centenary Year Royal Army Medical Corps Victoria Crosses 1898-1998	1998		—	£6.00
	ROYAL LEAMINGTON SPA				
25	Royal Leamington Spa	1971		20p	£3.50
	Album			—	£5.00
	ROYAL NATIONAL LIFEBOAT INSTITUTION				
M16	Lifeboats	1979		30p	£5.00
	ROYAL NAVY SUBMARINE MUSEUM				
M25	History of R.N. Submarines (including album)	1996		—	£12.00
	ROYAL SOCIETY FOR THE PREVENTION OF ACCIDENTS (RoSPA)				
24	Modern British Cars	1953		£2.40	£60.00
22	Modern British Motor Cycles	1953		£4.00	—
25	New Traffic Signs	1966		24p	£6.00
	Album			—	£20.00
24	Veteran Cars 1st Series	1955		£1.50	£36.00
24	Veteran Cars 2nd Series	1957		£2.00	£50.00
	Album			—	£20.00
	ROY ROGERS BUBBLE GUM				
M24	Roy Rogers — In Old Amarillo (plain back)	1955		25p	£6.00
M24	Roy Rogers — South of Caliente (plain back)	1955		25p	£6.00
	THE RUBY				
L10	Famous Beauties of the Day	1923		£11.00	—
L6	Famous Film Stars	1923		£11.00	—

Size & quantity	TRADE CARD ISSUES	Date	Handbook reference	Price per card	Complete set
	RUBY CARDS				
10	A Tribute to Dad's Army	2009		—	£5.00
	RUGBY FOOTBALL UNION				
50	English Internationals 1980-1991	1991		30p	£15.00
	RUGLYS				
L12	England Rugby Stars (Series Ref 1003)	2000		—	£6.00
L8	England Soccer Stars (Series Ref 1006)	2000		—	£4.00
L20	Manchester United Soccer Stars (Series Ref 1004)	2000		—	£10.00
L4	Shearer (Alan) Soccer Star (Series Ref 1005)	2000		—	£3.00
L8	Snooker Stars (Series Ref 1007)	2000		—	£4.00
L12	Wales Rugby Classics (Series Ref 1002)	2000		—	£6.00
L20	Wales Rugby Stars (Series Ref 1001)	2000		—	£10.00
	S. & B. PRODUCTS				
?69	Torry Gillicks's Internationals	c1950		£14.00	—
	S.C.M.C.C.				
15	Stoke's Finest Hour (1972 Football Cup Final)	2002		—	£6.00
	S.P.C.K.				
L12	Bible Promises Illustrated, Series VIII	c1940		£2.00	—
L12	Cathedrals of Northern England, Series VII	c1940		£2.00	—
L12	Palestine, Series II	c1940		£2.00	—
L12	Scenes from English Church History, Series V	c1940		£1.00	£12.00
L12	Scenes from Genesis, Series XI	c1940		£2.00	—
L12	Scenes from Lives of the Saints, Series VI	c1940		£1.50	£18.00
L12	Southern Cathedrals, Series XVI	c1940		£2.00	—
L12	Stories of Joseph and David, Series I	c1940		£2.00	—
	SSPC (USA)				
LT45	200 Years of Freedom 1776-1976	1976		—	£8.00
	SABAN ENTERTAINMENT (USA)				
	VR Troopers (Sectional Series):				
LT5	A J B Reese	1995		—	£3.00
LT5	B Jeb	1995		—	£3.00
LT5	C Kaitlyn Hall	1995		—	£3.00
LT5	D Ryan Steel	1995		—	£3.00
	SAINSBURY LTD				
M12	British Birds	1924		£9.00	—
M12	Foreign Birds	1924		£9.00	—
M144	Heroes (Disney, Pixar, Star Wars, Marvel)	2019		20p	£12.00
	Album			—	£10.00
M140	Lego Create the World	2017		20p	£12.00
	Album			—	£10.00
M140	Lego Create the World Amazingly	2020		—	£12.00
	Album			—	£10.00
M140	Lego Create the World Incredible Inventions	2018		20p	£12.00
	Album			—	£10.00
	SANDERS BROTHERS				
25	Birds, Poultry, etc	1924		£10.00	—
20	Dogs	1924		£4.00	£80.00
25	Recipes	1924		£5.00	—
	SANDERSON				
24	World's Most Beautiful Birds	c1925	HX-22	£11.00	—

Size & quantity	TRADE CARD ISSUES	Date	Handbook reference	Price per card	Complete set
	SANITARIUM (Australia)				
M20	Australian Test Cricketers (Weet-Bix)	1994		£1.25	—
	SANITARIUM HEALTH FOOD CO. LTD (New Zealand)				
EL12	Airliners of the 90's	1991		50p	—
M29	All Blacks Access (Rugby Union)	2012		—	£15.00
M30	All Blacks Code Black (Rugby Union)	2013		—	£12.00
M26	All Blacks Fuel Your Dreams (Rugby Union)	2014		—	£12.00
30	All Blacks Team Tags (3-D) (Rugby Union)	2010		—	£12.00
LT8	All Blacks Training Tips (Rugby Union)	2002		—	£6.00
EL12	Alpine Flora of New Zealand	1975		50p	—
EL12	Alpine Sports	1986		40p	£5.00
EL12	Amazing Animals of the World	1985		60p	—
LT8	Amazing Facts...	1998		50p	£4.00
EL12	Animals of New Zealand	1974		£1.00	—
M30	Another Look at New Zealand	1971		40p	—
M30	Antarctic Adventure	1972		40p	—
M20	The Aviation Card Series	1995		30p	£6.00
LT16	Babe & Friends — The Film	1999		—	£5.00
EL12	Ball Sports	1989		50p	£6.00
M4	Bee — 3D Motion Cards	1998		—	£3.50
EL12	Big Cats	1992		50p	£6.00
M20	Big Rigs	1983		20p	£3.50
M20	Big Rigs at Work	1986		20p	£4.00
M20	Big Rigs 3	1992		20p	£4.00
EL12	Big Sea Creatures	1994		50p	£6.00
L12	Boarding Pass (Landmarks Around the World)...	1998		50p	—
EL12	Bush Birds of New Zealand	1981		60p	—
M20	Cars of the Seventies	1976		35p	£7.00
LT20	Centenaryville	1999		25p	£5.00
EL12	Clocks Through the Ages	1990		50p	£6.00
M20	Conservation Caring for Our Land	1974		30p	£6.00
EL12	Curious Conveyances	1984		40p	£5.00
EL12	Did You Know	1994		40p	£5.00
M4	Discount Destination Passport	1991		—	£4.00
M20	Discover Indonesia	1977		20p	£3.50
M20	Discover Science With the DSIR	1989		20p	£3.50
EL12	Discovering New Zealand Reptile World	1983		50p	£6.00
EL24	Early Transport in New Zealand	1968		£1.00	—
M20	Exotic Cars	1987		30p	£6.00
M20	Exploring Our Solar System	1982		30p	—
M24	Famous New Zealanders	1971		30p	—
M20	Farewell to Steam	1981		40p	—
M30	Fascinating Orient	1966		20p	£4.00
EL12	Focus on New Zealand 1st Series	1982		50p	£6.00
EL12	Focus on New Zealand 2nd Series	1982		50p	£6.00
M24	Fuelling the Future All Blacks (Rugby Union)	2015		—	£15.00
LT12	Have You Had Your Weet-Bix (Sports)	1997		—	£5.00
EL12	High Action Sports	1994		40p	£5.00
EL12	Historic Buildings 1st Series	1982		50p	£6.00
EL12	Historic Buildings 2nd Series	1984		50p	£6.00
M30	The History of New Zealand Railways...	1968		60p	—
M20	History of Road Transport in New Zealand	1979		25p	£5.00
EL12	Horse Breeds	1990		50p	£6.00
LT15	Hunchback of Notre Dame (Disney)	1996		40p	£6.00
EL10	Hunchback of Notre Dame (Disney)	1996		—	£5.00
LT8	It's Showtime (Disney)	1997		—	£4.00
EL12	Jet Aircraft	1974		80p	—
M20	Kiwi Heroes...	1994		20p	£4.00

Size & quantity	TRADE CARD ISSUES	Date	Handbook reference	Price per card	Complete set

SANITARIUM HEALTH FOOD CO. LTD (New Zealand) (continued)

Size & quantity	Title	Date	Handbook reference	Price per card	Complete set
LT9	Kiwi Kids Tryathlon	1999	—	—	£4.50
M20	Kiwis Going for Gold	1992		20p	£4.00
EL12	The Lion King (Disney)	1995		40p	£5.00
M20	Living in Space	1992		50p	—
M20	Looking at Canada	1978		20p	£3.50
M20	Mammals of the Seas	1985		20p	£3.50
EL12	Man Made Wonders of the World	1987		40p	£5.00
M20	The Many Stranded Web of Nature	1983		30p	£6.00
M60	The Maori Way of Life	1969		50p	—
M30	Marineland Wonders	1967		50p	£15.00
M20	Motor Bike Card Series	1995		50p	—
EL12	Mountaineering	1987		40p	£5.00
LT10	Mr Men	1997		50p	£5.00
M25	National Costumes of the Old World	1968		60p	—
EL12	New Zealand Birds	1973		£1.00	—
EL12	New Zealand Butterflies and Insects	1972		£1.00	—
EL12	New Zealand Custom Vans	1994		—	£4.00
EL12	New Zealand Disasters	1991		35p	£4.00
EL12	New Zealand Hot Rods	1971		£1.00	—
EL12	New Zealand Inventions and Discoveries	1991		35p	£4.00
EL12	New Zealand Lakes 1st Series	1977		60p	—
EL12	New Zealand Lakes 2nd Series	1978		50p	£6.00
M30	New Zealand National Parks	1973		40p	£12.00
M20	New Zealand Reef Fish	1984		30p	£6.00
M20	New Zealand Rod & Custom Cars	1979		25p	£5.00
M20	New Zealand Summer Sports	1984		25p	£5.00
M30	New Zealand Today	1966		40p	£12.00
EL12	New Zealand Waterfalls	1981		50p	—
M20	New Zealand's Booming Industries	1975		20p	£3.50
M20	New Zealanders in Antarctica	1987		25p	£5.00
M20	New Zealanders on Top of the World	1991		20p	£4.00
M20	N.Z. Energy Resources	1976		20p	£4.00
EL12	N.Z.R. Steam Engines	1976		£1.00	—
M20	The 1990 Commonwealth Games	1989		20p	£4.00
M20	1990 Look How We've Grown	1990		20p	£3.50
EL12	Ocean Racers	1986		50p	£6.00
EL10	On the Wing Write 'N' Wipe	1985		£1.00	—
M30	100% All Blacks Jersey (3-D) (Rugby Union)	2011		—	£12.00
M20	100 Years of New Zealand National Parks	1987		20p	£4.00
EL12	Our Fascinating Fungi	1980		50p	—
M20	Our Golden Fleece	1981		20p	£4.00
M20	Our South Pacific Island Neighbours	1974		30p	£6.00
M20	Our Weather	1980		20p	£4.00
EL12	Party Tricks	1993		40p	£5.00
M20	Peanuts (Cartoon Characters)	1993		50p	—
M20	The Phonecard Collection	1994		25p	£5.00
EL12	Power Boats in New Zealand	1990		40p	£5.00
EL12	Robin Hood (Disney)	1996		50p	£6.00
M20	Saving the World's Endangered Wildlife	1991		20p	£4.00
EL12	Shipping in Our Coastal Waters	1988		50p	—
EL12	Silly Dinosaurs	1997		40p	£5.00
M8	Snow White & the Seven Dwarfs (3-D)	1997		—	£4.00
EL12	Spanning New Zealand	1992		40p	£5.00
M20	Spectacular Sports	1974		30p	£6.00
LT12	Speed	1998		40p	£5.00
L44	Stat Attack II New Zealand All Blacks (Rugby Union)	2008		—	£15.00
M20	The Story of New Zealand Aviation	1977		25p	£5.00
M20	The Story of New Zealand in Stamps	1977		35p	£7.00

Size & quantity	TRADE CARD ISSUES	Date	Handbook reference	Price per card	Complete set
	SANITARIUM HEALTH FOOD CO. LTD (New Zealand) (continued)				
M20	Super Cars	1972		50p	£10.00
50	Super Fourteen Super Flyers (Rugby Union)	2010		—	£15.00
EL12	Surf Life Saving	1986		40p	£5.00
LT12	Then & Now	1998		40p	£5.00
M20	Timeless Japan	1975		30p	£6.00
M20	Treasury of Maori Life	1980		30p	£6.00
EL12	Veteran Cars	1971		60p	—
M20	Vintage Cars	1973		40p	£8.00
M20	Weet-bix Stamp Album (Stamp Collecting)	1994		30p	£6.00
M30	What Makes New Zealand Different	1967		60p	£18.00
EL12	Wild Flowers of New Zealand	1979		50p	£6.00
EL12	Wildlife Wonders — Endangered Animals of NZ	1993		50p	£6.00
M20	The Wild South	1986		20p	£4.00
EL12	Windsports	1989		40p	£5.00
M20	Wonderful Ways of Nature	1978		20p	£3.50
EL12	Wonderful Wool	1988		50p	£6.00
M20	The Wonderful World of Disney	1993		50p	—
LT17	World Ball (Basketball)	1997		30p	£5.00
M20	World's Greatest Fun Parks	1990		25p	£5.00
M20	Your Journey Through Disneyland	1988		35p	£7.00
	SAVOY PRODUCTS				
M56	Aerial Navigation	c1925		£2.50	—
M56	Aerial Navigation Series B	c1925		£2.50	—
M56	Aerial Navigation, Series C	c1925		£3.50	—
M56	Famous British Boats	1928		£2.50	—
	SCANLEN (Australia)				
M208	Cricket Series No. 3	1984		—	£30.00
L84	Cricketers 1989/90	1989		25p	£20.00
L84	Cricketers 1990/91	1990		—	£20.00
L90	World Series Cricket	1981		25p	£20.00
	SCHOOL & SPORT				
M4	British Railway Engines	1922	HS-135.1	£7.50	—
M4	British Regiments	1922	HS-135.2	£7.50	—
M4	County Cricket Captains	1922	HS-135.3	£16.00	—
M4	Wild Animals	1922	HS-135.4	£7.50	—
	THE SCHOOL FRIEND				
LP6	Famous Film Stars	1927	HS-8	£11.00	—
EL10	Popular Girls of Cliff House School	1922		£10.00	—
L6	Popular Pictures	1923	HS-9	£4.50	—
	THE SCHOOL GIRL				
M12	Zoological Studies	1923	HS-21	£4.00	—
M4	Zoological Studies (anonymous)	1923	HS-21	£4.00	—
	THE SCHOOLGIRLS OWN PAPER				
12	Film Stars brown front (anonymous plain back)	1932	HS-10	£5.00	—
L3	Royal Family Portraits (anonymous)	c1925		£4.50	—
	THE SCHOOLGIRLS' WEEKLY				
L1	HRH The Duke of York	1922		—	£6.00
L4	Popular Pictures	1922	HS-17	£4.00	—
	SCORE (USA)				
LT47	Dallas Cowboys Cheerleaders	1993		—	£12.00
LT110	1991 NHL Rookie and Traded (Ice Hockey)	1991		—	£7.50

Size & quantity	TRADE CARD ISSUES	Date	Handbook reference	Price per card	Complete set
	SCORE CARD COLLECTABLES				
10	Score (Footballers of the 1970s) 1st Series	2011		—	£5.00
10	Score (Footballers of the 1970s) 2nd Series	2011		—	£5.00
	SCOTTISH DAILY EXPRESS				
EL24	Scotcard — Scottish Footballers	1973		£8.00	—
	SCOTTISH TOURIST BOARD				
L40	Places of Interest	1992		20p	£5.00
	THE SCOUT				
M9	Birds Eggs	1925		£8.00	—
M12	Railway Engines	1924		£8.00	—
	SCRAPBOOK MINICARDS				
27	Pendon Museum (model railway and village)	1978		20p	£4.00
	SCREEN ICONS				
10	Cary Grant	2013		—	£5.00
10	Frankie Howerd	2013		—	£5.00
10	Gregory Peck	2013		—	£5.00
10	Paul Newman	2013		—	£5.00
10	Robert Redford	2013		—	£5.00
10	Steve McQueen	2013		—	£5.00
	SEAGRAM				
25	Grand National Winners	1995		£1.20	£30.00
	SECRETS				
K52	Film Stars Miniature Playing Cards	c1930	HS-26	£2.00	—
	SELF SERVICE LAUNDERETTES				
50	150 Years of Locomotives	1955	HX-178	£6.00	—
	SELLOTAPE PRODUCTS LTD				
35	Great Homes and Castles	1974		60p	£21.00
	Album			—	£20.00
	SEMIC				
LT275	Equestrianism	1997		—	£20.00
	SEW & SEW				
25	Bandsmen of the British Army	1960	HX-62	£2.40	—
	A.J. SEWARD & CO. LTD				
40	Stars of the Screen	1935		£14.00	—
	SEYMOUR MEAD & CO. LTD (Tea)				
24	The Island of Ceylon	1961	HX-47	20p	£3.50
	SHARMAN NEWSPAPERS				
L24	Golden Age of Flying	1979		40p	£10.00
	Album			—	£3.00
L24	Golden Age of Motoring	1979		40p	£10.00
	Album			—	£3.00
L24	Golden Age of Steam	1979		40p	£10.00
	Album			—	£3.00

Size & quantity	TRADE CARD ISSUES	Date	Handbook reference	Price per card	Complete set
	EDWARD SHARP & SONS				
20	Captain Scarlet	c1970		£11.00	—
25	Hey Presto!	1968		20p	£3.50
100	Prize Dogs	c1925		£8.00	—
	T. SHELDON COLLECTIBLES				
L18	Central Lancashire Cricket League Clubs and Pavilions	1997		60p	£10.00
20	The Don (Reproductions of Don Bradman Cricket Cards) 2nd Series	2010		50p	£10.00
10	Famous Old Standians	2002		40p	£4.00
20	Fryer's Roses	1999		50p	£10.00
20	Kenyan Cricket I.C.C. World Cup	1999		40p	£8.00
L6	Mailey Master of His Art (Cricketers)	2003		65p	£4.00
L10	Match of The Day Aldershot Town v Accrington Stanley (10.8.03)	2004		—	£4.00
L10	Match of The Day Cwmbran Town v Maccabi Haifa (14.8.03)	2004		—	£4.00
L10	Match of The Day Rochdale v Yeovil Town (9.8.03)	2003		—	£4.50
20	Olden Goldies (Cricketers)	1998		—	£10.00
L18	Out of the Blue into the Red (Labour Politicians)	1997		40p	£7.00
18	Prominent Cricketers 1924 (reprint, G. Goode, Australia)	1999		—	£9.50
20	Stalybridge Celtic Football Club	1996		40p	£8.00
L18	We're Back Halifax Town A.F.C. 1998/99	1999		60p	
	SHELL (Oil)				
14	Bateman Series	1930		£10.00	—
EL20	Great Britons	1972	HS-34	£1.50	£30.00
	Album			—	£20.00
20	Historic Cars (metal coins)	1971	HS-36	£1.50	—
16	History of Flight (metal coins)	1970	HS-35	£1.50	—
M12	Olympic Greats including album	1992		—	£8.00
M16	3-D Animals	1971	HS-37	£1.50	—
M16	Wonders of the World	c1975		£1.50	—
	SHELL (Oil) (Australia)				
M60	Beetle Series (Nd 301-360)	1962		60p	£36.00
M60	Birds (Nd 121-180)	1960		70p	—
M60	Butterflies & Moths (Nd 181-240)	1960		75p	—
M60	Citizenship (Nd 1-60)	1964		50p	£30.00
M60	Discover Australia with Shell (Nd 1-60)	1959		70p	—
M60	Meteorology (Nd 361-420)	1963		50p	£30.00
M60	Pets (Nd 481-540)	1965		50p	£30.00
M60	Shells, Fish and Coral (Nd 61-120)	1959		50p	—
M60	Transportation (Nd 241-300)	1961		50p	£30.00
	SHELL (Oil) (New Zealand)				
M48	Aircraft of the World	1963		80p	—
M60	Cars of the World	1964		70p	£42.00
M40	Cars of the World	1992		—	£8.00
M20	The Flintstones (Film)	1994		50p	£10.00
M48	Racing Cars of the World	1964		80p	£40.00
M37	Rugby Greats (The All Blacks)	1992		—	£12.00
M40	World of Cricket	1992		30p	£12.00
	SHELLEY'S ICE CREAM				
25	Essex — County Champions (cricket)	1984		—	£9.00
	SHEPHERDS DAIRIES				
100	Shepherds War Series	1915	HX-200	£15.00	

Size & quantity	TRADE CARD ISSUES	Date	Handbook reference	Price per card	Complete set
	SHERIDAN COLLECTIBLES				
LT12	Bobby Jones at St Andrews (Golf)	1995		—	£7.00
LT12	The Bobby Jones Story (Golfer)	1993		—	£7.00
L6	Golf Adventures of Par Bear	1994		—	£4.00
LT25	Players of the Ryder Cup '93 (Golf)	1994		—	£10.00
L7	Railway Posters — Golf	1996		—	£5.00
LT12	The Tom Morris Story (Golfer)	1994		—	£7.00
L7	Underground Art — Football & Wembley	1996		—	£3.50
L7	Underground Art — Rugby	1996		—	£3.50
L7	Underground Art — Wimbledon (Tennis)	1996		—	£3.50
L7	Underground Art — Windsor	1996		—	£3.50
L12	Winners of the Ryder Cup 95	1996		—	£7.00
	SHERMAN'S POOLS LTD				
EL8	Famous Film Stars	1940	HS-39	75p	£6.00
EL38	Searchlight on Famous Players	1937	HS-40	£6.00	—
EL37	Searchlight on Famous Teams (Football):		HS-41		
	A 35 different	1938		£6.00	—
	B Aston Villa and Blackpool	1938		£1.00	£2.50
	W. SHIPTON LTD				
	Trojan Gen-Cards Series 1:				
5	Group 1 Famous Buildings	1959		£1.20	—
5	Group 2 Characters of Fiction	1959		£1.20	—
5	Group 3 Stars of Entertainment	1959		£1.20	—
5	Group 4 Fight Against Crime	1959		£1.20	—
5	Group 5 Prehistoric Monsters	1959		£1.20	—
5	Group 6 Railways	1959		£1.20	—
5	Group 7 Racing Cars	1959		£1.20	—
5	Group 8 Insect World	1959		£1.20	—
5	Group 9 Stars of Sport	1959		£1.20	—
5	Group 10 Animal World	1959		£1.20	—
5	Group 11 Nursing	1959		£1.20	—
5	Group 12 Under the Sea	1959		£1.20	—
5	Group 13 Ballet	1959		£1.20	—
5	Group 14 Wild West	1959		£1.20	—
5	Group 15 Motor Cars	1959		£1.20	—
	SIDELINES				
M23	19th Century Cricket Teams	1987		20p	£4.00
	SILVER KING & CO				
1	Advertisement Card	1905		—	£15.00
	SILVER SHRED				
6	British Medals	c1920	HR-25	£20.00	—
	SKETCHLEY CLEANERS				
25	Communications	1960		30p	£7.50
25	Nature Series	1960	HX-148	36p	£9.00
25	Tropical Birds	1960	HX-13.2	80p	—
	SKY ROCKET				
10	Euro Stars (Footballers of the 1960s and 1970s)	2016		—	£5.00

Size & quantity	TRADE CARD ISSUES	Date	Handbook reference	Price per card	Complete set
	SKYBOX (USA)				
LT90	The Adventures of Batman & Robin (Cartoon)	1995		—	£9.50
LT60	Babylon 5	1996		—	£10.00
EL10	Babylon 5 Posters	1996		—	£6.00
LT100	Babylon 5 Profiles	1999		—	£9.50
LT81	Babylon 5 Season Four	1998		—	£9.50
LT81	Babylon 5 Season Five	1998		—	£9.50
LT72	Babylon 5 Special Edition	1997		—	£9.50
EL70	Batman & Robin the Film	1997		—	£12.00
EL24	Batman & Robin Storyboards	1997		—	£12.00
LT90	Batman Master Series (Cartoon)	1995		—	£9.50
LT100	Batman Saga of The Dark Knight	1994		—	£12.00
LT94	Bill Nye The Science Guy	1995		—	£9.50
LT90	Blue Chips (Basketball Film)	1994		—	£9.50
LT90	Cinderella — Walt Disney Film	1996		—	£9.50
LT81	D C Bloodlines	1993		—	£9.50
LT45	D.C. Comics Stars	1994		—	£12.00
EL90	D.C. Comics Vertigo	1994		—	£9.50
LT100	D.C. Milestone (Comic Book Story)	1993		—	£9.50
LT100	Demolition Man — The Film	1993		—	£9.50
LT90	Disney's Aladdin	1993		—	£9.50
LT90	Free Willy 2 — The Film	1995		—	£9.50
LT75	Gargoyles Series 2	1996		—	£9.50
LT90	Harley Davidson Motor Cycles	1994		—	£9.50
LT101	Hunchback of Notre Dame — Disney Film	1996		—	£9.50
LT90	Jumanji — The Film	1995		—	£9.50
LT90	The Lion King 1st Series — Walt Disney Film	1995		—	£9.50
LT80	The Lion King 2nd Series — Walt Disney Film	1995		—	£9.50
LT90	Lois & Clark — New Adventures of Superman	1995		—	£9.50
LT100	The Making of Star Trek The Next Generation	1994		—	£12.00
LT90	Mortal Kombat The Film	1995		—	£9.50
LT101	101 Dalmations — The Movie	1996		—	£9.50
LT90	The Pagemaster (Film)	1994		—	£12.50
LT102	Pocahontas (Disney film)	1997		—	£9.50
LT100	The Return of Superman	1993		—	£9.50
LT100	Sea Quest DSV	1993		—	£12.00
LT90	Snow White and the Seven Dwarfs Series 1 (Red and yellow backs plus 11 cards turquoise back and front)	1993		—	£16.00
LT90	Snow White and the Seven Dwarfs Series 2 (White and blue backs)	1994		—	£12.50
LT100	Star Trek Cinema 2000	2000		—	£12.00
LT48	Star Trek Deep Space Nine	1993		—	£9.50
LT100	Star Trek Deep Space Nine	1993		—	£15.00
LT100	Star Trek Deep Space Nine Memories From the Future	1999		—	£9.50
LT82	Star Trek Deep Space Nine Profiles	1997		—	£9.50
EL60	Star Trek — First Contact	1996		—	£10.00
EL72	Star Trek — Generations	1994		—	£15.00
EL72	Star Trek — Insurrection	1998		—	£13.00
LT90	Star Trek Master Series 1st Series	1993		—	£14.00
LT100	Star Trek Master Series 2nd Series	1994		—	£12.00
LT39	Star Trek The Next Generation Behind the Scenes	1993		—	£9.50
LT82	Star Trek The Next Generation Profiles	2000		—	£12.00
LT108	Star Trek The Next Generation Season One	1994		—	£15.00
LT96	Star Trek The Next Generation Season Two	1995		—	£9.50
LT108	Star Trek The Next Generation Season Three	1995		—	£9.50
LT108	Star Trek The Next Generation Season Four	1996		—	£9.50
LT108	Star Trek The Next Generation Season Five	1996		—	£9.50
LT6	Star Trek The Next Generation Season Five foil embossed	1996		—	£24.00

Size & quantity	TRADE CARD ISSUES	Date	Handbook reference	Price per card	Complete set
	SKYBOX (USA) (continued)				
LT108	Star Trek The Next Generation Season Six	1997		—	£9.50
LT103	Star Trek The Next Generation Season Seven	1999		—	£12.00
LT90	Star Trek The Original Series, Series One	1997		—	£9.50
LT81	Star Trek The Original Series, Series Two	1998		—	£9.50
LT75	Star Trek The Original Series, Series Three	1999		—	£15.00
LT12/13	Star Trek The Original Series, Series Three Challenge Game (minus Letter C)	1999		—	£5.00
LT58	Star Trek The Original Series Character Log, 1st Series	1997		—	£12.00
LT52	Star Trek The Original Series Character Log, 2nd Series	1998		—	£12.00
LT48	Star Trek The Original Series Character Log, 3rd Series	1999		—	£12.00
LT100	Star Trek 30 Years Phase One	1995		—	£12.00
LT100	Star Trek 30 Years Phase Two	1996		—	£15.00
LT100	Star Trek 30 Years Phase Three	1996		—	£12.00
LT100	Star Trek Voyager — Closer to Home	1999		—	£13.00
LT90	Star Trek Voyager Profiles	1998		—	£14.00
LT98	Star Trek Voyager Season One, Series 1	1995		—	£9.50
LT90	Star Trek Voyager Season One, Series 2	1995		—	£9.50
LT100	Star Trek Voyager Season Two	1996		—	£9.50
LT3	Star Trek Voyager Season Two Xenobio	1997		—	£9.00
EL90	Superman Platinum Series	1994		—	£12.00
LT90	The Three Musketeers — The Movie	1997		—	£9.50
LT98	Toy Story — The Film	1996		—	£9.50
LT74	Toy Story 2 — The Film	1996		—	£9.50
LT100	Ultraverse	1993		—	£9.50
LT81	Wild Wild West — The Movie	1999		—	£9.50
	SKYFOTOS LTD				
48	Merchant Ships	c1965	HS-53	£3.80	—
	SLADE & BULLOCK LTD				
25	Cricket Series	c1925		£90.00	—
25	Football Terms	c1925		£50.00	—
	Modern Inventions:				
25	A Front light and dark blue	c1925		£15.00	—
25	B Front yellow and purple	c1925		£17.00	—
20	Now and Then Series	c1925		£17.00	—
25	Nursery Rhymes	c1925		£17.00	—
25	Science and Skill Series	c1925		£17.00	—
25	Simple Toys and How to Make Them	c1925		£17.00	—
24	World's Most Beautiful Butterflies	c1925	HX-23	£11.00	—
	SLOAN & GRAHAM				
L20	Magnificent Magpies 92/93 squad (Newcastle FC)	1993		—	£8.00
L5	Magnificent Magpies 92-93 2nd Series (Newcastle F.C.)	1993		—	£4.00
25	Newcastle All Time Greats (Football)	1993		50p	£12.50
L2	Newcastle Footballers (Keegan/Beardsley) Plain back	1993		—	£2.00
L12	Sunderland All Time Greats (Football)	1993		—	£8.00
L14	Sunderland Legends of '73 (Football)	1993		—	£8.00
	P. SLUIS				
EL30	Tropical Birds	1962	HS-54	£1.00	£30.00
	SMART NOVELS				
MP44	Cinema Stars (Anonymous plain back)	c1925	HS-56	£6.00	—
MP12	Stage Artistes and Entertainers	c1925	HS-58	£6.00	—

Size & quantity	TRADE CARD ISSUES	Date	Handbook reference	Price per card	Complete set
	SNAP CARDS PRODUCTS LTD				
L50	ATV Stars 1st Series	1958		£3.00	—
L48	ATV Stars 2nd Series	1960		£2.50	£125.00
L50	Associated Rediffusion Stars	1960		£3.50	£175.00
L25	Dotto (Celebrities) (photo)	1959		£2.50	—
L25	Dotto (Celebrities) (sketches)	1959		£2.50	—
	H.A. SNOW				
12	Hunting Big Game in Africa	c1920	HU-5	£9.00	—
	SOCCER BUBBLE GUM				
L48	Soccer Teams, No. 1 Series	1957		£2.50	—
	Album			—	£30.00
L48	Soccer Teams, No. 2 Series	1958		£3.50	—
	SOCCER STAR CARDS				
20	Soccer Star 1st Series	2010		—	£7.50
20	Soccer Star 2nd Series	2010		—	£7.50
20	Soccer Star 3rd Series	2010		—	£7.50
20	Soccer Star 4th Series	2010		—	£7.50
10	Super Soccer (Footballers from the 1950s to 1970s)	2018		—	£5.00
	SODASTREAM				
25	Historical Buildings	1957	HX-72	36p	£9.00
	SOLDIER MAGAZINE				
M24	The British Army	1993		—	£5.00
	SOLO CARDS				
10	Glamour Girls 1st Series (From the 1950s and 60s)	2016		—	£5.00
10	Glamour Girls 2nd Series (From the 1950s and 1960s)	2016		—	£5.00
10	Glamour Girls 3rd Series (From the 1950s & 60s)	2016		—	£5.00
10	Glamour Girls 4th Series (From the 1950s & 60s)	2016		—	£5.00
10	Glamour Girls 5th Series (From the 1950s & 60s)	2016		—	£5.00
10	Glamour Girls 6th Series (From the 1950s & 60s)	2016		—	£5.00
10	Glamour Girls 7th Series.(From the 1950s & 60s)	2016		—	£5.00
10	Glamour Girls 8th Series.(From the 1950s, 60s & 70s)	2017		—	£5.00
10	Glamour Girls 9th Series (From the 1950s, 60s & 70s)	2017		—	£5.00
10	Glamour Girls 10th Series (From the 1950s, 60s & 70s)	2017		—	£5.00
10	Glamour Girls 11th Series (From the 1950s & 60s)	2017		—	£5.00
10	Glamour Girls 12th Series (From the 1950s & 60s)	2017		—	£5.00
10	Glamour Girls 13th Series (From the 1950s, 60s & 70s)	2017		—	£5.00
10	Glamour Girls 14th Series (From the 1950s, 60s & 70s)	2017		—	£5.00
10	Glamour Girls 15th Series (From the 1950s, 60s & 70s)	2017		—	£5.00
10	Glamour Girls 16th Series (From the 1950s, 60s & 70s)	2017		—	£5.00
10	Glamour Girls 17th Series (From the 1950s, 60s & 70s)	2017		—	£5.00
10	Glamour Girls 18th Series (From the 1950s, 60s & 70s)	2018		—	£5.00
10	Glamour Girls 19th Series (From the 1950s, 60s & 70s)	2018		—	£5.00
10	Glamour Girls 20th Series (From the 1950s, 60s & 70s)	2018		—	£5.00
10	Glamour Girls 21st Series (From the 1950s, 60s & 70s)	2018		—	£5.00
10	Glamour Girls 22nd Series (From the 1950s, 60s & 70s)	2018		—	£5.00
10	Glamour Girls 23rd Series (From the 1950s, 60s & 70s)	2018		—	£5.00
10	Glamour Girls 24th Series (From the 1950s, 60s & 70s)	2018		—	£5.00
10	Glamour Girls 25th Series (From the 1950s, 60s & 70s)	2018		—	£5.00
10	Glamour Girls 26th Series (From the 1950s, 60s & 70s)	2019		—	£5.00
10	Glamour Girls 27th Series (From the 1950s, 60s & 70s)	2019		—	£5.00
10	Glamour Girls 28th Series (From the 1950s, 60s & 70s)	2019		—	£5.00
10	Glamour Girls 29th Series (From the 1950s, 60s & 70s)	2019		—	£5.00
10	Glamour Girls 30th Series (From the 1950s, 60s & 70s)	2019		—	£5.00

Size & quantity	TRADE CARD ISSUES	Date	Handbook reference	Price per card	Complete set
	SOLO CARDS (continued)				
10	Glamour Girls 31st Series (From the 1950s, 60s & 70s)...	2019		—	£5.00
10	Glamour Girls 32nd Series (From the 1950s, 60s & 70s)...	2019		—	£5.00
10	Glamour Girls 33rd Series (From the 1950s, 60s & 70s)...	2019		—	£5.00
10	Glamour Girls 34th Series (From the 1950s, 60s & 70s)....	2020		—	£5.00
	SOMPORTEX LTD				
L50	The Exciting World of James Bond 007	1965		£11.00	—
L60	Famous TV Wrestlers	1964		£5.00	—
L60	Film Scene Series James Bond 007	1964		£11.00	—
L72	John Drake — Danger Man	1966		£8.00	—
L72	The Saint	1967		£9.00	—
L26	Sean Connery as James Bond (You Only Live Twice) (real colour film, issued in strips of 3)	1967		£16.00	—
L72	Thunderball James Bond 007:		HS-65		
	A Complete set	1966		—	£425.00
	B 71 different (minus No. 24)	1966		£5.00	£355.00
L73	Thunderbirds (coloured)	1966		£8.00	—
L72	Thunderbirds (black and white):				
	A Size 90 × 64mm	1966		£4.00	—
	B Size 77 × 57mm	1966		£6.00	—
L36	Weirdies	1968	HS-66	£1.75	—
	SONNY BOY				
50	Railway Engines:				
	A White back	c1960		20p	£10.00
	B Cream back	c1960		20p	£10.00
	SOURCE GROUP/MORRISON ENTERTAINMENT (USA)				
LT48	Monster in My Pocket	1991		—	£9.00
LT24	Monster in My Pocket Island Sticker Poster Puzzle	1991		—	£4.50
	SOUTH WALES CONSTABULARY				
EL36	British Stamps	1983		—	£12.00
EL36	Castles and Historic Places in Wales	1988		40p	£15.00
EL36	City of Cardiff	1989		60p	—
EL35	The '82 Squad (rugby union)	1982		£1.25	—
EL36	Merthyr Tydfil Borough Council	1987		40p	£15.00
EL37	Payphones Past and Present	1987		70p	£25.00
EL36	Rhymney Valley District Council	1986		—	£15.00
EL20	South Wales Constabulary	1990		—	£12.00
M32	Sport-a-Card	1991		—	£18.00
	SOUTH WALES ECHO				
L36	Cardiff City Legends (Footballers)	2003		25p	£9.00
50	Great Welsh Rugby Players	1992		20p	£10.00
	SPACE VENTURES (USA)				
LT37	Moon Mars Space Shots (embossed)	1991		—	£10.00
LT110	Space Shots 1st Series	1990		—	£16.00
LT110	Space Shots 2nd Series	1991		—	£12.00
LT110	Space Shots 3rd Series	1992		—	£12.00
	SPAR GROCERS				
EL30	Walt Disney	1972	HS-67	£3.00	—
	SPILLERS NEPHEWS				
25	Conundrum Series	c1910		£25.00	—
40	Views of South Wales and District	c1910		£25.00	—

Size & quantity	TRADE CARD ISSUES	Date	Handbook reference	Price per card	Complete set
	SPOOKTASTIC CARDS				
10	Karloff (Boris Karloff Tribute to the Horror Legend) ...	2010		—	£5.00
	SPORT AND ADVENTURE				
M46	Famous Footballers	1922		£5.00	—
	SPORT IN PRINT				
M64	Nottinghamshire Cricketers	1989		—	£35.00
	SPORT IN VIEW				
25	Pro's and Poetry 1920s Football and Cricket 1st Series	2012		—	£12.50
M25	Pro's and Poetry 1920s Football and Cricket 2nd Series	2017		—	£7.00
	The Sporting Art of Amos Ramsbottom from 1900s:				
L16	Set 1 Football and Rugby	2012		—	£6.00
EL10	Set 2 Football	2012		—	£6.00
EL10	Set 3 Cricket	2012		—	£6.00
EL6	Set 4 Lancashire League Cricket	2012		—	£5.00
EL7	Set 5 Rugby Union	2012		—	£5.00
EL6	Set 6 Rugby League	2012		—	£5.00
EL5	Set 7 General Sport	2012		—	£4.50
	SPORT PHOTOS				
96	Smashers (Footballers)...	c1950		£18.00	—
	P. J. SPORTING				
L10	International Cricketers	2001		—	£8.00
	SPORTING PROFILES				
L8	Arsenal F.C. F.A. Cup Winners 1930 Programme Covers	2006		—	£5.00
L9	Arsenal F.C. F.A. Cup Winners 1971 Programme Covers	2006		—	£5.00
L13	Ashes Set Match Action — Cricketers...	2005		—	£6.50
L5	Ashes Set Match Action — Cricket Bonus Set Programme Covers.....	2005		—	£3.50
L10	Aston Villa F.C. European Cup Winners 1982 Programme Covers	2006		—	£6.00
L15	Ayrton Senna 1960-1994	2005		—	£6.50
L12	The Beatles Concert Posters Volume 1 UK Tour	2016		—	£6.00
L12	The Beatles Concert Posters Volume 2 USA Tour ...	2016		—	£6.00
L12	The Beatles Magazine Covers	2006		—	£6.00
L20	Bob Dylan Concert Posters	2009		—	£7.50
L15	Bon Jovi Concert Posters	2014		—	£6.50
15	Boxing Greats	2003		—	£5.00
L15	Bruce Lee Film Posters	2005		—	£6.50
L15	Bruce Springsteen Concert Posters	2009		—	£6.50
L20	Cardiff City F.C. European Adventure 1964-70 Programme Covers	2005		—	£7.50
L20	Carry On Up The Card Set (Carry On Film Stars)... ...	2005		—	£9.00
L16	Cassius Clay The Early Years	2002		—	£9.00
L10	Celtic F.C. 1967 European Cup Winners Programme Covers	2004		—	£6.50
L20	Charles Buchan's Football Monthly Magazine Covers	2004		—	£9.50
L10	Chelsea F.C. European Cup Winners 1971 Programme Covers...	2006		—	£6.00
L10	Chelsea F.C. F.A Cup Winners 1970 Programme Covers	2006		—	£5.00
L8	Circus Posters From Around 1900	2005		—	£5.00
L15	Classic Le Mans Posters	2007		—	£6.50

Size & quantity	TRADE CARD ISSUES	Date	Handbook reference	Price per card	Complete set

SPORTING PROFILES (continued)

Size & quantity	Title	Date	Handbook reference	Price per card	Complete set
L15	Classic Monaco Posters (Grand Prix)	2007	—		£6.50
EL8	Classic Teams Arsenal F.C.	2006	—		£4.00
EL8	Classic Teams Chelsea F.C.	2006	—		£4.00
EL8	Classic Teams Liverpool F.C.	2006	—		£4.00
EL8	Classic Teams Manchester United F.C.	2006	—		£4.00
EL8	Classic Teams Tottenham Hotspur F.C.	2006	—		£4.00
EL8	Classic Teams West Ham United F.C.	2006	—		£4.00
L15	The Cliff Richard Collection	2004	—		£7.50
L10	Dads Army	2006	—		£5.00
L15	David Bowie Concert Posters	2010	—		£6.50
L12	Depeche Mode (Concert Posters etc.)...............	2015	—		£6.00
L12	Elvis Concert Posters Volume 1	2016	—		£6.00
L12	England Players World Cup 1966	2007	—		£6.00
L6	England World Cup 1966 (Programme Covers, Posters & Ticket)...............	2006	—		£4.50
L9	Everton F.C. F.A. Cup Winners 1966 Programme Covers	2007	—		£5.00
L17	F.A. Cup Final Programme Covers 1923-1939	2001	—		£8.00
L20	F.A. Cup Final Programme Covers 1946-1965	2003	—		£8.00
L20	F.A. Cup Final Programme Covers 1966-1982	2004	—		£8.00
L21	F.A. Cup Final Programme Covers 1983-2000	2006	—		£8.00
L12	Fawlty Towers	2005	—		£6.50
L20	Frank Bruno Programme Covers	2005	—		£7.50
L9	The Golden Age of Middleweights 1980-1989	2006	—		£5.00
L15	Great British Cars of the 1950s	2004	—		£7.50
L12	The Greatest Cassius Clay Bonus Card Set Programme Covers 1958-1962	2010	—		£6.00
L50	The Greatest Muhammad Ali (Boxer)	1993	—		£12.00
L1	The Greatest Muhammad Ali Wild Card Ali v Marciano Computer Bout	1997	—		£1.00
L1	The Greatest Muhammad Ali Wild Card Clay v Lavorante	1997	—		£1.00
L4	Heavyweight Champions of the Naughty 1890s (Boxing)	2000	—		£2.50
L40	Henry Cooper (Boxer)	1997	—		£10.50
L20	Heroes of the Prize Ring	1994	—		£6.00
L14	Houdini Show Posters	2007	—		£6.50
L8	Ipswich Town F.C. F.A. Cup Winners 1978 Programme Covers	2007	—		£5.00
L15	Iron Maiden Concert Posters	2010	—		£6.50
L30	'Iron' Mike Tyson (Boxer)	2004	—		£10.00
L5	'Iron' Mike Tyson (Boxer) Bonus Series	2004	—		£2.50
L1	Iron Mike Tyson Additional Card Tyson v McBride ...	2005	—		£1.00
L20	Jack Nicklaus — Sports Illustrated	2005	—		£7.50
L25	Joe Louis A Career History (Boxer)	2000	—		£12.50
L1	Joe Louis A Career History Wild Card (Joe Louis v Billy Conn 1941)	2000	—		£1.00
L20	Johnny Cash Concert Posters	2009	—		£7.50
L20	The Krays	2009	—		£7.50
L36	Larry Holmes (Boxer) Programme Covers	2006	—		£10.00
L10	Led Zeppelin Album Covers	2006	—		£5.00
L8	Leeds United F.C. F.A. Cup Winners 1972 Programme Covers	2007	—		£5.00
L30	Lennox Lewis Programme Covers	2006	—		£10.00
L15	Liverpool F.C. Champions League Winners 2005 Programme Covers	2005	—		£6.50
L6	Liverpool F.C. European Cup Finals 1977-2005 Programme Covers	2006	—		£4.00

Size & quantity	TRADE CARD ISSUES	Date	Handbook reference	Price per card	Complete set

SPORTING PROFILES (continued)

Size & quantity	Title	Date	Handbook reference	Price per card	Complete set
L9	Liverpool F.C. F.A. Cup Winners 1974 Programme Covers	2008	—		£5.00
L10	Madonna (Concert Posters)	2015	—		£6.00
L7	Manchester City F.C. F.A. Cup Winners 1969 Programme Covers	2007	—		£5.00
L10	Manchester United 1968 European Cup Winners	2004	—		£6.50
L15	Marilyn Monroe	2006	—		£6.50
L20	Marvin Hagler (Boxer) Programme Covers	2006	—		£8.00
L30	Movie Idols — Alfred Hitchcock	2005	—		£10.00
L12	Movie Idols — Audrey Hepburn	2015	—		£6.00
L15	Movie Idols — Basil Rathbone is Sherlock Holmes	2004	—		£7.50
L30	Movie Idols — Errol Flynn	2004	—		£10.00
L10	Movie Idols — Fred Astaire & Ginger Rogers	2005	—		£5.50
L10	Movie Idols — Greta Garbo	2007	—		£5.00
L30	Movie Idols — Humphrey Bogart Film Posters	2003	—		£10.00
L15	Movie Idols — James Cagney	2008	—		£6.50
L20	Movie Idols — John Wayne Series 1 (Cowboy Films)	2007	—		£7.50
L30	Movie Idols — John Wayne Series 2 (Cowboy Films)	2006	—		£10.00
L15	Movie Idols — John Wayne Series 3 (War Films)	2010	—		£6.50
L30	Movie Idols — Marlon Brando	2004	—		£10.00
L12	Movie Idols — The Marx Brothers	2006	—		£6.00
L15	Movie Idols — Modern Gangster Classics	2008	—		£6.50
L15	Movie Idols — Paul Newman Classics	2010	—		£6.50
L15	Movie Idols — Steve McQueen Film Posters	2006	—		£6.50
L30	Muhammad Ali — Sports Illustrated	2002	—		£12.00
L10	The Muhammad Ali Story	2010	—		£6.00
L12	Newcastle United 1968/69 Fairs Cup Winners Programme Covers	2005	—		£7.00
L12	Nirvana Concert Posters	2016	—		£6.00
L10	Nottingham Forest European Cup Winners 1980 Programme Covers	2006	—		£6.00
L25	Olympic Posters — Summer Games	2003	—		£8.50
L1	Olympic Posters – Summer Games Bonus Card, Beijing 2008	2008	—		£1.00
L20	Olympic Posters — Winter Games	2003	—		£8.00
L15	Only Fools & Horses (Caricatures):				
	A Back white text on black background	2002	—		£12.00
	B Back black text on white background	2020	—		£9.00
L15	Only Fools & Horses Volume 1 (Scenes)	2003	—		£9.00
L20	Only Fools & Horses Volume II (Scenes)	2005	—		£7.50
L4	Only Fools & Horses Bonus Set A	2003	—		£2.50
L15	Pele (Footballer)	2005	—		£6.50
L12	Pink Floyd — Album Covers and Concert Posters	2008	—		£6.00
L20	Princess Diana Magazine Covers	2006	—		£7.50
L15	Queen Concert Posters	2010	—		£6.50
L12	Red Hot Chilli Peppers Concert Posters	2016	—		£6.00
L8	Rocky Marciano (Boxer)	2001	—		£5.00
L20	Rod Stewart Concert Posters	2013	—		£7.50
L13	The Rolling Stones Concert Posters	2006	—		£6.00
L20	Smokin' Joe Frazier — A Career History	2005	—		£9.00
L20	Steptoe & Son	2003	—		£9.00
L12	Stoke City F.C. 1972 League Cup Winners Programme Covers	2005	—		£6.00
L40	Sugar Ray Robinson (Boxer) Programme Covers	2017	—		£10.00
LT11	John L. Sullivan (Boxer) Cradle to Grave	1997	—		£6.00
L9	Sunderland F.C. F.A. Cup Winners 1973 Programme Covers	2007	—		£5.00

Size & quantity	TRADE CARD ISSUES	Date	Handbook reference	Price per card	Complete set
	SPORTING PROFILES (continued)				
L20	Team GB 19 Golds Beijing 2008 Olympics	2008	—		£7.50
L9	Tony Hancock	2002	—		£6.50
L8	Tottenham Hotspur F.A. Cup Winners 1961 Programme Covers	2008	—		£5.00
L9	Tottenham Hotspur F.A. Cup Winners 1967 Programme Covers	2008	—		£5.00
L9	Tottenham Hotspur F.A. Cup Winners 1981 Programme Covers	2008	—		£5.00
L6	Tottenham Hotspur League Cup Winners 2008 Programme Covers	2008	—		£4.50
L10	West Bromwich Albion F.A. Cup Winners 1968 Programme Covers	2007	—		£6.00
L7	West Ham United F.A. Cup Winners 1964 Programme Covers	2005	—		£5.00
L8	West Ham United F.A. Cup Winners 1975 Programme Covers	2007	—		£5.00
L8	West Ham United F.A. Cup Winners 1980 Programme Covers	2005	—		£5.00
L20	When Ali Met Pele	2007	—		£7.50
L20	The Who Concert Posters	2009	—		£7.50
L7	Wolverhampton Wanderers F.A. Cup Winners 1960 Programme Covers	2007	—		£5.00
L15	World Cup 1966 England	2002	—		£9.00
L17	World Cup Posters 1930-2002 (Football)	2002	—		£8.00
L4	The Young Ones (TV Comedy Show)	2006	—		£3.00
L20	Zulu The Movie	2014	—		£7.50
	SPORTS TIME (USA)				
LT100	The Beatles	1996	—		£16.00
LT100	Marilyn Monroe 1st Series	1993		20p	£16.00
LT10	Marilyn Monroe 1st Series Cover Girl Chromium Series	1993		£4.00	—
LT100	Marilyn Monroe 2nd Series	1995	—		£16.00
LT100	Miller Brewing Co. Adverts	1995	—		£9.50
LT100	Playboy Chromium Cover Cards Edition 1	1995	—		£20.00
	SPRATTS PATENT LTD				
K100	British Birds (numbered)	c1925	HS-77.1	£9.00	—
K50	British Birds (unnumbered)	c1925	HS-77.2	£6.00	—
42	British Birds	c1925	HS-78	£9.00	—
25	Bonzo Series	1924	HS-76	£6.50	—
36	Champion Dogs	c1930	HS-79	£15.00	—
K20	Fish	c1925	HS-21	£15.00	—
K100	Poultry	c1925	HS-82	£18.00	—
12	Prize Dogs (multi-backed)	c1910	HS-83	£50.00	—
12	Prize Poultry (multi-backed)	c1910	HS-84	£50.00	—
	THE STAMP CORNER				
25	American Indian Tribes	1962	HX-28	£3.00	—
	STAMP KING				
L7	Robin Hood	2002	—		£3.50
	STAMP PUBLICITY				
M40	1990 Cricket Tours	1990	—		£12.00
	Album		—		£10.00
	STAR CARDS				
LT99	Riders of the World (Equestrian)	1995		20p	£9.50

Size & quantity	TRADE CARD ISSUES	Date	Handbook reference	Price per card	Complete set
	STAR DISC ENTERPRISE (Canada)				
K58	Star Trek The Next Generation (circular)	1994		—	£9.50
	STAR INTERNATIONAL (USA)				
LT100	Venus Swimwear International Model Search	1994		20p	£9.50
	STAR JUNIOR CLUB				
10	Do You Know About Animals	1960		£1.50	—
10	Do You Know About Sports and Games	1960		£3.00	—
5	Do You Know About Sports and Games	1960		£3.00	—
	STAR PICS (USA)				
LT80	Alien 3 — The Movie	1992		—	£9.50
LT72	All My Children	1991		—	£9.50
LT6	All My Children Insert Set	1991		—	£3.50
LT80	Dinamation (Dinosaurs)	1992		—	£9.50
LT72	Playboy (Magazine)	1992		—	£12.00
LT150	Saturday Night Live	1992		—	£12.00
LT50	Troll Force (plus 6 stickers and advert card)	1992		—	£9.50
LT76	Twin Peaks (TV Series)	1991		—	£9.50
	STARLINE (USA)				
LT250	Americana (USA History)	1992		—	£18.00
LT125	Hollywood Walk of Fame Nos 1-125	1991		—	£9.50
LT125	Hollywood Walk of Fame Nos 126-250	1991		—	£9.50
	STATE OF THE ARTS				
L6	Sex, Drugs & Rock 'n Roll	1994		—	£7.50
	STAVELEY'S LUDGATE HILL				
24	World's Most Beautiful Birds	c1920	HX-22	£11.00	—
24	World's Most Beautiful Butterflies	c1920	HX-23	£11.00	—
	STERLING CARDS (USA)				
LT100	Country Gold (Country & Western Singers)	1992		—	£9.50
LT150	Country Gold (Country & Western Singers)	1993		—	£12.00
	STOKES & DALTON LTD				
M20	Dick Dalton in The Mystery of the Crimson Cobra	1950		£5.00	—
28	Dominoes (without the dot)	1939		20p	£5.00
	STOLL				
25	The Mystery of Dr. Fu-Manchu	c1930		£15.00	—
25	Stars of Today	c1930		£11.00	—
	STOLLWERCK				
L216	Animal World	c1910		£2.00	—
?93	Views of the World (multi-backed)	c1910	HS-93	£6.50	—
	STRICTLY INK				
LT100	The Avengers Series 1	2003		20p	£10.00
LT100	The Avengers Series 2 Season 4 and 5 1965-1967	2005		—	£15.00
LT54	The Avengers 3rd Series Additions The Archive Collection	2010		—	£9.50
LT100	CSI — Crime Scene Investigation Series 1	2003		—	£9.50
LT100	CSI — Crime Scene Investigation Series 2	2004		—	£9.50
LT72	CSI — Crime Scene Investigation Series 3	2006		—	£9.50
LT100	CSI Miami Series 1	2004		—	£9.50
LT72	CSI Miami Series 2	2007		—	£9.50

Size & quantity	TRADE CARD ISSUES	Date	Handbook reference	Price per card	Complete set
	STRICTLY INK (continued)				
LT72	CSI NY Series 1	2008		—	£9.50
LT10	Doctor Who Promotional Series	2000		—	£10.00
LT120	Doctor Who 1st Series	2000		20p	£12.00
LT120	Doctor Who 2nd Series	2001		20p	£15.00
LT120	Doctor Who 3rd Series	2002		20p	£12.00
LT200	Doctor Who	2006		—	£20.00
LT100	Doctor Who Big Screen	2003		20p	£12.00
	Doctor Who Big Screen Additions Collection:				
LT72	A Coloured	2008		—	£9.50
LT72	B Black and white	2008		20p	£9.50
LT100	Doctor Who 40th Anniversary	2003		20p	£12.00
LT54	Hammer Horror Series 2	2010		—	£9.50
LT72	The New Avengers Season 1	2006		—	£15.00
	SUGOSA				
12	Famous Footballers	1966		£10.00	—
	SUMMER COUNTY SOFT MARGARINE				
	Countryside Cards:		HB-95		
5	Birds	c1975		£2.00	—
5	Birds of Prey	c1975		£2.00	—
5	Butterflies	c1975		£2.00	—
5	Corn Crops	c1975		£2.00	—
5	Herbs & Berries	c1975		£2.00	—
5	The Hedgerow	c1975		£2.00	—
5	Horses & Ponies	c1975		£2.00	—
5	Mills	c1975		£2.00	—
5	Nocturnal Animals	c1975		£2.00	—
5	Trees	c1975		£2.00	—
5	Water Fowl	c1975		£2.00	—
5	Water Life	c1975		£2.00	—
5	Wild Animals	c1975		£2.00	—
5	Wild Flowers	c1975		£2.00	—
	SUMMER'S PRODUCTIONS				
EL3	War Effort Cartoons	1943		£10.00	—
	THE SUN				
M134	Football	1970		75p	£100.00
M52	Gallery of Football Action	1972	HS-106.2	£4.00	—
	6 different numbers			—	£6.00
M6	How To Play Football	1972	HS-106.3	£6.00	—
M54	Page 3 Playing Cards (Pin-Up Girls)	1979		—	£9.00
50	Soccercards — Nos 1 to 50	1979		25p	£12.50
50	Soccercards — Nos 51 to 100	1979		25p	£12.50
50	Soccercards — Nos 101 to 150	1979		25p	£12.50
50	Soccercards — Nos 151 to 200	1979		25p	£12.50
50	Soccercards — Nos 201 to 250	1979		25p	£12.50
50	Soccercards — Nos 251 to 300	1979		25p	£12.50
50	Soccercards — Nos 301 to 350	1979		25p	£12.50
50	Soccercards — Nos 351 to 400	1979		25p	£12.50
50	Soccercards — Nos 401 to 450	1979		25p	£12.50
50	Soccercards — Nos 451 to 500	1979		25p	£12.50
50	Soccercards — Nos 501 to 550	1979		25p	£12.50
50	Soccercards — Nos 551 to 600	1979		25p	£12.50
50	Soccercards — Nos 601 to 650	1979		25p	£12.50

Size & quantity	TRADE CARD ISSUES	Date	Handbook reference	Price per card	Complete set
	THE SUN (continued)				
50	Soccercards — Nos 651 to 700	1979		25p	£12.50
50	Soccercards — Nos 701 to 750	1979		25p	£12.50
50	Soccercards — Nos 751 to 800	1979		25p	£12.50
50	Soccercards — Nos 801 to 850	1979		25p	£12.50
50	Soccercards — Nos 851 to 900	1979		25p	£12.50
50	Soccercards — Nos 901 to 950	1979		25p	£12.50
50	Soccercards — Nos 951 to 1000	1979		25p	£12.50
EL50	3-D Gallery of Football Stars	1972	HS-106.1	£6.00	—
	SUNBLEST TEA				
25	Inventions and Discoveries 1st Series	1962	HX-131	70p	£17.50
25	Inventions and Discoveries 2nd Series:		HX-131		
	A Inscribed First Series (Nd 26 to 50)	1962		£2.00	—
	B Inscribed Second Series	1962		70p	£17.50
	Album for 1st and 2nd Series combined			—	£25.00
25	Prehistoric Animals 1st Series	1966	HX-151	36p	£9.00
25	Prehistoric Animals 2nd Series	1966	HX-151	36p	£9.00
	Album for 1st and 2nd Series combined			—	£25.00
	SUNBLEST (Australia)				
M25	Great Explorers	c1975		60p	£12.50
M24	Sports Action Card Series	c1975		—	£12.00
	SUNDAY STORIES				
M6	Flags (silk)	1915	HS-113	£16.00	—
M6	The King and His Soldiers (silk)	1916	HS-114	£16.00	—
	SUNNY BOY				
50	British Naval Series	c1960	HX-76	£3.00	—
	SUPER SOCCER STARS				
10	Super Soccer Stars (From the 1960s & 70s)	2019		—	£5.00
	SWEETACRES (Australia)				
48	Aircraft of the World	c1930		£5.00	—
36	Cricketers (back in red & green)	1926		£20.00	—
32	Cricketers – Test Match Record Nos. 1 to 32	1932		£6.00	—
32	Cricketers – Prominent Cricketers 2nd Series Nos. 33 to 64	1932		£6.00	—
24	Cricketers (Caricatures)	1938		£32.00	—
36	Footballers	c1930		£8.00	—
48	My Favourite Dogs	c1930		£6.00	—
48	Sports Champions	c1930		£7.00	—
48	Steamships of the World	c1930		£5.00	—
48	This World is Ours	c1930		£6.00	—
	SWEETULE PRODUCTS LTD				
25	Animals of the Countryside:		HX-9		
	A Short Design back 54mm long	1959		20p	£4.00
	B Long Design back 60mm long	1959		£1.50	—
25	Archie Andrews' Illustrated Jokes	1957		£11.00	—
25	Birds and Their Eggs ('Junior Service')	1955		20p	£4.00

Size & quantity	TRADE CARD ISSUES	Date	Handbook reference	Price per card	Complete set
	SWEETULE PRODUCTS LTD (continued)				
25	Birds and Their Eggs:		HX-102		
	A Black back	1959		20p	£5.00
	B Blue back	1959		20p	£5.00
25	Birds and Their Haunts	1958		£9.00	—
25	Birds of the British Commonwealth (Canada):				
	A Black back	1958		24p	£6.00
	B Blue back	1958		30p	£7.50
25	Do You Know?	1963	HX-166.2	20p	£5.00
25	Family Crests	1961		20p	£4.50
25	Famous Sports Records:				
	A Blue back	1956		90p	£22.50
	B Black back	1956		£1.60	—
25	Football Club Nicknames	1959		70p	£17.50
K18	Historical Cars and Cycles	1957		50p	£9.00
25	Junior Service Quiz	1958		20p	£4.00
50	Modern Aircraft	1954	HX-35	20p	£8.00
25	Modern Transport	1955	HX-125.2	30p	£7.50
50	Motor Cycles Old and New	1963		£2.00	—
30	National Flags and Costumes	1957		80p	£24.00
52	Natural History Playing Card inset	1961		50p	£25.00
25	Nature Series	1959	HX-148	20p	£3.50
25	Naval Battles	1959	HX-21	20p	£4.50
25	Products of the World	1960	HX-152	20p	£3.50
25	Sports Quiz	1958		24p	£6.00
25	Stamp Cards	1960		24p	£6.00
EL30	Trains of the World	1960	HX-121.1	£2.00	—
25	Treasure Island	1958		36p	£9.00
25	Tropical Birds:		HX-13.1		
	A Back with Series of 25	1954		£2.00	—
	B Back without Series of 25	1954		20p	£4.00
25	Vintage Cars	1964	HX-33	50p	£12.50
25	Weapons of Defence	1959		20p	£3.50
25	Wild Animals	1958	HX-160	20p	£3.50
25	Wild Flowers	1960	HX-124	20p	£3.50
25	The Wild West:		HX-55		
	A Black back	1960		80p	—
	B Blue back	1960		24p	£6.00
25	Wonders of the World	1956	HX-142	20p	£4.00
	Package Issues:				
18	Aircraft	1954		£7.00	—
M12	Coronation Series	1953		£8.00	—
M18	Home Pets	1955		£8.00	—
25	International Footballers	1959		£12.00	—
18	Landmarks of Flying	1958		£8.00	—
25	Racing Cars of the World	1960		£11.00	—
M18	Railway Engines	1956		£10.00	—
M18	Railway Engines Past & Present	1957		£10.00	—
24	The World of Ships	c1960		£10.00	—
	SWETTENHAM TEA				
25	Aircraft of the World	1959	HX-180	£1.00	—
25	Animals of the Countryside	1958	HX-9	20p	£3.50
25	Birds and Their Eggs	1958	HX-1.2	20p	£4.00
25	Butterflies and Moths	1960	HX-2	20p	£3.50
25	Evolution of the Royal Navy	1957	HX-90	20p	£4.50
25	Into Space	1959	HX-147	50p	£12.50
25	Wild Animals	1958	HX-160	30p	£7.50

Size & quantity	TRADE CARD ISSUES	Date	Handbook reference	Price per card	Complete set
	W. SWORD & CO.				
25	British Empire at Work	c1930	HX-113	£17.00	—
20	Dogs	c1930	HX-211	£20.00	—
20	Inventors and Their Inventions	c1930	HX-213	£20.00	—
25	Safety First	c1930	HX-199	£15.00	—
25	Sports and Pastimes Series	c1930	HX-225	£22.00	—
25	Vehicles of All Ages	c1930	HX-111	£16.00	—
25	Zoo Series (brown gravures)	c1930		£12.00	—
25	Zoo Series (coloured)	c1930	HX-186	£14.00	—
	SYMONDS CIDER (Scrumpy Jacks)				
M100	Sporting Greats (early 1900s) 10 pictures with 10 varieties on each	1994		75p	—
	76 Different including varieties			—	£57.00
	10 Pictures only without varieties			—	£7.50
	T C M ASSOCIATES (USA)				
LT100	Earthmovers 2nd Series (Tractors etc)	1994		—	£12.00
LT72	Santa Around the World (Premier Edition)	1994		—	£9.50
LT72	Santa Around The World 2nd Series (with snowflake border)	1994		—	£9.50
LT100	Winnebago (Mobile Homes etc.)	1994		—	£12.00
	T & M ENTERPRISES (USA)				
LT45	The Bikini Open	1992		—	£8.00
	TAMWORTH POLICE				
L18	Keepers of the Peace	1990		33p	£6.00
	Album			—	£5.00
	DES TAYLOR				
L20	My Favourite Fish	2000		—	£7.50
	TEA TIME ASSORTED BISCUITS (NABISCO)				
12	British Soldiers Through the Ages	1974		30p	£3.50
	Album			—	£5.00
	TEACARDS				
10	British Garden Birds	2020		—	£5.00
10	The Solar System	2021		—	£5.00
	TEACHERS WHISKY				
L12	Scottish Clans:		HT-2		
	A Back circular advert Teacher's Highland Cream:				
	i Thick card	1955		£6.00	
	ii Thin card	1955		£6.00	—
	B Back circular advert Teacher's Highland Cream Scotch Whisky	1955		£7.00	—
	C Back rectangular advert	1971		£3.50	£42.00
	TEASDALE & CO.				
25	Great War Series	1915		£30.00	—
	TELLY CLASSICS				
10	Telly Classics Nearest & Dearest 1960/70s Comedy with Jimmy Jewell & Hilda Baker	2009		—	£5.00

Size & quantity	TRADE CARD ISSUES	Date	Handbook reference	Price per card	Complete set
	TENNYSON ENTERPRISES (USA)				
LT100	Super Country Music	1992		—	£12.00
	TESCO				
EL6	Nature Trail	1988		—	£3.50
	TETLEY TEA				
48	British Birds...	c1975		£5.00	—
	TEXACO (Petrol)				
	Advertisement Cards issued with Cricket Series:				
1	A Free from Texaco Britannic Assurance Championship Voucher...	1984		—	25p
1	B Texaco Lucky Stars Win Line Try Again	1984		—	25p
12	Cricket	1984		40p	£5.00
	Folder/Album			—	£12.00
K24	England Squad 2006 (Football)	2006		—	£8.00
K5	England Squad 2006 Additions (Carson, Downing, Hargreaves, Lennon, Walcott) (Football)	2006		—	£5.00
K24	F.A. Cup Winners Hall of Fame	2007		—	£12.00
	Album and DVD	2007		—	£10.00
	D.C. THOMSON				
	Adventure Pictures:				
L10	Set 1 White borders, glazed	1922	HT-12.1	£4.00	—
L10	Set 2 White borders, matt	1922	HT-12.2	£4.00	—
L10	Set 3 Brown borders, glazed	1922	HT-12.3	£4.00	—
M16	Badges of the Fighting Fliers	1937	HT-14	£5.00	—
	Battles for the Flag:				
EL13	Inscribed 'Rover'	c1935	HT-15.1	£8.00	—
EL13	Inscribed 'Wizard' (different)	c1935	HT-15.2	£8.00	—
K80	Boys of All Nations	1936	HT-17	£1.75	—
LP11	British Team of Footballers	1922	HT-19	£3.50	—
L20	Canvas Masterpieces (silk)	1925		£10.00	—
16	Catch-My-Pal Cards	1938	HT-20	£3.00	—
M12	Coloured Photos of Star Footballers	c1930	HT-21	£9.00	—
16	County Cricketers (Adventure)	1957		£2.50	—
16	County Cricketers (Hotspur)	1957		£2.50	—
16	County Cricketers (Rover)	1957		£2.50	—
16	County Cricketers (Wizard)	1957		£2.50	—
	Cricketers:				
EL12	Inscribed 'Rover'	1924		£10.00	—
EL12	Inscribed 'Vanguard'	1924		£10.00	—
KP8	Cricketers	1923	HT-22	£4.50	—
EL16	Cup Tie Stars of All Nations (Victor)	1962	HT-24	£4.50	—
K28	Dominoes — School Caricatures	c1935		£2.50	—
MP35	Famous British Footballers:		HT-26		
	A 18 Different English Players	1921		£4.00	—
	B 17 Different Scottish Players...	1921		£12.00	—
K80	Famous Feats	1937	HT-27	£2.00	—
24	Famous Fights...	c1935		£3.00	—
24	Famous Footballers (Wizard)	1955		£2.40	—
25	Famous Footballers (Wizard)	c1955		£2.40	—
L32	Famous Ships	1931	HT-29	£5.00	—
EL12	Famous Teams in Football History	1961	HT-30	£5.00	—
EL16	Famous Teams in Football History 2nd Series (New Hotspur)	1962	HT-31	£5.00	—
K80	Flags of the Sea	1937	HT-33	£2.00	—

Size & quantity	TRADE CARD ISSUES	Date	Handbook reference	Price per card	Complete set
	D.C. THOMSON (continued)				
P40	Football Photos	c1925		£7.00	—
48	Football Stars (Adventure and Hotspur)	1957		£2.50	—
44	Football Stars of 1959 (Wizard)	1959		£3.00	—
K64	Football Team Cards:				
	A 63 Different (Minus No. 43)	1933		£1.75	—
	B Number 43	1933		£16.00	—
64	Football Tips and Tricks	1959		£1.10	—
L32	Football Towns and Their Crests	1931	HT-35	£8.00	—
KP137	Footballers:		HT-37		
	A 90 Different English Players	c1930		£1.75	—
	B 47 Different Scottish Players	c1930		£7.00	—
L8	Footballers	c1930	HT-38	£8.00	—
MP18	Footballers	1922	HT-36	£3.50	—
M12	Footballers (printed on metal)	1931	HT-137	£17.00	—
K52	Footballers — Hunt the Cup Cards	c1935	HT-41	£3.50	—
24	Footballers — Motor Cars (Double Sided)	c1930		£10.00	—
MP35	Footballers — Signed Real Photos:		HT-43		
	A 22 Different English Players	c1930		£3.00	—
	B 13 Different Scottish Players	c1930		£11.00	—
L12	Great Captains (Wizard)	c1970		£6.00	—
EL16	The Great Stars of Football	1968		£6.00	—
12	Guns in Action	1940		£3.00	—
M8	Hidden Treasure Clue Cards	1926		£15.00	—
EL16	International Cup Teams (Hornet)	1963	HT-51	£5.00	—
6	Ju-Jitsu Cards	1929		£6.00	—
24	Motor Bike Cards	1929		£7.00	—
K100	Motor Cars	1934	HT-53	£1.75	—
11	Mystic Menagerie	c1930	HT-56	£7.00	—
36	1930 Speedway Stars	1930		£9.00	—
K80	Punishment Cards	1936	HT-59	£2.25	—
	Puzzle Prize Cards:				
12	Dandy Dogs	1928		£8.00	—
12	Queer Animals	1928		£4.50	—
12	Speedsters of the Wilds	1928		£5.00	—
	Q Prize Cards:				
16	Cricket Crests	1929		£12.00	—
16	Flags of All Nations	1929		£4.50	—
16	Queer Birds	1929		£5.00	—
K80	Secrets of Cricket	1936	HT-62	£3.25	—
36	Spadger's Monster Collection of Spoofs	c1935		£3.50	—
48	Speed	1932		£1.50	—
M14	Star Footballers (printed on metal)	1932	HT-67	£16.00	—
EL22	Star Teams of 1961	1961		£4.00	—
24	Stars of Sport and Entertainment (Hotspur)	1958		£2.50	—
24	Stars of Sport and Entertainment (Rover)	1958		£2.50	—
L24	Superstars of '72 (Footballers) (Victor) (16 size 65 x 47mm, 8 size 95 x 65mm)	1972		£3.00	—
30	This Season's Latest Motor Cars (metal)	1926		£25.00	—
K25	This Year's Motor Car Crests	1925		£25.00	—
24	This Year's Top Form Footballers	1924		£4.00	—
EL12	Top Cup Teams	1964	HT-71	£6.00	—
10	Vanguard Photo Gallery	1923		£15.00	—
32	V.P. Flips (Adventure)	1932		£2.00	—
32	V.P. Flips (Rover)	1932		£2.00	—
32	V.P. Flips (Skipper)	1932		£2.00	—
24	Warrior Cards	1929		£3.00	—
K28	Warrior Cards (back with Dominoes)	1935		£2.20	—
K80	Warrior Cards	1937	HT-74	£2.00	—

Size & quantity	TRADE CARD ISSUES	Date	Handbook reference	Price per card	Complete set
	D.C. THOMSON (continued)				
K28	Wild West Dominoes	c1935		£2.50	—
	Wizard Series:				
20	British Birds and Eggs	1923	HT-18	£4.00	—
20	Easy Scientific Experiments	1923	HT-25	£3.50	—
20	Famous Liners	1923	HT-28	£4.50	—
20	Motor Cycles	1923	HT-54	£7.50	—
20	Why?	1923	HT-75	£4.00	—
20	The Wireless Telephone	1923	HT-76	£3.50	—
20	Wonders of the Rail	1923	HT-77	£5.00	—
20	Wonders of the World	1923	HT-78	£3.50	—
16	World Cup Footballers (Adventure)	1958		£3.50	—
16	World Cup Footballers (Hotspur)	1958		£3.50	—
16	World Cup Footballers (Rover)	1958		£3.50	—
16	World Cup Footballers (Wizard)	1958		£3.50	—
M72	World Cup Stars (Hornet/Hotspur)	1970		£3.50	—
32	The World's Best Cricketers (back in very dark green)	1932		£3.00	—
	The World's Best Cricketers:				
12	Inscribed 'Adventure' (back in mauve)	1930		£6.00	—
12	Inscribed 'Rover' (back in mauve)	1930		£6.00	—
12	Inscribed 'Wizard' (back in mauve)	1930		£6.00	—
18	The World's Best Cricketers (Adventure)	1956		£3.25	—
18	The World's Best Cricketers (Hotspur)	1956		£3.25	—
18	The World's Best Cricketers (Rover)	1956		£3.25	—
18	The World's Best Cricketers (Wizard)	1956		£3.25	—
EL12	The World's Biggest	1936		£10.00	—
	HY. THORNE & CO.				
25	Royalty	c1905	HT-82	£40.00	—
	THUNDER PRODUCTIONS (USA)				
LT100	Custom Motorcycles	1993		—	£9.50
	TIMARU MILLING CO. (New Zealand)				
M36	Focus on Fame	1948		£1.25	—
M37	Peace and Progress	1947		£1.25	—
M36	Victory Album Cards	1946		£1.25	—
	TIMES CONFECTIONERY CO. LTD				
M24	Roy Rogers — In Old Amarillo	1955		50p	£12.00
M24	Roy Rogers — South of Caliente	1955		50p	£12.00
	TITBITS				
K54	Pin-Up Girls (playing cards)	1976		40p	£22.00
M20	Star Cover Girls	1953	HT-84	£7.50	—
	CHOCOLAT TOBLER LTD				
12	Famaza Pedagogi (Famous People) Series 17	c1960		—	£3.50
50	Famous Footballers with 'Tobler' on front	c1937		£15.00	—
50	Famous Footballers without 'Tobler' on front	c1939		£15.00	—
12	Infanto En Arto (Children in Art) Series 21	c1960		—	£3.50
12	Planets and Fixed Stars, Series 45	c1960		—	£7.50
12	Infanto — Ludi (Children's Games) Series 52	c1960		—	£4.00
12	Tobler Posters 2nd Series, Series 58	c1960		—	£3.50
12	Different Ways of Travelling, Series 62	c1960		—	£6.00
L192	General Interest Series (28 sets of 6, 2 sets of 12)	c1900		£2.50	—

Size & quantity	TRADE CARD ISSUES	Date	Handbook reference	Price per card	Complete set
	TOBY				
24	Dogs 1st Series	c1920		£4.50	—
24	Dogs 2nd Series	c1920		£4.50	—
24	Sights of London	c1920		£4.00	—
24	Toby's Bird Series	c1920		£4.00	—
24	Toby's Ship Series	c1920		£4.00	—
24	Toby's Travel Series	c1920		£4.00	—
	TODAY NEWSPAPER				
LT14	Around Britain	1991		—	£3.50
	TOM THUMB (New Zealand)				
M24	Supercars (issued in strips of 3)	1980		£1.90	£15.00
	TOMMY GUN (Ideal Toys Ltd)				
50	Medals	1971		20p	£4.50
	TONIBELL (Ice Cream)				
M20	Banknotes of the World	1974		30p	£6.00
M12	Beautiful Butterflies	1977		35p	£4.00
M20	County Badge Collection	1976		20p	£4.00
L12	Did You Know	1976		£1.50	—
25	Did You Know?	1963	HX-166.2	20p	£3.50
EL12	England's Soccer Stars	1970	HT-86	£4.00	£50.00
L19	Famous Sports Trophies	c1970	HT-87	50p	£10.00
M12	Farmyard Stencils	1977		50p	£6.00
M24	1st Division Football League Club Badges	1972		£3.00	—
EL12	Horses in the Service of Man	1977		£1.00	£12.00
25	Inventions that Changed the World	1963	HX-18	20p	£3.50
EL10	Junior Champs	1979		£1.00	—
M24	Kings of the Road (car radiator badges)	1977		£1.25	—
M24	Pop Star Cameos (circular cards)	c1970		60p	£15.00
M10	Pop Stars (Star Shaped)	c1975		—	£15.00
K36	Team of All Time (English footballers)	1971		£2.25	£80.00
25	This Changing World:				
	A Black line under Tonibell	1963		40p	£10.00
	B Without black line under Tonibell	1963		40p	£10.00
25	Wonders of the Heavens	1963	HX-48	80p	£20.00
25	World's Passenger Liners	1963	HX-82	20p	£3.50
	TONIBELL & CADBURY				
12	Action Soldiers	1976		40p	£5.00
	TOP DRAW				
LT30	Cricket World Cup	1999		70p	—
	TOP PILOT (USA)				
LT17	Mach 1 Edition (Aircraft)	1989		—	£10.00
	TOP SELLERS LTD				
M54	Crazy Stickers	1975		—	£8.00
	TOP TRUMPS				
L30	Football South Africa 2010 World Cup Goalscorers	2010		—	£4.00
L30	Football South Africa 2010 World Cup Keepers & Defenders	2010		—	£4.00
L30	Football South Africa 2010 World Cup Legends	2010		—	£4.00
L30	Football South Africa 2010 World Cup Managers	2010		—	£4.00

Size & quantity	TRADE CARD ISSUES	Date	Handbook reference	Price per card	Complete set
	TOP TRUMPS (continued)				
L30	Football South Africa 2010 World Cup Moments	2010		—	£4.00
L30	Football South Africa 2010 World Cup Stadiums	2010		—	£4.00
L35	Prehistoric Monsters...	1979		—	£4.00
L33	Rockets	1980		—	£4.00
	TOPICAL TIMES				
EL8	Cricketers in Action	1937	HT-89	£20.00	—
M24	Footballers — English (Head and Shoulders)	1939	HT-98.1	£3.50	£85.00
	Album titled Great Players			—	£25.00
M24	Footballers — Scottish (Head and Shoulders)	1939	HT-98.2	£12.00	—
	Album titled Great Players			—	£40.00
L48	Footballers — English (size 125 x 46mm):				
	A First 24 Subjects...	1937	HT-97.1	£3.50	£85.00
	Album titled Panel Portraits			—	£25.00
	B Second — 24 Subjects	1938	HT-97.3	£3.50	£85.00
	Album titled Panel Portraits			—	£25.00
L48	Footballers — Scottish (size 125 x 46mm):				
	A First 24 Subjects	1937	HT-97.2	£12.00	—
	Album titled Stars of To-Day			—	£40.00
	B Second 24 Subjects	1938	HT-97.4	£12.00	—
	Album titled Stars of To-Day			—	£40.00
MP10	Footballers (2 players per card)	c1930	HT-92	£6.00	—
EL8	Footballers (3 players per card)	1937	HT-96.1	£7.00	—
EL8	Footballers (size 253 x 190mm), coloured	1936	HT-94.1	£7.00	—
MP6	Football Teams (card)	c1930	HT-91	£6.00	—
M6	Football Teams (metal)...	c1925	HT-90	£20.00	—
	Star Footballers Black and White:				
	English:				
EL12	1932 Issue size 245 x 89mm	1932	HT-99.1	£5.00	—
EL24	1932-33 Issue size 248 x 89mm 1932/33		HT-99.2	£5.00	—
EL28	1935 Issue size 250 x 95mm	1935	HT-99.3	£5.00	—
EL14	1938-39 Issue size 248 x 93mm 1938/39		HT-99.4	£5.00	—
EL16	1939-40 Issue size 249 x 92mm 1939/40		HT-99.5	£5.00	—
	Scottish:				
EL6	1932 Issue size 245 x 89mm	1932	HT-99.1	£15.00	—
EL12	1932-33 Issue size 248 x 89mm 1932/33		HT-99.2	£15.00	—
EL14	1935 Issue size 250 x 95mm	1935	HT-99.3	£15.00	—
EL14	1938-39 Issue size 248 x 93mm 1938/39		HT-99.4	£15.00	—
EL16	1939-40 Issue size 249 x 92mm 1939/40		HT-99.5	£15.00	—
	Irish:				
EL4	1932 Issue size 245 x 89mm	1932	HT-99.1	£35.00	—
EL20	1930s Issue size 248 x 89mm	1930s	HT-99.6	£35.00	—
EL16	Star Footballers – English Coloured size 250 x 94mm	1936	HT-95.1	£7.00	—
EL16	Star Footballers – Scottish Coloured size 250 x 94mm	1936	HT-99.2	£15.00	—
	TOPPS (Australia)				
LT63	Australian Cricket..	2000		—	£25.00
	TOPPS (Germany)				
LT99	Jurassic Park (including Sticker Set)	1993		—	£10.00
	TOPPS (UK)				
M80	Alf His Life and Times	1988		20p	£12.00
M88	American Baseball	1988		20p	£18.00
M88	American Baseball	1989		20p	£18.00
M88	American NFL Football..	1987		25p	£22.00
LT99	Autos of 1977	1977		£2.25	—

Size & quantity	TRADE CARD ISSUES	Date	Handbook reference	Price per card	Complete set
	TOPPS (UK) (continued)				
M132	Batman (size 77 x 55mm)	1989		20p	£9.50
M22	Batman stickers	1989		20p	£4.00
LT88	Batman Returns	1992		20p	£9.50
M10	Batman Returns stickers	1992		35p	£3.50
LT66	Battlestar Galactica (Nos 1-66) (white card)	1979		23p	£15.00
LT66	Battlestar Galactica (Nos 67-132) (white card)	1979		23p	£15.00
LT66	Bay City Rollers	1976		40p	—
LT132	Beavis and Butt-Head (No 6934 unissued, 7769 not on check list)	1994		20p	£12.00
LT88	Beverly Hills 90210	1991		20p	£9.50
M11	Beverly Hills 90210 stickers	1991		33p	£3.50
LT88	The Black Hole	1980		25p	£22.00
LT49	Comic Book Heroes (with copyright 1975)	1977		£2.50	
LT88	Desert Storm (white card)	1991		20p	£16.00
M22	Desert Storm Stickers	1991		20p	£3.50
LT60	England 2002 (Football)	2002		—	£18.00
LT10	England 2002 (Football) Electric Foil Series Nd. E1 to E10	2002		£1.00	—
EL30	English League Football Internationals	1980		£1.00	—
LT88	The Flintstones (The Movie)	1994		20p	£9.50
M11	The Flintstones (The Movie) stickers	1994		33p	£3.50
LT124	Football Premier Gold	2001		—	£25.00
LT125	Football Premier Gold	2002		—	£25.00
LT125	Football Premier Gold	2003		—	£25.00
LT125	Football Premier Gold	2004		—	£25.00
	Football Saint and Greavsie:				
M175	A Complete set	1988		20p	£25.00
M264	B Complete set plus varieties	1988		—	£30.00
LT132	Footballers, Nd 1-132 (red back)	1975		£2.00	—
LT88	Footballers, Nd 133-220 (red back)	1975		£2.00	—
LT88	Footballers, Scottish (blue back)	1975		£3.50	—
LT110	Footballers, Nd 1-110 (blue back)	1976		£1.50	—
LT110	Footballers, Nd 111-220 (blue back)	1976		£1.50	—
LT110	Footballers, Nd 221-330 (blue back)	1976		£1.50	—
LT132	Footballers, Scottish (red back)	1976		£3.50	—
LT110	Footballers, Nd 1-110 (red back)	1977		£1.50	—
LT110	Footballers, Nd 111-220 (red back)	1977		£1.50	—
LT110	Footballers, Nd 221-330 (red back)	1977		£1.50	—
LT132	Footballers, Scottish (yellow back)	1977		£2.50	—
LT132	Footballers, Nd 1-132 (orange back)	1978		60p	—
LT132	Footballers, Nd 133-264 (orange back)	1978		60p	—
LT132	Footballers, Nd 265-396 (orange back)	1978		60p	—
LT132	Footballers, Scottish (green back)	1978		£2.50	—
LT132	Footballers, Nos 1-132 (light blue back)	1979		£1.50	—
LT132	Footballers, Nos 133-264 (light blue back)	1979		£1.50	—
LT132	Footballers, Nos 265-396 (light blue back)	1979		£1.50	—
LT132	Footballers, Scottish (red back)	1979		£2.50	—
LT66	Footballers (pink back) (3 numbers per card)	1980		£1.25	£90.00
EL18	Footballers Posters	1980		£1.00	£18.00
LT65	Footballers (blue back) (3 numbers per card)	1981		£1.25	£80.00
	Album			—	£12.00
LT100	Footballers Stadium Club nos 1-100	1992		20p	£16.00
LT100	Footballers Stadium Club nos 101-200	1992		20p	£16.00
LT10/14	Footballers Stadium Club Promotional Series	1992		35p	£3.50
LT21	Funny Puzzles	1978		£2.00	—
M39	The Garbage Gang nd 1a-39a	1990		50p	—

Size & quantity	TRADE CARD ISSUES	Date	Handbook reference	Price per card	Complete set
	TOPPS (UK) (continued)				
M39	The Garbage Gang nd 1b-39b (except for subjects 15b & 39b, incorrectly numbered 15a & 39a)	1990		50p	—
M42	The Garbage Gang Nos 418A-459A	1991		50p	—
M41	The Garbage Gang Nos 460A-500A	1991		50p	—
M41	Garbage Pail Kids 1st Series A	1986		50p	—
M41	Garbage Pail Kids 1st Series B	1986		50p	—
M42	Garbage Pail Kids 2nd Series A	1986		50p	—
M42	Garbage Pail Kids 2nd Series B	1986		50p	—
M44	Garbage Pail Kids 3rd Series A	1987		50p	—
M37	Garbage Pail Kids 3rd Series B	1987		50p	—
M42	Garbage Pail Kids 4th Series A	1987		50p	—
M42	Garbage Pail Kids 4th Series B	1987		50p	—
M39	Garbage Pail Kids 5th Series A	1987		50p	—
M39	Garbage Pail Kids 5th Series B	1987		50p	—
M44	Garbage Pail Kids 6th Series A	1988		50p	—
M44	Garbage Pail Kids 6th Series B	1988		50p	—
M86	The Goonies	1986		30p	—
M15	The Goonies stickers	1986		30p	—
LT88	Gremlins 2 The Movie (white card)	1990		20p	£9.50
LT66	Home Alone 2 The Movie	1993		20p	£8.00
M11	Home Alone 2 The Movie stickers	1993		33p	£3.50
LT44	Home & Away	1990		20p	£6.00
LT99	Hook — The Film	1992		20p	£9.50
M11	Hook — The Film stickers	1992		33p	£3.50
LT88	Jurassic Park (without Topps on back)	1993		20p	£9.50
M11	Jurassic Park stickers	1993		33p	£3.50
LT66	Kings of Rap (including stickers)	1991		20p	£12.00
M111	Mad Cap Alphabet (including All Varieties)	1994		25p	—
LT49	Marvel Super Heroes (with copyright 1976)	1980		£1.70	£85.00
LT83	Match Attax Extra 2007/08 (red backs)	2008		20p	£9.50
LT20	Match Attax Extra 2007/08 Club Captains (foil fronts)	2008		—	£6.00
LT7	Match Attax Extra 2007/08 Hat-Trick Hero	2008		£2.00	—
LT10	Match Attax Extra 2007/08 Man of the Match	2008		£1.00	—
LT5	Match Attax Extra 2007/08 Player of the Month	2008		£1.00	—
LT92	Match Attax Extra 2008/09 (blue backs)	2009		20p	£12.00
LT20	Match Attax Extra 2008/09 Club Captains	2009		25p	£5.00
LT20	Match Attax Extra 2008/09 Fans Favourite (foil fronts)	2009		50p	£10.00
LT20	Match Attax Extra 2008/09 Man of the Match	2009		£1.00	—
LT1	Match Attax Extra 2008/09 100 Club Edwin Van Der Sar	2009		—	£6.00
LT112	Match Attax Extra 2009/10 (orange backs)	2010		20p	£9.50
LT20	Match Attax Extra 2009/10 Club Captains	2010		£1.00	—
LT6	Match Attax Extra 2009/10 Hat-Trick Hero	2010		£1.00	—
LT20	Match Attax Extra 2009/10 I-Card Chromium	2010		75p	—
LT20	Match Attax Extra 2009/10 Man of The Match	2010		£1.00	—
LT4	Match Attax Extra 2009/10 Managers	2010		—	£2.00
LT1	Match Attax Extra 2009/10 100 Club Wayne Rooney	2010		—	£6.00
LT76	Match Attax Extra 2014/15 (black border, red & blue backs)	2015		20p	£9.50
LT20	Match Attax Extra 2014/15 Captains	2015		25p	£5.00
LT20	Match Attax Extra 2014/15 Duo (foil fronts)	2015		50p	£10.00
LT3	Match Attax Extra 2014/15 Hat-Trick Hero (foil fronts)	2015		£1.00	£3.00
LT1	Match Attax Extra 2014/15 Hundred Club Diego Costa	2015		—	£6.00
LT20	Match Attax Extra 2014/15 Managers	2015		25p	£5.00
LT21	Match Attax Extra 2014/15 New Signings:				
	A 9 Different foil fronts	2015		24p	£4.50
	B 12 Different white fronts	2015		—	£3.00

Size & quantity	TRADE CARD ISSUES	Date	Handbook reference	Price per card	Complete set
	TOPPS (UK) (continued)				
LT68	Match Attax Extra 2015/16 Squad Updates (black back, blue & green border)	2016		20p	£12.00
LT20	Match Attax Extra 2015/16 Extra Boost	2016		30p	£6.00
LT9	Match Attax Extra 2015/16 Hat-Trick Hero	2016		£1.00	—
LT20	Match Attax Extra 2015/16 Magic Moments	2016		50p	£10.00
LT40	Match Attax Extra 2015/16 Man of the Match	2016		60p	—
LT20	Match Attax Extra 2015/16 Managers	2016		30p	£6.00
LT28	Match Attax Extra 2015/16 New Signings	2016		25p	£7.00
LT1	Match Attax Extra 2015/16 100 Club Sergio Aguero ...	2016		—	£6.00
LT20	Match Attax Extra 2015/16 Rising Stars	2016		30p	£6.00
LT224	Match Attax World Cup 2010 (red backs)	2010		20p	£12.00
LT32	Match Attax World Cup 2010 International Legends ...	2010		20p	£5.00
LT8	Match Attax World Cup 2010 International Masters (foil fronts)	2010		—	£5.00
LT28	Match Attax World Cup 2010 Man of the Match (foil fronts)	2010		60p	£17.00
LT16	Match Attax World Cup 2010 Managers	2010		30p	£5.00
LT4	Match Attax World Cup 2010 100 Club (foil fronts) ...	2010		£3.00	£12.00
LT6	Match Attax World Cup 2010 Star Legends (foil fronts)	2010		85p	£5.00
LT25	Match Attax World Cup 2010 Star Players (foil fronts)	2010		20p	£5.00
LT66	Michael Jackson	1984		50p	—
LT49	Monster in My Pocket	1991		20p	£7.50
LT66	Neighbours 1st Series	1988		20p	£6.00
LT66	Neighbours 2nd Series	1988		20p	£6.00
LT88	New Kids on the Block (white card)	1990		20p	£7.50
M11	New Kids on the Block stickers, red borders	1990		33p	£3.50
M11	New Kids on the Block stickers, yellow borders	1990		33p	£3.50
M64	Nintendo Games – Super Mario Bros, Punch Out, Zelda, Robowarrior etc	1992		20p	£13.00
LT66	Planet of the Apes (TV Series)	1974		£1.50	£100.00
LT90	Pokemon (TV animation series) 1st Series	2000		25p	£16.00
LT72	Pokemon (TV animation series) 2nd Series	2000		25p	£16.00
LT72	Pokemon (TV animation series) 3rd Series	2000		—	£16.00
LT72	Pokemon The Movie...	2000		25p	£16.00
LT72	Pokemon 2000 The Movie...	2000		—	£16.00
M75	Pro-Cycling	1988		20p	£15.00
M66	Put On Stickers (including varieties)	1992		20p	£15.00
LT50	Shocking Laffs (No.17 not issued, but two Nos 47):				
	A Grey card	1977		£2.50	—
	B White card	1977		£2.75	—
LT88	The Simpsons	1991		20p	£18.00
M22	The Simpsons Stickers	1991		40p	£9.00
LT66	Spitting Image	1990		20p	£12.00
LT88	Star Trek, The Motion Picture (white card)	1980		£1.50	£130.00
LT66	Star Wars, Nd 1-66	1978		£2.00	£130.00
LT66	Star Wars, Nd 1A-66A	1978		£3.00	—
LT80	Star Wars Attack of The Clones (white Star Wars on front)	2002		—	£15.00
LT10	Star Wars Attack of The Clones — Characters...	2002		—	£10.00
LT5	Star Wars Attack of The Clones — Planets	2002		—	£5.00
LT10	Star Wars Attack of The Clones — Vehicles	2002		—	£10.00
LT66	Stingray — Thunderbirds — Captain Scarlet	1993		20p	£9.50
M44	Stupid Smiles	1990		30p	—
	Super Mario Bros – Nintendo 1992 see Nintendo Games				
LT66	Superman The Movie 1st Series	1979		27p	£18.00
LT66	Superman The Movie 2nd Series	1979		24p	£16.00
LT66	Take That (Pop Group)...	1994		20p	£6.00
M11	Take That (Pop Group) stickers	1994		33p	£3.50

Size & quantity	TRADE CARD ISSUES	Date	Handbook reference	Price per card	Complete set
	TOPPS (UK) (continued)				
LT66	Teenage Mutant Hero Turtles	1990		20p	£6.00
M11	Teenage Mutant Hero Turtles Stickers	1990		50p	—
LT132	Teenage Mutant Ninja Turtles Movie	1990		20p	£9.50
M11	Teenage Mutant Ninja Turtles Movie Stickers	1990		33p	£3.50
M44	Terminator 2 (size 77 × 55mm)	1991		20p	£7.50
LT77	Toxic Crusaders	1993		20p	£9.50
M11	Toxic Crusaders stickers	1993		33p	£3.50
M54	Toxic High School	1991		35p	—
M23	Toxic High School Senior stickers	1991		20p	£4.50
M44	Trash Can Trolls nos 1A-44A	1993		50p	£22.00
M44	Trash Can Trolls nos 1B-44B	1993		50p	—
LT66	Trolls (glossy backs)	1992		20p	£8.50
M11	Trolls stickers	1992		33p	£3.50
LT38	Wacky Packages 1st Series	c1978		£1.50	—
LT38	Wacky Packages 2nd Series	c1978		£1.50	—
M30	Wacky Packages	1982		£1.00	—
LT42	Wanted Posters	1978		£1.75	—
LT66	World Championship Wrestling	1992		20p	£9.50
EL18	World Cup Supersquad England (Football)	1990		70p	£12.00
EL18	World Cup Supersquad Scotland (Football)	1990		£1.00	£18.00
	TOPPS (USA)				
LT66	The 'A' Team	1984		—	£9.50
LT11	The 'A' Team Stickers	1984		—	£4.50
LT84	Alien — The Movie	1979		—	£15.00
LT88	American Gladiators	1991		—	£9.50
LT66	Baby	1985		—	£8.50
LT88	Back to the Future Part II — The Film	1989		—	£15.00
LT11	Back to the Future II – The Film Stickers	1989		—	£4.50
LT72	Barb Wire (Pamela Anderson Film)	1996		—	£9.50
LT12	Barb Wire Embossed Series (Pamela Anderson Film)	1996		—	£5.00
LT132	Batman (size 89 x 64mm)	1989		20p	£9.50
LT90	Batman Begins — The Film	2005		—	£12.00
LT100	Batman Returns (Stadium Club)	1992		—	£12.00
LT72	The Blair Witch Project — The Movie	1999		—	£9.50
LT88	Buck Rogers in the 25th Century	1979		—	£18.00
LT66	Charlie's Angels 3rd Series	1977		—	£25.00
LT11	Charlie's Angels 3rd Series Stickers	1977		—	£6.00
LT66	Close Encounters of The Third Kind — The Movie	1978		—	£15.00
LT11	Close Encounters of the Third Kind – The Movie Stickers	1978		—	£5.00
LT72	Daredevil — The Movie	2003		20p	£12.00
LT72	Dark Angel 1st Series	2002		—	£9.50
LT88	Desert Storm 1st Series (Grey Card):				
	A Front Desert Storm in Brown	1991		—	£20.00
	B Front Desert Storm in Yellow	1991		—	£12.00
LT88	Desert Storm 2nd Series	1991		—	£9.50
LT88	Desert Storm 3rd Series	1991		—	£9.50
LT88	Dick Tracy — The Movie	1990		—	£8.50
LT11	Dick Tracy — The Movie Stickers	1990		—	£4.00
LT55	Dinosaurs Attack (including Set LT11 Stickers)	1988		—	£12.00
LT100	Doctor Who Extraterrestial Encounters	2016		—	£17.50
LT100	Doctor Who Timeless	2016		—	£17.50
EL72	Dragon Heart The Film — Widevision	1996		—	£9.50
LT33	Duran Duran (Stickers)	1985		—	£7.50
LT87	ET — The Extra Terrestrial	1982		—	£9.50
LT54	Goosebumps	1996		—	£8.50
LT99	Greatest Olympians	1983		—	£12.00
LT88	Gremlins 2 — The Movie (grey card)	1990		—	£9.50

Size & quantity	TRADE CARD ISSUES	Date	Handbook reference	Price per card	Complete set
	TOPPS (USA) (continued)				
LT66	Growing Pains (TV Series)	1988		—	£9.50
LT77	Harry and The Hendersons	1987		—	£9.50
LT90	Heroes Series 1	2008		—	£9.50
LT90	Heroes Volume 2	2008		—	£9.50
LT77	Howard The Duck	1986		—	£8.50
LT90	Image Universe (Chromium Issue) Comic Art	1995		—	£16.00
LT88	In Living Colour — Fox TV Series	1992		—	£9.50
LT72	The Incredible Hulk	2003		—	£9.50
EL72	Independence Day — The Film Widevision	1996		—	£9.50
LT90	Indiana Jones and The Kingdom of The Crystal Skull	2008		—	£9.50
LT90	Indiana Jones Masterpieces	2008		—	£12.00
LT59	Jaws 2	1978		—	£15.00
LT44	Jaws 3-D The Film	1983		—	£8.50
LT80	Kong The 8th Wonder of The World	2005		—	£9.50
LT88	Last Action Hero — The Film	1993		—	£9.50
LT44	Little Shop of Horrors	1986		—	£8.50
LT72	Lord of The Rings Evolution	2006		—	£9.50
LT90	Lord of The Rings Fellowship of the Ring Series 1	2001		—	£30.00
LT72	Lord of The Rings Fellowship of the Ring Series 2	2002		—	£12.00
LT90	Lord of The Rings Masterpieces Series 1	2006		—	£15.00
LT72	Lord of The Rings Masterpieces Series 2	2008		—	£15.00
LT90	Lord of The Rings The Return of the King Series 1	2003		—	£9.50
LT72	Lord of The Rings The Return of the King Series 2	2004		—	£12.00
LT90	Lord of The Rings The Two Towers Series 1	2002		—	£12.00
LT72	Lord of The Rings The Two Towers Series 2	2003		—	£12.00
LT72	The Lost World of Jurassic Park + Set LT11 Stickers	1997		—	£9.50
LT56	Mars Attacks	1962		—	—
EL72	Mars Attacks — Widevision	1996		—	£9.50
LT55	Mars Attacks Heritage	2012		—	£12.00
LT10	Mars Attacks Heritage Deleted Scenes	2012		—	£7.50
LT15	Mars Attacks Heritage Guide to the New Universe	2012		—	£8.00
LT66	Menudo (Pop Group)	1983		—	£9.50
LT33	Michael Jackson 1st Series	1984		—	£10.00
LT33	Michael Jackson 2nd Series	1984		—	£10.00
LT99	Moonraker James Bond 007	1979		—	£20.00
LT22	Moonraker James Bond 007 Stickers	1979		—	£6.00
LT99	Mork and Mindy	1978		—	£18.00
LT88	New Kids on the Block 1st Series (grey card)	1990		—	£9.50
LT88	New Kids on the Block 2nd Series (grey card)	1990		—	£9.50
LT11	New Kids on the Block 2nd Series Stickers (Nos. 12 to 22)	1990		—	£4.00
LT88	Nicktoons	1993		—	£9.50
LT50	NSYNC (Pop Group)	2000		—	£9.50
LT50	Outer Limits	1964		—	—
LT33	Pee Wee's Playhouse	1989		—	£7.50
LT55	Perlorian Cats	1982		—	£8.00
LT90	Planet of the Apes — The Movie	2001		—	£9.50
LT44	Return to Oz	1985		—	£12.00
LT55	Robin Hood Prince of Thieves — The Film	1991		—	£8.50
LT9	Robin Hood Prince of Thieves – The Film Stickers	1991		—	£4.00
LT88	Robocop 2 — The Film	1990		—	£8.50
LT99	The Rocketeer — The Film	1991		—	£8.50
LT99	Rocky II	1979		—	£12.00
LT90	The Shadow — The Movie	1994		—	£8.50
LT88	Star Trek Motion Picture (grey card)	1980		£1.00	£90.00
LT100	Star Wars Attack of The Clones (silver Star Wars on front)	2002		—	£16.00
EL80	Star Wars Attack of The Clones — Widevision	2002		—	£18.00
LT90	Star Wars Clone Wars	2004		—	£12.00

Size & quantity	TRADE CARD ISSUES	Date	Handbook reference	Price per card	Complete set
	TOPPS (USA) (continued)				
LT90	Star Wars The Clone Wars — The Film	2008	—		£9.50
EL80	Star Wars The Clone Wars (Widevision)	2009	—		£9.50
LT90	Star Wars Clone Wars Rise of The Bounty Hunters	2010	—		£8.50
LT132	Star Wars The Empire Strikes Back 1st Series	1980	—		£25.00
LT132	Star Wars The Empire Strikes Back 2nd Series	1980	—		£20.00
EL48	Star Wars The Empire Strikes Back 30th Anniversary (3-D) Widevision	2010	—		£15.00
EL80	Star Wars Episode 1 Series 1 — Widevision (red)	1999	—		£15.00
EL80	Star Wars Episode 1 Series 2 — Widevision (blue)	1999	—		£15.00
LT93	Star Wars Evolution	2001	—		£15.00
LT120	Star Wars Galaxy Series 4	2009	—		£12.00
LT120	Star Wars Galaxy Series 5	2010	—		£12.00
LT120	Star Wars Galaxy Series 6	2011	—		£12.00
LT110	Star Wars Galaxy Series 7	2012	—		£12.00
LT12	Star Wars Galaxy Lucas Art	1995	—		£15.00
LT120	Star Wars Heritage	2004	—		£12.00
LT90	Star Wars Jedi Legacy	2013	—		£9.50
LT132	Star Wars Return of The Jedi 1st Series	1983	—		£25.00
LT33	Star Wars Return of the Jedi 1st Series Stickers	1983	—		£8.00
LT88	Star Wars Return of The Jedi 2nd Series	1983	—		£20.00
LT90	Star Wars Revenge of The Sith	2005	—		£9.50
EL80	Star Wars Revenge of The Sith — Widevision	2005	—		£15.00
LT120	Star Wars The 30th Anniversary	2007	—		£12.00
EL72	Star Wars Trilogy — Widevision	1997	—		£16.00
LT72	Star Wars Vehicles	1997	—		£15.00
LT100	Stranger Things Season 1	2018	—		£12.00
LT44	Supergirl — The Film	1994	—		£7.50
LT88	Superman II — The Film	1980	—		£9.50
LT99	Superman III — The Film	1983	—		£9.50
LT22	Superman III – The Film Stickers	1983	—		£5.00
LT90	Superman Returns — The Film	2007	—		£9.50
LT44	T.2 — Terminator 2 — The Movie (size 89 × 64mm)	1991	—		£7.50
LT90	Terminator Salvation Movie	2009	—		£9.50
LT16	Three's Company (Puzzle Picture)	1978	—		£5.00
LT77	Tiny Toon Adventures plus LT11 Stickers	1991	—		£16.00
LT66	Trolls by Russ (matt backs)	1992	—		£9.50
LT11	Trolls by Russ Stickers	1992	—		£3.50
LT100	Walking Dead Season 5	2016	—		£16.00
LT100	Walking Dead Season 6	2017	—		£16.00
LT100	Walking Dead Season 7	2017	—		£16.00
LT90	Walking Dead Season 8	2018	—		£12.00
LT100	Walking Dead Evolution	2017	—		£16.00
LT100	Walking Dead Hunters and the Hunted	2018	—		£16.00
LT100	Walking Dead Road to Alexandria	2018	—		£16.00
LT72	WCW Nitro (Wrestling)	1999	—		£9.50
LT132	Who Framed Roger Rabbit — The Movie	1987	—		£9.50
LT100	Wild C.A.T.S Covert Action Teams by Jim Lee (2 different No. 66, No.68 not issued)	1983	—		£9.50
LT72	World Championship Wrestling Embossed	1999	—		£10.00
LT72	The X Files Fight for the Future	1998	—		£12.00
LT72	The X Files Season 1	1996	—		£9.50
LT72	The X Files Season 2	1996	—		£9.50
LT72	The X Files Season 3	1997	—		£9.50
EL72	The X Files Showcase — Widevision	1997	—		£12.00
LT72	X-Men — The Movie	2000	—		£9.50
LT72	X-Men 2 United — The Movie	2003	—		£9.50
LT72	Xena Warrior Princess Season 1	1998	—		£9.50
LT72	Xena Warrior Princess Season 2	2000	—		£12.00

Size & quantity	TRADE CARD ISSUES	Date	Handbook reference	Price per card	Complete set
	JOHN TORDOFF & SON				
K25	The Growth and Manufacture of Tea	c1930		£14.00	—
25	Safety First	c1930	HX-199	£14.00	—
	TOTAL UK				
L25	Return to Oz	1985		20p	£4.50
	Album			—	£5.00
	TOURISM RESOURCES				
L24	Historic Irish Houses	1993		—	£15.00
	TOURIST BOARD				
L40	Places to Visit Cumbria	1992		—	£4.00
L40	Places to Visit Cumbria	1993		—	£4.00
L40	Places to Visit Cumbria	1995		—	£4.00
L40	Places to Visit North West	1991		—	£5.00
L40	Places to Visit North West	1992		—	£5.00
L40	Places to Visit North West	1993		—	£4.00
L40	Places to Visit North West	1994		—	£4.00
L40	Places to Visit North West	1995		—	£4.00
L40	Places to Visit North West	1996		—	£4.00
L40	Places to Visit North West	1999		—	£4.00
L40	Places to Visit Stockport	1992		—	£4.00
L40	Places to Visit Stockport	1993		—	£4.00
L40	Places to Visit Stockport	1994		—	£4.00
L40	Places to Visit Trafford	1990		—	£4.00
L40	Places to Visit Trafford	1991		—	£4.00
L40	Places to Visit Wigan & District	1991		—	£4.00
L40	Places to Visit Wigan & District	1992		—	£4.00
	TOWER TEA				
24	Illustrated Sayings	c1910	HT-100	£34.00	—
	TRADE CARDS (EUROPE) LTD				
	(SEE ALSO FUTERA)				
LT90	Arsenal F.C. Fans Selection	1998		20p	£16.00
LT18	Arsenal F.C. Fans Selection (embossed)	1998		30p	£5.00
LT99	Arsenal F.C. plus Set LT9 embossed	1999		20p	£15.00
LT9	Arsenal F.C. Hot Shots (silver foil fronts)	1999		£2.00	£18.00
LT9	Arsenal F.C. Vortex (silver foil fronts)	1999		£2.00	£18.00
LT50	Arsenal F.C. Greatest	1999		—	£25.00
LT50	Arsenal F.C. Main Series	2000		20p	£9.00
LT50	Arsenal F.C. Main Series (silver foil front)	2000		—	£25.00
LT6	Arsenal F.C. Electric Series	2000		£3.00	£18.00
LT90	Aston Villa F.C. Fans Selection	1998		—	£17.50
LT18	Aston Villa F.C. Fans Selection (embossed)	1998		—	£5.00
LT18	Aston Villa F.C. Fans Selection (silver foil fronts embossed)	1998		£1.50	£27.00
LT99	Aston Villa F.C. plus Set LT9 embossed	1999		20p	£15.00
LT99	Aston Villa F.C. Player Edition (silver foil fronts)	1999		—	£30.00
LT9	Aston Villa F.C. Cutting Edge Player Edition (silver foil fronts)	1999		—	£18.00
LT9	Aston Villa F.C. Hot Shots (silver foil fronts)	1999		£2.00	£18.00
LT9	Aston Villa F.C. Vortex (silver foil fronts)	1999		£2.00	£18.00
LT90	Celtic F.C. Fans Selection	1998		20p	£17.50
LT18	Celtic F.C. Fans Selection (embossed)	1998		30p	£5.50
LT99	Celtic F.C. plus Set LT9 embossed	1999		20p	£15.00
LT99	Celtic F.C. Player Edition (silver foil fronts)	1999		—	£30.00

Size & quantity	TRADE CARD ISSUES	Date	Handbook reference	Price per card	Complete set
	TRADE CARDS (EUROPE) LTD (continued)				
LT9	Celtic F.C. Cutting Edge Player Edition (silver foil fronts)	1999		—	£18.00
LT9	Celtic F.C. Hot Shots (silver foil fronts)	1999		£2.00	£18.00
LT9	Celtic F.C. Vortex (silver foil fronts)	1999		£2.00	£18.00
LT50	Celtic F.C. Main Series	2000		20p	£9.00
LT50	Celtic F.C. Main Series (silver foil fronts)	2000		—	£25.00
LT4	Celtic F.C. Electric Series	2000		£3.00	£12.00
LT90	Chelsea F.C. Fans Selection	1998		20p	£17.50
LT18	Chelsea F.C. Fans Selection (embossed)	1998		32p	£6.00
LT99	Chelsea F.C. plus Set LT9 embossed	1999		20p	£15.00
LT9	Chelsea F.C. Hot Shots (silver foil fronts)	1999		£2.00	£18.00
LT9	Chelsea F.C. Vortex (silver foil fronts)	1999		£2.00	£18.00
LT50	Chelsea F.C. Greatest	1999		—	£25.00
LT90	Leeds United F.C. Fans Selection	1998		—	£17.50
LT18	Leeds United F.C. Fans Selection (embossed)	1998		—	£6.00
LT99	Leeds United F.C. plus Set LT9 embossed	1999		20p	£15.00
LT99	Leeds United F.C. Player Edition (silver foil fronts)	1999		—	£30.00
LT9	Leeds United F.C. Cutting Edge Player Edition (silver foil fronts)	1999		—	£18.00
LT9	Leeds United F.C. Hot Shots (silver foil fronts)	1999		£2.00	£18.00
LT9	Leeds United F.C. Vortex (silver foil fronts)	1999		£2.00	£18.00
LT50	Leeds United F.C. Greatest	1999		—	£25.00
LT50	Leeds United F.C. Main Series	2000		20p	£8.00
LT50	Leeds United F.C. Main Series (silver foil fronts)	2000		—	£25.00
LT4	Leeds United F.C. Electric Series	2000		£3.00	£12.00
LT99	Liverpool F.C. Main Series	1998		—	£16.00
LT99	Liverpool F.C. plus Set LT9 embossed	1999		20p	£15.00
LT99	Liverpool F.C. Player Edition (silver foil fronts)	1999		—	£30.00
LT9	Liverpool F. C. Cutting Edge Player Edition (silver foil fronts)	1999		—	£18.00
LT9	Liverpool F.C. Hot Shots (silver foil fronts)	1999		£2.00	£18.00
LT9	Liverpool F.C. Vortex (silver foil fronts)	1999		£2.00	£18.00
LT50	Liverpool F.C. Main Series	2000		20p	£10.00
LT6	Liverpool F.C. Electric Series	2000		£3.00	£18.00
LT100	Manchester United F.C.	1997		—	£20.00
LT90	Manchester United F.C. Fans Selection	1998		—	£16.00
LT18	Manchester United F.C. Fans Selection (embossed)	1998		—	£6.00
LT99	Manchester United F.C. Main Series	1998		—	£17.50
LT99	Manchester United F.C. plus Set LT9 embossed	1999		20p	£15.00
LT9	Manchester United F.C. Hot Shots (silver foil fronts)	1999		£2.00	£18.00
LT9	Manchester United F.C. Vortex (silver foil fronts)	1999		£2.00	£18.00
LT99	Manchester United F.C. Main Series	2000		20p	£15.00
LT9	Manchester United F.C. Electric Series	2000		£3.00	—
LT99	Newcastle United F.C. plus Set LT9 embossed	1999		20p	£15.00
LT99	Newcastle United F. C. Player Edition (silver foil fronts)	1999		—	£30.00
LT9	Newcastle United F. C. Cutting Edge Player Edition (silver foil fronts)	1999		—	£18.00
LT9	Newcastle United F.C. Hot Shots (silver foil fronts)	1999		£2.00	£18.00
LT9	Newcastle United F.C. Vortex (silver foil fronts)	1999		£2.00	£18.00
LT50	Newcastle United F.C. Greatest	1999		—	£25.00
	TRADING CARDS INTERNATIONAL (USA)				
LT50	Princess Diana 1961-1997	1997		—	£9.50
	TRAKS (USA)				
LT50	Richard Petty Motor Racing	1991		—	£8.00
	TREASURE				
L18	Zoo Time plus album	1966		—	£12.00

Size & quantity	TRADE CARD ISSUES	Date	Handbook reference	Price per card	Complete set
	TREBOR LTD				
M42	Space Series (Waxed Paper issue):				
	A Top 'Victory Bubble Gum'............	1964		£6.00	—
	B Top 'Trebor Zip Bubble Gum'	1964		£6.00	—
M48	V.C. Heroes (Waxed Paper issue):		HX-215		
	A Inscribed 'Zip'........................	1967		£6.00	—
	B Inscribed 'Zoom Bubble Gum'	1967		£6.00	—
	TREBOR BASSETT LTD (SEE GEO. BASSETT)				
	TREBOR/SHARP				
24	Famous Pets	1972		20p	£3.50
	Album			—	£5.00
	TRIBUTE COLLECTABLES				
10	Abbott and Costello	2010		—	£5.00
10	Anita Ekberg	2016		—	£5.00
10	Ann-Margaret	2017		—	£5.00
10	Astaire Legend of Dance (Fred Astaire)	2010		—	£5.50
10	Betty Grable	2016		—	£5.00
10	Carole Lombard	2015		—	£5.00
10	Charlie Parker	2014		—	£5.00
10	Count Basie	2016		—	£5.00
10	Cyd Charisse	2010		—	£5.50
10	Debbie Reynolds	2014		—	£5.00
10	Dizzy Gillespie	2014		—	£5.00
10	Ella Fitzgerald	2010		—	£5.50
15	Gina Lollobrigida	2014		—	£6.50
10	Ginger Rogers	2010		—	£5.50
10	Humphrey Bogart	2010		—	£5.50
10	Janette Scott	2017		—	£5.00
10	John Wayne A Tribute To The Duke	2010		—	£5.00
10	Josephine Baker (Dancer & Actress)	2010		—	£5.50
10	June Allyson	2015		—	£5.00
10	Marty (Marty Feldman Commemorating the British Comedy Star)	2010		—	£5.00
20	Paulette Goddard	2015		—	£9.50
10	Sammy Davis Jr.	2015		—	£5.00
15	Satchmo	2014		—	£6.50
10	Screamin Jay Hawkins	2015		—	£5.00
10	Screen Sirens — Veronica Lake	2015		—	£5.00
10	A Tribute to Danny Kaye	2010		—	£5.50
10	A Tribute to Dean Martin	2010		—	£5.00
10	A Tribute to Diana Dors	2010		—	£5.00
10	A Tribute to Fay Wray	2018		—	£5.00
20	A Tribute to Gene Kelly	2010		—	£9.00
10	A Tribute to Judy Garland	2010		—	£5.50
15	A Tribute to On The Buses (1970s TV Show) ...	2014		—	£6.50
10	Victor Mature	2010		—	£5.50
10	Yvonne De Carlo	2017		—	£5.00
	TRUCARDS				
M30	Animals	1970		20p	£3.50
M30	Battle of Britain	1970		20p	£5.00
M30	Flowers	1970		20p	£3.50
M30	History of Aircraft	1970		20p	£4.00
M30	Sport	1970		20p	£4.00
M30	Veteran and Vintage Cars	1970		20p	£4.00
M30	World War I	1970		20p	£4.00
M30	World War II	1970		20p	£4.00

Size & quantity	TRADE CARD ISSUES	Date	Handbook reference	Price per card	Complete set
	TUCKETTS SWEETS				
25	Photos of Cricketers	1926		£50.00	—
50	Photos of Film Stars	1939	HT-105	£10.00	—
25	Photos of Football Stars	1928	HX-188	£35.00	—
	TUCKFIELD (Australia)				
M32	Australiana Animals	c1970		£1.60	—
M48	Australiana Birds Nos 1-48	c1970		£1.00	—
M48	Australiana Birds Nos 49-96	c1970		£1.00	—
M48	Australiana Birds Nos 97-144	c1970		£1.00	—
M48	Australiana Birds Nos 145-192	c1970		£1.00	—
M48	Australiana Birds Nos 193-240	c1970		£1.00	—
M48	Australiana Birds Nos 241-288	c1970		£1.00	—
M48	Australiana Birds Nos 289-336	c1970		£1.00	—
M48	Australiana Birds Nos 337-384	c1970		£1.00	—
	TUFF STUFF (USA)				
LT33	Peanuts by Schulz	1992		—	£8.00
LT50	Remember Pearl Harbor	1991		—	£15.00
LT15	World War II Propaganda Diamond Edition	1991		—	£7.00
	W.E. TURNER				
20	War Pictures	1915	HX-122	£24.00	—
	21st CENTURY ARCHIVES (USA)				
LT50	The Comic Art Tribute To Joe Simon and Jack Kirby	1994		—	£8.50
LT100	National Lampoon	1993		—	£9.50
	TWININGS TEA				
30	Rare Stamps 1st Series	1958		£1.00	—
30	Rare Stamps 2nd Series				
	A No overprint	1960		20p	£5.00
	B Red overprint	1960		20p	£3.50
	TYPHOO TEA				
	(36 page Illustrated Reference Book — £4.50)				
25	Aesop's Fables	1924	HT-117	£3.60	£90.00
M12	The Amazing World of Doctor Who	1976		£2.25	£27.00
25	Ancient and Annual Customs	1924		£3.00	£75.00
L25	Animal Friends of Man	1927	HT-118	£6.00	—
L25	Animal Offence and Defence	1928		£2.00	£50.00
24	British Birds and Their Eggs	1914	HX-164	£15.00	—
L25	British Birds and Their Eggs	1936		£1.80	£45.00
	British Empire at Work:				
30	1 Normal set with pictures	1925		£2.00	£60.00
30	2 Wording only 'This is a Continuation Card'	1925		£7.00	—
1	3 The Last Chance Card	c1925		—	£10.00
25	Calendar 1934 (Dogs)	1933	HT-119	£40.00	—
25	Calendar	1936	HT-120	£25.00	—
L1	Calendar	1937		—	£10.00
L25	Characters from Shakespeare	1937		£1.40	£35.00
25	Common Objects Highly Magnified (multi-backed)	1925		£1.60	£40.00
25	Conundrums	1915		£25.00	—
24	Do You Know?	1962		20p	£4.00
	Album			—	£12.00
L25	Famous Voyages (multi-backed)	1933	HT-123	£2.00	£50.00

373

Size & quantity	TRADE CARD ISSUES	Date	Handbook reference	Price per card	Complete set
	TYPHOO TEA (continued)				
M20	Flags and Arms of Countries	1916	HT-124	£22.00	—
24	Great Achievements	1967		£1.60	£40.00
	Album			—	£20.00
L25	Historical Buildings	1939		£2.00	£50.00
L25	Homes of Famous Men (multi-backed)	1934		£1.40	£35.00
L25	Horses	1934		£1.80	£45.00
L25	Important Industries of the British Empire (multi-backed)	1938	HT-127	60p	£15.00
L25	Interesting Events in British History (multi-backed)	1938	HT-127	60p	£15.00
10	Nursery Rhymes	c1910	HT-130	£32.00	—
24	Our Empire's Defenders	c1915		£38.00	—
48	Puzzle Pictures	c1915		£38.00	—
L30	Robin Hood and His Merry Men:				
	A Back with Oval Imprint	1926		£10.00	—
	B Back without Oval Imprint	1926		£10.00	—
L25	Scenes from John Halifax, Gentleman	1931		£2.60	£65.00
L25	Scenes from Lorna Doone:		HT-132		
	A Lemon borders to picture side (multi-backed)	1930		£4.00	—
	B Orange borders to picture side (multi-backed)	1930		£4.00	—
L25	Scenes from a Tale of Two Cities by Charles Dickens:				
	A Back inscribed '897.1/31'	1931		£4.00	£100.00
	B Back inscribed '897.10/31'	1931		£4.50	—
L30	The Story of David Copperfield:				
	A Coupon inscribed 'until 30th September'	1930		£3.00	£90.00
	B Coupon inscribed 'until end of October'	1930		£6.00	—
	C With coupon cut off	1930		£2.50	£75.00
L25	The Swiss Family Robinson (multi-backed)	1935	HT-133	£2.00	£50.00
24	Travel Through the Ages	1961		20p	£3.50
	Album			—	£12.00
L25	Trees of the Countryside (multi-backed)	1937	HT-127	£1.00	£25.00
L25	Whilst We Sleep Series:				
	A Back with inscription '79610/10/28'	1928		£3.40	—
	B Back without inscription '79610/10/28'	1928		£3.00	£75.00
24	Wild Flowers	1963		36p	£9.00
	Album			—	£12.00
L25	Wild Flowers in Their Families 1st Series	1935		£1.20	£30.00
L25	Wild Flowers in Their Families 2nd Series	1936		£1.20	£30.00
L25	Wonder Cities of the World (multi-backed)	1933	HT-134	£2.00	£50.00
M24	Wonderful World of Disney	1975		£3.60	—
L25	Work on the Farm (No. 1 multi-backed)	1932	HT-135	£4.40	£110.00
25	Zoo Series	1932	HX-186	£1.60	£40.00

PACKAGE ISSUES:

(N.B. The prices are for full slides, slides cut to picture size are half catalogue price)

	Children's series of:				
L20	By Pond and Stream	1960		£1.00	—
L20	Common British Birds:				
	A With red framline	1954		£1.50	—
	B Without red framline	1954		£1.00	—
L20	Costumes of the World	1961		£2.00	—
L20	Famous Bridges	1958		£1.00	—
L20	Famous Buildings:				
	A With red framline	1953		£1.00	—
	B Without red framline	1953		£1.00	—

Size & quantity	TRADE CARD ISSUES	Date	Handbook reference	Price per card	Complete set
	TYPHOO TEA (Package issues continued)				
L20	Pets	1959		£1.00	—
L20	Some Countryside Animals:				
	A With red framline	1957		£1.25	—
	B Without red frameline	1957		£1.25	—
L20	Some Popular Breeds of Dogs:				
	A With red framline	1955		£2.00	—
	B Without red frameline	1955		£2.50	—
L20	Some World Wonders	1959		£1.00	—
L20	Types of Ships:				
	A With red framline	1956		£1.00	—
	B Without red frameline	1956		£1.25	—
L20	Wild Animals:				
	A With one red framline	1952		£1.00	—
	B With two red framelines	1952		£2.00	—
L24	Do You Know?	1962		£1.00	—
L24	Famous Football Clubs 1st Series	1964		£4.00	—
	Famous Football Clubs 2nd Series:				
L24	A With 'Second Series' in red above picture	1965		£4.00	—
L24	B Without 'Second Series' in red above picture	1965		£4.00	—
L24	Football Club Plaques	1973	HT-125	£12.00	—
L24	Football Stars, New Series:				
	A With football at top	1973		£6.00	—
	B Without football at top	1973		£6.00	—
L24	Great Voyages of Discovery	1966		£1.00	—
L24	International Football Stars 1st Series	1967		£4.00	—
L24	International Football Stars 2nd Series:				
	A Red border marked 2FS at base	1969		£5.00	—
	B White border marked 2nd Series at top	1969		£5.00	—
L24	100 Years of Great British Achievements:				
	A Full card with token and checklist	1972		£4.00	—
	B Full card with token without checklist	1972		£3.00	—
	C Cut card without token and checklist	1972		£1.50	—
	Album			—	£30.00
L24	Travel Through the Ages:				
	A With frameline around text	1961		£1.00	—
	B Without frameline around text	1961		£2.00	—
L24	Wild Flowers	1963		£1.50	—
	PREMIUM ISSUES:				
EL24	Famous Football Clubs 1st Series	1964	HT-121	£15.00	—
EL24	Famous Football Clubs 2nd Series	1965	HT-122	£12.00	—
EL24	Football Stars	1973	HT-126	£12.00	—
—	Great Voyages of Discovery Wall Chart with 24 stickers	1966		—	£40.00
EL24	International Football Stars 1st Series	1967	HT-128	£12.00	—
EL24	International Football Stars 2nd Series	1969	HT-129	£12.00	—
EL24	100 Years of Great British Achievements:				
	A Plain back	1972		£1.50	£36.00
	B Printed back	1972		£5.00	£125.00
	TYSON & CO. LTD				
28	Semaphore Signals	c1912		£20.00	—
	'UNION JACK'				
MP6	Monarchs of the Ring	1923		£10.00	—
M8	Police of All Nations	1922		£8.00	—

Size & quantity	TRADE CARD ISSUES	Date	Handbook reference	Price per card	Complete set
	UNITED AUTOMOBILE SERVICES				
	Kodak Views Series:				
25	Castles, Series No. 1	1925		£8.00	—
25	Churches, Series No. 2	1925		£8.00	—
25	United, Series No. 3	1925		£8.00	—
25	Places of Interest, Series No. 4	1925		£8.00	—
	THE UNITED CONFECTIONERY CO. LTD				
50	Wild Animals of the World	1905	HX-216	£13.00	—
	UNITED DAIRIES (Tea)				
25	Aquarium Fish	1964	HX-87	32p	£8.00
25	Birds and Their Eggs	1961	HX-1.3	£1.00	£25.00
25	British Uniforms of the 19th Century	1962	HX-78	£1.00	£25.00
25	The Story of Milk	1966	HX-3	30p	£7.50
25	The West	1963	HX-42	£1.00	£25.00
	UNIVERSAL AUTOMATICS LTD				
L30	Trains of the World	1958	HX-121	£1.75	—
	UNIVERSAL CCC				
15	Australian Cricket Team 1905	1986		—	£3.50
15	English Cricketers 1902	1987		—	£3.50
	UNIVERSAL PICTURES				
LT4	Snow White and the Huntsman (Film)	2012		—	£4.00
	UNSTOPPABLE CARDS				
LT72	The Avengers 50 (TV Series of the 1960s)	2012		—	£8.50
LT54	The Avengers The Complete Collection 1st Series (1960s TV Series)	2019		—	£9.50
LT54	The Avengers The Complete Collection 2nd Series (1960s TV Series)	2020		—	£9.50
LT54	Blake's 7 1st Series (1970/80s TV Series)	2013		—	£8.50
LT54	Blake's 7 2nd Series (1970s/80s TV Series)	2014		—	£8.50
LT54	Captain Scarlet	2015		—	£8.50
LT36	Captain Scarlet and the Mysterons 50 Years	2018		—	£8.50
LT54	Doctor Who and the Daleks (Movies)	2015		—	£8.50
LT54	Fireball XL5	2017		—	£8.50
LT6	Fireball XL5 Silver Foil Sub Set	2017		—	£4.50
LT18	Four Feather Falls	2018		—	£5.00
LT54	Joe 90	2017		—	£8.50
LT6	Joe 90 Silver Foil Sub Set	2017		—	£4.50
LT54	The Man Who Fell to Earth	2014		—	£10.00
LT36	My Favorite Martian	2015		—	£8.50
LT36	The Persuaders	2018		—	£8.50
LT36	The Prisoner 50th Anniversary	2018		—	£8.50
LT36	The Saint 1st Series (blue backs)	2017		—	£9.50
LT36	The Saint 2nd Series (green backs)	2018		—	£8.50
LT18	The Secret Service	2018		—	£5.00
LT54	Space 1999 1st Series (TV Series)	2016		—	£8.50
LT36	Space 1999 2nd Series (TV Series)	2018		—	£8.50
LT54	Stingray	2017		—	£8.50
LT6	Stingray Silver Foil Sub Set	2017		—	£4.50
LT54	Supercar	2017		—	£8.50
LT6	Supercar Silver Foil Sub Set	2017		—	£4.50
LT72	Terminator 2 Judgement Day T2	2017		—	£8.50
LT9	Terminator 2 Judgement Day T2 Silver Foil Sub Set	2017		—	£4.50

Size & quantity	TRADE CARD ISSUES	Date	Handbook reference	Price per card	Complete set
	UNSTOPPABLE CARDS (continued)				
LT54	Thunderbirds 50 Years (50th Anniversary)	2015		—	£9.50
LT54	UFO 1st Series (back grey panel at base)	2016		—	£9.50
LT36	UFO 2nd Series (back purple panel at base)	2018		—	£9.50
LT54	The Wicker Man	2014		—	£11.00
LT54	The Women of The Avengers	2014		—	£8.50
	UPPER DECK (Germany)				
LT45	Werder Bremen F.C.	1997		—	£7.50
	UPPER DECK (Italy)				
LT45	Italian Footballers World Cup	1998		—	£7.50
LT90	Juventus F.C. 1994/95	1994		—	£7.50
LT45	Juventus F.C. Centenary 1897-1997	1997		—	£7.50
	UPPER DECK (Spain)				
LT45	Spanish Footballers World Cup	1998		—	£7.50
	UPPER DECK (Sweden)				
LT224/225	Swedish Hockey League (minus No. 36) 1997/98	1997		20p	£15.00
LT30	Swedish Hockey League Crash Cards 1997/98	1997		—	£10.00
LT15	Swedish Hockey League Stickers 1997/98	1997		—	£5.00
LT15	Swedish Hockey League Update Series 1997/98	1997		—	£10.00
	UPPER DECK (UK)				
LT34	Digimon Digital Monsters	2000		—	£7.50
LT45	England's Qualifying Campaign (Football World Cup) 1st Series Nos 1 to 45	1997		—	£12.00
LT37	England's Qualifying Campaign (Football World Cup) 2nd Series Nos 46 to 82	1998		—	£12.00
LT135	Manchester United F.C. 2001	2001		20p	£17.50
LT14	Manchester United F.C. 2001 Legends of Old Trafford	2001		—	£14.00
LT7	Manchester United F.C. 2001 Magnificent 7's	2001		—	£7.00
LT7	Manchester United F.C. 2001 Strike Force	2001		—	£7.00
LT14	Manchester United F.C. 2001 We Are United	2001		—	£14.00
LT90	Manchester United F.C.	2002		—	£17.50
LT100	Manchester United F.C. Play Makers	2003		—	£20.00
LT100	Manchester United F.C. Strike Force	2003		—	£20.00
LT90	Manchester United Legends	2002		—	£20.00
LT45	Manchester United World Premiere	2001		—	£20.00
LT45	The Mini (Car) Collection	1996		—	£15.00
LT250	World Cup Football	1994		—	£25.00
LT17	World Cup Football nos 251-267 Unissued	1994		—	£10.00
LT30	World Cup Football All Stars	1994		—	£5.00
	UPPER DECK (USA)				
LT90	Adventures in Toon World	1993		—	£9.50
LT99	Anastasia — The Movie	1998		—	£8.50
LT90	Battlefield Earth — The Film	2000		—	£8.50
LT198	Beauty and the Beast	1992		—	£12.00
LT90	Black Panther The Movie	2018		—	£15.00
LT90	Congo The Film	1995		—	£9.50
LT89	Disney Treasures 1st Series	2003		—	£15.00
LT45	Disney Treasures 1st Series — Mickey Mouse	2003		—	£18.00
LT10	Disney Treasures 1st Series — Walt Disney Retrospective	2003		—	£4.00
LT90	Disney Treasures 2nd Series	2003		—	£12.00
LT45	Disney Treasures 2nd Series — Donald Duck	2003		—	£18.00

Size & quantity	TRADE CARD ISSUES	Date	Handbook reference	Price per card	Complete set
	UPPER DECK (USA) (continued)				
LT10	Disney Treasures 2nd Series The Lion King Special Edition	2003		—	£4.00
LT89	Disney Treasures 3rd Series	2004		—	£12.00
LT10	Disney Treasures 3rd Series Aladdin Special Edition	2004		—	£4.00
LT45	Disney Treasures 3rd Series — Winnie The Pooh	2004		—	£18.00
LT75	Disney Treasures Celebrate Mickey 75 Years of Fun	2004		—	£12.00
LT75	Iron Man 2 — The Film	2010		—	£8.50
LT55	Looney Tunes Olympics 1996	1996		—	£8.50
LT210	N.H.L. Hockey Players 1st Series 1997/98	1997		20p	£15.00
LT55	Princess Gwenevere and The Jewell Riders	1996		—	£8.50
LT90	Ricky Martin	1999		—	£15.00
LT60	Space Jam — The Film	1996		—	£7.50
LT120	The Valiant Era	1993		—	£12.00
LT120	World Cup Toons	1994		—	£9.50
	UPPER DECK/HOOLA HOOPS (UK)				
L40	Basketball Players (NBA) (No. HH1 to HH40)	1997		—	£10.00
	VAN DEN BERGHS LTD				
EL8	Birds	1974		50p	£4.00
LT24	Pirates	1968		£4.00	—
LT24	This Modern World	1968		£3.00	—
	VAUXHALL MOTORS				
L25	Vauxhall's 90th Anniversary Series	1993		—	£10.00
	VENORLANDUS LTD				
M48	Our Heroes, World of Sport	1979		60p	£30.00
	Album			—	£8.00
	VERKADE (Holland)				
L120	Cactussen (Cacti)	1931		25p	—
L140	De Bloemen en Haar Vrienden (Flowers and Their Friends)	1933		20p	£20.00
L140	De Boerderil (The Farm)	c1930		30p	—
L138	Hans de Torenkraai (Hans the Crow)	c1930		20p	£20.00
L132	Kamerplanten (House Plants)	1928		25p	—
L126	Mijn Aquarium (My Aquarium)	1925		30p	—
L132	Texel District	1927		30p	—
L126	Vetplanten (Succulents)	1932		20p	£25.00
	VICTORIA GALLERY				
L6	A Gathering of Spirits (Native North Americans)	1994		—	£3.50
L20	American Civil War Leaders	1992		—	£8.50
L25	Ashes Winning Captains (cricket)	1993		—	£8.50
L20	Boxing Champions 1st Series	1991		—	£10.00
L21	Boxing Champions 2nd Series	1992		—	£9.00
L6	British Birds of Prey by D. Digby	1994		—	£4.00
L6	British Birds of Prey 2nd Series	1996		—	£3.50
L20	Caricatures of the British Army 1st Series	1994		—	£7.50
L20	Caricatures of the British Army 2nd Series	1994		38p	£7.50
L6	Classic Motor Cycles (Harley Davidson)	1993		—	£3.50
50	Deep Sea Diving	1997		20p	£10.50
L20	Embassy Snooker Celebrities	1988		—	£7.50
L20	Endangered Wild Animals	1992		—	£7.50
L10	Formula One 91 (Cars)	1991		—	£10.00
L25	Hollywood Moviemen	1993		—	£8.50
L20	Legends of Hollywood	1991		—	£7.50
L25	Olympic Greats	1992		—	£8.50

Size & quantity	TRADE CARD ISSUES	Date	Handbook reference	Price per card	Complete set
	VICTORIA GALLERY (continued)				
L20	Partners (Film Stars)	1992		—	£7.50
L15	The Ryder Cup (Golf)	1987		—	£15.00
L25	The Ryder Cup 1991 (Golf)	1991		—	£15.00
L12	Samurai Warriors	1996		—	£10.00
L10	Spirit of a Nation (Native North Americans)	1991		—	£5.00
L12	Twelve Days of Christmas	1992		—	£6.00
L20	Uniforms of the American Civil War	1992		—	£7.50
L24	Uniforms of the American War of Independence	1993		—	£8.50
L12	Wild West — Frontiersmen	1993		—	£4.00
L12	Wild West — Indians	1993		—	£6.00
L12	Wild West — Lawmen	1993		—	£4.00
L12	Wild West — Outlaws	1993		—	£4.00
	VICTORIAN CRICKET ASSOCIATION (Australia)				
L20	Bushrangers Cricketers	1998		—	£6.00
L20	Bushrangers Cricketers	1999		—	£6.00
	VINCENT GRAPHICS				
M48	The Life and Times of Nelson	1991		50p	—
	VISION (USA)				
LT150	Generation Extreme (Extreme Sports)	1994		—	£15.00
	VOMO AUTOMATICS				
LT50	Flags of the World	c1960		£2.00	—
	WAKEFORD				
30	Army Pictures, Cartoons, etc	1916	HX-12	£120.00	—
	JONATHAN WALES LTD				
25	The History of Flight 1st Series	1963		£8.00	—
25	The History of Flight 2nd Series	1963		£8.00	—
	WALES ON SUNDAY				
L40	British Lions on Tour Australia (Rugby Union)	2001		20p	£8.00
L36	World Cup Heroes (Rugby Union Players)	1995		33p	£12.00
L24	World Cup Rugby Greats (including album)	1999		—	£12.00
	WALES ON SUNDAY/WESTERN MAIL				
EL13	Welsh Rugby Union — Graham Henry's Wales	2001		—	£4.00
	WALKER HARRISON AND GARTHWAITE LTD				
M15	Dogs	1902	HW-1	£28.00	—
	WALKERS SNACK FOODS				
K50	Looney Tunes — Tazos Nos 1-50 (circular)	1996		25p	—
K10	Monster Munch Tazos (circular)	1996		35p	£3.50
K35	Pokemon Tazos (circular)	2001		50p	—
K50	Star Wars Trilogy — Tazos (circular)	1997		30p	£15.00
	Album			—	£15.00
K20	World Tazos Nos 51-70 (circular)	1996		25p	£5.00
	T. WALL & SONS				
24	Do You Know?	1965		20p	£4.50
	Album			—	£25.00
36	Dr. Who Adventure	1967		£3.50	—
20	Incredible Hulk	1979		£1.25	£25.00

Size & quantity	TRADE CARD ISSUES	Date	Handbook reference	Price per card	Complete set
	T. WALL & SONS (continued)				
M6	Magicards — Prehistoric Animals	1971	HW-4	60p	£3.50
48	Moon Fleet	1966		35p	£17.50
EL6	Sea Creatures	1971		60p	£3.50
20	Skateboard Surfer	1978		25p	£5.00
20	Time Travel with Starship 4	1984		£5.00	—
	WALLIS CHOCOLATES				
24	British Birds	c1920		£16.00	—
	WALTERS' 'PALM' TOFFEE				
50	Some Cap Badges of Territorial Regiments	1938		50p	£25.00
	WAND CONFECTIONERY LTD				
EL10	Chubby Checker — How To Do the Twist	1964	HW-7	£10.00	
25	Commemoration Stamp Series	1962		£3.60	£90.00
EL35	Pop DJs	1967		£4.50	
25	They Gave Their Names	1963	HX-52	60p	£15.00
	F. WARNE & CO. LTD				
	Observer's Picture Cards (issued with Presentation Box)				
L32	Series I British Birds	c1955		£1.25	—
L32	Series II Wild Flowers	c1955		£1.25	—
L32	Series III British Wild Flowers	c1955		£1.25	—
L32	Series IV Dogs	c1955		£1.25	—
L32	Series V Domestic Animals	c1955		£1.25	—
L32	Series VI Trees	c1955		£1.25	—
L32	Series VII Flags	c1955		£1.25	—
L32	Series VIII Ships	c1955		£1.25	—
L32	Series IX Insects	c1955		£1.25	—
	WARUS (UK)				
10	The Beatles — Abbey Road	1998		—	£5.50
10	The Beatles — Beatles for Sale	1998		—	£5.50
10	The Beatles — Beatles for Sale No. 2 EP Series	2005		—	£5.50
10	The Beatles — Beatles Second Album	2005		—	£5.50
10	The Beatles — Beatles 65	2005		—	£5.50
10	The Beatles — EP Series	2005		—	£5.50
10	The Beatles — Hard Day's Night	1998		—	£5.50
10	The Beatles — Help	1998		—	£5.50
10	The Beatles — Hits EP Series	2005		—	£5.50
10	The Beatles — Let It Be	1998		—	£5.50
10	The Beatles — Long Tall Sally EP Series	2005		—	£5.50
10	The Beatles — Magical Mystery Tour	1998		—	£5.50
10	The Beatles — Meet The Beatles	2005		—	£5.50
10	The Beatles — Million Sellers EP Series	2005		—	£5.50
10	The Beatles — Nowhere Man EP Series	2005		—	£5.50
10	The Beatles — Please Please Me	1998		—	£5.50
10	The Beatles — Revolver	1998		—	£5.50
10	The Beatles — Rubber Soul	1998		—	£5.50
10	The Beatles — Sgt. Pepper	1998		—	£5.50
10	The Beatles — Something New	2005		—	£5.50
10	The Beatles — Twist and Shout EP Series	2005		—	£5.50
10	The Beatles — White Album	1998		—	£5.50
10	The Beatles — With the Beatles	1998		—	£5.50
10	The Beatles — Yellow Submarine	1998		—	£5.50
10	The Beatles — Yesterday and Today	2005		—	£5.50
10	The Beatles — Yesterday EP Series	2005		—	£5.50
10	The Rolling Stones Urban Jungle Tour	1998		—	£5.50

Size & quantity	TRADE CARD ISSUES	Date	Handbook reference	Price per card	Complete set
	WARWICK DISTRICT COUNCIL				
30	England's Historic Heartland	1980		20p	£4.00
	WATFORD BISCUITS				
KP48	Cinema Stars 1st Series	1955		£3.50	—
KP48	Cinema Stars 2nd Series	1956		£6.00	—
	JOHN WATSON				
M56	Norfolk Churches	2012		—	£15.00
M52	Taverns of East Anglia Series 1	2004		—	£15.00
M56	Taverns of Norfolk Series 2	2008		—	£15.00
	WEBCOSA & CO. LTD				
M48	Footballers (Waxed Paper issue with firms name upside down)	c1964		£6.00	—
EL20	Trail Town	1964	HW-15.1	£3.00	£60.00
M47	Treasure Trail (Anonymous Waxed Paper issue)	c1964	HW-15.2	£5.00	—
M48	Victoria Cross Heroes (waxed paper issue)	c1963		£5.00	—
	WEEKLY WELCOME				
12	'Lest We Forget' cards	1916		£14.00	—
	WEETABIX LTD				
L25	Animal Cards	1960		80p	£20.00
L28	Asterix — His Friends and Foes...	1976		£3.00	—
L18	Batman and Wonderwoman	1979		£3.00	—
L25	British Birds...	1962		£2.40	—
L25	British Cars	1963		£3.60	—
L25	Conquest of Space, Series A	1958		£2.60	£65.00
	Album			—	£25.00
L25	Conquest of Space, Series B...	1959		£2.60	£65.00
	Album			—	£25.00
L24	Dr. Who — Coloured background	1977		£6.00	—
L24	Dr. Who — White background	1975		£6.00	—
L8	ET The Extra Terrestrial	1988		£2.50	—
L18	Flash Gordon	1981		£2.50	—
L18	Huckleberry Hound	1977		£3.00	—
L8	Jurassic Park	1993		£2.50	—
L10	Just Do It (Weetabix Characters)	1987		£2.50	—
M12	Matchbox Performance Cars	1994		£3.00	—
L6	Neet Weet Beet Band	1983		£2.50	—
L25	Our Pets...	1961		80p	£20.00
L9	Pop Stars	1984		£2.50	—
L18	Robin Hood Characters from Walt Disney	1974		£3.00	—
L6	Scarry Stickers	1986		£3.00	—
L18	Star Trek	1979		£4.00	£70.00
L10	Star Trek The Next Generation	1994		£2.50	—
L18	Superman	1978		£2.50	—
L25	Thrill Cards	1961		£2.40	—
L18	Walt Disney Cartoon Characters	1978		£3.00	—
L5	Weet Olympix	1984		£2.50	—
L25	The Western Story	1959		£2.00	£50.00
L8	Where's Wally	1994		£2.50	—
M8	Wild Animals 3-D (London Zoo, Weetos issue)... ...	1994		£3.00	—
L25	Working Dogs	1960		30p	£7.50
L18	World of Sport	1986		£4.00	—
	WELSH RUGBY UNION				
50	Great Welsh Rugby Players	1980		20p	£9.00

Size & quantity	TRADE CARD ISSUES	Date	Handbook reference	Price per card	Complete set
	WEST BROMWICH ALBION FOOTBALL CLUB				
M25	West Bromwich Albion Footballers	1993		—	£17.50
L12	West Bromwich Albion Footballers Plus Folder (VE/VJ Day Issue)	1995		—	£6.00
	J. WEST FOODS LTD				
M8	Famous Sea Adventurers (inscribed series of 14, only 8 cards issued)...	1972		45p	£3.50
	WEST LONDON HOSPITAL				
EL1	Calendar 1947 (size 125 × 75mm)	1947		—	£1.50
	WEST LONDON SYNAGOGUE				
25	Hebrew Texts Illustrated	1960		£2.00	—
	WEST MIDLANDS COLLECTORS				
24	Busby Babes (Football)...	1990		50p	£12.00
12	Busby Babes Nos 25-36 (Football)	1991		25p	£3.00
36	Busby Babes (revised combined 1990/91 issues)	1994		40p	£15.00
2	Busby Babes Additional Cards Nos 24 & 25 Error Marked Series of 25 ... ...:	1991		—	£1.50
30	England Captains (Football)	1997		30p	£9.00
24	Golden Wolves (Football)	1989		30p	£7.50
EL1	Reproduction of Manchester United F.C. 37 Busby Babes Autographs c1957	1994		—	£5.00
24	Vintage Spurs (Football)	1993		60p	£15.00
	WEST MIDLANDS POLICE				
EL24	The Old Bill Collection	1990		20p	£5.00
	Album			—	£5.00
EL36	Pictorial History of Walsall and District	1986		50p	£18.00
EL8	Play Safe — Stay Safe (including Album)	1992		—	£6.00
	WEST RIDING COUNTY COUNCIL				
20	Health Cards	c1920		£8.00	—
	WEST YORKSHIRE FIRE SERVICE				
M29	Huddersfield Giants R.L.F.C.	1999		—	£10.00
	WEST YORKSHIRE POLICE				
EL20	Great Britain Rugby League Stars	2003		—	£6.00
	WESTCO				
K60	Westco Autocards	1954		£12.00	—
	WESTERN MAIL				
L36	Wales Grand Slam (Rugby Union)	2005		—	£6.00
L24	Wales Soccer Stars	2003		—	£6.00
	WESTON BISCUITS CO. LTD (Australia)				
50	Dogs	c1965		£4.00	—
M24	Veteran and Vintage Cars 1st Series	1961		£2.00	£50.00
	Album			—	£5.00
M24	Veteran and Vintage Cars 2nd Series	1962		30p	£7.50
	WHAT CAMERA				
EL12	Photocards	1988		—	£3.50

Size & quantity	TRADE CARD ISSUES	Date	Handbook reference	Price per card	Complete set
	R. WHEATLEY				
36	Animal Pictures	c1920		£10.00	—
	WHITBREAD & CO. LTD				
M1	The Britannia Inn Sign:				
	A Printed Back	1958		—	£65.00
	B Plain Back	1958		—	£45.00
M1	Duke Without a Head Inn Sign	1958		—	£10.00
M50	Inn Signs 1st Series (metal)	1951		£4.00	£200.00
M50	Inn Signs 2nd Series (metal)	1951		£4.00	£200.00
M50	Inn Signs 3rd Series:				
	A Metal	1951		£5.00	£250.00
	B Card	1952		£4.00	£200.00
M50	Inn Signs 4th Series (card)	1952		£4.00	£200.00
M50	Inn Signs 5th Series (card)	1953		£4.00	£200.00
M4	Inn Signs (special issue):				
	A Printed Back	1951		£8.00	—
	B No 2 with Red Overprint	1958		—	£30.00
M25	Inn Signs, Bournemouth	1973		£10.00	—
	Album			—	£25.00
M25	Inn Signs, Devon and Somerset	1973		£2.40	£60.00
	Album			—	£25.00
M25	Inn Signs, Isle of Wight	1974		£10.00	—
	Album			—	£25.00
M25	Inn Signs, Kent	1973		£10.00	—
	Album			—	£25.00
M15	Inn Signs, London:				
	A Complete set	1973		—	£170.00
	B 12 different (minus Nos 3, 10 & 13)	1973		£4.00	£50.00
	Album			—	£25.00
M10	Inn Signs, London	1974		£6.00	—
	Album			—	£10.00
M25	Inn Signs, Maritime	1974		30p	£7.50
	Album			—	£12.00
M25	Inn Signs, Marlow	1973		£10.00	—
	Album			—	£25.00
M25	Inn Signs, Portsmouth	1973		£11.00	—
	Album			—	£25.00
M25	Inn Signs, Stratford-upon-Avon	1974		£8.00	—
	Album			—	£25.00
M25	Inn Signs, West Pennine	1973		£10.00	—
	Album			—	£25.00
M1	The Railway Inn Sign	1958		—	£15.00
M1	The Startled Saint Inn Sign:				
	A With Printed in Great Britain	1958		—	£70.00
	B Without Printed in Great Britain	1958		—	£50.00
	THE WHITE FISH AUTHORITY				
25	Fish We Eat	1954		20p	£4.00
	WHITEHAVEN MUSEUM				
M6	The Port of Whitehaven	1978		85p	£5.00
	WHITEHEAD (NOTTINGHAM) LTD				
L25	Kings and Queens	1980		20p	£4.50
	WIKO (Germany)				
50	Soldaten Der Welt	1969		30p	£15.00

Size & quantity	TRADE CARD ISSUES	Date	Handbook reference	Price per card	Complete set
	WILCOCKS & WILCOCKS LTD				
25	Birds	1965	HX-71	£2.60	—
25	British Cavalry Uniforms of the 19th Century	1964	HX-43	£1.00	£25.00
25	Garden Flowers	1964	HX-46	24p	£6.00
24	The Island of Ceylon	1964	HX-47	£6.00	—
25	Passenger Liners	1967	HX-82	£1.00	—
25	People and Places	1967	HX-26	30p	£7.50
25	Tropical Birds	1965	HX-13	60p	£15.00
25	Wonders of the Deep	1965	HX-89	20p	£4.50
25	Wonders of the World (1st 25 cards only issued)	1971	HX-49	24p	£6.00
	A.S. WILKIN LTD				
25	Into Space	1960	HX-147	40p	£10.00
	W.R. WILKINSON & CO. LTD				
M25	Popular Footballers	c1955		£50.00	—
	WILKINSON SWORD LTD				
K4	Garden Tools (Firm's name in black on white background)	1961	HW-30	£2.50	£10.00
K2/4	Garden Tools (Firm's name in white on black background)	1961	HW-30	—	£2.00
K16	Regimental Swords	1995		£5.00	—
	Album			—	£25.00
	WILLARDS CHOCOLATE LTD (Canada)				
50	Indian Series	c1925		£12.00	—
	R.J. WILSON				
L5	B.R. Preserved Diesel-Electric Locomotives	2005		—	£5.00
LT6	British Birds	2005		—	£3.00
L10	British Steam Locomotives	2000		—	£6.00
L6	Eggs of British Birds	2004		—	£4.00
L6	Glamour Girls (Pin Up Girls)	2004		—	£4.00
L10	Hunting With the South Wold	2000		—	£7.00
LT6	Lincolnshire Village Churches 1st Series	2006		—	£5.00
LT6	Lincolnshire Village Churches 2nd Series	2007		—	£5.00
LT6	Nests and Eggs of British Birds 1st Series	2005		—	£4.00
LT6	Nests and Eggs of British Birds 2nd Series	2005		—	£4.00
LT6	Nests and Eggs of British Birds 3rd Series	2006		—	£4.00
LT6	Nests and Eggs of British Birds 4th Series	2007		—	£4.00
L6	Railway Engines	2004		—	£3.00
10	Railway Locomotives	2000		—	£5.00
L4	The South Wold (Lincolnshire) Foxhounds	2004		—	£3.00
L10	Traditional Lincolnshire Country Life	2001		—	£7.00
L6	Vintage Agricultural Traction	2003		—	£7.00
L6	Vintage Motive Power	2004		—	£5.00
L10	Vintage Tractors	2002		—	£5.00
LT6	Wilford Bowls Club	2007		—	£4.00
LT6	Young of British Birds	2007		—	£4.00
	WILTSHIRE LIBRARY				
EL13	Wiltshire Railcards 1st Series	1978		30p	£3.50
EL8	Wiltshire Railcards 2nd Series	1979		45p	£3.50
	WIMPY				
M20	Super Heroes Super Villains	1979		£1.50	£30.00

Size & quantity	TRADE CARD ISSUES	Date	Handbook reference	Price per card	Complete set
	WINGATE CARDS				
10	Team Line—Ups (1950/60s Football Teams)	2014	—		£5.00
	WINGS				
M5	Back to the Egg — Paul McCartney	c1980		£3.00	—
	WINTERLAND (USA)				
LT10	Backstreet Boys Awards	2000		—	£4.00
LT4	Backstreet Boys Black & Blue	2000		—	£3.00
LT15	Backstreet Boys Hot Shots	2000		—	£4.00
LT25	Backstreet Boys Millennium	2000		—	£5.00
	WIZARDS				
LT80	F.A. Premier League 2001-02 (Football)	2001		20p	£12.00
LT250	F.A. Premier League 2001-02 (Football)	2001		20p	£30.00
EL81	Harry Potter & The Sorcerer's Stone	2001		—	£20.00
	A Nos 1 to 40			30p	—
	B Nos 41 to 81			20p	£8.00
EL40	Harry Potter & The Sorcerer's Stone Parallel Series	2001		£2.00	—
	WOMAN'S OWN				
8	Film Stars	c1956	HW-45	£8.00	—
	WONDERBREAD (USA)				
LT24	Close Encounters of The Third Kind	1977		—	£15.00
	WONDERBREAD/TOPPS (USA)				
LT24	American Football Stars	1976		—	£7.50
	WOOD & CO				
24	Island of Ceylon	1964	HX-47	£6.00	—
	E. WOODHEAD & SONS				
25	Types of British Soldiers	1914	HX-144	£34.00	—
	WOOLWORTHS				
M24	Guinness Book of Records	1989		—	£7.50
	WOOLWORTHS-TOPPS (USA)				
LT33	Baseball Highlights	1988		—	£8.00
	WORLD CRICKET INC (New Zealand)				
LT18	New Zealand Cricketers 2007	2007		75p	—
LT27	New Zealand Cricketers 2008	2008		—	£9.50
LT25	New Zealand Cricketers 2009	2009		50p	—
	WORTHINGTON (BEST BITTER)				
36	Sportsmen from 1920 to 1940 (Reprints from various cigarette card issues)	1992		£1.25	£45.00
	WRIGHTS BISCUITS LTD				
24	Marvels of the World	1968	HX-234	20p	£3.50
24	Mischief Goes to Mars:				
	A 'Join the Mischief Club' at base	1954		20p	£5.00
	B 'Issued by Wright's Biscuits Ltd' at base	1954		40p	£10.00
	C Name at side, but not at base	1954		25p	£6.00

Size & quantity	TRADE CARD ISSUES	Date	Handbook reference	Price per card	Complete set
	YORKSHIRE FRAMING CO				
25	England World Cup 2006 (Football)	2006		—	£7.50
14	The 36th Ryder Cup	2006		—	£5.00
	YOUNG BRITAIN				
MP15	Favourite Cricketers Series (2 pictures per card)	1922		£9.00	—
	YOUR CLASSIC MAGAZINE				
50	Cars	c1980		£4.00	—
	ZELLERS (Canada)				
L24	Batman Returns	1992		—	£10.00
	ANONYMOUS				
50	Animals of the World	1954	HX-93	20p	£5.00
4	Birds, Nests and Eggs	c1960		75p	£3.00
25	Bridges of the World	1958	HX-132	20p	£3.50
25	British Coins and Costumes	1958	HX-191	20p	£3.50
25	British Uniforms of the 19th Century:		HX-78		
	A Black back	c1965		32p	£8.00
	B Blue back	c1965		20p	£4.50
20	Budgerigars (officially indented by issuer)	1957		60p	£12.00
25	Cacti	c1965	HX-133	20p	£3.50
M137	Caricatures of Cricketers (no Artist's signature)	c1990		—	£70.00
M50	Caricatures of Cricketers by 'Mac'	c1990		—	£25.00
M83	Caricatures of Cricketers by Mickey Durling	c1990		—	£42.00
25	Castles of Britain	c1960	HX-134	60p	—
25	Children of All Nations	1958		20p	£3.50
25	The Circus	1964	HX-79	60p	—
25	Family Pets	1964	HX-136	40p	—
? K300	Film & Entertainment Stars	c1960		50p	—
	A 10 Different Male Stars (size 44 x 28mm) (our selection)	c1960		—	£3.50
	B 10 Different Female Stars (size 50 x 25mm) (our selection)	c1960		—	£3.50
25	Flags and Emblems	c1965	HX-17	40p	—
25	Flowers	c1970		20p	£3.50
25	Football Clubs and Badges	c1960	HX-137	20p	£5.00
110	General Interest Series	c1970		—	£12.00
40	Greats from the States (Golf)	1994		60p	—
50	Jewish Life in Many Lands	c1960		£1.20	£60.00
	Jewish Symbols & Ceremonies:				
50	A Complete set	1961		£2.00	£55.00
25	B Numbers 1 to 25 only	1961		20p	£3.50
25	Modern Aircraft	1958	HX-219	40p	—
L12	Motor Cycles 1907-1950	1987		30p	£3.50
25	Musical Instruments	1967		20p	£3.50
25	Pigeons	1971		20p	£5.00
25	Pond Life	c1970	HX-81	20p	£3.50
1	Soldier — Bugler	c1970		—	£2.50
25	Sports of the Countries	c1970		80p	—
25	Tropical Birds	c1960	HX-13.1	20p	£4.50
1	Venice in London	c1970		—	£1.00

FILM AND ENTERTAINMENT ** STARS **

These miniature glossy photographs were issued anonymously around 1960 and we can supply the following at 50p each

Size approx 44 x 28mm

Pier Angelli
Brigitte Bardot
* Warren Beatty
Ann Blyth
Dirk Bogarde
Marlon Brando
Max Bygraves
* Eddie Byrnes
Rory Calhoun
Rosemary Clooney
Perry Como
Doris Day
Yvonne De Carlo
Diana Dors
* Duanne Eddy
Anita Ekberg
Vera-Ellen
Ava Gardner
* James Garner
Mitzi Gaynor
Richard Greene
Susan Hayward
Audrey Hepburn
* Jeffrey Hunter
Glynis Johns

Shirley Jones
Kay Kendall
Deborah Kerr
Frankie Laine
Mario Lanza (light suit)
Piper Laurie
June Laverick
Belinda Lee
Janet Leigh
Liberace
Gina Lollobrigida
Sophia Loren
Dennis Lotis
Virginia McKenna
Gordon Macrae
Jayne Mansfield
Dean Martin
Victor Mature
Virginia Mayo
* Sal Mineo
Guy Mitchell
Terry Moore
Kenneth More
George Nader
Sheree North

Kim Novak
Debra Paget
Laya Raki
Johnnie Ray
Debbie Reynolds (swimsuit)
Debbie Reynolds (head)
* Cliff Richard
Jane Russell
Janette Scott
Jean Simmons
* Roger Smith
* Tommy Steele
Maureen Swanson
Elizabeth Taylor
Mamie Van Doren
* Frankie Vaughan (h&s)
Frankie Vaughan (singing)
Esther Williams
Shelley Winters
Natalie Wood

Size approx 50 x 25mm

Lucille Ball
* Cyd Charisse
Jeanne Crain
* Linda Darnell (black top)
Linda Darnell (swimsuit)
Doris Day

Yvonne De Carlo
* Dale Evans (sitting)
* Dale Evans (standing)
Ava Gardner (black top)
* Ava Gardner (skirt)
* Gloria Grahame
Susan Hayward

* Hedy Lamarr
Ann Miller
* Gale Robbins
* Jane Russell
* Beryl Wallace
Esther Williams

SPECIAL OFFER:
The 10 male stars marked with an asterisk * for £3.50
The 10 female stars marked with an asterisk * for £3.50

TOP TRUMPS

We have available the following Top Trumps sets that were issued between 1978 and 1980. These sets of colour photos can also be used as a card game.

TOP TRUMPS (UK) (CARD GAMES)

L33	Dragsters (Series 7)	1978	£5.00
L33	Flowers (Quartets)	1978	£5.00
L33	Rockets	1980	£5.00

MINI TRUMPS SERIES 1

K25	Dragsters	1978	£4.00

MINI TRUMPS SERIES 2

* K25	Grand Prix Cars	1978	£4.00
* K25	Hot Rods	1978	£4.00
* K25	Jumbos and Jets	1978	£4.00
K25	Rally Cars	1978	£4.00
K25	Super Trains	1978	£4.00
K25	Vintage Racers	1978	£4.00

SUPER MINI TRUMPS SERIES 1

* M25	Dragster Bikes	1978	£4.00
* M25	Formula Cars	1978	£4.00
M25	Helicopters	1978	£4.00
* M25	Stock Cars	1978	£4.00

SUPER MINI TRUMPS SERIES 2

M25	Dragsters	1978	£4.00
* M25	H P Giants (Lorries etc)	1978	£4.00
* M25	Super Cars	1978	£4.00
* M25	Super Dragsters	1978	£4.00

SPECIAL OFFER:
The 9 sets marked with an asterisk * for £19.00 (saving £8.00)

SECTION 5

LIEBIG CARD ISSUES

Prices are for **Good Condition**. (More recent series will be of a higher quality.)
We do have a selection of sets from the 1-300 series. Please send a wants list and we will quote prices and condition of any we can supply.

In 1847, Justus von Liebig, an eminent German chemist at the Royal Pharmacy in Munich, published a treatise titled *Extractum Carnis* in which he described how a concentrated essence could be made from fresh meat. However, the cost of production was prohibitive until the vast herds of cattle on the grasslands of South America could be exploited

In 1863 an engineer, George Giebert, established a factory at Frey Bentos in Uruguay and began shipping low-cost extract to Liebig in Europe. After testing at a depot in Antwerp, the extract was sold in stone jars each with a distinctive label bearing the signature of Baron von Liebig who had been honoured for his contribution to science. The business expanded rapidly and in 1865 the Liebig's Extract of Meat Company Limited, with a capital of half a million pounds, was set up in London.

Trade cards had been circulating on the Continent since the 1850s, and the Liebig Company soon latched on to the fact that colourful cards were an excellent form of advertisement. In 1872, only a short time before the Baron died, the first cards or 'chromos' were published to show the production of Liebig extract. During the following 100 years, no fewer than 1863 different series were to be issued, ending in 1973, a few years after Liebig merged with Brooke Bond and became part of Brooke Bond Oxo.

Except for the earliest series issued before 1883, almost all the sets comprise six cards, although a few later issues were of 12 or 18. In a large format, approximately 110 x 70 mm, the cards were distributed in many countries and were printed in a number of languages, the most common of which were Italian, German and French, plus Bohemian, Danish, Dutch, Flemish, Hungarian, Russian, Spanish and Swedish. A few were in English, but these are rarely seen.

The cards were given away as complete sets in exchange for coupons. On the backs of many of the earlier cards was printed the signature 'J. v Liebig' in large blue script, a reflection of the number of imitation products which were marketed, some ending in protracted lawsuits. On one of the English language issues appears the words 'Caution. – A sort called 'Baron Liebig's Extract' with photo of Baron Liebig has no connection whatever with the Baron. Insist on having Liebig Company's Extract – avoid all imitation extracts.'

There is no doubt as to the authenticity of the cards, however. Printed on coated cardboard by the hand lithographic method using up to twelve colours, they are fine examples of the printer's art. The subjects cover almost every field of knowledge and human activity; the arts, places and scenes from many countries, historical events, the customs of different peoples, their fashions and occupations, ancient and colourful festivals, weapons of war and military uniforms, natural history in its many forms, bird, animal, insect and marine life, science, social and industrial life of past ages, various forms of transport old and new, sports and pastimes, etc. The Liebig 'chromos' provide very wide scope and a most fertile field for the specialist.

In the ensuing pages, we list all but the earliest three hundred series showing the number in the set, the internationally recognised 'Fada reference number', a translation of the subject description, an approximate date of issue, and the price per set. We do have a selection of sets from the 1-300 series. Please send a wants list and we will quote prices and condition of any we can supply. Only the 'Chromos' are covered, and collectors are referred to Section 4 Trade Card Issues for details of pre-war Oxo cards and the many post-war issues of Brooke Bond.

Incidentally, readers may be interested to know that the fascinating story of the Liebig Oxo Company and its card issues was published in numbers 484 to 486 of *Card Collectors News*, copies of which are still available @ £3.75 for the 3 copies plus £2.00 handling fee.

How to Use this Section

The series are listed in the same order as shown in the Italian-language Fada Liebig Catalogue, officially recognised by the Liebig Company. These are the 'F' reference numbers shown in the left-hand column. The second column shows the 'S' numbers which refer to the Sanguinetti Liebig listings which some collectors use for their numbering reference. The third column is the number of cards in the set, followed by an English language translation of the series title. The right-hand columns show the approximate date of issue and the price per set, in good average condition. Please see front of the catalogue for how to order cards etc

F No.	S No.	Qty	LIEBIG CARD ISSUES Title (English Translation)	Date	Set Price
301	293	6	Popular Songs	1891	£180.00
302	294	6	Playing Cards	1891	£140.00
303	295	6	Horses in the Circus	1891	£90.00
304	296	6	Child Clowns	1891	£140.00
305	297	6	Shells	1891	£90.00
306	299	6	Little Chefs III	1891	£250.00
307	298	6	Little Chefs IV	1891	—
308	300	6	National Dances II	1891	£80.00
309	303	6	Famous Explorers	1891	£110.00
310	304	6	Liebig in Africa	1891	£40.00
311	301	6	Where Liebig is Used	1891	£60.00
312	306	6	Adventures on the Railway	1891	—
313	307	6	Scattered Flowers	1891	£220.00
314	317	6	The Thieving Magpie (Opera by Rossini)	1891	£120.00
315	308	6	Nymphs with Sashes	1891	£80.00
316	309	6	Puzzle Pictures IX	1891	—
317	310	6	Puzzle Pictures X	1891	£100.00
318	320	6	Inventions of the 19th Century	1891	£75.00
319	311	6	Italian Plays	1891	£40.00
320	312	6	The Beautiful Melusina	1891	£45.00
321	313	6	Caricatures of Negroes	1891	£125.00
322	314	6	Marriage Costumes of different countries	1891	£125.00
323	318	6	Pierrot's Illness	1891	—
324	319	6	Food and Meals - menus	1891	£90.00
325	321	6	Proverbs II	1891	£100.00
326	322	6	The Illness of Pierrot	1891	£50.00
327	325	6	Symbols (Bird and People)	1891	£50.00
328	326	6	Coats of Arms	1891	—
329	327	6	Tea	1891	£50.00
330	329	12	Alphabet Girls	1892	£175.00
331	330	6	The Argonauts	1892	£75.00
332	355	6	Planets	1892	£150.00
333	332	6	The Bull	1892	£40.00
334	333	6	Songs IX	1892	—
335	334	6	The Coalman and The Englishman	1892	£450.00
336	335	6	Venetian Carnivals	1892	£50.00
337	336	6	Playing Cards IV	1892	—
338	337	6	The Ant and the Grasshopper	1892	£70.00
339	338	6	Father, Son and Donkey	1892	£55.00
340	339	6	Christopher Columbus II	1892	£60.00
341	340	6	National Dances III	1892	£100.00
342	341	6	National Dances IV	1892	£90.00
343	331	6	National Beauties II	1892	£80.00
344	342	6	Flower Girls IV	1892	£175.00
345	353	6	Faust (opera)	1892	£65.00
346	343	6	Gargantua (Giant)	1892	£85.00
347	344	6	Children's Games	1892	£75.00
348	345	6	Gnomes	1892	£100.00
349	365	6	The Trojan War	1892	£60.00
350	348	6	Puzzle Pictures XI	1892	£60.00
351	347	6	Puzzle Pictures XII	1892	£90.00
352	346	6	Puzzle Pictures XIII	1892	£70.00
353	349	6	Language of Flowers III	1892	£90.00
354	350	6	Natural Resources II	1892	£70.00
355	351	6	Christmas in Different Countries	1892	—
356	386	6	Christmas Customs in different countries	1892	£50.00
357	354	6	Geological Periods	1892	£50.00
358	356	6	Sleeping Beauty	1892	£50.00

F No.	S No.	Qty	LIEBIG CARD ISSUES Title (English Translation)	Date	Set Price
359	357	6	Problems II	1892	£75.00
360	358	6	Proverbs III	1892	£70.00
361	360	6	When you are alone and in Company	1892	£85.00
362	363	6	Puzzle Pictures VIII	1892	£110.00
363	362	6	Puzzle Pictures IX	1892	£110.00
364	361	6	Puzzle Pictures X	1892	£110.00
365	359	6	Grannie's Present, Mr. Punch	1892	£200.00
366	364	6	History of Writing I	1892	£50.00
367	366	6	Birds and Flowers	1892	£80.00
368	367	6	The Emperor William's Voyage	1892	£200.00
369	368	6	The Liebig Tree	1893	£50.00
370	369	12	Alphabet of Male Operatic Characters	1893	£110.00
371	375	6	Commerce, Industry and Culture	1893	£50.00
372	371	6	Calendar for 1893 January to June	1893	—
373	372	6	Charlemagne	1893	£50.00
374	373	6	Celebrated Castles	1893	£40.00
375	374	6	Famous Composers I	1893	£80.00
376	376	6	An Unfortunate Mistake	1893	—
377	377	6	Falstaff (Opera)	1893	£55.00
378	379	6	Symbolic Flowers	1893	£40.00
379	380	6	Flowers, Birds and Butterflies	1893	£50.00
380	370	6	Boats II	1893	£140.00
381	381	6	Puzzle Pictures XIV	1893	£75.00
382	382	6	Puzzle Pictures XV	1893	£60.00
383	383	6	Puzzle Pictures XVI	1893	£180.00
384	384	6	Puzzle Pictures XVII	1893	£125.00
385	388	6	Lohengrin Opera by Wagner	1893	£70.00
386	385	6	Italian Masquerade VIII	1893	£40.00
387	352	6	Shadowgraphs I	1893	£50.00
388	387	6	Shadowgraphs II	1893	£60.00
389	392	6	Precious Stones	1893	£50.00
390	393	6	Problems III	1893	£70.00
391	421	6	Proverbs IV	1893	£275.00
392	394	6	Picture Puzzle XI	1893	—
393	395	6	Picture Puzzle XII	1893	£175.00
394	391	6	Opera Scenes III	1893	£40.00
395	389	6	A Midsummer's Night Dream	1893	£35.00
396	396	6	States of America	1893	£110.00
397	397	6	Styles of Architecture	1893	£40.00
398	398	6	Story of France	1893	£45.00
399	399	6	The Magic Table	1893	£90.00
400	400	6	The Telephone	1893	—
401	401	6	The Trumpeter from Sakkingen	1893	£120.00
402	402	6	The Voyage of Mr. Durand	1893	£70.00
403	403	6	Travel Around the World	1893	£40.00
404	390	6	The Walkyries (Opera)	1893	£90.00
405	434	6	The Weather	1894	—
406	435	6	Adventure in the Congo	1894	—
407	405	6	Popular Songs X	1894	£60.00
408	436	6	Seaside Towns	1894	£90.00
409	406	6	Famous Composers II	1894	£60.00
410	407	6	The Legend of Frithjof	1894	£40.00
411	408	6	In Japan	1894	£55.00
412	409	6	Magic	1894	£90.00
413	410	6	Months of the Year	1894	£70.00
414	411	6	Children's Occupations	1894	£70.00
415	412	6	Scandinavian Mythology	1894	£70.00
416	413	6	The World of Children	1894	£60.00

F No.	S No.	Qty	LIEBIG CARD ISSUES Title (English Translation)	Date	Set Price
417	414	6	Monograms	1894	£45.00
418	415	6	The Dwarf Nose (Fairy Tale)	1894	£40.00
419	416	6	Christmas Scenes I	1894	£60.00
420	417	6	Marriage	1894	—
421	419	6	Theft IV (Pierrott)	1894	£100.00
422	420	6	Problems IV	1894	£40.00
423	422	6	Proverbs V	1894	£70.00
424	423	6	Puzzle Pictures XIII	1894	—
425	424	6	Puzzle Pictures XIV	1894	£130.00
426	404	6	Masked Ball	1894	—
427	425	6	Carnival Scenes	1894	£110.00
428	418	6	Opera Scenes IV (Caricatures)	1894	£50.00
429	431	6	Views of Venice	1894	£50.00
430	428	6	Leisure Sports	1894	£60.00
431	427	6	Theatre Scenes	1894	£60.00
432	426	6	The Story of Writing II	1894	£40.00
433	429	6	Story of France II	1894	—
434	430	6	History of Transport	1894	—
435	432	6	Around the Mediterranean	1894	£40.00
436	433	6	Arts and Crafts	1895	£45.00
437	438	6	Hunting	1895	£45.00
438	439	6	The Wild Hunter (poem by Wolff)	1895	£70.00
439	454	6	Carmen (Opera)	1895	£80.00
440	441	6	Circus Scenes with children	1895	£250.00
441	449	6	Letters of Liebig with Flowers	1895	£40.00
442	447	6	Times of the Day	1895	£60.00
443	444	6	Children's Faces with Flowers	1895	£55.00
444	445	6	Flower Girls' Bodies	1895	£50.00
445	459	6	On and Off Stage	1895	£65.00
446	446	6	Winged People	1895	£60.00
447	448	6	Puzzle Pictures XVIII	1895	£80.00
448	450	6	Madame Sans-Gene by Sardov	1895	£130.00
449	451	6	The Seven Wonders of the World	1895	£60.00
450	437	6	Barometer Children	1895	£225.00
451	452	6	Christmas II	1895	£90.00
452	453	6	Shipping Through the Ages	1895	£60.00
453	455	6	The Oyster and the Pilgrims	1895	£55.00
454	442	6	Children with Kitchen Utensils	1895	£90.00
455	456	6	Children Growing Up	1895	£90.00
456	457	6	Provinces of France III	1895	£70.00
457	458	6	Romeo and Juliet	1895	£45.00
458	443	6	Scenes in the Moonlight	1895	£75.00
459	460	6	Snow White and the Seven Dwarfs	1895	£100.00
460	461	6	Sport I (English)	1895	—
461	462	6	Sport II	1895	£120.00
462	494	6	Sports III	1895	£90.00
463	495	6	Winter Sports I	1895	£75.00
464	463	6	Till the Buffoon	1895	£60.00
465	464	6	Wine	1895	£50.00
466	485	6	The African (Opera)	1896	£55.00
467	465	6	The Arts II	1896	£45.00
468	467	6	The Hunt	1896	£350.00
469	468	6	Views of Cities	1896	£40.00
470	500	6	The Course of Life I	1896	£90.00
471	469	6	Ancient Gods	1896	£60.00
472	471	6	Women and Children in Different Countries	1896	£50.00
473	472	6	Mythological Scenes	1896	£50.00
474	473	6	Fables of La Fontaine II	1896	—

F No.	S No.	Qty	LIEBIG CARD ISSUES Title (English Translation)	Date	Set Price
475	474	6	Alpine Flowers	1896	£55.00
476	475	6	Flowers with Cupids	1896	£50.00
477	476	6	The Two Smokers	1896	—
478	477	6	Gargantua II (Giant)	1896	—
479	478	6	The Policemen and the Apple Thieves	1896	£60.00
480	488	6	People Young and Old	1896	£50.00
481	479	6	Hansel and Gretel	1896	£70.00
482	480	6	Puzzle Pictures XIX	1896	£45.00
483	481	6	Musical Instruments	1896	£65.00
484	482	6	The Kaethchen Von Hielbronn (Play)	1896	£50.00
485	490	6	Mountain People	1896	£50.00
486	484	6	Christmas III	1896	£50.00
487	487	6	German Town Halls	1896	£35.00
488	489	6	Celebrated Painters	1896	£35.00
489	491	6	Famous Queens	1896	£35.00
490	470	6	Old German Proverbs	1896	£50.00
491	492	6	French Provinces IV	1896	£40.00
492	493	6	The Valiant Tailor	1896	£90.00
493	466	6	Comic Animal Scenes II	1896	£70.00
494	483	6	Army on Manoeuvres	1896	£45.00
495	496	6	Bible Stories V	1896	£45.00
496	497	6	Wandering Musicians	1896	£80.00
497	486	6	Tannhauser (Opera)	1896	£50.00
498	498	6	Theatre of Berlin I	1896	£45.00
499	499	6	Theatre of Berlin II	1896	£55.00
500	501	6	Trees of Different Latitudes	1897	£30.00
501	502	6	Types of Warships	1897	£35.00
502	507	6	German Dramatists	1897	£45.00
503	504	6	Variety Acts	1897	£30.00
504	505	6	Popular Songs XI	1897	£60.00
505	506	6	The Carnival in Rome	1897	£25.00
506	508	6	Shells II	1897	£40.00
507	509	6	Cooper's Adventures with the Red Indians	1897	£40.00
508	510	6	Special Army Corps	1897	£25.00
509	511	6	Biggest Natural Phenomena	1897	£30.00
510	512	6	Crusades I	1897	£30.00
511	513	6	Crusades II	1897	£35.00
512	514	6	Famous Women in History	1897	£22.00
513	515	6	Natural Tricks of Light	1897	£30.00
514	516	6	Scenes from the time of the Caliphs	1897	£30.00
515	517	6	Journey into the Alps	1897	£23.00
516	518	6	Butterflies of Central Europe IV	1897	£35.00
517	519	6	Butterflies and Moths V	1897	£35.00
518	520	6	Flowers and Lovers	1897	£30.00
519	526	6	The Letters of Liebig with Flowers	1897	£50.00
520	521	6	Postage Stamps I	1897	£30.00
521	522	6	Fungi	1897	£32.00
522	523	6	In Japan II	1897	£25.00
523	524	6	The Discovery of the Route to the Indies	1897	£20.00
524	525	6	Puzzle Pictures XX	1897	£30.00
525	527	6	The Conquest of Mexico	1897	£25.00
526	529	6	Orders of Chivalry I	1897	£25.00
527	530	6	Pastimes for Winter and Summer	1897	£30.00
528	528	6	The Prophet (Opera)	1897	£22.00
529	533	6	Provinces of France V	1897	£25.00
530	539	6	The Pied Piper	1897	£55.00
531	503	6	Cattle Breeds	1897	£20.00
532	531	6	Types of Poultry	1897	£40.00

F No.	S No.	Qty	LIEBIG CARD ISSUES Title (English Translation)	Date	Set Price
533	532	6	The First Pipe Tobacco or Sweets	1897	£40.00
534	541	6	The Snow Ball	1897	£50.00
535	534	6	Famous Sculptors	1897	£30.00
536	535	6	The Five Senses II	1897	£25.00
537	536	6	History of France III	1897	£30.00
538	537	6	History of the Telegraph	1897	£30.00
539	538	6	Horse-drawn Carriages	1897	£45.00
540	540	6	Exotic Flowers and Birds VII	1897	£40.00
541	542	6	Signs of the Zodiac	1897	£70.00
542	543	12	The Alphabet (Male National Costumes)	1898	£50.00
543	545	6	Fishing for Whales	1898	£30.00
544	546	6	Hunting Scenes XII	1898	£25.00
545	547	6	Cantons of Switzerland	1898	£30.00
546	570	6	Children's Nursery Rhymes III	1898	£300.00
547	548	6	Popular Folksongs XIII	1898	£35.00
548	549	6	Carnival Serenades	1898	£22.00
549	550	6	Royal Castles of Bavaria	1898	£30.00
550	551	6	Children with Kitchen Utensils	1898	£35.00
551	552	6	Don Quixote	1898	£25.00
552	556	6	Flower Girls V	1898	£32.00
553	578	6	Uses of Liebig IV	1898	—
554	554	6	Flower Children	1898	£30.00
555	555	6	Moths of the Night of Central Europe	1898	£28.00
556	557	6	Rivers of Europe	1898	£25.00
557	558	6	Happy Children	1898	£30.00
558	559	6	Puzzle Pictures XXI	1898	£30.00
559	560	6	Puzzle Pictures XXII	1898	£30.00
560	561	6	National Musical Instruments II	1898	£25.00
561	562	6	The Book	1898	£25.00
562	563	6	Language of Flowers IV	1898	£25.00
563	564	6	Monuments of Ancient Rome	1898	£30.00
564	565	6	Children and Balloons	1898	£35.00
565	566	6	The Cultivation of Plants in Warm Countries	1898	£20.00
566	567	6	Celebrated Poets	1898	£20.00
567	568	6	Provinces of Spain	1898	£30.00
568	569	6	Provinces of Italy	1898	£24.00
569	572	6	Robezahl (Fable)	1898	£50.00
570	571	6	Nursery Rhymes IV	1898	£90.00
571	553	6	Elephant Tales	1898	£35.00
572	544	6	Snow White and Rose Red	1898	£55.00
573	574	6	Sport (Grand Ballet of L. Manzotti)	1898	£25.00
574	575	6	Styles of Architecture II	1898	£25.00
575	573	6	Scenes of Old France IV	1898	£30.00
576	576	6	Children's Natural History	1898	£30.00
577	577	6	Variety Actions	1898	£30.00
578	579	6	Modes of Travel	1898	£25.00
579	609	12	Alphabet (Female National Costumes) IV	1899	£80.00
580	602	6	Beasts of Burden	1899	£20.00
581	580	6	National Drinks	1899	£24.00
582	581	6	Bismark	1899	£25.00
583	582	6	The Naughty Dog	1899	£50.00
584	583	6	Famous Waterfall	1899	£20.00
585	596	6	Musical Celebrities	1899	£25.00
586	584	6	Views of European Cities	1899	£20.00
587	586	6	The Danube	1899	£24.00
588	585	6	Cuba	1899	£20.00
589	587	6	The Making of Iron	1899	£20.00
590	588	6	Popular Festivals Masked	1899	£20.00

F No.	S No.	Qty	LIEBIG CARD ISSUES Title (English Translation)	Date	Set Price
591	589	6	Postage Stamps II	1899	£35.00
592	590	6	Gnomes	1899	£40.00
593	591	6	The Development of Artificial Illuminations	1899	£20.00
594	592	6	Puzzle Pictures XXIII	1899	£25.00
595	593	6	National Anthems II (with music)	1899	£70.00
596	594	6	Inventors I	1899	£22.00
597	595	6	Marine Fauna	1899	£20.00
598	597	6	Orders of Chivalry II	1899	£22.00
599	598	6	The Tit Family	1899	£20.00
600	599	6	Fish and Fishing II	1899	£28.00
601	600	6	Famous Bridges	1899	£20.00
602	601	6	Art Forms	1899	£22.00
603	603	6	Richard III by Shakespeare	1899	£20.00
604	604	6	Sea Rescues	1899	£20.00
605	605	6	Comic Situations	1899	£22.00
606	606	6	In Transvaal	1899	£20.00
607	608	6	European Military Uniforms	1899	£20.00
608	607	6	Birds - Fowl	1899	£25.00
609	638	6	Hamlet (Opera)	1900	£20.00
610	610	6	Balloons	1900	£40.00
611	611	6	Children's Army	1900	£60.00
612	612	6	Doll Making	1900	£35.00
613	613	6	Country Children	1900	£25.00
614	629	6	Story of the Little Brother and Sister	1900	£40.00
615	614	6	At the Races	1900	£25.00
616	615	6	Breeds of Dogs I	1900	£50.00
617	616	6	Popular Songs	1900	£65.00
618	617	6	German Colonies	1900	£45.00
619	618	6	Colours II	1900	£32.00
620	619	6	Military Uniforms in Different Ages	1900	£25.00
621	620	6	National Dances V	1900	£22.00
622	651	6	In the World of the Birds	1900	£35.00
623	621	6	Famous Words of Schiller & Goethe	1900	£50.00
624	622	6	Asiatic Women	1900	£40.00
625	623	6	Duelling	1900	£20.00
626	624	12	World Exhibition 1900 Paris	1900	£75.00
627	625	6	Fable of La Fontaine III	1900	£40.00
628	626	6	Neapolitan Festivals	1900	£20.00
629	627	6	From Field and Forest	1900	£22.00
630	628	6	Postage Stamps III	1900	£30.00
631	630	6	Fruits and Women in Costume	1900	£20.00
632	631	6	Edible Fungi II	1900	£30.00
633	632	6	Gnomes and Elves	1900	£45.00
634	633	6	Grottos and Caves	1900	£25.00
635	634	6	William Tell	1900	£20.00
636	635	6	Inventors	1900	£65.00
637	636	6	The Philippine Islands	1900	£20.00
638	637	6	Monuments of Naval Heroes	1900	£20.00
639	639	6	Gold	1900	£20.00
640	640	6	The Poor Fisherman from 1001 Nights	1900	£35.00
641	641	6	Famous Regiments	1900	£25.00
642	642	6	Salt	1900	£20.00
643	648	6	Opera Scenes	1900	£25.00
644	643	6	The Swan Princess	1900	£40.00
645	644	6	Sinbad the Sailor	1900	£28.00
646	647	6	Bible Story VI	1900	£20.00
647	645	6	Dreams	1900	£25.00
648	646	6	Story of France V	1900	£20.00

F No.	S No.	Qty	LIEBIG CARD ISSUES Title (English Translation)	Date	Set Price
649	649	6	The World and its Inhabitants	1900	£20.00
650	650	6	Treasures of the Earth	1900	£20.00
651	652	6	The Glass Industry I	1900	£20.00
652	653	6	Volcanoes	1900	£20.00
653	654	6	The Manufacture of Sugar	1900	£20.00
654	667	6	Adventures of a Kite	1901	£65.00
655	657	6	Weapons of War through the Ages	1901	£20.00
656	658	6	Bicycle Games	1901	£40.00
657	664	6	What the Children Find in the Forest	1901	£50.00
658	659	6	Scenes of China I	1901	£20.00
659	660	6	Scenes of China II	1901	£20.00
660	661	6	Cyrano de Bergerac (Play)	1901	£18.00
661	662	6	Colours of the Rainbow	1901	£28.00
662	663	6	French Theatre	1901	—
663	689	6	The Course of Life	1901	£25.00
664	665	6	Easter Customs	1901	£18.00
665	666	6	Marriage Costumes	1901	£18.00
666	655	6	The Restaurant	1901	£20.00
667	668	6	Pheasants	1901	£25.00
668	669	6	Festivals of Ancient Times	1901	£20.00
669	675	6	Fidelio (Opera)	1901	£35.00
670	676	6	Der Freischutz (Opera)	1901	£18.00
671	685	6	The Two Envious Sisters from 1001 Nights	1901	£40.00
672	670	6	Seaside Children's Games	1901	—
673	671	6	The Island of Caroline	1901	£18.00
674	672	6	Famous Lakes	1901	£18.00
675	673	6	The Three Musketeers	1901	£20.00
676	656	6	The Christmas Tree	1901	£25.00
677	677	6	The Sparrow with Split Tongue (Japanese Fable)	1901	£18.00
678	678	6	Mountain Passes	1901	£18.00
679	679	6	Prince Achmed & Fairy Paribanu from 1001 Nights	1901	£45.00
680	680	6	The Rhine from Bingen to Coblenz	1901	£140.00
681	681	6	Course of the Rhine	1901	£18.00
682	682	6	The Rhine in History	1901	£18.00
683	683	6	Medieval War Scenes	1901	£18.00
684	674	6	Dutch Scenes	1901	£22.00
685	684	6	Composers	1901	£40.00
686	686	6	Famous Street Scenes from around the World	1901	£20.00
687	687	6	Johann Strauss and His Operas	1901	£18.00
688	688	6	Types and People of Hindustan	1901	£20.00
689	690	6	Unusual Trees	1902	£16.00
690	691	6	Special Armies	1902	£16.00
691	692	6	Architectural Art	1902	£16.00
692	694	6	Spa Towns	1902	£16.00
693	695	6	Famous City Ruins	1902	£40.00
694	715	6	Cultivation of Tobacco in Sumatra	1902	£16.00
695	696	6	Commerce	1902	£16.00
696	697	6	The Count of Monte Cristo	1902	£16.00
697	726	6	The Seven Ravens and the True Sister (Story)	1902	£35.00
698	728	6	Ancient Customs of the Provinces of France	1902	—
699	698	6	Whitsun Customs	1902	£16.00
700	699	6	Entertainments and Festivals in the Middle Ages	1902	£16.00
701	700	6	Spices	1902	£16.00
702	701	6	The Elephant	1902	£22.00
703	702	6	France in Olden Times	1902	£16.00
704	703	6	Game Bird Shooting	1902	£20.00
705	693	6	Famous Leaders	1902	£20.00
706	704	6	The Island of Samoa	1902	£16.00

F No.	S No.	Qty	LIEBIG CARD ISSUES Title (English Translation)	Date	Set Price
707	709	6	King Drosselbart	1902	£28.00
708	705	6	Naval Manoeuvres	1902	£24.00
709	706	6	Bread	1902	£16.00
710	707	6	Useful Plants	1902	£16.00
711	708	6	Homing Pigeon	1902	£20.00
712	710	6	Famous Rocks	1902	£16.00
713	711	6	Scenes from the History of Civilisation	1902	£16.00
714	712	6	Schools	1902	£16.00
715	713	6	Symbolic Flowers	1902	£40.00
716	714	6	History of France in the 16th Century VI	1902	£16.00
717	716	6	Treasures of the Sea	1902	£18.00
718	717	6	The Life of Verdi	1902	£17.00
719	752	6	The Life of a Director	1902	—
720	718	6	Culinary Art Through the Ages	1903	£16.00
721	719	6	The Art of Medicine	1903	£18.00
722	720	6	Feasts Through the Ages	1903	£16.00
723	722	6	Canals I	1903	£16.00
724	723	6	Canons Through the Ages	1903	£16.00
725	724	6	Horsemen I	1903	£16.00
726	761	6	Chasing the Butterfly	1903	£45.00
727	727	6	Constellations	1903	£25.00
728	729	6	The Heroines from Wagner's Operas	1903	£30.00
729	730	6	Various Scenes of the Uses of Liebig	1903	£28.00
730	731	6	Flower Festivals	1903	£16.00
731	732	6	Japanese Fable – The Mouse's Daughter	1903	£18.00
732	733	6	Rivers in France	1903	£16.00
733	734	6	Ice	1903	£16.00
734	735	6	Gulfs and Bays	1903	£16.00
735	725	6	Famous Conquerors 1st Series	1903	£16.00
736	765	6	Famous Conquerors 2nd Series	1903	£16.00
737	721	6	Types of Boats	1903	£18.00
738	736	6	Useful Insects	1903	£16.00
739	738	6	Alpine Troop Manoeuvres	1903	£16.00
740	739	6	Scenes with Gnomes	1903	£30.00
741	740	6	Flora and Fauna of the Alps	1903	£15.00
742	741	6	Monuments of Famous Captains	1903	£15.00
743	742	6	Monuments of Famous Scientists	1903	£16.00
744	743	6	La Muta dei Portici (Opera)	1903	£15.00
745	744	6	Sea Fishing	1903	£20.00
746	745	6	Use of Stone	1903	£15.00
747	746	6	Nomadic People	1903	£16.00
748	747	6	Clowns	1903	£25.00
749	737	6	Scenes from the Life of Liebig	1903	£15.00
750	748	6	Poisonous Snakes	1903	£20.00
751	750	6	Biblical Scenes VII	1903	£18.00
752	749	6	Sport	1903	£40.00
753	751	6	Drinking Vessels	1903	£15.00
754	754	6	The History of Needlework	1904	£15.00
755	755	6	Inns	1904	£16.00
756	758	6	Animals in Art	1904	£16.00
757	757	6	Famous Animals from History I	1904	£16.00
758	756	6	Famous Animals from History II	1904	£15.00
759	759	6	The Plough	1904	£16.00
760	784	6	The Elements II	1904	£25.00
761	760	6	Butter	1904	£16.00
762	762	6	Uncle Tom's Cabin	1904	£20.00
763	763	6	Cavaliers of Ancient Times II	1904	£18.00
764	764	6	Different Foods	1904	£40.00

F No.	S No.	Qty	LIEBIG CARD ISSUES Title (English Translation)	Date	Set Price
765	766	6	In Korea	1904	£15.00
766	767	6	Processions and Fetes	1904	£15.00
767	768	6	Ancient German Customs	1904	£15.00
768	769	6	Wedding Costumes	1904	£14.00
769	770	6	Dances Through The Ages	1904	£14.00
770	802	6	The Path of Life	1904	£25.00
771	772	6	The Seasons	1904	£22.00
772	774	6	In the Land of the Pharaohs	1904	£15.00
773	775	6	Trans-Siberian Railway	1904	£16.00
774	776	6	Popular Fetes	1904	£15.00
775	800	6	Harvest Ceremonies	1904	£40.00
776	777	6	Children Experimenting	1904	£30.00
777	778	6	Norwegian Fjords	1904	£16.00
778	782	6	The Glove	1904	£45.00
779	783	6	The Goose Girl	1904	£50.00
780	779	6	Water Creatures	1904	£16.00
781	780	6	Life in Japan	1904	£20.00
782	781	6	Cereals	1904	£15.00
783	753	6	Dwellings	1904	£55.00
784	785	6	The Italian Lakes II	1904	£16.00
785	786	6	The Letter	1904	£14.00
786	851	6	The Story of Mother Holle	1904	£50.00
787	787	6	Grandmothers	1904	£25.00
788	798	6	Birds and Their Nests	1904	£55.00
789	788	6	Parsifal (Opera)	1904	£100.00
790	790	6	Parliament Buildings	1904	£14.00
791	791	6	Plants in Decorative Art	1904	£14.00
792	792	6	Poisonous Plants	1904	£14.00
793	793	6	Precious Stones II	1904	£16.00
794	771	6	Scenes in the Lives of Famous Painters	1904	£14.00
795	794	6	Italian Renaissance Art	1904	£14.00
796	789	6	Operas IV	1904	£20.00
797	796	6	Scenes in Spain I	1904	£14.00
798	840	6	Scenes in Spain II	1904	£16.00
799	773	6	Children's Scenes	1904	£75.00
800	795	6	In Servia	1904	£14.00
801	797	6	Modes of Transport	1904	£60.00
802	799	6	Useful Birds	1904	£16.00
803	801	6	One Hundred Years of Travelling	1904	£45.00
804	803	6	Ducks	1905	£15.00
805	804	6	Antwerp in the Middle Ages	1905	£14.00
806	805	6	Dogs – (Head Silhouettes)	1905	£100.00
807	806	6	Views of Capital Cities	1905	£14.00
808	807	6	Rural Dwelling Places in Europe	1905	£14.00
809	808	6	Historic Castles	1905	£15.00
810	809	6	Life in Feudal Castles	1905	£14.00
811	810	6	Popular Customs of India	1905	£14.00
812	811	6	The Crusades	1905	£15.00
813	812	6	Emotions	1905	£25.00
814	813	6	Episodes in the History of Belgium 1st Series	1905	£15.00
815	814	6	Episodes in the History of Belgium 2nd Series	1905	£15.00
816	815	6	Factories of the Hanseatic Towns	1905	£45.00
817	816	6	The Fire in Artistic Industries	1905	£14.00
818	817	6	In Japan III	1905	£14.00
819	823	6	Types of Transport in Japan	1905	£14.00
820	839	6	Days of the Week	1905	£25.00
821	818	6	The War of the Roses	1905	£16.00
822	819	6	House Interiors	1905	£45.00

F No.	S No.	Qty	LIEBIG CARD ISSUES Title (English Translation)	Date	Set Price
823	820	6	Useful Trees	1905	£14.00
824	821	6	Places of Worship	1905	£14.00
825	822	6	Ancient War Machines	1905	—
826	824	6	Migration of People	1905	£14.00
827	825	6	Feminine Dress	1905	£25.00
828	826	6	Windmills	1905	£15.00
829	827	6	Wedding Procession	1905	£20.00
830	828	6	The Marriage of Figaro (Opera)	1905	£25.00
831	829	6	Oberon (Opera)	1905	£20.00
832	831	6	Medals Given to Females	1905	£16.00
833	832	6	Time Pieces	1905	£16.00
834	833	6	In Panama	1905	£16.00
835	834	6	The Fisherman and His Wife	1905	£40.00
836	836	6	Raphael	1905	£16.00
837	837	6	In Rumania	1905	£16.00
838	835	6	Opera Scenes – Leading Ladies	1905	£18.00
839	838	6	Famous Sculptors	1905	£25.00
840	841	6	History of France VII	1905	—
841	842	6	The Theatre - Old and New	1905	£16.00
842	830	6	Le Trouvere (Opera)	1905	£30.00
843	843	6	In Abyssinia	1906	£14.00
844	844	6	Dutch Head-Dress	1906	£16.00
845	846	6	Astronomers	1906	£17.00
846	847	6	Celebrated Colosseums	1906	£15.00
847	848	6	Popular Russian Costume	1906	£15.00
848	849	6	Heroes of Wagner's Operas	1906	£30.00
849	850	6	The Production of a Liebig Card	1906	£30.00
850	852	6	Gardens	1906	£14.00
851	853	6	In India	1906	£18.00
852	854	6	Views of Morocco	1906	£16.00
853	855	6	Materials for Artistic Industries III	1906	£14.00
854	856	6	Life of Mozart	1906	£20.00
855	857	6	Old Holland	1906	£14.00
856	859	6	Famous Italian Town Halls	1906	£14.00
857	860	6	Children in National Dress	1906	£25.00
858	861	6	Pompeii - Then and Now	1906	£15.00
859	862	6	Wells and Fountains	1906	£14.00
860	863	6	The Life of Rembrandt	1906	£14.00
861	864	6	History of Rome	1906	£14.00
862	858	6	Samson and Delilah (Opera)	1906	£18.00
863	845	6	Scenes of Africa	1906	£16.00
864	865	6	The Life of Shakespeare	1906	£16.00
865	866	6	Nymphs	1906	£15.00
866	867	6	Straits of Europe	1906	£15.00
867	868	6	Straits Outside Europe	1906	£16.00
868	869	6	In Sweden	1906	£14.00
869	870	6	The Simplon Tunnel	1906	£15.00
870	871	6	Famous Tragedies	1906	£15.00
871	872	6	Birds of Prey	1906	£15.00
872	873	6	Ensigns and Standards	1906	£15.00
873	874	6	Voyage in the Mediterranean	1906	£14.00
874	875	6	Ancient Dwellings	1907	£14.00
875	876	6	Sources of Water	1907	£14.00
876	877	6	In East Africa	1907	£14.00
877	878	6	Fruit Trees	1907	£14.00
878	879	6	Art in the Metal Industry	1907	£14.00
879	880	6	The Art of Different Races	1907	£14.00
880	881	6	Automobiles	1907	£30.00

F No.	S No.	Qty	Title (English Translation)	Date	Set Price
881	882	6	Cacti	1907	£14.00
882	883	6	The Carnival in Different Ages	1907	£14.00
883	884	6	Flourishing Towns in the Middle Ages	1907	£14.00
884	885	6	Guilds of Middle Ages	1907	£14.00
885	886	6	History of Female Dress	1907	£14.00
886	887	6	History of Male Costume	1907	£14.00
887	888	6	Berceaux Dynastiques	1907	£14.00
888	903	6	Don Juan (Opera)	1907	£25.00
889	889	6	Electricity	1907	£15.00
890	890	6	History of Belgium	1907	£12.00
891	891	6	Lighthouses	1907	£22.00
892	892	6	The Puppets Story	1907	£22.00
893	893	6	Popular Japanese Fetes	1907	£14.00
894	894	6	Markets and Fairs in Different Countries	1907	£14.00
895	895	6	In Finland	1907	£14.00
896	896	6	Flowers and Dragonflies	1907	£16.00
897	897	6	Roman Emperors	1907	£14.00
898	898	6	Inventions of the 19th Century	1907	—
899	899	6	Malta	1907	£20.00
900	900	6	Materials Used for Clothing	1907	£14.00
901	901	6	Famous Merchants	1907	£14.00
902	902	6	Parasols and Umbrellas	1907	£15.00
903	904	6	In Indo-China	1907	£14.00
904	905	6	In Persia	1907	£14.00
905	906	6	Medical Plants	1907	£14.00
906	907	6	In Spring	1907	£50.00
907	908	6	Queens	1907	£40.00
908	909	6	The Legend of Roland	1907	£50.00
909	910	6	In Scandinavia	1907	£14.00
910	911	6	Italian Scenes	1907	£14.00
911	912	6	The Story of Silk	1907	£14.00
912	913	6	On the Beach	1907	£22.00
913	914	6	In Turkistan	1907	£14.00
914	915	6	Views and Costumes in the Alps	1907	£15.00
915	916	6	In Venezuela	1907	£14.00
916	917	6	Afghanistan	1908	£12.00
917	918	6	The Hunter of Furs	1908	£20.00
918	919	6	In the Caucasus	1908	£15.00
919	920	6	In Chile	1908	£20.00
920	921	6	Money of Different Periods	1908	£15.00
921	922	6	Flowers of the Desert	1908	£15.00
922	923	6	Ancient Roman Buildings	1908	£15.00
923	924	6	The Manufacture of Perfume from Roses	1908	£17.00
924	925	6	In the Far West (Cowboys and Indians)	1908	£30.00
925	926	6	Aquatic Plant Life	1908	£20.00
926	927	6	Festival of Flowers II	1908	£15.00
927	928	6	Fetes in Olden Days	1908	£14.00
928	929	6	Flowers of the Night	1908	£15.00
929	930	6	The Flora in the Upper Mountain	1908	£14.00
930	931	6	Fruits and their Enemies in the Animal Kingdom	1908	£16.00
931	932	6	The Making of a Fire	1908	£14.00
932	933	6	Military Uniforms of Different Countries	1908	£16.00
933	934	6	Islands of the Mediterranean	1908	£15.00
934	935	6	The Feminine Arts	1908	£15.00
935	936	6	The Story of Steam Machines	1908	£20.00
936	937	6	Madagascar	1908	£16.00
937	939	6	The Merchant of Venice	1908	£16.00
938	940	6	In Mexico	1908	£16.00

F No.	S No.	Qty	LIEBIG CARD ISSUES Title (English Translation)	Date	Set Price
939	942	6	Mignon (Opera)	1908	£17.00
940	941	6	The Story of Nala and Damavanti	1908	£15.00
941	943	6	Historic Gateways to Cities	1908	£15.00
942	944	6	Harvesting in Different Countries	1908	£14.00
943	938	6	In the Domain of the Medusas (Jellyfish, etc)	1908	£14.00
944	945	6	The Sources Of Important Rivers	1908	£16.00
945	946	6	Birds Who Cannot Fly	1908	£15.00
946	947	6	Journey of Suen-Hedin to Tibet	1908	£20.00
947	948	6	Feminine Head-dress	1909	£20.00
948	949	6	In Burma	1909	£20.00
949	950	6	Famous Cloisters	1909	£14.00
950	951	6	French Colonies	1909	£15.00
951	952	6	The Culture of Cotton	1909	£14.00
952	953	6	The Coast of France	1909	£14.00
953	954	6	Curious and Ancient Writings	1909	£14.00
954	955	6	Episodes from Russian History	1909	£14.00
955	956	6	Children's Occupations	1909	£40.00
955A	956A	6	Children's Occupations	1909	£100.00
956	957	6	Episodes in the History of Famous Towns	1909	£14.00
957	958	6	Alpine Animals	1909	£20.00
958	959	6	Different Railway Systems	1909	£14.00
959	960	6	The Magic Flute (Opera)	1909	£30.00
960	961	6	Living in the Extreme North	1909	£14.00
961	962	6	Light and Illumination	1909	£14.00
962	963	6	Islands of New Guinea	1909	£14.00
963	966	6	Law Courts in Different Countries	1909	£17.00
964	967	6	Road Surfaces	1909	£14.00
965	968	6	Hobbies	1909	£14.00
966	969	6	Medicinal Plants	1909	£14.00
967	970	6	Useful Exotic Plants	1909	£14.00
968	971	6	Coastal Ports	1909	£15.00
969	973	6	In the Republic of Argentina	1909	£18.00
970	964	6	Robert the Devil (Opera)	1909	£15.00
971	974	6	Frederic de Schiller	1909	£18.00
972	975	6	Servicing at the Table in Ancient Times	1909	£14.00
973	976	6	Solanum (Plants)	1909	£14.00
974	977	6	Monarchs Among Their People	1909	£14.00
975	978	6	Styles of Furniture	1909	£14.00
976	979	6	The History of Weaving	1909	£14.00
977	965	6	La Traviata (Opera)	1909	£20.00
978	972	6	Picturesque Corners in Venice	1909	£14.00
979	981	6	Coaches and Carriages of the Ages	1909	£14.00
980	980	6	Old Customs of France	1909	£110.00
981	982	6	Life in Siam	1909	£18.00
982	983	6	Armies of the Balkan States	1910	£14.00
983	984	6	In Australia	1910	£18.00
984	985	6	In Bulgaria	1910	£14.00
985	986	6	Carnival Scenes	1910	£14.00
986	987	6	Rubber Cultivation	1910	£14.00
987	988	6	The Story of the Round Table	1910	£14.00
988	989	6	Colonies of European Origin	1910	£14.00
989	990	6	The Flight of the Dragon	1910	£14.00
990	991	6	Summer Pastimes	1910	£14.00
991	992	6	The Story of Nibelungen	1910	£20.00
992	993	6	Evolution of Commerce and Industry	1910	£14.00
993	994	6	Wedding Feasts in Different Countries	1910	£14.00
994	995	6	Garibaldi and His Expedition 1860	1910	£14.00
995	996	6	Episodes of the Thirty Years War	1910	£15.00

F No.	S No.	Qty	LIEBIG CARD ISSUES Title (English Translation)	Date	Set Price
996	997	6	The Delivery of Jerusalem	1910	£14.00
997	998	6	Winter in Sunny Countries	1910	£14.00
998	999	6	Pastimes at the Sea Side	1910	£25.00
999	1002	6	The Master Singers of Nuremberg (Opera)	1910	£22.00
1000	1000	6	Monuments of the Renaissance	1910	£14.00
1001	1001	6	The Nine Muses	1910	£20.00
1002	1003	6	History of Porcelain	1910	£14.00
1003	1004	6	In Portugal	1910	£14.00
1004	1005	6	Scenes of Egypt	1910	£18.00
1005	1006	6	Performing Monkeys	1910	£14.00
1006	1007	6	History of France VIII (Louis XIV 1643-1715)	1910	£14.00
1007	1008	6	Evolution of Musical Instruments	1910	£14.00
1008	1009	6	The Good Old Times	1910	£14.00
1009	1010	6	In Turkey	1910	£20.00
1010	1011	6	Famous Old Churches	1910	£15.00
1011	1012	6	Picturesque Algeria	1911	£14.00
1012	1013	6	Exotic Dolls and Games	1911	£14.00
1013	1014	6	Uses of Bells	1911	£14.00
1014	1015	6	Famous Castles of Italy (Laziali)	1911	£25.00
1015	1016	6	Famous Castles of Italy (Piemontesi)	1911	£25.00
1016	1017	6	Celebrated Italian Military Leaders	1911	£14.00
1017	1026	6	Le Cid (Opera)	1911	£20.00
1018	1027	6	The Damnation of Faust (Opera)	1911	£14.00
1019	1018	6	Dances of Different Countries VI	1911	£14.00
1020	1019	6	Scented Flowers	1911	£14.00
1021	1020	6	In the Kingdom of Flowers	1911	£22.00
1022	1021	6	Ancient Roman Leaders	1911	£14.00
1023	1022	6	Iceland	1911	£14.00
1024	1023	6	Mountain People	1911	£14.00
1025	1024	6	Famous Dwarfs	1911	£40.00
1026	1025	6	Aerial Navigation	1911	£26.00
1027	1029	6	The Age of Pericles	1911	£14.00
1028	1028	6	Sacred Plants	1911	£16.00
1029	1060	6	The French Riviera	1911	£85.00
1030	1030	6	The Dardanelles	1911	£14.00
1031	1031	6	The Truffle	1911	£14.00
1032	1032	6	Towers	1911	£14.00
1033	1033	6	In Hungary	1911	£15.00
1034	1034	6	The History of Glass	1911	£14.00
1035	1035	6	Curious Animals	1912	£14.00
1036	1036	6	Sacred Animals	1912	£15.00
1037	1040	6	Ancient Norwegian Costumes	1912	£14.00
1038	1037	6	The Art of Cooking in Different Ages	1912	£14.00
1039	1038	6	In Brittany	1912	£14.00
1040	1039	6	Corsica	1912	£14.00
1041	1057	6	Curious Natural Bridges	1912	£14.00
1042	1041	6	Gods of the Hindus	1912	£18.00
1043	1043	6	Buildings in Rome	1912	£12.00
1044	1044	6	Italian Celebrities in their Childhood	1912	£22.00
1045	1045	6	Military Manoeuvres in Italy	1912	£12.00
1046	1046	6	Italian-Turkish War	1912	£20.00
1047	1047	6	The Library Through the Ages	1912	£12.00
1048	1048	6	Macbeth	1912	£15.00
1049	1049	6	The Masque	1912	£12.00
1050	1050	6	History of Lace	1912	£16.00
1051	1051	6	Gothic Monuments	1912	£12.00
1052	1052	6	Buildings in Italy	1912	£14.00
1053	1054	6	Equatorial Countries	1912	£12.00

F No.	S No.	Qty	LIEBIG CARD ISSUES Title (English Translation)	Date	Set Price
1054	1055	6	Imperial Palaces in China	1912	£12.00
1055	1056	6	Historic French Town Halls	1912	£12.00
1056	1042	6	Places in Paris	1912	£14.00
1057	1058	6	Ports of France	1912	£14.00
1058	1053	6	The Queen of Sheba (Opera - Goldmark)	1912	£14.00
1059	1059	6	The Republic of Andorra	1912	£14.00
1060	1061	6	St. Louis King of France	1912	£14.00
1061	1062	6	The Champagne Industry	1912	£15.00
1062	1063	6	Sleighs in Different Countries	1912	£15.00
1063	1064	6	Ancient and Modern Villas	1912	£12.00
1064	1065	6	Camouflage with Insects	1913	£12.00
1065	1066	6	Courage and Discipline of Italian Army	1913	£22.00
1066	1067	6	History of Beer	1913	£20.00
1067	1068	6	The History of Paper	1913	£20.00
1068	1069	6	Chateaux and Forts of Italy	1913	£14.00
1069	1070	6	How Films are Made	1913	£22.00
1070	1071	6	Crowns and Coronations	1913	£15.00
1071	1072	6	The Cat Family	1913	£22.00
1072	1073	6	Memorable Journeys Across the Alps	1913	£18.00
1073	1074	6	Monuments in the Baroque Style	1913	£18.00
1074	1075	6	Monuments of Vittorio Emanuel II in Rome	1913	£16.00
1075	1076	6	Countries where Romany is Spoken	1913	£18.00
1076	1077	6	Vanished Civilisations	1913	£15.00
1077	1078	6	Robinson Crusoe	1913	£15.00
1078	1079	6	Scenes of Dutch Life	1913	£24.00
1079	1080	6	Historic Sicily	1913	£14.00
1080	1081	6	Fans of Different Countries	1913	£20.00
1081	1082	6	Verdi and His Works	1913	£22.00
1082	1083	6	Richard Wagner	1913	£20.00
1083	1084	6	The Provisioning of Armies on Campaign	1914-15	£15.00
1084	1085	6	Art Among Primitive People	1914-15	£15.00
1085	1088	6	Costumes of Servia	1914-15	£125.00
1086	1089	6	Costumes and Views of Austria	1914-15	£140.00
1087	1114	6	Gluck the Composer	1914-15	£350.00
1088	1094	6	Famous Navigators	1914-15	—
1089	1098	6	In Palestine	1914-15	£150.00
1090	1105	6	In Tunisia	1914-15	£375.00
1091	1106	6	Remains of the Roman Empire in Africa	1914-15	£14.00
1092	1086	6	The Panama Canal	1919-20	£25.00
1093	1113	6	Canals II	1919-20	£100.00
1094	1087	6	Cavaliers	1919-20	£20.00
1095	1090	6	Dante (Poet) I	1919-20	£30.00
1096	1116	6	Dante (Poet) II	1919-20	£18.00
1097	1091	6	The History of Iron	1919-20	£18.00
1098	1092	6	Mountain Railways	1919-20	£20.00
1099	1117	6	Foundries	1919-20	£40.00
1100	1093	6	Symbolic Stamps	1919-20	£30.00
1101	1095	6	Toothless Mammals	1919-20	£50.00
1102	1096	6	Gold Mines of Mont-Rose	1919-20	£14.00
1103	1097	6	Forges Throughout the Ages	1919-20	£15.00
1104	1099	6	Weights and Measures	1919-20	£50.00
1105	1100	6	Useful Plants and Their Promoters	1919-20	£40.00
1106	1101	6	The Winter's Tale (Shakespeare)	1919-20	£22.00
1107	1102	6	The Republic of San Marino	1919-20	£24.00
1108	1103	6	Scenes from Ural Mountains	1919-20	£25.00
1109	1104	6	Tramways Old and New	1919-20	£40.00
1110	1107	6	Travelling in Corsica	1919-20	£40.00
1111	1108	6	The Six Altitudinal Zones	1919-20	£24.00

F No.	S No.	Qty	LIEBIG CARD ISSUES Title (English Translation)	Date	Set Price
1112	1109	6	Ancient Commercial Centres	1921	£18.00
1113	1110	6	Famous Astronomers	1921	£50.00
1114	1111	6	Amateur Dramatics	1921	£22.00
1115	1112	6	In Canada I	1921	£50.00
1116	1115	6	Curious Experiments in Physics	1921	£40.00
1117	1118	6	The Story of Gas	1921	£35.00
1118	1119	6	Giants	1921	£125.00
1119	1120	6	The Pass of St. Gothard	1921	£30.00
1120	1121	6	Leonardo da Vinci	1921	£50.00
1121	1122	6	The Migration of Birds	1921	£22.00
1122	1123	6	The Pre-Historic Animal World	1921	£900.00
1123	1124	6	Animals in Human Situations	1921	£70.00
1124	1126	6	The Discoveries of Famous Scientists	1921	£60.00
1125	1127	6	Items of Yesterday and Today	1921	£45.00
1126	1128	6	Animals and Their Furs	1921	£30.00
1127	1125	6	Sapho (Opera)	1921	£30.00
1128	1129	6	Ruins in Sicily	1921	£45.00
1129	1130	6	Winter Sports	1921	£65.00
1130	1131	6	Zone Language in Italy	1921	£24.00
1131	1132	6	In East Africa II	1922-23	£22.00
1132	1133	6	Deep Sea Animals and Plants	1922-23	£20.00
1133	1134	6	Sacred Animals	1922-23	£22.00
1134	1135	6	Bees and Bee Keepers	922-23	£22.00
1135	1136	6	Roman Construction	1922-23	£22.00
1136	1137	6	Famous Women	1922-23	£22.00
1137	1138	6	Episodes in the History of the Middle Eastern Empire	1922-23	£22.00
1138	1139	6	The Founders of Large Empires	1922-23	£22.00
1139	1140	6	Uses of Fire	1922-23	£22.00
1140	1141	6	Episodes from the Lives of Famous Historians	1922-23	£22.00
1141	1142	6	The Glove as a Symbol	1922-23	£24.00
1142	1143	6	Lakes in Mountains	1922-23	£24.00
1143	1144	6	Flour Mills II	1922-23	£22.00
1144	1145	6	Military Music	1922-23	£30.00
1145	1146	6	The Origin of Different Colonies	1922-23	£22.00
1146	1147	6	Plants and Their Uses	1922-23	£22.00
1147	1148	6	Scenes from the Lives of Famous Painters	1922-23	£24.00
1148	1149	6	Birds in the Life of Man	1922-23	£22.00
1149	1150	6	People of Asia Minor	1922-23	£22.00
1150	1151	6	Torquato Tasso (Poet)	1922-23	£22.00
1151	1152	6	Remains of Bygone Civilisations	1922-23	£24.00
1152	1153	6	Famous Roman Villas	1922-23	£15.00
1153	1154	6	Water and the Ancient Romans and Egyptians	1924	£15.00
1154	1155	6	History of Culinary Art	1924	£10.00
1155	1156	6	Natural Catastrophes	1924	£10.00
1156	1157	12	Milan Cathedral	1924	£30.00
1157	1158	6	The Miller, His Son and the Ass	1924	£12.00
1158	1159	6	The Little Marat (Opera)	1924	£16.00
1159	1160	6	Robert the Bruce	1924	£15.00
1160	1161	6	Holy Shrines	1924	£20.00
1161	1162	6	Historic Military Expeditions	1924	£16.00
1162	1163	6	Famous Opera Houses	1924	£25.00
1163	1164	6	Holy Year 1925	1925	£10.00
1164	1165	6	Famous Italian Towers	1925	£9.00
1165	1166	6	Different Sleeping Places	1925	£12.00
1166	1167	6	Swiss Guard at the Vatican	1925	£10.00
1167	1175	6	Liebig Transported by Elephant (Humorous)	1925	£15.00
1168	1168	6	Natural Light Phenomena	1925	£16.00
1169	1169	6	Nero – Opera	1925	£16.00

F No.	S No.	Qty	LIEBIG CARD ISSUES Title (English Translation)	Date	Set Price
1170	1170	6	Famous Belgian Town Halls	1925	£12.00
1171	1171	6	Unusual Plant Life	1925	£14.00
1172	1172	6	Famous Italian Squares	1925	£10.00
1173	1173	6	Death and Burial of Tutankhamen	1925	£25.00
1174	1174	6	Picturesque Views of Spain	1925	£14.00
1175	1176	6	Rearing of Useful Creatures	1926	£14.00
1176	1177	6	Famous Diplomats and Ambassadors	1926	£14.00
1177	1178	6	Popular Fables	1926	£22.00
1178	1179	6	War in the Alps	1926	£15.00
1179	1180	6	Art in Japan	1926	£14.00
1180	1181	6	The Promised Bride by Manzoli	1926	£12.00
1181	1182	6	Greetings of Primitive Peoples	1926	£10.00
1182	1183	6	The Life of St. Francis of Assisi	1926	£16.00
1183	1184	6	Architectural Treasures of Latium	1926	£10.00
1184	1185	6	Leaning Towers	1926	£14.00
1185	1186	6	Historical Vehicles	1926	£15.00
1186	1187	6	Pictures of Olden Times	1926	£14.00
1187	1188	6	'L'Aiglon' - Drama by Rostand	1927	£14.00
1188	1203	6	Beethoven	1927	£14.00
1189	1189	6	'Boris Goudonov' by Mussorgsky	1927	£16.00
1190	1190	6	British Castles	1927	£15.00
1191	1191	6	'Cyrano de Bergerac' by Rostand	1927	£12.00
1192	1192	6	Sun Worshippers	1927	£12.00
1193	1193	6	Glaciers and Alpine Flowers	1927	£10.00
1194	1194	6	Gulliver's Travels in Lilliput	1927	£15.00
1195	1195	6	Gulliver's Travels in Brobdingnag	1927	£16.00
1196	1196	6	The Iliad - Roman Mythology	1927	£14.00
1197	1197	6	The Odyssey	1927	£12.00
1198	1198	6	The Story of Bread	1927	£12.00
1199	1199	6	Perseus	1927	£10.00
1200	1200	6	Rain	1927	£12.00
1201	1201	6	Famous Scenes from the Napoleonic Era	1927	£12.00
1202	1202	6	Sailing Ships Through the Ages	1927	£12.00
1203	1205	6	Diogenes	1928	£9.00
1204	1206	6	The Twelve Labours of Hercules I	1928	£12.00
1205	1207	6	The Twelve Labours of Hercules II	1928	£9.00
1206	1208	6	Historic Invasions of Italy	1928	£12.00
1207	1209	6	The Working of Copper and Bronze	1928	£8.00
1208	1210	6	The Legend of St. Nicholas	1928	£15.00
1209	1211	6	Women and Children of the World	1928	£9.00
1210	1212	6	Mohammed	1928	£10.00
1211	1213	6	Dangerous Occupations	1928	£8.00
1212	1215	6	Uses of Feathers	1928	£10.00
1213	1216	6	Sensitive Plants	1928	£7.00
1214	1204	6	Conquest of the North Pole	1928	£20.00
1215	1217	6	Unusual Outdoor Occupations	1928	£8.00
1216	1218	6	Arctic Russia	1928	£8.00
1217	1219	6	Schubert	1928	£12.00
1218	1232	6	Humorous Sports	1928	£12.00
1219	1220	6	Theseus	1928	£8.00
1220	1214	6	New Zealand Views	1928	£10.00
1221	1221	6	The Inhabitants of Tierra del Fuego	1929	£8.00
1222	1222	6	Scenes of Canada	1929	£10.00
1223	1224	6	Chocolate	1929	£10.00
1224	1225	6	Dante - Divine Comedy I The Inferno	1929	£8.00
1225	1226	6	Dante - Divine Comedy II Purgatory	1929	£10.00
1226	1227	6	Dante - Divine Comedy III Paradise	1929	£8.00
1227	1228	6	Cheese Industry in Different Lands	1929	£8.00

F No.	S No.	Qty	LIEBIG CARD ISSUES Title (English Translation)	Date	Set Price
1228	1229	6	Combat Formations	1929	£12.00
1229	1230	6	The Apple as an Historical Symbol	1929	£7.00
1230	1231	6	The Mediterranean Coast	1929	£7.00
1231	1233	6	Evolution of the Earth	1929	£14.00
1232	1234	6	The Life of Buddha	1930	£12.00
1233	1223	6	Famous Chemists	1930	£7.00
1234	1235	6	Belgian Churches	1930	£6.00
1235	1236	6	Confucius	1930	£7.00
1236	1237	6	Electing a Doge of Venice	1930	£8.00
1237	1238	6	Legend of Aeneid I	1930	£7.00
1238	1239	6	Legend of Aeneid II	1930	£7.00
1239	1240	6	Classical Italian Gardens	1930	£6.00
1240	1241	6	Gems of Sicilian Architecture	1930	£6.00
1241	1242	6	Historic Buildings and Gateways of Milan	1930	£25.00
1242	1243	6	Hindu Monuments	1930	£7.00
1243	1244	6	Microscopic Water Life	1931	£6.00
1244	1245	6	Great Greek Tragedies	1931	£6.00
1245	1246	6	Pictorial History of Switzerland	1931	£6.00
1246	1247	6	Mahabharata - Ancient Legend of India	1931	£8.00
1247	1248	6	Ancient Egyptian Monuments	1931	£10.00
1248	1249	6	Prehistoric Monuments	1931	£8.00
1249	1250	6	Famous Mosques	1931	£6.00
1250	1252	6	Ramayana - Ancient Legend of India	1931	£6.00
1251	1253	6	Bizarre Rocks	1931	£6.00
1252	1254	6	Scenes from Venetian History	1931	£6.00
1253	1255	6	The Story of Medieval Switzerland	1931	£6.00
1254	1256	6	Loading and Unloading Ships	1932	£6.00
1255	1257	6	Paper Making	1932	£7.00
1256	1258	6	Methods of Fixing a Position at Sea	1932	£7.00
1257	1259	6	Building a Liner	1932	£9.00
1258	1260	6	Faust I	1932	£7.00
1259	1261	6	Faust II	1932	£7.00
1260	1262	6	Aesop's Fables	1932	£8.00
1261	1263	6	Ants	1932	£8.00
1262	1264	6	Jupiter	1932	£6.00
1263	1251	6	Orpheus	1932	£6.00
1264	1265	6	Parasitic Plants	1932	£7.00
1265	1266	6	Transmission of News Among Primitive People	1932	£8.00
1266	1267	6	Bees	1933	£10.00
1267	1271	6	Hydroelectricity	1933	£6.00
1268	1270	6	Coal-Mining	1933	£8.00
1269	1272	6	Chateaux of the Loire	1933	£12.00
1270	1273	6	Castles of the Rhine	1933	£9.00
1271	1275	6	Story of China I	1933	£8.00
1272	1276	6	Story of China II	1933	£12.00
1273	1277	6	Climate and Vegetation	1933	£6.00
1274	1278	6	The Comedy of Aristophanes	1933	£10.00
1275	1281	6	Cloud Formations	1933	£6.00
1276	1280	6	Isis and Osiris - Ancient Egyptians	1933	£12.00
1277	1283	6	Symbiosis	1933	£8.00
1278	1284	6	Japanese Theatre	1933	£10.00
1279	1285	6	Living in the Alps	1933	£12.00
1280	1268	6	Apollo	1934	£8.00
1281	1286	6	Pre-Colombian Architecture in South America	1934	£12.00
1282	1269	6	Ancient Athens	1934	£35.00
1283	1287	6	The Isle of Capri	1934	£6.00
1284	1289	12	Medieval German Cathedrals	1934	£30.00
1285	1274	6	Swiss Chalets	1934	£7.00

F No.	S No.	Qty	LIEBIG CARD ISSUES Title (English Translation)	Date	Set Price
1286	1288	12	Chateaux of Belgium	1934	£35.00
1287	1290	6	How and Why Flowers Attract Insects	1934	£6.00
1288	1301	6	German Youth Movement	1934	£120.00
1289	1300	6	German Girls	1934	£150.00
1290	1291	6	Edda - Mythological Saga	1934	£9.00
1291	1292	6	Head Adornment in Primitive People	1934	£6.00
1292	1279	6	European Alpine Fauna	1934	£18.00
1293	1293	6	Match Making	1934	£10.00
1294	1295	6	Iceland	1934	£6.00
1295	1296	6	Geological Times	1934	£8.00
1296	1297	6	Fishing in the North Sea	1934	£8.00
1297	1298	6	Production of Petroleum	1934	£6.00
1298	1282	6	Carnivorous Plants	1934	£10.00
1299	1294	6	Preparation of an Illustrated Journal	1934	£6.00
1300	1299	6	Legend of Prometheus	1934	£6.00
1301	1302	6	Samarkand - (City of Tamerlane)	1934	£8.00
1302	1303	12	The Legend of Till Uilenspeigel	1934	£100.00
1303	1304	12	The Life of the People of the Congo	1934	£27.00
1304	1306	6	Strange Trees of the World	1935	£6.00
1305	1307	6	Arabian Scenes	1935	£6.00
1306	1308	6	Construction of Spiders' Webs	1935	£6.00
1307	1321	6	Types of Jellyfish	1935	£14.00
1308	1310	6	The Vatican City	1935	£6.00
1309	1311	6	Historical Aspects of Modern Cities	1935	£8.00
1310	1312	6	Travel in our Grandfather's Time	1935	£6.00
1311	1313	6	Conquering the Air I	1935	£20.00
1312	1314	6	Conquering the Air II	1935	£20.00
1313	1309	6	Evolution of Cacti	1935	£6.00
1314	1315	6	Tropical Butterflies and Beetles	1935	£14.00
1315	1318	6	Irish Scenes	1935	£16.00
1316	1305	6	Unusual German Youth Hostels	1935	£50.00
1317	1319	6	Great Engineering Feats of Modern Europe	1935	£5.00
1318	1320	6	Lhasa, Holy City of the Himalayas	1935	£10.00
1319	1322	6	Luxurious Ships of Bygone Days	1935	£6.00
1320	1324	6	Views of Tierra Del Fuego	1935	£5.00
1321	1325	6	Famous Abbeys of Belgium	1936	£8.00
1322	1327	6	Hamlet (Shakespeare)	1936	£15.00
1323	1330	6	Belfries of Belgium	1936	£9.00
1324	1329	6	Blooms of Aquatic Flowers	1936	£12.00
1325	1323	6	De Rozenkavalier (Opera)	1936	£18.00
1326	1337	6	'El Cid' Tragedy by Corneille	1936	£5.00
1327	1332	6	Hummimg Birds	1936	£12.00
1328	1333	6	Folk Dances of the World	1936	£6.00
1329	1334	6	Don Quixote II	1936	£7.00
1330	1316	6	The Coast of Europe	1936	£5.00
1331	1336	6	Landscaped Gardens	1936	£18.00
1332	1317	6	Great American Sky-Scrapers	1936	£16.00
1333	1338	6	Legend of Roland	1936	£6.00
1334	1339	6	Exotic Aquarium Fish	1936	£7.00
1335	1341	6	Processions and Pilgrimages in Belgium	1936	£7.00
1336	1342	12	King Albert of Belgium	1936	£23.00
1337	1346	12	The Life of Queen Astrid of Belgium	1936	£25.00
1338	1343	6	River and Maritime Signals	1936	£9.00
1339	1344	6	Distribution of Seeds by the Wind	1936	£8.00
1340	1345	6	Views of Submarine Life	1936	£7.00
1341	1347	6	Legend of Zarathustra	1936	£6.00
1342	1348	6	Unusual Dwellings	1937	£6.00
1343	1326	6	Climbing in the Alps	1937	£10.00

F No.	S No.	Qty	LIEBIG CARD ISSUES Title (English Translation)	Date	Set Price
1344	1349	12	Wild Animals of the Congo	1937	£45.00
1345	1328	6	The Antarctic	1937	£12.00
1346	1350	12	Chinese Art	1937	£40.00
1347	1351	6	Moroccan Art	1937	£17.00
1348	1331	6	Wooden Churches	1937	£7.00
1349	1335	6	Alpine Flowers	1937	£7.00
1350	1353	6	Life of a River	1937	£6.00
1351	1354	6	Flora of the Riviera	1937	£6.00
1352A	1356	6	The Italian Empire (Nos 1-6)	1937	£12.00
1352B	1356	6	The Italian Empire (Nos 7-12)	1937	£12.00
1352C	1356	6	The Italian Empire (Nos 13-18)	1937	£12.00
1353	1355	6	Joan of Arc II	1937	£9.00
1354	1359	6	Strange Mammals	1937	£7.00
1355	1361	6	Marvellous Grottoes of Belgium	1937	£8.00
1356	1362	6	Orchids	1937	£12.00
1357	1363	6	The Reign of Albert and Isabella	1937	£8.00
1358	1364	6	Lifestyle of Termites	1937	£6.00
1359	1365	6	Birds	1937	£14.00
1360	1368	6	Glass Industry II	1937	£9.00
1361	1366	6	Customs of Belgium	1937	£6.00
1362	1367	6	Old Houses	1937	£10.00
1363	1372	6	Belgium	1938	£6.00
1364	1385	6	German Town Halls	1938	£350.00
1365	1374	6	The Gods of Egypt	1938	£10.00
1366	1352	6	Animals and the Plants They Eat	1938	£6.00
1367	1376	6	The Fountains of Rome	1938	£6.00
1368A	1377	6	History of Japan (Nos 1-6)	1938	£6.00
1368B	1377	6	History of Japan (Nos 7-12)	1938	£6.00
1369	1378	6	Caesar	1938	£7.00
1370	1380	6	Famous Historical People of Latin America	1938	£6.00
1371	1381	6	The Grottoes of Postumia	1938	£11.00
1372	1386	6	William Tell (Opera)	1938	£15.00
1373	1358	6	Development of Insects from Water to Air	1938	£8.00
1374	1357	6	Water Insects	1938	£8.00
1375	1383	6	Justus Von Liebig	1938	£35.00
1376	1382	6	G. Marconi	1938	£24.00
1377	1360	6	Submarine Life at 500 Fathoms	1938	£12.00
1378	1384	6	Marriage Through the Ages	1938	£9.00
1379	1387	6	The Master Singers (Opera)	1938	£400.00
1380	1340	6	Women's Hair Styles	1938	£6.00
1381	1371	6	School of Horse Riding	1938	£15.00
1382	1388	6	Industries of Italy	1938	£22.00
1383	1375	6	History of the U.S.A.	1938	£10.00
1384	1390	6	Characteristic Houses of the Pacific Islands	1939	£5.00
1385	1369	6	Inside an Iron Foundry	1939	£5.00
1386	1391	6	Emperor Augustus	1939	£5.00
1387	1370	6	Farming Silk Worms	1939	£10.00
1388	1392	6	Benvenuto Cellini	1939	£5.00
1389	1394	6	Riders of the World	1939	£6.00
1390	1395	6	Famous Italian Knights	1939	£11.00
1391	1411	6	Coral	1939	£5.00
1392	1373	6	Crustacea	1939	£5.00
1393	1393	6	German Provincial Halls	1939	£125.00
1394	1397	6	Italian Festivals	1939	£6.00
1395	1389	6	The Life of a Glacier	1939	£5.00
1396	1403	6	Amber	1939	£160.00
1397	1379	6	Modern Drilling, Excavating and Dredging Plant	1939	£5.00
1398A	1400	6	History of India (Nos 1-6)	1939	£6.00

F No.	S No.	Qty	LIEBIG CARD ISSUES Title (English Translation)	Date	Set Price
1398B	1400	6	History of India (Nos 7-12)	1939	£6.00
1399	1399	6	Popular Games	1939	£6.00
1400	1401	6	Flax Industry in Belgium	1939	£6.00
1401	1404	6	Fishing III	1939	£6.00
1402	1398	6	Rivers of the Ardennes	1939	£6.00
1403	1406	6	Scipio and Hannibal	1939	£6.00
1404	1405	6	Skiing	1939	£25.00
1405	1402	6	Turandot (Opera)	1939	£15.00
1406	1409	6	Museums in Houses	1939	£7.00
1407	1396	6	Folk Costumes of Germany	1939	£140.00
1408	1412	6	Ancient Dwellings	1940	£6.00
1409	1413	6	Castles of Tuscany	1940	£6.00
1410	1414	6	Flora and Fauna of Ethiopia	1940	£8.00
1411	1415	6	Primitive Production and Uses of Fire	1940	£7.00
1412	1416	6	Giants	1940	£5.00
1413	1419	6	The History of the Post	1940	£10.00
1414	1417	6	Gastropods (Snails, etc.)	1940	£9.00
1415	1418	6	The Albert National Park, Africa	1940	£6.00
1416	1420	6	Rhine and Lake Boats	1940	£150.00
1417	1421	6	The Life of Rubens	1940	£5.00
1418	1422	6	Skiing II	1940	£60.00
1419	1407	6	Tobacco	1940	£10.00
1420	1408	6	Bearded Birds	1940	£9.00
1421	1424	6	Death Valley	1940	£5.00
1422	1425	6	Traditional Belgian Farmhouses	1940	£6.00
1423	1410	6	Life in an Ancient Village	1940	£5.00
1424	1423	6	Winter Sport	1940	£180.00
1425	1426	6	Animals Used for Fur	1941	£8.00
1426	1427	6	Bamboo	1941	£6.00
1427	1428	6	Exotic Wedding Costumes	1941	£5.00
1428	1429	6	Majesty of the Alps	1941	£12.00
1429	1430	6	Sea Mammals	1941	£8.00
1430	1431	6	Marco Polo	1941	£5.00
1431	1432	6	Molluscs and Oysters	1941	£6.00
1432	1433	6	Unusual Fish	1941	£7.00
1433	1434	6	Useful Plants of the Congo	1941	£5.00
1434	1436	6	Water Sports	1941	£9.00
1435	1435	6	Old Belgian Bridges I	1941	£8.00
1436	1437	6	Artistic Craftsman of the Congo	1942	£7.00
1437	1438	6	Famous Waterfalls	1942	£10.00
1438	1439	6	Dances of Ancient Greece	1942	£6.00
1439	1441	6	Belgian Windmills	1942	£5.00
1440	1447	6	Mosquitoes	1942	£5.00
1441	1442	6	Birds Nests	1942	£10.00
1442	1443	6	The Origin and History of Writing	1942	£6.00
1443	1444	6	Italian Bridges	1942	£8.00
1444	1440	6	Popular Festivals	1942	£5.00
1445	1445	6	The Discovery of America	1942	£6.00
1446	1446	6	Indian Temples	1942	£7.00
1447	1448	6	Legendary Beings	1943	£6.00
1448	1449	6	The Story of Gil Blas	1943	£5.00
1449	1455	6	Birds of Paradise	1943	£12.00
1450	1450	6	Sponge Fishing	1943	£6.00
1451	1451	6	Medicinal Plants II	1943	£6.00
1452	1452	6	The Four Sons of Aymon	1943	£5.00
1453	1453	6	The Sahara	1943	£5.00
1454	1454	6	Life in the Sahara Desert	1943	£8.00
1455	1456	6	Cephalopods (Shells)	1947	£22.00

F No.	S No.	Qty	LIEBIG CARD ISSUES Title (English Translation)	Date	Set Price
1456	1457	6	The Cheese Industry	1947	£20.00
1457	1462	6	History of Egypt	1947	£35.00
1458	1458	6	Insects of the Locust Family	1947	£20.00
1459	1459	6	The Kalevala	1947	£7.00
1460	1460	6	Water Mills	1947	£10.00
1461	1461	6	San Giovani Bosco	1947	£18.00
1462	1463	6	Italian Leaders and Events of 1848	1948	£12.00
1463	1464	6	Baudouin - Arms of Iron	1948	£8.00
1464	1465	6	Song of Hiawatha	1948	£8.00
1465	1466	6	Journey of a Rich Roman	1948	£8.00
1466	1467	6	Baby Mammals	1948	£18.00
1467	1468	6	Miguel of Cervantes	1948	£7.00
1468	1469	6	Applications of Science	1948	£6.00
1469	1471	6	The Life of Albert Durer	1948	£6.00
1470	1470	6	Old Arches	1948	£5.00
1471	1472	6	Picturesque Abruzzo	1949	£12.00
1472	1473	6	History of Christianity in Italy I	1949	£5.00
1473	1474	6	History of Christianity in Italy II	1949	£5.00
1474	1475	6	History of Christianity in Italy III	1949	£8.00
1475	1476	6	Beetles of Europe	1949	£6.00
1476	1477	6	Winter Plants	1949	£14.00
1477	1483	6	The Discovery of America	1949	£8.00
1478	1478	6	Famous Italian Navigators	1949	£12.00
1479	1479	6	Masks of the World	1949	£10.00
1480	1480	6	Street Tradesmen	1949	£8.00
1481	1481	6	The Life of Rembrandt	1949	£5.00
1482	1482	6	Reptiles	1949	£7.00
1483	1484	6	The Life of Socrates	1949	£5.00
1484	1485	6	Antonie van Dyck	1949	£4.00
1485	1487	6	Alexander, the Founder of the Empire	1950	£8.00
1486	1488	6	Cavalry	1950	£8.00
1487	1489	6	Sea Shells	1950	£8.00
1488	1490	6	Inhabitants of Mexico Before Colombo	1950	£8.00
1489	1491	6	Erasme	1950	£5.00
1490	1492	6	Edible Fungi II	1950	£15.00
1491	1493	6	Poisonous Fungi	1950	£12.00
1492	1494	6	Belgian Generals	1950	£6.00
1493	1496	6	The Gaules at War	1950	£8.00
1494	1507	6	The History of the Horse	1950	£7.00
1495	1501	6	Bread, Wine, Oil, made in Rome	1950	£5.00
1496	1497	6	Moths	1950	£6.00
1497	1498	6	Lusitanian's	1950	£6.00
1498	1499	6	The Life of Moliere	1950	£4.00
1499	1500	6	Palissy Bernard	1950	£4.00
1500	1502	6	Monuments	1950	£5.00
1501	1503	6	Plants in Ceremonies	1950	£6.00
1502	1504	6	Picturesque Portugal	1950	£5.00
1503	1495	6	The First Tour Around the World	1950	£5.00
1504	1505	6	The Retreat of the Ten Thousand	1950	£5.00
1505	1506	6	Robin Hood	1950	£12.00
1506	1508	6	History of Ceramics	1950	£12.00
1507	1510	6	Some Occupations of Belgians	1951	£5.00
1508	1509	6	Albanians and Volscions	1951	£5.00
1509	1511	6	Plant and Animal Life on the Heath	1951	£5.00
1510	1512	6	The Hunter and His Dog	1951	£8.00
1511	1514	6	'Cuore' E. De Amicis	1951	£7.00
1512	1516	6	Flowers of the Marsh	1951	£8.00
1513	1517	6	Gardens of Italy	1951	£7.00

F No.	S No.	Qty	LIEBIG CARD ISSUES Title (English Translation)	Date	Set Price
1514	1515	6	King Herod Antipas	1951	£5.00
1515	1522	6	The History of Anvers	1951	£5.00
1516	1523	6	The History of Flanders (West)	1951	£6.00
1517	1549	6	The History of Flanders (East)	1951	£5.00
1518	1524	6	The History of Hainault	1951	£4.00
1519	1548	6	The History of Brabant	1951	£5.00
1520	1525	6	History of Leige	1951	£5.00
1521	1526	6	The History of Limbourg	1951	£5.00
1522	1527	6	History of Luxembourg	1951	£5.00
1523	1550	6	The History of Namur	1951	£5.00
1524	1513	6	The Court of Bourgogne	1951	£4.00
1525	1530	6	The Life of Manzoni Alessanoro	1951	£5.00
1526	1521	6	The History of Pasta	1951	£18.00
1527	1518	6	Princesses Visiting Belgium	1951	£4.00
1528	1519	6	Occupations of Animals and Birds	1951	£8.00
1529	1520	6	Sports of the World	1951	£24.00
1530	1528	6	History of Italy I	1951	£7.00
1531	1529	6	Parasites and their Hosts	1951	£8.00
1532	1531	6	Admirals and Buccaneers of Belgium	1951	£7.00
1533	1532	6	Garden Shrubs	1952	£7.00
1534	1533	6	Italian Cars	1952	£8.00
1535	1541	6	The Masked Ball (Opera by Verdi)	1952	£12.00
1536	1535	6	Natural Catastrophes	1952	£7.00
1537	1534	6	Fishing and Hunting in the Belgian Congo	1952	£5.00
1538	1539	6	The Belgian Emperors in Constantinople	1952	£4.00
1539A	1554	6	Historical Battles (Nos 1-6)	1952	£8.00
1539B	1555	6	Historical Battles (Nos 7-12)	1952	£8.00
1540	1536	6	Large Flowers	1952	£6.00
1541	1537	6	Fruits	1952	£6.00
1542	1545	6	History of the Belgian Congo 1st Series	1952	£6.00
1543	1546	6	History of the Belgian Congo 2nd Series	1952	£6.00
1544	1547	6	History of the Belgian Congo 3rd Series	1952	£6.00
1545	1551	6	History of Luxembourg	1952	£5.00
1546	1538	6	Flowers	1952	£6.00
1547	1540	6	Mercator	1952	£4.00
1548	1542	6	Astronomy	1952	£9.00
1549	1543	6	Coastal Fishing	1952	£9.00
1550	1544	6	Flowers of the Meadow	1952	£8.00
1551	1552	6	History of Italy II	1952	£8.00
1552	1553	6	History of Italy III	1952	£7.00
1553	1556	6	The River Po Right Bank	1953	£6.00
1554	1557	6	Algae	1953	£4.00
1555	1558	6	Sites of Milan	1953	£7.00
1556	1559	6	The Antelope	1953	£4.00
1557	1560	6	Archimedes' Principles	1953	£4.00
1558	1561	6	Suez Canal	1953	£5.00
1559	1562	6	Mountain Songs	1953	£9.00
1560	1564	6	Carnivores	1953	£7.00
1561	1565	6	Sea Mammals	1953	£5.00
1562	1563	6	Charles-Joseph, Prince of Ligne	1953	£4.00
1563	1566	6	The Civilisation of Minoica	1953	£5.00
1564	1567	6	Mountain Costumes	1953	£7.00
1565	1568	6	Forest Flowers	1953	£4.00
1566	1569	6	William of Orange	1953	£4.00
1567	1577	6	Plant Life	1953	£5.00
1568	1570	6	The Production of Timber	1953	£7.00
1569	1571	6	Marsupials	1953	£5.00
1570	1580	6	Flightless Birds	1953	£8.00

F No.	S No.	Qty	LIEBIG CARD ISSUES Title (English Translation)	Date	Set Price
1571	1572	6	Wild Animals	1953	£6.00
1572	1575	6	Pierre Le Grand	1953	£4.00
1573	1574	6	House Plants	1953	£4.00
1574	1573	6	Freshwater Fish	1953	£9.00
1575	1576	6	Solomon the Great	1953	£7.00
1576	1578	12	Expanding the Colonies of Belgium	1953	£8.00
1577	1579	6	Trees and Their Blossom	1953	£4.00
1578	1581	6	Virgil the Poet	1953	£4.00
1579	1584	6	Ancient Boats	1954	£8.00
1580	1583	6	Fishing Craft of Belgium	1954	£7.00
1581	1586	6	Paddle Footed Carnivora	1954	£9.00
1582	1587	6	Catherine II of Russia	1954	£4.00
1583	1588	6	Nuptial Dances of Birds	1954	£12.00
1584	1589	6	The Fall of Constantinople in 1452/3	1954	£4.00
1585	1591	6	The Empire of the Incas	1954	£5.00
1586	1590	6	The Horse Family	1954	£9.00
1587	1585	6	Falconry	1954	£6.00
1588	1596	6	Oysters	1954	£4.00
1589	1593	6	Invasion of the Moors	1954	£4.00
1590	1594	6	The Use of Marble	1954	£6.00
1591	1595	6	Picturesque Lazio	1954	£5.00
1592	1610	6	Sea Birds	1954	£8.00
1593	1597	6	Fish and their Habitat	1954	£4.00
1594	1592	6	Insects and Molluscs of the Shore	1954	£4.00
1595	1598	6	Primates	1954	£7.00
1596	1599	6	Francois Rabaelais	1954	£4.00
1597	1600	6	Rodents	1954	£4.00
1598	1601	6	Rodents	1954	£6.00
1599	1602	6	Inventors of Belgium	1954	£4.00
1600	1603	6	Monkeys I	1954	£7.00
1601	1604	6	Monkeys II	1954	£5.00
1602	1605	6	The History of Italy IV	1954	£12.00
1603	1606	6	The History of Italy V	1954	£20.00
1604	1607	6	The History of Italy VI	1954	£5.00
1605	1608	6	The History of Italy VII	1954	£7.00
1606	1609	6	Tuscany	1954	£8.00
1607	1611	6	The Life of S. Ambrogioa	1954	£6.00
1608	1612	6	Australian Mammals	1955	£4.00
1609	1613	6	Architecture in Spain	1955	£4.00
1610	1582	6	Sailing Ships Through the Ages	1955	£5.00
1611	1616	6	Bats	1955	£9.00
1612	1617	6	New Varieties of Flowers	1955	£9.00
1613	1631	6	History of England	1955	£8.00
1614	1630	6	History of Germany	1955	£4.00
1615	1629	6	History of France	1955	£4.00
1616	1614	6	The Poems of Leopardi	1955	£5.00
1617	1628	6	The Storage and Use of Methane	1955	£4.00
1618	1619	6	Monster Sculptures of Bomarzo	1955	£5.00
1619	1634	6	Fish Eating Birds	1955	£8.00
1620	1620	6	Bears	1955	£5.00
1621	1621	6	Parrots	1955	£9.00
1622	1623	6	Fish and Fishing	1955	£5.00
1623A	1626	6	Natives of the Belgian Congo (Nos 1-6)	1955	£4.00
1623B	1626	6	Natives of the Belgian Congo (Nos 7-12)	1955	£4.00
1623C	1626	6	Natives of the Belgian Congo(Nos 13-18)	1955	£4.00
1624	1625	6	Desert Plants	1955	£4.00
1625	1624	6	Climbing Plants (White Borders)	1955	£6.00
1625A	1624A	6	Climbing Plants (Inner Coloured borders)	1955	£6.00

F No.	S No.	Qty	LIEBIG CARD ISSUES Title (English Translation)	Date	Set Price
1626	1622	6	Life in Sand-Dunes	1955	£4.00
1627	1627	6	Prosimiae - Tree Living Mammals	1955	£9.00
1628	1615	6	The Cultivation of Rice	1955	£6.00
1629	1618	6	Rice from Field to Table	1955	£6.00
1630	1632	6	Birds of the Congo	1955	£6.00
1631	1633	6	Social Birds	1955	£8.00
1632	1635	6	The River Po Left Bank	1956	£10.00
1633	1636	6	Dog, Friend of Man	1956	£6.00
1634	1648	6	Teaching Children to Walk	1956	£6.00
1635	1637	6	Harmful Insects of the Congo	1956	£4.00
1636	1638	6	Space Travel	1956	£8.00
1637	1639	6	Caterpillars	1956	£5.00
1638	1640	6	Cities of Switzerland	1956	£6.00
1639	1658	6	History of Spain	1956	£4.00
1640	1659	6	History of the U.S.A.	1956	£7.00
1641	1657	6	History of Holland	1956	£4.00
1642	1641	6	Indians of the North American Plains	1956	£10.00
1643	1642	6	North American Indians	1956	£10.00
1644	1644	6	Large Insects of the Belgian Congo	1956	£4.00
1645	1645	6	Insect Eaters	1956	£4.00
1646	1646	6	Ivan the Terrible	1956	£4.00
1647	1647	6	Pilgrimages	1956	£4.00
1648	1649	6	Features of the World I	1956	£6.00
1649	1650	6	Features of the World II	1956	£5.00
1650	1651	6	Places on Athos	1956	£4.00
1651	1652	6	The Career of Mozart	1956	£12.00
1652	1653	6	Jet Propulsion and Reaction	1956	£4.00
1653	1654	6	Holy Places	1956	£4.00
1654	1655	6	Rodents	1956	£4.00
1655	1656	6	Caving	1956	£4.00
1656	1660	6	History of Italy VIII	1956	£12.00
1657	1643	6	The Manufacture of Sulphur	1956	£5.00
1658	1670	6	Alaska	1957	£5.00
1659	1661	6	Types of Frog	1957	£4.00
1660	1665	6	Cradles of Different People	1957	£4.00
1661	1663	6	Armies from 1848	1957	£7.00
1662	1666	6	Cats	1957	£9.00
1663	1664	6	The Dolomites	1957	£6.00
1664	1681	6	History of Hungary	1957	£4.00
1665	1680	6	History of Portugal	1957	£4.00
1666	1667	6	Childhood of Jesus	1957	£4.00
1667	1668	6	Harmful Agricultural Insects of the Congo	1957	£4.00
1668	1669	6	Leopold I	1957	£4.00
1669	1673	6	Life in a Brook	1957	£4.00
1670	1671	6	Aromatic Plants	1957	£6.00
1671	1672	6	Scarce Plants	1957	£4.00
1672	1674	6	Plankton	1957	£4.00
1673	1662	6	Ancient Roman Buildings	1957	£6.00
1674	1675	6	Saladin	1957	£6.00
1675	1676	6	Siberia	1957	£4.00
1676	1677	6	History of Italy IX	1957	£7.00
1677	1678	6	History of Italy X	1957	£7.00
1678	1679	6	History of Italy XI	1957	£7.00
1679	1682	6	Jousting Tournament	1957	£4.00
1680	1683	6	Wind Flight	1957	£5.00
1681	1695	6	Spiders	1958	£4.00
1682	1684	6	Pirates	1958	£5.00
1683	1685	6	Doctors' Dress Through the Ages I	1958	£8.00

F No.	S No.	Qty	LIEBIG CARD ISSUES Title (English Translation)	Date	Set Price
1684	1686	6	Doctors' Dress Through the Ages II	1958	£6.00
1685	1687	6	Costumes of Sicily	1958	£5.00
1686	1688	6	Infantry	1958	£6.00
1687	1701	6	History of Italy	1958	£4.00
1688	1697	6	History of Denmark	1958	£4.00
1689	1702	6	History of Mexico	1958	£4.00
1690	1689	6	Parasites of Agriculture	1958	£4.00
1691	1690	6	The Legends of the Grottoes of Italy	1958	£6.00
1692	1691	6	Landscapes of Planets	1958	£9.00
1693	1692	6	National Parks	1958	£5.00
1694	1693	6	Living Prehistoric Plants	1958	£6.00
1695	1694	6	Creative Work by Well Known Belgians	1958	£4.00
1696	1696	6	Learned Men of Ancient Times	1958	£4.00
1697	1698	6	History of Italy XII	1958	£5.00
1698	1699	6	History of Italy XIII	1958	£8.00
1699	1700	6	History of Italy XIV	1958	£4.00
1700	1703	6	Tortoise	1958	£4.00
1701	1705	6	Living Prehistoric Animals	1959	£5.00
1702	1704	6	Luminous Animals	1959	£4.00
1703	1706	6	Artillery	1959	£6.00
1704	1707	6	The Grasshopper	1959	£5.00
1705	1708	6	How Children are Carried	1959	£4.00
1706	1709	6	Costumes of Sardinia	1959	£5.00
1707	1710	6	Dinosaurs	1959	£8.00
1708	1711	6	Letters and Numbers on Butterflies	1959	£10.00
1709	1712	6	Gaul Before Julius Caesar	1959	£4.00
1710	1713	6	Grenadiers of Sardinia	1959	£8.00
1711	1717	6	History of Argentina	1959	£4.00
1712	1723	6	History of Moscow	1959	£4.00
1713	1718	6	History of Poland	1959	£4.00
1714	1714	6	Leopold II	1959	£4.00
1715	1716	6	Aquarium Plants	1959	£4.00
1716	1715	6	Inedible Fish	1959	£4.00
1717	1719	6	History of Italy XV	1959	£8.00
1718	1720	6	History of Italy XVI	1959	£8.00
1719	1721	6	History of Italy XVII	1959	£8.00
1720	1722	6	History of Italy XVIII	1959	£7.00
1721	1724	6	Vincent van Gogh	1959	£4.00
1722	1725	6	Alchemy	1960	£4.00
1723	1749	6	The Alpine Brigade	1960	£14.00
1724	1726	6	Brillat-Savarin (18th century Personality)	1960	£4.00
1725	1727	6	The Story of Coffee	1960	£4.00
1726	1728	6	Famous Italian Benefactresses	1960	£4.00
1727	1758	6	Winged Gods and Heroes of Ancient Greece	1960	£4.00
1728	1733	6	Peer Gynt	1960	£4.00
1729	1743	6	History of Bulgaria	1960	£4.00
1730	1744	6	History of Ancient Greece	1960	£4.00
1731	1745	6	History of Rumania	1960	£4.00
1732	1746	6	History of Yugoslavia	1960	£4.00
1733	1730	6	Italian Lakes	1960	£10.00
1734	1731	6	Legends of Poland	1960	£4.00
1735	1736	6	Quentin Metsyr	1960	£4.00
1736	1732	6	Insect Nests	1960	£4.00
1737	1734	6	The Conquering Races of Asia	1960	£4.00
1738	1729	6	Parasites and their Hosts	1960	£4.00
1739	1735	6	National Prisons & Celebrated Historical Prisoners	1960	£4.00
1740	1737	6	San Carlo Borromeo	1960	£10.00
1741	1738	6	Artificial Satellites	1960	£8.00

F No.	S No.	Qty	LIEBIG CARD ISSUES Title (English Translation)	Date	Set Price
1742	1739	6	The Story of the Manger	1960	£12.00
1743	1740	6	History of Italy XIX	1960	£9.00
1744	1741	6	History of Italy XX	1960	£11.00
1745	1742	6	History of Italy XXI	1960	£18.00
1746	1769	6	History of Italy XXII	1960	£18.00
1747	1747	6	Songbirds of Europe I	1960	£12.00
1748	1770	6	Types of Italian Dwellings	1961	£6.00
1749	1748	6	Military Aircraft	1961	£12.00
1750	1751	6	Bilharzia - Lifecycle of a Parasite	1961	£4.00
1751	1753	6	Cavalry	1961	£14.00
1752	1752	6	Dogs	1961	£10.00
1753	1754	6	Cicero	1961	£4.00
1754	1755	6	Scottish Clans	1961	£6.00
1755	1756	6	The Conquest of Mountains by Climbers	1961	£9.00
1756	1757	6	Costumes of Doctors Through the Ages	1961	£10.00
1757	1762	6	The Daughters of Joric	1961	£8.00
1758	1760	6	Cable Cars	1961	£8.00
1759	1761	6	Owls	1961	£5.00
1760	1767	6	History of Finland	1961	£4.00
1761	1768	6	History of Czechoslovakia	1961	£4.00
1762	1776	6	Olden Day Children's Games	1961	£4.00
1763	1759	6	Butterflies	1961	£5.00
1764	1750	6	The Adventures of Pinnocchio	1961	£10.00
1765	1782	6	Regimental Paintings	1961	£11.00
1766	1763	6	Mountain Dwellings	1961	£6.00
1767	1764	6	Van Der Neyden (15th century Artist)	1961	£4.00
1768	1765	6	Mountain Chairlifts	1961	£5.00
1769	1766	6	Story of the Knights Templar	1961	£12.00
1770	1771	6	Songbirds of Europe II	1961	£10.00
1771	1772	6	Motorways of the World	1962	£5.00
1772	1777	6	Belgian Air Force Battles	1962	£5.00
1773	1773	6	Belgian Army Overseas	1962	£5.00
1774	1774	6	Great Dams	1962	£4.00
1775	1775	6	Textile Fabrics	1962	£4.00
1776	1778	6	Da Vinci's Inventions	1962	£4.00
1777	1779	6	The Dead Sea Scrolls	1962	£4.00
1778	1780	6	Aquarium Fish	1962	£6.00
1779	1781	6	Pierre Bruegel (16th century Artist)	1962	£4.00
1780	1783	6	Famous Bridges	1962	£6.00
1781	1784	6	Italian Ports	1962	£5.00
1782	1785	6	Predatory Submarine Life	1962	£6.00
1783	1786	6	History of the Gun	1962	£9.00
1784	1787	6	Story of the Army Engineers	1962	£8.00
1785	1788	6	Famous Italian Tunnels	1962	£5.00
1786	1789	6	Crossbows	1963	£5.00
1787	1790	6	Sea Creatures	1963	£9.00
1788	1791	6	Goldeni – Opera	1963	£9.00
1789	1792	6	Strange Insects	1963	£5.00
1790	1795	6	History of the Rifle	1963	£8.00
1791	1793	6	Riddles	1963	£7.00
1792	1794	6	History of String Instruments	1963	£9.00
1793	1796	6	Sea Birds	1963	£9.00
1794	1797	6	Tropical Birds	1963	£9.00
1795	1798	6	Lithographic Art	1964	£5.00
1796	1799	6	Beautiful Italian Islands	1964	£6.00
1797	1800	6	Famous Tall Buildings	1964	£6.00
1798	1801	6	Etruria (Ancient Italy)	1964	£6.00
1799	1802	6	Antique Guns	1964	£8.00

F No.	S No.	Qty	LIEBIG CARD ISSUES Title (English Translation)	Date	Set Price
1800	1803	6	The Story of Sail	1964	£8.00
1801	1804	6	Protected Birds (without Brooke Bond name)	1964	£8.00
1802	1806	6	The Life and Opera of Moliere	1964	£8.00
1803	1807	6	The Life and Opera of Vittorio Alfieri	1964	£7.00
1804	1808	6	Medieval Armour	1965	£10.00
1805	1811	6	The Inferno (Dante)	1965	£14.00
1806	1809	6	The Story of Jade	1965	£13.00
1807	1810	6	The Life of Dante	1965	£7.00
1808	1812	6	The Life of Galileo	1965	£7.00
1809	1813	6	The Life of Michelangelo	1965	£8.00
1810	1805	6	The Life and Work of Emilio Salgari	1965	£7.00
1811	1814	6	The World Cup (Football)	1966	£16.00
1812	1815	6	Religious Council	1966	£5.00
1813	1816	6	Antique Furniture	1966	£10.00
1814	1818	6	Paradise (Dante)	1966	£14.00
1815	1817	6	Purgatory (Dante)	1966	£7.00
1816	1819	6	History of the Motorcar	1966	£12.00
1817	1820	6	History of Photography	1966	£13.00
1818	1821	6	Cradles of the World	1967	£6.00
1819	1822	6	Famous Marriage Places	1967	£12.00
1820	1823	6	Massimo D'Azeglio	1967	£6.00
1821	1826	6	The Life and Work of Giotto	1967	£8.00
1822	1824	6	The Life of Pope Pius XII	1967	£8.00
1823	1825	6	The Life of Pope Giovanni XXIII	1967	£10.00
1824	1827	6	The First Aeroplanes	1968	£18.00
1825	1828	6	Italian Army	1968	£25.00
1826	1829	6	Philosophers and Scientists	1968	£10.00
1827	1830	6	Locomotives from 1815-1872	1968	£15.00
1828	1831	6	Old Military Dress I (without Brooke Bond name)	1968	£10.00
1829	1832	6	Old Military Dress II (without Brooke Bond name)	1968	£14.00
1830	1833	6	Old Military Dress III	1968	£16.00
1831	1834	6	Aircraft of the Future	1969	£10.00
1832	1835	6	Aircraft	1969	£10.00
1833	1836	6	Scenes Based on Chessmen	1969	£10.00
1834	1837	6	Locomotives	1969	£14.00
1835	1838	6	Principal Countries of the Middle East	1969	£16.00
1836	1839	6	The Life and Work of Rossini	1969	£15.00
1837	1840	6	Astronomy I	1970	£7.00
1838	1841	6	Astronomy II	1970	£10.00
1839	1842	6	Ancient Cavalry	1970	£8.00
1840	1843	6	Ancient Helmets	1970	£16.00
1841	1844	6	Giovanni Pascoli	1970	£8.00
1842	1845	6	Dangerous Occupations I	1970	£6.00
1843	1846	6	Dangerous Occupations II	1970	£8.00
1844	1847	6	Journey to the Moon I (without Brooke Bond name)	1971	£18.00
1845	1852	6	The Nativity	1971	£25.00
1846	1848	6	Crowns I	1971	£16.00
1847	1849	6	Crowns II	1971	£5.00
1848	1850	6	Bullfighting I	1971	£6.00
1849	1851	6	Bullfighting II	1971	£10.00
1850	1853	6	Self-Portraits of Famous Artists	1972	£8.00
1851	1854	6	Journey to the Moon II	1972	£10.00
1852	1855	6	Historical Fights	1972	£8.00
1853	1856	6	The Resurrection	1972	£18.00
1854	1857	6	History of the Typewriter	1972	£12.00
1855	1860	6	How Animals See I	1973	£8.00
1856	1862	6	Ludwig Van Beethoven	1973	£8.00
1857	1858	6	The Fight Against Microbes I	1973	£8.00

F No.	S No.	Qty	**LIEBIG CARD ISSUES** Title (English Translation)	Date	Set Price
1858	1861	6	How Animals See II	1973	£8.00
1859	1863	6	The Story of the Circus I	1973	£14.00
1860	1859	6	The Fight Against Microbes II	1973	£16.00
1861	1864	6	The Story of the Circus II	1974	£16.00
1862	1865	6	War at Sea	1974	£40.00
1863	1866	6	Animals	1974	£16.00
1867	1867	6	Journey to the Moon I (with Brooke Bond name)	1975	£13.00
1868	1868	6	Protected Birds (with Brooke Bond name)	1975	£12.00
1869	1869	6	Old Military Dress I (with Brooke Bond name)	1975	£12.00
1871	1871	6	Old Military Dress II (with Brooke Bond name)	1975	£45.00

2022 AUCTIONS

We have been auctioning for over 75 years cards to suit every collector

Monthly 360-lot postal auctions of cigarette and trade cards and associated items with estimated values from as little as £1 up to many hundreds. Lots to interest every collector and suit their pocket.

Postal Auctions for 2022 are as follows:

Monday,	4th January	Saturday,	25th June
Saturday,	29th January	Saturday,	30th July
Saturday,	26th February	Saturday,	27th August
Saturday,	26th March	Saturday,	24th September
Saturday,	30th April	Saturday,	29th October
Saturday,	28th May	Saturday,	26th November

Each postal auction finishes at midnight on the above dates.

A guide to how we assess condition and how to bid can be found on our bidding sheet which comes with the free auction catalogue, so it couldn't be easier if you are an 'auction beginner'. (Auction date could be subject to change.)

There are no additional charges to bidders for buyer's premium, so bidding is straightforward, with no 'hidden extras'.

Each lot is described with an estimate of its value reflecting the condition of the cards, ranging from poor right through to mint condition, and for over 75 years collectors have bid with complete confidence, knowing that every effort is made to describe the lots accurately.

Each auction contains a selection of rare sets, rare and scarce individual cards, pre-1918 issues, 1920-40 series, old and modern trade issues including Brooke Bond, errors and varieties, silks, albums, books, Liebigs, cigarette packets etc – in fact plenty to interest everyone.

Auction catalogues are available **FREE OF CHARGE**, 4 weeks before the date of sale from London Cigarette Card Company Limited, Sutton Road, Somerton, Somerset TA11 6QP
Telephone: 01458-273452   Fax: 01458-273515
E-mail: auctions@londoncigcard.co.uk

The Auction Catalogue can also be found on our website, which contains a preview of each auction as well as facilities for on-line bidding – visit www.londoncigcard.co.uk for further details or why not sign up to our **FREE E-mail Newsletter** to be reminded when new auctions become available online.

Also a copy of the auction catalogue is automatically sent each month to members of our Card Collectors Club
(membership details on page ii)

CARD COLLECTORS CLUB BY THE LCCC

A club for collectors from all over the world!!

With this prestigious club you will receive:

- 12 Free copies of Card Collectors News
- Free Type Cards with every issue
- Monthly Savings on over 100 sets
- Free Monthly Auction Catalogue
- A Special Discount on a Set of the Month
- Details on New Issues and Additions to Stock
- Reduced Handling Fees on orders
- Priority Order Despatch
- Reduced Price on our Cigarette and Trade Card Catalogues
- Loyalty Vouchers
- Competitions with Prizes
- Handy Membership Card with your own membership ID & renewal date.
- Free Newsletters via Email

ALL THIS CAN BE YOURS FOR JUST

£27 for UK Members
£54 for European Members
£66 for the Rest of the World

You can even become a **Digital Member** to this club for a cost of just **£20** regardless where you are in the world

(T & C's apply)